D0303661

Tall Tales about the Mind and Brain.

Separating fact from fiction

 B UNIVERSITY LIS

3042 00722 6796

Whilst every effort has been made to ensure that the contents of this book are as complete, accurate and up to date as possible at the date of writing, Oxford University Press is not able to give any guarantee or assurance that such is the case. Readers are urged to take appropriately qualified medical advice in all cases. The information in this book is intended to be useful to the general reader, but should not be used as a means of self-diagnosis or for the prescription of medication.

Tall Tales about the Mind and Brain.

Separating fact from fiction

Edited by

Sergio Della Sala

Human Cognitive Neuroscience-Psychology
University of Edinburgh

OXFORD
UNIVERSITY PRESS

MER
612.82 DEL
7 dy

OXFORD
UNIVERSITY PRESS

Great Clarendon Street, Oxford OX2 6DP

Oxford University Press is a department of the University of Oxford.
It furthers the University's objective of excellence in research, scholarship,
and education by publishing worldwide in

Oxford New York

Auckland Cape Town Dar es Salaam Hong Kong Karachi
Kuala Lumpur Madrid Melbourne Mexico City Nairobi
New Delhi Shanghai Taipei Toronto

With offices in

Argentina Austria Brazil Chile Czech Republic France Greece
Guatemala Hungary Italy Japan Poland Portugal Singapore
South Korea Switzerland Thailand Turkey Ukraine Vietnam

Oxford is a registered trade mark of Oxford University Press
in the UK and in certain other countries

Published in the United States
by Oxford University Press Inc., New York

© Oxford University Press, 2007

The moral rights of the authors have been asserted
Database right Oxford University Press (maker)

First published 2007

All rights reserved. No part of this publication may be reproduced,
stored in a retrieval system, or transmitted, in any form or by any means,
without the prior permission in writing of Oxford University Press,
or as expressly permitted by law, or under terms agreed with the appropriate
reprographics rights organization. Enquiries concerning reproduction
outside the scope of the above should be sent to the Rights Department,
Oxford University Press, at the address above

You must not circulate this book in any other binding or cover
and you must impose the same condition on any acquirer

British Library Cataloguing in Publication Data

Data available

Library of Congress Cataloging-in-Publication Data

Tall tales about the mind and brain separating fact from fiction / edited by Sergio Della Sala. – 1st ed.
     p.   cm.
   Includes bibliographical references and index.
   ISBN-13: 978-0-19-856876-6 (hardback: alk. paper)
   ISBN-13: 978-0-19-856877-3 (pbk.: alk. paper)   1. Brain–Miscellanea.   2. Neurosciences–Miscellanea.
3. Tall tales.   I. Della Sala, Sergio.
   QP376.T354   2007
   612.8′2–dc22

                                                                                    2007031708

Typeset by SPI Publisher Services, Pondicherry, India
Printed in Great Britain
on acid-free paper by
Biddles Ltd., King's Lynn

ISBN 0-19-856876-2   978-0-19-856876-6 (hb)
ISBN 0-19-856877-0   978-0-19-856877-3 (pb)

1 3 5 7 9 10 8 6 4 2

To Hans, a friend and a mentor

Contents

Tall tales on language and communication

Tall tales on the brain

Contributors

Mike Anderson
Department of Psychology,
The University of Western Australia,
Nedlands, Western Australia

Giovanni Berlucchi
Dipartimento di Scienze Neurologiche e
della Visione,
Sezione di Fisiologia, Università di
Verona, Verona, Italy

Barry L. Beyerstein
Department of Psychology,
Simon Fraser University,
Burnaby, British Columbia, Canada

Olaf Blanke
Laboratory of Cognitive Neuroscience,
Ecole Fédérale Polytechnique de
Lausanne,
Lausanne and Department of Neurology,
University Hospital, Geneva, Switzerland

Peter Brugger
Neuropsychology Unit, Department of
Neurology, University Hospital Zurich,
Zurich, Switzerland

David P. Carey
Department of Psychology,
University of Aberdeen, Old Aberdeen,
UK

Zhijian Chen
Department of Psychological Sciences,
University of Missouri, Columbia, MO,
USA

Eric H. Chudler
Department of Anaesthesiology,
University of Washington,
Seattle, WA, USA

Seema L. Clifasefi
Department of Psychology,
University of Washington
Seattle WA, USA

Michael C. Corballis
Department of Psychology,
University of Auckland,
Auckland, New Zealand

Cesare Cornoldi
Dipartimento di Psicologia Generale,
Università degli Studi di Padova, Padova,
Italy

Nelson Cowan
Department of Psychological Sciences,
University of Missouri, Columbia, MO,
USA

Rossana DeBeni
Dipartimento di Psicologia Generale,
Università degli Studi di Padova,
Italy

Sergio Della Sala
Human Cognitive Neuroscience,
Psychology,
University of Edinburgh, UK

Christopher C. French
Department of Psychology,

Goldsmiths College, University of
London, London, UK

Marion Funk
Neuropsychology Unit,
Department of Neurology,
University Hospital Zurich, Zurich,
Switzerland

Maryanne Garry
Department of Psychology,
Victoria University of Wellington,
Wellington,
New Zealand

Ken Gilhooly
School of Psychology,
University of Hertfordshire,
Hertfordshire, UK

Colin Gray
Department of Psychology,
University of Aberdeen, Old Aberdeen,
UK

James Handel
Simon Fraser University, Burnaby,
British Columbia,
Canada

Ray Hyman
University of Oregon,
Eugene, OR, USA

Peter Lamont
School of Philosophy,
Psychology and Language Sciences,
University of Edinburgh, Edinburgh, UK

Elizabeth Loftus
Department of Psychology & Social
Behaviour,
University of California, Irvine, CA, USA

Samantha Mann
University of Portsmouth,

Psychology Department,
Portsmouth, UK

Amina Memon
Department of Psychology,
University of Aberdeen, Old Aberdeen,
UK

Nick Miller
Speech and language Sciences,
University of Newcastle,
Newcastle on Tyne, UK

Candice C. Morey
Department of Psychological Sciences,
University of Missouri,
Columbia, MO, USA

David G. Myers
Department of Psychology,
Hope College
Holland, MI, USA

Massimo Polidoro
Comitato Italiano per il Controllo delle
Affermazioni sul Paranormale,
Padova, Italy

Wallace I. Sampson
Stanford University School of Medicine,
Palo Alto, CA, USA

Julia Santomauro
Department of Psychology,
Goldsmiths College, University of
London, London, UK

Fernando Saravi
Department of Morphology and
Physiology,
Universidad Nacional de Cuyo,
Mendoza, Argentina

Mark Solms
Departments of Neurology and

Psychology, University of Cape Town,
Cape Town, South Africa

Antonella Sorace
School of Philosophy, Psychology and
Language Science,
University of Edinburgh,
Edinburgh, UK

Zarka Stojanovic
Simon Fraser University, Burnaby,
British Columbia, Canada

Deryn Strange
Victoria University of Wellington,
Wellington,
New Zealand

Rachel Sutherland
Victoria University of Wellington,
Wellington,
New Zealand

Don Thomson
School of Social Science and Liberal
Studies

Charles Sturt University,
Bathurst, Australia

Gregor Thut
Department of Neurology,
University Hospital,
Geneva and Department of
Fundamental Neuroscience,
University Medical School, Geneva,
Switzerland

Oliver Turnbull
Centre for Cognitive Neuroscience,
School of Psychology,
University of Wales,
Bangor, UK

Aldert Vrij
Psychology Department,
University of Portsmouth,
Portsmouth, UK

Krissy Wilson
Department of Psychology,
Goldsmiths College, University of
London, London, UK

Preface

Mandy boasted her best smile 'How do you want your hair trimmed today, sir?', 'In silence, please'. She never stopped talking ever since. 'Hurowhat?' she enquired; 'Neuro, n-euro, neuroscience' muttered I, uptight. 'We are almost colleagues, you work a few millimetres above the scalp, I just below it'. She tittered and patiently showed me that talking and sharing, possibly with little contempt, feels refreshingly good. I enjoy now discussing with Mandy, my natural pomposity at bay. She always has penetrating questions, those rarely heard during scientific debates 'And, what would that be for?', or scathing probing like 'I have read on a magazine that anybody can learn to have a perfect photographic memory, if this is not true why nobody says so?'. Mandy was right.

People often derive their knowledge about the mind on conventional beliefs accepted as truth, but supported by little validation. Hence, this collection of essays which is geared at sharing with the interested lay people, students, and colleagues what we know, or we think we know, about how the brain and its product, the mind, work. We considered the questions that people who are curious about neurological and cognitive phenomena but based their knowledge on sources of information bragging about little proved claims are likely to ask at cocktail parties. Cocktail parties, you know, can be a strenuous experience for a brain scientist, sooner or later the inevitable question will crop up 'I have read that we should all learn to better use our right hemisphere, now what do you believe?'. Perhaps it is the word 'believe' that makes such instances beyond the pale, or perhaps the certainty that you will never convince somebody that things are not as they think simply by using null-hypothesis arguments. If one claims to have invented a hat which keeps the dinosaurs at large, and presents as evidence that indeed no dinosaur can be found nearby when one is wearing the hat, and people queue to buy the anti-dino hat, how can I argue against it, if not by showing that even my tennis hat scares the dinosaurs away? Then what if people want to by my tennis hat as well?

Aim of this book is to discuss the evidence on which such claims are based. The take-home message is that understanding how the brain functions can be a rewording and creative endeavour, unsubstantiated beliefs are tedious. The purpose of this book is not to teach anything to anybody. I berate the concept of public understanding of science (PUS for short). I do not think that everybody should know everything, I do not want to know anything about linguistics, I do not want to understand it, I decided to delegate to experts in that area. I trust that linguists know what they are doing because we share a common method for accruing knowledge. We all accept that the scientific method should be used in improving our knowledge of scientific matters. Then anybody is free to believe in whatever madcap assumptions please them. Indeed, being a scientist does not protect us from sustaining the most wacky ideas in fields outwith our area of expertise. Consider

Linus Pauling's petition in favour of magadoses of Vitamin C to prevent cancer, Kary Mullis's belief in astrology, or Brian Josephson's praise of telepathy: Nobel laureates with brilliant minds believing in more bogus than the Lewis Caroll's Queen of Heart. And I am sure that I am not exempt.

The different chapters collected in this book will give you the opportunity to read what experts have to say about mind and brain matters that we hear on the telly about. I enjoyed reading the various contributions to this volume, I trust that you also will find some useful information in it, even though I am fully aware that the IKEA catalogue is more practical, colourful and easier to read. Of course most of what is reported in this volume will prove wrong in a few years, but this is the fascination of science, its absence of dogmatism, and its ability to change. Neuroscience, the science of the brain, is no exception. Nevertheless it was, I hope, a fruitful endeavour for which I have many people to thank.

First I am grateful to Barry Beyerstein and all the authors who accepted with enthusiasm my suggestion that they write a chapter for this book. I also thank Gillian Leslie, who persuaded me that is was worthwhile to concoct a second collection of chapters for a book to follow Mind Myths, the volume with a similar theme that I edited for Wiley in 1999, and of course the people at the Oxford University Press who made the project possible, in particular Martin Baum, commissioning editor, Carol Maxwell, assistant commissioning editor, and Angela Butterworth, senior production editor. Finally, I would like to thank Supri Rajiv, who assisted me with my editorial work for this book, and who makes my working life easy and my office life pleasant.

It is tradition (please check) that prefaces of scientific books should round off with moving words of thanks for the spouse and sons of the author/editor who claims that their dedication to the book almost wrecked their family life. You would be glad to know that my family did not even notice.

Sergio Della Sala

Introduction: The myth of 10% and other Tall Tales about the mind and the brain

Sergio Della Sala and Barry Beyerstein

It seems safe to say that most people are of two minds about the mind. On the one hand, they dutifully don their helmets before hopping on their motorbikes and change their diets to avoid clogging their cerebral arteries—because they know that damage to the brain from accident or disease will wreak havoc on their ability to think, perceive, and respond. At some level, they are acknowledging that the brain is the organ of consciousness and that having an intact one is necessary for any semblance of normal mental activity. In this way, they are further conceding, whether they realize it or not, that if the brain is a physical organ, whose operations are bound by well-established physical, physiological and psychological principles, then certain cherished beliefs about the mind and its alleged powers are on rather shaky ground. On the other hand, many of these same people shove this inconvenient implication—which is as well-supported as any in science—aside and line up to buy any doctrine, course, exercise, or gadget that offers to mitigate this unpalatable corollary of the proposition that mind equals brain function. Consequently, entrepreneurs rarely go broke selling books or documentaries that assert that minds can leave bodies and still see, hear and remember, or that powerful spiritual entities can play us like unseen puppeteers. So the president of the United States signs a law forbidding termination of nutritional life support for a patient in a persistent vegetative state (see below) whose brain is damaged beyond any hope of regaining her sentience. This because he, like the unfortunate woman's family, fervently wants to believe in the dualistic doctrine that says her mind abides intact in some supernatural realm despite insufficient neural tissue to support even minimal awareness. After all, a strong appeal of most religions is their promise that one's personality will survive in another existence, long after the brain is dead and decomposed. Moreover, poll after poll attests that a substantial majority believes that people can bend spoons with their bare minds and 'see' through walls and the barrier of time. Hucksters successfully peddle power drinks, mental exercises and devices that purportedly create superbrains, even though such claims fly in the face of most up-to-date evidence in modern neuroscience. Note the inconsistency here: dualists who fundamentally believe that the mind is a spiritual rather than a physical, brain-produced phenomenon, trying to enhance their immaterial minds by refurbishing their material brains. Claims of this sort seldom disappear, of course, because they offer substantial comfort to the believer. Thus, profitable but ridiculously tall tales of the mind and brain recycle endlessly despite the best efforts of the scientific community to debunk them. Hope really does spring eternal it seems.

This book tackles a variety of tall tales about the mind and the brain, though it is by no means exhaustive. Additional examples can be found in sibling volumes like *Mind Myths*[1] or *The Fountain of Myth*.[2] These myths pervade our culture and converging commercial and evangelical interests will undoubtedly provide new variations on these themes to provoke the sceptics' ire. Most of these unsubstantiated whoppers are innocuous enough, annoying though they may be to the scientifically literate. Some, however, could have dire consequences, such as, for instance, when an allegedly scientific handwriting analyst besmirches someone's reputation with unfounded character slurs or recommends that he or she not be hired or granted a loan on the basis of techniques with no more validity than palm reading (see Chapters 15 and 16). These pseudoscientific character readers feel qualified to pronounce on strangers' abilities, inclinations, and moral stature because, as they say, 'handwriting is brainwriting'.

Many popular views are seen as either true or false, whereas science is largely probabilistic. Moreover the probabilistic conclusions of science often do not match our intuitive views, making many scientific explanations difficult to accept (see Chapters 1, 2 and 3). Of course, phony stories and misinformation are not the exclusive prerogative of the tabloid press or prime time TV; they occasionally mar the scientific debate as well. How often have you seen serious textbooks reporting, as hard evidence, the alleged discovery that untrained flatworms can learn a task by eating other, previously trained, worms, or that scientists have achieved nuclear fusion on the laboratory bench (so-called 'cold fusion')? The former is, in effect, merely another rehash of the old 'cellular memory' hypothesis criticized below. In the same vein, hardly a week goes by without a triumphant claim that scientists have discovered a new drug that will cure heroin addiction. This, despite the fact that such a desirable but unlikely solution is predicated upon the popular but seriously flawed notion that addiction is purely a biochemical and physiological problem to be solved by some 'magic bullet' from the chemist's bench. This ignores the fact that most users of cocaine or heroin do not become addicted and some people become addicted without using enough of the drug to cause long-term biochemical changes in their bodies—not to mention the fact that a goodly proportion of addicts simply quit with no help from the medical or psychological professions.[3,4] If substituting another chemical were all it took to overcome drug addiction, cigarette smokers who use nicotine patches should have a much higher rate of successful quitting than they typically do.[5]

Brain matters are fashionable and rightly fascinating to the public. Unfortunately, simplistic accounts abound, spawning numerous pseudoscientific products in the New Age marketplace. Sad to say, the arrogant, elitist attitude of many academics prevents them from taking the trouble to explain to the intelligent layperson why such claims fall short. For instance, readers who have travelled recently with KLM may have noticed several nonsensical assertions, without expert rebuttal, in the airline's glossy in-flight magazine (May, 2006 issue). Therein, passengers were advised that if their creative juices are running a bit dry, they can capitalise on the 'Mozart Effect' (see Chapter 10) to unlock their creative impulses. Allegedly, this panacea, which involves the thoroughly delightful, but hardly therapeutic, effects of listening to the master's music, is based on 'compelling evidence'. The same airline publication also extols the dictates of one Angela Zakon, a self-styled 'life coach' who maintains that people would fare much better if only they learned to breathe through their left nostril to stimulate the right side of the brain, allegedly its fount of creativity. Elsewhere in the present volume there are discussions of legitimate research demonstrating functional specializations of the right and left hemispheres of the brain (see Chapter 18). These scientifically documented differences bear little resemblance to the fanciful speculations of the pop psychology industry concerning alleged left-brain/right-brain specializations, however.

Despite its lack of scientific support, self-help advice of this sort oozes from almost every popular magazine and Sunday weekly, not to mention numerous primetime television 'documentaries'. These inspiring but unfounded messages soon insinuate themselves into much of our friendly everyday chitchat as well. Scientific opinion differs as to whether these myths should be challenged vigorously or just ignored with appropriate disdain. The contributors to this volume feel it is worth taking time from our various professional pursuits to at least voice our reasons for maintaining that claims of this sort do not hold water. Naturally, in so doing, we will be breathing through our right nostril to stimulate the rational approach of our left hemisphere.

In the remainder of this introductory chapter, we will briefly introduce some controversial brain/mind topics not fully covered in the rest this book. Here are a few additional Tall Tales to consider.

The myth of ten per cent

Those with intelligence below average, please raise your hand. Few will. We all like to think about ourselves as bright, lovable people. Myths about intelligence are deeply ingrained in our culture (see Chapters 8 through 12). Probably the most durable brain myth of all time is the pervasive belief that normal people only use ten percent of their brains. This assertion is disputed by virtually every datum of modern brain research.[6] E.g., powerful functional neuroimaging scanners show no 'dead spots' awaiting reassignment. Likewise, tissue losses due to strokes or head injury always impair some kind of psychological function, no matter where in the brain they occur; and losses of far less than ninety percent have devastating effects on consciousness, personality, emotions, abilities, and movements. Electrical or chemical stimulation of nerve cells elicits some kind of mental or physical activity regardless of where in the brain it is targeted. In other words, we normally use it all (though different parts contribute to differing degrees to various mental tasks).

If you think about it, even a basic knowledge of evolutionary biology should have deflated this myth long ago. Brains are very expensive, biologically speaking, to grow and to run. Natural selection, a stingy process at the best of times, seems very unlikely to have permitted wasting precious resources shaping and maintaining such a massively underutilized organ. Would you keep paying exorbitant power bills to heat all ten rooms of your house if you never ventured out of the kitchen?

Despite much contrary data and its affront to logic, this hoary myth refuses to die, no doubt because of (you guessed it) the considerable uplift and encouragement it affords (not to mention the profit it generates for those who hawk self-improvement products that exploit the myth). If ninety percent of the brain were really a cerebral spare tire, as many of these hucksters claim, learning to tap its unused capacity could be the route to fabulous achievement, riches and fame—even, according to many New Age entrepreneurs, the pathway to psychic powers and transcendent bliss. As Mark Twain said, 'It ain't the things we don't know that gets us in trouble, it's the things we know that just ain't so.'

The ten-percent myth likely sprang from a misinterpretation of a metaphorical statement contained in a public pronouncement in the early 1900's by the pioneering psychologist, William James. It received its biggest later-day boost when the popular adventurer Lowell Thomas misquoted James in his foreword to the 1936 first edition of Dale Carnegie's all-time best seller, *How to Win Friends and Influence People*. James actually said he doubted that most people use more than 10% of their *potential*, not their brains. In his day, Carnegie was the most successful in a long line of self-help advisors, many of whom have tried to gild the lily by misappropriating the latest breakthroughs in brain science to add unearned credibility to their endlessly recycled commonsense maxims. Some of these, unfortunately, have been propagated and misinterpreted by accredited sceptics as well.[7] Let us look at a few more-recent examples.

Neurolinguistic Programming and other 'personal growth' training

As we have seen, the longevity of the ten percent myth owes much to the promotion it has received from descendants of the self-improvement and positive thinking movements that swept America in the mid-nineteenth century.[6] Much of what these advisors peddled was useful, if overblown, advice of the sensible sort your wise old grandmother could have given you for free. Many of these personal make-over coaches, however, attempted to add additional punch to their come-ons by justifying their recipes for achieving health, wealth, and happiness with pseudoscientific distortions of valid brain research and by turning to the mystical and occult lore for magical assistance.[8]

As the philosopher Dale Beyerstein has observed, 'nonsense often piggy-backs on reliable knowledge'. The personal enhancement method called Neurolinguistic Programming (NLP) is a case in point. It began with some now outmoded information from legitimate psychology, linguistics, and neuroscience that even most experts accepted back in the 1960's, when NLP first arrived on the scene. The nice thing about real science, as opposed to pseudoscience, is that the former eventually corrects its mistakes as new discoveries emerge. NLP remains mired in the past or the never-was.

Not surprisingly, assumed but now discredited left-brain/right-brain differences top the list of NLP's dubious roots. Its mental typologies, and the remedies for personal shortcomings derived from them, are not to be found in any reputable psychology textbook. NLP promoters claim that each of us has a Primary Representational System (PRS), a tendency to think in specific modes: visual, auditory, kinaesthetic, olfactory or gustatory. A person's PRS can supposedly be exposed by observing the kinds of words and metaphors he or she tends to use in everyday conversation (e.g., 'I see what you mean,' as opposed to 'I hear what you're saying'). NLP's quirky ideas about the significance of the directionality of one's eye movements also play a prominent role in their diagnoses and treatment of problems. NLP therapists claim they can achieve better rapport with clients, and cure them more successfully, if they address them with the appropriate PRS. None of this has been adequately supported by the scientific literature. Nonetheless, NLPs advertising makes extraordinary claims, such as instant cures for phobias or miraculously quick and easy acquisition of new abilities, with no credible research to back them up. For example:

> Changing the quality of your life is the focus of NLP. You will deal with—vanquish—anything that may be holding you back from utilizing the force that can instantly change your life. Empower yourself with the keys to extraordinary achievement. Discover within yourself the force that can change everything.

As Carl Sagan wisely advised, 'Extraordinary claims demand extraordinary evidence.' A variety of fair-minded critics have looked at the evidence for NLP's vaunted effectiveness and found it wanting.

NLP became one of several objects of scrutiny when the U.S. Congress appealed to the National Research Council (NRC) to advise it as to which performance-enhancement methods could or could not live up to the advertising promoters were using to pitch their wares to the armed services and numerous government agencies. The NRC struck a panel of eminent psychologists and neuroscientists to look into heavily promoted products that ranged from NLP and various 'positive thinking' and 'brainstorming' courses to sleep learning devices, biofeedback, subliminal audiotapes (containing hidden but supposedly effective self-help messages that are impossible to hear), various 'memory boosters,' and even courses offering to develop workers' powers of ESP (extrasensory perception). The NRC panel first combed the world's scientific literature to look for (a) evidence that the underlying rationale for each of these self-improvement products was based on sound psychological and neurological data, and (b) evidence from properly-conducted outcome tests to support claims that these expensive interventions really work. Just to be sure they had not missed anything, the NRC panel invited the promoters of the various performance enhancement products to supply them with any supporting evidence that might have been missed in their review of the scientific literature—virtually none was forthcoming. The panel even visited the offices of most of these promoters to get a feel for their scientific acumen. None, including NLP, was able to convince the NRC's assessors that their products were a sound buy for improving worker efficiency or well-being.[9] In this regard, the NRC panel might well have quoted the famous physicist Wolfgang Pauli, who, in rejecting an article he was reviewing, told its author, 'What is true in your paper is not new. What is new in your paper is not true.'

In the May 2001 edition of *The Training Journal*, which vets the sorts of extravagant training programs touted to industry and government, Gary Platt showed in detail how weak the corroborative evidence for NLP is. In Platt's article, he quotes the noted British psychologist and sceptic, Dr. Michael Heap, from the Sheffield Health Authority, who has published extensive critiques of NLP.

> He [Heap] can find virtually no substantive evidence to support the claims made for NLP, and writes:
>
> 'The present author is satisfied that the assertions of NLP writers concerning the representational systems have been objectively and fairly investigated and found to be lacking. These assertions are stated in unequivocal terms by the originators of NLP and it is clear from their writings that phenomena such as representational systems, predicate preferences and eye-movement patterns are claimed to be potent psychological processes, easily and convincingly demonstrable on training courses by tutors and trainees following simple instructions, and, indeed, in interactions in everyday life. Therefore, in view of the absence of any objective evidence provided by the original proponents of the PRS hypothesis, and the failure of subsequent empirical investigations to adequately support it, it may well be appropriate now to conclude that there is not, and never has been, any substance to the conjecture that people represent their world internally in a preferred mode which may be inferred from their choice of predicates and from their eye movements'.

Personal growth is desirable and can be achieved without resorting to convoluted pseudo-scientific exercises. The bottom line: When it comes to self-improvement, specific training in task-relevant skills, hard work, practice, and attention to detail, seem to be the only reliable routes to success. So sayeth the NRC.

Subliminal learning

Like most other human abilities, there are many popular but false beliefs about the nature of memory. These misconceptions arise largely because each of us feels that we have a privileged insight into how our own mind works (see Chapters 4, 5, 6 and 7). We mentioned above the claim that audio tapes with repeated suggestions played while we are asleep can help us to give up smoking, stop drinking, think creatively, increase confidence or make friends. As the abovementioned NRC panel reported, these tapes clearly do not work as their promoters claim. Tapes played during sleep that do not contain these motivational messages appear to promote exactly the same results as the ones that do. That is, if you do end up smokeless, or with a new circle of friends, it is not because of the messages on the tape but because you were already motivated to stop smoking or to become more gregarious and the same motives led you to buy and use the tapes.

Along the same lines, a well-publicised case reported in 1957 by James Vicary, an advertising consultant, popularized the notion that visual or auditory messages, played while we are awake—but too weakly or rapidly to be consciously perceived—could still affect consumer or voter preferences and produce therapeutic changes in people's behaviour. The technique is called 'subliminal messaging'.[10] Vicary claimed that by flashing the message 'Eat Popcorn' or 'Drink Coke' on a cinema screen, too briefly for it to be noticed by the theatre patrons, he had dramatically increased subsequent sales at the snack bar. However, the assertion turned out to be a complete hoax. Vicary had, in fact, collected little or no evidence of this kind, and later attempts to replicate his alleged effect failed conclusively. Similarly, accusations that anti-social recording artists were inserting subliminal messages in their pop music albums to persuade unsuspecting fans to adopt particular political or social views, to start taking drugs, or to commit suicide have also been shown to be total fabrications.[10,11]

Subliminal audiotapes whose promoters claim they will help you improve your memory have been shown to lead to people *reporting* that their memory is better. However, a clever study that the promoters ought to have done themselves before selling such products to the public involved giving people subliminal audiotapes that were mislabelled to indicate that they were for memory improvement but were, in fact, ones that the manufacturers actually claimed would enhance one's self-esteem instead. Most people given the mislabelled self-esteem tapes were convinced that their memory had improved, but when tested, their abilities were no better than they had been before listening to the tapes (British Psychology Society—Working Party Report, 1992).[12,13] Needless to say, none reported that their self-esteem had been unexpectedly boosted. Similar findings have been published for evaluations of self-help tapes for losing weight: people who were given the 'subliminal' slimming tapes lost no more weight when they went on a diet than did those who merely tried to reduce their intake without playing the tapes[14]. The power of the simple control group is an awesome tool.

Implicit processing

Sometimes truth really is stranger than fiction. What makes it so much fun for academics like those of us who have contributed this volume to come in to work each morning is that the field of brain-behaviour research is always expanding and changing. As you will see throughout this volume, these discoveries often pour cold water on cherished and comforting beliefs that many people would rather not have challenged. However, they sometimes confirm ideas that were frequently dismissed as 'old wives' tales' (please pardon the sexism in quoting this old expression—the evidence, of course, is that men are every bit as gullible). Here are a few 'tall tales' that have withstood the cold, hard scrutiny of scientific investigation. As the Nobel prize-winning novelist and scientist Primo Levi so nicely put it, 'Science respects what is.'

Our earlier casting of doubt on the powers of subliminal persuasion was not intended to deny that implicit processing occurs in the brain (i.e., that there are mental operations that we are not consciously aware of). Indeed, the human brain expends a great deal of energy controlling activities that we do not perceive directly, such as those of other organs involved in circulation, digestion, or emotional reactions, including heart rate and sweating. Moreover, we know that the brain can also deal with certain cognitive activities non-consciously. Psychologists have shown that non-conscious processes are not only involved in normal cognition but also in producing many experiences that people interpret as supernatural, because they haven't the foggiest idea where they came from (the recesses of their own brains, of course—see Chapter 19). Examples that have helped reveal how this works involve patients who suffer from so-called 'hemi-spatial neglect' or from 'blindsight'.

On 25th September, 1919, the US President Woodrow Wilson suffered a stroke while addressing an audience in Colorado. As a result, he was paralysed and lost sensation on the left side of his body. In the following few days, it became clear that the president also had a range of deficits that seemed quite bizarre. For example, his wife (who essentially ran the country during his incapacitation) requested that any visitors be led to the right side of his bed or wheelchair. This was done to 'ensure that he would not ignore people on his left side'. [14,p.357] In a detailed discussion of Wilson's impairments, Sigmund Freud described the problem in psychoanalytic terms, as a rather strange form of neurosis.[15] However, it seems much more likely that the deficits arose from a lesion in the parietal lobe of the right hemisphere. Indeed, Weinstein argued that President Wilson must have been suffering from what is now known as 'unilateral spatial neglect', in addition to his physical paralysis.[14]

Hemi-spatial neglect is a condition in which brain-damaged patients fail to detect or to respond to events, people or objects on one side of their body, normally on the left. Typically, it arises from damage to the right parietal lobe of the brain (about half way down on the right side towards the rear). When asked to describe the layout of the room, such patients will omit details on their left side and, in severe cases, will eat from only the right half of their plate. This deficit does not arise from a failure of vision, nor from a general intellectual impairment.

Interestingly, even although these patients seem unaware of information presented to their left, there is evidence that they can 'implicitly' process some stimuli in the 'neglected' field. Marshall and Halligan[16] presented patients suffering from neglect with a series of paired houses, drawn one above the other. The two houses were identical except that one member of each pair was drawn with flames coming from either the left or the right side of the building. For each pair presented, patients were asked to decide whether the two houses were the same or different. When the flames came from the right of one of the houses, they could readily detect the difference, but when the flames came from the left, patients maintained that the two were identical. However, when asked in which of the houses they had perceived as identical they would rather live, patients tended to point to the one without the flames. Of course, they were unable to say why they felt that one was preferable. Several other examples have been reported of this kind of non-conscious processing of visual information in patients with hemi-spatial neglect. Although scientists are still debating as to the explanation for this phenomenon, there is general agreement that covert processing of information is perfectly possible. The brains of these patients seem to know better even if they can't say why!

You may think, this condition is asymmetrical, only the left space is neglected. The strange case of blindsight addresses this issue. Blindsight arises following damage to the areas of the brain responsible for making sense of what we see.[17] People with this kind of brain damage are essentially blind in the affected area of their visual field (see also Chapter 22), although their eyes and visual tracts to the brain remain healthy. Oddly enough, when shown points of light, moving stimuli, pictures, or objects, they can often 'guess' at a better than chance level what has been presented, although they remain totally unaware that they are accurate. For example, when shown a vertical or horizontal line, they can guess its orientation without being aware that a line is present. When presented with a small object in the blind area, such patients deny being able to see anything, but they can form their hand into the appropriate shape for grasping an object of that sort. The conclusion from studying these patients is that there is more than one route into the higher parts of the brain from the eyes, and that one of these routes does not rely on the primary visual areas in the occipital cortex (at the back of the brain), the ones that are damaged in patients who exhibit blindsight. This alternative pathway does not give rise to conscious awareness, but does allow some processing of the visual information which is sufficient to support a plausible guess.[18] When there are so many fascinating things of this sort that our brain has to reveal, so many secrets to uncover, so much to study and discover, why should we accept Mumbo Jumbo instead of the real thing? Here's some more of that Mumbo Jumbo to avoid.

Brain tuners

Predictably, the amazing advances in cognitive neuroscience (the interdisciplinary field that studies brain-behaviour relationships) have spawned a variety of doubtful gizmos, vigorously marketed to the over-stressed and spirituality-seeking public. Sellers of these devices offered shortcuts to enjoyment, relaxation, enlightenment, and creativity, as well as improved health and mental performance—all allegedly produced by rewiring brain circuitry from the outside.[8,19] The first devices of this genre sprang from early electroencephalographic (EEG) studies showing that highly practised meditators showed copious amounts of the EEG frequencies called alpha waves (6–12 Hz) while they were meditating. Completely forgetting that correlation does not imply causation, many in the New Age self-help industry jumped to the doubtful conclusions that (a) alpha waves occur when, and only when, somebody is meditating, and (b) training one's self to enhance one's output of alpha waves by use of a technique called 'biofeedback' would rapidly bring the trainee the same benefits that allegedly accrue to those who devote countless hours learning to meditate. Biofeedback, another fad that has failed to live up to expectations, uses an electronic detector to monitor bodily functions of which we are normally not consciously aware. By sounding a signal when bodily organs, including the brain, produce potentially beneficial physiological changes that we are unable to sense directly, the supposition was that voluntary control of these desirable states could be achieved. E.g., in its heyday, biofeedback aficionados confidently predicted that in the near future diabetics would be curing themselves by teaching their sluggish pancreas to ramp up its insulin production.

The so-called 'alpha state,' when the EEG registered primarily alpha waves, was supposed to be one of these enjoyable and beneficial states that one could learn to turn on at will through biofeedback, in this case by alpha wave feedback employing cheap home EEG devices of questionable quality. The disappointing truth of the matter is that alpha waves are found to accompany a variety of mental states, many of which are far removed from meditative bliss (they are really an indication of how much you are attending to visual information from the world around you or to mental images generated from memory).[19] Meditators, who have learned to regulate the attention they pay to inner and outer stimulation, might well produce substantial amounts of alpha waves while meditating, but this in no way guarantees that learning to produce alpha waves is equivalent to meditation. Rainfall will probably induce you to open your umbrella, but opening your brolly on a sunny afternoon is unlikely to produce a downpour.

Moreover, institution of simple control groups that the original claimants ought to have included in their studies, showed that the alleged relaxation and bliss attributed to being in a so-called 'alpha state' were entirely due to expectation on the part of the trainee. The second author of this chapter demonstrated this by secretly re-wiring an alpha feedback device to sound the signal when users were actually *suppressing* their alpha waves.[19] Those seekers who believed promoters' claims that the alpha state was relaxing and blissful were just as effusively happy with the results of the training as those who had attached themselves to the nice little blue box before the big, bad psychologist crossed the wires. Can you spell P-L-A-C-E-B-O, boys and girls?

Since that time, various other 'brain tuners', offering to enhance other allegedly beneficial EEG rhythms, have appeared on the self-help market. Like the trail-blazing alpha conditioners, they too have failed to deliver the goods.[8] Moreover, promoters of the ones that promised to rocket users into the highly beneficial states that are allegedly produced by meditation would have done well to look more carefully at the scientific literature on meditation itself before hitching their wagons to this particular star. It is hardly controversial any more that prolonged stress can have adverse health consequences and that anything overworked urbanites do to promote relaxation and reduce autonomic over-arousal can benefit their long-term health. If learning to meditate facilitates this kind of lifestyle improvement for any given individual, so be it. But, a cold, dispassionate look at the best research in the field strongly suggests that the specific mental exercises and subjective experiences of meditation, per se, add little if anything to the benefits to be gained from any other relaxation technique, or even simple rest. Anything that removes the stressed-out person from the pressures of the 'rat race' and gets his or her mind off his or her pressing sources of anxiety for a while each day will produce equivalent results.[20] The claims of the sellers of the particular technique called Transcendental Meditation that if one percent of the population in a locality adopts their methods, the crime rate will drop and the weather will improve are too far-fetched to be taken seriously by anyone who has not a financial or emotional stake in the teachings of Transcendental Meditation.

Near-Death Experiences and Reawakening from Coma

The physician and clergyman Raymond Moody coined the term Near-Death Experience (NDE) to describe a set of sensations and experiences felt by a substantial minority of people who are resuscitated from almost fatal accidents, cardio-pulmonary arrest ('heart attack'), or while going into or coming out of anaesthesia for major surgery[21,22]. Reports of these sorts of experiences are far from new. Plato, in *The Republic*, told the story of a soldier, Er, son of Armenius of Pamphylia, who, having fallen in battle, came back to tell of his NDE. On the twelfth day after his 'death' he came to life as he was lying on the pyre. 'When he had revived, he told them what he had seen yonder. His soul, he said, departed from him, and journeyed along with a great company, until they arrived at a certain ghostly place where there were two openings in the earth side by side, and opposite them and above two openings in the heaven.' In the twentieth century, Carl Jung had his own NDE following a heart attack, during which he 'bathed in a glorious blue light' and witnessed 'the whole phantasmagoria of earthly existence'. The feeling of the self being outside, looking down at the lifeless body, which is typically the first stage of an NDE, is referred to as an 'out of body experience,' or OBE, for short (see Chapters 21 and 26).

Many who require more than mere faith to sustain their belief in an afterlife interpret the OBE/NDE with its joyful, carefree state of consciousness and the feeling of being propelled down a long tunnel toward a bright light, as a privileged glimpse of the hereafter. Doubters point out, however, that similar sensations occur in situations where people are not on the verge of death and that the elements of the OBE/NDE are components of many other subjective states that are widely accepted as hallucinatory. Most important of all is the fact that none of these NDE patients had actually died—or more properly, they had not reached the terminal state of brain death, which occurs many minutes after heartbeat and breathing cease. The fact that brains continue to work, albeit in a degraded fashion, during such traumatic incidents and that they can construct elaborate dream-like sequences that can be recalled after the person is resuscitated is not particularly surprising. As discussed in Chapters 19 and 26, it is well-documented in the scientific literature that various types of trauma can temporarily disrupt the brain's ability to construct our experience of external reality from sensory information, and that complex hallucinations that seem very real often ensue. The brain, like nature, abhors a vacuum and when trauma impedes the normal sensory input to consciousness, complex images from the brain's memory banks temporarily fill the void.

Those who want to believe in the dualistic notion that minds are spiritual and brains are physical—and hence the former can really leave and return to the body, and probably survive death as well—point to various anecdotes where some people who experience NDEs allegedly 'come back' from their OBEs with information that they supposedly could not have gained by any means other than having really been out of their bodies. In debates with prominent advocates of this position, the second author of this chapter was repeatedly confronted with the case of 'Maria' who, during a cardio-pulmonary arrest, supposedly left her body, floated outside the hospital and spied a red running shoe on the roof. So the story went, when she told this to sceptical listeners after her resuscitation, they ran to the roof and discovered the highly improbable shoe, just as Maria had described it. If this story were true, exactly as told and re-told in countless books and documentaries aiming prove the existence of an afterlife, it would indeed cause problems for those who say the OBE/NDE is nothing but a complex hallucination. Consequently, Barry Beyerstein and two of his students decided to investigate the Maria story that believers had repeatedly told him was the most compelling proof they can muster for their interpretation of the NDE.[22] Upon investigation, it emerged that the story had been greatly embellished in its numerous re-tellings and that most of the alleged 'facts' were debatable at best. There turned out to have been many prosaic ways in which Maria could have obtained her supposedly miraculous knowledge—starting with the fact that the running shoe (which wasn't red, by the way) had been on a plainly visible window ledge, not the roof as the canonical version of the story would have it.

The popular appeal of OBE/NDE stories is easy to understand. They are among the strongest support for mind-body dualism, which offers much comfort to those who want to believe that humans have an immaterial soul that survives death of the body. The experience can seem so real and emotionally charged that many who undergo it state that it fundamentally changed their metaphysical outlook. The prominent philosopher Sir Alfred Ayer, one of the most vocal atheists of his generation, had such an experience. It was so profoundly moving that it caused him to question his life-long rejection of the likelihood of an afterlife—at least until some of his scientific friends explained that NDEs can be explained by physiological mechanisms, after which he resumed his earlier stance. The contrary position that NDEs really involve the self or soul exiting the physical body, has recently been revamped by Pim van Lommel, a Dutch cardiologist who claims that about one in five people undergoing resuscitation following cardiac arrest report NDE episodes that cannot be accounted for by purely physiological interpretations. Most psychologists and neuroscientists are satisfied, however, that physiological interpretations adequately account for the observed phenomena.[20,21] Readers who want details of the debate on this issue between soul-brain dualists on the one hand and the vast majority of the neuroscience community on the other, can find them in a two-part article in *Skeptic* magazine dedicated to this controversy (Volume 18, issues no. 1 and 2).

Of course, the existence of adequate naturalistic explanations for the OBE/NDE do not disprove the possible existence of an afterlife. Doubters merely assert that these dramatic subjective experiences offer no scientific support for personal survival after death either. Those who accept the existence of an afterlife as an article of faith rather than scientific proof will receive no guff from the present authors, even if they cannot accept the belief in a hereafter themselves.

So what would it take to convince sceptics that OBEs really involve separation of mind and body? One such blockbuster would be positive results from an experiment that has been tried in a number surgical wards in the US and the UK. Patients are told before their procedures, 'If at any time you should feel like your mind has left its body and you are floating above, looking down on the proceedings, would you please float over to this ledge in the uppermost corner of the operating theatre, well above normal eye-level. On the ledge is a five-digit number. Please look at it, memorize it, and tell us what it is when you return to your body.' So far, no one has 'come back' with the number.

Coma Folklore

In movies such as *Kill Bill*, patients often awaken after long periods in a coma, appearing mentally alert and behaviourally ready to take on the world. Unfortunately, this is rarely the case in real life. When real patients emerge from a coma, they are usually confused, emaciated, and require months of physical therapy. Periodically, the media highlight a story of a patient who miraculously emerges from a lengthy coma, but this kind of uplifting saga often turns out to be misleading when it is explored more thoroughly. It is usually the case that the patient, although responding at a low physical and cognitive level, had in fact been interacting to some minimal degree with his/her environment for some time, prior to what media exuberance describes as a 'miraculous awakening.' Routine caregivers for these patients, who are said to be in a 'minimally conscious state' often failed to notice that small incremental improvements were gradually taking place.

By using the term 'coma' indiscriminately, media accounts often confuse neurological conditions that are quite different from one another and have different prospects for recovery (e.g., coma proper, minimally conscious state, locked-in syndrome, persistent vegetative state, brain death). Prevalent confusion about the meaning of these terms makes possible unlikely tales such as an instantaneous resuscitation from a deep coma state, thanks to some improbable stimulus. In a recent movie, a comatose mother is shocked into awakening by 'seeing' her son kissing a woman of whom she disapproves while they are visiting her in the hospital. This kind of unlikely scenario was typical of the sort of misrepresentation of coma in the movies that prompted Dr. Eelco Wijdicks to review thirty Hollywood and international films that depicted comatose people in their plots. Dr. Wijdicks, a neurologist at the Mayo Clinic, published his findings in a 2006 issue of the journal *Neurology* (www.mayoclinic.org/news2006-rst/3367.html). He had become concerned that a large portion of the public was developing unrealistic expectations based on these fictional accounts, leading families to make unwise decisions regarding loved ones who were in a comatose state and thereby placing excessive demands on the healthcare system. 'What we found was there were only two movies [out of thirty] that were accurate,' Dr. Wijdicks told reporters. 'Patients in a coma and their neurologists are portrayed inaccurately, and so are almost all awakenings after coma,' he continued.

Coma is defined as a deep state of unconsciousness from which the person cannot be aroused, even by intense stimulation. Comatose patients are not brain dead (which is indicated by a total lack of electrical activity in the higher cerebral centres of the brain), but their eyes remain closed and they cannot move or respond to the environment. A coma usually does not last for more than a few weeks, after which the patient typically begins to revive.

A persistent vegetative state (PVS) involves deeper depression of brain function, usually due to more severe brain damage, and it is more unremitting and long-lasting. Even though patients in a PVS lose all higher brain functions, their so-called 'vital functions' (breathing, circulation and digestion) remain relatively intact. This is because the latter are controlled by brain centers deep beneath the cerebral hemispheres, which are responsible for thought and self-awareness. With artificial feeding and other physical support, such patients have been known to remain technically 'alive' for a decade or more, but with none of the mental attributes that define human life as opposed to mere biological life. After three months in a PVS, regaining consciousness is highly unlikely—after a year, this virtually never occurs. Loved ones are often falsely encouraged, however, because spontaneous movements can occur and the eyes may open in response to external stimuli. Patients in a PVS may even occasionally grimace, cry, or laugh, but all this is purely reflexive. Although individuals in this state may appear to exhibit some awareness of their surroundings, such as tracking objects that move in front of them, they cannot speak or respond to commands and they show no objective evidence of higher cognitive functions. In the case of Terri Schiavo, where President Bush intervened to prevent the removal of her feeding tube as ordered by the courts, an autopsy was performed after higher courts intervened and the tube was removed. It showed that the incident that had caused her to lose consciousness more than fifteen years earlier had destroyed huge parts of the higher parts of her cerebral hemispheres that are essential for maintaining consciousness.

A persistent vegetative state is different from the so-called 'locked-in syndrome', a rare neurological disorder characterized by complete paralysis of all voluntary muscles except for those that control eye movements. It can result from traumatic brain injury, a drug overdose, or diseases that destroy the white matter of the brain or its blood supply. Patients with locked-in syndrome are mute and paralyzed, but mentally aware of their environment. In a scenario reminiscent of a Stephen King novel, they are able to think, remember, hear, see, and feel emotions, though they have no conventional way of expressing it. Communication may be possible, however, by using a code comprised of eye-blinks, sort of like the Morse code used by telegraphers.

Some people, perhaps buoyed by fictional accounts such as those criticised by Dr. Wijdicks, believe they can awaken patients from a coma or PVS by constantly stimulating them with familiar voices calling their name, playing their favourite music, parading familiar pictures in front of their opened eyelids, etc. This technique is called sensory coma stimulation or coma arousal therapy. Visual, auditory, smell, taste, touch, and body movement stimulation has been employed in this way, but researchers and medical professionals have differing, though mostly negative, opinions on its effectiveness. Proponents claim that with intense and repeated stimulation of this sort a patient will awaken earlier, and return to a higher level of functioning. A review of the small number of properly-conducted studies of this therapy concluded that there is no reliable evidence to support the effectiveness of multisensory stimulation programs for patients in a coma or vegetative state.[23]

A Hearty Mistake

In hopes of acquiring their valour, warriors in some pre-literate cultures used to eat the hearts of conspicuously brave opponents they had bested in battle. Similarly, the brains of particularly astute deceased elders were often ceremonially devoured to pass on their brilliance to the feasting descendents. The latter had at least figured out that it is the brain, not the heart, that is the organ of consciousness. English expressions such as 'a broken heart,' 'learning something by heart,' and Barry Goldwater's famous campaign slogan, 'In your heart you know he's right,' are holdovers from the pre-scientific era when many believed that the heart was the seat of the mind and soul. It would be hard to think of a more thoroughly discredited idea, but there are still some today who believe it and even claim that heart transplant patients come to resemble the organ donor psychologically—because, according to the believers, our thoughts and memories reside in tissues throughout the body. This is another case of belief in so-called 'sympathetic magic,' (things once in contact with another object allegedly acquire the latter's characteristics by magical 'sympathy' and these absorptions can, in turn, rub off on the next person or thing they encounter). This is described further in Chapter 16, which deals with the pseudoscience of handwriting analysis. It also relies on a form of sympathetic magic.

Although modern neuroscience has convincingly shown that laying down new memories or skills involves 'hardening in' selected synaptic pathways among large networks of active nerve cells (neurons) in the brain, rather than by creating 'memory molecules' inside individual neurons (let alone cells in other bodily organs), the idea of cellular memories, which could be transferred wholesale from a trained donor to a naïve recipient by cannibalism or surgical transplantation, refuses to die. Routine transplantation of hearts, lungs, livers, kidneys, appendages and, recently, even whole faces, has emboldened the mystically inclined who assert that pulp fiction novels and grade-B movies with plots involving transfer of knowledge, inclinations, and abilities in this way were more than mere fantasy. On his excellent sceptics' website, the philosopher Robert Carroll (http://www.skepdic.com/cellular.html) reviews many books and movies of this genre, such as *Brian's Song*, an allegedly true story:

> In that [1971] film, the 26-year old [football player, Brian] Piccolo (played by James Caan) is dying of cancer when Gayle Sayers (played by Billy Dee Williams), his friend and Chicago Bears teammate, visits him in the hospital. Piccolo had been given a transfusion and he asks Sayers if he had donated any blood. When Sayers [a man of colour] says yes, Piccolo remarks that that explains his [sudden and unprecedented] craving for chitlins.

Carroll traces many modern versions of the nonsensical idea that memories, motives, and personality are anything but functions of the brain to the novel, *Les Mains d'Orlac* by Maurice Renard (1875–1939). Therein, a concert pianist has his hands severed in an accident and receives the hands of a murderer in a transplant operation that would have been totally in the realm of science fiction in Renard's day. Upon recovery, the pianist is suddenly overcome by inexplicable murderous impulses. Renard's story found its way into several motion picture versions between 1935 and 1991. In one of the latest re-tellings, a prison psychiatrist suffers an amputation of his arm. He receives in replacement the arm of an executed psychopathic killer. The arm then develops a mind of its own.

Claims that such things are more than the stuff of pulp fiction received a boost from the assertions of Claire Sylvia, a heart-lung transplant recipient. In her fanciful book, *A Change of Heart*, Silvia tries to account for a number of changes in her personality and predilections after she recovered from her operation.[24] One was a sudden craving for beer, which she had previously hated. Silvia assumed that it must have acquired it along with the organs she received from her donor, an 18-year old male who died in a motorcycle accident.

While amateurs may be easily seduced by this kind of magical thinking, and be unaware of various prosaic explanations for the sorts of effects Sylvia experienced, it is more disconcerting when professionals with post-graduate degrees buy into such doubtful propositions. Paul Pearsall, who holds a doctoral degree in educational psychology, authored *The Heart's Code*, in which he adopts the idea of cellular memory to explain why the heart can allegedly think and remember and is able to transfer characteristics of the organ donor to the transplant recipient.[25] As if anything more were needed to discredit cellular memory, let it be noted that L. Ron Hubbard, the founder of that pernicious pseudoscience, Scientology, was a strong supporter of the concept. Robert Carroll, in his previously recommended website, offers a detailed and trenchant critique of this notion one would have thought would have been dispelled by the last hundred years of brain research. As professors whose job it is to relay to others, by more conventional means, what is in our brains, we take some comfort in the fact that devouring our cerebral parts would probably do would-be diners little good.

We all believe at least six strange things before breakfast

So far in this introduction, as throughout the rest of this book, we have concentrated primarily on tall tales that originated outside the scientific community, often the products of untutored pseudoscientists who adopted the outward trappings of legitimate sciences but not the rigorous methods most likely to produce reliable data. We must acknowledge, however, that genuine scientists, sometimes even brilliant ones, occasionally go off the rails too. Despite important contributions to their fields, for which they deserve to be remembered with respect, some famous scientists have tarnished their reputations by refusing to abandon discredited theories long after new discoveries had proved them wrong—or worse yet, mistakenly announced dubious 'breakthroughs' of their own, or lent their prestigious support to claptrap advanced by lesser lights.

Critics, such as the postmodernists and deconstructionists (a minority of academics from fields such as sociology and literary criticism who deny the existence of objective truth—see Haack[26]), resent the special deference our society accords to science. Extreme relativists of this stripe often point to scandals of the abovementioned sort as evidence that science, despite its claims to objectivity, is just one of many competing politically-driven bodies of opinion vying for social acceptance and power. E.g., the late philosopher Paul Feyrabend once asserted that science has no more special call on our belief than 'other ways of knowing' such as intuition and witchcraft. We, of course, reject such claims, and side with the compelling refutations of this view by scholars who, though admitting that science is an imperfect enterprise carried out by fallible human beings, assert that it is far more likely to lead to a true understanding of the world than the subjective, 'anything goes' methods advocated by the postmodernists.[26,27,28] It is the self-correcting nature of science, along with its insistence on objective, replicable evidence, that place it in starkest contrast to political and religious dogma with which the post-modernists wish to equate it. Nonetheless, just as members of other professions occasionally fail to live up to the highest ideals of their calling, scientists sometimes stray from the strict methods of observation, experimentation, and replication that were instituted by the pioneers of their craft. Their forebears invented these safeguards, of course, precisely to reduce our human tendency to jump to hasty conclusions that reinforce our pre-existing world view, enhance our self esteem, or merely make us feel good. The early practitioners of science realized the need to protect us all, themselves included, from our strong need to enchant ourselves.

As the psychologist James Alcock[29] reminds us, our brains were shaped by natural selection into machines for enhancing survival and reproduction, not for automatically seeking the truth. A false belief that happens to serve these evolutionary ends is more functional, biologically speaking, than a true one that lessens our fitness in the struggle to survive and reproduce. For similar reasons, quick-and-dirty reckoning techniques that arrive at an approximation of the right answer enough of the time were favoured over strictly rational ways of reasoning that require more time and effort.[30] This is not an entirely bad thing, because much of our decision-making in everyday life involves making an informed guess, since we rarely have the twin luxuries of complete information or sufficient time to ponder it in a strictly logical manner. Faced with the frequent need to guess-timate, quickly and on the basis of fragmentary data, our brains have evolved to think in quasi-logical ways that are generally useful but nonetheless likely to lead us to grossly wrong conclusions in many situations. As a consequence, superstitious beliefs abound because our brains come wired for magical thinking as the 'default mode'.[29] Critical thinking and logical ways of deliberating are add-ons that must be painstakingly learned. They are fragile and easily over-ridden when there is prestige, monetary gain or emotional satisfaction to be won by accepting a false but self-serving belief. Even those who have learned that correlation does not imply causation, or that we need control groups to rule out possible alternative explanations, and that we must have objective measurements that are carefully checked by others in order to avoid falling prey to expectancy and the will to believe, are prone to abandon such cautionary protections when the tangible or the psychological pay-offs are sufficiently valuable.[29,30] It is deviations of this sort that can often be found when famous scientists venture into pseudoscientific pursuits.

The psychologist Ray Hyman[31] has long been fascinated by the clever ways in which very smart people can fool themselves and remain quite unaware of the fact they have done so. Both errors of reasoning, such as those described above, and more subtle emotional pay-offs can often be found to underlie these case histories. In some instances, such as several of the famous scientists who endorsed mediums and spiritualism in the 19th century (e.g., Sir William Crookes, Alfred Russel Wallace, Sir Oliver Lodge), the motive was largely to find a way of salvaging their Christian beliefs in the face of the advances of science that were beginning to raise serious doubts about the literal truth of the Bible.[32] In many instances it was a fervent desire for proof to bolster their faith that dead loved ones continued to exist, happy and secure, in the afterlife.

In other cases, national pride played a role, such as when the distinguished French physicist Rene Blondlot felt driven to match the German, Roentgen's recent discovery of X-rays with his own, imaginary N-rays (critics were unanimously of the opinion that it was self-delusion rather than fraud on Blondlot's part). Likewise many top palaeontologists and anatomists in the UK endorsed the transparent hoax of Piltdown man, in part because Britain had no comparable fossil finds to match prestigious German, French and Chinese discoveries in the race to find 'the missing link'. Again, the sincerity of those such as Sir Arthur Smith Woodward, Sir Eliot Grafton Smith, Sir Arthur Keith, Sir Ray Lankaster, and many other luminaries who endorsed the crudely faked fossil remains has not been questioned.[31] That such accomplished men of science could have failed to notice for so long the blatant signs of chicanery staring them in the face, speaks to the power of the psychological factors, discussed above, to shape our beliefs—when we want to believe, that is.[31] We should all heed Bertrand Russell's warning: 'What is wanted is not the will to believe, but the will to find out, which is the exact opposite.'

Likewise, personal ambition often plays a part when some of the best and brightest scientists run amok. A number of these excellent researchers who astonished their colleagues by championing highly questionable theories were lucky enough to achieve well-deserved fame early in their careers. The strong desire to repeat the adulation and emotional satisfaction of their early triumphs mixed dangerously with overconfidence bred by years of effusive praise for the astuteness that led to their earlier breakthroughs. This can nurture the fatal flaw of invulnerability—becoming incapable of believing that someone as obviously brilliant as one's self could be mistaken. This often produces embarrassing lapses, obvious to others but oblivious to the perpetrator, such as tortuous special pleading to explain away clearly disconfirming evidence amassed by fair and competent critics. Just think about the simple-mindedness shown by the otherwise brilliant chemist Kary B. Mullis (Nobel Prize, 1993) who confessed in his autobiography that he began 'to think about astrology after a ten-year-old neighbour correctly classified [him] as a Capricorn'. Or consider the resolute Brian Josephson (Nobel Prize for Physics in 1973) who uncritically endorses telepathy. An important lesson here is that brilliance in one area does not automatically confer equal perspicacity in other areas where one has failed to do one's homework. It is interesting that we rarely see psychologists trying to advise physical scientists about their own fields of specialization, but the latter often feel qualified to blunder into conceptual minefields in the realm of psychology. As we lamented earlier, many people, including highly talented ones, tend to think that naïve introspection is all that is needed to understand how our minds work.

Tragic blindspots of this kind have also been suggested to explain the odd behaviour that occurred in the careers of two giants of 20th-century science. The two-time Nobel laureate Linus Pauling went to his grave dismissing numerous failures by others to confirm his belief that massive doses of vitamin C could alleviate cancer and the common cold. In a similar case of hubris, the French immunologist Jacques Benveniste literally rewrote the textbooks in his field with discoveries very early in his career, but he died an object of pity and ridicule in the scientific community for his espousal of the thoroughly discredited field of homeopathy. Colleagues speculated that hunger for another achievement of stellar magnitude may have helped steer him into support for this bizarre treatment. The brainchild of a German doctor, Samuel Hahnemann (1755–1843), homeopathy asserts that in order to cure a disease, one must take a substance that would actually cause the symptoms one wishes to alleviate. However, this substance must first be diluted, one part to ten parts of pure water, and then shaken (or 'secussed' as homeopathists say) exactly one hundred times. The resulting potion must then be diluted again in a similar 1:10 fashion and secussed once more. According to Hahnemann, it works better if this is conducted in moonlight. This procedure is repeated dozens of times until the statistical probability that there is even one molecule of the original substance in the elixir is virtually zero. Hahnemann could not have been expected to know this but, ever since Amedeo Avogadro (1776–1856), every high school chemistry student should have been well aware of the fact. To accept that such a dilute solution could have any chemical effect at all, let alone the opposite of the one it would have had if taken in concentrated form, one would have to abandon virtually every important principle of modern chemistry. Nonetheless, some positive clinical reports made it into the medical literature. They have been highly criticised on methodological grounds and a 2005 meta-analysis published in *The Lancet* declared that placebo effects alone could account for these apparent successes.[33] An accompanying editorial in the journal declared, perhaps over-optimistically given the will to believe, 'the end of homeopathy.'

We are guilty of similar sins when we praise in skeptical publications unsubstantiated claims solely because they come from our friends; cases in point are Susan Blakemore's memes or Richard Wiseman's luck factor. Fascinating as these ideas may be, are they supported by the kind of evidence that we would demand for propositions coming from authors outside our own circle of trusted colleagues?

Scientific breakthroughs almost always result from patient preparation and long, hard work, rather than from blinding illumination in a moment of creativity. Moreover, as we said earlier, because there is so much to know before one can usefully contribute to a field, scientists can be expert in only a minuscule field of knowledge. Nonetheless, it is widely believed that most major advances come from inspired outsiders whose genius is ridiculed by the hidebound and uncomprehending establishment. But, as Carl Sagan said, '... the fact that some geniuses were laughed at does not imply that all who are laughed at are geniuses. They laughed at Columbus, they laughed at Fulton, they laughed at the Wright brothers. But they also laughed at Bozo the Clown.' The bottom line is that we must leave the door sufficiently ajar so that the oddballs who are the rare but true unsung geniuses, the ones who will revolutionize our view of the world, will be able to present their data to the scientific community. If the case is good enough, it will eventually be accepted, but because scientists are human beings, not always as quickly or as magnanimously as it should.

Enough of belittling

If you previously believed some of the tall tales you are about to encounter in this book, do not feel bad. We all carry around with us a plethora of false beliefs, especially if we cannot or will not subject them to careful scrutiny and demand for evidence. Many times, we simply accept dubious beliefs on presumed authority, and there are many who have a stake in convincing us to believe. Research has shown that sceptics are just a susceptible to being fooled, and to fooling themselves, as believers. The same goes, as we have just seen, for exceptionally smart people. The main difference between sceptics and believers is that the former realize how vulnerable we all are and try to take precautions against being fooled. If sceptics fail to engage their critical thinking abilities, because it would be so nice if the proposition were true or too threatening to accept that it isn't, they are as likely as anyone else to waltz gleefully down the garden path. As a general rule of thumb, it is always wise to keep in mind that if it sounds too good to be true, it probably *is* too good to be true.

So, now relax, magnetise your wine, and enjoy the rest of the book.

References

1. **Della Sala S**, ed. *Mind myths: Exploring everyday mysteries of the mind and brain.* John Wiley and Sons, Chichester, UK. 1999.
2. **Lilienfeld S, Lynn S, Beyerstein B.** *The fountain of myth.* Blackwell, London, UK. To appear 2007.
3. **Zinberg NE.** *Drug, set, and setting: The basis for controlled intoxicant use.* Yale University Press, New Haven. 1984. (available on-line at: http://www.druglibrary.org/schaffer/lsd/zinberg.htm)
4. **Alexander BK.** The disease and adaptive models of addiction: A framework evaluation. *Journal of Drug Issues*, 1987; 17:47–66. (summary available at: http://en.wikipedia.org/wiki/Rat_Park).
5. **Hadaway P, Beyerstein BL, Kimball M.** Addiction as an adaptive response: Is smoking a functional behaviour? *Journal of Drug Issues*, 1986; **16**:371–390. (Available on-line at: www.sfu.ca/psyc/faculty/beyerstein)
6. **Beyerstein BL.** Whence cometh the myth that we only use ten percent of our brains? In S Della Sala, ed. *Mind myths: Exploring everyday mysteries of the mind and brain.* John Wiley and Sons, Chichester, UK. 1999:1–24.
7. **Angela P.** Quanto cervello usiamo? *Scienza & Paranormale*, 2006; **65**:16–17.
8. **Beyerstein BL.** Pseudoscience and the brain: Tuners and tonics for aspiring superhumans. In, S. Della Sala, ed. *Mind myths: Exploring everyday mysteries of the mind and brain.* John Wiley and Sons, Chichester, UK. 1999: 59–82.
9. **Druckman D, Swets J,** eds. *Enhancing human performance: Issues, theories, and techniques.* National Academy Press, Washington, DC. 1988.
10. **Pratkanis AR.** How to sell a pseudoscience. *Skeptical Inquirer*, 1995; **19**:19–25.

11. **Moore TE.** Subliminal self-help auditory tapes: An empirical test to perceptual consequences. *Canadian Journal of Behavioral Science*, 1995; **27**:9–20.

12. **Merikle PM, Skanes, H.** Subliminal self-help audio tapes: A search for placebo effects. *Journal of Applied Psychology*, 1992; **77**: 772–776.

13. **Pratkanis, AR, Eskenazi, J, Greenwald AG.** What you expect is what you believe (but not necessarily what you get): A test of the effectiveness of submliminal self-help audio tapes. *Basic and Applied Social Psychology*, 1990; **15**:251–276.

14. **Weinstein EA.** *Woodrow Wilson: A medical and psychological biography*. Princeton University Press, Princeton, NJ. 1981.

15. **Freud S, Bullitt WC.** *Thomas Woodrow Wilson, twenty-eighth president of the United States: A Psychological Study*. Weidenfeld and Nicolson, London. 1967.

16. **Marshall JC, Halligan, PW.** Blindsight and insight in visuo-spatial neglect. *Nature*, 1988; **336**: 766–767.

17. **Weiskrantz L.** Blindsight revisited. *Current Opinion in Neurobiology*, 1996; **6**: 215–220.

18. **Stoerig P, Cowey A.** Blindsight in man and monkey. *Brain*, 1997; **120**: 535–559.

19. **Beyerstein BL.** The myth of Alpha Consciousness. *Skeptical Inquirer*, 1985; **10**: 42–59. (Available on-line at: www.sfu.ca/psyc/faculty/beyerstein)

20. **Blackmore S.** Is meditation good for you? *The New Scientist*, 6 July, 1991; 30–33; 61.

21. **Blackmore S.** *Dying to live: Near-death experiences*. Prometheus Books, Amherst, NY. 1993.

22. **Ebbern H, Mulligan S, Beyerstein BL.** Maria's near-death experience: Waiting for the other shoe to drop. *Skeptical Inquirer*, 1996; **20**: 27–33. (Available on-line at: www.sfu.ca/psyc/faculty/beyerstein)

23. **Lombardi F, Taricco M, De Tanti A, Telaro E, Liberati A.** Sensory stimulation of brain-injured individuals in coma or vegetative state: Results of a Cochrane systematic review. *Clinical Rehabilitation*. 2002; **16**:464–72.

24. **Sylvia C.** *A change of heart: A memoir*. Warner Books, New York. 1997.

25. **Pearsall P.** *The heart's code*. Broadway Books, New York. 1999.

26. **Haack S.** Science, scientism, anti-science in the Age of Preposterism. *Skeptical Inquirer*. 1997; **21**: 37–42. (Available on-line at: http://www.csicop.org/si/9711/preposterism.html).

27. **Gross PR, Levitt N.** *Higher superstition: The academic left and its quarrels with sfience*. Johns Hopkins University Press, Baltimore. 1998.

28. **Sokal A, Bricmont J.** *Intellectual impostures*. (second edition) Profile Books, London. 2003.

29. **Alcock JE.** The Belief Engine. *Skeptical Inquirer*. 1995; **19**: 255–263. (Available on-line at: http://www.csicop.org/si/9505/belief.html).

30. **Sutherland S.** *Irrationality: Why we don't think straight*. Rutgers. University Press. New Brunswick, NJ. 1992.

31. **Hyman R.** How smart scientists goof. *Humanist Perspectives*. (in press, 2006)

32. **Alcock, JE.** Parapsychology: Science of the anomalous or search for the soul? *Behavioral and brain sciences*, 1987; **10**: 553–565.

33. **Shang A, Huwiler-Muntener K, Nartey L.** Are the clinical effects of homoeopathy placebo effects? Comparative study of placebo-controlled trials of homoeopathy and allopathy. *Lancet*, 2005; **366**:726–32.

Where do tall tales about the mind and the brain come from?

Chapter 1

Cognitive factors underlying paranormal beliefs and experiences

Christopher C. French and Krissy Wilson

Introduction

Interest and belief in the paranormal and related phenomena are today as high as ever, and may, if anything, be on the increase. In a poll published in *USA Today*, Yankelovich Partners compared levels of belief in 1997 with those recorded in 1976.[1] The results, shown in Table 1.1, indicated that levels of belief in the paranormal appeared to be on the increase between these two dates. This trend was confirmed in a more recent Gallup poll, the results of which were released in 2001. In the last decade of the previous millennium, increases in levels of belief in the American population were noted for a wide range of paranormal beliefs including haunted houses, ghosts, witches, extraterrestrial visitations, psychic healing, telepathy and clairvoyance.[2]

Despite such high levels of belief, sceptics remain unconvinced by the scientific evidence put forward in support of paranormal claims. It is clear, however, that most members of the general public are not basing their opinions upon such scientific evidence in the first place. Instead, maintenance of such beliefs is more likely to be due to the influence of the media, of testimony from trusted others and from personal experiences.[3]

The generally positive and uncritical media coverage of paranormal claims and reports of all manner of anomalous events and experiences may have a powerful influence over a largely uncritical audience. Television programmes, such as *The X Files*, *Most Haunted* and *Crossing Over*, present a seductive and intriguing view that we can talk to our dead relatives, that we can move objects with the power of the mind alone and that we can foresee the future. Seldom do these programmes provide a critical or sceptical approach. The sheer volume of such programmes creates an atmosphere of acceptance that paranormal phenomena must and do exist.

A second, and perhaps more persuasive, factor underlying belief in the paranormal is that these beliefs are often based on personal experiences, either our own or those of trusted others. Indeed, evidence has shown that there is a clear and established correlation between belief in and experience of the paranormal.[4–6] As one might expect, not everyone who believes in the paranormal claims to have had personal experience of it, but a sizeable minority do. The fact that this holds in all known societies can only mean one of two

Table 1.1 Percentage of American population samples responding positively to the question 'Which if any of the following do you believe at least to some degree?' in 1976 and 1997.

Belief	1976	1997
Spiritualism	12%	52%
Faith healing	10%	45%
Astrology	17%	37%
UFOs	24%	30%
Reincarnation	9%	25%
Fortune telling	4%	14%

1976 $n = 8709$; 1997 $n = 1000$; margin of error $= \pm 3$–5%.

things: either at least some of these experiences are based upon genuine paranormal phenomena, or people are misinterpreting non-paranormal situations as involving forces currently beyond the traditional scientific worldview.

One possible factor underlying such misinterpretations is the potential role played by cognitive biases. Cognition in its broadest sense relates to all mental activities that are involved in the processing of information and includes thinking, problem solving, memory and perception. Although our cognitive systems are the most sophisticated that we know of, it is also recognized that we are prone to various cognitive biases that can systematically distort our thinking. In a paper written over a decade ago, French[3] presented an overview of the way in which cognitive biases might lead people to believe that paranormal forces do exist even if in fact they do not. Research has produced considerable support for this notion.[7–18] He also considered the possibility that believers in the paranormal may be more prone to such biases than non-believers. In 1992, he concluded that, 'the limited evidence available suggests that this is a real possibility' (p. 298). This chapter will provide an overview of the additional research that has been carried out in this area since the early 1990s.

Review of relevant cognitive factors

The reader should bear in mind, when reading the following, that any attempt to categorize the relevant studies in this area under convenient subheadings will inevitably be something of an oversimplification. It is recognized that many of the studies reported could have been included under more than one subheading and that the categories themselves are by no means mutually exclusive or comprehensive. However, it is hoped that the attempt to categorize the studies will at least enhance the readability of the review. It should also be borne in mind that it is a mistake to conceive of paranormal belief as a unidimensional entity. Different cognitive biases are likely to be correlated with different aspects of paranormal belief and experience.

Critical thinking

It has been suggested that believers in the paranormal tend to perform poorly on tests of critical thinking. However, the evidence is mixed. Royalty,[19] for example, correlated scores from the Cornell Critical Thinking Test[20] and scores from the Belief in the Paranormal Scale.[21] The Cornell Critical Thinking Test is a comprehensive, 52-item, multiple-choice test that assesses performance on a variety of skills including, induction, deduction, value judgements and credibility. Although a significant correlation was found between belief in and experience of the paranormal, belief was not shown to be a significant predictor of performance on the critical thinking test.

Roe[22] rightly criticized, on methodological grounds, earlier studies that claimed that believers were poorer at critical thinking than non-believers.[23] In his own study, participants were asked to rate brief experimental reports, matched for study quality, that were either sympathetic or unsympathetic towards parapsychology. No differences were found between believers and non-believers in terms of critical thinking, but there was an overall tendency for participants to give lower quality ratings to studies where the results were incongruent with their own beliefs. Overall then, there is no clear evidence that believers in the paranormal are inferior to non-believers in terms of critical thinking ability.

Syllogistic reasoning

A great deal of experimental evidence exists that conclusively demonstrates that human beings are prone to systematic errors for certain types of deductive reasoning.[24,25] Given that poor reasoning may lead us to draw faulty conclusions from available evidence, it has been suggested that believers in the paranormal may be poorer at deductive reasoning than non-believers. One approach to this issue has involved the use of syllogistic reasoning tasks. Typically, researchers will use a syllogistic reasoning questionnaire and correlate the results with scores from a measure of belief in the paranormal. A syllogism is a structured logical argument consisting of two assumed or given propositions that function as premises, followed by a third which functions as a conclusion. A typical example would be:

All men are mortal.

No gods are mortal.

Therefore no men are gods.

An example with paranormal content might be:

All cheats are immoral.

This psychic is a cheat.

Therefore this psychic is immoral.

The syllogisms above are examples of categorical reasoning, in that the premises and conclusions deal with entities belonging to or excluded from particular categories. Another type of syllogism is known as a conditional syllogism. An example would be:

If it is raining then the pavement will get wet.

It is raining.

Therefore the pavement will get wet.

It is trivially easy to affirm that the reasoning in this example is valid, that is to say that the conclusion must be true if the premises are true. However, other examples are not so obvious. People are particularly prone to make the error known as affirmation of the consequent, illustrated by the following example:

If the government is engaged in a cover-up of the existence of UFOs then they will deny that UFO landings have taken place.

The government does deny that UFO landings have taken place.

Therefore the government is engaged in a cover-up of the existence of UFOs.

People often erroneously judge that syllogisms such as that presented above are valid. The error made here is based upon interpreting the 'if' to mean 'if and only if'. Although the government would indeed deny that UFO landings were taking place if they were engaged in a conspiracy to conceal the existence of UFOs, there are alternative reasons why they might deny that UFO landings have taken place, the most obvious being that no such landings have in fact occurred.

In studies of syllogistic reasoning, participants are typically presented with sets of syllogisms and asked to judge whether or not they reflect valid or invalid reasoning. Wierzbicki[26] produced some support for the argument that believers in the paranormal are poorer at deductive reasoning when he found a significant correlation between paranormal belief, as assessed using the Belief in the Paranormal Scale,[27] and the number of reasoning errors made on syllogisms with paranormal content. However, this correlation did not hold for non-paranormal syllogisms. Irwin,[28] on the other hand, failed to find any difference between believers and non-believers on a syllogistic reasoning task regardless of the syllogism type, having assessed paranormal belief using Tobacyk's Revised Paranormal Belief Scale.[29]

Irwin suggested that previous studies indicating a negative correlation between levels of paranormal belief and performance on reasoning and critical thinking tasks may have produced biased results due to the context in which they were carried out. If the researchers carrying out the studies were known to have a sceptical approach to paranormal claims, it may be that the more intelligent amongst their participants would be less forthcoming in admitting to their own paranormal beliefs. Since Irwin is known to adopt a more sympathetic attitude towards paranormal claims, his student participants may have felt more comfortable in admitting the strength of their beliefs. Thus, in Wierzbicki's study, the brighter students would tend to appear to be more sceptical, even if in reality they were not, and would also do better on the syllogistic reasoning task simply because they were more intelligent. No such artefactual bias would affect Irwin's results.

Although Irwin's suggestion is interesting and plausible, there are other possible reasons for his failure to replicate Wierzbicki, as pointed out by Roberts and Seager.[30] In particular, Roberts and Seager criticize the syllogistic reasoning task used by Irwin, pointing out that it differed in important ways from that used by Wierzbicki. Using a brief conditional reasoning task of their own design, consisting of both abstract and paranormal syllogisms, Roberts and Seager replicated the negative correlation found by Wierzbicki between paranormal belief, as assessed using the Belief in the Paranormal Scale of Jones et al.,[27] and syllogistic reasoning ability for both types of syllogism. The fact that they used the same scale to measure paranormal belief as that used by Wierzbicki raises the possibility that the choice of scale used to measure paranormal belief may be critical.

However, a recent study by Watt and Wiseman[31] has shown that at least some experimenters can produce results which show a negative correlation between paranormal belief, as assessed by the same as scale that used by Irwin (Tobacyk's Revised Paranormal Belief Scale), and a subset of the same syllogisms that Irwin used. Because of time constraints, Watt and Wiseman had to omit some of the syllogisms used by Irwin. In light of the fact that Wierzbicki only obtained significant correlations with syllogisms that had paranormal content, it seems odd that it was this type of syllogism that Watt and Wiseman chose to omit. Watt and Wiseman's experiment was an attempt to test the idea that different experimenters might obtain different patterns of results even though they were following identical procedures. Caroline Watt is known to be sympathetic towards paranormal claims, whereas Richard Wiseman is a well-known sceptic. The two experimenters did indeed produce different patterns of results, as Irwin might have predicted. Unfortunately for Irwin's hypothesis, it was the sceptic Wiseman who failed to find any correlation between paranormal belief and problems with syllogistic reasoning, whereas the more pro-paranormal Watt found the largest negative correlation between these two variables that has been reported to date. This is the exact opposite of what Irwin's hypothesis predicts. Note that Merla-Ramos[32] also found a negative correlation between paranormal belief and syllogistic reasoning ability, but only for syllogisms with paranormal or religious content, not for neutral syllogisms.

Smith, Foster and Stovin[33] report another attempt to test Irwin's hypothesis regarding the possible relationship between testing context and participants' willingness to express their true levels of paranormal belief. They reasoned that if Irwin's hypothesis was correct, we might expect to find that more intelligent participants would be more willing to give pro-paranormal responses on Tobacyk and Milford's Paranormal Belief Scale in a pro-paranormal context and less willing in an anti-paranormal context, producing relatively more positive and negative correlations between intelligence and expressed paranormal belief in the pro- and anti-paranormal contexts, respectively. Intelligence was measured using the Advanced Progressive Matrices Test,[34] and then context was manipulated by asking participants to read a pro-paranormal or an anti-paranormal statement prior to completing the Paranormal Belief Scale. A third group of participants, acting as a control group, did not receive any statement regarding the paranormal. As predicted, the context did have a significant effect upon the expressed levels of paranormal belief, with the highest levels being reported for the pro-paranormal context and the lowest for the anti-paranormal. However, context did not affect the correlations reported between intelligence and paranormal belief, as would be predicted upon the basis of Irwin's hypothesis. In fact, intelligence was found to be negatively correlated with paranormal belief in all three groups, significantly so in all but the control group. Such negative correlations between paranormal belief and intelligence have been reported elsewhere,[35] but other studies have reported no correlation between intelligence and paranormal belief[36] and some have even reported positive correlations.[27] Irwin[37,38] presents a convincing case that there is no straightforward correlation between lower intelligence and paranormal belief.

In summary, it appears that the correlation between paranormal belief and a deficit in syllogistic reasoning is fairly robust, with only two published failed attempts to date to find such an effect (one from a believer, one from a sceptic). Irwin's interesting hypothesis regarding the possible effects of context has fared less well in empirical tests.

Probabilistic reasoning

In addition to our problems with certain aspects of syllogistic reasoning, we are also very poor at estimating probabilities in a variety of everyday situations. This could be another important factor in leading people to misinterpret certain situations as involving paranormal forces when in fact the explanation lies elsewhere. We often hear reports of people having dreams that then appear to come true. Is it possible that dreams can sometimes provide us with a mysterious insight into future events in defiance of the conventional scientific worldview? Another fairly common experience is that of thinking about a friend that one has not seen for a long time, only to be interrupted by a telephone call from that very person. Does this really provide evidence of a telepathic link? Maybe it does, maybe it does not. If people are not very good at estimating probabilities, it follows that they may well be reluctant to accept the sceptic's standard response to such stories: 'It was just a coincidence!' But maybe the sceptics are right.

John Allen Paulos,[39] an American mathematician, illustrates the fact that we should expect many reports of apparently 'precognitive' dreams every year purely on the basis of coincidence. For the sake of argument, let us suppose that we define a dream as 'apparently precognitive' if the chances of the dream matching some future event in one's life are as low as one chance in 10 000. Surely, all of us would be impressed if we were the person who had such a dream? Again, we will simplify matters by assuming that each person has one dream per night (in fact, we all have a lot more). The probability that any one dream will not be apparently precognitive is high (0.9999). The probability that over a whole year one will not have a dream that appears to predict the future is given by

$$(0.9999)^{365} = 0.9642(\text{approximately})$$

In other words, even over a whole year, the chances are that you will not have such a dream. However, around 3.6 per cent of the population will have at least one such dream! This amounts to 9 million people in the USA alone. Furthermore, any single person, over a 19-year period, will have a slightly better than even chance of one such dream. Even if you think that 1 in 10 000 is too high, and opted say for odds of 1 in 100 000 before classing a dream as 'precognitive', you would still have 900 000 reports per year in the USA without any need to invoke psychic powers whatsoever. In fact, of course, it is likely that other non-paranormal factors are often involved in people having ostensibly precognitive dreams, e.g. dreaming of an elderly relative dying when one already knows that they are ill.

Blackmore and Troscianko[40] found that generally believers in the paranormal performed more poorly on various tasks of probability estimation compared with non-believers, sometimes significantly so. Amongst the tasks that they gave to their participants was the famous 'Birthday Problem': how many randomly selected people would you need to have at a party to have a 50:50 chance that two of them share the same birthday (ignoring year)? The correct answer is 23, which comes as a surprise to most people. Matthews and Blackmore[41] presented evidence supporting the idea that people are often inappropriately surprised by coincidences such as this because the intuitive way in which they estimate probability is based upon an incorrect application of linear scaling. However, no differences were found in this study between believers and non-believers in the paranormal. Roberts and Seager, despite finding that believers were poorer on syllogistic reasoning tasks as reported above, failed to find differences between believers and non-believers amongst student participants on probabilistic reasoning tasks.

Blackmore[42] attempted to test the 'probability misjudgement' theory of paranormal belief further by means of a large-scale newspaper survey with 6238 respondents. She hypothesized that individuals who underestimate the probability that something that is true for them would also be true of others may be more likely to be impressed by statements made by psychics that just happened to be true for them (e.g. 'There is someone called Jack in your family'). She presented 10 statements that might be produced by psychics and asked people to state whether they were true for the respondent personally and to estimate the number that would be true for other people. Her hypothesis, that believers would tend to underestimate the number of statements true for other people more than disbelievers, was not supported. Unexpectedly, however, it was found that believers did claim that more of the statements were true for them personally.

Musch and Ehrenberg[35] investigated the relationship between probability misjudgement and paranormal belief, but also considered the possibility that if any relationship were to be found it might simply reflect the possibility that both paranormal belief and problems with probabilistic reasoning might both be associated with lower general cognitive ability. They gave their student participants at the University of Bonn a probabilistic reasoning test battery and a paranormal belief scale partly based upon previously used scales. Cognitive ability was assessed in terms of the secondary school completion grade achieved by each student. A significant correlation was found between paranormal belief scores and error rates on the probabilistic reasoning battery, but this correlation disappeared when cognitive ability was controlled for. The authors concluded that paranormal beliefs were more likely to be due to lower general cognitive ability rather than specific difficulties with probabilistic reasoning (but note that, as previously stated, Irwin[37,38] has cast serious doubt upon the reliability of such a negative correlation between intelligence and paranormal belief).

Bressan[43] presented data that she feels undermine the idea that people interpret coincidences as paranormal because of problems with probability estimation. Across two studies, she asked participants to complete a series of probability problems, a questionnaire about the frequency of meaningful coincidences in the participants' lives and a specially constructed measure of paranormal belief. Analyses were carried out both for the samples as a whole as well as for student and non-student subsamples. Although performance on several of the types of probability problem was indeed found to correlate negatively with paranormal belief across the entire sample, the correlations typically held for the non-student subsample but not for the students. A significant correlation between paranormal belief and self-reported frequency of meaningful coincidences, on the other hand, was found to hold regardless of educational level. Furthermore, the frequency of meaningful coincidences did not correlate with scores on the probability estimation task, as would be predicted by probability misjudgement theories of paranormal belief. Bressan argues that the results are most parsimoniously explained by assuming that more frequent experience of coincidences and a more biased representation of randomness are both the result of a stronger tendency to find connections between separate events in believers in the paranormal compared with non-believers.

If Bressan's suggestion is correct, it would account for the results reported by Wiseman and Smith[44] using tests that did not directly involve probability estimation. Two experiments were reported, both based upon conceptually similar designs. In the first experiment, participants were asked to rate so-called 'target' and 'control' horoscopes in terms of how accurate and specific they were deemed to be. The target horoscopes were said to be based upon the participant's birth details whereas the control horoscopes were not. In fact, all horoscopes were randomly allocated. One possibility is that participants who believe in astrology would judge the so-called target horoscopes as more accurate and specific than the so-called controls because they were motivated to find support for their belief in astrology. An alternative possibility, in line with Bressan's suggestion, is that believers may give a higher rating to the target readings than controls simply because they are better at finding connections, in this case between the readings and their own lives. If this explanation is correct, we would expect them to also give higher ratings to the control horoscopes than non-believers. The results of Wiseman and Smith's first experiment clearly supported the latter explanation. These two competing explanations were further explored in a second experiment in which participants were asked to judge the outcome of a fictional ESP experiment. They were told that a psychic had been asked to divine the contents of a sealed envelope containing a drawing. They

Fig. 1.1 *Cartoon by Steve Yesson.*

were presented with the drawings made by the fictional psychic along with a 'target' picture that the psychic had allegedly been concentrating upon and a 'control' picture. In fact, the choice of label as 'target' and 'control' was randomly determined. Once again, the believers gave higher ratings for correspondence to the target picture than did the non-believers, but once again they also gave higher ratings for the control picture than did the non-believers. Both sets of results are in line with Bressan's suggestion and not in line with an explanation in terms of belief bias.

In summary, the probability misjudgement theories of paranormal belief have received at best modest support from empirical investigations. Some studies have failed to find differences between believers and non-believers with respect to probability judgement and, in some of the studies that have found such differences, there are alternative explanations in terms of both paranormal belief and problems with probability judgement both being correlated with a third factor (e.g. intelligence or the tendency to find connections between separate events).

Biased concepts of randomness and meaningfulness

A number of the studies referred to in the previous section included in their batteries of probabilistic reasoning tasks attempts to replicate an effect first investigated by Brugger *et al.*[45] These investigators had argued that believers may be more likely than non-believers to read meaning into random patterns and sequences and thus be more likely to be impressed by everyday coincidences. Such coincidences would seem to believers to require some explanation other than mere chance and they would therefore be more prone to opt for a paranormal explanation. One aspect of a biased representation of randomness is that people typically avoid repetition of elements when trying to generate random sequences. In three experiments, Brugger *et al.* showed that believers demonstrate this repetition-avoidance bias to a greater extent than non-believers in tasks involving both the recognition and generation of random strings. Attempts at replication have sometimes been successful[35,43,46,47] and have sometimes failed,[40,48] possibly due to variations in methodology.

Brugger and colleagues have developed the notion that paranormal belief is associated with the tendency to see meaning in more or less random patterns.[49,50] Two types of error can be made when searching for patterns and meaning in the world around us. The first (type I error or false alarms) is to see meaning in randomness due to the adoption of very loose criteria in assessing evidence. Believers in the paranormal are more likely to be prone to such errors, but on the positive side this cognitive style is likely to be associated with creativity. According to Brugger, the right hemisphere is dominant for such thinking due to its tendency to make remote associations (see next section). Gianotti *et al.*[51] produced evidence showing that believers in the paranormal produce more original responses than non-believers on a word association task. The second type of error that can be made is to miss meaning and patterns that really do exist (type II error). Sceptics, with strict criteria for assessing evidence, are more likely to make this type of error. The claim that believers require less evidence before they jump to a conclusion is supported by evidence from a variety of sources, and arguably is consistent with evidence that delusions are generally associated with a bias towards jumping too readily to conclusions.[52]

Brugger and Graves[53] produced support for this model using a computer game in which a mouse was moved from the lower left corner of the screen to a trap in the upper right corner. At that point, participants were either rewarded with cheese or punished by the closing of the trap. Participants were asked to determine 'how the game worked' over 100 trials. Unbeknown to them, rewards and punishments were entirely based upon the delay between starting and finishing a trial. If it was less than 4 s, they were punished. Believers in the paranormal tested fewer hypotheses during the task but ended up believing more.

Perceptual biases

Perception itself can often be influenced by our expectations, particularly in less than perfect observational conditions. Obvious examples include the tendency to see threatening ghostly forms in dark spooky houses. Some people might more readily conclude that they had seen something in such viewing conditions, whereas others might be more cautious and withhold judgement. Again, we might expect differences to be found between believers and disbelievers in this respect. Blackmore and Moore[54] have presented evidence supporting this in a study involving the brief presentation of a series of pictures ranging from indistinct blobs to clear outlines of identifiable objects. After each brief presentation, participants were asked if they had seen anything and, if so, what. As predicted, believers reported seeing forms earlier in the series than disbelievers, but were in fact no more accurate in their attempts at identification.

Brugger *et al.*[55] presented random dot patterns briefly to the left or right visual fields, telling participants that the experiment was an investigation of subliminal perception and that about half of the stimuli would contain some meaningful information. Participants were not required to report what they had seen. Believers reported seeing 'something meaningful' on significantly more trials than disbelievers, and it was also found that left visual field presentations led to more such claims than right visual field presentations. Brugger *et al.* argue that this suggests a possible link between right hemisphere processing and delusional perception and beliefs. According to Brugger and Taylor,[50] relative overactivation of the right cerebral hemisphere compared with the left is also indicated by the fact that higher levels of paranormal belief are associated with leftward deviation on a tactile rod bisection task[56] and on an implicit line bisection task.[57] Brugger and colleagues also claim that this hypothesized link between relative right hemisphere overactivation and paranormal belief is supported by the results of divided visual field studies of lexical processing. Brugger *et al.*[58] reported that, compared with the typical pattern of left hemisphere (i.e. right visual field) superiority for lexical decision shown by non-believers, believers in the paranormal show a bias towards right hemisphere processing.[59] Furthermore, Pizzagalli *et al.*[60] report that the resting electroencephalogram (EEG) patterns of believers show more right hemisphere activation than those of disbelievers. Evidence for a link between right hemisphere processing and the capacity to find connections between remotely associated stimuli (cf. Bressan[43]) was provided in the study of Pizzagalli *et al.*[61] showing that the believers' capacity to appreciate indirectly related information was specifically related to left visual field (i.e. right hemisphere) presentation.

The accumulated evidence thus strongly suggests that believers in the paranormal may well have a stronger tendency to see patterns and meaning in noisy, and even totally random, stimulus arrays. This may be based upon a more distorted concept of true randomness and a tendency more readily to connect remotely associated concepts.

Anomalous sensations

It is possible that believers and non-believers in the paranormal differ with respect to the degree to which they experience mildly anomalous sensations such as sensing a presence, sudden changes in temperature and dizziness, and the degree to which they opt for a paranormal interpretation of such sensations. There is also evidence to suggest that believers may be more suggestible than non-believers. These possibilities were examined in an investigation of the alleged haunting of Hampton Court Palace by Wiseman *et al.*[62] A large number of visitors to this site ($n = 678$) completed questionnaires measuring belief in ghosts, anomalous experiences they had had in the past and whether they attributed these experiences to ghosts. As expected, believers reported more such experiences and were more likely to believe they were caused by ghosts. Participants then visited specific locations within the Palace and recorded any unusual experiences they had during that time. Prior to visiting the locations, half of the participants had been told that there had recently been an increase in the frequency of unusual phenomena in that location (positive suggestion) and half were told the opposite (negative suggestion). As predicted, believers reported more anomalous experiences during their visit and were more likely to attribute such experiences to ghosts that non-believers. Furthermore, the believers reported significantly more unusual experiences than the non-believers in the positive suggestion condition, but no differences were found in the negative suggestion condition.

A second report[63] presents further analysis of the data from the Hampton Court investigation, as well as new data collected during an investigation of the South Bridge Vaults in Edinburgh, another supposedly haunted location. In both cases, it was found that participants were more likely to report unusual phenomena in those parts of the haunted sites that already had a reputation for being haunted. Furthermore, this effect could not be explained as being just due to the power of suggestion as the same pattern of results was found for those participants with no specific knowledge regarding which parts of the site were supposed to be the most haunted. This suggests that there may be certain environmental factors that tend to trigger the anomalous sensations that are interpreted as ghostly activity in susceptible individuals. Data collected at the site suggested that variance in local magnetic fields and lighting levels may well be such factors.

Memory biases

French[64] has presented a comprehensive review of relevant studies relating to the unreliability of eyewitness testimony and also to the formation of false memories as they relate to reports of anomalous experiences. With respect to the unreliability of eyewitness testimony, it has long been accepted that accounts of staged or actual crimes are often very unreliable,[65] but there are also now a number of relevant studies of the accuracy of eyewitness accounts of ostensibly paranormal events. For example, Wiseman et al.[66] investigated the accuracy of eyewitness accounts of events that took place in a staged séance (cf. similar studies by Davey, as cited by Hyman,[67] and by Besterman[68]). In Experiment 1, the suggestion was made that a stationary table was moving. Approximately a third of the participants reported that the table did move even though it did not, and this tendency was stronger for believers in the paranormal than for non-believers. In a second fake séance, it was found once again that believers were more susceptible to suggestion than disbelievers, but only when the suggestion was consistent with their pro-paranormal beliefs. Overall, one-fifth of the participants believed they had witnessed genuinely paranormal phenomena. It should be noted here that it is often unclear whether, in such experiments, one is dealing with an actual memory bias or a perceptual bias. It is possible that some participants actually erroneously perceived the table to move at the time the suggestion was made. Indeed, given that both memory and perception are constructive processes, both processes are likely to be susceptible to distortion as a result of suggestion.[64,69] The end result, however, is the same: sincere but unreliable eyewitness reports of ostensibly paranormal events.

Wiseman and Morris[70] presented participants with pre-recorded pseudo-psychic demonstrations (i.e. conjuring tricks), such as metal bending. Unsurprisingly, believers in the paranormal were found to rate the demonstrations as more 'paranormal' than disbelievers, but they also tended to have poorer memories for the details of the demonstrations, particularly for important clues as to how the effects might have been achieved by sleight of hand. For example, believers were less likely to notice that a key went out of sight during a demonstration. This was important because on this occasion the effect was achieved by switching a bent key for the original straight one.

Smith[71] considered how both paranormal belief and prior mental set might affect what is remembered from a viewing of an ostensibly paranormal event (in this case, a demonstration of alleged psychic surgery in which a blood clot is removed from the back of a patient). Mental set was manipulated by introducing the video clip as either an authentic demonstration of a paranormal phenomenon or else as involving trickery. The participants who viewed the video with the latter mental set were significantly more accurate, but no differences were found between believers and non-believers.

Wiseman and Greening[72] have recently reported further investigations of the psychology of apparent psychokinesis. In two experiments, participants were shown a videotape of the pseudo-psychic bending of a key achieved by sleight of hand, but in one condition participants also heard the pseudo-psychic suggest that the key was 'still bending' after he had put it down whereas those in a second condition did not hear this suggestion. Objectively, the key did not bend any further after it had been put down, but around 40 per cent of the participants in the suggestion condition reported that it did. Only one participant out of 71 did so in the no-suggestion condition. Interestingly, participants who reported that the key continued to bend were more confident about the accuracy of their recall and also less likely to remember the actual verbal suggestion made by the pseudo-psychic. No differences between believers and non-believers in the paranormal were found in these experiments.

Summing up these studies of the unreliability of eyewitness testimony for ostensibly paranormal experiences, we can see that it would be wise to treat all such testimony with caution. Furthermore, there is evidence to suggest that both prior mental set and pre-existing levels of paranormal belief will influence subsequent reports and in particular that believers may be more suggestible in certain contexts. It should be borne in mind that it is often impossible to say whether such distorted reports are actually the result of memory bias or the more or less accurate reporting of biased perception of the event in question.

French[64] also draws attention to the relevance of recent research into the formation of false memories to assessing reports of anomalous experiences. A strong case can be made that many reports of apparent alien abduction and of hypnotic past-life regression are probably based upon false memories.[73–78] Furthermore, a number of psychological variables that have been shown to correlate with susceptibility to false memories (e.g. imagery ability,[79] hypnotic susceptibility[80] and dissociativity[81]) have also been shown to correlate with paranormal belief and tendency to report ostensibly paranormal experiences.[82–84] This raises the possibility that many reports of ostensibly paranormal events may in fact be based upon false memories.

Most of the direct attempts to date to investigate whether believers in the paranormal are more susceptible to false memories than non-believers have failed to find evidence to support the hypothesis.[85–87] These studies have typically employed so-called reality monitoring tests in which participants are presented in phase one with words and pictures of common objects. On word trials, participants are instructed to form a mental image of the object. Memory is subsequently tested in a second recognition phase during which

Fig. 1.2 *Cartoon by Steve Yesson.*

participants are presented with a list of stimuli and have to indicate whether they were presented in phase one and, if so, whether they were presented as words or pictures. One measure of susceptibility to false memories would be poorer reality monitoring on a test like this, e.g. the tendency to say that pictures of objects had been presented when in fact they had only been imagined.

The results of Clancy et al.,[88] using a different experimental approach, are worth noting. They compared three groups of participants in terms of their susceptibility to false memories using the word list paradigm of Roediger and McDermott.[89] This involves presenting participants with lists of words in which every word on any particular list is strongly associated with a critical target word that is not itself presented. During subsequent testing, these critical lures are often falsely recalled or recognized. Using this technique, Clancy et al. found that participants who had conscious memories of having been abducted by aliens were more susceptible to false memories than either participants who believed themselves to have been abducted by aliens but had no conscious memory for the event or participants who did not believe that they had been abducted by aliens.

The search for direct links between susceptibility to false memories, paranormal belief and the tendency to report false memories certainly merits further effort. There are now many different techniques available to measure susceptibility to false memories, and the choice of technique may well have a crucial bearing upon the pattern of results obtained. In fact, it is intuitively quite surprising that Clancy et al. obtained the results that they did, given the fact that falsely remembering particular words in an experimental task appears to be very different from having detailed memories of having been abducted by aliens. Recent research by the current authors[90] using what would appear to be a more ecologically valid measure of susceptibility to false memories has produced further evidence for the claim that paranormal belief is indeed associated with such susceptibility.

Non-conscious processing

Research has shown that most human information processing occurs outside of conscious awareness. This fact has potentially important implications in terms of both explaining the maintenance of belief in the paranormal, and for explaining certain types of ostensibly paranormal experiences. Wilson,[91] for example, suggests that perception without awareness (also known as subliminal perception) offers 'a possible mechanism for many experiences in which people claim to have been influenced by some "unknown" or anomalous means' (p. 272). Experimental evidence from cognitive psychology shows that we may well be influenced by information presented to us so briefly that it is beyond conscious awareness. It is fair to suggest that someone who believes in the paranormal may well interpret information that has come to them by non-conscious means as having come from a paranormal source. Wilson illustrates this argument with the hypothetical example of a woman who regularly crosses a suspension bridge on her way to work each day but one day decides, apparently on a whim and for the first time ever, to walk to work via an alternative route. She later learns that the suspension bridge collapsed just at the time she would normally have been crossing it. A startling example of precognition? Perhaps. However, it is also possible that, as she approached the bridge, she sensed that something was different about it—perhaps the way it was swaying in the wind—and that was enough to prompt her actions even though she was not consciously aware of it. This possibility is supported by recent research by Rensink[92] in which it was shown that if participants are presented with a sequence of displays alternating between an image of a scene and a slightly changed image of the same scene, they often sense that something has changed even though they have no conscious visual experience of it.

As long ago as 1940, Miller[93] showed that, in an experimental context, the effects of perception without awareness could be interpreted by participants as evidence for telepathy.

The results of a more recent study by Crawley, French and Yesson[94] also support this claim. In this study, participants were under the impression that they were engaged in a computerized ESP task in which they had to guess which of five symbols would be randomly chosen by the computer on each trial. They were presented on the computer screen with an image of the back of a playing card and then had to guess the symbol chosen. What they did not know was that on half the trials, the correct answer was subliminally 'primed' as it was flashed up very briefly prior to the appearance of the back of the card. Furthermore, on the basis of a questionnaire, participants were divided into those who scored high on 'transliminality' and those who scored low. Transliminality is a concept developed by parapsychologist Michael Thalbourne[95] and is defined as 'a hypothesised tendency for psychological material to cross (*trans*) the threshold (*limen*) into or out of consciousness' (p. 31). It is hypothesized that individuals differ in terms of the permeability of the threshold between that which is typically conscious and that which typically is not. In line with our hypothesis, we found that transliminality was correlated with the number of hits on the primed trials, but not on the unprimed trials. No evidence for actual ESP was obtained, but it would not be surprising if high transliminals misinterpreted their better than average performance as evidence of ESP. Transliminality correlates strongly with paranormal belief.[96]

The role of non-conscious (or subliminal) processing in accounting for ostensibly paranormal experiences is clearly one that merits further research in light of the promising results obtained in the few studies to date which have directly addressed this issue.

Conclusion

Since the early 1990s, a considerable amount of research has been carried out investigating possible cognitive biases underlying paranormal belief and experience. It is clear that a wide range of situations exist that can potentially lead people to believe that they have experienced the paranormal when in fact they have not. The question regarding possible differences between believers and non-believers in the paranormal in terms of proneness to cognitive biases can now be answered rather more definitively than was possible then. Although believers and non-believers do not seem to differ reliably in terms of critical thinking, and inconsistently reported differences in probabilistic reasoning ability may have alternative explanations, many of the other postulated cognitive biases do seem to be reliably related to paranormal belief and experience. Thus believers in the paranormal tend to be poorer at syllogistic reasoning, have a more distorted concept of randomness leading them to see meaning where there is none, are more susceptible to experiencing anomalous sensations and are, in certain circumstances, more suggestible. Memory biases in the accuracy of eyewitness testimony for ostensibly paranormal events have also often been reported, and evidence is beginning to accumulate that believers may be more prone to false memories. Believers may also show a tendency to interpret the products of non-conscious processing as evidence of paranormal activity.

References and notes

1. Nisbett, M. (n.d.). New poll points to increase in paranormal belief. Available from: http://www.csicop.org/articles/poll/ (Accessed 26 February 2005)
2. Karr, B. (2001). Gallup: Paranormal belief increase since 1990. Available from: http://www.csicop.org/list/listarchive/msg00227.html (Accessed 26 February 2005)
3. French CC. Factors underlying belief in the paranormal: do sheep and goats think differently? *The Psychologist*, 1992; 5:295–299.
4. Blackmore SJ. A postal survey of OBEs and other experiences. *Journal of the Society for Psychical Research*, 1984; 52:225–244.
5. Glicksohn J. Belief in the paranormal and subjective paranormal experience. *Personality and Individual Differences*, 1990; 11:675–683.
6. Clarke D. Experience and other reasons given for belief and disbelief in paranormal and religious phenomena. *Journal of the Society for Psychical Research*, 1995; 60:371–384.
7. Alcock JE. *Parapsychology: science or magic?* Pergamon, Oxford. 1981.
8. Blackmore S. The lure of the paranormal. *New Scientist*, 1990:62–65.
9. Blackmore S. Psychic experiences: psychic illusions. In K Frazier, ed. *Encounters with the paranormal: science, knowledge, and belief*. Prometheus, Amherst, NY. 1998:201–211.
10. Dawes RM. *Everyday irrationality: how pseudo-scientists, lunatics, and the rest of us systematically fail to think rationally*. Westview, Boulder, CO. 2001.

11. Gilovich T. *How we know what isn't so: the fallibility of human reason in everyday life.* Free Press, New York. 1991.
12. Hyman R. *The elusive quarry: a scientific appraisal of psychical research.* Prometheus, Buffalo, NY. 1989.
13. Marks D. *The psychology of the psychic*, 2nd edn. Prometheus, Amherst, NY. 2000.
14. Myers DG. *Intuition: its powers and perils.* Yale University Press, New Haven and London. 2002.
15. Sutherland S. *Irrationality: the enemy within.* Constable, London. 1992.
16. Vyse SA. *Believing in magic: the psychology of superstition.* Oxford University Press, New York. 1997.
17. Wiseman R. *Deception and self-deception: investigating psychics.* Prometheus, Amherst, NY. 1997.
18. Zusne L, Jones WH. *Anomalistic psychology*, 2nd edn. Lawrence Erlbaum Associates, London. 1989.
19. Royalty J. The generalizability of critical thinking: paranormal beliefs versus statistical reasoning. *Journal of Genetic Psychology*, 1995; **156**:477–488.
20. Ennis RH, Millman J. *Cornell Critical Thinking Test—level Z.* Midwest Publications, Pacific Grove, CA. 1985.
21. Tobacyk JJ, Milford G. Beliefs in paranormal phenomena: assessment instrument development and implications for personality functioning. *Journal of Personality and Social Psychology*, 1983; **44**:1029–1037.
22. Roe CA. Critical thinking and belief in the paranormal: a re-evaluation. *British Journal of Psychology*, 1999; **90**:85–98.
23. Gray T, Mill D. Critical abilities, graduate education (biology vs. English), and belief in unsubstantiated phenomena.*Canadian Journal of Behavioural Science*, 1990; **22**:162–172.
24. Evans J, StB T. *Bias in human reasoning: causes and consequences.* Psychology Press, Hove, UK. 1989.
25. Evans J, StB T, Newstead SE, Byrne RMJ. *Human reasoning: the psychology of deduction.* Psychology Press, Hove, UK. 1993.
26. Wierzbicki M. Reasoning errors and belief in the paranormal. *Journal of Social Psychology*, 1985; **125**:489–494.
27. Jones WH, Russell DW, Nickel TW. Belief in the Paranormal Scale: an objective instrument to measure belief in magical phenomena and causes. *JSAS Catalog of Selected Documents in Psychology*, 1977; **7**:100.
28. Irwin HJ. Reasoning skills of paranormal believers. *Journal of Parapsychology*, 1991; **55**:281–300.
29. Tobacyk JJ. A Revised Paranormal Belief Scale. Unpublished manuscript, Louisiana Tech University, Ruston, LA. 1988.
30. Roberts MJ, Seager PB. Predicting belief in paranormal phenomena: a comparison of conditional and probabilistic reasoning. *Applied Cognitive Psychology*, 1999; **13**:443–450.
31. Watt C, Wiseman R. Experimenter differences in cognitive correlates of paranormal belief and in psi. *Journal of Parapsychology*, 2002; **66**:371–385.
32. Merla-Ramos M. Belief and reasoning: the effects of belief on syllogistic reasoning. *Dissertation Abstracts International: Section B: The Sciences and Engineering*, 2000; **61**:558.
33. Smith MD, Foster CL, Stovin G. Intelligence and paranormal belief: examining the role of context. *Journal of Parapsychology*, 1998; **62**:65–77.
34. Raven JS. *Raven's matrices: the advanced progressive matrices set 1.* Oxford Psychologists Press, Oxford. 1976.
35. Musch J, Ehrenberg K. Probability misjudgement, cognitive ability, and belief in the paranormal. *British Journal of Psychology*, 2002; **93**:169–177.
36. Thalbourne MA, Nofi O. Belief in the paranormal, superstitiousness and intellectual ability. *Journal of the Society for Psychical Research*, 1997; **61**:365–371.
37. Irwin HJ. Belief in the paranormal: a review of the empirical literature. *Journal of the American Society for Psychical Research*, 1993; **87**:1–39.
38. Irwin HJ. *An introduction to parapsychology*, 4th edn. McFarland & Co., Jefferson, NC. 2003.
39. Paulos JA. *Innumeracy: mathematical illiteracy and its consequences.* Penguin, London. 1988.

40. Blackmore SJ, Troscianko T. Belief in the paranormal: probability judgements, illusory control, and the 'chance baseline shift'. *British Journal of Psychology*, 1985; **81**:455–468.
41. Matthews R, Blackmore S. Why are coincidences so impressive? *Perceptual and Motor Skills*, 1995; **80**:1121–1122.
42. Blackmore SJ. Probability misjudgement and belief in the paranormal: a newspaper survey. *British Journal of Parapsychology*, 1997; **88**:683–689.
43. Bressan P. The connection between random sequences, everyday coincidences, and belief in the paranormal. *Applied Cognitive Psychology*, 2002; **16**:17–34.
44. Wiseman R, Smith MD. Assessing the role of cognitive and motivational biases in belief in the paranormal. *Journal of the Society for Psychical Research*, 2002; **66**:157–166.
45. Brugger P, Landis T, Regard M. A 'sheep–goat' effect in repetition avoidance: extra-sensory perception as an effect of subjective probability? *British Journal of Psychology*, 1990; **81**:455–468.
46. Brugger P, Baumann AT. Repetition avoidance in responses to imaginary questions: the effect of respondents' belief in ESP. *Psychological Reports*, 1994; **75**:883–893.
47. Brugger P, Regard M, Landis, T, Graves RE. The roots of meaningful coincidence. *Lancet*, 1995; **345**:1306–1307.
48. Lawrence TR. Subjective random generations and the reversed sheep–goat effect. *European Journal of Parapsychology*, 1990–1991; **8**:131–144.
49. Brugger P. From haunted brain to haunted science: a cognitive neuroscience view of paranormal and pseudoscientific thought. In J Houran and R Lange, ed. *Hauntings and poltergeists: multidisciplinary perspectives*. McFarland and Company, Inc., Jefferson, NC. 2001:195–213.
50. Brugger P, Taylor KI. ESP: Extrasensory perception or effect of subjective probability? *Journal of Consciousness Studies*, 2003; **10**:221–246.
51. Gianotti LR, Mohr C., Pizzagalli D, Lehmann D, Brugger P. Associative processing and paranormal belief. *Psychiatry and Clinical Neurosciences*, 2001; **55**:595–603.
52. Garety PA, Freeman D. Cognitive approaches to delusions: a critical review of theories and evidence. *British Journal of Psychology*, 1999; **38**:113–154.
53. Brugger P, Graves RE. Testing vs. believing hypotheses: magical ideation in the judgement of contingencies. *Cognitive Neuropsychiatry*, 1997; **2**:251–272.
54. Blackmore SJ, Moore R. Seeing things: visual recognition and belief in the paranormal. *European Journal of Parapsychology*, 1994; **10**:91–103.
55. Brugger P, Regard M, LandisT, Cook N, Krebs D, Nederberger J. 'Meaningful' patterns in visual noise: effects of lateral stimulation and the observer's belief in ESP. *Psychopathology*, 1993; **26**:261–265.
56. Brugger P, Graves RE. Right hemispatial inattention and magical ideation. *European Archives of Psychiatry and Clinical Neuroscience*, 1997; **247**:55–57.
57. Taylor KI, Zäch P, Brugger P. Why is magical thinking associated with leftward deviation on an implicit line bisection task? *Cortex*, 2002; **38**:247–252.
58. Brugger P, Gamma A, Müri R, Schäfer M, Taylor KI. Functional hemispheric asymmetry and belief in ESP: towards a 'neuropsychology of belief'. *Perceptual and Motor Skills*, 1993; **77**:1299–1308.
59. Leonhard D, Brugger P. Creative, paranormal, and delusional thought: a consequence of right hemisphere semantic activation? *Neuropsychiatry, Neuropsychology, and Behavioral Neurology*, 1998; **11**:177–183.
60. Pizzagalli D, Lehmann D, Gianotti L, Koenig T, Tanaka H, Wackermann J, Brugger P. Brain electric correlates of strong belief in paranormal phenomena : intracerebral EEG source and regional Omega complexity analyses. *Psychiatry Research: Neuroimaging*, 2000; **100**:139–154.
61. Pizzagalli D, Lehmann D, Brugger P. Lateralized direct and indirect semantic priming effects in subjects with paranormal experiences and beliefs. *Psychopathology*, 2002; **34**:75–80.
62. Wiseman R, Watt C, Greening E, Stevens P, O'Keeffe C. An investigation into the alleged haunting of Hampton Court Palace: psychological variables and magnetic fields. *Journal of Parapsychology*, 2002; **66**:388–408.

63. Wiseman R, Watt C, Stevens P, Greening E, O'Keeffe C. An investigation into alleged 'hauntings'. *British Journal of Psychology*, 2003; **94**:195–211.
64. French CC. Fantastic memories: the relevance of research into eyewitness testimony and false memories for reports of anomalous experiences. *Journal of Consciousness Studies*, 2003; **10**:153–174.
65. Loftus EF. *Eyewitness testimony*. Harvard University Press, Cambridge, MA. 1979.
66. Wiseman R, Greening E, Smith M. Belief in the paranormal and suggestion in the séance room. *British Journal of Psychology*, **94**:285–297.
67. Hyman R. A critical historical overview of parapsychology. In P Kurtz, ed. *A skeptic's handbook of parapsychology*. Prometheus, Buffalo, NY. 1985:3–96.
68. Besterman T. The psychology of testimony in relation to paraphysical phenomena: report of an experiment. *Proceedings of the Society for Psychical Research*, 1932; **40**:363–387.
69. French CC. *Paranormal perception? A critical evaluation*. Institute for Cultural Research, London. Monograph Series, No. 42, 2001.
70. Wiseman R, Morris RL. Recalling pseudo-psychic demonstrations. *British Journal of Psychology*, 1995; **86**:113–125.
71. Smith MD. The effect of belief in the paranormal and prior set upon the observation of a 'psychic' demonstration. *European Journal of Parapsychology*, 1992; **9**:24–34.
72. Wiseman R, Greening E. 'It's still bending': verbal suggestion and alleged psychokinetic ability. *British Journal of Psychology*, 2005; **96**:115–127.
73. Baker RA. *Hidden memories: voices and visions from within*. Prometheus, Buffalo, NY. 1992.
74. French CC. Alien abductions. In R Roberts, D Groome, ed. *Parapsychology: the science of unusual experience*. Arnold, London. 2001:102–116.
75. Holden KJ, French CC. Alien abduction experiences: clues from neuropsychology and neuropsychiatry. *Cognitive Neuropsychiatry*, 2002; **7**:163–178.
76. Spanos NP. *Multiple identities and false memories: a sociocognitive perspective*. American Psychological Association, Washington, DC. 1996.
77. Spanos NP, Menary E, Gabora NJ, DuBreuil SC, Dewhirst B. Secondary identity enactments during hypnotic past-life regression: a sociocognitive perspective. *Journal of Personality and Social Psychology*, 1991; **61**:308–320.
78. Spanos NP, Burgess CA, Burgess NF. Past-life identities, UFO abductions, and Satanic ritual abuse: the social construction of memories. *International Journal of Clinical and Experimental Hypnosis*, 1994; **42**:433–446.
79. Dobson M, Markham R. Imagery ability and source monitoring: implications for eyewitness memory. *British Journal of Psychology*, 1993; **84**:111–118.
80. Barnier AJ, McConkey KM. Reports of real and false memories: the relevance of hypnosis, hypnotisability, and test control. *Journal of Abnormal Psychology*, 1992; **101**:521–527.
81. Hyman IE Jr, Billings FJ. Individual differences and the creation of false childhood memories. *Memory*, 1998; **6**:1–20.
82. Diamond MJ, Taft R. The role played by ego-permissiveness and imagery in hypnotic responsivity. *International Journal of Clinical and Experimental Hypnosis*, 1975; **23**:130–138.
83. Palmer J, Van Der Velden I. ESP and 'hypnotic imagination': a group free-response study. *European Journal of Parapsychology*, 1983; **4**:413–434.
84. Pekala RJ, Kumar VK, Marcano G. Anomalous/paranormal experiences, hypnotic susceptibility, and dissociation. *Journal of the American Society for Psychical Research*, 1995; **89**:313–332.
85. Blackmore SJ, Rose N. Reality and imagination: a psi-conducive confusion? *Journal of Parapsychology*, 1997; **61**:321–335.
86. Rose N, Blackmore SJ. Are false memories psi-conducive? *Journal of Parapsychology*, 2001; **65**:125–144.
87. Roe CA. Revisiting false memories as a vehicle for psi. *Journal of the Society for Psychical Research*, 2003; **67**:281–295.

88. **Clancy SA, McNally RJ, Schacter DL, Lenzenweger MF, Pitman RK.** Memory distortion in people reporting abduction by aliens. *Journal of Abnormal Psychology*, 2002; 111:455–461.
89. **Roediger HL III, McDermott KB.** Creating false memories: remembering words not presented on lists. *Journal of Experimental Psychology: Learning, Memory, and Cognition*, 1995; 21:803–814.
90. **Wilson K, French CC.** The relationship between susceptibility to false memories, dissociativity, and paranormal belief and experience, in press in Personality and Individual Differences.
91. **Wilson S.** Psi, perception without awareness, and false recognition. *Journal of Parapsychology*, 2002; 66:271–289.
92. **Rensink R.** Visual sensing without seeing. *Psychological Science*, 2004; 15:27–32.
93. **Miller JG.** The role of motivation in learning without awareness. *American Journal of Psychology*, 1940; 53:229–239.
94. **Crawley SE, French CC, Yesson SA.** Evidence for transliminality from a subliminal card guessing task. *Perception*, 2002; 31:887–892.
95. **Thalbourne MA.** Transliminality: a review. *International Journal of Parapsychology*, 2000; 11:1–33.
96. **Thalbourne MA, Houran J.** Transliminality as an index of the sheep–goat variable. *European Journal of Parapsychology*, 2003; 18:3–14.

Chapter 2

Critically thinking about paranormal belief

Peter Lamont

In 1864, the Davenport brothers (see Fig. 2.1) came to Britain. They performed on stage as spirit mediums, and many people came to believe they were genuine. The Davenports would sit inside a large cabinet, which contained musical instruments, and they would be tied to their chairs with rope. When the doors of the cabinet were closed, the instruments would be heard playing, and then would be seen flying out from the top of the cabinet, as if they had been thrown. When the doors were opened, however, the brothers would still be tied up as before and, therefore, apparently not responsible for what had happened. As a result, many people believed that these bizarre occurrences must be the work of departed spirits.

A few months later, John Nevil Maskelyne began his career. He would become the most famous conjuror in Britain, and the most public debunker of spiritualism. He began, however, by duplicating the Davenports' performance, and without the aid of spirits. He assured the public that what he did was precisely what the Davenports did, and that they were not conjuring spirits, but were merely performing conjuring tricks. That was enough for most people, but it was not enough for everyone, for spiritualists continued to argue that the Davenports were genuine mediums. Even when the Davenports were actually caught cheating, spiritualists maintained that it was not their fault, but was the work of evil spirits, or they claimed that even if the brothers did cheat occasionally, they were nevertheless genuine on other occasions. One of the Davenport brothers' staunchest supporters was Benjamin Coleman, a successful stockbroker and a prominent spiritualist. He went to see Maskelyne perform the same cabinet routine, and became quite convinced that what Maskelyne did was similar to what the Davenports did. He therefore came to the conclusion that the Maskelyne performance was also the work of spirits.[1]

There are many examples of believers in spiritualism (or, more recently, psychic and paranormal phenomena) coming to similarly strange conclusions. They can be seen as glaring illustrations of how people can base their beliefs upon a lack of critical thinking, and as evidence to support a very old argument that continues to this day: that belief in the paranormal is the product of ignorance, gullibility and wishful thinking. It is an argument of which Coleman was well aware, but one that he adamantly rejected. In that

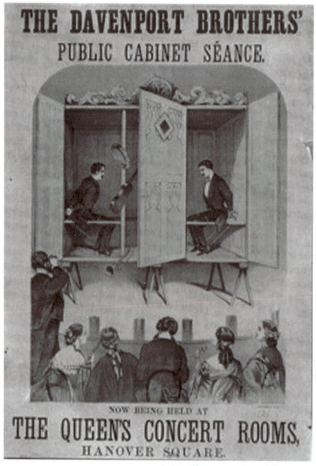

Fig. 2.1 The Davenport brothers: conjuring spirits or conjuring tricks?

sense at least, Coleman was right. For, as we shall see, despite the existence of illustrations such as these, it is not a satisfactory explanation.

A history of uncritical thinking about the paranormal

What we would now call paranormal phenomena have long been dismissed as the product of ignorance, gullibility and wishful thinking, but the theme really got going in the nineteenth century. One classic text appeared in 1832, when David Brewster, an expert on optics (and the inventor of the kaleidoscope), wrote a book called *Letters on natural magic*. The book exposed the various ways in which fake supernatural phenomena had allowed tyrants to rule past civilizations, how they had exploited the fear and ignorance of primitive populations by the ingenious use of acoustics, hydrostatics, mechanics and optics. Concave mirrors, he explained, had been used to make heathen gods appear in ancient temples, and acoustic illusions had allowed the gods to speak. For Brewster, the ignorance of earlier peoples was no longer to be tolerated in the modern era of 1832. As far as he was concerned, scientific wonders were only inexplicable miracles to 'less gifted minds'.[2] The idea, of course, was that nineteenth century minds were superior to those of yesteryear, that the growth of scientific knowledge was evidence that they knew better than their forebears.

This was a common view in nineteenth century Britain and, as the British dismissed their ancestors as superstitious, so they dismissed many of their contemporaries in a similar fashion. Contemporary India, for example, was regarded as primitive in much the same way as Europe had been in the past. Regular accounts of Indian idolatry and superstition appeared in the *Times*, for example, paraded as evidence that the colonized could only benefit from the rational influence of the West. From the point of view of the modern West, they lived in a more knowledgeable and sceptical age, one that was not so ignorant, not so gullible and not so prone to wishful thinking as either the primitive past or the primitive Eastern present.

The problem, however, is that this view regularly accompanied belief in the miracles of the Bible, espoused as it often was by Christian missionaries who felt that *their* miracles were more plausible. This, despite the fact that the evidence for these miracles came from the ancient 'primitive' past of the 'primitive' East. Furthermore, this was not simply the view of missionaries, because the mainstream press took the same view, as did most scientists. When Brewster dismissed the miracles of past and present, he took a quite different position when it came to the miracles of the Bible. In fact, he even complained of a colleague who, '[i]n his anxiety to account for every thing miraculous by natural causes, he has ascribed to the same origin some of those events in sacred history which Christians cannot but regard as the result of divine agency'.[3] The modern view of the early nineteenth century was, for the most part, to reject all miracles as impossible, except for the ones in the Bible.

As the century progressed, most Victorians would have agreed with such a position, but then critical thinking and the rejection of miracles did not always amount to the same thing. This became clear with the arrival of Modern Spiritualism, when countless Victorians sat round tables, placed their hands lightly on top of it, and watched as it moved back and forward apparently without any human influence. This was all too much for some scientific observers, and *Chambers' Journal* declared that '[i]f this be a world of natural law, as most enlightened persons believe it to be, it is impossible that such things can be realities: they can only be some form of delusion or fallacy'.[4] The anonymous writer had not witnessed such things, but dismissed the reports as untrue on the grounds that they could not be true. Such a view, based as it was upon ignorance and wishful thinking, was not shared by his editor, Robert Chambers. Chambers was a prolific writer who had already published a controversial theory of evolution (many years before Darwin). When Chambers heard about these table movements, he went along to investigate, became quite convinced that the phenomena were indeed possible, and spent a great deal of time trying to reconcile spiritualism to theories of evolution.[5]

Michael Faraday took a different line. Faraday was probably the most influential scientist of the period, and he approached the subject in an experimental frame of mind. His hypothesis was that sitters were inadvertently pushing the table via unconscious muscular movement, provoked by a desire for it to move. He therefore designed an experiment in which he placed a moveable board on top of the table, and sitters placed their hands upon the board. As a result, it was the board that moved rather than the table. The experiment thus demonstrated the power of wishful thinking, it was well publicized in the *Times*, and Faraday was regularly held up as an exemplar of critical scientific thinking.[6] However, Faraday was not only a scientist, he was also a fundamentalist Christian, whose primary problem with Spiritualism was that it was blasphemous.[7] He believed that the Bible was literally true and, given that this was being increasingly challenged by both theologians and some scientists at the time, he could easily be accused of being guilty of wishful thinking himself.

This does not negate the worth of his experiment, but the notion that he approached miraculous phenomena in a critical manner can only be applied to that experiment. After all, spiritualist phenomena were often far more impressive, particularly in the case of the famous medium, Daniel Dunglas Home. According to eyewitnesses, Home's séances included the movement of large and heavy tables, and all manner of other objects and furniture, often without any contact at all. However, when Faraday was invited to investigate Home, he refused. Indeed, throughout Home's career, despite the most extraordinary phenomena being reported, and despite regular invitations to scientists to investigate, the vast majority not only declined but also denounced the phenomena as fraudulent without any investigation whatsoever. As a result, no adequate explanation ever emerged for how Home did what he did. This does not mean that his phenomena were necessarily genuine, and perhaps the scientists were technically correct, but, correct or not, their position was nevertheless one that was based upon ignorance.

There were, however, a few scientists who attended séances with Home, and their positions are even more insightful. In 1855, David Brewster himself was invited along by a sceptical friend, in order to 'find out the trick'. According to Brewster's own account, 'the table actually rose from the ground when no hand was upon it', and a hand-bell 'actually rang, when nothing could have touched it'. This he reported in a private letter to his sister shortly after the séance, in which he described the various feats, and concluded that 'we could give no explanation of them, and could not conjecture how they could be produced by any kind of mechanism'. When he later wrote to the press, however, he claimed he had seen 'several mechanical effects', that he 'saw enough to satisfy myself that they could all be produced by human hands and feet and to prove to others that some of them, at least, had such an origin'. The hand-bell, he now claimed, 'did not ring'. As for the secret of the phenomena, the only reason he could not provide the details was because the table was 'covered with copious drapery, beneath which nobody was allowed to look'.[8] All of this was flatly contradicted by the other witnesses present, who pointed out that he had not only been allowed to look under the cloth, but that he had actually done so! Brewster's account was later contradicted by his own hand, when the private letter to his sister was published posthumously.[9] So, it seems, that it was Brewster who was ignorant of what was going on, who was thus guilty (by his own definition) of gullibility, and who accused others of deception while misleading the public himself.

Whatever the truth about séance phenomena, it is clear that those who accused spiritualists of ignorance, gullibility and wishful thinking were often themselves guilty of precisely the same vices. Furthermore, those who accused mediums of deceiving their audiences were equally capable of misleading the public. Brewster was by no means unique, for the press often made false accusations that mediums had been exposed when they had not been, and conjurors regularly misled the public on the question of whether they knew the secrets of the séance room . All of this while in the very process of accusing others of being untrustworthy. Scientists other than Brewster were equally misleading, most notably when the eminent chemist, William Crookes, carried out experiments with Home. Crookes was a Fellow of the Royal Society, who had already received financial support from that society and would later become its president. Following experiments with Home, however, Crookes announced the existence of a new 'psychic' force, and invited senior members of the Royal Society to witness the experiments for themselves. They not only declined the invitation, then dismissed his findings as nonsense (despite being unable to provide an adequate alternative explanation), but also went on to mislead the public about how the experiments had been conducted, and even about the scientific competence of Crookes himself.[10]

The man most responsible for this was W. B. Carpenter, the most prominent scientific critic of spiritualism and, as it happens, a pioneer of the psychology of belief. Carpenter spent much of his career explaining reported séance phenomena in terms of self-deception and unreliable testimony, and he stressed the importance of distinguishing between belief and knowledge.[11] Nevertheless, he also accused mediums of fraud and witnesses of gullibility, even when he himself had no knowledge of how the phenomena had been faked, and he occasionally misrepresented evidence in order to make spiritualist phenomena seem less impressive.[12] For example, when Daniel Dunglas Home reportedly floated out of a third-floor window in front of three witnesses, and two of them publicly declared that he had done so, Carpenter claimed that the witnesses had imagined things. He maintained that, since the third 'sceptical' witness had declared he had seen nothing, it showed how the imagination of believers could be influenced by wishful thinking.[13] The third witness, however, had said nothing of the sort (indeed, when asked, he confirmed what the other two had reported). Thus, the great naturalist (and spiritualist), Alfred Russell Wallace, suggested it was Carpenter whose wishful thinking had led him to imagine things.[14]

This tradition was continued by Joseph Jastrow, one of the most important of early psychologists. Like Carpenter, Jastrow was intrigued by how seemingly supernatural phenomena might be the result of self-deception or deception by others. In his attempts to convince the public, he presented them with 'the confession of an exposed medium, D. D. Home', in which the medium admitted how he had disguised himself as a spirit by wearing a disguise.[15] Home, however, had never confessed to fraud. On the contrary, this was the confession of an entirely different medium, and it was actually Home who had exposed this to the public.[16] Since Jastrow must have got this information (directly or indirectly) from Home's own book, it is hard to imagine how he was not aware of this. At the very least, it was an extremely naive error. Rather like his own criticisms of spiritualism, then, either Jastrow was guilty of deliberate deception, or else he had come to a sincere (but mistaken) belief as the result of a lack of critical thinking.

The problem of dismissing spiritualist beliefs as the product of a lack of critical thinking is not only that 'sceptics' could be equally uncritical (in their thinking if not in their language), but also that spiritualists often rejected miraculous phenomena, detected fraudulent mediums and even exposed the secrets of conjuring tricks. Roman Catholic miracles, for example, were denounced by spiritualists as the product of 'a country where superstition is made a trade to bring pence to its mendicant priests, and where a small proportion of true spiritual phenomena have been eked out by nine-tenths of impostures, in the shape of winking Madonnas [and] bleeding pictures'.[17] This was, as it happens, a position not so unlike that of the great sceptic, David Brewster. Furthermore, mediums were often caught cheating by spiritualists themselves and, while many spiritualists conjured up convoluted explanations to account for such exposures, others were clearly more sceptical. George Sexton, for example, became frustrated at the attempts of conjurors (such as John Nevil Maskelyne) to dismiss spiritualists as gullible fools. He therefore figured out Maskelyne's tricks and, much to the frustration of the conjuror, exposed the secrets to the public.[18] Whatever reasons Sexton had for believing that the feats of mediums were genuine, he can hardly be accused of gullibility.

It was not just the Victorians who dismissed spiritualist beliefs in this way, as historians since have tended to explain them as the result of the so-called 'crisis of faith'. According to this version of events, the emergence of Biblical criticism and the rise of scientific knowledge (such as geological findings and Darwinian theory) increasingly challenged people's faith in the accuracy of the Bible, and provoked in many a crisis of faith. Spiritualism was thus the refuge of individuals desperate to replace their dwindling faith in orthodox Christianity. That has been the general explanation of historians, but it was not what spiritualists said themselves. Time and again, they declared that they had been converted from a position of scepticism by the evidence of the séance room. Furthermore, when the contemporary evidence is actually studied, it becomes clear that neither scientists nor conjurors were able to explain certain reported séance phenomena.[19] No doubt there were many Victorian spiritualists whose desire to believe led them to be deceived, but then nobody denied that there were fraudulent mediums. The question was whether there were any genuine phenomena, and it is the case that some reported phenomena eluded explanation even by the most ardent opponents of spiritualism (who were presumably not suffering from a crisis of faith). Perhaps the phenomena were genuine, or perhaps they were tricks that fooled even the experts. However, either way, the crisis of faith does not adequately explain spiritualist beliefs.

Nevertheless, for the majority of Victorians themselves, belief in spiritualist or psychic phenomena would have been explained in much the same way as magic beliefs in 'primitive' countries, or in their own primitive past. Such beliefs were the product of ignorance, gullibility and wishful thinking, which had no place in the modern world. Yet the rejection of these beliefs was itself often based upon a lack of knowledge, an inability to explain how the 'tricks' were done, and accompanied by belief in other miracles for which it was often admitted there was less supporting evidence. There can be little doubt that many mediums were fooling their audiences with tricks, but there were also reported phenomena for which no adequate explanation was provided, and the only scientists who actually tested Home concluded he was genuine. Whether any of these mediums were genuine or not, the disbelief of the majority of Victorians often rested upon no greater degree of critical thinking than the belief of the minority.

A legacy of ignorance, gullibility and wishful thinking

Belief in the paranormal has persisted, of course, and similar explanations continue to be provided. According to Gilovich (1991), questionable beliefs (such as belief in ESP) are attributed to cognitive, motivational and social *determinants*. People believe in the paranormal because, for example, they misinterpret information, they see what they want to see, and they believe what they are told.[20] Few would question that people are capable of such errors, but the idea that they *determine* paranormal belief is questionable itself. For one thing, such errors are by no means the monopoly of believers in the paranormal. Just as in the past, people who reject the paranormal can do so on the basis of no greater knowledge. As the psychoanalyst, Ernest Jones, pointed out back in 1930, '[t]he average man of today does not hesitate to reject the same evidence of witchcraft that was so convincing to the man of three centuries ago, though he usually knows no more about the true explanation than the latter did'.[21] Both the 'average man' (and the average woman) of today is undoubtedly more sceptical about magic and witchcraft than in the past, but their own beliefs are not necessarily based upon firmer foundations. All of us attribute many wonders to science and technology without knowing how they actually work, and we do so for good reason. After all, we cannot be experts on such a variety of specialist knowledges, and we need only assume that there are others who know such things, expert authorities who can be trusted.

In the case of the paranormal, one group of authorities are magicians, who regularly assure the public that paranormal phenomena are often simply tricks. The specialist knowledge that magicians possess is often directly relevant to how ostensibly paranormal feats can be faked, and thus ignorance of such knowledge may lead people to believe that something is paranormal when it is not. However, this does not mean that knowledge prevents deception. Magicians are quite capable of being deceived by methods of which they are well aware, and knowledge (rather than ignorance) can actually be a contributory factor. One informal experiment that makes this clear took place at the Magic Circle in London, and was filmed for a BBC science programme. An audience of 12 (six magicians and six non-magicians) was invited to watch a card trick. A card was chosen, then replaced in the middle of the pack. The magician snapped his fingers and the card appeared on the top of the pack. It was replaced in the centre of the pack, he once again snapped his fingers, and it reappeared on the top. Once again it was placed in the centre, once again it reappeared at the top. Members of the audience were then interviewed individually, and asked how the trick was done. The non-magicians correctly concluded that all the cards were the same. Yet all six magicians came to a different conclusion, i.e. that the secret was due to sleight-of-hand, and that it would take significant time to learn.[22]

The reason for their error was that they thought they recognized the trick (because the magician performed it in such a way that it looked as if he was using sleights with which they would be familiar). What is particularly interesting, however, is that the trick always begins by showing the audience that the cards are different (otherwise they would simply assume, as the lay audience did here, that all the cards were the same). The magicians were so convinced that they knew what was going on, however, they missed the crucial fact that they were never shown the faces of the cards. It has been often pointed out that magicians regularly fool each other with new tricks or new sleights, and with ingenious uses of familiar ploys.[23] But they can also be fooled by tricks that do not fool the public, even when they actually know the method, and are given clues to how it might be done. This is not, therefore, a matter of ignorance, nor even of gullibility. It is simply a matter of exploiting assumptions, and all of us have assumptions.

Our assumptions can certainly lead us to misperceive or misinterpret events, but disbelievers in the paranormal are perfectly capable of making such errors. A wonderful illustration of this is when Arthur Ellison, a Professor of Engineering at City University, London, and a senior member of the Society for Psychical Research, levitated a bowl of flowers. He claimed he would use paranormal powers, but secretly used an electromagnetic device. Nevertheless, five out of six sceptics present denied it had actually moved.[24] The fact is that we are all capable of basing our beliefs upon a lack of knowledge, of being deceived, and of misinterpreting the world in line with what we want or what we expect. Sometimes such errors lead to paranormal belief and sometimes they do not. Both believers and sceptics are guilty of such errors, and the paranormal has been both supported and rejected by appealing to erroneous evidence. Ignorance, gullibility and wishful thinking may underlie questionable beliefs but, if they can lead not only to belief in the paranormal but also to disbelief in the paranormal, their role as determinants is clearly somewhat complicated.

It may be, of course, that people who believe in the paranormal are, *on the whole*, more ignorant, more gullible and more prone to wishful thinking than those who do not. There have been studies that suggest believers may be more suggestible than disbelievers in certain respects, and there have been others that suggest believers may be worse at certain types of critical thinking.[25] These findings, however, are not conclusive, as there are also some studies that suggest no difference.[26] In one experiment, for example, people were shown a video of an individual apparently bending a key by psychokinesis. The feat was a trick, but after the key had been placed upon the table, the performer stated that it was still bending. Later, many observers stated that the key had indeed continued to bend, but disbelievers did this to the same extent as believers.[27] Whatever the overall differences between believers and disbelievers, it is not a simple case of one group being more ignorant, more gullible and more prone to wishful thinking than the other. After all, there have been many investigations into the differences between the two groups, yet no consistent findings have been found in relation to their scientific education, their performance in intelligence tests or their accuracy in probability misjudgements.[28]

It may be that believers in the paranormal are more likely than disbelievers to interpret a pseudo-psychic demonstration as a paranormal event.[29] Indeed, the most recent study concluded that 'belief in paranormal phenomena has a major effect on the reception of pseudo-psychic demonstrations'. In each experiment of this study, subjects were first asked questions about whether paranormal phenomena exist, then shown a demonstration of an ostensibly paranormal phenomenon. The result was that 'believers in paranormal phenomena . . . have a greater tendency to categorize the presentation as paranormal than do sceptics'.[30] However, perhaps it is not surprising that believers are more likely to regard an event as paranormal than people who do not believe in the paranormal. After all, it is not unusual for people to interpret events in line with their beliefs. Furthermore while it may be that, generally speaking, disbelievers are more observant, or better at recalling details, again there are no conclusive findings.[31] Thus, disbelievers may correctly interpret the demonstration as a trick, but they do not necessarily have any greater knowledge of how it is actually accomplished.

The reason why believers are assumed to be prone to misinterpretation is, of course, that paranormal experiences are assumed to be erroneous, and such experiences are often described as the basis for paranormal belief. Indeed, when asked, people cite personal experience as the main reason for their belief not only in ESP but also in a variety of other paranormal phenomena.[32] It may be that certain types of people are more prone to paranormal experiences and, therefore, to paranormal belief. For example, childhood trauma and encouragement of fantasy in childhood have been suggested as possible causes of fantasy-proneness, which in turn may lead to such experiences and associated belief, though again there have been no conclusive findings to date.[33] Perhaps paranormal beliefs are functional, providing an individual with a greater sense of control over his or her life. But while this may be a partial explanation for why people believe in the paranormal, there are probably a range of psychological reasons not only why some people believe, but also why others do not. Indeed, in the case of those who strongly reject the paranormal, one expert on paranormal belief has suggested that 'the existence of the paranormal is unacceptable very largely for emotional reasons'.[34] Clearly, things are more complicated than believers being guilty of wishful thinking.

One of the reasons for the relative lack of conclusive findings may be the process through which one measures paranormal belief in the first place. Psychologists generally use questionnaires to find out what individuals believe, but these differ significantly in the questions that they ask. They can include expressions of belief about a diverse range of phenomena, from extrasensory perception and psychokinesis to witchcraft, UFOs and the Loch Ness Monster. One of the most popular of questionnaires has been the subject of significant debate concerning, amongst other things, its definition of the paranormal, the appropriateness of its questions and the statistical validity of the factors being studied.[35] It has also been pointed out that participants' responses may be influenced by the context of measurement. Studies have suggested that responses are influenced by the experimenter's attitude towards the paranormal, and by prior exposure to statements about the paranormal.[36] In other words, if the subject thinks the experimenter is a believer, or if the subject is provided with information that supports the existence of the paranormal prior to being given the questionnaire, he or she may be more inclined to express a similar belief.

To some extent, then, paranormal belief can mean different things, and different contexts can produce different expressions of belief. Perhaps there is nothing particularly surprising about this, since the paranormal is inherently ambiguous, and beliefs are necessarily based upon limited knowledge. However, some psychologists would argue that there are more fundamental problems with how one measures belief.[37] After all, a belief is regarded as an enduring internal mental state, yet it is measured by using responses to questions. This may, of course, be unavoidable, but the problem of assuming that a person's response represents their internal mental state is not merely a question of whether it might be skewed by the context of measurement, perhaps resulting in a response bias. After all, if responses can vary in different contexts, then how does one elicit an unbiased response? When an individual states, 'I'm not a racist but...', it is often followed by a comment that others might regard as racist. Which of these represents the unbiased expression? Does the statement 'I'm not a racist' represent an internal position? Of course, one could ask more specific questions, about immigration or inter-racial marriage, but why should responses to these questions be taken as any more accurate, and can we then over-rule the subject and accuse him or her of being racist when s/he explicitly denies it? Whatever the answer to these questions, the issues surrounding measurement of such beliefs are equally relevant to measurements of paranormal belief.

There are, then, a variety of disputed questions, as well as inconclusive answers, when it comes to the question of paranormal belief. It may be that further questionnaire research will provide more conclusive results, but questionnaires are not the only way to record and analyse what people say about the paranormal. Rather than rely upon restricted responses, we can give individuals more time to describe and explain their views about the paranormal. By recording and analysing more lengthy accounts, certain patterns do emerge. For example, when individuals describe paranormal experiences, the way in which they do so regularly takes the from of 'I was just doing X, ... when Y'. X refers to a normal event, such as making a pot of tea, and Y refers to the ostensibly paranormal event, such as a poltergeist. When subjected to minute analysis, the way in which such accounts are presented shows a high degree of complexity, as the individual builds up the reality of an extraordinary story by placing it within an ordinary context. Thus, the paranormal experience is made more convincing to the listener.[38] Such analysis is radically different from the quantitative measures in questionnaires, and shows the importance of function, rather than accuracy, in individual accounts of paranormal experience. When people talk about paranormal experiences, they no doubt want to be believed, and so describe such experiences in a convincing way. Similarly, when asked what they believe, people may want to be agreeable, to avoid appearing either narrow-minded or gullible; indeed, their responses may be shaped by a whole host of interests. To assume that a particular response to a particular person at a particular time and place amounts to a genuine, enduring internal state of mind is to miss the enormous variety of ways in which humans can articulate experiences and beliefs in different situations.

The history of the paranormal illustrates that there are all sorts of people who believe in the paranormal, as there are all sorts of people who disbelieve. We can, of course, fall back on the assumption that such beliefs are wrong, and therefore must be the product of ignorance, gullibility and wishful thinking. That, if nothing else, would be in line with tradition. However, as we have seen, disbelief in the paranormal has also been based upon ignorance, gullibility and wishful thinking, and paranormal phenomena have been not only supported but also rejected by appealing to misleading evidence. It may be that there is an overall difference between believers and disbelievers in terms of how they observe and think, but the findings at present are, at best, inconclusive. Considering the variety of issues concerning how one measures belief in the paranormal, perhaps an adequate understanding will require a range of approaches. For the moment, however, there is no simple answer.

Acknowledgements

The author would like to thank Professor Richard Wiseman for his feedback on a previous version of this paper.

References and notes

1. **Podmore F.** *Modern spiritualism: a history and criticism.* Methuen, London. 1902:61.
2. **Brewster D.** *Letters on natural magic.* John Murray, London. 1832.
3. **Brewster, 1832:6.**
4. **Anon.** 'The spirit faith in America'. *Chambers' Journal*, 1856; 5:83.
5. **Oppenheim J.** *The other world: spiritualism and psychical research in England, 1850–1914.* Cambridge University Press, Cambridge. 1998.
6. **Winter A.** *Mesmerized: powers of mind in Victorian Britain.* Chicago University Press, Chicago. 1998.
7. **Cantor G.** *Michael Faraday: Sandemanian and scientist: a study of science and religion in the 19th century.* Macmillan, Basingstoke, UK. 1991.
8. **Podmore, 1902:142–4.**
9. **Gordon M.** *The home life of Sir David Brewster.* Edmonston and Douglas, Edinburgh. 1870.
10. **Lamont P.** Spiritualism and a mid-Victorian crisis of evidence. *Historical Journal*, 2004; 47:785–808.
11. See, for example: Carpenter W. On the psychology of belief. *Contemporary Review*, 1873; 23:123–145; Carpenter, W. On the fallacies of testimony in relation to the supernatural. *Contemporary Review*, 1875; 27:279–295.
12. **Carpenter W.** Spiritualism and its recent converts. *Quarterly Review*, 1871; 131:301–353; Carpenter W, 1875; p. 286; Carpenter W. Psychological curiosities of spiritualism. *Fraser's Magazine*, 1877; 16:541–564; Wallace AR. Psychological curiosities of skepticism, *Fraser's Magazine*, 1877; 16:694–706.
13. **Carpenter, 1875:286.**
14. **Wallace, 1877:697.**
15. **Jastrow J.** The psychology of spiritualism. *Popular Science Monthly*, 1889; 34:721–732.

16. **Home DD.** *Light and shadows of spiritualism.* Virtue and Co., London. 1877.

17. *Spiritual Magazine,* 1877; 5:64

18. **Sexton, G.** *Spirit-mediums and conjurors.* James Burns, London. 1873.

19. **Lamont,** 2004.

20. **Gilovich T.** *How we know what isn't so: the fallibility of human reason in everyday life.* The Free Press, New York. 1988.

21. **Thomas K.** *Religion and the decline of magic.* Penguin University Books, London. 1973:774.

22. **Edmondson M.** Are you superhuman? *The Young Magician,* 2001; 10.

23. **Lamont P. Wiseman R.** *Magic in theory: an introduction to the theoretical and psychological elements of conjuring.* University of Hertfordshire Press, Hatfield. 1999.

24. **Inglis B.** *The hidden power.* Jonathon Cape, London. 1986:266–267.

25. On the former, see Haraldsson E. Interrogative suggestibility and its relationship with personality, perceptual defensiveness and extraordinary beliefs. *Personality and Individual Differences,* 1985; 6:765–767; Hergovich A. Field dependence, suggestibility and belief in paranormal phenomena. *Personality and Individual Differences,* 2003; 34:195–209; Wiseman R, Greening E, Smith M. Belief in the paranormal and suggestion in the séance room. *British Journal of Psychology,* 2003; 94:285–297. On the latter, see Alcock JE. Otis LP. Critical thinking and belief in the paranormal. *Psychological Reports,* 1980; 46:479–482; Wierzbicki M. Reasoning errors and belief in the paranormal. *Journal of Social Psychology,* 1985; 125:489–494.

26. **Irwin H.** Reasoning skills of paranormal believers. *Journal of Parapsychology,* 1996; 55:281–300; Roe C. Critical thinking and belief in the paranormal: a re-evaluation. *British Journal of Psychology,* 1999; 90:85–98; Wiseman R, Greening E. 'It's still bending': verbal suggestion and alleged psychokinetic ability. Proceedings of the Parapsychological Association Convention, Vienna, 2004.

27. **Wiseman and Greening,** 2004.

28. **Irwin H.** Belief in the paranormal: a review of the empirical literature. *Journal of the American Society for Psychical Research,* 1993; 87:1–39; Blackmore S. Probability misjudgment and belief in the paranormal: a newspaper survey. *British Journal of Psychology,* 1997; 88:683–689; Roe, 1999.

29. **Singer B. Benassi V A.** Occult beliefs. *American Scientist,* 1981; 69:49–55; Wiseman R, Morris RL. Recalling pseudo-psychic phenomena. *British Journal of Psychology,* 1995; 86:113–125; Hergovich A. The effect of pseudo-psychic demonstrations as dependent on belief in paranormal phenomena and suggestibility. *Personality and Individual Differences,* 2004; 36:365–380.

30. 30. Hergovich, 2004.

31. **Jones W, Russell D.** The selective processing of belief disconfirming information. *European Journal of Social Psychology,* 1980; 10:309–312; Smith MD. The effect of belief in the paranormal and prior set upon the observation of a 'psychic' demonstration. *European Journal of Parapsychology,* 1992;9:24–34; Wiseman and Morris, 1995; Wiseman and Greening, 2004.

32. **Blackmore S.** A postal survey of OBEs and other experiences. *Journal of the Society for Psychical Research,* 1984; 52:225–244; Clarke D. Experience and other reasons given for belief and disbelief in paranormal and religious phenomena. *Journal of the Society for Psychical Research,* 1995; 60:371–384.

33. **Irwin H.** *An introduction to parapsychology,* 3rd edn. McFarland & Co., Jefferson, NC. 1999.

34. **Irwin H.** On paranormal disbelief: the psychology of the sceptic. In G Zollschan, JF Schumaker, GF Walsh, ed. *Exploring the paranormal: perspectives on belief and experience* Prism Press, Bridport, UK. 1989:305–312.

35. **Lawrence T.** How many factors of paranormal belief are there? A critique of the Paranormal Belief Scale. *Journal of Parapsychology,* 1995; 59:3–25; Tobacyk J. What is the correct dimensionality of paranormal beliefs? A reply to Lawrence's critique of the Paranormal Belief Scale. *Journal of Parapsychology,* 1995; 59:27–46.

36. On the former, see Layton BD, Turnbull B. Belief, evaluation and performance on an ESP task. *Journal of Experimental Social Psychology,* 1975; 11:166–179; Crandall JE. Effects of favorable and unfavorable conditions on the psi-missing displacement effect. *Journal of Parapsychology,* 1985; 79:27–38. On the

latter, see Fishbein M, Raven BH. The AB scales: an operational definition of belief and attitude. In M Fishbein, ed. *Readings and attitude theory and measurement*. Wiley, New York. 1967:183–189; Smith MD, Foster CL, Stovin G. Intelligence and paranormal belief: examining the role of context. *Journal of Parapsychology*, 1998; **62**:65–78; Watt C, Baker IS. Remote facilitation of attention focusing with psi-supportive versus psi-unsupportive experimenter suggestions. *Journal of Parapsychology*, 2002; **66**:151–168.

37. **Potter J, Wetherell M.** *Discourse and social psychology: beyond attitudes and behaviour.* Sage, London. 1987.

38. **Wooffitt R.** *Telling tales of the unexpected: the organisation of factual discourse.* Harvester Wheatsheaf London. 1992.

Chapter 3

The magic in the brain: how conjuring works to deceive our minds

Massimo Polidoro

'Conjuring' is a word that indicates the ancient art of making sensorial or optical illusions appear as real. It is a form of entertainment in which, by the use of trickery, the conjurer appears to be able to control and violate the laws of nature.

'Magic' is a synonym, and so is 'prestidigitation'. This last term, in particular, was created in 1815 by French magician Jules de Rivère in order to indicate manual dexterity, or sleight of hand. It was commonly thought then, and often still is today, that magic tricks work because 'the hand is quicker than the eye', or because magicians use tricked apparatus or 'they do it with mirrors'. However, this is not exactly the case.

Equipment may play an important part in the trick or may be inconsequential. What is always true, however, is that a considerable part of the success of a magician's performance is based on the use of psychology. It is not enough to know how a trick works in order to both entertain and deceive an audience, what is needed above all is an understanding of how the human mind works.

Misdirection

A lot of things that modern neuroscientists know today about the brain's mechanisms have been used for centuries by unwitting magicians. At the basis of every magic trick, for example, there is the ability of the performer in controlling the attention of the audience.

This is what is usually termed 'misdirection', and it consists essentially in directing the attention of the spectator towards non-significant aspects of the performance, distracting it from the relevant ones. It is the most crucial tool in the bag of the magician and, as Jean Hugard[1] said, 'The principle of misdirection plays such an important role in magic that one might say that Magic is misdirection and misdirection is Magic'.

A magician asks a person to hold a different coin in each hand, then he turns his back and invites the person to 'think' about one of the two coins, by bringing the hand with it to his own forehead. After a few seconds, the magician turns around, asks the spectator to show him both coins and then he guesses correctly which is the one thought of by the spectator. In reality, the magician does not look at the coins but observes the hands of the spectator: the one that was held at the forehead is paler than the other, since less blood circulated in it. You will notice, however, that the magician did not say 'Raise a hand and I will guess whci one it was'; this would have given the trick away.

Several magicians, including Hugard,[1] distinguish between 'physical' and 'psychological' misdirection. By using 'physical misdirection', as Lamont and Wiseman[2] put it, the magician may direct what the spectator perceives by controlling where he looks. By using 'psychological misdirection', the magician may direct what the spectator thinks by controlling his suspicion.

More specifically. In physical misdirection, the performer needs to direct *where* the spectator is looking, by creating some new stimulus: a sudden sound, an unfamiliar object, a quick move or a facial expression. He also needs to direct *when* the spectator is looking, by reducing or increasing the level of attention. He would try to reduce it when the trick is being put into action, and increase it when the 'magic' has to be shown.

In psychological misdirection, the object of the magician is in reducing or diverting the spectator's suspicion. This can be done through various techniques, such as making unnatural moves appear natural or 'inducing the audience to attribute the effect produced to any cause rather than the real one'[3].

Let us say, for example, that the magician needs to make a coin disappear from his hand. He would first show the coin with his right hand, then drop it in his left which closes in a fist; take some magic powder from his coat pocket with his right fingers, sprinkle it on the left fist, then open the fist and show that the coin is no more.

The trick is very simple, the coin never leaves the right hand, it is falsely transferred to the left hand and then it is dropped in the pocket when the right hand reaches for the 'magic powder'. Knowing the trick, however, is near to nothing. In order to make it look like magic, the false transfer has to be learned to perfection by the magician, who will rehearse it many times in front of a mirror. The action has to look perfectly natural, and in order to learn how a natural pass of a coin from one hand to the other looks, he will maybe spend days just looking at his hands really passing a coin from one hand to the other. Then he has to learn how to hold the left hand in a convincing fist, and how to hide the coin in the right hand without raising suspicions.

When the technical part is learned, it is time to concentrate on the psychological aspects of the performance. In order to misdirect *where* the spectator will look when the pass is done, the magician can make good use of eye contact. As Andrew Galloway[4] said: 'If you want somebody to look at something, look at it. If you want somebody to look at you, look at them'. So, when he first shows the coin in his right hand, the magician looks at it and the spectators will do the same. Then, when he has to make the false transfer, he will raise his eyes and look at the audience, maybe asking something or making a joke related to what he is doing.

By taking the attention away from his hands, the magician is also signalling that nothing of importance is happening, thus reducing the level of attention of the audience.

When the coin appears to have been transferred to the left hand the magician not only looks at the left fist, but also raises it upward. The human eye is automatically drawn to movement, and the fact that the magician is looking at the left moving hand as well reinforces the need for the audience to look at it.

By again putting the focus on the left hand, the magician is also signalling that now the magic will take place and everybody has to pay attention, thus raising the level of attention. However, the 'move' has already taken place.

Meanwhile, the right hand secretly holding the coin, reaches for the right coat pocket. It drops the coin there and takes out some 'magic powder' (it could be anything, from salt to glittering powder). Taking the powder gives the magician a rationale for putting his hand inside his pocket: an action that, without the excuse of the powder, would look extremely suspicious.

Finally, he sprinkles the powder on the closed fist and then opens it slowly. He can also create a momentary false solution to the effect by opening the hand but keeping the third and fourth fingers tightly together, as if clipping the coin behind them. This immediately raises suspicion from the audience, and draws it away from the real method. When the hand is shown to be perfectly empty, the audience is left with no solution to the mystery.

Cognitive short cuts

Some of the most formidable illusions rely on the human tendency to reach a conclusion with insufficient data. 'Seeing is believing' is an old truism. 'I saw it with my own eyes' is an expression of confidence about the reality of what was experienced. People learn to trust their sensory experiences, and usually that is a practical approach. Their interpretation of the world, based on analysis of incoming sensory information, is accurate enough for most purposes. But how can anyone know that what he sees or hears is 'reality'?[5]

Our brain is not blank and passive. Because of its anatomical and physiological make-up, the brain processes sensory information in pre-determined ways. As experiences multiply, they set up certain expectancies in terms of what is valued and what is rejected. Past experiences bias the brain toward experiencing the world in a certain way.[6]

We learn to perceive things in certain ways which allow us to function appropriately in the physical world around us. This, however, can also lead us to wrong conclusions.

Consider this example by James Randi[7]. A magician produces from his inner jacket pocket a brand new deck of cards. He removes the cellophane wrapper, breaks the seal and removes the pack. The end-cards (extra Joker, guarantee, etc.) are discarded, and he commences to shuffle the cards thoroughly. The deck is handed to a spectator, who continues the shuffling, and then squares up the deck and returns it to the magician, who refuses it, asking only that it be placed back in his inner pocket, without the box, exactly as it left the hands of the spectator.

All sounds fair. Yet now the magician is able to look away from his pocket and announce the identities of four or five cards in a row, in advance of his reaching in and removing them. He names a card, then reaches in and removes it, tossing it face-up on the table. He repeats this several times, then invites the spectator to reach in, remove the rest of the deck, and add the 'divined' cards to the pack. The whole thing can then be examined freely. The deck proves to be intact, unmarked and ordinary.

What happened?

It's all very easy, once you know the trick. The magician has previously opened the pack, removed the four or five cards he wishes to 'divine', and replaced the other cards, with seal and wrapping restored. The few selected cards are memorized in order, and placed in the inner shirt pocket, adjacent to the inner jacket pocket.

The simple fact of seeing a deck still wrapped in cellophane and sealed induces in the spectators the idea that it has not been tampered with. To make the illusion more powerful, however, misdirection must be brought in as well. If the pack was given to the spectator and he was allowed to open it, some impact would be lost. Sounds illogical? Actually, as it was said, an important strategy to divert suspicion consists of deliberately raising suspicions about false solutions and then demolishing them in a casual way. This happens when the performer removes the pack from the inner pocket and opens it himself. The spectator accepts, with reservations, what he sees, but has a need to handle the deck. The magician in fact hands it over casually, asking that it be further shuffled '... if you wish'. This offer is never refused. The casual approach completely disarms the spectator. It looks as if none of this procedure is really important at all. He has, after all, been given free handling of the cards, and he himself places them into the pocket again. Thus he relaxes and, without realizing it, gets ready to be fooled...

Ambiguity

A fundamental rule in magic states that the magician should never tell the audience what he intends to do: this would completely ruin the surprise and alert the spectators to focus more closely on what is relevant to the effect. Ambiguity, then, plays a central role in magic and, as with everything else we perceive, it is the context that strips this ambiguity away and furnishes a meaning.

How powerful is the context in directing cognitive reasoning can be deduced by the following story as told by Barton Bowyer[9]. A group of magicians goes to the theatre to watch a colleague perform. During the performance, a man stands up from the audience and challenges the magician to accomplish a specific magical number for which he is famous: the growth of a flower from an empty pot. The magician accepts the challenge and invites the man on stage. He takes a pot and gives it to the man so that he can check it thoroughly. Once the spectator is satisfied, the magician fills the pot with sand, then places it on top of a table. Slowly, a flower rises out from the pot to the amazement of the challenger, who returns to his seat stumped. The public applauds wildly and the magicians in the audience have no clue to how their friend could perform such a miracle.

Once the show is over, they reach their friend backstage and ask him the 'secret', since no known method could be used to introduce the flower inside the pot under such strict conditions. The performer, bemused, explains that, in fact, the flower was not introduced by him in the pot, but by the spectator checking it! Engaged by the situation,

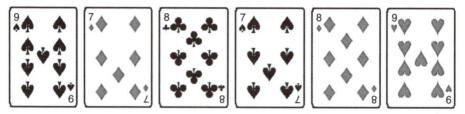

Fig. 3.1A

the magicians had not been able to detach the friend–challenger context and realize that the challenger (actually an accomplice of the magician) had actively contributed to the success of the illusion.

Ambiguity also allows the magician to alter the ending of the trick according to the responses he gets from the audience.

On a table, there are two small piles of cards. The magician shows an envelope where he has sealed a 'prediction' of something that will happen shortly. He then invites a spectator to choose one of the two piles. Having done so, the envelope is opened and in it is clearly stated which pile is chosen.

Again, a very simple method: one pile is comprised of six different cards, the other one is comprised of the four sixes (hearts, clubs, spades and diamonds). The prediction reads: 'The spectator will choose the pile of six'. If he chooses the one with six cards he is correct, because counting the cards in each pile (without turning their faces), it can be seen that one has four and the other six cards. On the contrary, if he chooses the one with the four sixes, the magician is still correct, for he only has to turn the cards over and show (without counting them) that one pile has indifferent cards, and the other one has all four sixes.

Perceptual limitations

This is a pre-cognitive test done through this book. Look at these six cards (see Fig. 3.1A).

Now, mentally select any one of the cards at random. Have you got one? Good, then memorize it. Do not just look at the card, I want you to stare at it, become one with it, whisper its name (but not too loud, the book may hear it ...) Now remember the name of your card and do not forget it.

You think you had a free choice but I actually knew exactly what you would choose. You don't believe me? You are still free to change your mind one last time if you wish. Do you want to change the card? Do it now. Done? Perfect. Now memorize your card and be ready to be amazed. Turn to page 41

Now that you have been properly amazed, you will probably be even more surprised when you take a good look at the cards above and then again at the cards at page 41 (Fig. 3.1B). Did you notice anything odd? If not, look again very carefully ...

Exactly. The six cards you saw here are all different from the ones on page 40. You did not see your card and so you thought that I had correctly guessed it. The truth is that you did not see that all of the cards were different. How can this be possible?

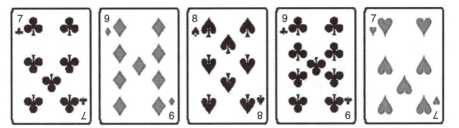

Fig. 3.1B You have a card in your mind: well, since I knew you would choose that one, I took it off from the six cards I showed you and so here are the remaining five cards: You card has disappeared, hasn't it? Do you want to know how I did it? Then, go back to page 40.

Recent studies have shown that under certain circumstances, very large changes can occur in full view in a visual scene without observers noticing them. You may have seen a quite famous 'candid camera' video where one actor asks a person he stops on the street for directions. Almost immediately, two workers carrying a big, wide board, pass rudely in front of the actor so that he can leave and another actor, quite different in appearance, takes his place and continues asking the same information. Interestingly, approximately 50 per cent of the subjects fail to notice that they are talking to a different person after the board passes.

This phenomenon has been called 'Change Blindness'[10] and psychologists at Harvard[11–13] have collected some startling examples of this.

In one of the most surprising tests, subjects are invited to watch a short video clip where two teams of players, dressed in black and white, have a basketball each and pass it around to their own players. Subjects watching the clip are given the task of counting the number of passes made by the white team. The clip lasts about half a minute and, at one point, a person dressed as a black gorilla walks in the middle of the players, thumps his chest and walks off. The extraordinary thing is that most of the people watching the clip do not see the gorilla.

This change blindness depends on the focus of attention. When observers are attending to another object or event, they are less likely to notice the unexpected event.

Though not recognized as such, it is however interesting to consider that magicians, as well as artists, have for centuries traded on precisely these and other familiar perceptual limitations.

Memory alterations

One last tool in the bag of every good magician is the ability to tamper with the spectators' memory of what they saw. Usually, when somebody witnesses a magic performance, he or she will later try to reconstruct what happened in order to guess the method behind the magic.

Misdirection and ambiguity help a lot in making it difficult for an audience to remember a performance correctly. We also know how fake psychics are used to recapitulate what happened in a way that never happened. A magician may do the same. He may take a deck of cards and give it to a spectator. Then ask him or her to shuffle it, take a card out, look at it, and place it back. The magician may just cut the deck in half once and then leave it there on the table, asking the spectator to shuffle it even more. He will then proceed to guess the card correctly.

All through this procedure he may repeat a few times that he does not want to 'touch the deck' and, before revealing the card thought of, he may recapitulate what happened stating that he 'never touched the deck'. Most of the people will later be convinced that he really never touched the deck, whereas the trick could only have been possible when he touched it to cut it.

Sometimes, the magician does not even need to do anything, since the spectator will misremember events all by himself. Lamont and Wiseman[2] cite some examples of this, as in the experiment by Triplett[14] in which a magician threw a ball into the air twice, then secretly ditched the ball and pretended to throw it into the air. Seventy-eight out of 165 spectators later remembered seeing the ball go up and disappear, stating various points at which it vanished. Also they cite another experiment[15] in which a magician performed a number of tricks, but only described a coin transposition effect. Weeks later, 80 per cent of the audience remembered actually seeing the transposition effect.

In the end, then, it appears as if the performer on stage is certainly a good artist and actor, but the real magician is the one that hides inside our heads . . .

References and notes

1. **Hugard J.** Misdirection. *Hugard's magic monthly*, March, 1960:115.
2. **Lamont P, Wiseman R.** *Magic in theory.* University of Hertfordshire Press, Hatfield, UK. 1999.
3. **Robert-Houdin JE.** *Secrets of conjuring and magic* (transl. Professor Hoffmann). Routledge, London. 1878.
4. **Galloway A.** *The Ramsay legend.* Goodliffe Publications, Birmingham. 1969.
5. **Alcock JE.** *Parapsychology: science or magic?* Pergamon Books, Oxford. 1981.
6. **Zusne L, Jones WH.** *Anomalistic psychology.* Lawrence Erlbaum Associates, Hillsdale, NJ. 1989.
7. **Randi J.** The psychology of conjuring. *Technology Review*, January, 1978:56–63.
8. **Rampin M.** *L'arte dell'impossibile.* Asolo Edizioni, Treviso, Italy. 2004.
9. **Bowyer B.** *Cheating: deception in war & magic, games & sports, sex & religion, business & con games, politics & espionage, art & science.* St Martin's Press, New York. 1982.
10. **McConkie GW, Currie CB.** Visual stability across saccades while viewing complex pictures. *Journal of Experimental Psychology: Human Perception and Performance,* 1996; 22:563–581.
11. **Simons DJ, Levin DT.** Change blindness. *Trends in Cognitive Sciences,* 1997; 1:261–267.
12. **Simons DJ, Levin DT.** Failure to detect changes to people in a real-world interaction. *Psychonomic Bulletin and Review,* 1998;5:644–649.
13. **Simons DJ, Chabris CF.** Gorillas in our midst: sustained inattentional blindness for dynamic events. *Perception,* 1999; 28:1059–1074.
14. **Triplett N.** The psychology of conjuring deceptions. *The American Journal of Psychology,* XI, 1900;4:439–510.
15. **Siegel, L.** *Net of magic: wonders and deceptions in India.* University of Chicago Press, Chicago. 1991.

Tall tales on memory and learning

Chapter 4

The legend of the magical number seven

Nelson Cowan, Candice C. Morey and Zhijian Chen

Origin of the legend of seven

Individuals who know very little about experimental psychology are still likely to have heard or read that people can keep in mind about seven items. Telephone numbers were developed with some concern for people's ability to remember the numbers, and local calls in the USA typically require dialling seven digits (and, in some countries, just six digits). Intelligence test batteries include a test called *digit-span* in which one is to repeat a list of random digits in the presented order; the digits in the list change from one trial to the next, and the length of the list keeps increasing every few trials until the tested individual cannot repeat any lists correctly. Normal adults typically can repeat lists of about seven digits. This maxim of seven has often been applied to daily life. For example, some self-help sources proclaim that a good oral presentation should include up to seven points on the outline. The number seven appears in dinner-party talk, along with other psychological folk wisdom such as the best way to raise children or how to bargain with salespeople effectively.

How did this information become established in the public mind? It goes back to a seminal journal article by George Miller[1] that was published in 1956, in the formative days of a new field that came to be known as *cognitive psychology*, the experimental study of thought processes such as memory, attention, imagery, and language comprehension and production. Miller's article was written in a very engaging and entertaining fashion, in part because it began as an hour-long conference presentation before it was moulded into a written article. It begins with the author's humorous confession that he has been persecuted by the integer seven. He goes on to discuss three types of psychological task in which this number has emerged.

The first and most obvious task is *immediate memory*, such as the digit-span task or similar tasks in which lists are presented and must then be repeated without delay in the presented order. No matter whether the stimuli are words, letters or digits, lists of only about seven of them can be recalled. This differs somewhat from one individual to the next and from one type of memoranda to the next and, indeed, the title of Miller's article included the phrase, 'the magical number seven, plus or minus two'.

In a second type of task that Miller discussed, *absolute judgement*, a single stimulus is presented and its correct label has to be recalled. This is tough when the stimuli are simple and differ in only one dimension, such as a series of lines of different lengths or a series of tones of different pitches, each with a different label. It turns out not to matter whether the stimuli differ only slightly or whether they differ a lot. So long as they differ enough that the research participants can see or hear the differences between them when they are placed side by side (or, for sounds, in close succession), the same memory limit applies. The task of identifying an isolated stimulus can be accomplished adequately only when there are no more than about seven stimulus choices, again varying depending on the exact context.

A third type of task that Miller discussed is the *span of attention*. In the relevant task, a set of haphazardly arranged objects (or perhaps dots on a computer screen) must be *enumerated* as quickly as possible, i.e. the participant must indicate how many objects are present. Now, your own experience probably tells you that enumerating the objects in a set of, say, two is a very different experience from enumerating objects in a larger set of, say, 11. The two objects can be enumerated very quickly, on the basis of rapid recognition or attention to both at once, without counting. It is a different matter with 11 objects. One must carefully keep track of which ones have been counted while one is in the process of counting the others. Miller said that sets of up to about six or seven objects are enumerated rapidly, whereas, with higher numbers, the time to give an answer begins to rise steeply with each added object in the set.

These three phenomena not only comprised an impressive display of evidence; they comprised evidence central to the newly developing field of cognitive psychology. In an earlier era, philosophically oriented psychologists such as William James had pointed out that there were several types of memory. James[2] distinguished between the small amount of information that is or recently was in one's conscious mind, which he termed *primary memory*, and the large storehouse of knowledge that one collects over a lifetime, which he termed *secondary memory*. If cognitive psychology was to become scientific, though, there had to be a way to measure and characterize these types of memory. The estimate that about seven items could be held in primary memory would be a giant step toward that end. In the era when Miller wrote, psychologists from the behaviourist tradition, counter to James, were advising that one should study stimuli and responses only, and should avoid making statements about unobservable entities inside the human head such as memory or mental imagery. On the basis of Miller's article and other, converging work published at around the same time, that sentiment was overturned for cognitive psychologists. Regarding Miller's findings, if people could recall about seven items, there must be some holding mechanism in the brain, corresponding to James' primary memory, that could hold about seven items at once but not much more. The well-described findings were repeated often by psychologists and they eventually reached the general public, in much the same way that concepts from Sigmund Freud earlier had reached the public.

The intent behind the legend

There are aspects of Miller's 1956 article[1] that have left the careful reader with a bit of confusion regarding what he intended to say. He does not actually make the claim that memory span, absolute identification and enumeration tasks call upon the same faculty of the mind limited to seven or so items. Instead, he ends with a note on the mystery of the convergence of many phenomena:

> What about the seven-point rating scale, the seven categories for absolute judgment, the seven objects in the span of attention, and the seven digits in the span of immediate memory?...Perhaps there is something deep and profound behind all of these sevens, something just calling out for us to discover it. But I suspect that it is only a pernicious, Pythagorean coincidence (p. 96).

Often when one ponders a legend and learns more, the supporting evidence can be seen to have different implications from what one might have thought according to the legend that developed. In this case, it turns out that Miller was not very interested scientifically in the number seven. Perhaps if he had been, he would not have attached the adjective 'magical' to it. As he explained in an autobiographical essay,[3] he was asked to give an hour-long presentation at a point in his career when he did not feel that he had any one research topic developed enough to take up that time period. He did, however, have some research on immediate memory and on absolute judgement. He did not want to give two unconnected reports of these research topics and at first saw no common theme between them. However, he then discovered that they shared the number seven in terms of research participants' limits in performance. He decided to make that limitation a theme of the talk to tie them together and, to add an air of legitimacy, threw in the research on enumeration. However, the reference to 'plus or minus' two was supposed to convey the humorous notion that a magical number could have a margin of error. This is an amazing way for a scientific legend to be born.

One concept that was more important to Miller[1] was the concept of *chunking*. This means taking multiple items and putting them together to form new groups or chunks. Before Miller, psychologists tried to measure information in *bits*, a term frequently used in computing, meaning a choice between two options. Two bits equals 2^2 or four options, three bits equals 2^3 or eight options, and so on. For example, how many yes/no questions would it take you to guess which English letter a friend is thinking of? With your first question (eliciting one bit of information), you could ask if the letter comes before N in the alphabet, narrowing the choices down to 13 of 26 letters, or half of the alphabet; with your second question (eliciting a second bit), you could narrow the choices down to approximately half of that half; and so on, until you could determine which letter it was. There also is a mathematical definition of bits on a scale that includes fractions; without going into this definition, it is enough here to give the example that 2.6 bits is something more than 2 bits but smaller than 3 bits. If one considers digits from the set 0–9, there are 10 choices so each digit conveys somewhere between 3 and 4 bits of information. If one considers the 26 English letters, each letter conveys somewhere between 4 bits

($2^4 = 16$ choices) and 5 bits ($2^5 = 32$ choices). There are many thousands of English words, so the bit measure for an English word would be considerably higher.

However, it turned out that bits did not matter for actual research participants. Memory span is about the same number of items when the items are random digits, random letters or random words. It appears that immediate memory should be measured not in bits, but in units that are psychologically meaningful. Each meaningful unit is called a chunk. In this regard, human memory appears to operate in a manner quite different from computer memory, which is composed of many locations that can be turned on or off, each worth 1 bit of information.

One might have thought that bits would be important for humans, given that each nerve cell is in a firing or non-firing state at any moment and therefore may convey only 1 bit of information. Apparently, though, this binary property of individual nerve cells is not what is important for immediate memory limits. Perhaps that is because large portions of the brain's memory system can participate in immediate memory; not just a relatively small, dedicated portion of the memory locations as in a computer. What may be important is limitations in the firing patterns that nerve cells can take on at any moment, such that only a few ideas can be actively represented concurrently.

Miller and one of his colleagues found that stimuli can be transformed in a way that makes them easier to remember, by reducing the number of chunks. In the binary numerical system that is used to encode computer memory locations using only the digits 0 and 1, the rightmost digit reflects how many 1s there are, the next digit to the left reflects how many 2s, and the next digit to the left of that reflects how many 4s; so 001 = 1; 010 = 2; 011 = 3; 100 = 4; 101 = 5; 110 = 6; and 111 = 7. It would be difficult to remember the binary string 011–111–101–110, yet much easier to remember the familiar decimal numerical equivalent, 3–7–5–6. If one knows the binary system, one can recode the binary string into its decimal equivalent. In the example given here, recoding reduces the load on immediate memory from 12 chunks (the binary digits shown) down to only four chunks (the digits 3, 7, 5 and 6). Another example that makes the concept clear is memorization of the letter string *USAFBICIA*. This looks like nine chunks (single, unrelated letters) but they can be reduced to three acronyms: USA (United States of America), FBI (Federal Bureau of Investigation) and CIA (Central Intelligence Agency). For someone who knows these acronyms by heart and notices these patterns, there are only three chunks to be remembered.

In sum, it was not the number seven *per se* that fascinated Miller, but rather the processes that were used to encode information and the nature of the units that were meaningfully encoded. This was intimated in the tone of the closing comments in his 1956 article[1] and was made clear in his later autobiographical discussion.[3] People could recall about seven chunks, regardless of the processes that were involved in deriving those chunks from the stimuli to be recalled.

The formation of chunks in immediate or primary memory often made use not only of the information present to the research participant, but also of prior knowledge that was already present in long-term or secondary memory. It is worth noting that there have been demonstrations that practically anything can be held in immediate memory, if there is enough knowledge to back it up. Anders Ericsson[4] and colleagues trained an individual to increase his digit span from the usual seven or so up to 80 digits, in the course of a year. This individual was an athlete who already had memorized many record running times. This made it easier to transform digits into multidigit chunks. For example, 3.98 might be the record time in minutes to run a mile on a certain type of track. This could be supplemented with new chunks, such as 85.7 as the age of a fairly old man. Grouping sets of three and four digits together to form new chunks, over a period of months this special individual (or was he just specially motivated?) learned to repeat lists of about 20 digits, presumably organized into 5–7 larger chunks. Then, somehow he learned to combine several chunks into even larger super-chunks, so that he eventually could repeat series of about 80 digits. This skill did not generalize; his memory for letters or words remained at about seven.

Similarly, Jeffrey Rouder and colleagues[5] recently found that, with extended practice, absolute judgements for line lengths could be extended considerably beyond the seven or so distinct labels that Miller noted. We do not know just how chunking is involved in absolute judgements but one possibility is that there is a limit in how many categories can be kept distinctly in mind during the test, which might be overcome through extended familiarity with the categories.

Problems with the number seven

There were findings resulting in seven or so items remembered, and these findings require some explanation. Still, one might question whether seven actually is a fundamental number of immediate memory. Consider this. If people are able to perceive multiple items in terms of chunks that they already know (such as the acronym IRS), might it not also be possible for them to form new chunks rapidly? Why is it, for example, that the seven digits in a telephone number are typically presented in two groups, in the form # # # – # # # #? It seems reasonable to suppose that some rapid grouping process goes on to ease the process of recall by reducing the number of independent units that have to be recalled. These questions did not get a great deal of immediate attention, however. One reason was that, after 1956, George Miller's career seemed to veer more into the study of language and categorization, as opposed to primary memory.

Published just 4 years after Miller's famous article, a 1960 article by George Sperling[6] became another lasting classic in the field of cognitive psychology and yielded a different answer about primary memory. The study's main point was that a large amount of information about how a visual stimulus looks is stored in the mind for a very short time, but the study also provided information about primary memory. On each trial, a spatial array of characters (such as letters) was flashed on the screen briefly. The task was to record all of the characters in the array, or some part of the array. A large amount of elegant experimental work was included in the article. It was found that if the row of the array to write down was indicated by a tone presented quickly enough, before sensory memory had faded, it was possible to write down most of the characters in that row. This showed that sensory memory could hold visual information from at least 12 characters at once. However, if there was no tone cue and the entire array had to be written down, there was a more severe limit in performance so that only about four of the items could be written down. The theoretical model for this task was that information had to be processed, from a visual form in sensory memory into a more categorized or labelled form in primary memory, before it could be reported. Either primary memory could hold only about four items, or sensory memory did not last long enough to allow more than four items to be processed. One can imagine an analogy in which a painter must paint objects onto a canvas of limited size (like primary memory) using an open tray of paint that is plentiful but dries up extremely rapidly (like a fading sensory memory). The number of objects that can be painted onto the canvas depends on both the size of the canvas and the time available before the paint becomes too dry to use. We will return to this issue later.

There also were studies indicating that people could recall roughly four clusters or chunks of objects, though experts could recall chunks comprising more objects. This research involved people's ability to recall the pieces on a chessboard, as a function of their expertise in chess.[7] Work continuing along this line[8] has suggested that even the notion of a chunk is often an oversimplification for what can be a broad network of associations between items, or template.

There were a few studies by other investigators looking at the issue of grouping in immediate recall. For example, Tulving and Patkau[9] carried out a study in which people were asked to remember strings of 24 words that were in jumbled order, or that resembled coherent English to varying degrees (e.g. 'The best grain stamps made in America you beast that see something...'), or that were perfectly coherent English sentences. The task was to recall the words in any order (*free recall*). Whenever runs of several words were recalled in the same order in which they were presented, each such run counted as a single chunk. Many more words were recalled in the sequences that were better approximations to English, but the measured number of chunks recalled remained fixed across conditions, at 4–6 chunks. It was just that more coherent strings of words led to *larger* chunks recalled, not *more* chunks. Other methods were invented in attempts to identify chunks clearly, such as making the assumption that the task of recalling lists in order (*serial recall*) would proceed relatively smoothly within a chunk but would be more likely to encounter difficulty between chunks.[10] Overall, though, the magical number seven was neither seriously questioned nor put to many stringent tests in the early days. Some investigators lived by it, and others probably were sceptical and ignored it, perhaps taking their cues from the ending of Miller's article in which it was said that the magical number seven was probably just a coincidence.

The year 1975 was, in hindsight, an important one for the study of immediate memory. By this year, the magical number seven had been recognized as a classic finding that had withstood the test of time. Yet, two papers were published that also have had a lasting impact and have cast doubt on the magic of the number seven.

First, Alan Baddeley and colleagues[11] showed that it is not simply the number of meaningful units that mattered in immediate recall; word length mattered. Lists of words that took longer to pronounce were not recalled as well as lists of the same number of words that could be pronounced more quickly. The explanation of that finding was that people refresh their verbal memories by rehearsing the words (i.e. imagining saying the words to themselves), a process that can be carried out more efficiently for short words. If the entire list were rehearsed over and over, for example, the time between one rehearsal of a particular word and the next rehearsal of the same word would be shorter if the words were shorter, leaving less time for forgetting. It may be that rehearsal takes place in a more complex or piecemeal manner than that but, in any case, many such methods of rehearsal would lead to the expectation of the word-length effect that actually was obtained. Baddeley has amassed a large amount of information about primary memory in subsequent work, and a time-related limit remains an important part of the theorization that has become predominant in the field of what is now called *working memory*, or primary memory as it is used to help do work such as solving problems and comprehending and producing language.

Secondly, rehearsal aside, in a 1975 book chapter,[12] one of the founding fathers of the field of cognitive psychology, Donald Broadbent, began to question how fundamental the number seven actually was in primary memory. The logic of this challenge was similar to what has been stated above. It was pointed out that although people typically could remember up to about seven items, perhaps a more meaningful number was the number of items that people could remember flawlessly (because presumably those items are recalled without relying on a mental strategy that can fail). For sets of only three items, memory was nearly flawless. Adding a fourth or fifth item resulted in a set that could usually be recalled correctly; adding more made the situation worse. It therefore appeared that three was a basic capacity limit and that rehearsal, grouping or other strategies or mental tricks might be used sometimes to increase the number recalled beyond that basic capacity. As analogies for these strategies, a juggler can keep multiple balls off the ground by repeatedly renewing their upward momentum (like rehearsing), and a person can keep multiple balls off the ground by putting several of them together on a plate (like chunking). However, jugglers sometimes make mistakes and balls sometimes roll off of plates. Broadbent pointed out other phenomena to support the notion that the magical number was not seven, but three. For example, when one attempts to recall items from a category in secondary memory, one tends to recall in bursts of three items. Try, for example, to name countries of the world as quickly as possible and you will notice that they tend to be produced in spurts of just several countries at a time.

Is there a magical number after all?

Much more recently, one of the present authors (Nelson Cowan) wrote a literature review[13] that examined Broadbent's hypothesis more broadly and systematically. It suggested that, across many types of experiment, something like a semi-magical number

NAPIER   SITY L.I.S.

four (plus or minus two, varying across individuals and situations) actually exists. To find this result, one must include only procedures in which the items are well known and in which it is impossible to form larger chunks from the items. This can be accomplished, for example, by presenting many items in an array, like Sperling,[6] with the array presented only briefly so that there is not enough time to think about all of the items in a way leading to extensive chunking. In a particularly compelling demonstration of this, called multiobject tracking,[14] there are multiple objects on the computer screen and then several of them momentarily are marked to stand out (for example by flashing). When this stops, so that all the items look alike again, they wander around the screen randomly, in different directions. When they stop, the research participant is quizzed regarding whether a certain object was one of the previously marked objects, or not. People typically can follow or track a maximum of four objects, and sometimes fewer.

Formation of new chunks also can be prevented by presenting lists of spoken items in a situation in which attention is diverted to another task at the time that these items are presented, making rehearsal impossible. Then the spoken items have to be recovered from the stream of auditory sensory memory when a cue to recall them is presented, just after the list in question has ended. If chunking is not possible, it is assumed that each item remains a single chunk in primary memory. Under such circumstances, about four items (i.e. presumably, single-item chunks) can be recalled. Similar results are obtained if the spoken items are attended but covert verbal rehearsal is prevented by requiring that the participant at the same time repeats a meaningless phrase during the testing, a procedure known as *articulatory suppression*.

Could it be shown that this capacity limit of about four chunks, observed in so many circumstances when chunks were presumably limited to one item each,[13] also applies when chunking is possible? If so, then this capacity limit will gain considerable generality. This does seem to be the case with some of the previous results.[7,9] However, the question has so rarely been studied that it cannot be considered to have been decided.

The reason for the limit of about four chunks also has not been determined. One reason it could occur is that the chunks have to be held in the focus of attention, which is limited in capacity. Another possibility is that the chunks do not have to be held in a region of the mind that is limited in capacity, but that the chunks interfere with each other if they include similar features or concepts.

In the final section of this chapter, we will illustrate the ongoing controversy and how it might be resolved in the future, by reporting on some recent work on capacity limits.

Some recent studies on immediate memory capacity limits

Recently, work has been conducted to help ascertain that there really are capacity limits in immediate memory, and also to determine what the reasons for capacity limits might be.

One recent study conducted to ascertain the capacity limit[15] went back to the standard technique to study immediate memory that was discussed by Miller,[1] serial recall. Instead of preventing chunking (as in Cowan's[13] previous approach), steps were taken to control

Training Conditions (including 4 presentations of each word)
1. Words presented 4 times as singletons, but never paired (0-pairing)
2. Words presented 3 times as singletons, and 1 time paired (1-pairing)
3. Words presented 2 times as singletons, and 2 times paired (2-pairing)
4. Words never presented as singletons, but 4 times paired (4-pairing)
Presentations were randomly mixed as in *box, hat, dog-shoe, box, girl, desk, tree-brick, hat, dog-shoe...*

Serial Recall Test:
For each training condition, a list of 4 pairs of words was presented using known pairs.
Pairs from a condition were randomly arranged in a list, as in *tree-brick, dog-shoe, man-tank, rock-coin.*

Cued Recall Test (before or after the serial recall test)
The first word in a pair was presented and the correct response was the second word, as in *dog - ???*

Fig. 4.1 Illustration of a procedure used by Cowan *et al.*[15] to examine the capacity limit of serial recall expressed in chunks.

chunking. In a training session that preceded serial recall, words were presented either singly or in pairs. Each word was presented four times but a proportion of those presentations involved consistent pairs of words. For example, within the training sequence of words, the words *brick* and *hat* might each be presented twice by themselves, and twice in the consistent pair *brick–hat*. This mixture was termed the 2-pairing condition. The different training conditions (the 0-, 1-, 2- and 4-pairing conditions) used with different words are outlined in Fig. 4.1. The 0-pairing condition involved no training with word pairs *per se* whereas, at the other end of the continuum of training conditions, the 4-pairing condition involved consistent training with words in pairs. The expectation was that more frequent pairing would increase the likelihood that the pair would be remembered as a single chunk in serial recall, rather than as two separate words. There also was a cued-recall test in which, for example, the word *brick* was presented and the correct response was *hat*, if that was a pair that had been presented.

To encourage the recall of learned pairs, items within the eight-word lists to be recalled were presented in pairs. Each list included words from a single training condition. Each list that was composed from words in the 1-, 2- or 4-pairing condition included only pairs that were already familiar from training. For example, somewhere within an eight-word list of words from the 2-pairing condition, the pair *brick–hat* would appear, if it happened to be part of this training condition for a certain participant (as in the example above). Results of this experiment are depicted in Fig. 4.2. The triangles show that the number of words recalled in the correct list positions increased markedly as a result of more paired training.

The circles in Fig. 4.2 show the number of chunks recalled, using one of several measures of chunking. This reflects the sum of one-word chunks, or singletons, and two-word chunks, or learned pairs. (Several methods were used to ascertain which pairs had been learned.) The clear finding was that the number of chunks recalled stayed constant across learning conditions, at an average of about three and a half chunks, even though the number of words recalled increased with pair training.

Another, very different research procedure[16] will now be introduced, not only to show the variety of procedures leading to a capacity limit, but also to permit a discussion of

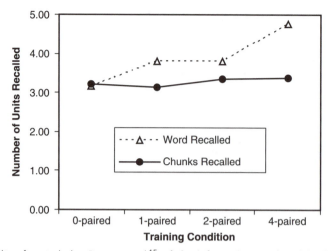

Fig. 4.2 Results of a study by Cowan et al.[15] of the information produced in the serial recall of eight-word lists. The results are averaged over two experiments. The triangles show that the average number of words recalled in the correct serial positions increased as a function of the amount of training with pairs of words. (A similar trend was observed for words recalled regardless of the serial positions.) The circles show that the average number of chunks that were recalled nevertheless remained constant across these training conditions. Chunks included words recalled as singletons, and also pairs of words that were presented together within the list and recalled together with the pair intact.

some recent research on the question of why the capacity limit occurs. In this procedure, a haphazard array of coloured squares is briefly presented and is followed, after a short break of about a second, by another array of squares that is identical to the first one or differs in just the colour of one of the squares. The task is to indicate whether the array has changed or not; half the time, the correct answer is 'yes' and half the time it is 'no'. To make the decision easier, a circle can appear surrounding one square, the participant having been instructed that, if anything changed, it was the colour of the circled square. The procedure is illustrated in Fig. 4.3.

This task is easy with up to four squares in the array, but it becomes progressively harder as the number of squares in the array (called the *set size*) increases beyond four. There is a way to use the results of the experiment to estimate the number of squares from the first array that had to be held in primary memory, taking into account guessing (Cowan[13], p. 166). For all set sizes above four, the estimate comes out to be about three and a half items. If we can assume that the arrays are flashed too briefly for multi-item chunks to be formed, this means an average of three and a half chunks.

This array comparison procedure may be helpful in understanding capacity limits and what factors cause them, because it is a non-verbal procedure. In a verbal procedure, the process of rehearsal may get in the way of understanding the fundamental capacity limit, as discussed above. In a non-verbal procedure, as we will show, this can be less of an issue.

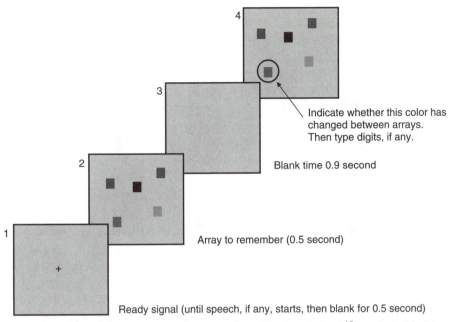

Indicate whether this color has changed between arrays. Then type digits, if any.

Blank time 0.9 second

Array to remember (0.5 second)

Ready signal (until speech, if any, starts, then blank for 0.5 second)

Fig. 4.3 Illustration of the array comparison procedure of Luck and Vogel[16] as adapted by Morey and Cowan.[17] (*See colour plate section*)

Recall that one explanation for the capacity limit is that some information in primary memory must be held in the focus of attention, as William James[2] implied in his writing long ago. It is clear that the focus of attention is limited; perhaps it is the focus of attention that has a capacity of three or four chunks of information. To examine this possibility, one recent study[17] used a dual task in which a spoken list of digits was to be retained and recited aloud during the reception and retention of the first array on the trial. Given that spoken digits and visual arrays have very different features, they need not interfere with one another unless both of them require the same resource that is severely limited in capacity, such as the focus of attention and its potential ability to hold information.

There were four different conditions. In one condition, there was no digit recitation. In two memory load conditions, a random two- or a seven-digit number had to be recited. The fourth condition was a control to make sure that it was not recitation *per se* that hurt recall. In this condition, it was the participant's own seven-digit telephone number that had to be recited during the trial. Because the number was known, it did not impose a load on primary memory. However, it involved digit recitation comparable with the seven-digit load condition. Thus, it was only the seven random digit condition that imposed the kind of load that should make demands on the focus of attention, in addition to articulation.

The results of this study are shown in Fig. 4.4 in terms of the estimated capacity in each condition (averaged across different array sizes). As expected according to the theory that the capacity limit is in the focus of attention, performance was impaired by the

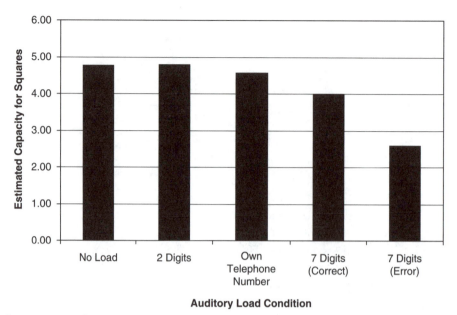

Fig. 4.4 Results of a study of the effect of a verbal memory load on the retention of an array of coloured squares to be compared with a second array.[17] A formula (Cowan[13], p. 166) was used to estimate visual memory capacity expressed as the number of squares retained, which was then averaged across arrays with four, six or eight squares. The key finding is that although repeating a seven-digit load had a strong effect, especially when the load was repeated incorrectly, repeating a known seven-digit number (the participant's own telephone number) had little effect. Therefore, it was the demand on attention rather than articulation *per se* that disrupted retention of the array of coloured squares.

seven-digit memory load, but not by the other recitation conditions. The effect of the memory load was especially great when the load was recited incorrectly, in which case the valiant attempts to retrieve the verbal information were probably distracting in and of themselves.

Recent studies differ in their conclusions. In one study,[18] the interference between visual arrays and digit lists was considerably less than in the study shown in Fig. 4.4. One possibly important difference between the studies was that only in the study that showed more interference[17] was the digit memory load to be recited aloud in the time between the two visual arrays. Other recent work suggests that the retention of verbal information can require attention even if it is to be held silently, provided that two conditions are met. The information must be beyond the amount that can be conveniently and silently rehearsed, yet it must be unstructured enough that it cannot be greatly simplified or chunked using information from long-term memory.[19]

Other recent research has tied the visual array procedure to neural functioning. Individuals with a larger capacity for the coloured squares appear to show electrical signals emanating from the brain that increase more as the number of squares per array increases from two to four.[20] Images of neural responses to stimulation based on functional magnetic resonance imaging (fMRI) show select areas of the brain that respond in a manner similar to the capacity limits observed in behavioural work.[21]

There are many different experimental procedures and each one has to be analysed carefully before we will know whether a similar 'magical number' truly applies to all of them, and for the same reason. In one sort of procedure, a visually presented list of words is followed by a probe word, which has to be judged to be present in the list or absent from it. The reaction time to the last word in the list is shorter than the reaction time to the other words, leading to the possible conclusion that, actually, only one item is held in the focus of attention in such situations.[22] If this is the case, then the capacity limit of 3–4 items might not apply to such situations. However, further work has shown that the fast reaction time spreads from one item to four items as the participants become highly practised.[23] Perhaps, therefore, when the task is novel or difficult, the focus of attention adjusts and zooms in to capture fewer than four chunks, so as to leave more attention free to carry out the task itself. With practice, the task becomes more automatic and attention can be used to hold more chunks at once. A slightly different suggestion[24] is that the focus of attention itself only holds one chunk, but there is a mental region associated with that focus that holds up to four chunks.

Some procedures are highly controversial. Let us return to the enumeration procedure discussed by Miller.[1] Subsequent work has set the limit for rapid enumeration without counting, called *subitizing*, not at seven but at about four objects.[25] Some have suggested that subitizing has nothing to do with a limit in primary memory capacity, but rather with the observation that spatial patterns can be more easily recognized when they consist of fewer objects because, as the number of objects in the display increases, the number of distinguishable patterns skyrockets.[26] This might explain why primitive skills of enumeration of small numbers exist even in infants and non-human animals.[27] However, some research argues against that interpretation. It has been found that elderly individuals cannot subitize as many objects as young adults can,[28] yet there is no reason to suspect that the elderly lose the ability to detect known patterns; a great deal of previous research does suggest, though, that their primary memory capacity is diminished relative to young adults.

Has one legend been replaced by another?

In this chapter, we began by discussing a simple answer to the question of what primary memory capacity is: that primary memory can hold seven chunks or meaningful units. This answer was shown to have some basis in the facts, but overall it was shown not to be a general rule, and therefore was said to be a legend.

However, it should be said that simple answers are not, in principle, bad. One of the goals of science is to find simple rules to explain the available evidence in a comprehensible manner. What makes the simple rules unacceptable is just when they are shown not to match the facts. By analogy, in the realm of physics, it was not a bad move for Isaac

Newton to propose a simple law of gravitational force, because it helped explain the data of planetary motion collected by Tycho Brahe and the regularities of planetary motion derived from the data by Johannes Kepler. The laws of gravity could be clearly observed only in situations in which wind resistance was eliminated or taken into account; just as, the capacity of primary memory can be clearly observed only in situations in which rehearsal and chunking have been eliminated or taken into account as we have suggested.

Just as the more comprehensive understanding of gravity by Albert Einstein eventually displaced the simpler gravitational law of Newton, a more comprehensive understanding of primary memory capacity is bound to come along and replace the simple generalization[12,13] that people can remember on average three or four chunks of information. Until that time, however, the limit of three or four serves as a useful guideline for research and theory, as did the gravitational constant for many years. What is likely to advance us to the next level, beyond a new legend of three or four, is a better understanding of the long-term memory processes involved in chunking, a topic emphasized in the seminal work that launched the modern research on primary memory: the article published by George Miller[1] in 1956, about 50 years before the present chapter went to print.

References and notes

1. Miller GA. The magical number seven, plus or minus two: some limits on our capacity for processing information. *Psychological Review*, 1956; 63:81–97.
2. James W. *The principles of psychology.* Henry Holt, New York. 1890.
3. Miller GA, George A Miller. In L Gardner, ed. *A history of psychology in autobiography*, Vol. VIII. Stanford University Press, Stanford, CA. 1989:391–418.
4. Ericsson KA, Chase WG, Faloon S. Acquisition of a memory skill. *Science*, 1980; 208:1181–1182.
5. Rouder JN, Morey RD, Cowan N, Pfaltz M. Learning in a unidimensional absolute identification task. *Psychonomic Bulletin and Review*, 2004; 11: 938–944.
6. Sperling G. The information available in brief visual presentations. *Psychological Monographs*, 1960; 74:1–29.
7. Chase W, Simon HA. The mind's eye in chess. In WG Chase, ed. *Visual information processing.* Academic Press, New York. 1973:215–281.
8. Gobet F, Simon HA. Expert chess memory: revisiting the chunking hypothesis. *Memory*, 1988; 6:225–255.
9. Tulving E, Patkau JE. Concurrent effects of contextual constraint and word frequency on immediate recall and learning of verbal material. *Canadian Journal of Psychology*, 1962; 16:83–95.
10. Johnson MF. The role of chunking and organization in the process of recall. In GH Bower, JT Spence, ed. *Psychology of learning and motivation*, Vol. 4. Academic Press, Oxford. 1969: 171–247.
11. Baddeley AD, Thomson N, Buchanan M. Word length and the structure of short-term memory. *Journal of Verbal Learning and Verbal Behavior*, 1975; 14:575–589.
12. Broadbent DE. The magic number seven after fifteen years. In A Kennedy, A Wilkes, ed. *Studies in long-term memory.* Wiley. 1975:3–18.
13. Cowan N. The magical number 4 in short-term memory: a reconsideration of mental storage capacity. *Behavioral and Brain Sciences*, 2001; 24:87–185.
14. Pylyshyn ZW, Storm RW. Tracking multiple independent targets: evidence for a parallel tracking mechanism. *Spatial Vision*, 1988; 3:179–197.
15. Cowan N, Chen Z, Rouder JN. Constant capacity in an immediate serial-recall task: a logical sequel to Miller (1956). *Psychological Science*, 2004; 15:634–640.

16. **Luck SJ, Vogel EK.** The capacity of visual working memory for features and conjunctions. *Nature*, 1997; **390**:279–281.
17. **Morey CC, Cowan N.** When visual and verbal memories compete: evidence of cross-domain limits in working memory. *Psychonomic Bulletin and Review*, 2004; **11**:296–301.
18. **Cocchini G, Logie RH, Della Sala S, MacPherson SE, Baddeley AD.** Concurrent performance of two memory tasks: evidence for domain-specific working memory systems. *Memory and Cognition*, 2002; **30**:1086–1095.
19. **Jefferies E, Lambon, Ralph MA, Baddeley AD.** Automatic and controlled processing in sentence recall: the role of long-term and working memory. *Journal of Memory and Language*, 2004; **51**:623–643.
20. **Vogel EK, Machizawa MG.** Neural activity predicts individual differences in visual working memory capacity. *Nature*, 2004; **428**:749–751.
21. **Todd JJ, Marois R.** Capacity limit of visual short-term memory in human posterior parietal cortex. *Nature*, 2004; **428**:751–754.
22. **McElree B.** Working memory and focal attention. *Journal of Experimental Psychology: Learning, Memory, and Cognition*, 2000; **27**:817–835.
23. **Verhaeghen P, Cerella J, Basak C.** A Working-memory workout: how to expand the focus of serial attention from one to four items, in ten hours or less. *Journal of Experimental Psychology: Learning, Memory, and Cognition*, 2004; **30**:1322–1337.
24. **Oberauer K.** Access to information in working memory: exploring the focus of attention. *Journal of Experimental Psychology: Learning, Memory, and Cognition*, 2002; **28**:411–421.
25. **Mandler G, Shebo BJ.** Subitizing: an analysis of its component processes. *Journal of Experimental Psychology: General*, 1982; **111**:1–22.
26. **Logan GD, Zbrodoff NJ.** Subitizing and similarity: toward a pattern-matching theory of enumeration. *Psychonomic Bulletin and Review*, 2003; **10**:676–682.
27. **Gallistel CR, Gelman R.** Non-verbal numerical cognition: from reals to integers. *Trends in Cognitive Sciences*, 2000; **4**:59–65.
28. **Basak C, Verhaeghen P.** Subitizing speed, subitizing range, counting speed, the Stroop effect, and aging: capacity differences and speed equivalence. *Psychology and Aging*, 2003; **18**:240–249.

Chapter 5

Setting the record (or video camera) straight on memory: the video camera model of memory and other memory myths

Seema L. Clifasefi, Maryanne Garry and
Elizabeth Loftus

> Whatever one believes to be true either is true or becomes true in one's own
> mind
>
> John C. Lilly

A fascinating group of individuals to study are those who believe that they have been
abducted by aliens.[1] Is there something special about these people? One observation is
that they do not have any elevated psychological problems, relative to the rest of the
population, but they are a group who tends to believe in the idea of extraterrestrials.[2]
We do not know, of course, whether believing in extraterrestrials made these individuals
more prone to interpret ambiguous experiences as if they involved UFOs, or whether
the individuals, after coming to believe they had seen UFOs or had been abducted,
became believers as a result of their false beliefs. One thing is clear: our beliefs drive our
experiences. For instance, if you believe that you can recover memories from before you
were born, you are also more likely to engage in special memory techniques to try and
recover these pre-birth memories than people who believe that these types of memories
are nonsense.[3] In other words, the actions you take, the memories you recall and the way
you experience the world are shaped by your beliefs about the way the world works. That
is why it is important to set the record straight when it comes to mistaken beliefs about
memory.

  One of the most pervasive—but inaccurate—beliefs about memory is that it operates
like a video camera, storing information in the brain in something like a permanent video
library. There are at least three important corollaries of this belief. First, subscribing to
the video camera view of memory means subscribing to the belief that we do not forget
something so much as we temporarily cannot find where we have stored the information
in our mental library. Secondly, with this view comes the belief that the right techniques

might help us to tidy up the video library and find whatever it is we are trying to remember. Thirdly, holding this view of memory also means that one believes that once we find the missing video, remembering is a simple matter of replaying the information etched into the memory records.

There is no scientific support for these views, yet so many people subscribe to them. Why? One idea is that the video recorder notion of memory is comforting. After all, our memories are just that: *ours*. Our unique experiences affect the way that we think and act, for better or for worse. Some memories are sharp lessons in life that we hope never to forget. Other memories tie us to people or places that we love. These memories define us and give us our identity. To believe in the permanence of memory protects us against loss of self-identity in the same way that believing in heaven protects us against loss of life after death. However, just as believing in an afterlife is an article of faith, so are these views of memory.

Ironically, the enduring myths about memory are a little like the myth that memory is a collection of mental videotapes: some of them disappear for a while, but are never really gone. Eventually they come back. Memory myths have a sense of permanence about them that fly in the face of scientific support. In this chapter, our goal is to erase those myths about the way memory works and replace them with more scientifically sound information. Let us begin by rewinding the tape.

Rewinding the tape side A: remembering

When people subscribe to the video camera model of memory, they implicitly assume that to remember an event is to 'rewind the tape' and replay the memory. Each time they replay the tape, the same thing happens, just as reliably as when we play the collector's edition DVD of the Titanic: every time, the battered ship sinks like a stone into the ocean, and every time, Leonardo Dicaprio dies. However, remembering is not like that at all. Remembering is not a movie; instead, it is improvisational theatre with rough script, and what we remember changes with each retelling. We embellish, edit and revise to suit our audience, even when that audience is ourselves. As the psychologist Daniel Schacter noted:

We often edit or entirely rewrite our previous experiences—unknowingly and unconsciously—in light of what we now know or believe. The result can be a skewed rendering of a specific incident, or even of an extended period in our lives, that says more about how we feel now than about what happened then[4] (p. 7).

Thus, without knowing it, we can modify our own history. Most of these historical revisions have little or no consequences. However, sometimes changing memories can have grave consequences. For example, in a courtroom, eyewitness memory can mean the difference, quite literally, between life and death.

In fact, our legal systems rely heavily on the accuracy of memory. One of the most compelling moments in a court of law is when a testifying eyewitness singles out the defendant in the courtroom and says, 'It was him, I *saw* him do it'. For Gary Graham, these words were his death sentence. Graham was executed by the state of Texas on 22 June 2000 based primarily on the evidence of one eyewitness, Bernadine Skillern, who claims she saw him shooting the victim from a distance of 30–40 feet away. Although we may never know whether Graham was the person Ms Skillern saw commit murder, we know of at least 156 people in the US judicial system who have been wrongfully convicted due in large part to faulty eyewitness testimony.[5] Let us take a look at the history of eyewitness memory research to see how these errors might occur.

History of eyewitness memory research

Eyewitness researchers have known how easy it is to misidentify someone or something for almost a century. In one of the first reported studies of eyewitness memory, a professor by the name of Hugo Munsterberg carefully staged a crime in his classroom and then asked his students to report what they could remember. The results from this classroom demonstration showed that even the most accurate eyewitness report still contained a significant amount of error.[6]

If memory does not operate like a video recorder, how does it work? Although scientists are still a long way away from fully understanding the inner workings of memory, the past 30 years of research has shed significant light on the issue. We know, for example, that information that people encounter after witnessing an event can distort their original memory of the event. In one of the first demonstrations of what has now come to be widely known as the *misinformation effect*, Elizabeth Loftus and John Palmer showed that the wording of a question could alter and even add to people's original memories of an event.[7] In their study, subjects first witnessed a film of a car accident. After some delay, the witnesses were asked questions about what they saw in the film. When witnesses were asked, 'About how fast were the cars going when they *smashed* into each other?' they estimated that the car was going faster than when the word smashed was replaced with either *collided, bumped, contacted* or *hit*. In addition, people in the 'smashed' condition were more likely to report having seen broken glass in a later recall test, even though there was no broken glass in the original scene.

In a related study, Loftus and Guido Zanni reported a similar distortion arising from the use of innocuous words such as, 'a' and 'the' embedded in questions asked after the event had occurred.[8] For example, after witnessing the accident, people who were asked the question, 'Did you see *the* broken headlight?' were more likely to later report seeing a broken headlight, as opposed to subjects who were asked the question, 'Did you see *a* broken headlight?' even though there was never a broken headlight in the original scene. Thus, even the subtle use of definite and indefinite articles in post-event questioning can affect how a person later comes to report the scene of a crime.

In another experiment, Loftus found that asking people misleading questions could lead them to remember not only little details such as non-existent broken glass, but also big details such as non-existent buildings.[9] Subjects witnessed a videotape of a car driving along the countryside. In one condition, they were asked how fast the car was travelling when it passed the barn, whereas in another condition the question did not mention a barn. In fact, no barn was featured in the videotape. A week later, significantly more of the subjects fed the barn misinformation reported having seen a barn compared with subjects who were not fed the barn misinformation.

The critical finding in these three early eyewitness studies is that when people are fed slight suggestions, these suggestions can have a significant impact on how they remember an event, i.e. information encountered after an event cannot only alter the remembered details of a previously witnessed event, it can also cause a person to report seeing objects that never existed in the first place. These studies provide evidence that memory does not work like the video recorder suggests it does, recording information verbatim. Instead, thousands of studies since the first demonstration of the misinformation effect have shown that it is relatively easy to distort memories for witnessed events. These types of studies cast a shadow of reasonable doubt on the accuracy of eyewitness testimony.

Interestingly, research has also shown that it is not just the misinformation itself that leads to memory distortion, but also social factors—such as *who* delivers the misinformation—that play an important role in causing memory distortions. For example, in one study, people first witnessed a car accident and then were later tested on their memory for the accident. Before the memory test, the witnesses read statements about the accident. Half of the people were told that the person who caused the accident prepared the statement, while the other half were told that a neutral witness prepared the statement. In fact, there was only one statement (prepared by the experimenter) and it was always the same misinformation-riddled account of the accident. The people who read the statement prepared by the supposed neutral witness were more likely to buy into the misinformation-riddled account of events than the people who read the statement prepared by the supposed person who caused the accident. In other words, the more reliable people considered the witness who prepared the statement, the more likely they were to be misled by that witness.[10]

In another study evaluating social factors on memory distortions, people witnessed a slide sequence of a young man shoplifting several items from a store. After a delay, everyone listened to a speaker describe the shoplifting. Half of the people heard the speaker describe the shoplifting in a New Zealand accent while the other half of the people heard the speaker describe the shoplifting in a North American accent. The information in both descriptions of the shoplifting was virtually identical except for the accent in which it was delivered and a few New Zealand colloquialisms ('elevator' in the North American version was changed to 'lift' in the New Zealand version). Participants were then asked to rate the speakers on various characteristics, trying to describe what she was like on the basis of her voice. For example, the participants were asked to rate how prestigious, trustworthy, dependable and friendly they thought the speaker to be. Finally, everyone took a memory test asking them to recall what they had seen in the original slide sequence. When people rated the speaker high on traits of prestige, trust, dependability and friendliness, they were more likely to buy into the misinformation-riddled account, as opposed to when they did not rate the speaker high on these traits.[11] Other studies have shown social factors such as age, profession and status influence the extent to which one experiences memory distortions.[12-14] Thus, when a police officer questions a witness, the extent to which that officer misleads a witness may depend on how the witness perceives authority figures.

If memory can be so easily distorted, how do we know when to judge it as fact or fiction? For instance, we know that if an eyewitness confidently describes her experiences, relays a high level of detail and emotion, and consistently delivers her testimony, others will judge her memory report as more accurate compared with an eyewitness who is unconfident, vague and inconsistent. Although intuitively this logic seems to make sense, the truth of the matter is that relying on these traits to make judgements about how accurate or real a memory is can ultimately lead to miscarriages of justice.

Confidence

There is ample evidence to suggest that how confident an eyewitness seems is one of the most important factors in whether or not jurors will believe that eyewitness, regardless of accuracy.[15] For example, consider one well-known real world case demonstrating how confident, yet wrong, an eyewitness can be. A young college student named Jennifer Thompson was raped in her apartment in an attack that lasted almost an hour. When she saw Ronald Cotton in a photo spread, she deliberated, but picked him out as her attacker. When she later saw him in a live lineup she was emphatic that he was the man who broke into her apartment and raped her. When the case made it to court, the jury saw a woman totally convinced that she had correctly identified the perpetrator. As a result, the jury had no difficulty finding Cotton guilty. Cotton spent 11 years in jail before DNA evidence exonerated him and implicated the real criminal, Bobby Poole. Thompson was astounded to discover that she had identified the wrong man.

Clearly, in Thompson's case, there was no link between the intensity of her belief and the accuracy of the belief. However, that is not to say that confidence and accuracy are never related. In one study examining the relationship between confidence and accuracy, Steve Lindsay and his colleagues showed that under the right conditions, eyewitnesses could be both confident and accurate about their positive identification.[16] For example, when people had a good view of the perpetrator and saw the perpetrator for a lengthy period of time, they were indeed more accurate and confident about their choice, compared with when they had a poor view and less exposure to the perpetrator. Interestingly, Lindsay and colleagues also showed that the same conditions that led people to identify a target suspect more accurately also led them to be more confident, even when they identified the wrong person. This latter finding leads us to our cautionary point: just because we are confident about something, does not always mean that we are right.

In fact, there are many ways in which an eyewitness can become more confident about her initial testimony. For example, Gary Wells and colleagues have conducted several studies that have shown that when a witness identifies a suspect and then receives feedback about it, the feedback can change her confidence.[17] For example, simply telling an eyewitness, 'Good, you identified the suspect'—even when the suspect is not in the lineup—is enough to make an eyewitness more confident that her wrong identification is right. However, positive feedback has ripple effects: it can also lead witnesses to think their view of the suspect was better than it really was, and that they identified him more quickly and easily than they really did. Thus, a simple offhand comment can lead people to misremember details about an event and become more confident about their memory reports.

Detail

Another common misconception about memory is the idea that the amount of detail in a memory is related to the accuracy of that memory. Indeed, studies have shown us that the degree of detail contained in an eyewitness statement is an important factor in jurors' decision-making processes. For example, when mock jurors were presented with conflicting eyewitness testimony about an incident from two fictitious witnesses, they assigned higher credibility to the testimony of the witness who provided a greater level of detail.[18,19] Similarly, when eyewitnesses provide greater detail, they are judged not only to be more credible, but also to have a better memory for the culprit's face and other relevant details, and to have paid more attention to the culprit.[20] Cumulatively, these studies show that the level of detail in a witnesses' testimony can sway jurors, typically favouring the witness who provides the higher level of detail.

Consistency

Another criterion often used by jurors to determine witness credibility is the extent to which an eyewitness is consistent in her testimony. Imagine a courtroom scenario where jurors listen to two different witnesses testify about the fact that they saw the perpetrator threatening a store clerk with a *knife*. During cross-examination, the opposing lawyer draws attention to previous statements made by each of the respective witnesses. The jury learns that Witness A has always maintained that the weapon was a knife. In contrast, the jury learns that Witness B in an earlier deposition described the weapon not as a knife, but instead as a *gun*. Clearly, jurors will judge Witness B as a less credible witness than Witness A, and may even discount Witness B's later testimony rationalizing that if she was wrong about the weapon, how could she be right about anything else. In fact, attorneys often try to discredit witnesses by uncovering the inconsistencies in their statements from one session to another (i.e. from deposition to courtroom). However, there are some interesting and complex findings in the psychological literature that concern consistency that are not as intuitive as we may think.

Ronald Fisher and colleagues have been studying the relationship between inconsistency and accuracy in eyewitness testimony for many years. In one study, he and Brian Cutler organized for a staged crime to occur in front of a group of people. Afterwards, the witnesses were asked to describe the perpetrators responsible for the crime, and they did so again a few days later. After giving this second description, the witnesses were asked to identify the perpetrator from either a photo spread or a physical lineup. Interestingly, there was virtually no relationship between the consistency of witnesses' description of the perpetrator and whether or not they could correctly identify the perpetrator.[21] In other words, when eyewitnesses' descriptions differed from one telling to another, it was not highly predictive of that witnesses' ability to choose the offender correctly. In another study, subjects were asked to watch a video of a bank robbery and then were later tested about their overall memory for the crime. Overall accuracy for the crime memory was not related to how well one remembered one particular aspect of the event. Put another way, just because you correctly remember what the get away car looked like, it does not mean that you are more likely to be correct about the perpetrator's face.[22] Thus, just because an eyewitness may inaccurately describe one aspect of an incident, it does not mean she is inaccurate about other details of that incident.

Emotional intensity

Most people also believe that if a person has an intense emotional reaction to a memory, it is strong evidence that the event happened to them. In fact, although lie detector tests are inadmissible evidence in US courts, many people still look to these physiological types of test as evidence for a person's guilt or innocence. However, we know from the psychological research that physiological responses can occur in response to both real and false events. Richard McNally and his colleagues investigated whether recollection of highly improbable traumatic experiences (such as alien abductions) provoked intense emotional reactions in the same way as real, verifiable traumatic events (such as war) provoked emotional reactions in veterans. In their study, they measured various physiological reactions such as heart rate and skin conductance responses of people who claimed that they had been abducted by aliens compared with control participants who had not reported abductions. Both groups of people were read scripts of the reported alien encounters, and then measured on these various physiological tests. Interestingly, alien abductees rated much higher on all the physiological measures compared with people who did not purport to be abducted by these extraterrestrial creatures.[23] McNally and colleagues concluded that the belief that one has been traumatized is enough to evoke intense emotional reactions similar to those seen with those who actually have been traumatized. Thus, to someone who believes that he has been abducted by aliens, his memory can look and feel like a real recollection of the event. Thus, real and false memories cannot be distinguished by intense emotional reactions.

Taken together, the research evaluating confidence, detail, consistency and emotion in relation to memory accuracy has significant implications for law enforcement officials. For example, legal systems rely heavily on the accuracy of memory. Police officers are under pressure to reconstruct many situations accurately. They can recreate situations from their own observations and speculations, and/or from questioning eyewitnesses. Although they may think they have the potential pieces of the puzzle solved—the equivalents of the barn, or the smashed headlights in the previous examples, if they are unaware of the likelihood of inaccuracy (as demonstrated by Munsterberg) and the possibility of distortion through the use of misleading questioning (as demonstrated by Loftus), then it is highly likely that inaccurate facts reach the courtroom. In addition, if the jury members and then judges also adhere to the video camera concept or have other inaccurate beliefs about memory, then it is also likely that there could be wrongful convictions. Unfortunately, as we have already described, if we look at our judicial history, this injustice is precisely what has occurred.

The research conducted over nearly two decades tells us that mistaken eyewitness evidence is the leading cause of wrongful convictions.[24] For all the studies that have been conducted showing the fallibility of memory, our criminal justice system still relies heavily on eyewitness memory. With the advent of new technologies, such as improved DNA testing and the rising number of post-conviction DNA exonerations, technology is confirming what psychological science has been saying for the past hundred years about memory: that even witnesses who testify with great confidence, emotion, detail and consistency can still be wrong. No one can make this point better than one who has experienced the consequences of memory distortions. Jennifer Thompson, the college student whose mistaken testimony sent Ronald Cotton to prison, wrote to the *New York Times* when she heard about the potential upcoming execution of Gary Graham:

> I was certain, but I was wrong... If anything good can come out of what Ronald Cotton suffered because of my limitations as a human being, let it be an awareness of the fact that eyewitnesses can and do make mistakes... I know that there is an eyewitness who is absolutely positive she saw Gary Graham commit murder. But she cannot possibly be any more positive than I was about Ronald Cotton. What if she is dead wrong?[25]

Eyewitness testimony is not the only type of memory that has put the accuracy of memory on trial; there is another type of memory—'recovered repressed memory'—that has also seen its day in court. This type of memory is one that even science cannot prove exists beyond a reasonable doubt.

Playing back the tape (side B: repression and recovery)

Sometimes, no matter how hard we try, we just cannot seem to remember information we want to remember. Proponents of the 'video camera' analogy of memory believe that all you should have to do to recover a memory is to play back the tape of that memory. In other words, recovering a forgotten memory is just a matter of finding the tape from our video library collection and playing it back in our mind's eye. If this assumption about memory is correct, how do we go about finding a specific tape? Proponents of this belief will tell you that with the right techniques, you can recover even those memories locked far away in the trenches of the mind.

Repression, the idea that we banish traumatic memories from conscious awareness to protect our mind from psychological damage, is a concept originally developed by the early twentieth century psychologist, Sigmund Freud. Although the concept of repression was first popularized by Freud, in recent years many proponents of the recovered memory movement have recreated their own interpretation of Freud's theory on repression and ignored the ambiguities and contradictions presented in his writings.[26,27]

There are two ideas underlying the twenty-first century concept of repression. First, there is the idea that our mind intentionally represses a difficult memory, but that the emotions from the memory seep out and contaminate the individual's mind, resulting in some form of mental ailment. Secondly, there is the idea that the difficult and forgotten memory can be recovered in therapy and appropriately dealt with, thus leading to better mental health. To put it another way, the idea is that these repressed traumatic memories can be summoned from our mind's own video library collection by using the 'right' hunting technique. When that video is found, that memory will re-emerge in perfect form. Some therapists argue that by remembering the memory and dealing with the original trauma, the individual would recover from her secondary symptoms that are a result of the traumatic experience.

In fact, it is this belief—that a memory is forever archived in our mind's library—that has allowed movements such as that of the recovered repressed memory of the late 1980s and 1990s even develop to in the first place. The recovered memory movement began as a feminist backlash against those who denied the reality and frequency of childhood sexual abuse (CSA).[26,27] With the rise of feminism in the 1970s, the cultural climate surrounding CSA began to change. Women were no longer afraid to admit their abuse and began sharing their personal experiences of CSA through writings and books. The word was getting out: CSA happened and it was more common than once believed. CSA prevention programmes mushroomed in North America from the mid-1980s onward.[28] Self-help books were springing up in an effort to empower people to regain control of their lives. In one such book, the *Secret Survivors*, the author, E. Sue Blume, included a checklist that readers could complete to find out if they were likely survivors of incest. Among the 34 items included on the list were: the fear of being alone in the dark, avoidance of mirrors, poor body image and crying uncontrollably for no reason. The author implied that if you had several of these symptoms, that it was likely that you were abused as a child but had probably repressed the incident.[29] In another self-help book, *The Courage To Heal*, Ellen Bass and Laura Davis encouraged women to face their fears and get to the root of their problems by digging deep into their memories to remember their abuse and their abusers. They write:

> Children often cope with abuse by forgetting it ever happened. As a result you may have no conscious memory of being abused.... To say, *I was abused*, you don't need the kind of proof that would stand up in a court of law. Often the knowledge that you were abused starts with a tiny feeling, an intuition...If you genuinely think you were abused and your life shows the symptoms, there's a strong likelihood that you were[30] (p. 26).

In essence, people like Blume, Bass and Davis helped kick-start a fevered media focus on the theory of repression.

On the sidelines, many academics were growing increasingly concerned about the concept of repression and its treatment. Knowing how easy it was to distort memories after a short period of time, they were afraid that many of the 'memories' women were uncovering were at best, distorted, and at worst entirely false. Of particular concern to some researchers was that like Bass and Davis' checklist, some therapists used techniques, such as dream therapy, bodywork or hypnosis, that were extremely suggestive. During the late 1980s, throughout the mid- to late 1990s, many women left therapy with recovered memories of horrific abuse (primarily by fathers, uncles, brothers, occasionally mothers and sometimes even satanic cults). A conservative estimate suggests that by 1988 at least 1 million people had been helped to 'recover' repressed memories of CSA.[26,27] Some of these women filed criminal and civil lawsuits against alleged perpetrators, and this divided families and communities into those who wanted to punish wrongdoers and those who refused to believe that the memories were true and the accused guilty. One such case occurred in November 1990. George Franklin Sr was convicted of raping and murdering 8-year-old Susan Nason 20 years earlier in 1969. Franklin's conviction was based entirely on the testimony of his daughter Eileen's 'recovered repressed memory'. Susan 'recovered' the memories of the rape and murder of her best friend during therapy for unrelated issues.

Thus, with these types of convictions being brought to the courtroom, it became critical to separate the myths from the truths. However, this was no easy task. What bothered researchers in the field of memory was that these 'uncovered' memories were being accepted as fact, without any sense of whether there were alternative routes to producing them. Researchers faced the scientific challenge of proving that something does not exist. Just as it is practically impossible to prove or disprove the existence of God, it is also effectively impossible to prove or disprove the authenticity of a recovered memory. Instead, researchers tried to illustrate the malleability of the mind by using their own techniques of suggestibility to implant and recover 'memories' that they could prove were not true.

The bonus remixed track: creating false memories in the laboratory

The eyewitness literature shows us that we can distort memories of factual events, but when it came to understanding repression, the more important question was whether we could create entirely new memories from scratch and then get people to believe the event happened to them? A number of studies have investigated this question, and the answer is yes. Loftus and Pickrell (1995) were the first to show that entire false memories could be implanted.[31] They used techniques in which they would 'suggest' events to see if people would take hold of them as their own memories. The people who took part in the study were asked to recall events that were described to them earlier by a 'confederate'—a family member who helped out the experimenters on the sly. Three of the events were true, but one—being lost in a shopping mall or other public place at the age of 5—was false. The study consisted of three sessions separated by a week. In the first session, people were given booklets describing the events and were instructed to write down what they could. The second and third sessions were live interviews. By the end of the third session, 25 per cent of people remembered at least some aspect of the suggested false event. Since then, other studies have repeatedly shown us that memories can be created through suggestive techniques. For example, after false suggestions, people have come to 'remember' being attacked by a vicious animal, spilling punch on the parents of the bride at a wedding, having a skin sample taken for a health test or even kissing a frog.[32-35]

Some critics argued that many of the false events used in the early implantation studies are so familiar that it is easy to understand how with a little suggestion a scene could be created, personalized and then 'remembered'. For instance, they argued that events like being lost in a public place were very plausible and could well be part of any person's autobiography. To illustrate their point, researchers tried unsuccessfully to get people falsely to remember having a rectal enema as a child: an experience that is not very common for the everyday child, and of course more ethical than attempting to implant false memories of CSA.[36] These researchers concluded that the reason subjects could not be swayed into believing they received a rectal enema was related to the plausibility of the event. They reasoned that of course, it is easy to make someone believe they got lost when they were young, we all know and are taught about this concept at a very young age. In contrast, they maintained that events that are rare, bizarre or implausible are not easily planted because if people have never experienced the event in question how would they have enough knowledge about the event to report details about it. In other words, they reasoned that subjects were unable to generate enough information about the rectal enema event for it to seem real.

Note, however, that two assumptions are made in this argument. First, that a person needs to have experienced CSA to have an idea of how that storyline goes. That assumption is disputable, given that since the early 1980s, children as young as 2 or 3 begin learning about the difference between 'good touch' and 'bad touch'.[28] Meanwhile, parents see photos of missing children on milk cartons, and the whole family can tune into any talk show and hear yet another presentation of the prevalence of CSA. Such a phenomenon may be nothing more than an expression of cognitive availability, in that when we talk about CSA and think about CSA and wonder about CSA, we think it is more likely to happen.[37]

The second assumption that is made in relation to why people may or may not come to remember certain events, is that people's notion of plausibility do not change. However, Gulianna Mazzoni and her colleagues[38] showed that plausibility is a characteristic that can be manipulated. In one study, people were asked to rate how plausible they thought certain events were, and also to rate the likelihood that these events had personally happened to them in childhood. Then, half the people read what they thought were real scientific articles describing demonic possessions and their relative frequency, but the articles were phonies concocted by the experimenters. Next, in what appeared to be a seemingly unrelated task, the people in the study were again asked to rate how plausible they thought certain events were—one of which was a demonic possession— and rate the likelihood that these events happened in their childhood. People who had read the demonic possession stories subsequently rated demonic possessions as more plausible than they had initially reported on the first questionnaire. Moreover, these same people were more likely to say that they had personally witnessed a demonic possession in their childhood compared with people who did not read articles about demonic possession. Thus, believing that an event is plausible is one important and necessary step in determining whether one will later come to remember the event as having happened. More to the point, these results suggest that the more our culture talks about demonic possessions, alien abductions, satanic ritual abuse cases, and the more familiar we become with these types of stories, the more easily people are able to create their own stories, and hence come to falsely 'remember' these types of events.

However, false memories can develop from more causes than just suggestion. For a false memory to grow, you need to find something plausible, and then you need to become more confident that it happened to you. Research tells us that we can also come to believe more confidently that certain things happened to us simply by imagining those things.[39] In one study investigating how confidence about childhood events can develop, people rated their confidence on a scale from 1 (being the least confident) to 8 (being the most confident) that each of a series of possible childhood events had happened to them before the age of 10. Then, these people imagined certain items from the list as though they had in fact happened. Finally, they provided new confidence ratings after the imagination task. When people imagined an event, they later came to be more confident that the event had occurred in their childhood. This effect was coined, 'imagination inflation'. Since then, numerous studies have shown similar findings. In fact, similar inflation in confidence can be produced with other sorts of techniques. Simply exposing people to the event might be enough: inflation in confidence can happen when people paraphrase the event, unscramble a word that has to do with the event and, interestingly, even see an ad related to the event.[40–43]

In a set of studies examining the effects of false advertising on childhood memory, people were shown one of two ads and asked to rate it for various characteristics. The participants either saw an ad with Bugs Bunny at a Disney theme park, or they saw an ad at the theme park without any cartoon characters. After some delay—and in what appeared to be a different study—participants were asked to rate how confident they were that they had met and shook hands with Bugs at a Disney Theme park in their childhood. Subjects who had previously been exposed to the Bugs at Disney ad were more likely to report shaking hands with, hugging the rabbit and hearing him say, 'What's up Doc?' than those who saw the ad without any cartoon characters. Why are these studies fascinating? Bugs Bunny is a Warner Brothers character, so he would have never been caught at a Disney theme park. Combined, this line of work shows that false advertising can lead to false memories for childhood events.

Memory distortions: the digitally re-mastered edition

Advancing technology allows us to explore what happens if subjects are presented with what they think is evidence that the event happened: photos. People often remark that a picture is worth a thousand words. They see photos and *remember the time when...*

Kimberley Wade and her colleagues showed people four photographs and asked them to recall the events in the photo.[44] What participants did not know was that one of the photos in the picture was a fake, created using digital technology. The false photograph depicted the participant, usually with another family member, taking a hot air balloon ride—an event that family members verified did not happen in the participant's childhood. After three interviews where people were shown the hot air balloon photo, and asked to imagine what it would have been like to be in the balloon, 50 per cent of them came to remember some aspect of the hot air balloon ride that they never took.

Another study used photography to 'jog' people's memories of childhood events that never happened. Steve Lindsay and collaborators used a real childhood photo to help cultivate a false memory. The false memory that they tried to plant had to do with school children getting into trouble with their teacher. Specifically, the suggested that the participant, along with a friend, was caught putting slime (a bright gooey play-dough equivalent) in his teacher's desk and were punished by having to sit in the corner of the classroom facing the wall.[45] Some participants were then shown a real class photograph corresponding to the alleged year that the 'Slime incident' took place. When participants viewed the class photo—even though it had nothing to do with the slime event—65 per cent of them came to remember the slime incident compared to 45 per cent of participants who came to remember the slime incident after only reading about it.

Although the early memory implantation studies showed that just thinking about an event and how it might have happened could elicit some kind of memory about that event, the photo studies showed that photographs may also be powerful memory joggers that can lead to remembering events that never happened. So, when someone tells you that a picture is worth a thousand words, you can respond by telling them it may also be worth, '...a thousand lies'[44] (p. 597).

The final track (summary)

Is there a lesson to learn from all this? If you do not want to be abducted by aliens, you need only to make sure that you do not believe in extraterrestrial creatures. The beliefs that we have about memory and how it works drive the way in which we remember, what we remember as well as the decisions that we make when judging other people's memories. Many prosecutors urge witnesses to use common sense when making their decision about a defendant's guilt. However, as we have demonstrated throughout this chapter, scientific reality sometimes flies in the face of common sense.

In this chapter, we have challenged the notion that memory is permanent by presenting evidence that when we remember experiences, we often incorporate new information or interpret things in line with what we believe to be true now. We have demonstrated that people can be confident, emotional, detailed and consistent in their eyewitness testimony and still be wrong about their memories. We have shown that false memories can be created precisely because they are not entirely false. They are made up of some true things and some false things combined together to make a false event. They are not spun out of whole cloth so much as woven from the idiosyncrasies of our lives.

People give more credit to memory and think it is capable of more than it is. For the most part, if you believe that you wore a blue T-shirt last Friday when really you wore a white T-shirt, no harm is done by your belief. However, as our own judicial history has revealed, sometimes mistaken beliefs about memory can have more serious consequences, such as in the cases of Ronald Cotton, George Franklin or Gary Graham. When faced with legal decisions, if we continue to rely on common sense intuition rather than on scientific evidence, then we run the risk of living in a world where life and death decisions are based on whimsical feelings. What a sorry state medicine would be in if physicians accepted the same imprecision in their diagnostic and treatment procedures.

One of the most popular and pervasive myths surrounding memory is that it records our experiences verbatim in the same way that a video camera might. Here, we have provided ample evidence to dispel this myth, and hopefully set the record, or shall we say—video camera, straight on other mistaken beliefs about memory.

References and notes

1. **Clancy SA, McNally RJ, Schacter DL, Lenzenweger MF, Pitman RK.** Memory distortion in people reporting abduction by aliens. *Journal of Abnormal Psychology*, 2002; 111:455–461.
2. **Spanos N, Cross PA, Dickson K, DuBreuil SC.** Close encounters: an examination of UFO experiences. *Journal of Abnormal Psychology*, 1993; 102:624–632.
3. **Garry M, Loftus EF, Brown SW, DuBreuil SC.** Womb with a view: beliefs about memory, repression, and memory-recovery. In P Conrad, ed. *Intersections in basic and applied memory research.* Lawrence Erlbaum Associates, Hillsdale, NJ. 1997:233–255.
4. **Schacter D.** *The seven sins of memory: how the mind forgets and remembers.* Houghton Mifflin Company, Boston, MA. 2001.
5. Innocence Project.org
6. **Munsterberg H.** *On the witness stand: essays on psychology and crime.* The McClure Company, New York. 1908.
7. **Loftus EF, Palmer JC.** Reconstruction of automobile destruction: an example of the interaction between language and memory. *Journal of Verbal Learning and Verbal Behavior*, 1974; 13:585–589.
8. **Loftus EF, Zanni G.** Eyewitness testimony: the influence of the wording of a question. *Bulletin of the Psychonomic Society*, 1975; 5:86–88.
9. **Loftus EF.** Leading questions and the eyewitness report. *Cognitive Psychology*, 1975; 7:560–572.
10. **Dodd DH. Bradshaw JM.** Leading questions and memory: pragmatic constraints. *Journal of Verbal Learning and Verbal Behavior*, 1980; 19:695–704.
11. **Vornik LA, Sharman S.J, Garry M.** The power of the spoken word: sociolinguistic cues influence the misinformation effect. *Memory*, 2003; 11:101–109.
12. **Ceci S, Bruck M.** Suggestibility of the child witness: a historical review and synthesis. *Psychological Bulletin*, 1993; 113:403–439.
13. **Lindsay DS.** Misleading suggestions can impair eyewitnesses' ability to remember event details. *Journal of Experimental Psychology: Learning, Memory and Cognition*, 1990; 16:1077–1083.
14. **Loftus EF, Levidow B, Duensing S.** Who remembers best? Individual differences in memory for events that occurred in a science museum. *Applied Cognitive Psychology*, 1992; 6:93–107.

15. Cutler BL, Penrod SD, Dexter HR. Juror sensitivity to eyewitness identification evidence. *Law and Human Behavior*, 1990; **14**:185–191.
16. Lindsay DS, Read JD, Sharma K. Accuracy and confidence in person identification: the relationship is strong when witnessing conditions vary widely. *Psychological Science*, 1998; **9**:2215–2218.
17. Wells GL, Olson, EA, Charman SD. Distorted retrospective eyewitness reports as functions of feedback delay. *Journal of Experimental Psychology: Applied*, 2003; **9**:42–52.
18. Bell BE, Loftus EF. Degree of detail of eyewitness testimony and mock juror judgments. *Journal of Applied Social Psychology*, 1998; **18**:1171–1192.
19. Jones M. Preventing the application of stereotypic biases in the courtroom: the role of detailed testimony. *Journal of Applied Social Psychology*, 1997; **27**:1767–1784.
20. Bell BE, Loftus EF. Trivial persuasion in the courtroom: the power of (a few) minor details. *Journal of Personality and Social Psychology*, 1989; **56**:669–679.
21. Fisher RP, Cutler BL. The relation between consistency and accuracy of eyewitness testimony. In G Davies, S Lloyd-Bostok, M McMurran, C Wilson, ed. *Psychology, law, and criminal justice: international developments in research and practice*. Walter De Gruyter, Oxford. 1996:21–28.
22. Mitchell T, Haw R, Fisher RP. Eyewitness accuracy: can accuracy for one statement be predictive of more 'global' accuracy? Poster presented at European–American Psychology–Law Society, July 2003.
23. McNally RJ. *Remembering trauma*. Cambridge University Press, Harvard, MA. 2003.
24. Radelet ML. Introduction: wrongful convictions of the innocent. *Judicature*, 2002; **86**:67–68.
25. Thompson J. I was certain, but I was wrong. *New York Times*, Op-Ed. 2000.
26. Crews FC. The revenge of the repressed: part I. *New York Review of Books*, 1994; **41**:54–60.
27. Crews FC. The revenge of the repressed: part II. *New York Review of Books*, 1994; **41**:49–58.
28. Krivacska J. Antisexualism in child sexual abuse prevention programs—good touch, bad touch... don't touch? *Issues in Child Abuse Accusations*, 1993; **5**:78–82.
29. Blume ES. *Secret survivors: uncovering incest and its aftereffects in women*. John Wiley & Sons, Inc. 1990.
30. Bass, E, Davis, L. *The courage to heal: a guide for women survivors of child sexual abuse*, 3rd edn. HarperCollins Publishers, Inc. 1994.
31. Loftus EF, Pickrell JE. The formation of false memories. *Psychiatric Annals*, 1995; **25**:720–725.
32. Hyman I E Jr, Husband TH, Billings FJ. False memories of childhood experiences. *Applied Cognitive Psychology*, 1995; **9**:181–197.
33. Mazzoni G, Memon A. Imagination can create false autobiographical memories. *Psychological Science*, 2003; **14**:186–188.
34. Porter S, Yuille JC, Lehman DR. The nature of real, implanted, and fabricated memories for emotional childhood events: implications for the recovered memory debate. *Law and Human Behavior*, 1999; **23**:517–537.
35. Thomas AK, Bulevich JB, Loftus EF. Exploring the role of repetition and sensory elaboration in the imagination inflation effect. *Memory and Cognition*, 2003; **31**:630–640.
36. Pezdek K, Finger K, Hodge D. Planting false childhood memories: the role of event plausibility. *Psychological Science*, 1997 **8**:437–441.
37. Tversky A. Kahneman D. Availability: a heuristic for judging frequency and probability. *Cognitive Psychology*, 1973; **5**:207–232.
38. Mazzoni GA, Loftus EF, Kirsch I. Changing beliefs about implausible autobiographical events: a little plausibility goes a long way, *Journal of Experimental Psychology: Applied*, 2001; **7**:51–59.
39. Garry M, Manning C, Loftus EF, Sherman S. Imagination inflation: imagining a childhood event inflates the confidence that it occurred. *Psychonomic Bulletin and Review*, 1996; **3**:208–214.
40. Bernstein DM, Whittlesea BWA, Loftus EF. Increasing confidence in remote autobiographical memory and general knowledge: extensions of the revelation effect. *Memory and Cognition*, 2002; **30**:432–438.

41. **Braun KA, Ellis R, Loftus EF.** Make my memory: how advertising can change our memories of the past. *Psychology and Marketing*, 2002; **19**:1–23.
42. **Grinley MJ.** Effects of advertising on semantic and episodic memory. Unpublished Masters Thesis. University of Washington, Seattle. 2002.
43. **Sharman SJ, Garry M, Beuke C.** Repeated imagination or repeated exposure causes imagination inflation. *American Journal of Psychology*, 2004; **117**:157–168.
44. **Wade KA, Garry M, Read JD, Lindsay DS.** A picture is worth a thousand lies: using false photographs to create false childhood memories. *Psychonomic Bulletin and Review*, 2002; **9**:597–603.
45. **Lindsay DS, Hagen L, Read JD, Wade KA, Garry M.** True photographs and false memories. *Psychological Science*, 2004; **15**: 149–154.

Chapter 6

The myth of the incredible eyewitness

Amina Memon and Don Thomson

Visual identification plays an important role in the investigation and detection of many crimes, and conviction of many suspects.[1] However, as detailed by Clifasefi *et al.* (Chapter 5, this volume), the reconstructive nature of our memories means that an eyewitness's evidence cannot always be relied upon. Research shows that one in five witnesses mistakenly identifies a volunteer at identity parades, despite warnings that the culprit may not be present.[2,3] Mistaken eyewitness testimony from victims and bystanders has to date been held responsible for two-thirds of the cases ($n = 110$) of wrongful convictions in the USA following new DNA evidence.[4] Further cases are pending examination. The current chapter examines whether research on the factors that influence the quality of visual evidence from eyewitnesses can inform police investigators and the courts about the reliability of witness evidence under different conditions. We also consider the extent to which there is a consensus in the research findings (and hence in expert opinion). Finally, we briefly examine what laypersons or potential jurors know about the factors influencing eyewitness evidence.

As early as 1933, problems associated eyewitness identification were identified by two judges of the High Court of Australia. In a minority judgement the two judges said:

> An honest witness who says 'The prisoner is the man who drove the car', whilst appearing to affirm a simple, clear and impressive proposition, is really asserting: (1) that he observed the driver, (2) that the observation became impressed on his mind, (3) that he still retains the original impression, (4) that such an impression has not been affected, altered or replaced, by published portraits of the prisoner, and (5) that the resemblance between the original impression and the prisoner is sufficient to base a judgment, not on resemblance, but of identity. It therefore became necessary in the present case, to pay attention to the following circumstances:- (1) Whether the witness was a stranger to the driver of the car, (2) whether the driver had any special peculiarities which, at the time, impressed themselves upon the witness, (3) the length of time which elapsed between December 14th and (a) the time when the witness first described the driver or (b) the time when the witness first saw the accused person, (4) the description of the driver given by the witness *before* seeing the prisoner, and (5) the circumstances under which the witness was first seen and identified by the witness as the driver.[5]

In an appeal before the High Court of Australia 4 years later, the court identified one of the circumstances which rendered eyewitness identification as suspect: dock identification. The court said:

But where, before the occasion with which it is sought to connect the person accused or suspected, the witness has seldom or never seen him, experience has led the English court to the greatest care to avoid a mistake or prejudice. They treat it as indisputable that a witness, if shown the person to be identified singly and as the person whom the police have reason to suspect, will be much more likely, however fair and careful he may be, to assent to the view that the man he is shown corresponds to his recollections.[6]

It was not until nearly 40 years on that identification once again became the focus of attention, in USA in the case of *Neil v Biggers*[7], in the UK in R *v Turnbull*[8] and in Australia in *Alexander v R.*[9] In England following the 1976 Devlin Inquiry into mistaken identification, the Court of Appeal in Turnbull's case spelled out factors to be taken into account when eyewitness identification is a key issue. These factors were: the length of time a witness had to observe an offender, the distance the witness was from the offender, the prevailing perceptual conditions and whether or not the offender is a stranger to the witness. Since that time, extensive psychological research on the factors influencing eyewitness reliability has been conducted.[10] Notwithstanding the explicit recognition by the courts in the case of Biggers, in Turnbull's case, and in Alexander's case of factors that may vitiate the reliability of eyewitness identification courts, mistaken identification continues to be a significant source of wrongful convictions.

Although courts in most common law jurisdictions have acknowledged that there is a significant risk that identification evidence is unreliable and that the circumstances under which eyewitnesses viewed the offender and made their identification should come under close scrutiny, there has been a great reluctance on the part of the courts to allow expert witnesses to testify about factors germane to the reliability of the eye-witnesses' identification of the accused. The chances are high that the courts will rule the expert evidence as inadmissible on the basis either that admitting such evidence offends against the common knowledge rule, i.e. that eyewitness identification is a matter of common sense and judges and jurors are not assisted by expert opinion. However, in cases where eyewitness identification evidence plays a key role, courts in common law jurisdictions in cases are required to include as part of the judicial instructions to jurors, warnings about the potential unreliability of eyewitness identification. Such an instruction clearly undermines the validity of the claim that eyewitness identification is a matter of common sense. Further, warning jurors about the potential unreliability of eyewitness identification after all the evidence has been given and all the arguments made may be too late, as by that stage jurors may have already made up their minds that the accused is the offender. Thus, there is a strong argument for experts to testify about factors affecting the reliability of eyewitness identification so that the trier of fact, be it a judge or a jury, can better assess the reliability of any identification evidence.

If expert evidence on factors affecting eyewitness identification is permitted, it is crucial that that evidence be reliable and relevant to the case at hand. So let us now turn to some of the factors that psychological research has identified as influencing the reliability of an eyewitness.

Variables that influence eyewitness accuracy

There are many reasons why errors in eyewitness evidence can occur. For example, a witness who has seen a crime take place from a considerable distance and late at night is less likely to make an accurate identification of the perpetrator than a witness who has had more favourable viewing conditions. On the other hand, the witness may have made a wrong identification because the police conducted a lineup which was biased in some way.

In order to test eyewitness performance under various conditions, researchers have employed staged events, post-event manipulations and various types of identification procedures (see below). Experimental studies have been supplemented by a number of archival studies. A host of variables have been associated with an increase in mistaken identification. Wells and Loftus[11] have suggested that a useful way of organizing the research findings is to categorize the variables into those relating to witness characteristics (e.g. age, race), those relating to the witnessed event (e.g. length of exposure, presence of weapons), post-event factors (e.g. exposure to mugshot photographs, discussion with other witnesses), the nature of the identification task (e.g. the type of identification parade) and any information or feedback that a witness encounters post-identification (see Clifasefi et al., Chapter 5, this volume). While the legal system has no control over witness characteristics and conditions at the time the event is witnessed, post-event influences can be controlled to some extent. Moreover, knowledge about the most effective procedure for eliciting an accurate identification decision from eyewitnesses can also be applied.

Witness characteristics

One witness characteristic that could influence accuracy of identification is the race of the witness and the race of the person that they are trying to recognize. A witness is more likely to recognize a person of their own race accurately than a person from a different racial group.[12] Ninety per cent of the experts we surveyed said the so-called cross-race identification effect (or own-race bias) was robust enough to present in court,[13] and mock juror research suggests the layperson is insensitive to the effect.[14] The cross-race effect has been supported by archival research. Behrman and Davey[15] in their analysis of 271 police cases in California found higher suspect identifications for own-race faces. Wright et al.[16] conducted a field study of the cross-race effect in South Africa and England. In each country, they asked a black or white male confederate to approach either a black or white member of the public in a shopping centre to enquire if they had seen some jewellery that they had lost. A few minutes later, another confederate asked questions about the stranger and asked if they could identify him from a lineup. An own-race bias was found in response to questions about the target as well as the ability to identify the target accurately from the lineup. One hypothesis as to why the own-race bias occurs is a lack of contact and hence familiarity with other race facial features. Wright et al. suggest that it would be interesting to track the own-race bias in South Africa as the races become more integrated to support the notion that racial integration will decrease the own race bias.[12]

Another factor that can influence visual identification evidence is the age of the witness. The typical finding in laboratory studies of unfamiliar face recognition (the recognition of faces seen only once before) is that older adults (60–80 years) are more likely to make false alarms.[17] In order to examine the recognition performance in eyewitness identification situations, a series of studies comparing young (18–32 years old) and older (60–80 years old) adults were conducted in Aberdeen, Scotland and Dallas, Texas. Searcy, Bartlett and Memon[18] presented mock witnesses with a crime video followed by a lineup of photographs and asked them if the culprit (target) was present. While there were no differences in correct identification rates, older witnesses made more erroneous foil choices regardless of whether the target was present or absent in the lineup. The age-related increase in false identifications was replicated in subsequent studies.[19] One factor that may be responsible for the age-related increase in false alarms to faces that have not been seen before is that older adults rely on 'familiarity' as a basis for responding. Ageing is typically associated with a reduction in cognitive resources[20] and an increased reliance on 'automatic' familiarity processes as opposed to a 'conscious' effortful recollection process.[21] Accurate recollection of source information is critical in an eyewitness setting as illustrated in the section on post-event influences. Thus older adults may rely more on non-analytical strategies such as 'availability' and 'fluency' when making identification.[17] Searcy, Bartlett and Memon[22] manipulated availability by presenting participants with a crime-relevant or -irrelevant narrative shortly after young and older witnesses viewed a simulated crime and prior to a target-absent lineup (the perpetrator was not present in the lineup). As expected, false identification rates for older adults increased when they were presented with the crime-relevant narrative. Contrary to what one might expect older adults who recalled more details about the culprit were actually *more* likely to make false identifications than younger adults.

Characteristics of the event

A good illustration of the impact of situational variables on eyewitness memory comes from an appeal case that came before the high courts in Australia.[23] The accused was charged with attempted murder. The appeal case was based on appellant claims that the trial judge misdirected the jury on the issue of the identification of the gunman by failing to give specific warnings concerning various features of the evidence of an eyewitness to the shooting. There were a number of weaknesses in the identification evidence. At the time of the shooting, the witness claimed she did not know the appellant. Nearly 9 months elapsed before she formally identified him from photographs which had been altered to show the appellant wearing a wig and a false moustache. By that time, the appellant was a definite suspect, the witness had seen him on television on a number of occasions and allegedly in the vicinity of her home.

The conditions of witnessing were as follows for the witness in this case. When she saw the gunman, he was some distance away. She was hiding behind another vehicle. He was leaning across the passenger's seat and he was disguised. Her opportunity to observe him was fleeting. Moreover, her first observation of the gunman took place after about

30 shots had been fired in her direction, after she had seen her husband shot through the hand and after her husband had physically pushed her head down. As a result of the shooting, she suffered shock. The direction the judge gave to the jury was as follows:

His Honour told the jury that 'sudden and unexpected acts of violence such as Mrs F described in this case, can affect people caught up in the events in different ways. The terror of the occasion can serve to impress indelibly on the minds of some people the features of anyone they see involved in it. With other people the effect may be to obscure their judgment and their later recollection'.

The judge's directions were deemed inadequate in *Dominican v Queen*,[23] the appeal was allowed, the conviction quashed and a new trial ordered.

If an expert on eyewitness testimony had been permitted to give evidence in this case, what factors could they have drawn the jury's attention to? A review of studies that have examined the effect of stress on eyewitness memory leads to the conclusion that heightened stress has a detrimental effect on the ability to recognize a perpetrator as well as to recall details of the crime.[24]

A good illustration of the effect of emotional arousal at the time of witnessing is the research on the so-called weapon-focus effect. A crime is typically classed as emotionally arousing on the basis of the presence of emotional stimuli at the crime scene (e.g. a gun). Research on 'weapon focus' has found that memory for some details (e.g. the face) is impaired but memory for other details (e.g. a weapon) is enhanced.[25] There are two explanations for the weapon-focus effect: (1) that it increases level of arousal in the witness and (2) that it focuses attention on the weapon such that other more central details are not attended to.[26] The effects were convincingly shown by Maass and Köhnken.[27] Participants were approached by an experimenter who was holding at hip level either a syringe or a pen and who threatened the participant. Later on, the participants were asked to identify the experimenter in a target-absent lineup and to recall details about the experimenter's face and hand. Twice as many participants in the syringe-present condition (64 per cent) than in the pen-present condition (33 per cent) made a false identification in the lineup task. Moreover, the more fear that participants had self-reported about injections prior to the study, the more hand cues and the less facial cues they accurately recalled.

More recently, researchers have critiqued the method used to manipulate emotional arousal.[28,29] Laney *et al.* argue that prior studies have manipulated emotion by using a salient visual stimulus which could serve as an attention magnet (e.g. showing people blood, injuries, a weapon, and so on). They argue that a more naturalistic manipulation of arousal is to examine witness involvement and empathy with an unfolding event. Laney *et al.* have examined how participants recall events that involve arousal that is induced thematically (e.g. by using a script that accompanies the stimulus that increases empathy with the victim). These data show that emotional arousal measured in this way improves memory for all aspects of the emotional event. In contrast, Morgan *et al.*[30] found no relationship between eyewitness accuracy and stress-induced symptoms of dissociation. In the Morgan *et al.* study, military participants were subjected to highly stressful interrogation for an extended period. No differences in accuracy in identifying the interrogator were found as a function of the level of stress experienced by the participants. One of the problems with the literature on the effects of stress on memory is that studies differ in the way they define the stress and arousal. Researchers have also neglected the role of individual differences in state or trait anxiety, neuroticism and physiological responses.[24,31]

How do the laboratory studies compare with actual cases? An archival study of witnesses of a single shooting incident in Canada involving 21 witnesses (of which 13 were corroborated) noted that eyewitnesses gave detailed and accurate information about actions and objects. However, there were numerous errors in person descriptions. The estimates of the height, weight and age of the offender had only a 50–50 chance of being correct. At the initial interview, three out of the 13 witnesses either were unable to describe or wrongly described hair colour. Four out of the 13 were unable to describe or wrongly described hairstyle. In an analysis of capital cases of rape and robbery in Germany, Sporer[32] examined the data from 100 witnesses. Again, the quantity of person descriptions was poor and only 30 per cent of witnesses described the face of the perpetrator. Interestingly, the quantity and pattern of descriptions found in this archival study resembled those of a staged event study in which a confederate interrupted a lecture to remove a slide project.[33] These findings suggest that the stress associated with being a victim or witness of a rape/robbery does not increase errors in person descriptions any more than witnessing an innocuous staged event. Person descriptions tend to be rather poor in both cases.

Finally, a recent archival study reports null effects of stress on the accuracy and completeness of person descriptions,[34] questioning the generalizability of some laboratory studies.

Post-event influences

A commonly used procedure to test the visual identification ability of an eyewitness early in the investigative process is to show the witness a mugshot of a suspect or to ask the witness to review a book of photographs. This can range for a dozen or so photographs[35] to hundreds of photographs.[36] One of the problems of exposing witnesses to mugshots is that they may later be asked to identify the suspect at a formal identification parade. There are two types of biases that could ensue. The first is a source-monitoring error— a face appears familiar because of a prior encounter. The familiarity from seeing the face in a mugshot photo is incorrectly attributed to the crime context. Alternatively, if a face is selected from a mugshot album and the same face selected again in the formal identification parade, what might be occurring is what Dysart et al.[36] refer to as the commitment effect (a social bias to choose the same face as chosen before). However, Memon et al.[35] found that any choice made from mugshots shown earlier (even if it was not the suspect that was chosen) increased the tendency for witnesses to make a choice from a subsequent identification parade. Contrary to predictions, Memon et al.[35] found that older adults were no more susceptible to mugshot-induced biases than younger adults. A real world example of the potential dangers of mugshot-induced biases comes from the case of Gary Graham, a convicted murderer whose case relied primarily on eyewitness evidence. Gary was identified from a live parade a day after the witness had been exposed to his face in a mugshot album. Now the witness may have been accurate, but we will never know for certain because Gary was executed in Texas in 2000.[37]

Showups

A showup is when a single photograph of a suspect is presented to the witness for identification with the option to identify the person as the perpetrator or not. This form of identification has been described as 'suggestive'[38] and 'biased'.[15] The witness is placed under added pressure to make an identification because they believe the police have evidence that the person in the photo is the culprit; or because they believe the showup is the only opportunity they will have to identify the perpetrator. These suggestive mechanisms hold equally for the similar practice of a visual identification of the perpetrator—standing in the dock of a courtroom. A recent field study of 271 actual cases using files from the Sacramento Police Department reported higher rates of suspect identification from showups than photographic lineups.[15] One of the consequences of using a showup therefore is that it increases a bias to choose a suspect from an identity parade or lineup.

An analysis of multiple studies[39] comparing identification accuracy in showups and lineups reports no differences in rates of correct identifications (when the real perpetrator is present in a lineup). In a situation where the perpetrator is not in the lineup or is not the person in the showup (i.e. in the eventuality that the police have arrested an innocent person), showups can increase false identifications. In other words, showups are inferior to photo-lineups when it comes to protecting the innocent. Several studies have reported an increase in false identifications when showups are used.[40–42] Moreover, there are some conditions (e.g. alcohol intoxication) under which witnesses are even more likely to make false identifications from showups.[43]

In Scotland, in-court identifications (also referred to as dock identifications) are seen as a necessary element in establishing evidence of eyewitness identifications. A recent case, *Holland v HMA*,[44] identifies the intrinsic problems associated with pre-trial identification and subsequent dock identifications at the trial. The accused, in this case, was charged with two counts of armed robbery and assault at a private dwelling and at a newsagent. Eyewitness testimony was the sole form of identification evidence led at the trial. There were several witnesses. One witness (Mr L) was blind in one eye and could not see well out of the other. Two of the other witness (Miss G and Mr S) had identified the accused from police photographs but selected two foils from the live parade. Miss G's son had identified the accused from the live parade but there was some dispute as to whether this was an identification or a statement that the accused resembled the robber. During the trial, the Crown led no evidence about the identification parades but relied solely upon Miss G and her son who identified the accused in the dock. No identification evidence from Mr L was led. An air pistol found in the accused's flat at the time of the arrest was identified by all of the above eyewitnesses as 'similar in appearance' to that used in the robbery. In 2005, the Judicial Committee of the Privy council considered the Holland case and accepted that identification parades offer safeguards that are not available when a witness is asked to identify the accused in court. They conviction was overturned but the principle of dock identification was upheld.

In the Holland case, dock identifications of the accused were corroborated by the description of the weapon used and the two crimes associated using the *Moorov* Principle.[45] Essentially, the principle permits single sources of evidence, such as one eyewitness or one fingerprint, to be corroborated by evidence from other sources such as a second eyewitness. However, corroborating evidence from two witnesses is of little value unless it has been obtained independently and the procedures are not flawed.

Live lineups and use of video

A typical identification parade consists of one suspect and known non-suspects (foils). The witness's task is to decide if one of the people in the lineup is the culprit.

Slater[46] recorded the outcome of identification attempts by 843 witnesses in England who inspected 302 live lineups. Suspects were identified by 36 per cent of witnesses, foils were identified by 22 per cent, and 42 per cent of witnesses made no positive identification. Also in England, Wright and McDaid[2] examined the outcome of 616 live lineups involving 1561 witnesses, the suspect was identified by 39 per cent, a foil by 20 percent, with 41 per cent making no identification. More recently, Valentine *et al.*[3] analysed data from 640 attempts to identify the perpetrator from 314 lineups conducted by the Metropolitan Police (London) recording characteristics of the victim, suspect, witness's viewing condition and type of crime. Consistent with some of the laboratory findings, data analysis revealed that a suspect is more likely to be identified by younger witnesses (under 30 years), that white European suspects (as opposed to Afro-Caribbean) are more often recognized and that witnesses who gave a detailed description had viewed the suspect for more than 1 min. The witnesses who gave a detailed description also made their choice more speedily from the lineup and made more identifications of the suspect. These findings are not consistent with the results of laboratory studies which typically find no relationship between person description quality and identification performance.[47]

As pointed out by Valentine *et al.* the identities of the suspect and culprit are not necessarily the same in these field studies as investigators cannot be certain how many lineups contain the culprit.

In England and Wales, the preferred method of identification, a live parade, has remained unchanged until recently. The Home Office has recently revised codes of practice (2002, 2003) to allow greater use of video to collect formal identification evidence. This is largely as a result of the promising research findings that have emerged following preliminary research using a video identification system (VIPER).

West Yorkshire Police in England developed VIPER and it has several potential benefits compared with live parades. Use of video could make identification evidence more effective by dramatically reducing the time it takes to organize an identity parade. Furthermore, the use of a large database of video clips from which to select 'foils' could make lineups fairer to the suspect. Video is also less threatening to victims.[1] Previous research showed that VIPER video lineups from actual criminal cases were fairer to the suspects than conventional 'live' lineups,[48] and VIPER parades produced a higher rate of positive identifications (39 per cent) than live parades (35 per cent).[1] Subsequent research on the fairness of VIPER parades found that VIPER video lineups were equally fair to white European and African-Caribbean suspects.[49] Currently, 27 police forces in England are connected to VIPER, with 1500 VIPER users in the UK. The system is also currently being piloted in Scotland. Research is currently underway to compare VIPER with the North American photo-lineup procedure and to see what advantages a moving image and various foil selection strategies will have.[50]

Foil bias

A suspect in a lineup deserves a fair test, i.e. a test in which the suspect does not stand out inappropriately from the other innocent people ('foils') in the lineup. Although this sounds obvious, biased lineups do occur. One of the most notorious examples is when a black suspect appeared in an all-white lineup used by police in Minneapolis.[51] The police justified this lineup by explaining that there were no other blacks in the building when the lineup was constructed and that there were few blacks in Minneapolis so the lineup was representative for the population! Constructing a fair lineup is not an easy task. For example, on what basis do you select the lineup foils? According to Wells et al.,[52] selecting foils who fit a comprehensive description of the suspect could result in the selection of near 'clones', which might make the recognition of the actual culprit too difficult. Selecting foils on the basis of the verbal description of the witness guarantees more variability amongst the members of the lineup because there will be some differences between witnesses in their choice of descriptors and in the amount of detail, and a wider range of foil faces can be used to match the description. Clark and Tunnicliff[53] also recommend that when constructing a perpetrator-absent lineup for the purposes of research, the innocent foils should be selected on the basis of a match to a description of the perpetrator and not to match to the suspect. They found the false identification rate was lower in the former situation.

There are several problems associated with a match to description technique however. For example, if the suspect has a distinctive feature which the witness did not describe, the foils may not have that feature. In such a case, the suspect will stand out. Also, certain features of the suspect might be in witness' memory but not reported in a pre-lineup description. Furthermore, as illustrated earlier, the witness might give a very vague description of the culprit. Another problem is that the witness's description of the culprit could sometimes be so specific that finding a reasonable set of distracters is virtually impossible.

It is obvious that the suspect should not stand out from the foils. It is therefore recommended that all members of the lineup wear similar clothes. But should they all wear clothes similar to those worn by the perpetrator at the scene of crime? In one of the first studies to address this question, Thomson et al.[54] found strong effects on accuracy of recognition of presenting people in the same clothes at study and test. This fits both with common sense and encoding specificity theory which predicts that the more of the original event is re-instated[55] the more likely one will hit upon a feature which the witness has encoded. However, Lindsay et al.[56] found in an eyewitness simulation study that the guilty suspect was not chosen any more often when he wore the same clothes as in the crime scene. The innocent person wearing the clothing used in the crime scene was chosen significantly more often however. Lindsay et al.[57] in addition found that witnesses who had identified the clothing worn by the guilty suspect were more likely to identity the guilty suspect than the innocent suspect. This led to subsequent research on the use of body lineups to obtain eyewitness evidence[58] and the diagnostic value of multiple identifications by the same witness from different types (voice, body, face) lineups.[59] We concur that independent visual, voice and gait movement identification will allow courts to be in a better position to assess whether the defendant is the offender.

Investigator bias

If the person conducting the lineup (e.g. a police officer) knows which member of the lineup the suspect is, he/she may, perhaps unintentionally, pass on this information to an eyewitness through his non-verbal behaviour. For example, when the witness is observing the suspect, the investigator may at that moment become anxious about whether or not the witness will recognize the suspect. This anxiety could change his/her behaviour which in turn will lead the witness to believe that this particular person is the suspect.[60] Indeed, a lineup administrator's knowledge of a suspect's identity can increase false identifica-tion rates.[61] Moreover, lineup administrators' beliefs about a culprit's position within a lineup have been found to affect witnesses' confidence in their lineup choices.[62] Post-identification feedback has similar effects (see Clifasefi et al., Chapter 5, this volume).

Is it common sense?

Several prior surveys have tried to gauge the knowledge of jurors on factors affecting the reliability of eyewitness testimony. The surveys were all conducted in North America and relied primarily on jury-eligible college students. For example, Shaw et al.[63] conducted a study to look at common sense knowledge about eyewitness testimony 15 years ago using college students. While the students were aware of factors such as length of exposure, age of witness and delay, they had no idea about how different test procedures, questioning tactics of the police, and so on can influence the accuracy of eyewitness testimony. Garry et al.,[64] in a survey of beliefs about memory, found a large number of individuals had erro-neous beliefs about memory (see Clifasefi et al., Chapter 5, this volume). More recently, Wise and Safer[65] surveyed 160 US judges about their knowledge and beliefs about eyewit-ness testimony. Their findings suggest there are some issues related to eyewitness memory that judges had incorrect beliefs about such as the relationship between confidence and accuracy and the ability to distinguish accurate from inaccurate witnesses. Even where judges were able to give the correct response to a question about an eyewitness's ability, they felt that that average juror would not know the correct answer.

Another method that has been used to study juror knowledge is the post-diction method. During post-diction studies students and laypersons read written summaries of an eyewitness identification experiment and then post-dict the eyewitness identification accuracy rates of the participants in the original experiment. The comparison of post-dicted identification accuracy with actual experimental results enables researchers to assess the sensitivity of prospective jurors to specific factors manipulated in the study. Research conducted using this methodology has found that laypersons often predict higher identification rates than are generally found among participants of eyewitness research.[66]

Expert testimony

The impact of expert psychological testimony on jurors has been examined by varying the presence and type of expert testimony and examining juror conviction rates across conditions.[67,68] Although early research showed that the presence of expert psychological testimony reduced conviction rates, it was unclear whether this was a result of a simple increase in juror scepticism or a tendency to disbelieve or doubt an eyewitness, or due to juror sensitivity or increased knowledge of the factors influencing eyewitness memory.

In a study assessing the impact of expert testimony on juror verdicts with respect to the level of violence associated with a crime and presence/absence of expert testimony, Loftus[69] found that exposure to expert testimony led to increases in juror scepticism and sensitivity. Wells et al.[70] found that mock jurors exposed to expert testimony prior to the eyewitnesses' testimony were less likely to believe eyewitnesses (41 per cent) than mock jurors not exposed to expert testimony (62 per cent). The participants were also found to be sensitive to the effect of witnessing conditions on identification accuracy, but there was no reliable increase in juror sensitivity.

Devenport et al.[71] also assessed the impact of expert psychological testimony on juror common sense knowledge. By manipulating both lineup suggestiveness and presence of expert testimony in the simulated video trial, the authors were able to assess the impact of scientific knowledge regarding factors that influence eyewitness identification accuracy on jurors' evaluation of lineup suggestiveness. The authors report that jurors were sensitive to foil and instruction biases when asked about them directly but insensitive to the harmful effects of these factors when rendering verdicts. Moreover, expert testimony did not improve juror sensitivity to foil, instruction or presentation biases.

In conclusion, while the presentation of expert scientific knowledge can make jurors more sensitive to the factors influencing eyewitness identification performance, it does not appear to improve juror common sense knowledge of factors influencing lineup biases.[71]

Conclusions

In his 2005 text on the legal system's misconceptions and misuse of psychological research, James Doyle, a litigator whose cases ranged from death row appeal and murder to civil cases, traces the history of the battle for eyewitness research to have a place in the courtroom. He provides a good summary of the current state of play:

> In the late 1990s, after absorbing nearly a century of hostility, derision and patronising neglect from the legal system, research psychologists seized on DNA exoneration cases and launched one more effort to make the case that the science of memory must count in police stations and courtrooms[37] (p. 7).

In this chapter, we have drawn attention to characteristics of the witness and witnessing situation that can increase the likelihood of a mistaken identification. On the whole, psychologists have no control over these variables. We have also drawn attention to factors on which the legal system could exert some influence to increase the likelihood of an accurate eyewitness report. These post-event variables include the conditions at the time a witness's memory is tested as well as mechanisms that could be put in place to reduce contamination of witness evidence. So while the battle for expertise on eyewitness issues goes on in the courts, researchers continue to make progress in dispelling myths about eyewitnesses.

References and notes

1. **Pike G, Brace N, Kynan S.** *The visual identification of suspects: procedures and practice.* Home Office, Briefing Note, 02/02.
2. **Wright DB, McDaid AT.** Comparing system and estimator variables using data from real lineups. *Applied Cognitive Psychology*, 1996; 10:75–84.
3. **Valentine T, Pickering A, Darling S.** Characteristics of eyewitness identification that predict the outcome of real lineups. *Applied Cognitive Psychology*, 2003; 17:969–993
4. **Scheck B, Nuefeld P, Dwyer J.** *Actual innocence.* Random House, New York. 2000.
5. Craig v The King (1933) 49 CLR 429
6. Davies v The King (1937) 57 CLR 170
7. **Neil v. Biggers**, 409 us 188 (1972).
8. **R v Turnbull** (Launcelot) (1977) 65 Cr App R 242
9. Alexander v The Queen (1981) CLR 395
10. **Memon A, Vrij A, Bull R.** *Psychology & law: truthfulness, accuracy and credibility of victims, witnesses and suspects*, 2nd edn. Wiley, Chichester, UK. 2003.
11. **Wells GL, Loftus EF.** Eyewitness memory for people and events. In A Goldstein, ed. *Comprehensive handbook of psychology, forensic psychology.* John Wiley and Sons, New York. 2002.
12. **Meissner CA, Brigham JC.** Thirty years of investigating the own-race bias in memory for faces: a meta-analytic review. *Psychology, Public Policy, and Law*, 2001; 7:3–35.
13. **Kassin S, Tubb A, Hosch HM, Memon A.** On the 'general acceptance' of eyewitness testimony research: a new survey of experts. *American Psychologist*, 2001; 56:405–416.
14. **Abshire J, Bornstein B.** Juror sensitivity to the cross-race effect. *Law and Human Behaviour*, 2003; 27:471–480.
15. **Behrman B, Davey S.** Eyewitness identification in actual criminal cases: an archival analysis. *Law and Human Behaviour*, 2001; 25:475–491.
16. **Wright DB, Boyd CE, Theroux CG.** Inter-racial contact and the own-race bias for face recognition in South Africa and England. *Applied Cognitive Psychology*, 2003; 17:365–73.
17. **Bartlett JC, Strater L, Fulton A.** False recency and false fame of faces in young adulthood and old age. *Memory and Cognition*, 1991; 19:177–188.

18. **Searcy JH, Bartlett JC, Memon A.** Age differences in accuracy and choosing in eyewitness identification and face recognition. *Memory and Cognition*, 1999; 27:538–552

19. **Bartlett JC, Memon A.** Eyewitness memory in young and older adults. In R Lindsay, R Ross, D Read, M Toglia, eds. *Handbook of eyewitness psychology: Memory for people.* Mahwah, NJ: Lawrence. 2006; 2:309–338.

20. **Craik FIM, Byrd M.** Aging and cognitive deficits: the role of attentional resources. In FIM Craik, S Trehub, ed. *Aging and cognitive processes.* Plenum, New York. 1982:191–211.

21. **Jacoby LL.** Ironic effects of repetition: measuring age-related differences in memory. *Journal of Experimental Psychology: Learning, Memory and Cognition*, 1999; 25:3–22.

22. **Searcy JH, Bartlett JC, Memon A.** Relationship of availability, lineup conditions and individual differences to false identification by young and older eyewitnesses. *Legal and Criminological Psychology*, 2000; 5:219–236.

23. Domican v The Queen (1992) 173 CLR 555 f.c. 92/011

24. **Deffenbacher KA., Bornstein BH, Penrod SD, McGorty, EK.** A meta-analytic review of the effects of high stress on eyewitness memory. *Law and Human Behavior*, 2004; 28:687–706.

25. **Steblay NM.** A meta-analytic review of the weapon focus effect. *Law and Human Behavior*, 1992; 16:413–424.

26. **Christianson SA.** Emotional stress and eyewitness memory: a critical review. *Psychological Bulletin*, 1992; 112:284–309.

27. **Maass A, Köhnken G.** Eyewitness identification: simulating the 'weapon effect'. *Law and Human Behaviour*, 1989; 13:397–408.

28. **Laney, C., Heuer, F., Reisberg, D.** Thematically-induced arousal in naturally-occurring emotional memories. *Applied Cognitive Psychology*, 2003; 17:995–1004.

29. **Laney C, Campbell HV, Heuer F, Reisberg D.** Memory for thematically arousing events. *Memory and Cognition*, 2004; 32:1149–1159.

30. **Morgan CA III, Hazlett GA, Doran A, Garrett S, Hoyt G, Thomas P, Baraoski M, Southwick SM.** Accuracy of eyewitness memory for persons encountered during exposure to highly intense stress. *International Journal of Law and Psychiatry*, 2004; 27:265–279.

31. **Hulse L, Allan K, Memon A, Read JD.** Investigating post-stimulus elaboration as a mechanism for emotional arousal effects on memory. Now in press in American Journal of Psychology.

32. **Sporer SL.** An archival analysis of person descriptions. Paper presented at the Biennial Meeting of the American Psychology–Law Society in San Diego, California. 1992.

33. **Sporer SL.** Post-dicting eyewitness accuracy: confidence and decision times and person descriptions of choosers and non-choosers. *European Journal of Social Psychology*, 1992; 22:157–180.

34. **Wagstaff GF, MacVeigh J, Boston R, Scott L, Brunas-Wagstaff J, Cole J.** Can laboratory findings on eyewitness testimony be generalised to the real world? An archival analysis of the influence of violence, weapon presence and age on eyewitness accuracy. *Journal of Psychology: Interdisciplinary and Applied*, 2003; 137:17–28.

35. **Memon A, Hope L., Bartlett, J., Bull, R.** Eyewitness recognition errors: the effects of mugshot viewing and choosing in young and old adults. *Memory and Cognition*, 2002; 30:1219–1227.

36. **Dysart J, Lindsay RCL, Hammond R, Dupuis P.** Mug shot exposure prior to lineup identification: interference, transference and commitment effects. *Journal of Applied Psychology*, 2001; 86:1280–1284.

37. **Doyle J.** *True witness: cops, courts, science and the battle against misidentification.* Palgrave MacMillan, 2005.

38. **Malpass RS, Devine PG.** Research on suggestion in lineups and photospreads. In GL Wells, EF Loftus, ed. *Eyewitness testimony: psychological perspectives.* Cambridge University Press, New York. 1984:64–91.

39. **Steblay N, Dysart J, Fulero S, Lindsay RCL.** Eyewitness accuracy rates in police showup and lineup presentations: a meta-analytic comparison. *Law and Human Behaviour*, 2003; 27:523–540.

40. Dekle DJ, Beale C, Elliot R, Huneycutt D. Children as witnesses: a comparison of lineups vs. showup methods. *Applied Cognitive Psychology*, 1996; 10:1–12.
41. Lindsay RCL, Pozzulo JD, Craig W, Lee K, Corber S. Simultaneous lineups, and showups: eye-witness identification decisions of adults and children. *Law and Human Behaviour*, 1997; 21:391–404.
42. Yarmey AD, Yarmey MJ, Yarmey AL. Accuracy of eyewitness identifications in showups and lineups. *Law and Human Behaviour*, 1996; 20:459–477.
43. Dysart JE, Lindsay RCL, MacDonald TK, Wicke C. The intoxicated witness: effects of alcohol on identification accuracy. *Journal of Applied Psychology*, 2002; 87:170–175.
44. Holland v HM Advocate, Privy Council DRA No. 1 of 2004.
45. Duff P. Towards a unified theory of 'similar facts evidence' in Scots law: relevance, fairness and the reinterpretation of Moorov. *Juridical Review*, 2002; 143–181.
46. Slater A. *Identification parades: a scientific evaluation*. Police Research Awards Scheme, Home Office. 1994.
47. Meissner CA, Sporer SL, Schooler JW. Person descriptions as eyewitness evidence. In R Lindsay, R Ross, D Read, M Toglia, eds. *Handbook of eyewitness psychology: Memory for people*. Mahwah NJ: Lawrence Erlbaum and Associates. 2006; 2:3–34.
48. Valentine T, Heaton P. An evaluation of the fairness of police line-ups and video identifications. *Applied Cognitive Psychology*, 1999; 13:S59-S72.
49. Valentine T, Harris N, Colom Piera A, Darling S. Are police video identifications fair to African-Caribbean suspects? *Applied Cognitive Psychology*; 17:459–476.
50. Memon A, Valentine T, Darling S, Franssens D. Enhancing eyewitness identification accuracy with video parades. Paper presented at the Australian Psychological Association Annual Conference, Sydney, 30 September 2004.
51. Ellison KW, Buckhout R. *Psychology and criminal justice*. Harper & Row, New York. 1981.
52. Wells GL, Small L, Penrod S, Malpass RS, Fulero SM, Brimacombe CAE. Eyewitness identification procedures: recommendations for lineups and photospreads. *Law and Human Behavior*, 1998; 22:603–647.
53. Clark S, Tunnicliff J. Selecting foils in eyewitness identification experiments: experimental control and real world simulation. *Law and Human Behaviour*, 2001; 25:199–216.
54. Thomson DM, Robertson SL, Vogt R. Person recognition: the effects of context. *Human Learning*, 1982; 1:137–154.
55. Tulving E, Thomson, DM. Encoding specificity and retrieval processes in episodic memory. *Psychological Review*, 1973; 80:352–373.
56. Lindsay RCL, Nosworthy GL, Martin R, Martynuck C. Using mugshots to find suspects. *Journal of Applied Psychology*, 1994; 79:121–130.
57. Lindsay RCL, Wallbridge H, Drennan D. Do the clothes make the man? An exploration of the effect of lineup attire on eyewitness identification accuracy. *Canadian Journal of Behavioral Science*, 1987; 19:463–547.
58. Pryke S, Lindsay RCL. Multiple independent identification decisions: a radical alternative to current lineup methods. Unpublished PhD thesis. Queen's University, Kingston, Ontario, Canada.
59. Pryke S, Lindsay RCL, Dysart JE, Dupuis P. Multiple independent identification decisions: a method of calibrating eyewitness identifications. *Journal of Applied Psychology*, 2004; 89:73–84.
60. Rosenthal R. *Experimenter effects in behavioral research*. Irvington Press, New York. 1976.
61. Phillips M, McAuliff B, Kovera M, Cutler B. Double-blind photoarray administration as a safeguard against investigator bias. *Journal of Applied Psychology*, 1999; 84:940–51.
62. Garrioch L, Brimacombe E. Lineup administrators' expectations: their impact on eyewitness confidence. *Law and Human Behavior*, 2001; 25:299–315.
63. Shaw J, Garcia L, McClure K. A lay perspective of the accuracy of eyewitness testimony. *Journal of Applied Social Psychology*, 1999; 29:52–71.

64. **Garry M, Loftus EF, Brown SW, DuBreuil SC.** Womb with a view: beliefs about memory, repression and memory-recovery. In DG Payne, FG Conrad, ed. *Intersections in basic and applied memory research.* Lawrence Erlbaum Associates, Hillsdale, NJ. 1997:233–236.

65. **Wise RA, Safer MA.** What U.S. judges know and belief about eyewitness testimony. *Applied Cognitive Psychology*, 2004; **18**:427–444.

66. **Brigham JC, Bothwell R.** The ability of prospective jurors to estimate the accuracy of eyewitness identifications. *Law and Human Behavior*, 1983; 7:19–30.

67. **Fox S, Walters H.** The impact of general versus specific eyewitness testimony and eyewitness confidence upon mock juror judgement. *Law and Human Behaviour*, 1986; **10**:215–228.

68. **Maass A, Brigham, West S.** Testifying on eyewitness reliability: expert advice is not always persuasive. *Journal of Applied Social Psychology*, 1985; **15**:207–229.

69. **Loftus E.** The impact of expert psychological testimony on the unreliability of eyewitness identification. *Journal of Applied Psychology*, 1980; **65**:9–15.

70. **Wells GL, Lindsay R, Tousignant J.** Effects of expert psychological advice on human performance in judging the validity of eyewitness testimony. *Law and Human Behaviour*, 1980; 4:275–285.

71. **Devenport J, Penrod S, Cutler B.** Eyewitness identification evidence: evaluating commonsense evaluations. *Psychology, Public Policy and Law*, 1997; 3:338–361.

Chapter 7

We have got the whole child witness thing figured out, or have we?

Rachel Sutherland, Deryn Strange and Maryanne Garry

Throughout the 1980s and 1990s, numerous scientific papers on children's eyewitness testimony hooked their audiences in with descriptions of high profile sexual abuse cases. The cases were horrific and created panic throughout communities. In the end, it became clear that many of the cases developed because overzealous investigative interviewers were leading children to make false claims of abuse. It is now 2006, and these high profile cases have disappeared from the headlines. You could be forgiven for thinking that—after more than 20 years of research on the reliability and accuracy of child witnesses—the reason there are no headlines is because we have thoroughly scrutinized the evidence, identified the problems and developed new methods to gather evidence properly from children. To a certain extent you would be right: the massive body of scientific research published during the last 20 years has answered many of the most critical questions about child witnesses. However, the purpose of this chapter is to get you off your comfortable armchair: there are new problems.

Of course, let us not forget how far we have come since the 1980s. Because of research by psychological scientists, we now know the conditions most likely to elicit accurate and reliable accounts from young children, as well as those most likely to elicit false reports.[1,2] Academics and professionals alike have banded together and developed the best practice in interview protocols, and those protocols have led to significant policy changes in several countries, including the USA, Canada, the UK, Australia and New Zealand. Indeed, a quick scan through more recent academic publications reveals a noticeable decline in articles describing children's abilities to serve as witnesses, and the extent of their suggestibility. Perhaps more importantly, in recent years there has also been a noticeable decline in the number of child sexual abuse cases capturing media headlines, presumably because there has been a decline in contaminated evidence reaching the courtroom.

So, considering the decline in both research and media coverage, you could be forgiven for assuming that we have got evidential interviews all figured out. You could be forgiven for thinking that changes to courtroom procedure mean that we can weed out unreliable child witnesses before they take the stand. You could also be forgiven for thinking that once on the stand, cross-examination reveals unreliable child witnesses for what they are.

In short, you could be forgiven for thinking that—as far as the whole child witness thing goes—we have got it all figured out. However, in this chapter, we review three areas of research covering the major phases of the justice system relevant to child witnesses. The bottom line: to assume that we have got it all figured out just might be unforgivable.

We have figured out how investigative interviews should be done

The first stage of any criminal case means gathering evidence: investigators need to develop a clear picture of what happened, and to do that they must interview all known witnesses to a crime. It is these interviews that have received so much research attention. The daycare child abuse cases that dominated the media and the courts in the 1980s and 1990s were the product of suggestive interviewing techniques.[1,2] In their attempts to persuade children to disclose abuse, investigative interviewers were, in fact, creating the very crimes they rallied against.

After years of research, scientists have been able to dispel many of the widespread myths about how children and interviewers behave in investigative interviews. For example, recent work by Bruck and Ceci[3] shows that, contrary to popular belief, sexually abused children do not typically hide their abuse because they feel ashamed, guilty or fearful of the consequences. Instead, most children will disclose details of their unpleasant experiences when they are initially asked about them. In addition, we also know that it does not take a series of suggestive interviews for a child's report to become distorted and inaccurate. Instead, children can incorporate false details into their memories of an event from minimal feedback or a few, seemingly innocuous, leading questions asked in a single interview.[4] We also know that it is not possible to classify an interview as 'suggestive' simply by counting up the number of Hollywood-style leading questions. In reality, what makes an interview suggestive is much more insidious than the number of leading questions. As Bruck and Ceci[3] note, biased interviewers, i.e. those who harbour suspicions about what probably happened to a child, carry out biased interviews. They often construct the interview to draw out evidence to support their suspicions; and it will, regardless of whether or not the interviewer's suspicions are based in fact.

After much research, we now know that they key component of a good investigative interview is that the interviewer begins with open-ended questions (such as, 'Would you like to tell me what happened when you went to the park?') followed by more open-ended prompts ('Tell me more about that' or 'is there anything else you can remember about that day?'). More specifically, the interviewer should extend an open-ended invitation to the child to recall the experience in his or her own words. Of course, such a technique necessarily means that the interviewer should also delay specific, focused questions for as long as possible. If specific questions become necessary, then once interviewers use them, they should revert immediately to open-ended questioning, to allow children to elaborate in their own way. This kind of 'funnel' or 'stepwise' structure forms the basis of most good investigative interview protocols[2,5−9].

You might be wondering why is it so important to begin with open-ended questions. The answer is that the research consistently demonstrates that open-ended questions (such as, 'tell me everything you can remember about X') elicit the most accurate information from children.[2,10,11] The most likely reason that open-ended questions reduce inaccuracies is that open-ended questions allow children to describe the event in their own words, reducing the likelihood that they will unwittingly include suggested information in their report. Of course, improving interviewer practice is not as easy as simply asking interviewers to change the type of questions they ask. The research also consistently shows that the information children provide in response to open-ended questions is typically less detailed than investigators would like. As a result, it is understandable that interviewers often resort to more specific questions to bring out the seemingly more helpful, specific details. However, the difficulty with specific questions is that they can telegraph to the child the 'correct'— or at least the preferred—answer. Not wanting to disappoint the interviewer, the child may simply offer the answer the interviewer expects. That answer may be at odds with the way the child remembers the event. There is only a limited way out of this quagmire, because sometimes interviewers genuinely need to use specific questions. The caveat is that they need to return to open-ended questioning as soon as they can.

Have investigative interviewers got it figured out?

Unfortunately, to assume that investigative interviewers actually follow these best practice guidelines would be wrong. Despite the almost unanimous agreement regarding the best way to interview children, the research suggests that the guidelines are, more often than not, simply ignored.[12−16]

In fact, evaluations of real-life investigative interviews show that the standard of interviewer behaviour is best described as poor, with relatively few interviewers using good questioning techniques. For example, instead of relying on open-ended questioning, interviews are frequently dominated by potentially leading specific questions. Gilstrap[17] reported that on average, 40–50 per cent (and in some cases, as many as 60 per cent) of questions asked during their sample of real-life investigative interviews were specific and (potentially) leading. In addition, Warren and colleagues[16] found that only 31 per cent of the questions asked during the abuse-related section of a series of investigative interviews were open-ended questions that could be answered by more than one- or two-word responses. In contrast, nearly two-thirds of all questions asked during the interviews required a yes/no answer, or other specific response. These statistics would suggest that the potential for error to creep in to children's reports is high and unacceptable.

Unfortunately, other research suggests that even if interviewers do begin interviews by asking open-ended questions, they quickly revert to asking more specific questions. One study found that, on average, investigative interviews lasted 46 min. Of those 46 min, on average only 76 s was taken up by open-ended questioning.[12] In other words, only 2 per cent of the total interview time was spent on open-ended questions. To make matters worse, still other research shows that children had provided only 8 per cent of their total report before the investigative interviewer initiated specific questioning.[15]

With statistics like these, you could be forgiven for concluding that interviewers are not being trained properly, and that the blame lies squarely with those responsible for ensuring that interviewers are aware of, and skilled in, proper interview techniques. Unfortunately, this assumption would also be wrong.

It is certainly possible that some of the investigative interviewers in the studies above were unaware of the recommended procedures, or perhaps had not been trained properly. After all, some of the interviews analysed in those studies were conducted in the late 1980s, before many of the better interview protocols were published. However, even more recent studies of interviewer behaviour have produced similarly disappointing results.[14,15] In fact, these more recent studies suggest there is a far more worrying problem, one that is sure to lull you off of your comfortable armchair: there is good reason to believe that interview training programmes have no long-term benefit.

Recent research shows that training programmes actually have little effect on investigative interviewers' actual behaviour when they go out in to the field. A series of studies have shown that, despite intensive and thorough theoretical and practical training, and despite the fact that interviewers come out of their training with an increased under-standing of the need for good interview practices, this increase in understanding does not translate into more appropriate behaviour. Interviewers continue to rely heavily on specific questions.[12,14,16,18–20] In other words, while interviewers perform in the way they should in the confines of a training programme, they do not do so when they leave.

So what is going on? Many of these training programmes, although intensive, were one-off courses, conducted over several days. Research by Lamb and his colleagues has highlighted that while brief one-off courses are sufficient to teach more appropriate techniques and the reason for them, regular supervision and detailed feedback is incredibly important for maintaining improvements in interviewing technique.[15,18,21]

Interviewers who were trained in the structured NICHD interview protocol and par-ticipated in monthly supervision sessions showed marked improvements in their inter-view technique. They asked more open-ended questions, fewer suggestive questions, and showed a greater tendency towards delaying their specific (potentially suggestive) ques-tions until later in the interview. Nevertheless, even though interviewers participated in monthly supervision sessions for *a year*, their old habits returned as soon as supervision stopped.[18] Apparently, ongoing supervision was essential for maintaining the positive changes these interviewers had made after their training. The research suggests that with-out continuous support, investigative interviewers are unable to adhere to recommended interviewing procedures.

Clearly then, we do not have investigative interviews all figured out. There is a funda-mental gap between what researchers and investigative interviewers know to be important elements of safe interviewing practice and the actual use of those elements in the field. Of course, researchers recognize that it is not always a practical option for organiza-tions to provide ongoing and intensive supervision and feedback when resources are stretched.[18,22] However, the obvious question to consider is which is the greater cost: the cost involved in training and supervising interviewers to avoid risky interview practices, or the cost of obtaining unreliable evidence from a child witness?

We have got the judicial process all figured out

Once the investigation is over, the next step is often the courtroom. Once a case has made it to court, we rely on judicial process to ensure that the evidence presented in court is truthful and accurate. In this section, we look at two components of the judicial process relevant to child witnesses—the truth/lie discussion (TLD) and cross-examination—both of which are based on the assumption that, when it comes to children's testimony, we have got the justice system all figured out.

Truth/Lie discussions (TLD)

In most countries, child witnesses are not required to take an oath 'to tell the truth, the whole truth, and nothing but the truth' before giving evidence. Instead, children are often required to demonstrate that they understand the difference between the truth and a lie, and what it means to tell the truth. In many countries, children are now able to deliver evidence via video taped interviews so that they do not have to appear in court. Because the judge is not present during these interviews, it becomes the investigative interviewer's responsibility first, to demonstrate that the child understands the need to tell the truth; and secondly, to obtain a promise from the child to tell the truth. Failure to satisfy these requirements typically means that the child's evidence will not be admissible. For example, one New Zealand judge excluded a child's evidence because the interviewer failed to conduct a discussion about truth and lies. The judge ruled:

> Nothing whatever was said by the interviewer to show that she had determined that the boy understood the necessity to tell the truth. At no stage did she discuss the concept of truth with him.

The judge went on:

> The breach cannot now be cured....Nor could the boy himself now be called to determine the issue. It is now more than nine months later. His understanding today has no relevance to his understanding then.[23]

There are two main reasons why the courts require children to show that they understand the difference between the truth and a lie. The first and most obvious reason for the TLD is to determine whether a child is able to give accurate evidence in court. Of course, here we assume that children who understand the difference between the truth and a lie will provide more accurate testimony than those who do not. The second reason for the TLD is that we assume a TLD will increase the likelihood that children will tell the truth during their testimony.[2,24] In other words, we assume that the promise to tell the truth will make children more likely to tell the truth.[24] This line of thinking parallels our assumption that adults who take the oath to 'tell the truth, the whole truth, and nothing but the truth' will actually do so because they understand the consequences if they do not. Of course, whether these assumptions are actually correct or not is an empirical question. If they are correct, then requiring lawyers to assess a child's competence before the child gives evidence—by assessing children's understanding of truth and lies—is a worthwhile exercise. If these assumptions are correct, then the TLD is a useful tool for excluding children from testifying who are more likely to provide inaccurate evidence.

Unfortunately, research suggests that once again our assumptions are wrong. Studies show that there is, in fact, no relationship between a child's performance in a TLD and the accuracy of their evidence. Indeed, children who demonstrate an understanding of the difference between the truth and a lie are no more likely to report events that they were witness to than children who fail to show any understanding.[25–28] Moreover, children's level of understanding is unrelated to the overall accuracy of their reports.[24,26,27]

Take, for example Pipe and Wilson's[27] study. They examined 6- and 10-year-old children's memory for a novel event. During the event, an experimenter 'accidentally' spilled some ink, and made the children promise not to tell anyone about it. Later, at the beginning of the memory interview, the interviewer conducted a TLD, based on those used in actual investigative interviews. Pipe and Wilson were interested in whether or not the TLD would encourage children to report the incident with the ink. Unfortunately, the answer was no. Pipe and Wilson found that the TLD had no effect on children's reports: the TLD neither increased the overall accuracy of children's reports, nor encouraged children to report the accident. In other words, there was no relationship between children's understanding of truth or lies and their accuracy or honesty in the interview.

Pipe and Wilson's findings are not unique. Goodman and colleagues[25] reported similar findings with younger (3- to 6-year-old) children, and Talwar and colleagues[28] found something even more surprising. Talwar and colleagues asked 3- to 7-year-old children to play a simple game with an experimenter. At one point during the game, children were explicitly told not to peek at a toy while the experimenter was out of the room. Not surprisingly, the majority of children did peek. However, the more interesting result was that later, when the children were asked about whether they had peeked, about 80 per cent of the peekers lied, saying they had not. Across several studies, Talwar and colleagues found no relationship between children's understanding of truth and lies and their tendency to tell the truth. In the only study that did show a relationship, it was in the opposite direction—children who correctly recognized that a fictitious character's statement was a lie were *more* likely to lie about their own behaviour. Taken together, research suggests that despite our faith in TLDs, they have little, if any, predictive power with regard to the accuracy or honesty of children's testimony.

Despite the fact that TLDs fail to predict whether a child's testimony will be accurate, most guidelines for investigative interviews still recommend that a TLD is conducted at the beginning of an interview. Over and above this recommendation, however, there seems to be no consistent means of conducting the discussion.[2] This ambiguity about what constitutes a TLD is perhaps one reason why investigative interviewers seem ambivalent about including it in their interviews. Warren and Larson,[24] for example, examined 132 transcripts of investigative interviews to determine the frequency and content of TLDs, and found a TLD present in only 56 per cent of the sample. In contrast, Sternberg and colleagues[15] reported that interviewers trained in the highly structured NICHD interview protocol (where a TLD is recommended) initiated TLDs in almost all (96 per cent) interviews. In contrast, among those who had not received the comprehensive training, only 36 per cent included a TLD spontaneously.

So what should a TLD look like? Typically, TLDs are short, with only a few questions.[24] Often the discussion begins with an open-ended question where children are asked to distinguish between the truth and a lie, followed by one or two concrete examples, such as, 'if I said my shoes were blue, would that be the truth or a lie?' Indeed, Warren and Larson[24] reported that the majority of questions children were asked in actual TLDs were yes/no questions. Interestingly, only 20 per cent of the questions asked children to provide a definition of the truth and a lie.

However, research on the development of children's understanding about truth and lies suggests that children's understanding is actually more sophisticated than simply being able to recognize the truth or a lie accurately when they hear it. Children are also able to distinguish between lies and mistakes, and to take a speaker's intentions into account when deciding whether a statement is a lie or not.[24] What these results suggest is that the over-reliance on specific yes or no questions in TLDs may actually underestimate what children know about the truth and lies. The result could be that competent child witnesses are being denied the opportunity to testify.[26,28]

However, once again there is no simple solution: other research suggests that open-ended questions requiring children to provide a definition of the truth may be beyond a child's ability. Six and 10-year-olds in the study by Pipe and Wilson[27] could answer yes or no questions about truth and lies, but only 8 per cent of 6-year-olds and 31 per cent of 10-year-olds could provide an adequate definition when asked an open-ended question. In addition, Warren and Larson[24] found that only 22 per cent of children provided a definition of the truth when asked. These studies clearly show that if children were required to provide a verbal description distinguishing the truth from a lie, then the number of children eligible to testify would drastically diminish.

In response to these obvious difficulties in defining what a TLD should be, several researchers have attempted to develop more developmentally appropriate versions of the TLD.[24,26] Unfortunately, these studies have also had mixed success. Warren and Larson,[24] for example, found that a developmentally appropriate TLD promoted accuracy in children's reports. They compared children's accuracy following a standard TLD or an extended TLD. In the extended version, children were provided with hypothetical scenarios and were asked questions that assessed their level of moral understanding and what the consequences of lying typically are. Children in the extended discussion condition were more accurate than children in the standard discussion condition and children who did not have a TLD. Thus we could conclude that an extended discussion about truth promotes children's accuracy when they give evidence. However, in a similar study, London and Nunez[26] found that simply participating in a TLD, regardless of the length of the discussion, was enough. Children who participated in a TLD were less likely to lie about their own transgression during a game, compared with children who did not participate in a TLD. In contrast, the research of Talwar and colleagues[28] suggests that simply discussing the truth is *not* enough to promote accuracy. Only when the TLDs included a promise to tell the truth did children show a decrease (from 75–79 to 57–59 per cent) in lying behaviour.

Clearly then, the utility of the TLD is still unclear. Taken together, these studies suggest that the assumption that children will be more accurate or honest if they understand the difference between the truth and a lie has little empirical support. Briefly discussing the truth does not typically affect the accuracy or honesty of child witnesses. Also, successfully demonstrating an understanding of the difference between the truth and a lie does not predict whether a child will be more honest. The fact that some researchers have failed to find a positive relationship between TLDs and accuracy means that some children are likely to have been excluded from testifying who could have done so accurately; while others have been allowed to testify when they should not have. In short, the TLD in its current form has little, if any, predictive value when it comes to the accuracy of children's testimony, and thus is potentially hampering, rather than helping, the justice system. So it seems that we have not yet figured out a way to determine which children will be more accurate in court, nor how to encourage them to be more honest.

Cross-examination

Wigmore[29] once said that, 'Cross-examination is beyond a doubt the greatest legal engine ever invented for the discovery of truth'. For many years we have operated under the assumption that this statement is entirely true: that cross-examination uncovers the real truth. As a result, we have come to expect cross-examination to identify unreliable witnesses who slip through the cracks of the judicial process and make it to the witness stand. Unfortunately, once again, our assumptions may be wrong. Research suggests that sometimes when it comes to children, cross-examination can actually do more harm than good.

In fact, cross-examination may be the last in a long list of suggestive interviewing practices: it may make a child's testimony more inaccurate. A moment's reflection should make this point clear. Cross-examination is the antithesis of a good interview. In what can only be described as ironic, the criminal justice system goes to great lengths to discourage leading questions... yet encourages them under the guise of cross-examination.

Research examining court transcripts consistently shows that the language used during cross-examination is far beyond what the typical child can understand. For example, the questions are usually more complex: they are more likely to have multiple parts, contain more double-negatives, contain more complex vocabulary or concepts, and are more likely to be closed or leading than questions asked during direct examination.[30-35] In two recent studies, researchers analysed the transcripts from a series of court cases involving child witnesses and found strikingly similar results.[31,35] Compared with prosecution lawyers, defence lawyers ask far fewer appropriate questions. They ask more leading questions ('and you went somewhere else after that?'), use more complex vocabulary or concepts ('Is it your evidence that ...') and use a more confusing sentence structure (e.g. 'Was it in the car that there was talk about the things you would do for money?').

You may be asking yourself why researchers are so interested in the way lawyers ask questions during cross-examination. After all, if all goes according to plan, the child has already given their testimony to the best of their ability. Any suggestive questions at this point in the process are surely not going to have as much of an impact. Unfortunately that is not quite true. We know that children are especially likely to accept an answer suggested by a leading question.[36] We also know that children have difficulty monitoring or signalling when they have not understood a question, and that they will attempt to provide an answer even if the question makes no sense to them.[33,37-39] In short, we know that children trust adults to ask questions that have real answers and we know that children learn to expect adults only to ask questions that they, as the adult, already have an answer to. Keeping all of these facts in mind, it is easy to see how the cross-examination style of questioning —'lawyerese' if you will—would seem unexpected and complicated and why, ultimately, it might affect the accuracy of children's evidence.

Although a number of studies have criticized the language used during cross-examination, very few have actually gone on to examine the impact of 'lawyerese' on the accuracy of children's evidence. One study, by Perry and colleagues,[33] asked 5- to 16-year-olds, as well as adults, a series of questions that were phrased either in 'lawyerese' or in a simplified, developmentally appropriate way. For example, subjects were either asked a question in the simple form, 'Did you see Katie and Sam hug each other?' or in the lawyerese form, 'Was there a display of affection between the two participants?' Perry and colleagues found that regardless of age, subjects were less accurate when they were asked the questions in lawyerese than when asked the simplified version. Interestingly, all subjects, even the adults, had difficulty repeating the question verbatim back to the interviewer. In other words, even adults had difficulty understanding and answering these complex questions that even young children are expected to understand and answer.

More recently, Zajac and colleagues[35] examined actual court transcripts of the direct examination of child witnesses and compared them with their cross-examination. They were interested both in the way the lawyers' asked children questions and how children answered those questions. Just like the earlier research, they found that the language used by defence lawyers during cross-examination was consistently more complex and less developmentally appropriate than the language used by prosecution lawyers. However, what was most interesting about their study was that children were less consistent during cross-examination: three-quarters of the children changed at least part of their testimony. In contrast, no child changed their statement when questioned by prosecution lawyers.

As Zajac and colleagues[35] pointed out, this finding is particularly alarming because any change in testimony implies that some aspect of the child's testimony is inaccurate: either the child initially made an inaccurate statement that was subsequently corrected under cross-examination, or an accurate statement was then changed to an inaccurate statement under cross-examination. In the first instance, cross-examination might have successfully reduced the errors in children's evidence, leading them towards the truth. However, in the second instance, cross-examination may actually have introduced inaccuracies, leading children away from the truth. Whichever the direction of the change, the consequences are serious.

Because it was impossible to determine whether cross-examination increased or decreased the accuracy of the children's testimony in their earlier study, Zajac and Hayne[40] conducted a second study. This time 5- and 6-year-old children participated in a staged event, so that the accuracy of their statements could be verified. After children had participated in the event, they were interviewed about what had happened—the equivalent of a direct examination. Six months later, they were re-interviewed—the equivalent of a cross-examination. The interviewers asked questions during this phase that were modelled on the cross-examination questions found in their earlier study.[35] Consistent with their earlier findings, 85 per cent of the children changed at least one part of their direct testimony under cross-examination. Of course the real question is whether those changes were towards or away from the truth. Unfortunately, the answer is alarming. Children were just as likely to change an answer from wrong to right, as they were to change their answer from right to wrong. In other words, cross-examination caused children to change their testimony, regardless of the accuracy of their original testimony.[40]

Taken together, the research on cross-examination raises difficult questions for us as citizens. It turns out that cross-examination is just as likely to create inaccuracies as it is to uncover earlier inconsistencies. In other words, sometimes cross-examination actually does more harm than good.

Conclusion

So, have we got the child witness thing all figured out? The scientific research suggests that the answer is no, on all counts. In theory, we have got investigative interviews all figured out. We know which questions elicit the most reliable information from children, and which kinds of questions to avoid. In principle, investigative interviewers know it too. In practice, however, it seems that interviewers only adhere to recommended investigative interview procedures when someone is looking over their shoulder. Apparently, old habits do die hard, and the evidence demonstrates that we just do not have investigative interviews figured out at all. The fundamental link between knowledge and application is missing, and the challenge for researchers now is not to figure out how to teach old investigators new tricks, but how to make those new tricks stick.

As for the judicial process—do children tell the truth, the whole truth and nothing but the truth when they are in the witness stand? Perhaps. But it seems that assessing children's understanding of the difference between the truth and a lie is not the way to determine whether children are able, or indeed inclined, to actually do so. Even children who understand what it means to tell the truth can lie. Moreover, cross-examination can cloud the waters further. While in some cases cross-examination can make children who are inaccurate become more accurate, in other cases it can make children who are accurate become inaccurate. So evidently we do not have the judicial process all figured out, either.

Mark Twain once said, 'Truth is mighty and will prevail. There is nothing the matter with this except that it ain't so'. So it goes for our chapter. Given that researchers have dedicated the best part of 20 years to the reliability and accuracy of child witnesses—how to interview children, how to obtain accurate testimony, how to facilitate their giving of evidence in court— you could be forgiven for making the mighty assumption that 'we have got the child witness thing all figured out.' You could be. The truth is, it just ain't so.

References and notes

1. Ceci SJ, Bruck M. *Jeopardy in the courtroom: a scientific analysis of children's testimony.* American Psychological Association, Washington, DC. 1995.
2. Poole DA, Lamb ME. *Investigative interviews of children: a guide for helping professionals.* American Psychological Association, Washington, DC. 1998.
3. Bruck M, Ceci S. Forensic developmental psychology. *Current Directions in Psychological Science,* 2004; 13:229–232.
4. Garven S, Wood JM, Malpass RS. Allegations of wrong-doing: the effects of reinforcement on children's mundane and fantastic claims. *Journal of Applied Psychology,* 2000; 85:38–49.
5. American Professional Society on the Abuse of Children. *Guidelines for psychosocial evaluation of suspected sexual abuse in young children.* 1990; 3:136–147.
6. Lamb ME, Sternberg KJ, Esplin PW. Conducting investigative interviews of alleged sexual abuse victims. *Child Abuse and Neglect,* 1998; 22:813–823.
7. *Memorandum of good practice.* Her Majesty's Stationary Office, London. 1992.
8. Obach Y, Hershkowitz I, Lamb ME, Sternberg KJ, Esplin PW, Horowitz D. Assessing the value of structured protocols for forensic interviews of alleged child abuse victims. *Child Abuse and Neglect,* 2000; 24:733–752.
9. Wilson JC, Powell, MB. *A guide to interviewing children.* Allen and Unwin Sydney, Australia. 2000.
10. Dent HR, Stephenson GM. An experimental study of the effectiveness of different techniques of questioning child witnesses. *British Journal of Social and Clinical Psychology,* 1979; 18:41–51.
11. Ornstein PA, Gordon BN, Larus DM. Children's memory for a personally experienced event: implications for testimony. *Applied Cognitive Psychology,* 1992; 6:49–60.
12. Aldridge J, Cameron S. Interviewing child witnesses: questioning techniques and the role of training. *Applied Developmental Science,* 1999; 3:136–147.
13. Davies GM, Westcott HL, Horan N. The impact of questioning style on the content of investigative interviews with suspected child sexual abuse victims. *Psychology, Crime and Law,* 2000; 6:81–97.
14. Sternberg KJ, Lamb ME, Davies GM, Westcott HL. The memorandum of good practice: theory versus application. *Child Abuse and Neglect,* 2001; 25:669–681.
15. Sternberg KJ, Lamb ME, Orbach Y, Esplin PW, Mitchell S. Use of a structured investigative protocol enhances young children's responses to free-recall prompts in the course of forensic interviews. *Journal of Applied Psychology,* 2001; 86:997–1005.
16. Warren AR, Woodall CE, Hunt JS, Perry NW. 'It sounds good in theory, but...': do investigative interviewers follow guidelines based on memory research? *Child Maltreatment,* 1996; 1:231–245.
17. Gilstrap LL. A missing link in suggestibility research: what is known about the behavior of field interviewers in unstructured interviews with young children? *Journal of Experimental Psychology: Applied,* 2004; 10:13–24.
18. Lamb ME, Sternberg KJ, Orbach Y, Esplin PW, Mitchell S. Is ongoing feedback necessary to maintain the quality of investigative interviews with allegedly abused children? *Applied Developmental Science,* 2002; 6:35–41.

19. Stevenson KM, Leung P, Cheung KM. Competency-based evaluation of interviewing skills in child sexual abuse cases. *Social Work Research and Abstracts*, 1992; **28**:11–16.
20. Warren AR, Woodall CE, Thomas M, Nunno M, Keeney J, Larson S, Stadfeld J. Assessing the effectiveness of a training program for interviewing child witnesses. *Applied Developmental Science*, 1999; **3**:128–135.
21. Lamb ME, Sternberg KJ, Orbach Y, Hershkowitz I, Horowitz D, Esplin PW. The effects of intensive training and ongoing supervision on the quality of investigative interviews with alleged sex abuse victims. *Applied Developmental Science*, 2002; **6**:114–125.
22. Powell MB. Specialist training in investigative and evidential interviewing: is it having any effect on the behaviour of professionals in the field? *Psychiatry, Psychology and Law*, 2002; **9**: 44–55.
23. R v MEF [1992] 2 NZLR 372.
24. Warren AR, Larson SM. Discussing truth and lies in interviews with children: whether, why, and how? *Applied Developmental Science*, 1999; **3**:6–15.
25. Goodman GS, Aman C, Hirschman J. Child sexual and physical abuse: children's testimony. In SJ Ceci, MP Toglia, DG Ross, ed. *Children's eyewitness memory*. Springer-Verlag, New York. 1987:1–23.
26. London K, Nunez N. Examining the efficacy of truth/lie discussion in predicting and increasing the veracity of children's reports. *Journal of Experimental Child Psychology*, 2002; **83**:131–147.
27. Pipe M, Wilson JC. Cues and secrets: influences on children's event reports. *Developmental Psychology*, 1994; **30**:515–525.
28. Talwar V, Lee K, Bala N, Lindsay RCL. Children's conceptual knowledge of lying and its relation to their actual behaviours: implications for court competence examinations. *Law and Human Behavior*, 2002; **26**:395–415.
29. Yarmey AD. *The psychology of eyewitness testimony*. Free Press, New York. 1979.
30. Brennan M. Brennan R. *Strange language: child victims under cross examination*. Charles Sturt University-Riverina, Wagga Wagga, New South Wales, Australia. 1998.
31. Davies E, Seymour FW. Questioning child complainants of sexual abuse: analysis of criminal court transcripts in New Zealand. *Psychiatry, Psychology and Law*, 1998; **5**:47–61.
32. Goodman DS, Taub PEP, Jones DPH, England P, Port LK, Rudy L, Prado L. Testifying in criminal court. *Monographs of the Society for Research in Child Development*, 1992; **57**:1–161.
33. Perry NW, McAuliff B, Tam P, Claycomb L, Dostal C, Flanagan C. When lawyers question children: is justice served? *Law and Human Behavior*, 1995; **19**:609–629.
34. Saywitz K J, Nathanson R, Snyder LS. Credibility of child witnesses: the role of communicative competence. *Topics in Language Disorders*, 1993; **13**:59–78.
35. Zajac R, Gross J, Hayne H. Asked and answered: questioning children in the courtroom. *Psychiatry, Psychology and Law*, 2003; **10**:199–209.
36. Ceci SJ, Bruck M. Suggestibility of the child witness: a historical review and synthesis. *Psychological Bulletin*, 1993; **113**:403–439.
37. Carter CA, Bottoms B L, Levine M. Linguistic and socio-emotional influences on the accuracy of children's reports. *Law and Human Behavior*, 1996; **20**:335–358.
38. Hughes M, Grieve R. On asking children bizarre questions. *First Language*, 1980; **1**:149–160.
39. Waterman A, Blades M, Spencer C. Do children try to answer nonsensical questions? *British Journal of Developmental Psychology*, 2000; **18**:211–226.
40. Zajac R, Hayne H. I don't think that's what really happened: the effect of cross-examination on the accuracy of children's reports. *Journal of Experimental Psychology: Applied*, 2003; **9**:187–195.

Tall tales on intelligence

Chapter 8

Is bigger really better? The search for brain size and intelligence in the twenty-first century

David P. Carey

Introduction

The starting point for this chapter was an advert that I saw in a British newspaper, *The Guardian*, on 29 December 2003 (see Fig. 8.1). When I saw it I was immediately reminded of the excellent chapters by Berrystein (on that old myth that we use 10 per cent of our brains) and by Corballis (on that marketing man's dream, that you can train yourself up to use *more* of your left or your right hemisphere) from *Mind myths: exploring popular assumptions about the mind and brain*.[1] One common theme of both of these chapters is the idea that, for only £9.99 plus postage and handling, you can unlock the secrets of being smarter, having a better memory, being more creative, using more of your brain, etc., etc., etc. The light-hearted implication of the advert reproduced in Fig. 8.1 is that you will emerge from one of our stellar British MBA programmes with a larger brain than when you started.

Around the same time, I read a commentary (a tongue-in-cheek, I thought at first) by Richard Dawkins and R. Elisabeth Cornwell,[2] which in effect suggests that perhaps it would be dangerous to give 16-year-olds the vote, as they have underdeveloped frontal lobes—'the part of the brain that makes us human'. What links the MBA advert and 'Dodgy frontal lobes, y'dig?'? Commentary for the commoner? Tongue-in-cheek satire, or perhaps a metaphor for what surely is a truism: bigger brains are better, or in current currency, bigger frontal lobes are better?

But are they? Vague recollections of Stephen Jay Gould's *The mismeasure of man*[3] and repressed memories of Jean Phillippe Rushton's twentieth century attempts to resurrect some racists' ideas about brain size began to bubble about in my subconscious. Surely nobody believes that bigger brains *necessarily* mean superior intellect, spatial skill, political acumen? Or do they?

The brain size and intelligence debate has been around for a long time in a number of different guises, and I will not review many of them here. Suffice it to say, in one guise, some serious scientific effort is still trying to decipher *species* similarities and differences in brain size and brain structure.[4] Most authors who attempt such comparisons are well

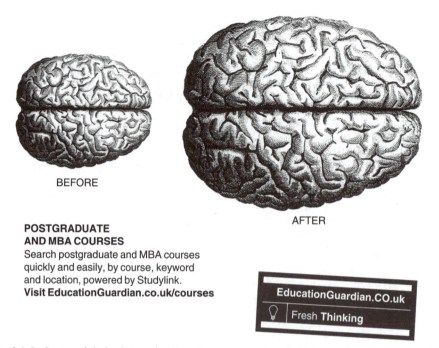

BEFORE

AFTER

**POSTGRADUATE
AND MBA COURSES**
Search postgraduate and MBA courses
quickly and easily, by course, keyword
and location, powered by Studylink.
Visit EducationGuardian.co.uk/courses

EducationGuardian.CO.uk

Fresh **Thinking**

Fig. 8.1 Brain growth in business administration, anyone? An advert for *The Guardian*'s Education supplement in December, 2003.

aware of some complex issues such as the importance of factoring body size into the equation (i.e. brain allometry: the relationship of an animal's body size to an animal's brain size). Mice have small brains, in part because they are small animals. In primates, our order, the relationship between brain size and body size is pretty strong, until we examine the brains of the great apes: orangutans, gorillas, chimpanzees, bonobos and that naked ape, us. As Sesame Street characters sing 'One of these things is not like the other' and that is of course, us. Depending on who you read, *Homo sapiens* have a brain that is three times larger than you would predict for an average primate of our body size. The poor gorilla, so demonized in the nineteenth century before Dian Fossey[5] in the twentieth, has a brain size as much as 40 per cent smaller than you would predict for a primate of that body size. Of the great apes, we are particularly big headed, literally.

Many sensible and sober arguments have been raised against previous incarnations of the brain size and intelligence debate, usually in the between-group context (i.e. race or sex; two powerful examples) as the dangers therein are perhaps the most obvious. So why in the early twenty-first century does there seem such little opposition to the current resurrection of this long-standing myth? Three independent developments in the last decade or so have rekindled interest in relating brain size to cognitive ability both within and across different species. The first has to do with the rapid spread of neuroimaging technology, the second is the explosive growth in a field which I will call behavioural genetics, and the third is a renewed interest in comparative cognition.

Neuroimaging

For the first decade or so when neuroimaging came into vogue as a neuroscientitfic tool, many of the studies focused on localizing functions in intact brains for which the only evidence previously available came from studies of abilities lost due to brain damage. These techniques allow neurologists, radiologists and even psychologists to look at brain structures in some detail (more on that below) or to use so-called functional magnetic resonance imaging (fMRI) or positron emission tomography (PET) to view metabolic changes in the brain while participants perform various tasks with their head in a brain scanner. As the techniques for analysing data from such brain scanners have improved, some of the scientists have boldly gone where no one has gone before—relating brain *structures* or *activations* to particular skill on some sort of task. The mysterious frontal lobes have been a popular target of this sort of enterprise. Also, suffice it so say, as a second wave of neuroimaging work, there is a lot of it.

Some of it is wrapped up in serious developmental work, designed to help understand the effects of malnutrition or poor environmental conditions on development of different structures in the brain, in human and non-human animals. Others are more about heritability of brain 'morphology' (i.e. size, shape, structure)—if your mother and father were big brained in one way or another, what are your chances of similar cerebral endowment? Behind some of these experiments is the implicit assumption that bigger is better, faster and brighter, and that brain size could be a relatively direct *physical* measure of intelligence—which for many Western scientists is a construct called Spearman's '*g*'.

What is intelligence, and how might you measure it?

It is called *g* because it seems to be a general ability that explains performance (good, average or poor) across a whole number of tests of mental ability. So-called intelligence quotient (IQ) tests usually require participants to solve problems and answer questions in verbal and non-verbal domains, and people who tend to perform well on one subtest tend to perform well on most or all of the others, hence *g*. It is a 'psychometric' construct, meaning related to theory and quantitative measurement of psychological entities such as memory, perception or social cognition. Evidence for *g* is very strong, as something that falls out of statistical analysis of many tests performed by many people. The statistical technique crucial for *g* is called 'factor analysis'. Factor analysis of the performance of many people on many tests can 'extract' a construct which explains much of the variability of the test scores.[6] Remaining variance can be accounted for by so-called 's' factors (meaning specific), each one explaining some of the remaining variability for a specific test, but its *g* which tells you about good or bad performance across all of the tests in your battery. Some people think that much of *g* can be understood as a general problem-solving ability that can be used for many different purposes. This view sometimes refers to such abilities as 'fluid' intelligence, as opposed to culture-specific knowledge that we gain through education, environment, books, TV etc., the so-called 'crystallized' intelligence.

The popularity of g as a construct does not mean that it is without a whole list of caveats, first and foremost the idea that g is culturally biased towards European-styled education. In fact, even the so-called 'culture fair' tests such as Raven's Matrices have been criticized in the same way.[7] Some of the concerns are political in the sense that horrific economic inequities on national and even international scales can be 'rational-ized' (I mean this in the very negative sense as making up self-satisfying but incorrect explanations) by suggesting that nothing can be done about individuals or groups which have low g. These arguments belong in a slightly different kind of chapter from this one (see Chapter 9 of this volume) but I have other science-based concerns about the whole enterprise, which I will outline below. The idea of g is so seductive that I find it hard to banish completely from my Zeitgeist, mainly because the construct is such a useful shorthand for the folksy beliefs we hold about relative abilities of friends, family and colleagues. It is much easier to hold on to and work with a belief that your favourite niece is 'as sharp as a tack' than 'she is a gifted reader and verbally precocious, but her trigonometry is not quite up to scratch and she has the social skills of your caveman brother, her father'. However, because an idea is a useful shorthand in day-to-day life does not necessarily mean it would relate in an obvious, direct way to a biological process, let alone a biological structure. Being in love depends on many biological structures and processes including the lungs, for example, because without respiration there is not a lover or a person to be loved. This clearly is not what the intelligence–brain size scientists have in mind.

The existence of g as a psychometric construct is fact. What it really means is less clear, and how we should use and study it even less so, but now let us delve into some reasons why scientists attempt to measure g (or some aspect of g) and relate it to the size of the brain (or of some subunit of the brain). Such experiments ultimately seek to establish some causal relationship for brain size and some cognitive measure, within *H. sapiens* right here, right now. Relying on comparisons with different species, even ancestors of our own, is interesting but not the 'raison d'etre' of the brain–intelligence proponents. Is there any evidence that bigger brains are better *within our species*? A good place to start is the idea that intelligence is partly or mainly genetically inherited from our parent (see Chapter 9 of this volume). After that, we will examine the case for the 'heritability' of brain size. If both of these are heritable in large part, then brain size measures may be a sensible place to look for the biological basis of intelligence.

Is intelligence inherited?

There is some evidence, although it is not without controversy, that intelligence as measured by psychometric tests is heritable. In essence, if you measure g in parents and their offspring, you tend to get correlations of about 0.45.[8] Fortunately for science, and unfortunately for all of you twins out there, Sir Francis Galton[9] recognized in the 1880s that any kind of relationship between parent and child ability could be explained by what we know now as 'heritability', but could just as easily be explained by a common environment which deprives or enriches the skills of the individuals within it. Hence, the twin study was born. The really good but hard to do experiments compare 'monozygotic' and 'dizygotic' twins reared together with twins reared apart. Monozygotic (MZ) twins share nearly identical DNA inherited from the parents, while dizygotic (DZ) twins, like brothers and sisters, share roughly 50 per cent of their DNA, on average. For example, in one study, say that the relationship between MZ twins' g scores is $r = 0.50$, and that of siblings or DZ twins is $r = 0.30$ (a correlation coefficient of 1.0 would mean a perfect relationship between the two variables). Such data suggest some genetic component (as the value is closer to 1.0 in the MZ twins), but such a study only shows that there is some genetic component that accounts for variability in intelligence *beyond environment*.

What most good studies do is use specialized statistics that calculate a measure called the heritability quotient (h^2), which uses data from MZ and DZ twins to get rid of the variance in intelligence accounted for by that stimulating, nutritionally sound environment that parents who tend to have higher IQs presumably produce (the opposite case is assumed, but somewhat more complicated by factors outside parental control, for one thing). An h^2 of 0.40 suggests that 40 per cent of the variability in some trait is more associated with genetics than it is with environment. Large h²s mean that the same trait is more highly correlated in MZ twins than in DZ twins (or siblings who are not twins). In the example above, MZ = 0.5 and DZ = 0.3 gives an $h^2 = 0.40$. You can use data from children and their biological parents, who share roughly 50 per cent of their genes ($r = 0.45$), and contrast those with the data of biological siblings raised apart ($r = 0.25$) in a similar way, which gives a heritability estimate of 0.40.[8] However, always keep in mind what heritability estimates do—they do not let you predict the IQ of a person based on the IQ of the parents or any such thing. All they tell you about is how much of the differences in IQ or g within a group is related to genes or to all the non-genetic factors, all lumped together.

Many published scientific articles and book chapters suggest that variability accounted for by genes in psychometrically measured intelligence is roughly 50 per cent.[10] Anderson (Chapter 9, this volume) pays particular attention to two large-scale twin studies. Remarkably, one of them suggests heritability of 0.50 while the other suggests something closer to 0.80. That is a difference of 30 per cent of the variability, and to date no one has explained why there is such a discrepancy between these two large sample studies. Anderson suggests that some of the differences depend on the ages of the samples. Paradoxically, although you might expect that as people get older the environment will have had more and more opportunity to influence traits, heritability studies suggest the opposite. Again, keep in mind that that does not mean that genes somehow have greater influences on people when they are adults than when they are children. It means that more of the variability of some trait is accounted for by genes in older rather than younger samples.

In addition to the age of the participants in any twin study, a more dramatic caveat for the whole heritability of intelligence business is suggested by work on groups who differ in socio-economic status (SES). A recent report[11] suggests that heritability of IQ is high in a higher SES group ($h^2 = 0.72$) but falls to essentially zero ($h^2 = 0.10$) in a lower SES group. In the higher SES group, the r values were MZ = 0.87 and DZ = 0.51, while in the lower group they were MZ = 0.68 and DZ = 0.63. If this finding holds true, it is encouraging for the scientists and politicians who are interested in interventions for the socially disadvantaged, but problematic for the mainstream research efforts on the heritability of IQ. Nobody thinks that the rules of genetic inheritance somehow differ across socio-economic status. Remember heritability estimates tell us about the amount of variance in a trait; perhaps environmental differences can play large roles on peoples' IQ scores in low SES groups, but in the higher SES groups, environmental effects such as good nutrition, schools, parental attitudes and so on lead to IQs near 'ceiling'—so high that small effects of genes on whatever IQ tests measure get a chance to show themselves and 'gobble up' more of the variability from person to person. Alternatively, these data could be due to some sort of complex interaction between environment and the genome which accounts for this large difference in heritability. Furthermore, as the vast majority of intelligence research is done with university students, their parents and their siblings, it may be that the heritability of IQ has been grossly overestimated by researching middle and upper SES families. For more on this topic, see Chapter 9 of this volume.

Is brain size inherited?

Some studies began this work by looking at measures of intelligence and brain size as estimated from brain scans in samples of unrelated volunteers.[12] Of course, such studies cannot sort out the heritability issues *per se*, because some of the variability in brain size and in intelligence will depend on environmental issues such as diet, education and SES. What is really needed are the kinds of MZ/DZ twin studies like those done in the genetics and intelligence field, mentioned above.

Of course, such studies have been done.[13] An early twin study of this sort has found that brains of identical twins are indeed more alike in size and shape than are those of fraternal twins.[14] However, the sample size in this study was somewhat small for its type: 10 MZ and 10 DZ twin pairs were examined. A later study[15] examined relationships between brain size, amount of white matter and amount of grey matter in 54 MZ twins, 58 DZ twins and 34 of their siblings. Estimates of heritability were close to 0.9 for all measures of brain size. Height was measured in the same participants, and although it was also highly heritable, it only appears to have counted for 22 per cent of the variance in overall brain size.[16] So, maybe big or small brains are indeed heritable. But what might that mean, vis-à-vis intelligence?

A problem with the 'big ones are better' perspective is that larger brains may actually have fewer neurons in them than smaller brains. Well, that is if by larger you mean thicker cortex (the convoluted outer layer of neurons of the brain). Apparently Einstein himself had rather thin cerebral cortex, but he had more neurons in it than some *almost* age-matched control brains (they were mostly younger than Einstein at time of death). It is hard to see how we can reconcile thinner is better (or at least as good as) than thicker cortex with the big brains/intelligence research.[17]

A more recent approach is to use complex multivariate statistics on MZ and DZ twin brain scans and compare many brain grey and white matter volumes. Then heritability estimates can be calculated for all of them to see which are the most heritable, i.e. the difference in the correlation coefficients between MZ and DZ twins is the greatest, with of course the MZ correlation being higher. In a 2001 paper,[18] Thompson and his colleagues suggest cautionary interpretation of their data (in the rather complex methods section, at least) as the study only used 10 MZ and 10 DZ twin pairs, but they conclude that brain structure is 'largely under genetic control'. For example, they link h^2 estimates that are greater than zero for frontal, sensorimotor and anterior temporal cortex with 'significant genetic control'. Technically h^2 estimates above 0 can be statistically significant, yes, but if they are small they are not terribly scientifically significant, if you catch my meaning.

Even so, this study 'comes to the rescue' of some of the big brains are better contradictions, by playing down the role of grey matter (i.e. neurons—a controversial position as they are the building blocks of the networks of the brain) and emphasize the connections between the neurons (the white matter) and intelligence. Thompson and his colleagues report correlations between frontal lobe white matter volume and a measure of intelligence of 0.45 in MZ twins and 0.37 in DZ twins, using a procedure that claims to be rather conservative (but difficult to understand).[19]

There is evidence in humans as well as non-human animals that suggests that the actual amount of grey matter decreases between birth and puberty but that the proportion of white matter increases up until age 20. (That commentary mentioned in the introduction about 'underdeveloped frontal lobes' was in fact referring to white matter connections.) That proportional increase is not completely accounted for by the decreases in grey matter. A popular interpretation of this type of finding is that in brain development too many neurons are produced pre-natally and that developmental experience 'prunes away' the ones that are not used (so proportionally we might be even bigger brained in this sense as youngsters!). The ones that are used by various sensory, cognitive and movement systems tend to strengthen their connections and the unused nerve cells and their connections die their natural deaths.[20] This model supports the idea that attempts to measure intelligence and brain structure might very well have been misguided when they overlooked the white matter. Only time will tell, although as a caveat there was a time, not that many years ago, when the corpus callosum, the thick white matter bundle that interconnects the two cerebral hemispheres, was thought of as connective tissue, whose major role was to hold the two halves of the brain together to keep them from sloshing around in the sea within our skull. Surely nobody believes that do they? (stay tuned for my contribution to Mind Myths III).

More white matter could (or should, in the minds of these scientists) mean more 'functional connectivity' between different brain regions. Unsurprisingly, some of these studies suggest that more white matter anywhere in the brain is correlated with greater g, but others suggest that it is the white matter in the frontal lobes that is really important. (remember: 'It's what makes us human, y'dig?'). These structural studies are beginning to concentrate more on the frontal lobes for several reasons, including the fact that functional imaging scientists have been making some claims about metabolism and intelligence there.

OK, brain size, or maybe brain white matter, or maybe frontal lobe white matter, and intelligence are heritable, sort of. Does that mean brain size (etc.) is directly related to intelligence?

One way to try to get a handle on an unbiased estimate of the relationship between brain size and various cognitive measures is to do a so-called 'meta-analysis'. These techniques look at many studies which have measured both brain size and intelligence, and use data such as sample size (more people means a more accurate estimate, ideally) and the variability of those scores to calculate an aggregate estimate of the brain size and intelligence estimate. A very interesting property of meta-analysis is that it can let you estimate publication bias. Publication bias in this context would mean, since many scientists who do this work believe that there is a strong brain size–intelligence relationship—it could be harder to publish a study where you do not find one— hence, publication bias. McDaniel has recently published a meta-analysis of the brain size and intelligence literature, and his title gives away his result: 'Big-brained people are smarter: a meta-analysis of the relationship between *in vivo* brain volume and intelligence'.[21] He suggests that the average size of the relationship is $r = 0.33$, from 37 different studies which examined brain size and intelligence in 1530 people. Additional analysis using figures called funnel plots (which give a pictorial view of how much noisier the r value is with small sample studies than with large sample studies) strongly suggests that the relationship is not a consequence of publication bias.

Other studies find a positive relationship between brain size and intelligence of about 0.40. If we accept this more generous figure, it implies that about 16 per cent of the variability of performance on the intelligence tests is accounted for by differences in brain size (this might not sound a huge amount, but in psychometric circles it is not too bad at all). One problem that these studies (like with the heritability and g studies mentioned above) often have is that when they compare individuals from different families, there will be substantial differences in many different factors that might affect how any person performs on a cognitive test but have nothing to do with one another. For example, there is evidence that enriched environmental conditions improve cognitive performance. There is ample evidence that many environmental factors (i.e. poor nutrition pre- and postnatally) adversely affect brain development. Therefore, two factors, although completely independent of one another, can create the spurious suggestion that people with bigger brains do better on cognitive tests than people with smaller brains because of their brains, and nothing else.[22]

An approach to these problems is to do so-called 'within-family comparisons'. In other words, calculate difference scores between two siblings, older minus younger. (Remember, even though siblings share 50 per cent of their genes on average, there is still room for variability in brain size and intelligence.) Over many pairs of siblings you can calculate an average estimate of the differences between brain size and cognitive test performance. Any directional differences (i.e. bigger brain, higher estimate of g) you get cannot be obviously accounted for by effects of SES and the like (as, aside from being Mum's favourite, we assume that schooling, diet, neighbourhoods and PlayStations are all more or less alike for siblings). A recent study endorsing this method showed that the relationships between brain size and cognitive test performance disappeared when you compared within-family estimates with between-family estimates.[23] Even though this procedure may be statistically overly conservative, if we believe even part of this story we need to rethink our estimates of the brain size–intelligence relationship.

Does intelligence depend upon the brain? Of course it does. In some sense all of our thoughts, emotions, beliefs etc., depend upon our brains.[24] The life experiences that have helped determine a person's, say, political affiliation, must reflect themselves through inputs, processing and outputs of the brain. Does political affiliation depend upon the brain? Yes, but only somewhat more directly than it does on the liver or on the lungs. Is political affiliation heritable? Probably in part—in so far as personality factors are roughly 50 per cent heritable[25] and shared environmental factors (i.e. parents, friends and community) probably make up a good chunk of the rest. Will we one day do an fMRI scan to determine the relevant difference between George Bush's and John Kerry's brain? (An interesting thought, that.)

Besides what is a bigger brain made of, in any case? Neurons are but one source of the stuff which makes the volume of your brain—other cells such as glia play a role in supporting neurons in various clean up/metabolic ways, but probably are not directly involved in the signal processing duties of the central nervous system. Maybe larger brains have more glial cells and the same number of neurons. One recent study suggests that male brains have on average 23 billion neurons, while female brains have on average 19 billion neurons, and that these differences are not accounted for by differences in body size.[26] Does this mean that men are 16 per cent smarter than women[27] (if only it were so, the male author concluded, after some deliberation).

In summary, there is good evidence that overall brain size has a heritable component. Nevertheless, given the earlier results suggesting that SES modulates the heritability of intelligence, I worry somewhat about the highly educated, middle- and upper-class participants who routinely put their heads into MRI scanners for the imaging experiments that make up the bulk of the evidence for these claims. These people are even more selected than the majority of those who have participated in the various IQ studies which suggest high heritability of g. One last caveat—although one study did measure height in their study of brain size, I would like to see an unconfounded estimate of body size taken in the broader SES sample brain size/g experiment. By unconfounded, I mean that a person's size as specified by genes is probably masked somewhat by diet so, for those of us who indulge a bit too much, estimates of percentage body fat could be used to calculate a standardized body mass (i.e. where you normalize all weights to the same percentage of body fat, say 15 per cent).[28] This kind of study could be important for understanding how much of brain size is really accounted for by body size within *H. sapiens*.

Is the size of a certain part of the brain related to intelligence?

An alternative approach is to give up on the overall brain size question and concentrate on specific structures, and/or to use functional imaging to examine possible brain processes that might be predictive of *g*. Functional imaging allows the scientists to look for relative changes in cerebral activity during some task, and is also being used to search for biological 'correlates' of intelligence. Some recent experiments attempt to relate some aspects of *g* to specific brain activations, as opposed to estimates of overall brain size. Information from the functional imaging research might then inform the structural scientists on what regions of the brain to focus on in the search for the big bright[29] brain region. For example, John Duncan and colleagues[30] used PET (a technique, like fMRI, for looking at brain activation in one condition compared with another) when participants performed in three very different complex tasks (which could require more *g*) relative to control tasks of similar type but which were easier (requiring less *g*, in theory). They found that, despite the facts that the tasks differed (i.e. verbal, spatial and 'perceptuo-motor'), all three difficult tasks resulted in higher activations of the lateral parts of the prefrontal cortex (regions anterior to the motor parts of the frontal lobes).

A later study claims that individual differences in performance on a difficult working memory task (which may depend upon *g*) were correlated with brain activation patterns in prefrontal cortex.[31] Nevertheless, there are a few questions I have about these findings and, as always in science, the strength of the effects from original sources should always be carefully scrutinized (which is more difficult for busy scientists who often believe the summaries of studies that they read in learned reviews—more learned that this one, mind!). First, the measure of *g* (Raven's matrices) was taken outside of the scanner and was compared with a different 'hard' task in the scanner by using correlation. They found a relationship between the intelligence test and the hardest cognitive task of 0.36— meaning that only 13 per cent of the variability in performance on the hard task within the scanner is accounted for by the outside scanner measure of *g*. This result means that the measure of individual intelligence which is correlated with brain activation is not the one that the participants did when they were actually being scanned. I will spare you the other details but the statistical evaluation of the data could be criticized (they did not control for the sheer number of pairwise correlations they performed—the more you do, the more chance you have of seeing a relationship for any single comparison) and they did not show the relevant data on a scatterplot which might have helped make the story more convincing.[32]

A common assumption in the morphological studies is that bigger is better. In these functional activation studies, it is the relative change in blood flow from one task to another that is the unit of analysis, so the equivalent measure in these experiments is more activation in a given area (which might predict better performance on the cognitive test). However, it seems just as sensible to argue the exact opposite: in an adult who is particularly skilled at a certain task, *less* brain would be required than in an individual who struggles. In fact, some early PET studies found an inverse relationship between skill acquisition and brain metabolic rate, and in later studies, between an estimate of *g* and overall metabolic rates.[33] This type of study led some to argue for 'neural efficiency'— if you are better at it, you use less (think of the tiny lightweight laptop you have now versus the one you had 10 years ago). It is hard to reconcile this view with the bigger is better perspective—unless of course those of you with big brains use a little at a time! (We have now come full circle to Beyerstein's review of the 'we use only 10 per cent of our brains' myth.) A few attempts to get around this problem have been suggested, including the idea that during task performance people with high abilities may show greater brain activations but for a shorter time, and with the poor temporal resolution of fMRI you would never see such an effect.[31] Evidence from a technique with better temporal resolution, event-related potentials, might speak to this slim possibility. However, at least one study has suggested that smarter brains do not 'run hotter' in any way that shows up in extracellular recordings made from the skull surface.[34]

One popular assumption about the frontal lobes (in particular the so-called prefrontal cortex—all the frontal lobes that are anterior to the primary motor cortex) is that, proportionally, we have a lot of it relative to our primate cousins. The claims can get pretty grand: anthropologist Terrence Deacon says 200 per cent more, for example.[35] A more recent study of one prefrontal cortex subregion (area 10) says about 2× more.[36] Ralph Holloway, who knows more about these issues than most, suggests that even the above is an overestimate, given our body size: for example, *H. sapiens* area 10 volume is pretty much exactly as you would predict for an ape with our brain size.[37] Sadly, for the '*g* is frontal' story, other authors find that differences in brain metabolism that are related to *g* have little to do with the frontal lobes and instead are seen in parietal cortex. The conclusion of one such study suggests that high and low *g* subjects may activate different circuits, depending on the task.[38] Such a claim is a far cry from the more specific claims about prefrontal cortex, and not easily reconcilable with a bigger is better story in any case.

The authors of the '*g* is frontal' studies are often beguiled by the intriguing accounts of behavioural abnormalities in human patients with damage to this region of the brain. For example, deficits have been described that include poor planning, inappropriate social behaviour, poor prospective memory and impulsiveness. One little caveat for the '*g* is frontal' camp; frontal lobe lesions tend not to impair performance on standard intelligence tests. This is one of the facts that has intrigued neuropsychologists about them in the first place—what does this 'vast' region of the brain do, when lesions produce *little effect* on general sensation and perception, movement and *intelligence*? Indeed.

The brain size–intelligence story may also interact with gender in some way. For example, some interesting new studies are suggesting that, although male brains tend to be bigger than female brains (remember about the scaling with body size that I mentioned earlier—men are bigger than women), females may have proportionally more 'grey matter' (that is the bodies of the nerve cells, that most scientists think are doing most of the serious brain work) than 'white matter', the fatty sheathed connections between cells.[39] What is going on here? Hard to say exactly, but thank goodness, gentlemen, for those studies that say the action is all in the white matter! ('He says tomato, she says tomato, he says potato, she says potato . . . ').

Perhaps it is slightly unfair to poke fun at these very serious scientists in such a way. After all, many able scholars used to think that the earth was the centre of the universe, but that is hardly a reason to doubt the current state of astronomy and cosmology. Of course, I would hate to imply in some way that the size of a brain is irrelevant. Brain development is a crucial part of our evolutionary heritage as a species, and is a worthy topic for comparative psychology and physical anthropology.

What does the big brain of *Homo sapiens* really mean then?

So, if you believe me so far, then you will not be afraid of having your brain scanned at a local hospital—if your brain is not quite gigantic you are probably coping just fine all the same (think of poor thin-brained Einstein). But what does science tell us about why our species are bigger brained than our closest primate cousins? Well one thing is for sure: claims that our bigger brains are mostly more prefrontal cortex than other species need to be rethought. 'The part that makes us human'? I am probably in the minority,[40] but I remain unconvinced.

Some interesting suggestions about human brain size have been made by comparative psychologists who are comfortable talking about evolution and about us as primates. These people argue that the advantages of group living for a species can work against the 'every gene for itself' world of natural selection. Food sharing, reproductive success and competition, the costs to an individual of altruistic acts and the like have created complex social structures in the primate world which largely balance competition with cooperation.[41] In this account, social intelligence and the pressures of group living have been the driving force behind brain development in the great apes and their ancestors. If this view of primate brain evolution is correct, then what sort of measure of 'social complexity' should best predict the systematic growth in brain size across the primates? What do chimpanzee (relatively big brained) societies have that gorilla societies do not? Group size, grooming partner number, the degree of 'Machiavellian intelligence' (i.e. behaviours suggesting tactical use of information at the expense of others) and social commodities exchange are all possibilities that are receiving some treatment early in the twenty-first century. However, I cannot imagine that any of these comparative psychologists would dream of predicting social skill (or network size, or political acumen or whatever) in an *individual* based on the size of her brain.

There are some very credible data on the rapid expansion of relative brain size in ancestral species of *Homo* relative to the other bipedal apes of the time (who have long since gone the way of the Dodo, probably at the expense of our ancestral groups who did not).[42] Many anthropologists and comparative psychologists argue that this big brain of ours (which comes with many costs to the species—think of your poor mother in childbirth with that slimmed down bipedal pelvis and your ridiculous large baby head) must have brought with it many 'adaptive' benefits—helping individual members of a species survive and pass the adaptive traits onto their offspring, who have a (slight) advantage relative to members of the species who do not have the gene and associated trait, and so on.

So far so good, but suddenly the argument is extended to members within a species at a given point in geological time, and then it is less much convincing. To borrow an analogy from Stephen Pinker, running around measuring brain size and trying to relate it to performance on some cognitive test or another is a bit like trying to measure spatial ability in elephants and correlating it with the lengths of their trunk. Perhaps there are unfortunate pachyderms with genetic disorders who have pathologically short or long trunks (hard to imagine what a too long trunk would be like, but for a stretch of an analogy, use your WWW browser and search on the 'Irish elk') which might be maladaptive.

In any case, evolution by natural selection works on geological time scales and in all likelihood with adaptations which follow from genetic mutations in individuals or genetic drift in small groups of isolated members of a species. A mutation in an individual and its genetic relatives may just happen to provide an advantage related to some change in the environmental conditions, and, *over geological time*, a new species radiates from an older one. The specialized bill of a Flamingo ancestor had morphological advantages relative to an earlier species which either died out or themselves adapted (in un-Flamingo-like ways) to different environmental pressures. The Flamingo's bill is beautifully adapted for filtering small marine animals out of water. The upper and lower bills are angled downwards, which enables the bird to flex its head until it is virtually upside down in the water, capturing nutritious crustaceans and other food. But would we really want to go around measuring the curvature of Flamingo bills (like Professional ice hockey sticks, which can be too curved for the rules[43]) at a single point in time and try to make some predictions about any individual's reproductive success, feeding acumen, future Flamingo evolution or anything else for that matter? Of course Flamingo bills vary in size and shape somewhat, for genetic and environmental reasons, but is a slight difference in a bill going to be related to some serious advantage for that individual?

There are some instances where individual phenotypic traits do predict something about the Darwinian fitness of that individual. For example, for the purposes of advertising one's health to potential mates, males of some species have elaborate displays, such as the tail of a peacock, metabolically costly to grow and potentially a bit of a pain for fast movement, avoiding predators, and so on. Most scientists believe that such ornaments in fact signal information about their health and vigour to potential mates.[44] Much of the recent excitement seems to be about the tail of the male guppy![45] These phenotypic traits, if you believe that they play a role in sexual selection, are obvious external markers that have to be visible to the female and are directly related to measures of health, such as testosterone levels or immune system competence. The links between brain size and other measures of health, mental or physical, or even of Darwinian fitness, remains somewhat tenuous, *within H. sapiens*.

So there is the rub: within-species variability versus between-species variability. Compared with many other mammals, one of our obvious phenotypic characteristics is that as a species we have relatively large brains (so do chimps, orangs and bonobos, relative to other species). In virtually every textbook just-so story of how humans have evolved, that big brain is right up there along with bipedalism, dextrous hands and language. The evidence available in the early twenty-first century suggests that *H. sapiens*, in more or less our current form, may have been around for as long as 200 000 years.[46] The type of intraspecies competition for food, shelter and access to possible mates was probably quite different under those conditions in Eastern Africa from what it is today, when Spearman's g is allegedly a good predictor of success. If a time machine could drop an infant clone of Bill Gates into a small tribe of humans 200 000 years ago, would you predict that he would fair as well as he has in the twenty-first century? Whatever you think of Bill's g[47] and how he has used it, it is the product of his biology interacting with a very complex environment which has little to do with the selective pressures which led to *H. sapiens*. Well the genome has not changed all that much in 200 000 years we suspect, so why would genetic control over brain size (which is incomplete) predict anything about performance on intelligence tests?[48] Or why do we think that performance on intelligence tests would tell you anything about brain size in the members of our species today?

Conclusions

Much to my surprise, the brain size–intelligence debate is alive and well in the twenty-first century. To be fair, virtually all of the scientists doing the work above are well aware of the dangers of racist (or 'class'-ist) misuse of data and theory which continues in small pockets to this day.[49] Nevertheless, the lack of a clear cogent scientific agenda for much of this work gives me cause for concern. Some authors comment on how these studies are important for understanding the biological basis of more specific cognitive abilities, but in fact much of that good work continues apace outside of the intelligence–brain size community. The reason that g captivates interest is that it appears to explain ability across broad swathes of thinking and reasoning, so this argument alone is not sufficient.

A second rationale is that understanding biological bases of intelligence could provide some insights into why individuals differ in whatever it is that intelligence tests measure.[50] However, the evidence from some almost 40 years of such work that looks at brain electrical activity to date has been mixed—some correlates with g have been found but other studies have been less successful. Perhaps these measures are too indirect, but one wonders if it will take 40 years of structural and functional imaging work to come to a similar conclusion.

Another rationale for the work is that identifying the appropriate brain structure associated with both genetics and g might help constrain the geneticists who look for gene groups that control specific behaviours. My gut reaction to this perspective is, effectively, that that seems a rather complicated and indirect way to do it, unless you believe that intelligence is largely genetic, in fact more so than more specific cognitive abilities that are less contentious and easier to measure. Of course, sensible scientists know that environment gene–interaction is important and that environment alone can have seriously beneficial consequences for cognitive development across many specific and non-specific abilities (like *g*), and they tend to say so in their scientific work. However, when they say that genes 'specify a range' and environment determines where you fall in that range, suddenly the size of the range is important. Also if the range is equated to our 'potential', then it is all too easy to conclude that 'our potential is predetermined'.[51,52] If that is potential for a range of scores (after all there is always measurement error) on a test which is not particularly culturally fair and is an imperfect measure of several different capacities, OK, not unreasonable. Nevertheless, sometimes the implications of the usual interpretations seem more serious than this more cautious conclusion.

The obvious conclusion at this stage seems to be that the range of scores on an IQ test of one sort or another is constrained, by the nature of the test, the difficulty of the items, the background and attitudes of the test taker, the time limits imposed for some subtests, and the fact that we have human brains, eyes and hands (all which limit how quickly you process information and respond to it). The relationships between what intelligence tests actually test and their prediction of real-world success is pretty confounded with some amazing environmental disasters as well as success stories. The evidence that links brain size with *g* directly is limited to date, in spite of some good data linking brain size to genes, and separate studies that link performance on some intelligence tests to genes. The debates about faster brains, using less or more if one excels at a task, grey or white, etc., have left me relatively unconvinced. As a neuroscientist myself, I am not at all uncomfortable with relating behaviour to brain function, but to date I cannot yet conclude that brain size is really yoked to intelligence in any largely meaningful way. For now, as a large-bodied male (who probably has a large brain, but I have never actually had it checked), I have little confidence that looking at a sophisticated twenty-first century brain scan (in any number of impossibly sophisticated ways) of a collaborator, competitor or any old conspecific is going to tell me anything meaningful at all about their capacities to perform in any cognitive way, psychometric or not.

References and notes

1. **Della Sala S.** (ed.) *Mind myths: exploring popular assumptions about mind and brain.* John Wiley & Sons, Chichester, UK. 1999.
2. **Dawkins R, Cornwell RE.** Dodgy frontal lobes, y'dig? *The Guardian*, 12 December 2003.
3. **Gould SJ.** *The mismeasure of man.* WW. Norton and Co, New York. 1996.
4. **Falk D, Gibson KR.** *Evolutionary anatomy of the primate cerebral cortex.* Cambridge University Press, Cambridge. 2001.
5. Immortalized by Sigourney Weaver in the 1988 film, 'Gorillas in the Mist' (USA, Michael Apted, Director). A less known fact is that Fossey, and the more famous Jane Goodall (who studied chimpanzees at Gombe in Tanzania), were actually sent out on their comparative quests by Richard Leakey,

a physical anthropologist with no small interest in comparisons between *Homo sapiens*, our extinct ancestors and the extinct ancestors of our closest cousins, the other great apes.

6. For example, in a sample of 1000 people, some of the variability in weight can be accounted for by variability in height—taller people weigh more in general. In fact, the correlation between height and weight is approximately 0.5. Correlation (the most common form is symbolized by a lower case r, i.e. $r = 0.50$) is a measure of how a given change in one measure affects another measure. A correlation of 1.0 (or -1.0, if one measure goes down in perfect proportion to the other measure going up) implies a perfect relationship between the two variables. A neat property of correlation is that by squaring the r value (or 'correlation coefficient'), you can estimate how much variability in one measure is explained by variability in another measure. In our weight to height example, $r = 0.50$, 0.50 squared $= 0.025$, which means 25 per cent of the variance in weight is accounted for by variance in height. In this example, it makes more sense to interpret the relationship in this direction, but in many cases either variable can be the predictor or the predicted. That is, a given person's performance on one sub test is correlated with their performance on many of the other subtests.

7. **Sternberg RJ, Grigorenko EL, Kidd KK.** Intelligence, race and genetics. *American Psychologist*, 2005; 60:46–59.

8. Reviewed in several places, including **Plomin R, Petrill SA.** Genetics and intelligence: whats new? *Intelligence*, 1997; 24:53–77.

9. A rather notorious character in this whole business: **Gilham NW.** *A life of Sir Francis Galton from African exploration to the birth of eugenics.* Oxford University Press, Oxford. 2001.

10. **Deary IJ.** Human intelligence differences: a recent history. *Trends in Cognitive Sciences*, 2001; 5:127–130.

11. **Turkheimer E, Haley A, Waldron M, D'Onofio B, Gottesman II.** Socioeconomic status modifies the heritability of IQ in young children. *Psychological Science*, 2003; 14:623–628.

12. For example, see **Wickett JC, Vernon PA, Lee DL.** In vivo brain size, head perimeter, and intelligence in a sample of healthy adult females. *Personality and Individual Differences*, 1994; 16:831–838.

13. Reviewed in **Toga AW, Thompson PM.** Genetics of brain structure and intelligence. *Annual Review of Neuroscience*, 2005; 28:1–23.

14. **Bartley AJ, Jones DW, Weinberger DR.** Genetic variability of human brain size and cortical gyral patterns. *Brain*, 1997; 120:257–269.

15. **Baaré WFC, Hulshoff Pol HE, Bootsma DI, Posthuma D, De Geus EJC, Schnack HG, van Haren NEM, Kahn RS.** Quantitative genetic modelling of variation in human brain morphology. *Cerebral Cortex*, 2001; 11:816–824.

16. Although the authors did not use any statistical techniques (that I could glean anyway) to 'partial out' the effects of height on brain size, which was certainly possible using their data.

17. In fact, another claim is that Einstein may have had less language-related prefrontal cortex, which one group suggests could explain his delayed speech development as a child! **Witelson SF, Kigar DL, Harvey T.** The exceptional brain of Albert Einstein. *The Lancet*, 1999; 353:2149–2153. Noted neurologist Albert Galaburda reviewed Einstein's brain, and concluded 'The search for gross anatomical markers for greatness will go on, I am sure, but I suspect that it will continue to be as unproductive as it has been in the past'. Indeed. No need to write this chapter, really that says it all. Galaburda AM. Albert Einstein's brain. *The Lancet*, 1999; 353:1821. Witelson and her colleagues reply in the same issue.

18. **Thompson PM, Cannon TD, Narr KL, van Erp T, Poutanen VP, Huttunen M, Lonnqvist J, Standertskjold-Nordenstam CG, Kaprio J, Khaledy M, Dail R, Zoumalan CI, Toga AW.** Genetic influences on brain structure. *Nature Neuroscience*, 2001; 4:1253–1258.

19. **Thompson and Toga** provide more details in their 2005 review paper (note 14), but the statistics are still remarkably difficult to understand and the methods require much more technical expertise than I could bring to the table. A visit to Paul Thompson's website gives a feeling for this very ambitious scientist and his team's work: http://www.loni.ucla.edu/~thompson/thompson.html.

20. **Hutchins JB, Barger SW.** Why neurons die: cell death in the nervous system. *Anatomical Record*, 1998; **253**:79–90.

21. **McDaniel MA.** Big-brained people are smarter: a meta-analysis of the relationship between in vivo brain volume and intelligence. *Intelligence*, 2005; **33**:337–346.

22. Of course, the 'flip side' of this argument is that any study which says environment accounts for all the variance of a trait has to be careful with between-family comparisons. Imagine showing a strong relationship between parental reading time and children's reading ability—across families. What is forgotten by some is that those children raised in the high or low reading homes also inherited their genes from their parents. More eloquently put in **Bouchard TJ Jr, McGue M.** Genetic and environmental influences on human psychological differences. *Journal of Neurobiology*, 2003; **54**:4–45.

23. **Schoenemann PT, Budinger TF, Sarich VM, Wang WS.** Brain size does not predict general cognitive ability within families. *Proceedings of the National Academy of Sciences of the USA*, 2000; **97**:4932–4937.

24. An interesting article distinguishes between a weak form of biologism and a strong form, where actual causal mechanisms are worked out. The weak form is not so scientifically interesting as in some sense everything psychological has some partial genetic contribution to it. **Turkheimer, E.** Heritability and biological explanation. *Psychological Review*, 1998; **105**:782–791.

25. **Bouchard TJ Jr, Lykken DT, McGue M, Segal NL, Tellegen A.** Sources of human psychological differences: the Minnesota study of twins reared apart. *Science*, 1990; **250**:223–228.

26. **Pakkenberg B, Gudersen HJG.** Neocortical neuron number in humans: effect of sex and age. *Journal of Comparative Neurology*, 1997; **384**:312–320.

27. No. For example, see **Colom R, Juan-Espinosa M, Abad F, García LF.** Negligible sex differences in general intelligence. *Intelligence*, 2000; **28**:57–68. Although having said that, many tests when constructed would have questions that one sex or the other performed more poorly on removed by the test makers.

28. Some studies have used height or weight as covariates in between-family experiments and have claimed that they only modestly affect the brain–IQ relationship. They did not correct for differences in body fat, nevertheless. References in **Egan V, Wickett JC, Vernon PA.** Brain size and intelligence: erratum, addendum, and correction. *Personality and Individual Differences*, 1995; **19**:113–115.

29. This is a pun, for all my neuroimaging pals out there. Both of them.

30. **Duncan J, Seitz RJ, Kolodny J, Bor D, Herzog H, Ahmed A, Newell FN, Emslie H.** A neural basis for general intelligence. *Science*, 2000; **289**:457–60.

31. **Gray JR, Chabris CF, Braver TS.** Neural mechanisms of general fluid intelligence. *Nature Neuroscience*, 2003; **6**:316–322.

32. Sadly most studies in these domains do not show you the raw data on a scatterplot; they rely on statistics almost exclusively. The more complex the statistics, the more you should worry, in my opinion.

33. **Larson GE, Haier RJ, LaCasse L, Hazen K.** Evaluation of a mental effort hypothesis for correlations between cortical metabolism and intelligence. *Intelligence*, 1995; **21**:267–278.

34. **Posthuma D, Neale MC, Boomsma DI, De Geus EJC.** Are smarter brains running faster? Heritability of alpha peak frequency, IQ, and their interrelation. *Behaviour Genetics*, 2001; **31**:567–579. For a more positive review of electrophysiology and intelligence research, see Deary IJ, Caryl PG. Neuroscience and human intelligence. *Trends in Neurosciences*, 1997; **20**:365–371.

35. **Deacon T.** *The symbolic species: the co-evolution of language and the brain.* W.W. Norton & Co., New York. 1997.

36. **Semendeferi K, Armstrong E, Schleicher A, Zilles K, Van Hoesen GW.** Prefrontal cortex in humans and apes: a comparative study of area 10. *American Journal of Physical Anthropology*, 2001; **114**:224–241.

37. **Holloway R.** How much larger is the relative volume of area 10 of the prefrontal cortex in humans? *American Journal of Physical Anthropology*, 2002; **118**:399–401.

38. **Haier RJ, White NS, Alkire MT.** Individual differences in general intelligence correlate with brain function during nonreasoning tasks. *Intelligence*, 2003; **31**:429–441.

39. See note 18. However, note that the same result is not found in the data of Pakkenberg and Gundersen (note 26). For other problems with relating male and female brain sizes with IQ, see Peters MJ. Does brain size matter? A reply to Rushton & Ankney. *Canadian Journal of Experimental Psychology*, 1995; **49**:570–576.

40. Many psychologists so fascinated with the frontal lobes actually have very with little training in brain science. Next one you meet at a cocktail party—ask about the neural connections of 'medialis dorsalis'.[52]

41. Many of the main players in this area are referred to in **Barrett L, Henzi P, Dunbar R.** Primate cognition: from 'what now?' to 'what if?' *Trends in Cognitive Sciences*, 2003; **7**:494–497.

42. One problem in any 'linear increase in brain size' story in the Homo lineage is the even bigger brain of the Neanderthal: Holloway RL. Volumetric and asymmetry determinations on recent hominid endocasts: Spy I and II, Djebel Ihroud I, and the Sale Homo erectus specimens, with some notes on Neanderthal brain size. *American Journal of Physical Anthropology*, 1981; **55**:385–393. Holloway suggests it might have been due to their increased muscle mass, but in any event the bigger is better story may not even work across species.

43. An opposing coach can stop the game and ask for a stick to be measured. If it is too curved, the player gets 2 min in 'the sin bin'. If it is not, the coach's team has to sit a player for 2 min in the sin bin.

44. **Emlen ST, Oring LW.** Ecology, sexual selection, and the evolution of mating systems. *Science*, 1997; **197**:215–223.

45. **Brooks R,Endler JA.** Direct and indirect sexual selection and quantitative genetics of male traits in guppies (*Poecilia reticulata*). *Evolution*, 2001; **55**:1002–1015.

46. **McDougall I, Brown FH, Fleagle JG.** Stratigraphic placement and age of modern humans from Kibish, Ethiopia. *Nature*, 2005; **433**:733–736.

47. It could be as high as 160, where 100 = average. http://www.aceviper.net/aceviper_net/ace_intelligence/ aceviper_questions_and_answers/aceviper_interesting_intelligence_related_questions _and_answers.html

48. 'If the history of empirical psychology has taught researchers anything, it is that correlations between causally distant variables cannot be counted on to lead to coherent etiological models' (see Turkheimer, 1998, note 24).

49. **Lieberman L.** How 'caucasoids' got such big crania and how they shrank. From Morton to Rushton. *Current Anthropology*, 2001; **42**:69–95.

50. **Deary and Caryl,** 1997, cited in note 34.

51. **Toga and Thompson,** 2005, cited in note 13.

52. The nucleus of the thalamus which provides the principle thalamic input to the prefrontal cortex (real neuropsychologists know such things about the brain).

Chapter 9

Biology and intelligence—the race/IQ controversy

Mike Anderson

The hypothesis that races may differ in intelligence pre-dates modern psychology, but was revamped in scientific terms in the late 1960s. Jensen[1] argued that part of the reason why black Americans did not fare as well in school as white Americans might be because of genetic differences in intelligence between the races. The resulting furore set back the scientific study of intelligence at least 15 years and halted the progress of human behaviour genetics, even though very few behaviour geneticists studied racial differences.[2] Just as things seemed to be settling back down and quiet progress was made in both disciplines, the publication of *The bell curve* put race and IQ back on the socio-political agenda, and once again ignited the explosive mixture of science and politics that has bedeviled research into human intellectual differences.[3] Such a climate is a veritable breeding ground for myths. The most important examples are:

1. IQ tests measure nothing other than social advantage.
2. There are so many different kinds of intelligence that everyone is 'intelligent' in some way.
3. There is no good evidence that there is a genetic basis for differences in IQ.
4. The genetics of intelligence has established that race differences in IQ are genetically based.

These are false beliefs widely held by many, and often by those who should know better. In this chapter, I want to present arguments and data that challenge these myths by establishing that:

1. IQ tests are good measures of intelligence.
2. There is a large unitary factor called general intelligence that accounts for most of the differences in IQ and that is based on biological differences between individuals.
3. Individual differences in IQ are, in large part, genetically inherited.
4. There is no good reason to believe that the difference in group means that exist between black and white Americans in measured IQ is either genetically based or based on race differences in biology. Rather, the weight of the current evidence

suggests that the difference between these populations is caused by socio-cultural factors.

Before I argue for these propositions, let us first consider why there are so many myths in this area of research.

The most obvious reason is that there is genuine confusion about what is meant by intelligence. A pre-requisite for myth debunking is some coherent scientific theory of what intelligence is. There are theories that might do this (and I will present an outline of one that I believe to be optimal later in the chapter), but there is no current consensus on which of these theories is likely to be closer to the truth. In no small part, this is because discussions of 'truth' or 'facts of the matter' have been clouded by an aversion on the part of scholars to the moral–political stance taken by their counterparts, to the point where the purpose of the research seems to be to support or refute political stances on race. As Kurt Vonnegut was fond of saying, so it goes . . .

Where science and politics become interwoven, myths will flourish because they map onto wider beliefs about how we, and society, ought to be, i.e. they are extensions of, and used as justifications for, more deeply held moral and political philosophies. Nowhere is this more clearly seen than in *The bell curve*.

In many ways, *The bell curve* is a tour de force of argument and data. Stripped down, the argument runs as follows:

- Intelligence, as measured by IQ, is a good predictor of social outcomes (poverty, unemployment, single parenthood, criminality, and so forth).
- Differences in intelligence cause these social outcomes rather than the other way around.
- Differences in intelligence are largely biologically-based, consequently so are social outcomes.
- Race differences in social outcome are explained by race differences in intelligence.
- Conjunction of the previous points mean that race differences in social outcome are caused by biological differences and consequently unchangeable.

The subtext (as Phil Donahue once put it to Charles Murray) of *The bell curve* is that society should be organized in a way that reflects these inherent and unchangeable differences between the races. Clearly, this is potent stuff.

The cultural context of intelligence research

It is the battle between two political ideologies and their different views on social engineering that has threatened to turn the science of intelligence into a swamp. Broadly speaking, these two ideologies are aligned historically with different views of human nature. To simplify. On the libertarian right there is a desire to believe that human beings are largely the product of their inherited potential, and any social inequalities (in Western democracies at least) are largely the result of inequalities of nature and, consequently, are just.[4] On the left, there is a desire to believe that human beings are to all extents and purposes infinitely socially, psychologically and culturally malleable. Consequently, any social inequalities are regarded as unjust, being the result not of inborn differences but social forces which can and should be changed. But so what? Why does this matter for the science of intelligence? It matters because of the role given to science in the political debate. *The bell curve* has put the case for the political right: *if it is true* that there are individual differences in inborn human intelligence and these map reasonably directly onto social outcomes, then there is no point in spending money to relieve social inequalities because they are consequences of inborn differences not causes. So this is the importance of science, for is it not science that will tell us whether or not this is indeed true?

The impact of ideology has been asymmetric. While the right have been most active in garnering supposed scientific justifications for political action, perhaps paradoxically, the most enduring negative consequence for the science of intelligence has come from the political posturing of the left. The major strategy of refutation from the left has been to attack the credibility of any scientific research that has been used by the right to argue for biological influences on intelligence. Those attacks have not been fuelled by counter evidence (for there isn't any) but by a fear that *if it were true* that there are biological influences on intelligence, then the right's recipe for social engineering would be vindicated. This strategy, of course, colludes with the game plan of the right by endorsing the scientific facts of the matter as the rightful arbiter of how society ought to be organized. By adopting the battle plan of denying any scientific merit to the study of differences in IQ, minor skirmishes may be won on some local battle fields but the war will assuredly be lost. The data have been amassed over 20 years and, as we shall see, it is no longer credible to deny that differences in IQ depend in some measure on inherited biological differences between individuals.

Meanwhile the Achilles heel of the right is being ignored. Political consequences should not hinge on the answer to the scientific question, and the sooner we decouple them the better. Science tells us the way the universe is, not the way it ought to be. This is not to say that science cannot inform us of constraints on our options, but that does not determine our choice. When we decide how society should be organized then science can help us to select paths that might attain those ends. In the case of race differences, if we were to accept a real and genetically caused difference in IQ we could respond either by increasing resources to black schoolchildren to 'compensate' them for their 'bad luck' in the genetic draw,[5] or we could stop spending any money at all on black children as it might be 'better spent' elsewhere, or we could ignore the race difference and allocate resources to children that best matches their individual needs. Which of those options we choose will depend on wider moral and political beliefs and science cannot tell us which is the 'correct' choice.

The discussion in this chapter is aimed at identifying what the science of intelligence has established about the nature and cause of human intellectual differences once we delve beneath the political grandstanding. The arguments are presented in four sections, each addressing one of the myths outlined above. In the first section I will present data and arguments that suggest that IQ tests are good measures of intelligence. In the second section I present a case for the construct of general intelligence. In the third section I will explain how behaviour geneticists calculate heritability and show that IQ differences are in large part heritable. In the fourth section I will turn to the crux of the matter and show that, despite a high heritability for IQ differences, it is unlikely that the difference in IQ between black and white populations in the USA is genetic in origin. In a fifth and final section I will present a theory of intelligence that reconciles the key facts of intelligence and points to the boundary between science and politics.

Intelligence and IQ tests

Myth 1: IQ tests measure nothing other than social advantage.

Quite the contrary: Alfred Binet created the intelligence test in response to a request to identify children in need of special education. His *explicit* aim was to develop tests that would depend as little as possible on the educational background or social circumstances of the children. He hit on the very clever idea of using the average age that children could correctly answer a question as a measure of its difficulty. In this way he constructed a scale of test item difficulty that became a measure of *mental age* (MA). It was Stern[6] who first thought of converting an assessment of mental age into an intelligence quotient (IQ) using the classic formula IQ = MA/chronological age × 100; IQ could then be thought of as how intelligent a child was compared with his or her same-age peers. In addition, Binet considered on *a priori* grounds that intelligence would be best reflected in the higher faculties; for example, memory, the nature of mental images, comprehension and perceptual skill in spatial relations. These faculties were not and are not the province of any school syllabus (i.e. attributable to explicit education) but relate to hypothetical fundamental properties of 'mind'.

However, while the tests inspired by Binet were not designed to be biased against the socially disadvantaged, it could still be that over time this has happened unintentionally during their development. However, there are a number of reasons for believing that this has not happened.

The construction of an intelligence test is a highly technical matter that guards against the introduction of social bias. One feature of the test is that items can be arranged from the easiest to the most difficult. It turns out that the item difficulties *do not systematically change across different social groups*, something you might expect to happen if particular knowledge was available to one group but not another. Further, if we look at a varied intelligence test battery, the most obviously culturally loaded items tend to be the verbal items (vocabulary, testing verbal comprehension, and so forth) rather than the non-verbal problem-solving items. But if anything, differences between black and white Americans tend to be greatest on the non-verbal than on the verbal items, something that seems to run counter to the prediction of cultural bias.[7] While measures of the predictive validity of IQ tests (e.g. do the tests predict success at school or work or university) have an element of tautology about them, it is not the case that the predictive validity of tests is different for different groups, again something you might expect if the tests were systematically biased. Indeed, some have argued that because IQ tests tend to overpredict outcomes for black Americans (they do worse in the real world than you would predict from their test scores) that if anything the tests are biased *in favour* of black Americans.[3,8] Personally, I think it is more sensible to conclude that the world is biased against black Americans. Finally, recent evidence seems to suggest that other cultural groups are outperforming the white Caucasian groups for whom we might assume the tests were designed to favour.[9]

None of this is to say that differential access to educational aids might not give an edge on some items or even some tests. But it is to say that there is precious little hard evidence, despite many years searching, that such effects are anything other than accidental and of little consequence to performance on intelligence tests as a whole.

Despite Binet's laudable intentions, there is, nevertheless, no doubt that intelligence tests have been misused. Every psychology student knows of the policy of Eugenics, where it is advocated that high IQ individuals should be encouraged to reproduce and low IQ individuals discouraged to reproduce so that society as a whole can be improved. As recently as the 1970s Nobel laureate William Shockley advocated a financial incentive scheme where individuals would be paid not to breed and the amount of payment increased as IQ decreased. Intelligence tests were also central to the control of immigration to the USA in the early part of this century, leading to the restriction of entry to certain nationalities on the (plainly ludicrous) grounds that the average IQs of their population were supposedly in the feeble-minded range. Examples such as these are testimony to the potential social impact of intelligence tests and explain why the science of intelligence is regarded with such suspicion and has found it difficult to shake free from political ideology.

It is not surprising, then, that some seem to believe that the only point of IQ tests is to justify social stratification. The left, appalled at the potential social consequences drawn from some advocates of IQ testing, have responded by criticizing the idea that there is a single 'thing' or capacity that we can label intelligence and summarize with a single index such as IQ, with the aim of pulling the rug from under the feet of those who use tests.[10,11] Consequently, and unfortunately, the idea of a single thing called intelligence is considered by many to be a myth invented by designers of intelligence tests to provide a pseudo-scientific validity for their use. While the notion of g is a central issue for the science of intelligence, the issue of its existence has diverted attention away from the real issue of the ethical use of tests, which is independent of the status of g in any case.

The notion of general intelligence as a property of the brain

Myth 2: there are so many different abilities that everyone is 'intelligent' in some way.

A somewhat paradoxical idea (because it is held by many who also argue that IQ is overly narrow) is that IQ measures an amalgam of a plethora of different abilities rather than a general proclivity for acquiring knowledge.[12,13] Gardner has argued that intelligence itself (as opposed to IQ) is composed of a number of autonomous intelligences each with their own developmental and evolutionary history.[14] If Gardner is right, then using IQ as a summary of intelligence does two things. First it masks the importance of special abilities in areas in which other cultures may excel, in favour of a narrow Western conception of intelligence (usually portrayed as varieties of logical-deductive ability). Secondly, if there are many intelligences and they are uncorrelated, then indeed taking an average IQ is meaningless; it would be like taking the average of your height, income, and the distance you live from the centre of town as an index of some unitary essence of yourself. The alternative, that intelligence is not simply the sum of what we know but rather represents an underlying capacity, is, however, a hypothesis with overwhelming support.[15−19]

Of course, the contrary view to both of these positions is that intelligence is largely unitary. Charles Spearman called this essence general intelligence, or g.[20] The existence or non-existence of g has become the central issue of the scientific validity of IQ.

The basic evidence for the existence of g is that if a heterogeneous set of cognitive tests are given to a random sample of the population, performance on these tests will correlate. For example, individuals who are better than average on tests of vocabulary will be better than average on tests of mechanical reasoning. They will also be better at solving analogies, better at making inferences, better at arithmetical calculations, know more general information, be faster at substituting digits for other symbols, and so forth. It is an indisputable fact that a remarkably wide range of cognitive abilities have something in common. For example, the original British Ability Scales contained no fewer than 23 subtests specifically designed to measure the plethora of different cognitive domains and yet it contains a single general intelligence factor as large as in any other test battery.[21] Unfortunately, far from being a method of settling the dispute about the reality of g, the fixation on the statistical method of factor analysis has obscured this fact about intelligence.

It turns out that quite different models of intelligence (e.g. those with or without a g factor) are supported by different methods of factor analysis, each of which can account for the intelligence test data equally well. The details of the debate about methods of factor analysis have been dealt with extensively elsewhere.[10,15,22] Suffice to say that the issue of whether general intelligence is 'real' or not can only be settled by some validation of g from data other than the pattern of intelligence test scores.

One hypothesis is that because g is associated with all intelligence tests yet devised, it must be a property of neural functioning[23,24] or at least be a property of the implementation of knowledge acquisition mechanisms rather than a property of knowledge itself.[15,25] The favoured contender for this property is the speed with which the brain processes information. This hypothesis has led to the development of new kinds of measures and methods that may settle the issue of the reality of g.

IQ and speed of processing

In the 1970s, Arthur Jensen began a research programme investigating the possibility that g may have its basis in the speed we process information, with more intelligent

Fig. 9.1 Jensen's reaction time procedure. The subject lifts his finger off the home button to press the button below the illuminated target. From Anderson[49] (Fig. 3.1). Reprinted with permission.

people processing information more quickly. To measure speed of processing Jensen used a reaction time procedure, illustrated in Fig. 9.1. Subjects hold down a home key until one of the surrounding lights is illuminated. They must then move their finger from the 'home' button to press a button immediately below the light. In such a procedure there are two principal measures. Decision time is the length of time between the onset of the stimulus light and the time at which the subject lifts his or her finger off the home button. Movement time is the time from the offset of the home button to the press of the button below the stimulus light.

This task is so simple that the instructions are easily understood by people of all levels of ability, even those in the mentally retarded ranges of IQ. There is little room for differences in knowledge, let alone culturally biased knowledge, to influence performance. There appears to be only one performance strategy—move as fast as possible once the target light has been identified. Thirty years ago few psychologists would have predicted that intelligence, the *doyen* of human rationality, would be correlated with performance on such a simple task: but it is. IQ is correlated with both the mean and variability of decision times,[26] i.e. those with higher IQs respond faster and with fewer very long responses. Importantly, movement time is usually uncorrelated with IQ, suggesting that the relationship is specific to the time it takes to make a decision rather than the time it takes to move to the target. Jensen claims that these studies show that the basis of individual differences in intelligence is to be found in the speed of processing a single unit of information, and has conjectured that this may depend on the rate of oscillation of excitatory and inhibitory phases of neuronal firing.[24] While Jensen's interpretation of reaction time data is not unchallenged, the speed of processing hypothesis has received support from a quite different task.[27]

In an *inspection time* task, a subject is required to make a perceptual discrimination at different exposure durations of a stimulus (see Fig. 9.2). For example, in a visual inspection time task, a test stimulus, usually two lines of markedly different length which are joined at the top with a short horizontal bar, is presented for a short duration before being obscured by a 'masking' stimulus that prevents any further processing of the test stimulus. The subject is required to make a discriminative judgement (is the longer line

Fig. 9.2 A stimulus is presented for a variable interval before the onset of a masking stimulus. From Anderson[49] (Fig. 3.2). Reprinted with permission.

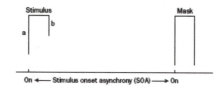

on the left or the right?) and his or her accuracy is compared with the amount of time the test stimulus was visible before being obscured. At longer exposures (about 500 ms) everyone's performance is virtually error free. At shorter exposures errors become more frequent. Inspection time is taken to be the stimulus exposure duration required by an individual to maintain a given level of accuracy, usually 70 per cent. In considered reviews of many studies, both Nettelbeck[28] and Kranzler and Jensen[29] came to the conclusion that inspection time and IQ correlate, negatively, at about 0.5. In other words, the speed at which an individual can process a 'simple' unit of information can predict about 25 per cent of the variance in performance on intelligence tests.

The search for a speed of processing basis for g has resulted in a great deal of research on a variety of more 'direct' measures of the speed or efficiency of neural processing that may be related to IQ differences. Correlations with nerve conduction velocities, with parameters of evoked potentials recorded by electrodes on the scalp, with parameters of positron emission tomography (PET) and nuclear magnetic resonance imaging (NMRI) brain scans, and even with good old cranial capacity are regularly reported.[30] Needless to say, there have also been a number of sceptical reviews.[31,32]

The correlations with neural processes are of modest size and variable replicability. However, taken together with the data on the correlation between IQ and virtually knowledge-free tasks, and with the data that we have not yet considered on the genetics of IQ, the overwhelming weight of evidence suggests that there are differences in neural functioning that result in individual differences in knowledge acquisition and problem solving and, ultimately, differences in IQ. The data so far make it *most likely* that g results from a property of neurons and hence there is a biological basis to differences in IQ. This has not been proved. Indeed, in a court of law the evidence may yet be deemed circumstantial. However, in any case such a conclusion need not be feared as we shall see in the remainder of the chapter.

The heritability of IQ

Myth 3: there is no good evidence that there is a genetic basis for differences in IQ.

To decide whether there is a genetic basis to differences in IQ, we need to understand what heritability means. Understanding heritability will require some knowledge of the technicalities of its measurement. The essential idea is to estimate how much variability in a trait,[33] such as height or intelligence, is due to genetic and or environmental factors. So first we have to consider what is meant by genetic and what is meant by environmental.

Our *genotype* is our genetic complement, coded in DNA, that we inherit from our parents. No two people have identical genotypes except identical twins. The expression of those genes in traits that we can measure is called our *phenotype*. Phenotypes can vary because of genotypic differences and/or they can vary because the environment affects gene expression during development. So it is possible in some instances for identical genotypes to have different phenotypes and, in other cases, for different genotypes to have the same phenotype because of environmental influences. It is also possible that some traits have no genetic contribution, for example, belief in God,[34] and no signifi- cant environmental contribution to traits (or *differences* in phenotypic expression), for example finger-ridge count.[35]

The influence of the environment on phenotypes comes in two main forms. There are differences that exist *between families* (levels of income, parental rearing style, number of books in the home, and so forth) that serve to make children brought up in that home more similar to each other than to children brought up in different homes. This source of differences (or variance) is often called the effect of the common, or shared, environment. The second kind of environmental influence are differences that exist in the environment *within* the same family (differences in birth order, children's friends, school teachers, and so forth). These effects serve to make children in the same family different from each other and is called unique, or non-shared, environment. Necessarily, this kind of influence is idiosyncratic to each child's development.

Given these different sources of phenotypic variation in traits, how are heritabilities actually estimated? In essence the methods make use of two quasi-experimental variables. The first variable is the degree of genetic relatedness. If a trait is in any part heritable then individuals who are more genetically related will be more similar for that trait. Identical twins represent a special case because they have identical genotypes. If genetic differences contribute to any particular trait, such as intelligence, then pairs of identical twins should be more similar to each other than other kinds of relatives, because there are no differences in their genotypes. The most interesting comparison is with non- identical twins, who on average have 50 per cent of their gentoype in common (compared with the baseline 0 per cent of a set of randomly selected individuals[36]). Therefore the difference in similarity for any trait between identical and non-identical twins (100–50 per cent) estimates half the contribution of genetic differences to that trait. Doubling the difference in similarity (technically doubling the difference in size of correlation for that trait) gives the measure of heritability. For example if the correlation for identical twins for a particular trait is 0.6 and the correlation for non-identical twins is 0.4, then double the difference $(0.2 \times 2) = 0.4 =$ heritability. A heritability (or h^2) of 0.4 means that 40 per cent of the variance in that trait can be attributed to genotypic differences. The maximum heritability is 1.0 (100 per cent of the differences is heritable) and the minimum is 0 (none of the difference is due to genotypic differences).

You will probably have thought of a snag with the analysis so far. The logic that individuals who are more genetically related will be more similar phenotypically if the trait is in part heritable, neglects the fact that genotypic relatedness tends to correlate with similarity in shared environment. That is, full siblings usually have more similar shared environments than say cousins; identical twins may be treated more similarly than non-identical twins, and so forth. This is where the second quasi-experimental variable comes in. We can measure the influence of the common, or shared environment, by comparing individuals who are reared together or apart. The extent to which pairs of individuals are more similar when they are brought up in the same home is a measure of the importance of the common or shared environment. If the home environment makes a difference then it should increase the similarity of, for example, identical twins when they are reared together compared with when they are reared apart (i.e. when they are adopted into different homes).

The combination of these two variables gives us the major studies that can be used to estimate heritabilities of traits. The twin study can compare identical and non-identical twins who are reared together or reared apart. If the twins are reared together, they have both genes and shared environment in common. If they are reared apart, then they have only genes in common. In this case, any similarity between the twins can only be attributed to genetic factors. Adoption studies are complementary to the twin method (the latter, of course, constitute a special subset of the former) where we can look at the similarity of individuals who are genetically unrelated but who share the same environment. If there is no effect of common environment then those individuals will be no more similar than individuals paired at random. In addition, we can contrast the similarity between the adopted children and their adoptive parents and siblings, with the similarity to his or her biological parents and siblings. Again this pits the relative influence of genetic and environmental differences and similarities against one another. So what do the data on the heritability of intelligence say?

The studies are in broad agreement. Intelligence, as measured by IQ tests, has a substantial heritability. Estimates of heritability vary between 50 and 80 per cent.[35,37] Hence, even the more conservative estimates argue that the influence of genetic differences is not trivial—they are at least as important as environmental differences and maybe more so. The Bouchard study of identical twins reared apart is already a 'classic'.[35] It is a classic because these researchers measured a number of variables that potentially can confound twin studies, and attempts were made to determine their influence on the estimate of heritability. For example, they measured the length of time the twins were together before they were separated and how similar the environments were for any twin pair (correlated placement reduces the estimates of the effect of the environment), and used these measures to adjust their estimates of heritability. It turns out that these effects are minor (contributing at most 3 per cent of the estimate of 70–80 per cent heritability). The many studies from the Colorado Adoption Project estimate the heritability of intelligence at about 50 per cent.[2] Their data also tell us something interesting about the environment. It turns out that the common environment is most influential early in development. The correlation between adopted children and their biologically unrelated siblings for IQ is about 0.2–0.3 during their early years. However, over the lifespan it seems that the most important environmental differences are those that are unique (or not shared amongst members of the same family). So rather than the major socio-economic variables (a large part of the shared, or common, environmental variance) being the principal environmental contributor to difference in intelligence, it is unique life events that happen to individuals that make up the major environmental contribution. Indeed, Sandra Scarr in a review of adoption and twin studies has estimated that the contribution of the shared environment to differences in IQ is approximately zero by adulthood.[38] Presumably, this genetic influence contributes in no small way to the remarkable stability of IQ differences across the lifespan.[39]

If, as I would claim, the data are watertight and there is a substantial genetic contribution to differences in intelligence, then where does all the heat in the debate about the heritability of IQ come from? The debate still rages, in my view, because heritability is poorly understood, and this misunderstanding is promoted, often disingenuously, by those who have a political rather than a scientific goal. *Perhaps the greatest disingenuity is that a high heritability means that race differences in IQ are almost certainly genetic in origin.*

How should heritability be interpreted?

The central point is that heritable is not synonymous with genetic, so many of the arguments surrounding 'genetic' influence are irrelevant to the issue of heritability, and vice versa. *Every* human characteristic is in some part genetically and environmentally caused. The issue surrounding heritability is: what difference does having a particular set of parents make for a trait and is any observed difference caused by genetic *or environmental* transmission from one generation to another? Confusing these different meanings of genetic has led to a debate awash with hubris, polemic, claimed truisms and obscurantism—again from both sides of the political spectrum. My two favourite examples are as follows

From the right: because many human traits are heritable, it is seen as 'obvious' that a trait such as intelligence, depending as it does on a physical brain, must be heritable too (why *bother* doing the careful behaviour genetic studies?). Such a conclusion is invalid as it betrays a misunderstanding of what heritable means. Because genes build brains, it does not follow that *differences* between genotypes contribute to *observed differences* in phenotypic traits. As far as we know, we need a brain to believe and not to believe in God. However, it seems that whether we do or not depends on our environment rather than differences in genotypes. If intelligence depends on a physical brain and that brain is constructed by genes, then it does not follow that intelligence is heritable. Another simple example should make this clear. Eyes are indisputably built by genes. Yet having two eyes is not heritable. Having two eyes is innate. It is not heritable because almost everyone has two eyes so there are no differences to which genes can contribute. In other words, having two eyes does not depend on who our parents are, any will do.

From the left: it is a truism that there can be no phenotype without both an environment and a genotype. This particular truism is often gravely meted out by geneticists or evolutionary biologists to their more biologically ignorant psychologist colleagues, leading to statements about how an individual is necessarily an inextricable combination of both genes and environment. A favourite analogy offered to psychologists, in the hope that they might finally grasp the point, is that of the cake. To make a cake requires both ingredients (genes) and an environment (ovens and so forth). Calculating heritabilities is like trying to estimate how much of the cake is due to the ingredients and how much is due to the cooking environment—according to these biologists, a self-evidently stupid and wrong-headed question, not least because it is not answerable. However, all this is yet more obscurantism because this is not what heritability means. A high heritability for a trait, such as height, does not mean that you can have height without an environment or that for any individual we can assign the cause of his or her height to 90 per cent genetic and 10 per cent environment (or whatever). Heritability refers to the genetic contribution to *differences between people* not the cause of structures *within individuals*. To use the cake analogy again. The question asked, and answered, is what proportion of the differences we see in cakes (in a particular cake population) is due to differences in ingredients and what proportion is due to differences in cooking conditions. This analysis does not imply that we can disentangle the effects of the ingredients from the effects of the temperature of the oven for any individual case. The fact that genotypes and environments are inextricably combined within individuals is irrelevant to the question of whether differences between individuals can be attributed to genetic or environmental differences. It is simply disingenuous to claim that this fundamental aspect of human nature renders the notion of the heritability of IQ meaningless.

The argument is that the complexities of genotype–environment interactions during development are so great (in effect the phenotypes are so variable) that quantification of the 'main' (independent) effects of genes and environment is impossible. However if this were true, then the twin and adoption data would not generate such ordered and reliable correlations—there would be no regularity of relationship with gentoype. It is certainly incumbent on those who argue that heritability is meaningless to list (even fanciful) examples of real human environments that might lead to the plethora of genotype–environment interactions that are so far not evident in any data set on intelligence that has been published. Testable hypotheses about the differential influence of human environments are preferable to the tedious sermons about the temperature sensitivity of the development of eyes in *Drosophila*, or experiments with Californian plants.[40]

I hope I have established a number of important facts. To summarize: there is such a thing as general intelligence; it is likely to be grounded in the neurophysiology of the brain; it is certain that differences in general intelligence have a substantial genetic cause. All of these facts are likely to be met by cheers from the ideological right. *Yet nothing that has been established so far gives any credence to the argument that race differences in IQ are genetically based.* To see why this is so, we finally turn to the intersection between the scientific data and the political polemic of the race debate.

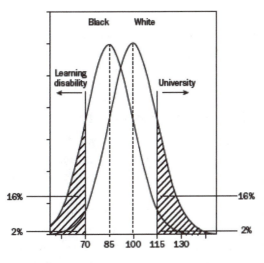

Fig. 9.3 The consequence of a one standard deviation difference in the mean of the black and white populations for a set criterion based on IQ.

Race differences in IQ

Myth 4: The genetics of intelligence has established that race differences in IQ are genetically based.

The tyranny of the mean

As with g, the central fact is not in dispute. Black Americans score around 15 points, or one standard deviation, lower than the white American population on intelligence tests. This difference is important if we: (1) believe in intelligence; (2) believe that IQ tests measure it; and (3) believe that intelligence should be the crucial variable for determining entry to some of society's institutions. If, for example, we set IQ cut-offs for both entry to university and eligibility for special education, then we will dramatically distort the representativeness of the different populations. Figure 9.3 shows the consequence of this mean (average) difference for a normally distributed variable (*The* bell curve) such as IQ.

In the case of entry to university we see that we cannot expect the equal ratio of whites to blacks (adjusting for base rate of numbers of whites and blacks in the population). On the basis of IQ alone, we would expect to see whites over-represented compared with blacks by 8 to 1. If we estimate that the ratio of whites to blacks in the population is 5 to 1, we can see that in fact there will be 40 whites at university for every black or 97 per cent of the university will be white—selected, colour-blind, on the basis of IQ. In the case of special education classes, the case is reversed, with an 8-fold over-representation of blacks compared with whites. Clearly, then, the location of the mean of a population can have large consequences when the variable is important. However, the crucial question for our discussion is what is likely to have caused this difference.

Given the robust difference in means and after all we have said about the nature of intelligence, does this not make it likely that black Americans have poorer/fewer genes for intelligence? Possible, yes; but likely? No. The reason this can be stated so boldly is because heritability says nothing about differences in means *between* populations. Heritability is an index of the genetic contribution to variability *within* a population. Understanding this is the key to unlocking the tangle of the scientific debate. Before I explain this fully, let us discuss the three major options for explaining why the difference in IQ might arise. I want to do this because one seems a non-starter yet continues to create myths that are damaging to those of us who use IQ differences to study intelligence.

Three major hypotheses for race differences in IQ

Hypothesis 1: IQ tests measure social advantage not intelligence. This hypothesis is the non-starter. We have already seen in this chapter that there are many good reasons to believe that in our society IQ tests do indeed measure an attribute of the information-processing capacity of the brain and that this capacity is probably highly heritable. Of course, this does not mean that there is no test item or test that is not in some way biased against a particular group and which would lower unfairly the mean for that group. However, in the absence of any hard evidence for this across the full gamut of intelligence tests, this explanation for the one standard deviation difference seems incredibly trite.

Hypotheses 2 and 3 are complementary. The second hypothesis accepts that the tests are valid measures of intelligence (so the black population does 'really' have a lower average) but proposes that the differences between the populations are environmental in origin. The third possibility concurs that the tests are valid, but says that the difference is genetic. The claim is that this is the most likely hypothesis *because IQ differences are highly heritable.* So we now come to the crux of the whole issue.

The second hypothesis at first blush looks extremely likely. What does it mean to compare the population averages? Let us forget about race and think instead of social class differences within a white population. Let us suppose that differences in IQ in this population have a substantial heritability. Let us further suppose that IQ is correlated with social class (which it is). Now let us take the mean of the IQ scores of the individuals with the lowest social class and compare that with the mean of the population as a whole. It is not hard to imagine that we would find a similar difference between the means of the two white populations to that found between black and white Americans. How easy is it to imagine that the difference in IQ between the working class and the rest of the population is genetic as opposed to the result of social disadvantage?[41] Is this harder to imagine than it is to imagine that the difference between black and white populations might be genetic? I think that, for many, the latter is easier to imagine than the former just because skin colour, which is obviously genetic, predisposes us to expect other genetic differences between the populations. But imagine in the case of our white working class population that we find that their mean height is also lower. Even though there is a large genetic contribution to differences in height, I do not think many would use this link to argue that the associated difference in intelligence is genetic in origin. Yet there is no more reason to believe that the genes for intelligence are more associated with those for skin colour than they are with those associated with height (in fact, a better case could be made for the opposite). Just as we might want to jump at environmental factors associated with lower social class to explain our social class difference in IQ within the white population, it seems more obvious to go looking for the very same factors that might be associated with the difference between black and white Americans. Now, the authors of *The bell curve* have thought of this. However, I want you to think of it, if only because it should remove the 'it is obvious' default for the genetic case that many people seem to have.

So, what do the authors of *The bell curve* make of this argument. What they make of it is the substantive content of the whole book. They deliberately pit the example used above (that social class causes IQ differences) with their own, that IQ differences cause social class, and they do so using some of the arguments that we are already familiar with and a new argument from a novel treatments of data. Let us deal with the new treatment of the data before we return to the old arguments.

Pitting social class against IQ

The problem with trying to assess the influence of IQ on a social outcome measure such as probability of employment, being an unmarried mother, going to jail, and so forth, is that IQ is correlated with other variables, in particular social class, that in turn are correlated with the social outcome variable. How do we know whether IQ has any effect on a social outcome variable, when it could be its association with social class that leads to the correlation? To give one example: suppose lower IQ people are more likely to go to prison. Further suppose those from the lower social classes are more likely to go to prison *and* to have a lower IQ. Is it that lower IQ causes an increased risk of going to prison and more lower class people go to prison only because more of them have lower IQs. Or could it be that it is the socio-economic circumstances associated with the lower social classes that causes the increased risk of going to prison and it just so happens that the lower classes have lower IQs? The proposal in *The bell curve* is that using statistics such as multiple regression or partial correlation can distinguish these options.[42] These techniques allow the influence of a variable on another to be adjusted for the influence of a third correlated variable. This is a method of statistical control, i.e. trying to see what would happen in an experiment if we could hold one variable constant while allowing the other to vary. Which variable would turn out to be 'more important' for explaining differences in social outcome?

The authors of *The bell curve* have no doubts. With social class differences held constant (or partialled out) IQ still predicts social outcome. However, if we repeat the analysis the other way round, when the effect of IQ is held constant there is very little influence of social class (see, for example, *The bell curve*, p. 149 for an example of the effect of each variable on the probability of dropping out of high school). In other words, social class is only associated with outcome variables because of its association with IQ. It is IQ that is the important causal variable.

This is a powerful analysis, but there are many potential problems in the use of such statistics. Gould has pointed out that while their analysis shows that IQ has the edge over social class in many comparisons, it still explains very little of the differences found.[11] So while there is an effect, it is a small one. However, the most serious problem for the conclusions of Herrnstein and Murray[3] has been eloquently discussed by Hunt.[16] In a nutshell, Hunt argues that the IQ predictions clearly hold at low IQ (below 85) but it is not clear that IQ has a linear positive effect on social outcome in the 85+ range which constitute the bulk of the population. In other words, a *low* IQ, irrespective of social class, is a risk factor for negative social outcomes, but there is not much evidence that there is a significant and systematic decrease in risk with rising IQ for the remaining 84 per cent of the population. This is a very different scenario from that painted in *The bell curve*.

Despite these objections, it is my view that the data in *The bell curve* have been dismissed in too cavalier a fashion. While I doubt that they substantiate the majority of the claims made by Herrnstein and Murray, they do deserve to be taken more seriously. A serious treatment like that of Hunt is better than a reflex dismissal. In any case, the central weakness in the race argument, as presented in *The bell curve*, is not the treatment of data but (1) the real possibility that it is not social class *per se* that may be an important environmental cause of race differences; and (2) the fact that no evidence is presented that the race difference in IQ is genetic.

The argument from heritability

The arguments for the genetic cause of race differences in *The bell curve* are re-hashes of the ones we have already met: (1) IQ differences are largely heritable; and (2) shared environment counts for little of the environmental variance anyway. Consequently, the most probable cause of the race differences in IQ is genetic.

Given the centrality of heritability to this argument, it is time to remind ourselves what heritability means and what the data on IQ differences tell us. Between 50 and 80 per cent of the differences in IQ in Western society is accounted for by genetic differences. To examine how the distinction between population means and population variance is crucial, let us take height as an easy to understand example.

It is well known that differences in height are highly heritable. The fact that the majority of differences in height between individuals in our population are based on differences in genotypes has not stopped the mean height of the population rising throughout most of recent history. It is highly unlikely that this change in mean is caused by changes in the gene pool (this would mean that smaller people are more likely to die before reproducing)—the rise this century alone is far too great for that. Rather, it is far more probable that environmental changes (improvements in nutrition and health) have caused everyone's height to increase. *Differences* in height within generations, however, are still largely genetically caused. The mean difference in height between the current generation and a generation from the nineteenth century is likely to be caused by environmental change, and the high heritability of height within generations has nothing to do with the generational difference in means.

However, is this not fanciful when it comes to intelligence? Surely we are not really any more intelligent than our parents' generation—better educated on the whole, maybe, but not more intelligent? Well, if by intelligence you mean IQ test score then our increase in height *has* been matched by an increase in intelligence this century. Flynn has estimated that most intelligence tests have shown a standard deviation improvement in performance per generation this century.[43] Working backwards, this argues that the average intelligence of the population before the Second World War was at the level of the mentally retarded by today's standards. Even if you do not find this idea intrinsically ridiculous then you must at least concede that this change is unlikely to be caused by a change in the gene pool. Substitute black compared with white mean performance for generational changes in performance and we see two things: (1) a high heritability is simply irrelevant when considering differences between the means of two populations; and (2) a large *change* over generations in a population's mean is unlikely to be genetic in origin, and it is just as unlikely that large *differences* between populations are genetic in origin. In any case, even on the high estimate of 80 per cent for the heritability of IQ, there is more than enough room for environmental influences that could shift a population mean by a standard deviation, particularly if these were pervasive and long-lasting. Before we turn from the logic of the situation which is so poorly understood to look again at some 'facts', let us finally hit the idea on the head (pun coming up) that it is obvious that race differences must be in part genetic in origin.

Let us conduct a thought experiment.[44] Suppose the dictator of a brave new world decided that in order to create a caste of workers we should hit every 10th baby on the head with a hammer (note that this is an *environmental* effect; many others such as lead poisoning, radiation, viral implants, etc., could be substituted). The babies are hit hard enough so that there is enough brain damage to cause a lowering of IQ by 15 points, but not so hard that it leaves any obvious mark. To make the choice of baby efficient, it was decided to select babies with red hair since they made up about 10 per cent of this particular population. What would the consequences of this be? I have simulated this situation,[45] and the results are presented in Table 9.1.

Imagine prior to the Hammer regime that the heritability of IQ was 80 per cent. The new regime then implements its head-hammering policy for red-haired babies. What would we find? We can see from Table 9.1 that this drastic step would only reduce the population mean by some 1.5 IQ points and increase the standard deviation by half a point. The heritability of IQ which was 79.9 per cent lowers to 74 per cent. So we see

Table 9.1 IQs of the population and red-haired children before and after the Hammer regime

			Before Hammer	After Hammer
Population				
	IQ	Mean	100.05	98.55
		SD	15.01	15.65
	Heritability		79.9%	74%
Red hair				
	IQ	Mean	–	85.24
		SD	–	15.17

in the post-hammer years that IQ is still highly heritable. Suppose someone happens to notice a preponderance of people with red hair in schools for the learning disabled and calculates their IQ separately for the red-haired population. They would find that the mean was 85.24, while the mean for the population who did not have red hair is 100.05. Let me draw the lessons from this thought experiment. The heritability of IQ in this brave new world is very high at 74 per cent. Those babies unlucky enough to have red hair (which, it is true, is caused by genetic differences) have a mean IQ one standard deviation less than the population mean. They have a lower IQ NOT because they have fewer of the good genes that contribute to the heritability of intelligence but because they had the genes for red hair and consequently they were subject to an environmental event—being hit on the head with a hammer.

Let us now suppose that being born black in American society is equivalent to being hit over the head with a hammer (i.e. being born black means exposure to pervasive social disadvantage from birth by virtue of the colour of their skin) as far as measured intelligence is concerned. I am sure that any fair-minded student of American society would have little trouble in coming up with educationally relevant variables that might be correlated with skin colour. Note that being black in American society is not a socio-economic variable in the conventional sense. Nor is it the kind of variable that could contribute to the estimates of 'shared environment' in a typical adoption or twin study. Rather, it is a variable that carries consequences (what Flynn calls an information-bearing trait[46]) that are unavoidable and last for a lifespan. This thought experiment demonstrates that a high heritability with an environmentally caused mean difference between two groups is not only theoretically possible but a highly plausible hypothesis for race differences in IQ.

Data on race differences

Pertinent data on possible sources of race differences are found in studies that have observed the influence of dramatically altering the social conditions of black children. The best known of these studies is the Minnesota Transracial Adoption Study by Scarr and Weinberg which reported IQ data on 101 adoptive families where a black child was placed in a white middle-class home.[47] The major finding of this study was that the average IQ of these black children was about 20 points higher than the population mean (85) expected for those children. A follow-up study 10 years later showed that, although the IQ advantage had narrowed somewhat, the black adoptees were still about 12 points (or nearly one standard deviation) above their expected mean.[48] The results of both studies allow Weinberg et al. to conclude that the results demonstrate 'persistent beneficial effects of being reared in the culture of the schools and the IQ tests' (p. 131).

An interesting feature of the data in these studies is that the white non-adopted children in these families have higher IQ scores than the black adopted children. There are at least two likely reasons for this.

First, this difference is to be expected because the adoptive parents in this study have a mean IQ around 120. The white children benefit from both the better environment and the genes provided by their high IQ parents. On the assumption that the black children would inherit 'average genes' from their parents (as opposed to the above average genes inherited by their white adoptive siblings in this selected sample), this suggests that the adoptive placement removed some of the negative impact of being raised in black as opposed to white culture. In other words, these children are doing as well as we would expect of 'average' white children adopted into such a home.

Secondly, the black children have in common a non-shared environmental difference with their white adopted siblings! Simply put, they are black not white, and this means that their effective environment cannot possibly be the same as their white siblings despite shared socio-economic circumstances.

I hope I have demonstrated that not only is it theoretically possible that the race difference in IQ could be cultural in origin, despite a high heritability for IQ in our society, but that data on transracial adoption make this the most likely explanation. It is now time to turn back to theoretical conceptions of the nature of intelligence. When we do so we shall see again that there is no inherent contradiction between a genetic constraint on individual differences in intelligence and environmentally caused differences in means between populations.

Anderson's theory of the minimal cognitive architecture underlying intelligence and development

This theory gives a central role to a biological constraint on intelligence, but at the same time acknowledges there is more to intelligence than differences in neural functioning.[49] I want to outline the architecture and explore some of its implications for understanding the relationship between biology and culture in shaping 'intelligence'.

The theory of the minimal cognitive architecture, outlined in Fig. 9.4, allows for two routes to knowledge acquisition which, roughly, cleaves individual differences in intelligence from cognitive development. Individual differences in intelligence are attributed to variations in speed of processing and developmental changes in cognitive competence to the maturation of modular functions. The two routes are as follows.

Route 1 knowledge acquisition (thought): knowledge that is acquired by the implementation of an algorithm generated by a specific processor. Problem-solving algorithms generated by two specific processors, one specialized for verbal representations and the other for spatial, are implemented by a basic processing mechanism which varies in its speed of processing. The higher the speed of the basic processing mechanism, the more complex the algorithms that can be implemented. The speed of this mechanism can be estimated by measures such as inspection time. When an algorithm generated by a specific processor is implemented, we can be said to be thinking, the process by which most knowledge is acquired. The basic processing mechanism represents a knowledge-free, biological, possibly genetic, constraint on thought. Variation in the speed of the basic processing mechanism is the primary cause of individual differences in intelligence as measured by IQ. However, I hypothesize that speed of processing does not change with development.

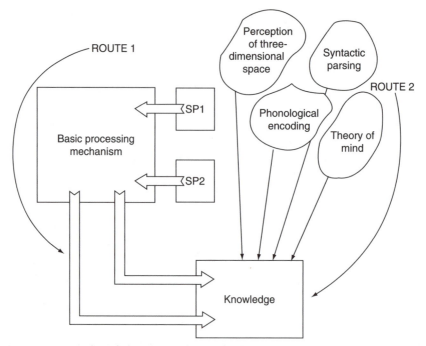

Fig. 9.4 Two routes to knowledge. Route 1 knowledge is acquired by thinking. Route 2 knowledge is directly given by modules that mature at different times in development. From Anderson[49] (Fig. 6.1). Reprinted with permission.

Route 2 knowledge acquisition: knowledge that is directly given by dedicated modules. Modules are dedicated, computationally complex, mechanisms whose function is to provide us with evolutionarily prescribed information which could not be furnished by general purpose problem solvers (i.e. by the specific processors). The computations of modules are not constrained by the speed of the basic processing mechanism and they are, therefore, unrelated to individual differences in intelligence. The maturation of modules is the primary cause of cognitive development in children and affords, in effect, new cognitive competences. Therefore, cognitive development and individual differences in intelligence are caused by different and unrelated cognitive mechanisms.

IQ tests work by measuring knowledge. We can see from the theory that differences in only certain kinds of knowledge are subject to the constraint of the basic processing mechanism—knowledge gained through thought. This predicts, for example, that some individuals of low IQ should be capable of certain kinds of complex knowledge acquisition, such as acquiring language, because it is modularly based (and, of course, they are). Further, we can demonstrate that the mentally retarded, while slow to process abstract information, can process ecologically relevant information (such as the perception of human movement) as fast as individuals of normal IQ.[50] Not only are there hidden talents in the mentally retarded suggested by this architecture, but it follows that there is more than one reason for being unintelligent or scoring poorly on IQ tests. For example, one hypothesis is that individuals with autism, who mostly have low IQs, have impairments in one or more modular systems (principally, a 'theory of mind' module[51]) but are unimpaired in speed of processing.[52] Autistics have low IQs because of the general consequences of a damaged crucial cognitive module and not because of slow speed of processing, as is the case for the generally mentally retarded.[53]

Distinguishing between knowledge and the mechanisms responsible for acquiring that knowledge *using this particular architecture* allows us to set a theoretical arena for discussing the relationship between biological constraints and environmental influences.

Clearly such an architecture argues that there is more to intelligence than a single variable such as speed of processing. Indeed, there are two quite distinct senses of the word intelligence; that which refers to individual differences, and that which refers to cognitive development. Because my hypothesis is that speed of processing does not change with development but 'intelligence' indisputably does, there is no incompatibility with a general biological constraint on knowledge acquisition and the malleability of 'intelligence'. In this model, intelligence is malleable through the kinds of knowledge environments made available to individuals and, inevitably, through the mechanisms underlying cognitive development.

Having said that intelligence is in some sense multifaceted, this does not imply open slather for the existence of a plethora of multiple intelligences, either within or between races, nor does it imply the demise of g. There is a domain general biological constraint on the acquisition of knowledge through thought. However, the knowledge we ultimately acquire will also be influenced by the kinds of knowledge environments we find ourselves in and, moreover, by non-intellectual factors such as our attitudes to acquiring knowledge (more prosaically for children this boils down to attitude to school). It should be clear from this theory that the biological constraint means that there is some knowledge that is too complex for most of us to acquire. However, the norm will surely be that we all underachieve for a variety of reasons; and some of those reasons for underachievement may be more salient for some social groups than others.

It is worth repeating that IQ tests measure knowledge, and while individual differences in knowledge acquisition are constrained by biological variables, a huge influence on knowledge itself is history and culture. Such influences could push up the mean knowledge of a population without implying that differences within the population are predominantly socially determined.

Finally, the history of science has shown that well articulated and, dare I say it, true theories open up new avenues for application and change. In this case, a well articulated theory that does embrace a fact of nature (that knowledge acquisition is constrained by biological differences) gives a new way in which we can think about enhancing knowledge acquisition. Acknowledging known constraints and armed with a detailed theory, we might yet be able to devise genuine educational interventions that might succeed in 'raising IQ' where all before have failed.

To date, we have looked at what is known about race differences in intelligence. We have managed to do this without recourse to advocacy on social policy and that is how a scientific discussion should proceed. To end and to reinforce the point, I would like to consider the situation that for many would be the apocalyptic one. Supposing through the use of some techniques not yet known to us we can establish that it is the case that the difference between blacks and whites in mean IQ is genetically based. What would we make of this for (1) politics and (2) science?

Politics

The political agenda of *The bell curve* is prefaced on Richard Herrnstein's old idea that IQ differences are the cornerstone of a meritocracy and a meritocracy is a good thing.[54] Charles Murray, being a political economist, has simply put numbers on Herrnstein's gut feelings and shown (given some assumptions underlying economic rationalism in capitalist industrial economies) the 'dollar value' of IQ. Accepting this analysis means accepting a whole host of other political values, none of which have anything to do with whether or not social class or race differences are biologically based. For example, we would have to believe that it is fair and just that a more intelligent, yet lazy and deceitful, individual should earn more money than a less intelligent but hardworking and honest individual. This is not a view that is universally held. Even on its own terms, if the argument in *The bell curve* coincides with your own preferred political recipe then what is important is not the colour of a person's skin or even their genotype, but their 'IQ'—however they came by it. Flynn discusses another concrete example of one of the options before us.[46] He cogently argues that if we accept that black people (as individuals) suffer because the colour of their skin leads to disadvantageous treatment on the basis of this group membership (and no one argues that it does not), then black people (as a group) should be compensated for this injustice through schemes of affirmative action. No matter what the cause of any group difference might be, there is a whole range of political options open to us.

Science

It is clear that the debate on race and intelligence is not going to go away. Indeed there has been a recent resurgence in the interest in brain size and intelligence and how that might mediate race differences[55] (see Carey, Chapter 8 of this volume). One of the problems I have with those who defend the study of race differences in IQ on the basis of scientific freedom is that it is not always made clear what kind of science this research serves. Why should we study race differences in IQ? My own view is that the argument from curiosity, 'because they are there', is not enough justification.[56] As we have seen, what might be harmless curiosity when applied to other topics can have profound and negative consequences on individual lives when the subject matter is racial differences. From the point of view of the theory of intelligence outlined in above, data on race differences are of little or no interest. I might just as well be interested in data that show that tall adults are more intelligent than small adults (I do not know if there is any difference). Either way, this information adds nothing to my understanding of the mechanisms underlying intelligence and development—for this purpose, one *savant* is worth more than *The bell curve's* 12,686 subjects put together.[57] From my point of view, then, the study of race differences is, in principle, irrelevant but in practice is a distraction that hampers scientific advance. So the study of race differences is not defensible on the grounds that they add to our scientific understanding of the nature of intelligence. Sociologists or politicians may well want to study race differences scientifically, but that is another matter and another defence.

Given the way I have framed this chapter, you might feel it is incumbent on me to confess my own political position. Despite the fact that I abhor the obscurantism, not to say Orwellianism, in the ravings about the social construction of psychological knowledge,[58] should you think my own political opinions are relevant to any of my arguments please feel free to ask.[59] More generally, my view is that it is the job of science to uncover nature; and clearly what is natural is not necessarily good. However, we fear that what is 'natural' is not only immutable but *must be*, and this, I submit, is the real source of antagonism against the idea of general intelligence and the genetics of IQ differences. In his new edition of *The mismeasure of man*, Stephen J. Gould[11] confesses that originally he was going to call the book 'Great is our sin' after a quote from Darwin's *Voyage of the Beagle*, 'If the misery of the poor be caused not by the laws of nature, but by our institutions, great is our sin'. Therein the fear is revealed. But it is a needless fear. The misery of the poor is *always* caused by social institutions and *never* by the laws of nature, and it is ridiculous to think that any scientific fact could say otherwise.

References and notes

1. Jensen AR. How much can we boost IQ and scholastic achievement? *Harvard Educational Review*, 1969; 39:1–123.
2. Plomin R. *Nature and nurture: an introduction to human behaviour genetics*. Brooks/Cole, Pacific Grove, California. 1990.
3. Herrnstein RJ, Murray CA. *The bell curve: intelligence and class structure in American life*. Free Press, New York. 1994.
4. Brand CR. The importance of intelligence in western societies. *Journal of Biosocial Science*, 1996; 28:387–404.
5. Even if we supposed that IQ differences were entirely heritable, given the moderate sized correlation between IQ and educational outcome there is no reason to believe that black children could not 'overperform' with special encouragement. In any case, as we shall see, a high heritability does not mean an absence of malleability.
6. Stern W. *Die psychologische methoden der intelligenzprufung*. Barth, Leipzig. 1914.
7. It is worth noting that not being culture-free (which is just about impossible for any test) is not the same thing as being culturally biased.
8. Jensen AR. Chronometric analysis of mental ability. *Journal of Social and Biological Structures*, 1981; 3:181–224.
9. Lynn R. *Cross-cultural differences in intelligence and personality*. Plenum Press, New York. 1995.
10. Gould SJ. *The mismeasure of man*. Pelican, Harmondsworth, UK. 1981.
11. Gould SJ. *The mismeasure of man*. Revised and expanded. Norton, New York. 1996.
12. Howe MJA. Intelligence as an explanation. *British Journal of Psychology*, 1988; 79:349–360.
13. Howe MJA. *The origins of exceptional abilities*. Blackwell, Oxford. 1990.
14. Gardner H. *Frames of mind: the theory of multiple intelligences*. Heinemann, London. 1983.

15. **Anderson M.** Intelligence. In AP Smith AP, DM Jones, ed. *Handbook of human performance*, Vol. III. Academic Press, London. 1992:1–24.

16. **Hunt E.** The role of intelligence in modern society. *American Scientist*, 1995; **83**:356–368.

17. **Neisser U.** Intelligence: knowns and unknowns—Report of a task force established by the Board of Scientific Affairs of the American Psychological Association. *APA Science Directorate*, Washington, DC. 1995.

18. **Nettelbeck T.** Intelligence does exist. *The Psychologist: Bulletin of the British Psychological Society*, 1990; **3**:494–497.

19. **Sternberg RJ.** Explaining away intelligence: a reply to Howe. *British Journal of Psychology*, 1988; **79**:527–533.

20. **Spearman C.** 'General intelligence' objectively determined and measured. *American Journal of Psychology*, 1904; **15**:201–293.

21. **Elliott CD.** *British Ability Scales: technical handbook*. NFER-Nelson, Windsor, UK. 1983.

22. **Carroll JB.** Reflections on Stephen J. Gould's *The mismeasure of man* (1981): retrospective review. *Intelligence*, 1995; **21**:121–134.

23. **Eysenck HJ.** The theory of intelligence and the psychophysiology of cognition. In RJ Sternberg, ed. *Advances in the psychology of human intelligence*. Lawrence Erlbaum Associates, Hillsdale, NJ. 1986:1–34.

24. **Jensen AR.** Reaction time and psychometric *g*. In HJ Eysenck, ed. *A model for intelligence*. Springer-Verlag, Berlin. 1982:93–132.

25. **Anderson M.** Individual differences in intelligence. In K Kirsner, C Speelman, M Maybery, A O'Brien-Malone, M Anderson M, C MacLeod, ed. *Implicit and explicit mental processes*. London, Lawrence Erlbaum. 1998.

26. **Jensen AR.** Test validity: g versus the specificity doctrine. *Journal of Social and Biological Structures*, 1984; **7**:93–118.

27. **Longstreth LE.** Jensen's reaction time investigations of intelligence: a critique. *Intelligence*, 1984; **8**:139–160.

28. **Nettelbeck T.** Inspection time and intelligence. In PA Vernon, ed. *Speed of information processing and intelligence*. Ablex, New York. 1987:295–346.

29. **Kranzler JH, Jensen AR.** Inspection time and intelligence: a meta-analysis. *Intelligence*, 1989; **13**:329–348.

30. **Deary IJ, Caryl PG.** Neuroscience and human intelligence differences. *Trends in Neuroscience*, 1997; **20**:321–372.

31. **Burns NR, Nettelbeck T, Cooper CJ.** The string measure of the event-related potential, IQ, and inspection time. *Personality and Individual Differences*, 1996; **21**:563–572.

32. **Mackintosh NJ.** The biology of intelligence? *British Journal of Psychology*, 1986; **77**:1–18.

33. A trait is an attribute of individuals that varies or differs in the population.

34. **Loehlin JC, Nichols RC.** *Heredity, environment and personality*. University of Texas Press, Austin, TX. 1976.

35. **Bouchard TJ, Lykken DT, McGue M, Segal NL, Tellegen A.** Sources of human psychological differences: the Minnesota study of twins reared apart. *Science*, 1990; **250**:223–250.

36. These percentages refer to the percentage of genes that contribute to individual variation in a population. The majority of genes are of course common across all members of a species.

37. **Plomin R, Daniels D.** Why are children in the same family so different from each other? *Behavioral and Brain Sciences*, 1987; **10**:1–16.

38. **Scarr S.** Developmental theories for the 1990s: development and individual differences. *Child Development*, 1992; **63**:1–19.

39. **Deary IJ, Whalley LJ, Lemmon H, Crawford JR, Starr JM.** *The stability of individual differences in mental ability from childhood to old age: follow-up of the 1932 Scottish Mental Survey. Intelligence*, 2000; **28**:49–55.

40. **Schiff M, Lewontin R.** *Education and class: the irrelevance of IQ genetic studies.* Clarendon Press, Oxford. 1986.

41. The far right probably would not have a problem imagining this (and indeed *The bell curve* implies this too), but I am assuming (1) that you have an open mind; (2) while you might imagine this, I suspect it is not as easy as imagining that black–white differences are genetically based.

42. Actually it is logistical regression but this distinction does not matter for the argument that follows.

43. **Flynn JR.** Massive IQ gains in 14 nations: what IQ tests really measure. *Psychological Bulletin*, 1987; **101**:171–191.

44. I am indebted to John Morton for a comment he made in an E-mail exchange that provoked the idea of this thought experiment.

45. **Anderson M, Reid CL.** Intelligence. In M Hewstone, FD Fincham, J Foster, ed. *Psychology*. BPS Blackwell, Oxford. 2005:268–290.

46. **Flynn JR.** Group differences: is the good society impossible? *Journal of Biosocial Science*, 1996; **28**:573–585.

47. **Scarr S, Weinberg RA.** IQ test performance of black children adopted by white families. *American Psychologist*, 1976; **31**:726–739.

48. **Weinberg RA, Scarr S, Waldman ID.** The Minnesota Transracial Adoption Study: A follow-up of IQ test performance at adolescence. *Intelligence*, 1992; **16**:117–135.

49. **Anderson M.** *Intelligence and development: a cognitive theory.* Blackwell, Oxford.

50. **Moore DG, Hobson P, Anderson M.** Person perception: does it involve IQ-independent perceptual processing? *Intelligence*, 1995; **20**:65–86.

51. **Leslie AM, Thaiss L.** Domain specificity in conceptual development: neuropsychological evidence from autism. *Cognition*, 1992; **43**:225–251.

52. **Scheuffgen K, Happé F, Anderson M, Frith F.** High 'intelligence', low 'IQ'? Speed of processing and measured IQ in children with autism. *Development and Psychopathology*, 2000; **12**:83–90.

53. **Anderson M.** Inspection time and IQ in young children. *Personality and Individual Differences*, 1986; **7**:677–686.

54. **Herrnstein RJ.** *IQ in the meritocracy.* Atlantic-Little Brown, Boston, MA. 1973.

55. **Rushton JP, Jensen AR.** Wanted: more race realism and less moralistic fallacy. *Psychology, Public Policy and Law*, 2005; **11**:328–336.

56. **Loehlin JC.** Should we do research on race differences in intelligence? *Intelligence*, 1992; **16**:1–4.

57. **Anderson M, O'Connor N, Hermelin B.** A specific calculating ability. *Intelligence*, 1998; **26**:383–403.

58. **Butler PV.** Psychology as history, and the biological renaissance: a brief review of the science and politics of psychological determinism. *Australian Psychologist*, 1998; **33**:40–46.

59. My E-mail is mike@psy.uwa.edu.au

Chapter 10

The Mozart effect: it's time to face the music!

Colin Gray and Sergio Della Sala

Ah, but a man's reach should exceed his grasp,
Or what's a heaven for?
                    Robert Browning, Andrea del Sarto (1855); I.27

Introduction
Boosting your brainpower: a pipe dream?

Have you ever wished you were more intelligent? If we are to judge from the autobiographies of the famous, even the most able of us longs, at least occasionally, for greater intellectual power. Oh, to be able to read even the most difficult books twice as fast as we can at present, absorbing and retaining the material effortlessly; how gratifying to perform lightning feats of mental arithmetic! Such wish-fulfilling fantasies are recurring themes in fiction and in drama. In the film *Phenomenon*, George Malley (played by a grievously miscast John Travolta), having been struck by a beam of light from outer space, finds himself with an intellect of galactic proportions. Charlie Gordon, the mentally challenged protagonist in Daniel Keyes' *Flowers for Algernon* (and the Oscar-winning film Charlie), having undergone brain surgery similar to that which produced a supermouse called Algernon, awakens to a new life as a genius. Such transformations, of course, open up great dramatic possibilities and make for a thoroughly enjoyable evening's entertainment.

Reality is less entertaining. For most of us, maturity brings the realization that we can raise our intellectual performance only within limits: strategy and tactics can be improved, but not fire-power. This personal insight is confirmed by scientific research: psychometricians have gathered large data sets showing that, relative to one's age group, performance on intelligence tests remains more or less constant throughout life.[1]

From time to time, of course, there have been claims that received wisdom and psychometric research have got it wrong: far from being confined by such glass ceilings, each of us actually have vast reservoirs of untapped mental power, just waiting to be harnessed! This myth of mental plasticity has been fully exploited by the modern media, and we are now inundated with advertisements offering to teach us foreign languages while we sleep, improve our memories and intellects—even change our entire personalities.

The authors wish to thank William P. Brown for reading the manuscript and making several helpful comments.

Now we cannot deny that those prepared to cross palms with silver may have received a useful tip or two on the use of mnemonics or examination strategy; but whether their general intellectual capacities really increased as a result of taking the course is doubtful. Should a curious investigator enquire into the nature of the evidence upon which such a claim is based, he or she will doubtless be regaled with further advice on how to be smarter, more creative or whatever. Scientific evidence for the efficacy of the method, however, has never yet been forthcoming.[2] These days, the promised key to Aladdin's cave invariably turns out to be yet another DVD, with a few lines of glib nonsense in the accompanying manual.

Experimental studies have demonstrated dramatic placebo effects in this area. Those who have used tapes claiming to improve memory through the use of subliminal input believe that they work; but so also do those who have used tapes which, although actually devised to raise self-esteem, were labelled as memory-expanding. In neither case was there any real improvement in memory (British Psychological Society Working Party Report, 1992). Subliminal input is, in general, of doubtful efficacy: people who dieted and received subliminal input from tapes lost no more weight than those who dieted but did not play the tapes.[3]

If you believe you can make yourself more intelligent by listening to something, you might as well buy some good music. What about Mozart's piano concertos for instance? That, however, brings us to the principal focus of this chapter.

The power of music

Those of us who love music are more than ready to accept that this most human (some would say divine) of creations has great beneficial properties. Science has demonstrated beyond doubt that music produces characteristic response patterns in the brain;[4] but what is the nature of the powerful effect that music has upon us? The traditional view has been that the effects of even the most complex music upon the ordinary listener are primarily—indeed, exclusively—emotional, rather than intellectual. Music enriches our lives in many ways: music can lift our spirits, raise our morale—even inspire some of us to great achievements. However, if elevated mood promotes elevated ideas, there is no inference that the music has influenced the thought process itself.

Great music, of course, is the product of great minds; and the analysis of the structure and harmony of a great musical work will fully exercise the intellectual powers of the most discerning scholar or critic. This ineluctable fact, however, carries no implication that listening to music actually *enhances* the intellect: musical composition and appreciation are simply fields which attract and challenge those of high intelligence.

The 'Mozart effect'

In recent years, the view that the effects of music are conative rather than cognitive has come under attack, with the advent of what Don Campbell has termed the 'Mozart effect'.[5] In the early 1990s, at the University of California, researchers at the Center for the Neurobiology of Learning and Memory, under the directorship of Gordon Shaw, began to study the effects of music upon college students and children. In 1993, Shaw and his colleagues (F. H. Rauscher and K. N. Ky) published a letter to the scientific journal *Nature* reporting that listening for only 10 min to some music by Mozart had enhanced the spatial IQs of some of their college students.[6]

The news of this result spread fast, and the repercussions, as educators and politicians jumped on the bandwagon, were dramatic. One immediate and worthy beneficiary was the teaching of music in schools, which enjoyed an instant fillip. Other developments, however, were more questionable. In some US states (Tennessee and Georgia, for example), legislation was introduced which provided all new parents with free Mozart tapes to play to their infants to enhance their intelligence. In Florida, several nurseries play 30 min of music each day to steepen the children's learning curves. In some rooms of the library of the Hudson Valley Community College, Mozart is played in the background to improve concentration and reading effectiveness. The 'Mozart effect' has attracted phenomenal interest: our Google search made over 248,000 hits. Amazon offers over 35 books (in English) with 'Mozart effect' in their titles.

According to Campbell, the Mozart effect is: 'the power of music to heal the body, strengthen the mind, and unlock the creative spirit' (see the subtitle of Campbell's book[5]). It is clear from this definition that the powers attributed to music range far beyond intellectual enhancement. According to Campbell, listening to music can also cure physical ailments—in animals as well as in humans. In monasteries in Brittany, for instance, monks have discovered that '... cows serenaded with Mozart give more milk' (p. 14). (It is not clear whether the music of other great composers similarly boosts milk output nor, indeed, whether giving more milk is good for the cows.) It appears, though, that some merino sheep in Australia, whose special diet of premium grains and hay was supplemented by an input of opera, produced the world's finest wool (see http://reuters.myway.com 26 January 2006). Some of Campbell's assertions, however, stretch credulity beyond breaking point, such as the claim that Beethoven's music improves the rising of bread (Campbell 1997[5], p. 14). Even microorganisms, it would seem, benefit from exposure to music.

In 2000 (3 years after the appearance of Campbell's book), Shaw published his own book, *Keeping Mozart in mind*, in which he describes his own research programme and gives further information about the *Nature* experiment.[7] At the outset, Shaw dissociates himself from many of the claims made under the umbrella of the Mozart effect: 'Note that neither my colleague Frances Rauscher nor I have been associated with them or endorsed them in any manner' (Preface, ix). In this chapter, we too shall confine ourselves to the scientific work. The purpose of this chapter is to consider this evidence in some detail, to see whether it really does justify the claim that listening to music enhances intelligence.

The Rauscher experiment

Rauscher, Shaw and Ky[6] reported that 36 college students, after listening to Mozart's Sonata for Two Pianos in D Major (K488) for only 10 min, achieved scores on standard spatial tasks from the Stanford–Binet intelligence test[8] which were fully 8–9 IQ points above the levels they achieved either after listening to a relaxation tape or experiencing complete silence for the same length of time.

The spatial tests used in Rauscher's experiment consisted of a pattern analysis test, a matrices test and a test of imaginary paper-folding and cutting. Test norms from the Stanford–Binet manual were used to transform the participants' raw scores into standard age scores (SAS) with a mean of 50 and a standard deviation of 8, so that the scores on the three different tests could be included in the same analysis. (This transformation was necessitated by the design of the experiment, which we shall consider in more detail below.) The mean SAS scores achieved by the participants for the Music, Relaxation and Silence conditions were 57.56, 54.61 and 54.00, respectively. A statistical analysis of the SAS scores confirmed that the mean SAS score under the Music condition was significantly higher than the mean for either the Relaxation or the Silence condition; the means for those two conditions did not differ significantly.

As the authors themselves note, the effect of the music was short lived: 'The enhancing effect of the music condition is temporal [sic], and does not extend beyond the 10–15 minute period during which subjects were engaged in each spatial task' (p. 611, final paragraph). Rauscher's result, therefore, hardly supports the claim that listening to music has permanent effects upon cognition. Taken at its face value, nevertheless, her result is still very surprising. To educators, it held out the exciting possibility that, with more extensive exposure to music, especially during the formative years of childhood, the benefits might be more long-lasting.

The IQ dimension

In the analysis reported in Rauscher et al.,[6] the SAS scores were converted to IQ equivalents, the means of which, for the Music, Relaxation and Silence conditions, were 119, 111 and 110, respectively. The mean IQ achieved by the participants after the Music condition, therefore, was 8–9 points higher than the mean IQ they achieved after either of the other two conditions. It was surely the transformation of the SAS scores to IQs that gave the Rauscher experiment its huge impact. To the general reader, the term IQ is highly emotive and carries a heavy baggage of what philosophers of science call 'surplus meaning'. No reader of Rauscher's report can avoid concluding that listening to music made her participants, at least for a short time, more 'intelligent', in both the everyday and psychometric senses of the term.

Rauscher's result, when expressed in IQ equivalents rather than SAS scores, is all the more remarkable when it is considered that standardized intelligence tests were developed specifically for the purpose of measuring functions that maintain essentially constant levels of performance throughout most of the lifespan, provided that no special coaching has been given. With test-sophisticated populations, in fact, special coaching has been shown to have relatively little effect. In the past, substantial gains in individual IQs on re-test have been obtained only with people from isolated regions: the increases in IQ that have been reported in recent years have taken place over generations, rather than within an individual's lifespan.[9] Yet here is an experiment which seems to have shown that an experimental manipulation lasting merely 10 min produced a dramatic (albeit temporary) improvement!

Should the SAS scores have been converted to IQs?

In Rauscher's experiment, each participant was tested on only ONE of the three spatial tests after each experimental condition. From the participant's score on the test, an IQ was calculated, so that, during the course of the experiment, each participant's IQ was calculated three times. We should also note that the IQs that Shaw's team calculated were not obtained in the manner prescribed by the Stanford–Binet manual, which requires the user to input scores by the same individual on *three* spatial tests. In order to calculate an IQ from just one score, the authors had to multiply the SAS score on that particular test by three. This procedure is highly questionable, because it produces a composite score which, since it is two-thirds notional, cannot legitimately be compared with the Stanford–Binet performance norms, which are based upon actual performance on three tests at a single sitting—without, moreover, the interpolation of any experimental conditions.

Replicating the Mozart effect

The Stanford–Binet intelligence scale, which was the first test to yield an IQ, would be a natural choice for researchers working at Stanford's next-door neighbour. Unlike later intelligence tests, however, the Stanford–Binet scale was constructed on the basis of the concept of mental age which, since test performance does not improve after the age of 16 years or so, is of limited value for the purposes of measuring cognition in adults. Moreover, the radical claim that listening to music boosts intelligence should rest on an evidential base more substantial than the performance of some highly intelligent adults on just one intelligence test—indeed, a small selection of items from one intelligence test. In fact, as we shall see, the whole case for intellectual enhancement turns out to rest upon performance on only *one* of the three tests used by Rauscher and her colleagues.

Other studies

There have been several attempts to reproduce the Mozart effect using other non-verbal intelligence scales, such as the Raven's Advanced Progressive Matrices. Generally speaking, such attempts have been unsuccessful.[10] In a meta-analytic study, Chabris reviewed 16 studies on the Mozart effect (with a total of 714 participants) and found that there was no effect whatsoever.[11] (Among the very few positive results in the literature, however, some are puzzling: for example, the memories of monkeys would appear to be adversely affected by exposure to Mozart's music[12]) If music has an effect upon cognition, one might also expect other measures of executive functioning, such as backward digit span, to show enhancement after listening to music; however, no such enhancement has been reported.

Several aspects of the design and implementation of Rauscher's experiment can be questioned. Newman *et al.*[10] suggest that the music merely maintained the cognition of the participants at normal level; whereas the Silence and Relaxation conditions, far from serving as adequate controls, actually dampened the participants' cognitive processes. Rauscher *et al.*,[6] anticipating the possibility that a change in arousal might have affected performance, had taken their participants' pulse rates before and after each condition. While there was no evidence that the pulse had changed after any of the three conditions, Newman's interpretation cannot be excluded and the adverse effects of monotony should always be taken into consideration in this type of research.

In Rauscher's experiment, each participant was tested only once after each condition (three times during the entire experiment). Had there been a pre-test on the same spatial test before each condition, each participant could have served as his or her own control, thus reducing the noisiness of the data and permitting more powerful statistical tests. Had the difference between the pre-test and post-test means for the Mozart condition been markedly greater than the same difference for the control conditions, we should have had at least some evidence of a genuine enhancement.

Rauscher's adoption of a within-subjects strategy may have been intended to reduce data noise. The use of a different test after each of the three experimental conditions, however, made it impossible to compare the same participants on exactly the same tests across the three experimental conditions. This problem cannot be remedied by transforming the raw scores on the three spatial tests to the same SAS scale. In our view, a between-subjects strategy should have been followed, with random assignment of the participants to the three experimental conditions. Each participant could then have been given the same spatial test after each condition. The statistical tests could have been given sufficient power by running more participants.

Many researchers avoid pre-testing because of the interpretational difficulties arising from practice effects. In the worst scenario, ceiling effects can vitiate comparisons among the post-test means for the different experimental conditions. In this case, however, practice could have been reduced by using equivalent forms of the same test at pre- and post-test and interposing a verbal distractor task after the pre-test.

In our own laboratories, Huw Thomas investigated the effects of music upon Raven's Advanced Matrices (APM) performance with an experiment of between-subjects design, in which equivalent forms of the APM were used at pre- and post-test. (The two forms, Form A and Form B, were constructed by selecting alternate items from the original 36 questions making up the APM, producing two equivalent 18-item tests.) The tests were timed, in order to avoid ceiling effects (cf. Newman *et al.*[10]).

As in the Rauscher experiment, there were three experimental conditions; but, instead of listening to a relaxation tape, participants in the 'Minimalist' condition of Thomas's experiment listened to some monotonous music by Philip Glass. As in Rauscher's experiment, the participants in the music condition listened to part of the Mozart Sonata for

Table 10.1 Results of Thomas's experiment: mean scores on equivalent selections of APM items at pre-test and post-test

Condition	Pre-test	Post-test
Mozart	10.20 (2.10)	11.30 (1.95)
Minimalist	11.10 (2.42)	12.10 (1.79)
Silence	11.00 (2.94)	11.40 (2.80)

Standard deviations are given in parentheses.

Two Pianos in D Major (K448). To minimize practice effects, the participants, after their pre-test with one form of the Raven's Matrices, listened to a short story before undergoing the experimental condition to which they had been assigned.

The results of Thomas's experiment are summarised in Table 10.1, from which it can be seen that the post-test mean for the Mozart condition was less than the mean for either the Minimalist or the Silence condition.[13] The differences among the three post-test means were not significant: $F(2,27) = 0.445$; $P = 0.645$.

Table 10.1 also shows a small practice effect: the mean scores at post-test are (for the two music conditions) about a point higher than those at pre-test; and the difference is even smaller for the Silence condition. None of the differences between pre-test and post-test is statistically significant. There is no evidence here for the enhancement of spatial performance by Mozart's music. As with other experiments that have used the Raven's Matrices as the dependent variable, Thomas's experiment failed to demonstrate the Mozart effect.

What really happened in the Rauscher experiment?

The scientific journal *Nature*, while subjecting submitted articles and scientific letters to a rigorous reviewing process, also imposes a strict length limit upon publications. It was probably for this reason that crucial details of the experimental design and the results were omitted from Rauscher's article.

It is stated explicitly[6] that the experiment was of within-subjects design: each participant was run under all three conditions (Music, Relaxation and Silence). After each experimental condition, however, the participant was tested on only ONE spatial test: pattern analysis, matrices or paper-folding and cutting (PFC). The order of presentation of the three conditions, therefore, would have been counterbalanced across individuals, so that the Music, Silence and Relaxation conditions were each experienced first, second and third equally often across the 36 participants. The presentation of the three spatial tests (PFC, matrices and pattern analysis) would also have been balanced across conditions, so that each test would have been taken by a third of the participants after each condition. The 36 SAS scores obtained under each condition must therefore have consisted of 12 scores on pattern analysis, 12 on matrices and 12 on PFC. While none of this is stated explicitly in the *Nature* article, failure to incorporate such arrangements would have vitiated the results of the experiment, so we can assume that the necessary counterbalancing was implemented.

The reader of the article by Rauscher et al.[6] would certainly form the impression that the music improved performance on all three spatial tasks, an impression strengthened by the authors' observation that: '... these three tasks correlated at the .01 level of significance. We were thus able to treat them as equal measures of abstract reasoning ability'.[6] The existence of positive correlations among the three tests, however, does not imply that the performance profiles of the three tests were identical across the three experimental conditions. In fact, they were not.

In his book,[7] Shaw (p. 162) supplies further details of the results of the Rauscher experiment which were omitted from the *Nature* paper. On re-analysis of the data, Shaw found that the higher average level of performance on the spatial tasks following the music condition derived from a higher mean score *on the PFC only*. The differences across the three experimental conditions for the matrices and pattern analysis tests, which Shaw represents in a clustered bar chart (p. 163), are negligible. We should also note that the means on the PFC for the three experimental conditions were calculated from the scores of three different groups, each consisting of 12 different participants. The effect of music upon spatial performance, therefore, turns out to be much more specific than the reader of the *Nature* article alone might suppose; moreover, the database showing this pattern is uncomfortably small.

Explaining the fact that only PFC is boosted by listening to music, Shaw argues that, of the three tasks, only PFC is a valid test of spatial–temporal reasoning: 'Theoretically, of the three tasks from the Stanford–Binet test used in our first experiment, ... only the PF&C explicitly tested spatial–temporal reasoning, and experimentally the dominant effect ... came from this task' (p. 164). That music should enhance PFC performance only is, Shaw argues, explainable in terms of the trion theory of cerebral functioning.[14]

In the PFC, the solver is shown a series of diagrams depicting a piece of paper being folded vertically and horizontally (in the more difficult items, several times) into a smaller rectangle or square (Fig. 10.1). Further pictures show the folded sheet with cuts that could be made with a pair of scissors, e.g. a corner could be cut off; a notch could be cut into one side. Finally, the solver is asked to choose from several pictures of what the entire sheet of paper might look like when unfolded, with varying patterns of creases and cut-out shapes.

The unusual nature of the PFC, which imposes heavy demands on visual memory and imagery, sets this test apart from many others and underlines the need for caution when generalizing to spatial tests in general.

Rauscher's follow-up experiment

Since he had found that PFC alone had been boosted by exposure to music, Shaw's team ran a more extensive follow-up experiment using PFC as the dependent variable. This experiment, which is also described in Shaw's book (p. 163),[7] ran over several days and demonstrated progressively greater enhancement of PFC performance in a group of

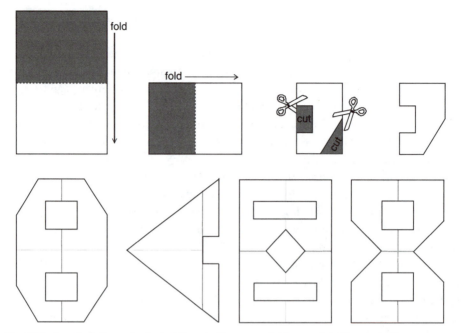

Fig. 10.1 An adaptation of a typical item in the paper folding and cutting test. The upper row shows (from the left) a sequence of imaginary folding and cutting operations: a dashed line represents a fold; a bold solid line represents a cut. The lower row presents the solver with a choice from four pictures of what the sheet of paper might look like when unfolded, with different patterns of creases, indentations and interior cut-out shapes.[15]

participants who listened to Mozart, in comparison with a Silence group and a Mixed group, who listened to repetitive music.

It would appear, therefore, that PFC may indeed be enhanced by exposure to some kinds of music. To demonstrate musical enhancement of performance on only one spatial test, however, falls far short of showing that music enhances spatial intelligence.

Conclusion

The impact of the 'Mozart effect' has been phenomenal. Judging from the publicity, its potential as a panacea would appear to be almost unlimited. In the cognitive domain, music is now used to stimulate fetuses and neonates, to treat epilepsy and to ameliorate memory loss in Alzheimer patients. A careful examination of the experimental evidence for the claim that listening to music enhances cognition, however, fails to provide the necessary support.

Intelligence is a hypothetical construct, a supposed general ability underlying any and every cognitive activity, including reasoning, attention and recall. As such, it has been measured by instruments that sample widely (and varyingly) from the domain of cognitive activities. The scientific research, as we have seen, has shown that listening to

Mozart's music may enhance performance on one particular spatial–temporal task (the PFC) but on no other.

While we strongly approve of giving children access to music at the earliest possible stage and encouraging their interest and participation in this most worthy and rewarding of human activities, the case for the enhancing effects of music upon intelligence has, in our view, yet to be made. As part of the celebrations and discussions for Mozart's 250th anniversary, Lucasta Miller wrote in *The Guardian* (January 21, 2006, Review, p. 8): 'Bounded by his legendary years as a child prodigy and his romantically early death, Mozart's life has offered itself up to myth-makers more than that of any other composer'. Sadly, it would appear that the Mozart Effect is yet another of these myths.

References and notes

1. See, for example, Deary IJ, Whiteman MC, Starr JM, Whalley LJ, Fox HC. The impact of childhood intelligence on later life: following up the Scottish mental surveys of 1932 and 1947. *Journal of Personality and Social Psychology*, 2004; **86**:130–147.
2. **McCrone J.** Mental gymnastics. *The New Scientist*, 2001; **2314**:30–34.
3. **Merikle PM, Skanes H.** Subliminal self-help audio tapes: a search for placebo effects. *Journal of Applied Psychology*, 1992; **77**:772–776.
4. See, for example, Peretz I, Zatorre RJ. Brain organization for music processing. *Annual Review of Psychology*, 2005; **56**:89–114.
5. **Campbell D.** *The Mozart effect: tapping the power of music to heal the body, strengthen the mind, and unlock the creative spirit.* Hodder & Stoughton, London. 1997.
6. **Rauscher FH, Shaw GL, Ky KN.** Music and spatial task performance. *Nature*, 1993; **365**: 611.
7. **Shaw GL.** *Keeping Mozart in mind.* Academic Press, London. 2000.
8. **Thorndike RL, Hagen EP, Sattler JM.** *The Stanford–Binet scale of intelligence.* Chicago University Press, Riverside. 1986.
9. See Flynn JR. The mean IQ of Americans: massive gains from 1932 to 1978. *Psychological Bulletin*, 1984; **95**:29–51; and Flynn JR. Massive IQ gains in 14 nations: what IQ tests really measure. *Psychological Bulletin*, 1987; **101**:171–191.
10. These studies include: Newman J, Rosenbach JH, Burns KL, Latimer BC, Matocha HR, Rosenthal-Vogt E. An experimental test of the 'Mozart effect': does listening to his music improve spatial ability? *Perceptual and Motor Skills* 1995; **81**:1379–1387; Steele KM, Brown JD, Stoecker JA. Failure to confirm the Rauscher and Shaw description of recovery of the Mozart effect. *Perceptual and Motor Skills*, 1999; **88**:843–848; Stough C, Kerkin B, Bates T, Mangan G. Music and spatial IQ. *Personality and Individual Differences*, 1994; **17**:695.
11. **Chabris CF.** Prelude or requiem for the 'Mozart effect'? *Nature*, 1999; **400**:826–827.
12. **Carlson S, Rama P, Artchakov D, Linnankoski I.** Effects of music and white noise on working memory performance in monkeys. *Neuroreport*, 1997; **8**:2853–2856.
13. The pre-test mean for the Mozart condition, on the other hand, was slightly less than those for either the Minimalist condition or Silence, which probably accounts for the fact that the Mozart post-test mean has the lowest value.
14. There is, incidentally, no mention of the special theoretical significance of paper-folding and cutting in the *Nature* article.
15. We are grateful to Peter Bates, School of Psychology, University of Aberdeen, for drawing the picture of the paper-folding experiment depicted in Fig. 10.1.

Chapter 11

The powers and perils of intuition

David G. Myers*

You don't know your own mind.

Jonathan Swift, *Polite conversation*, 1738

Even after spending a career pondering the connections between feeling and fact, intuition and reality, I am predisposed to welcome unbidden hunches. I once took an instant liking to a fellow teen, to whom I've now been married more than 40 years. Upon meeting job applicants, my gut reactions sometimes run ahead of my head's rationality. As a sign in Albert Einstein's office is rumoured to have read, 'Not everything that can be counted counts, and not everything that counts can be counted'.

However, I also know that my intuition—my effortless, immediate, unreasoned sense of truth—sometimes errs. My geographical intuition tells me that Reno is east of Los Angeles, Rome is south of New York, and Atlanta is east of Detroit; but I am wrong, wrong and wrong. 'The first principle', said Einstein's fellow physicist Richard Feynman, 'is that you must not fool yourself—and you are the easiest person to fool'.

So, what *are* intuition's powers? And what are its perils? When hiring, firing and investing, should we plug into our 'right brain' premonitions? Or with bright people so often believing demonstrably stupid things, do we instead need more 'left brain' rationality?

My message in a nutshell: psychological science reveals some astounding powers of intuition, and some notable perils. Creative yet critical thinkers will appreciate both.

Does comprehending intuition's powers and perils matter? I contend it matters greatly. Consider:

1. Judges' and jurors' intuitions determine the fate of lives. (Is she telling the truth? Will he do it again if released? Does applying the death penalty deter homicide?)

2. Investors' intuitions affect fortunes. (Has the market bottomed? Are tech stocks due for another plunge? Is it time to shift into bonds?)

3. Coaches' intuitions guide their decisions about whom to play. (Does she have the hot hand tonight? Is he in a batting slump?)

* Social psychologist David G. Myers professes psychology at Hope College (USA) and is author of *Intuition: its powers and perils* (Yale), from which this chapter is adapted.

4. Clinicians' intuitions steer their practice. (Is he at risk for suicide? Was she sexually abused?)

Intuitions shape our fears (do we fear the right things?), impressions (are our stereotypes accurate?) and relationships (does she like me?). Intuitions influence prime ministers in times of crisis, gamblers at the table and personnel directors when eyeing applicants.

Intuition's powers

Intuition's powers are widely acclaimed. 'I work through instinct, and instinct is my best counselor', declared Princess Diana in her last interview.[1] 'I'm a gut player. I rely on my instincts', said George W. Bush shortly before launching the Iraq War.[2] 'Buried deep within each and every one of us, there is an instinctive, heart-felt awareness that provides—if we allow it to—the most reliable guide', agreed Prince Charles. We need, he believes, 'to listen rather more to the common sense emanating from our hearts'.[3]

The princess, president and prince have plenty of company. Writers, counsellors and speakers galore offer to develop our sixth sense, to harness our inner wisdom, to unlock the power of our subconscious mind. Books (see Table 11.1) guide us toward intuitive healing, learning, selling, investing and managing.

Deciding what to make of this intuition industry is tricky. 'Intuitives'—intuition authors and trainers—seem largely oblivious to new scientific explorations of how the human mind processes information. Are their intuitions about intuition valid? Is consciousness often invaded by uninvited truth, there to grasp if we will but restrain our

Table 11.1 Books on intuition

Intuitive healing	Intuitive business
The intuitive healer: accessing your inner physician	*The intuitive manager*
Dr. Judith Orloff's guide to intuitive healing	*The intuitive trader*
The intuitive heart	*The intuitive business woman*
Intuitive cooking	*Intuitive selling*
Intuitive eating	*Intuition at work*
Intuitive learning	**Intuitive spirituality**
The intuitive principal	*Intuitive thinking as a spiritual path*
Understanding and teaching the intuitive mind	*Intuitive techniques for getting thru to your soul*
The intuitive approach to reading and learning abilities	*Divine intuition*
The wise child: a spiritual guide to nurturing your child's intuition	**Intuitive living**
Intuitive living: a sacred path	*The intuitive edge*
	The intuitive way
	You already know what to do

Table 11.2 From Daniel Kahneman's Nobel Lecture

Intuition	Reasoning
System 1	System 2
Fast	Slow
Parallel	Serial
Automatic	Controlled
Effortless	Effortful
Associative	Rule-governed
Slow-learning	Flexible
Emotional	Neutral

Most judgments and actions are governed by System 1. They are unproblematic, skilled and adequately successful.

rational thinking and attune to the still small voice within? Or are intuitives' writings perpetuating mind myths? Are they to cognitive science what professional wrestling is to athletics?

Today's cognitive science *is* revealing a fascinating unconscious mind that Freud never told us about. Thinking occurs on stage, but more so off stage, out of sight. Studies of (excuse some jargon) automatic processing, subliminal priming, implicit memory, heuristic judgements, spontaneous trait inference, right-brain processing, instant emotions, non-verbal communication, implicit attitudes and creativity unveil our intuitive capacities. The bottom line: thinking, memory and attitudes all operate on two levels— the conscious/deliberate and the unconscious/automatic. 'Dual processing', researchers call it (see Table 11.2). We know more than we know we know. Intuition does, indeed, have remarkable powers.

The extent to which our everyday thinking, feeling and acting operate outside conscious awareness is difficult for people to appreciate and accept, report psychologists John Bargh and Tanya Chartrand.[4] Our consciousness is biased to think that its own intentions and deliberate choices rule our lives; but consciousness over-rates its own control.

The automaticity of everyday living

We can recognize 'the automaticity of everyday living' (to use a Bargh–Chartrand phrase). Just compare our effortful control when first learning to drive, with total concentration, with our now well-practised intuitive driving skill. While our mind is making plans or engaging in conversation, our hands and feet, as if managed by an unseen mind inside our mind, will take us where we need to go. Or consider simple speech. Most of us could easily explain to a non-English speaker how we form the words 'dad' (with the tongue) and 'pad' (with the lips); but how would we teach the difference between 'pad' and 'bad'? Most of us cannot explain the difference. However, intuitively our mouths know. Moreover, strings of words effortlessly spill out our mouths with near-perfect syntax. It is as if there were servants upstairs, busily hammering together sentences that get piped down to the mouth and larynx and fluidly shoved out.

Even as these words spill onto my computer screen, my fingers gallop across the keyboard under instructions from . . . somewhere. If a person enters my office while I am typing, the cognitive servants running my fingers will finish the sentence while I start up a conversation. We have, it seems, two minds: one for momentary awareness and executive decisions, the other for everything else.

Reading thin slices

Do you ever, after but a moment's observing someone, form a lasting impression from their animation, gestures and voice? Such 'thin slices' of someone's behaviour can reveal much, report Nalini Ambady and Robert Rosenthal.[5] They invited people to view three thin slices—mere 10-s clips—of college professors' teaching, and from nothing more than this to rate the professors' confidence, energy and warmth. With remarkable accuracy, these ratings predicted end-of-term ratings by the professors' students. Thinner slices—three 2-s clips—yielded ratings that were similarly congruent with student evaluations. To form a reasonable accurate sense of someone's personality, 6 s will often do.

Even micro-thin slices tell us something. When John Bargh flashed an image of an object or face for just two-tenths of a second, his New York University students evaluated it instantly.[6] 'We're finding that everything is evaluated as good or bad within a quarter second', he reports. Before engaging in any rational thought, we may find ourselves mildly loathing or loving a portrait, a person or a poodle.

There is biological wisdom to this express link between perception and response. When meeting a stranger in the wilderness, one needed to decide instantly: friend or foe? Those who could read a person quickly and accurately were more likely to survive and leave descendants. That helps explain why we today can distinguish at a glance between facial expressions of anger, sadness, fear and pleasure.

Indeed, thanks to emotional pathways that run from the eye to the brain's emotional control centres—bypassing the cortex—we often react emotionally before we have had time to interpret the situation consciously. Below the radar of our awareness, we intuitively process threatening information in milliseconds. Then, after the cortex has had time to interpret the threat, the thinking brain asserts itself. In the forest, we jump at the sound of a cracking twig, leaving the cortex to decide later whether the sound came from the wind, a squirrel or a predator.

Clearly, human intelligence is more than logic and comprehension is more than conscious awareness. Cognitive psychologist George Miller offers a metaphor for this truth: 'There sure is a lot of water in the ocean', said one ship passenger to another. 'Yes' said the other, 'and we've only seen the top of it'.[7]

Gender and intuition

Shortly after Jackie Larsen left her Minnesota church group one April morning, she encountered Christopher Bono, a clean-cut, well-mannered youth whose car had broken down. Larsen invited him to use her shop telephone to call for assistance. When he later appeared, she felt a stomach pain. Sensing that something was wrong, she insisted they talk outside. 'I can tell by your manners that you have a nice mother', she explained. 'I don't know where my mother is', Bono replied.

Larsen directed Bono back to the church, then called the police and suggested they trace his licence plate. Discovering the car registered to his mother, Lucia Bono, who lived several hundred miles away, they sent local police to her apartment. There they discovered her dead in the bathtub. Bono, 16, was charged with first-degree murder.

Does Jackie Larsen's accurate intuition that something was awry illustrate what so many believe—that women have superior intuition? When surveyed, women are far more likely than men to describe themselves as empathic, as being able to feel what another feels. To a lesser extent, the self-reported empathy gap extends to behaviour. Women, for example, are more likely to cry or report distress at another's distress. This empathy gap helps explain why both genders report that their friendships with women are more intimate, enjoyable and nurturing than are their friendships with men. When seeking understanding, both men and women usually turn to women.

Underlying the empathy gap is women's seemingly superior skill at reading others' emotions. In an analysis of 125 studies of social sensitivity, Judith Hall discerned that women generally surpass men at decoding emotional messages.[8] When shown a silent, 2-s film clip of an upset woman, women more often than men accurately guess that she is discussing her divorce rather than criticizing someone. Women's non-verbal sensitivity also gives them an edge in spotting lies, and in discerning whether a male–female couple is genuinely romantic or a posed, phony couple.

The gender intuition gap often gets overstated. 'Activating intuition always starts with a shift into softness and silence', suggests Penny Peirce in *Intuition* magazine; it tunes down 'the linear, left-brained masculine mind'. Actually, some men are more empathic and sensitive than the average woman. Even so, the modest but apparently real gender difference is celebrated by some feminist scholars as one of 'women's ways of knowing'. Women more often base knowledge on intuitive and personal grounds. Slightly more than half of the intuition books in Table 11.1 are written by females. In contrast, among books in the 'science and the paranormal' section of a recent Prometheus books catalogue— all offering a rational, sceptical perspective—I counted 110 male and but four female authors.

Psychologists debate whether the intuition gap is truly intrinsic to gender. Whatever the reason, Western tradition has historically viewed rational thinking as masculine and intuition as feminine, notes feminist historian Evelyn Fox Keller. Women's ways of knowing give greater latitude to subjective knowledge, argues Mary Field Belinky. She contends that women winnow competing ideas less through hostile scrutiny than by getting inside another's mind, and often by way of friendly conversation. On the popular Myers–Briggs personality test, nearly six in 10 men score as 'thinkers' (claiming to make decisions objectively using logic), while three in four women score as 'feelers' (claiming to make decisions subjectively based on what they feel is right).

Women and men are more alike than different. However, it is the small differences that capture our fascination, one of which is women's seeming somewhat more empathic and intuitively sensitive to non-verbal cues.

Intuitive expertise

As a mushrooming mountain of evidence plainly indicates, we have two minds—two ways of knowing, two kinds of memory, two levels of attitudes—one above the surface in our moment-to-moment awareness, the other below, operating the autopilot that guides us through most of life. We see the results of those unseen cognitive workers in the social intuitions they slip into our awareness, and also in our developing expertise and creative inspirations. Through experience, we gain practical intuition—subtle, complex, ineffable knowledge that aids our problem solving.

From your two eyes your brain receives slightly differing images of an object. In a microsecond, it analyses their difference and infers the object's distance. Even with a calculator at hand, your conscious mind would be hard pressed to make the same computation. No matter, your intuitive mind already knows. Indeed, we know much that is too complex for our conscious minds to understand.

What you know, but do not know you know, affects you more than you know. That is the bottom line of more than 300 experiments on our powers of unconscious learning (or 'non-conscious' learning, as the cognitive scientists often prefer to call it, lest their concept be confused with Freud's idea of a seething unconscious mind). The multitasking non-conscious mind is not just tending to housekeeping details, reveal experiments by Pawel Lewicki. No, the mind is quick, agile, perceptive, and surprisingly capable of 'detecting complex patterns of information'.[9]

An example: you know which of these two phrases sounds better—'a big, red barn' or 'a red, big barn'—but your conscious mind struggles to articulate the rule that you intuitively know. Likewise, say Lewicki et al., 'the seemingly simple act' of recognizing an object's shape and size and placing it 'in three-dimensional space requires a set of sophisticated geometrical transformations and calculations that go far beyond what most perceivers could articulate or even comprehend'.[10] Don't bother to ask chess masters to explain their next move, or poets where the image came from or lovers why they're in love. 'All they know is that they just do it'.

The Tulsa experiments reveal that people's non-conscious learning can anticipate patterns 'too complex and too confusing to be consciously noticed'. In one study, some students watched (others did not) as the numeral '6' jumped around a computer screen, from quadrant to quadrant. Although it seemed like a random order—no one consciously detected any rule—those who had seen the earlier presentations were quicker to find the next 6 when it was hidden among a screen full of numbers. Without knowing how they did it, their ability to track the number from one quadrant to another was improving. When the numbers' movement became truly random, their performance declined.

Lewicki repeated the experiment with his quick-witted psychology professor colleagues, who knew he was studying non-conscious learning. They, too, gained speed in locating the target's next position, and they too did not know why. When the experimenters switched to a random sequence and performance declined, the professors conjectured reasons for the decline (threatening subliminal messages, perhaps?). To students who had displayed unconscious learning, Lewicki even offered US$100 if they could uncover the hidden pattern. Some spent hours trying to decipher the sequence. None succeeded.

In 1998, World Checkers (draughts) Champion Ron 'Suki' King of Barbados set a new record by simultaneously playing 385 players in 3 h and 44 min. While his opponents often could leisurely plot their moves, King could devote only about 35 s to each game— barely more than a glance at the board for each move. Yet he still managed to win all 385 games.[11] How did he do it? How are car mechanics, physicians and swimming coaches (all of whom have been subjects of study) often able to diagnose problems instantly?

Compared with novices, experts know much more. In a classic study, William Chase and Herbert Simon found that chess experts, unlike the rest of us, could often reproduce a chess board layout after a mere 5 s glance.[12] Unlike a poor chess player who has few stored patterns in memory, a good player has 1000 and a chess master has roughly 50,000.[13] A chess master may also perceive the board in several chunks—clusters of positions they have seen before. A quick look at the board is therefore all it takes to recognize many layouts—unless the pieces are placed randomly, in which case the experts' memory becomes slightly *worse* than that of novices. Chess masters can therefore play by intuition at 5–10 s a move, without time for analysis of alternatives, and without much performance decline.

Physicians and mechanics likewise can often make intuitive diagnoses, as if thinking, 'This reminds me of symptoms I have seen before, when the problem was X'. The diagnosis is not dictated by logic—other ailments could produce the same symptoms. However, it is quick and usually right.

Even quicker and more astoundingly accurate are professional chicken sexers. Poultry owners once had to wait 5–6 weeks before the appearance of adult feathers enabled them to separate cockerels (males) from pullets (hens). Egg producers only wanted to buy and feed pullets, and were intrigued to hear that some Japanese had developed an uncanny ability to sex day-old chicks. Although even poultry farmers cannot tell male from female organs in a newborn chick, the Japanese experts could do it at a glance. Hatcheries elsewhere then gave some of their workers apprenticeships under the Japanese experts, by watching them do it and then beginning to sort on their own, with feedback on their accuracy. After months of training and ensuing experience, the best Americans and Australians could almost match the Japanese, by sexing 800–1000 chicks per hour (about one a second) with 99 per cent accuracy.[14] But don't ask them how they do it. The sex difference, as any chicken sexer can tell you, is too subtle to explain.

When experienced gourmet cooks say they 'just use experience and intuition' in mixing ingredients, they are stating 'the theory of expert performance that has emerged in recent years'. noted Simon. 'In everyday speech, we use the word *intuition* to describe a problem-solving or question-answering performance that is speedy and for which the expert is unable to describe in detail the reasoning or other process that produced the answer. The situation has provided a cue; this cue has given the expert access to information stored in memory, and the information provides the answer. Intuition is nothing more and nothing less than recognition'.[15] Although we do not know what they are sensing, chicken sexers are intuitively recognizing subtle indicators of sex.

Creativity builds upon intuitive expertise. The solution to many a stubborn scientific or mathematical problem, such as Andrew Wiles' solution of Fermat's Last Theorem, have appeared unbidden, like a website pop-up ad. Poets, novelists, composers and artists readily recognize intuition's role in creativity. 'You get your intuition back when you make space for it, when you stop the chattering of the rational mind', counsels writer Anne Lamott.[16]

So try to calm down, get quiet, breathe and listen. Squint at the screen in your head and, if you look, you will see what you are searching for, the details of the story, its direction—maybe not right this minute, but eventually. If you stop trying to control your mind so much, you will have intuitive hunches about what this or that character is all about. It is hard to stop controlling, but you can do it. If your character suddenly pulls a half-eaten carrot out of her pocket, let her. Later you can ask yourself if this rings true. Train yourself to hear that small inner voice.

The perils of intuition

Thanks to the three pounds of wet neural tissue folded and jammed into our skulls, we are the world's greatest wonder. With circuitry more complex than the planet's telephone networks, we process boundless information, consciously and unconsciously. Right now your visual system is disassembling the light striking your retina into millions of nerve impulses, distributing these for parallel processing, and then reassembling a clear and colourful image. From ink on the page to a perceived image to meaning, all in an instant.

Our species, give us credit, has had the genius to invent cell phones and harvest stem cells; to unlock the atom and crack and map our genetic code; to travel to the moon and tour the sunken Titanic. Not bad, considering that we share 90 per cent of our DNA with a cow. Just by living, we acquire intuitive expertise that makes most of life effort-less. Understandably, Shakespeare's Hamlet extolled us as 'noble in reason! ... infinite in faculties! ... in apprehension how like a god!' We are rightly called *Homo sapiens*—wise humans.

However, as Pascal taught 300 years ago, no single truth is ever sufficient, because the world is complex. Any truth, separated from its complementary truth, is a half-truth.

It is true that our intuitive information-processing powers are impressive for their efficiency, yet also true that they are prone to predictable errors and misjudgements. With remarkable ease, we form and sustain false beliefs. Just as understandably, T. S. Eliot called us 'the hollow men ... headpiece filled with straw.' We wise humans are sometimes fools.

In July 2002, a Russian airliner's computer guidance system instructed its pilot to ascend as another jet approached in the sky over Switzerland. At the same time, a Swiss air traffic controller—whose computerized air traffic system was down—offered a human judgement: descend. Faced with conflicting advice, the pilot's intuitive response was to trust another human's intuition. Tragically, the two planes collided, killing everyone onboard, including 45 children.

The history of science tells story after story of challenges to human intuition. To our ancestors, the sun's daily travels had at least two plausible explanations: either the sun was circling Earth, or Earth was spinning while the sun stood still. Intuition preferred the first explanation. Galileo's scientific observations demanded the second.

Psychology, too, is replete with compelling examples of how people fool themselves. Even the most intelligent people make predictable and costly intuitive errors; coaches, athletes, investors, interviewers, gamblers and psychics fall prey to well-documented illusory intuitions. It is shocking how vulnerable we are to forming false memories, misjudging reality and mispredicting our own behaviour. Our intuition errs.

In *Intuition: its powers and perils* I describe predictable flaws in people's intuitions about reality (including intuitions about elementary principles in physics and mathematics) and in people's intuitions about their own past and future and abilities. Here is but one example—a well-documented problem in our intuitive predictions of our own emotions.

Intuiting our future feelings

Many of life's big decisions require intuiting our future feelings. Would marrying this person lead to lifelong commitment? Would entering this profession make for enduring satisfaction? Would going on this vacation produce happy memories? Or would the more likely results be divorce, burnout and disappointment?

Sometimes our intuitions are on target. We know how we will feel if we fail that exam, win that big game or soothe our tensions with a 3 mile jog. Our intuitions more often fail in predicting an emotion's intensity and duration. In recent studies of 'affective forecasting', people have mispredicted the durability of their emotions after a romantic break up, losing an election, winning that game and being insulted.[17]

To introduce this 'durability bias', Harvard psychologist Daniel Gilbert and his colleagues invite us to 'Imagine that one morning your telephone rings and you find yourself speaking with the King of Sweden, who informs you in surprisingly good English that you have been selected as this year's recipient of a Nobel prize. How would you feel and how long would you feel that way?' Might you not expect a 'sharp and lasting upturn' in your well-being? Now imagine that the telephone call is from your college president, who regrets to inform you (in surprisingly good English) that the Board of Regents has dissolved your department, revoked your appointment, and stored your books in little cardboard boxes in the hallway. How would you feel and how long would you feel that way?' Most people facing this personal catastrophe, say Gilbert and his colleagues, would expect the emotional wounds to be enduring.

Such expectations are often wrong. Gilbert *et al.* offer examples:[18]

♦ When shown sexually arousing photos, then exposed to a passionate date scenario in which their date asks them to 'stop', many male youths admit that they might not stop. If not first aroused by the pictures, they more often deny the possibility of sexual aggression. When not aroused, one easily mispredicts how one will feel and act when sexually hot—a phenomenon that leads to professions of love during lust, to unintended pregnancies, and to repeat offences among sex abusers who have sincerely vowed 'never again'.

♦ Researchers have documented what obstetricians know—that women in labour sometimes reverse their stated preference for anaesthetic-free delivery.[19] When we mispredict intensity, pain as well as pleasure can hijack our intentions. As George MacDonald wrote in 1886, 'When a feeling was there, they felt as if it would never go; when it was gone, they felt as if it had never been; when it returned, they felt as if it had never gone'[20]

♦ Shoppers do more impulse buying when hungry than when shopping after dinner. When hungry, one mispredicts how gross those deep-fried doughnuts will seem when sated. When sated, one mispredicts how yummy a doughnut might be with a late-night glass of milk.

Our intuitive theory seems to be: we want. We get. We are happy. If that were true, this chapter would be shorter. In reality, note Gilbert and Timothy Wilson, we often 'miswant'. People who imagine an idyllic desert island holiday with sun, surf, and sand may be disappointed when they discover 'how much they require daily structure, intellectual stimulation, or regular infusions of Pop Tarts'. We think that if our candidate or team wins we will be delighted for a long time. However, study after study reveals that the emotional traces of good tidings evaporate more rapidly than we expect. Attention shifts, and in hours, days or weeks (depending on the extremity of the good or bad happening) the feelings subside and we recalibrate our ups and downs around the new reality.

It is after negative events that we are especially prone to durability bias—to mispredicting the durability of emotions. When people being tested for HIV predict how they will feel 5 weeks after getting the results, they expect to be feeling misery over bad news and elation over good news. Yet 5 weeks later, the bad news recipients are less distraught and the good news recipients less elated than they anticipated.[21] When Gilbert and his colleagues asked assistant professors to predict their happiness a few years after achieving tenure or not, most believed a favourable outcome was important for their future happiness.[22] 'Losing my job would crush my life's ambitions. It would be terrible'.

Yet when surveyed several years after the event, people who had been denied tenure were about as happy as those who had received it.

Let us make this personal. Gilbert and Wilson invite us to imagine how we might feel a year after losing our non-dominant hand. Compared with today, how happy would you be?

Thinking about this, you perhaps focused on what the calamity would mean: no clapping, no shoe tying, no golf, no speedy keyboarding. Although you probably would forever regret the loss, your general happiness some time after the tragedy would be influenced by 'two things: (1) the event; and (2) everything else'.[23] In focusing on the negative event, we discount the importance of everything else that matters, and so overpredict our enduring misery. 'Nothing that you focus on will make as much difference as you think', concur fellow researchers David Schkade and Daniel Kahneman.[24]

Moreover, say Gilbert and Wilson, people neglect the speed and power of their 'psychological immune system', which includes their strategies for rationalizing, discounting, forgiving and limiting trauma. Being largely ignorant of this emotional recovery system— this 'immune neglect', as they call it—we accommodate to disabilities, romantic break ups, exam failures, tenure denials, and personal and team defeats more readily than we would expect. 'Weeping may tarry for the night, but joy comes in the morning', reflected the Psalmist.[25] Ironically, Gilbert and his colleagues report, major negative events (which activate our psychological defences) can be less enduringly distressing than minor irritations (which do not activate our defences).[26] We are more resilient than we know.

Intuitively fearing the wrong things

For me the most fascinating chapters in my book *Intuition* are those exploring intuition's powers and perils in specific practical realms: sports intuitions, investors' intuitions, interviewers' intuitions, clinical intuition, gamblers' intuitions, psychic intuition and intuitions about risk. Here is a single example, drawn from our perilous intuitions about risk.

With 9/11 images etched on their memories and the media dramatizing orange-level warnings, travellers have had terrorists on their minds. 'I'm going Greyhound rather than fly to California', my Baltimore cousin explains. 'Al Qaeda's not so likely to target a bus'. Others, fearing the worst, have elected to drive rather than fly to that Florida vacation.

However, people's fears are often misaligned with the facts. The U.S. National Safety Council reports that from 2000 through 2002, Americans were, mile for mile, 39.5 times more likely to die in a vehicle crash than on a commercial flight.[27] Terrorists, perish the thought, could have taken down 50 more planes with 60 passengers each in 2001 and— had we kept flying (speaking hypothetically)—we would still have finished 2001 safer in planes than on the road.[28] If flying is scary (531 people died on US scheduled airlines in 2001, none in 2002), driving the same distance should be many times scarier.

In a late 2001 essay for the American Psychological Society, I calculated that if we now flew 20 per cent less and instead drove half those unflown miles, about 800 more people would die in traffic accidents in the next year. In a follow-up article in *Psychological Science*, German psychologist Gerd Gigerenzer[29] confirms that the last 3 months of 2001 indeed produced 350 more American traffic fatalities than normal for those months. Long after 9/11, the terrorists were still killing us in ways unnoticed.

Why do we intuitively fear the wrong things? Why do so many smokers (whose habit shortens their lives, on average, by about 5 years) fret before flying (which, averaged across people, shortens life by 1 day)? Why do we fear violent crime more than clogged arteries? Why do we fear terrorism more than accidents—which kill nearly as many per *week* in just the USA as did worldwide terrorism in all of the 1990s. Even with the horrific scale of 9/11, more Americans in 2001 died of food poisoning (which scares few) than terrorism (which scares many).

Psychological science has identified four influences on our intuitions about risk. First, we fear *what our ancestral history has prepared us to fear*—which includes confinement and heights, and therefore flying.

Secondly, we fear *what we cannot control*. Driving we control, flying we do not. 'We are loathe to let others do unto us what we happily do to ourselves', noted risk analyst Chauncey Starr.[30]

Thirdly, we fear *what is immediate*. Teens are indifferent to smoking's toxicity because they live more for the present than the distant future. Likewise, the dangers of driving are diffused across many moments to come, each trivially dangerous.

Fourthly, we fear *what is most readily available in memory*. Horrific images of United Flight 175 slicing into the World Trade Center form indelible memories; and availability in memory provides our intuitive rule for judging risks. Thousands of safe car trips (for those who have survived to read this) have largely extinguished our anxieties about driving. A thousand massively publicized anthrax victims would similarly rivet our attention more than yet another 30 000+ annual gun deaths. If a surface to air missile brings down a single American commercial airliner, the result will be traumatic for the aviation industry. Probabilities will not matter—the human mind has trouble grasping the infinitesimal odds of its being a plane you will be on. Images will rule the mind.

We therefore fear too little those threats that will claim lives undramatically, one by one (rather than in bunches). Smoking kills 400 000 Americans a year, yet we subsidize tobacco growers. Although killing many fewer, terrorists kill in ways that cause more terror; and as George Orwell's *1984* long ago recognized, it serves those in power to keep our attention focused on perceived external threats. Many a social psychology experiment confirms the principle: a perceived external enemy serves to quell dissent and unify a group.

Ergo, we will spend tens of billions to save future thousands, yet are reluctant to spend a few billion to save millions. Ten billion dollars a year would spare 29 million world citizens from developing AIDS by 2010, according to a joint report by representatives of the United Nations, the World Health Organization and others. Also, a few tens of billions spent converting cars to hybrid engines and constructing renewable energy sources could help avert the anticipated future catastrophe of global warming and its associated surging seas and extreme weather. In 2003, reports the World Meteorological Organization, Western Europe experienced its hottest weather ever, with 14 802 heat-related deaths in France alone. May of 2004, the warmest May in world history, brought the USA 562 tornados, easily breaking the previous monthly record of 399. Without making too much of one year's extreme weather, climatologists warn us that global warming will be a genuine weapon of mass destruction.

The moral: it is perfectly normal to fear purposeful violence from those who hate us. When terrorists strike again, we will all recoil in horror. However, smart thinkers will also want to check their intuitive fears against the facts, and to resist politicians who serve their own purposes by cultivating a culture of fear. To be prudent is to be mindful of the realities of how humans die. By so doing, we can take away the terrorists' most omnipresent weapon: exaggerated fear. If our fears cause us to live and spend in ways that divert our attention from tomorrow's biggest dangers, then we surely do have something to fear from fear itself.

Conclusion

Intuition is bigger than we realize. Intuition feeds our automatic behaviours, our creativity and our spirituality. Intuition is a wonder. But intuition is also perilous. Today's cognitive science aims not to destroy intuition but to fortify it, to sharpen our thinking and deepen our wisdom. Scientists who expose intuition's flaws note that it works well in some areas, but needs restraints and checks in others. In realms from sports to business to risk assessment, we now understand how perilous intuitions often go before a fall, and how we can therefore think smarter, even while listening to the creative whispers of our vast unseen mind.

References and notes

1. Diana: quoted by Roger Cohen, Collision course: how Diana's life ended. *New York Times*, September 6, 1997 (www.nytimes.com).
2. George Bush: quoted by Bob Woodward, *Bush at war*. Simon & Schuster, New York. 2002.
3. Prince Charles: Reith Lecture. http://news.bbc.co.uk/hi/english/static/events/reith_2000/lecture6.stm.
4. **John AB, Tanya L.** Chartrand: 'the unbearable automaticity of being'. *American Psychologist*, 1999; 54:462–479.
5. **Nalini A, Robert R.** Thin slices of expressive behavior as predictors of interpersonal consequences: a meta-analysis. *Psychological Bulletin*, 1992; 111:256–274. Half a minute: predicting teacher evaluations from thin slices of nonverbal behavior and physical attractiveness. *Journal of Personality and Social Psychology*, 1993; 64:431–441. See also JA Hall, F Bernieri, ed. *Interpersonal sensitivity: theory and measurement*. Erlbaum. Mahwah, NJ. 2002.
6. **John Bargh:** quoted by Bath Azar, split-second evaluations shape our moods, actions. *Monitor*. American Psychological Association. 1998:13.
7. **George AM.** *Psychology: the science of mental life*. Harper & Row, New York. 1962.
8. **Hall JA.** *Nonverbal sex differences: communication accuracy and expressive style*. Johns Hopkins University Press, Baltimore, MD. 1984.

9. Detecting complex patterns: Lewicki P. Conclusions of the research on nonconscious information processing (a quick 'non-technical' summary). www.personal.utulsa.edu/~pawel-lewicki/simple.html.

10. Recognizing a shape: Lewicki P, Hill T, Czyzewska M. Nonconscious acquisition of information. *American Psychologist*, 1992; **47**:796–801. A synopsis and citations of Lewicki's other research can be found here.

11. Ron 'Suki' King: Hamill D. Checkers king crowned. *Games*, 1998:6.

12. **William GC, Herbert AS.** Perception in chess. *Cognitive Psychology*, 1973; **4**:55–81. Also, Herbert AS, William GC. Skill in chess. *American Scientist*, 1973; **6**:394–403.

13. 5000 chess patterns: Jean B, Michelene THC. Expertise. *Current Directions in Psychological Science*, 1992; **1**:135–139.

14. Chicken sexers: Dreyfus HL, Stuart ED. *Mind over machine: the power of human intuition and expertise in the era of the computer.* Free Press, New York. 1986:196–197, and Gazza's Poultry Page, 'Chicken Sexing' www3.turboweb.net.au/~garrys/poultry/chickensexing.html.

15. **Herbert AS.** What is an 'explanation' of behavior? *Psychological Science*, 1992; **3**:150–161.

16. **Anne L.** *Bird by bird: some instructions on writing and life.* Anchor Books/Random House, New York, 1994:112–113.

17. Mispredicted: Gilbert DT, Jenkins JE. Decisions and revisions: the affective forecasting of changeable outcomes. *Journal of Personality and Social Psychology*, 2002; **82**:503–513.

18. Examples: Loewenstein G, Schkade D. Wouldn't it be nice? predicting future feelings. In D Kahneman, E Diener, N Schwarz, ed. *Understanding well-being: scientific perspectives on enjoyment and suffering.* Russell Sage Foundation, New York. 1999:85–105; Gilbert DT, Wilson TD. Miswanting: some problems in the forecasting of future affective states. In J Forgas, ed. *Feeling and thinking: the role of affect in social cognition.* Cambridge University Press, Cambridge. 2000; Wilson TD, Wheatley TP, Meyers JM, Gilbert DT, Axsom D. Focalism: a source of durability bias in affective forecasting. *Journal of Personality and Social Psychology*, 2000; **73**:821–836.

19. Women in labor: Christensen-Szalanski JJ. Discount functions and the measurement of patients' values: women's decisions during child birth. *Medical Decision Making*, 1984; **4**:47–58.

20. **MacDonald G.** *What's mine's mine.* 1886.

21. HIV patients: Sieff EM, Dawes RM, Loewenstein GF. Anticipated versus actual responses to HIV test results. *American Journal of Psychology*, 1999; **112**:297–311.

22. Assistant professors: Gilbert DT, Pinel EC, Wilson TD, Blumberg SJ, Wheatley TP. Immune neglect: a source of durability bias in affective forecasting. *Journal of Personality and Social Psychology* 1998; **75**:617–638.

23. Two things: Gilbert DT, Wilson TD. Miswanting: some problems in the forecasting of future affective states. In J Forgas, ed. *Feeling and thinking: the role of affect in social cognition* Cambridge University Press, Cambridge. 2000.

24. **Schkade DA, Kahneman D.** Does living in California make people happy? a focusing illusion in judgments of life satisfaction. *Psychological Science*, 1990; **9**:340–346.

25. Psalmist: Psalm 30:5.

26. Minor irritations: Gilbert DT, Lieberman MD, Morewedge CK, Wilson TD. The peculiar longevity of things not so bad. *Psychological Science* 2004; **15**:14–19.

27. Commercial flight: Fearn KT. Personal correspondence from the National Safety Council's Research and Statistics Department, October 3, 2005.

28. Safer in planes: Myers DG, For calculation see www.davidmyers.org/Brix?pageID=65.

29. **Gigerenzer G.** Dread risk, September 11, and fatal traffic accidents. *Psychological Science*, 2004; **15**:286–287.

30. **Starr C.** Social benefit versus technological risk. *Science* 1969; **165**:1232–1238.

Chapter 12

Creative thinking: the mystery myth

Ken Gilhooly

Introduction

There is a widespread myth that creative thinking is intrinsically mysterious, inexplicable and not open to empirical study. In contrast, psychologists generally hold to the belief that creative processes are explicable and are composed of similar ingredients to those entering into less exalted forms of thinking. It is the working assumption of the cognitive psychology of creative thinking that creative products result from many small information-processing steps carried out by limited capacity cognitive systems that suffer from all the normal limitations of cramped working memory and imperfect retrieval from long-term memory; supernatural interventions in the form of 'daemons' or 'divine sparks' are ruled out.

Matters of definition loom quite large in this area, and so before discussing creative processes, it is necessary briefly to consider what is meant by the term 'creative' and its associate 'creativity'. It is perhaps easiest to start by defining creative products. Creative products, whether they are poems, scientific theories, paintings or technological advances, are both novel and acknowledged to be valuable or useful in some way. Whether a product is novel or not is relatively easy to determine, although an element of judgement does enter, in that some products are more obviously derived from previous developments than others. Objective measurement of novelty is possible in laboratory settings, since the same task can be given to a large number of people (e.g. 'think of ways of improving a doorknob'), and the degree of novelty of proposed solutions can be readily assessed by counting their frequencies of occurrence. In real life, however, only the 'creator' may be working on a given self-set problem and so frequency of production is not always available as a criterion. When we turn to the quality of a product, subjective judgement looms still larger than in the case of judging novelty. In science and technology, the criteria for quality are clearer than in the arts. A new theory or gadget can be seen to 'work' if it covers more phenomena with no more assumptions than its predecessors (e.g. Einstein's theory compared with Newton's) or meets the function for which it was devised (e.g. the first telephone). Notoriously, there is usually less agreement about the merits of artistic productions, both at the time of their emergence and over history. Initial reactions may well be negative to artistic products that either depart too far from established styles or, at the other extreme, are too conventional. Later generations are more likely to appreciate the boldness of developments that their ancestors decried as 'insane', e.g. Surrealism, Cubism, Expressionism, etc.

It may also be suggested here, that judgements of 'novelty' or 'unusualness' will presumably relate to the degree to which the product can be fitted into an established style (in the arts) or 'paradigm' (in the sciences). Highly creative products signal and exemplify a new style or paradigm.[1,2] Subsequent work within a given style or paradigm would generally be regarded as less creative than the initial style-defining work.

The above comments should serve to indicate what is meant here by a creative product. What of 'creativity'? 'Creativity' is an attribute ascribed to those individuals who show a long-term tendency to generate novel products that are also influential.[3] With a few extremely rare exceptions (such as Leonardo Da Vinci), most 'creatives' display their valued characteristic within a particular speciality—but within that speciality they are marked for their combination of productivity (e.g. Picasso) and high quality of work (as indexed by its influence). Of course, in real life, for someone to be acknowledged as displaying 'creativity' involves social processes, as well as purely within-individual cognitive processes. To become known, creative individuals must 'promote' their products and convince enough others who control the communication media that these products should be presented to a larger audience.[4,5] Given that wider presentation, further social processes leading to widespread acceptance and influence, or to apathy or rejection can begin. A similar point is made by Simonton[6] who argues that creativity is a form of leadership in that it entails personal influence over others. Just as a leader must have followers to be classed as a leader, so a creator must have appreciators to be classed as an effective creator. It has been suggested that instead of asking '*What* is creativity?' one should ask '*Where* is creativity?'.[7] It is proposed that creativity emerges out of a three-way process between an individual, his or her domain of work and the audience of knowledgeable peers and judges. This chapter, however, will focus on within-individual cognitive processes which are essential in any creative work.

In the rest of this chapter, I will discuss some of the main approaches and findings that have arisen in the study of creative processes. First, I will outline the individual differences approach, which considers in what ways individuals acknowledged to be creative might differ in cognitive, personality or biographical characteristics from others. Secondly, there is the approach via personal accounts by artists and scientists of how the process seemed to them, and this leads on to stage models for creative thinking based on personal accounts. Next, we turn to laboratory-based approaches that have examined ways of stimulating idea production. Finally, there will be a discussion of theoretical approaches and a brief summing up.

Studies of creative individuals

It may be that highly creative individuals differ from less creative people because of personality or biographical characteristics. A number of early studies were made of people acknowledged to be creative, (e.g. Roe's[8] study of scientists, MacKinnon[9] on architects, and Barron[10] on writers and artists). These studies were aimed at uncovering any common background or personality characteristics of these unusual groups of people.

In one of the earliest investigations of its kind, Ann Roe[8] studied 64 American scientists who had been rated as eminent in their fields by expert panels. The 64 were roughly evenly split amongst physicists, biologists and social scientists. Each individual was subjected to long interviews, projective personality tests (TAT and Rorschach) and a conventional intelligence test. On the basis of this investigation, Roe gave the following composite picture of the average eminent scientist in the 1950s. The average eminent scientist was a first-born son in a middle-class Protestant family, with a professional man as a father. He was likely to have often been ill in childhood or to have lost a parent early. He had a very high IQ and began reading avidly at an early age. He felt 'lonely' and different from his school mates, did not have much interest in girls and married late (27 years old on average). He usually decided on his career as a professional scientist as a result of a student project involving individual research. He worked hard and persistently, very often 7 days a week with few holidays.

Similar evidence on personality characteristics of creative people was gathered by Cattell and his colleagues. Before actually testing any 'live' scientists, Cattell[11] scanned the biographies of many famous scientists and noted that the typical eminent scientists seemed to be introverted and stable. Although introverted, they were generally independent and self-sufficient. They also tended to be solemn or restrained and rather dominant in personal relationships.

Cattell and Drevdahl[12] selected groups of about 45 eminent researchers in physics, biology and psychology and asked them to complete the 16 Personality Factors (16 PF) test. Compared with the general population, the eminent researchers were more introverted, intelligent, dominant and inhibited; they were also more sensitive emotionally and more radical. These findings are in line with the suggestion of biographies and with the results of Roe's investigation.

Also of interest is Mitroff's[13] study of scientists engaged in the analysis of lunar samples as part of the Apollo moon project. Mitroff noted a strong tendency toward a style of thinking often labelled 'convergent'.[14] Any open-ended question put to the scientists would be quickly transformed into a narrower, more tightly defined one. This tendency fits in with Hudson's[14] finding that those boys who performed better on convergent (one answer) test questions than on divergent items (multiple possible answers) tended to specialize in science subjects. It was also noted that the lunar scientists strongly identified with the traditionally conceived 'masculine' characteristics. They believed in hard work, dedication and striving, and did not disapprove of a touch of ruthlessness. Intriguingly, and contrary to earlier reports, Mitroff found evidence in his interviews of strongly aggressive tendencies. In discussing other scientists and rival groups, the desire to win glory at the expense of others and a fear of their rivals' overaggressive tactics (e.g. idea stealing) were evident. Aggressiveness was also clear in their attitude to promoting their own ideas. As one scientist remarked, 'if you want to get anybody to believe your hypothesis, you've got to beat them down with numbers: you've got to hit them again and again over the head with hard data until they're stupefied into believing it'[13] (p. 144). Mitroff suggested that the scientists were somewhat one-sided in emotional expression and he found that they were far less free in displaying softer emotions as against harsh or aggressive ones. The notion that science is an aggressive activity was also expressed in Freud's self description. He wrote '... I am not really a man of science, not an observer, not an experimenter, and not a thinker. I am nothing but by temperament a conquistador—an adventurer, ... with the curiosity, the boldness, and the tenacity that belong to that type of being'[15] (p. 227).

A study of artists and writers[16] using Cattell's 16 PF test yielded a profile rather similar to that of the scientists.[12] The artistic group were more emotionally sensitive than the scientists and exhibited more inner tension—but were otherwise similar.

Readers may well have come across John Dryden's famous lines from his eighteenth century poem *Absalom and Achitopel* (Pt I. 156)—'Great wits are sure to madness near allied/And thin partitions do their bounds divide'—and some recent studies do indeed suggest a dark side of artistic creativity that manifests in a higher incidence than normal of manic-depressive and depressive pathology.[17-21] Jamison reviews seven studies of acknowledged creative writers and artists, which have found rates of depression 8–10 times, of manic-depression 10–20 times and of suicide up to 18 times those of the general population. These studies have included both living and dead artists and writers. In the case of dead artists and writers, pathology was inferred from their biographies or from records of their medical treatment while alive. Although the association should not be overinterpreted—not all artists and writers display pathology and not all sufferers from depression/manic-depression are highly creative—nonetheless a statistical association is present. Could such mood disorders conceivably assist in artistic work? Mania, and especially its mild form, hypomania, do have features that could be conducive to creative thinking. Indeed, one of the diagnostic criteria for hypomania is 'sharpened and unusually creative thinking and increased productivity'. Hypomanic subjects tend to use rhyme, other sound associations and unusual words in their speech and are markedly faster at giving synonyms and word associations than normals. The condition then seems to involve a speeding of thought and a tendency to use uncommon associations and ideas. These tendencies could well be helpful in creatively bringing together unusual combinations of ideas. During manic periods, the person tends to be extremely confident and filled with energy, which would also facilitate the completion of creative work. While little overt progress is normally made during periods of pathological depression, it is conceivable that experience of such states gives a broader range of contrasting experiences to draw on in normal periods than would be otherwise available. An alternative interpretation of the relationship between manic-depression and creativity has been advanced by Shapiro and Weisberg[22] who argued that marked mood swings may be a normal by-product of creative work. Progress in creative work could lead to highly positive affective states, while lack of progress or criticism could lead to negative affective states.

Links between productivity and mood states have been found in studies of individual artists. In a study of the composer Robert Schumann, Weisberg[23] found that the quantity and quality of Schumann's compositions per year were correlated with the composer's changes of mood on the basis of his diaries and letters and the recollections of his contemporaries. Similar results were also found in studies of the productivity and affective states of the writers Emily Dickinson and Nicolai Gogol.[24,25]

Some interesting points emerged from a study of the ages at which creative accomplishments tend to occur. Data gathered by Lehman[26,27] revealed that in many fields the most highly regarded contributions were produced between 30 and 40 years of age. The average age was younger in some subjects, e.g. in chemistry it was at 25–30 years, and older in others, such as painting, psychology, philosophy, novel writing and architecture. Although these age trends were detectable, it should be noted that good work was evident in all fields at a very wide range of ages. The 32-year-old chemist is not necessarily 'finished' as far as creative work is concerned. The declines from peak productivity tend to be gradual and to remain well above initial levels, even late in life.[28] Precociously early achievement in a number of fields has been found to have an unfortunate link with early death[29,30] which may reflect an association of 'Type A' personalities with both achievement motivation and premature death.

The differences between fields in ages of peak achievement seem to reflect an advantage of youth for relatively abstract and well-defined fields and an advantage for age in more concrete and less well-defined fields. It may be noted that peak ages of creative production can change over historical periods. Galenson and Weinberg[31] report an analysis of peak ages of creative work by American artists in the twentieth century and found that the peak ages of creative production were markedly younger for artists born between 1921 and 1940 than for those born in 1900–1920. The explanation seems to be a shift in the art market after around 1960 to favour conceptual innovation in art over the slower process of developing expressive techniques, and this change favoured younger artists.

Personal accounts of creative problem solving—stages and incubation

Many scientists and artists have provided accounts of their experiences in creatively solving complex problems (see, for example, Ghiselin,[32] Koestler[33] or Vernon[34]). These personal accounts are of interest for evidence they contain about features common to the creative process in a wide range of difficult tasks. Fairly consistent patterns do seem to emerge, and these patterns have served as the bases for various analyses into stages of both creative thinking and more routine problem solving. It is interesting to note that some well-known thinkers have disclaimed any ability to tell us how they solved problems or thought creatively. For example, Bertrand Russell was once asked to contribute to a book on how to think clearly. He replied that he could not help because, for him, thinking was instinctive, like digestion. He said that he simply filled up with relevant information, went about his business, doing other things and later, with time and good luck, he found that the work had been done. Perhaps Russell was too modest on this occasion. His brief account broadly matches those of others who have tried to be more detailed. It is only possible to consider a small number of these more detailed reports here, and I have selected two typical accounts given by Poincaré and Helmholtz.

Poincaré's account

Henri Poincaré was a prominent French mathematician of the nineteenth century. He reported[35] once struggling for a long time to prove a certain theorem without getting any results. One evening he drank black coffee before going to bed and it seemed to him that ideas of possible ways of solving the problem combined and recombined in one way after another before he finally got to sleep. In the morning, he clearly saw how the problem was to be solved, and after 2 h had completed the detailed proof. The solution to the initial problem raised further problems and Poincaré noted that these problems were solved as a result of ideas that occurred while he was not actively engaged on them, e.g. while riding in a bus, walking along a street or beach.

Helmholtz's account

The nineteenth century scientist Herman Helmholtz who contributed to physics, neurology and psychology, volunteered the following report of his problem-solving experience in a speech made at a dinner in honour of his seventieth birthday in 1896[36] (p. 838).

> So far as my experience goes, 'happy thoughts' never came to a fatigued brain and never at the writing desk. It was always necessary, first of all, that I should have turned my problem over on all sides to such an extent that I had all its angles and complexities 'in my head' and could run through them freely without writing. To bring the matter to that point is usually impossible without long preliminary labour. Then, after the fatigue resulting from this labour had passed away, there must come an hour of complete physical freshness and quiet well being, before the good ideas arrived. Often they were there in the morning when I awoke, just according to Goethe's oft cited verses, and as Gauss also once noted. But they especially liked to make their appearance while I was taking an easy walk over wooded hills in sunny weather.

On the basis of reports such as those of Poincaré, Helmholtz and others, and on the basis of his own experiences as a university teacher, administrator and writer, Graham Wallas[37] proposed a four-stage analysis of creative problem solving in a book entitled *The art of thought*. In this book, Wallas was concerned with the natural course of thought and with how thinking might be made more effective. So, in addition to proposing certain typical stages, he also offered advice on how these stages could be made more fruitful. The stages extracted by Wallas were as follows.

1. *Preparation.* In this stage, the problem solver familiarizes himself with his problem and engages in conscious, effortful, systematic and usually fruitless work on the problem. Although this stage may well not lead to a solution in itself, it is widely believed to be very important in influencing the likelihood that the next stage will result in a useful idea. Much personal testimony indicates that inspiration will not be forthcoming without this preliminary labour or, as Edison, the prolific inventor, is reported to have said, 'No inspiration without perspiration'.

2. *Incubation.* This is a period during which the task is set aside. No conscious work is done on the problem during this stage. Poincaré and others have hypothesized that unconscious work is carried out during this phase. On the other hand, it may be that this is simply a necessary rest period which enables a later period of conscious work to proceed more effectively than it would have without the break. Wallas suggested that this phase could be made more or less effective, depending on the intervening activity. Light work on minor problems or duties could be beneficial. Better still he thought, was complete mental rest, coupled with mild exercise. He felt that the habit of filling every spare minute with reading was especially detrimental.

3. *Illumination or inspiration.* This is the point when a fruitful idea, or 'happy thought' in Helmholtz's phrase, occurs to us. The inspiration is not usually a complete solution to the problem but points in the direction in which the complete solution may be found.

4. *Verification.* This stage is much like preparation, in that conscious work must be done in order to develop and test the inspiration.

These four stages are visible in the personal reports of Helmholtz, Poincaré and others.

The incubation stage suggests a low effort way to reach creative solutions when conscious work has reached an 'impasse'.[38] Most people would probably endorse the reality of incubation from their own experience, and the basic effect has been demonstrated in a number of laboratory-based studies. A recent review by Dodds *et al.*[39] identified 39 relevant experiments in the literature since 1938 of which 26 (about 75 per cent) successfully demonstrated incubation effects. An example study will now be outlined.

Murray and Denny[40] investigated the effects of giving an incubation opportunity to subjects of high and low problem-solving ability. Subjects were divided into high and low ability on the basis of the Gestalt Transformation Test. This test requires the selection of objects for unusual uses, e.g. 'From which object could you make a hose: a tree, cigarette, shirt, bicycle, eye glasses?' Subjects were also divided into control and experimental groups. Both were given a rather complicated problem devised by Saugstad, in which the subject is given a nail, pliers, a length of string, a pulley, some elastic bands and several newspapers.

Eight feet from the subject was a glass containing metal balls and standing on a movable frame. Next to the glass was a steel cylinder. The subject had to find a way of transferring the steel balls from the glass to the cylinder without going nearer than 8 ft to the glass or the cylinder.

The solution involves two stages. First, bend the nail into a hook, attach the hook to the string and throw it into the frame. The frame can then be dragged back to the line and the balls removed. The second stage is to construct a long hollow tube by rolling up the newspapers and connecting them telescope fashion by elastic bands, and then roll the balls down the tube to the steel cylinder.

Control subjects were given 20 min continuously to solve the problem, while the experimental subjects worked 5 min on the task, then had 5 min on an unrelated pencil and paper task. They were then given a further 15 min on the main task.

Neither incubation nor ability level significantly affected the frequency of solutions—but there was a significant interaction in that high ability solvers were hindered by incubation opportunity while low ability solvers were aided by an incubation opportunity. Murray and Denny interpreted these results by suggesting that low ability subjects quickly became fixated, and incubation allowed their inappropriate sets to die out, while the high ability subjects may have been working more systematically through various possibilities, without fixation, but this orderly process was disrupted by an incubation opportunity. Murray and Denny suggest, then, that incubation will be most effective when the problem is very difficult for the solver—as for their low ability subjects tackling the tube and balls problem and, presumably, for famous scientists and artists tackling major problems and projects.

Given that incubation opportunities are sometimes useful, how might any benefits be brought about? Three main ideas that have been put forward, are those of (1) *unconscious work*, (2) *the decay of inappropriate sets* and (3) *spreading activation during incubation*.

Poincaré[35] provided a graphic attempt at describing possible unconscious work during incubation periods. He proposed that the course of unconscious activity would be influenced by prior preparation or conscious work. Imagine ideas to be like hooked atoms, then Poincaré suggests that conscious work selects certain atoms/ideas as relevant to the problem and tries to organize them to reach a solution. When the problem is put aside, the atoms continue to move about hooking up with each other and with other atoms not activated during conscious work. Eventually, a solution combination may be reached—but it will generally involve at least one of the atoms/ideas which were selected during conscious work. In contrast, Woodworth and Schlosberg[36] suggested that incubation simply involves a decay in misleading tendencies that interfere with problem solution. Consistent with the decay of misleading tendencies or sets view, Smith and Blankenship[41] were able to demonstrate benefits from an incubation period in people solving verbal problems to which they had initially been given misleading cues. Presumably the disruptive effects of misleading cues had decayed over time. The spreading activation approach[42–44] proposes that when an unsuccessful attempt is made at a problem, activation spreads from information activated by the problem statement and eventually may weakly activate or 'prime' solution-relevant information in long-term memory. If a hint or relevant accidental cue arises in the environment, then the weakly activated solution information may be activated above threshold and an 'insight' will be experienced. Seabrook and Dienes[45] found some support for the spreading activation hypothesis in that a change of context including relevant cues following an incubation period benefited participants solving anagrams more than the relevant context alone without an incubation period. Further recent support for this idea has come from a study of children's problem solving by Howe et al.[46] in which it was found that prior group attempts to understand conceptual problems regarding why some objects float and some do not primed later use of relevant cues to understanding.

Increasing idea production

Are there any ways of increasing the production of novel ideas? Although numerous proposals have been put forward for stimulating the idea production stage of creative thinking, probably the most famous, and certainly the most researched, method is that known as 'brainstorming'.

Brainstorming

In the 1940s and 1950s, a practical businessman, Alex Osborn, developed a package of recommendations known as the brainstorming method. This was intended mainly for use in group problem solving and as a means of increasing idea production. The method can be adapted for individual use and is described in Osborn's[47] book *Applied imagination*. Brainstorming has been taken up quite widely in a variety of organizations and has also been extensively investigated in laboratory settings.

Osborn adopts the standard view that problem solving and creative thinking involve (1) problem formulation, (2) idea finding and (3) evaluation of ideas to find a likely solution. Brainstorming aims at facilitating the middle, idea-finding, stage and it can be summarized as involving two main principles and four rules.

Principles

1. Deferment of judgement.
2. Quantity breeds quality.

Rules

1. Criticism is ruled out.
2. Free wheeling is welcomed.
3. Quantity wanted.
4. Combination and improvement sought.

The 'Deferment of judgement' principle meant that evaluation of ideas was to be postponed until a set period of idea production had elapsed. The untutored thinker will tend to evaluate each idea as it is produced. Osborn suggests that this can be inhibiting and may lead to premature abandonment of ideas that, although not useful in themselves, may lead on to possible solutions. The 'Quantity breeds quality' principle states that the more ideas produced the larger the absolute number of useful ones there are likely to be, even if the proportion is very low. The rules listed above remind 'brainstormers' not to criticize their own ideas or those of others, to free associate to ideas already produced, to aim for quantity and to combine and improve already generated suggestions.

The method was originally devised for group use but can be adapted for individual applications. A number of questions arise, e.g. does the method lead to better productivity

(1) for groups and (2) for individuals? Does group brainstorming lead to better results than would be obtained by pooling the ideas produced by the appropriate number of individual brainstormers?

Numerous studies support the hypothesis that groups using brainstorming produce more ideas than similar groups working along conventional lines. Brainstorming instructions strongly affect the quality of ideas produced and, although effects on average quality are not so evident, reports of more high quality ideas have been obtained (as would be expected by virtue of the 'quantity effect'). An example study is the following by Meadow et al.[48]. They compared the effects of brainstorming instructions with the effects of instructions that stressed the quality of ideas produced. The tasks set the subjects were to think of as many uses as they could for (1) a broom and (2) a coathanger. Ideas were rated independently for uniqueness (the degree to which the suggested use differed from normal use) and for value (social, economic or aesthetic). 'Good' ideas were defined as those rated highly on both uniqueness and value. The results indicated that significantly more good ideas were produced with the brainstorming instructions than with the non-brainstorming instructions. Favourable results on individual brainstorming have also been reported by Parnes and Meadow.[49]

Given that both individual and group brainstorming seem to be effective, the question arises of whether brainstorming in a group produces better results than would be obtained by pooling results from individual brainstormers. It could be argued either that the group procedure would lead to beneficial mutual stimulation or, alternatively, that participants would be inhibited by fear of implicit criticism even though overt criticism is not permitted.

Taylor et al.[50] tackled this question with an experiment in which 12 groups of four men and 48 individuals followed the basic rules of brainstorming while working on the same three problems. The problems were (1) 'think of as many ways as possible of encouraging European tourists to visit the USA'; (2) 'what would be the consequences if all future children were born with an extra thumb on each hand?' (a diagram of the new hand structure was provided); and (3) 'how could the education system cope with the effects of a "bulge" in the school age population?' (as was being experienced at the time of the study).

After the idea production stage, the 48 individual subjects' data were assigned to 12 nominal groups of size four. The performance of each such nominal group was then scored as though the members had in fact worked together. The achievement of such nominal groups provided a baseline level of performance which would be achieved if group work were neither facilitating nor inhibiting. The nominal groups produced (1) more unique ideas than the real groups and (2) more distinct 'good' ideas—largely by virtue of a quantity effect. It was concluded from these data that group participation in brainstorming inhibited creative thinking relative to individual brainstorming. The 'nominal group superiority effect' first revealed in Taylor et al.'s experiment, has held up over a number of studies[51–53] and seems to be very robust. Perhaps individuals fear implicit criticism even when open criticism was not permitted. Also, individuals working in a real group are more likely to develop the same set or direction in their thinking than the same number of individuals working alone. Individuals working alone will probably develop 'sets', but these sets are likely to differ from person to person.

A further possible negative effect of working in real groups is that of 'production blocking' caused by participants having to wait their turns to provide ideas which could cause forgetting and distraction by other's ideas.[54] Better group productivity has been found with *electronic groups* in which participants can enter their ideas at any time into a common electronic database rather than waiting their turns and so do not suffer from response blocking.[55,56] Indeed, large electronic groups ($n > 9$) have been found to outperform nominal groups[55]—in contrast to the robust finding that group size increases the nominal group effect in standard face to face conditions.

Lateral thinking

De Bono[57] has popularized the notion of lateral thinking as an aid to effective creativity and has developed instructional materials aimed at teaching lateral thinking skills. Lateral thinking involves re-representing a problem while, in contrast, normal ('vertical') thinking involves working within a given problem representation. Vertical thinking is seen as logical, sequential, predictable and habit-bound, while lateral thinking would be characterized by the opposite attributes. De Bono has devised a set of instructional materials known as the CoRT programme (named after de Bono's Cognitive Research Trust). These materials are intended to increase individuals' skills in lateral thinking. The programme involves six units each consisting of ten 35-min lessons. The six units are outlined in de Bono[57] and may be summarized as follows: CoRT1, 'Breadth', stresses thinking about problems in different ways; CoRT 2, 'Organization', aims at effective control of attention; CoRT 3, 'Interaction', focuses on questions of evidence and arguments; CoRT 4, 'Creativity' provides strategies for producing unusual ideas; CoRT 5, 'Information and Feeling', considers affective factors related to thinking; CoRT 6, 'Action', presents a general framework for tackling problems. De Bono suggests that CoRT 1 should be taught first, after which the other units can be used in any order. Broadly speaking, the CoRT lessons involve using 'operators' which are given to help students retrieve and apply the operators when needed. Sample operators are 'consider all factors' or 'CAF', and 'positive, negative and interesting points', or 'PNI'.

De Bono[58] reports studies in which students who had undergone CoRT instructions produced more ideas than control groups. This certainly suggests a 'quantity' effect; whether average quality was improved is unclear. The test questions were similar to the exercises in the training material and so the extent of transfer of training is also unclear. Edwards and Baldauf[59] carried out an instructional study using CoRT 1 and found that various measures of quantity and quality of divergent thinking improved after the CoRT 1 course. Transfer of training in CoRT 1 to performance in high school Physics was investigated, but no clear indication of transfer emerged.

Rather stronger evidence supporting the CoRT programme comes from a Venezuelan study.[60] Large groups of children received training in a version of the CoRT programme for periods of 1–3 years. Control subjects of similar background did not receive these lessons. Pre- and post-tests with divergent problems similar to those used in training showed significantly larger gains on quantity and quality measures for the experimental subjects compared with the controls. Interestingly, the relative gains increased with the number of years of training.

The results, particularly those of the Venezuelan study, were quite encouraging for the CoRT programme, even though these studies left open questions regarding transfer to dissimilar tasks. However, more recent studies have shown beneficial effects of lateral thinking instructions on creative problem solving in a range of applied areas such as nursing[61] and engineering.[62,63]

Theoretical approaches

In this section I will consider some attempts to explain creative processes within the frameworks of theoretical approaches established in other areas. The approaches dealt with here are those of associative and information processing theory, and indicate how creative processes could be explained in terms of normal cognitive processes.

Simonton's chance-configuration theory

Simonton[6,28] builds on a previous earlier blind-variation and selective-retention model of creative processes.[64] Campbell's[64] model involved the following three basic propositions:

1. The solution of novel problems requires some means of generating *ideational variation*. This process is 'blind' in that the problem tackler cannot know in advance of testing a new idea whether it will help or not.
2. The idea variations are subject to a fixed *selection process* that retains advances and rejects non-advances.
3. The selected variations must be *retained*.

Campbell's model of idea generation, selection and retention is clearly analogous to Darwinian evolutionary theory. Simonton builds on this model in his chance-configuration theory by introducing concepts of (1) the chance permutation of mental elements, (2) the formation of stable configurations and (3) the communication and acceptance of those configurations.

Simonton proposes that the creative process operates on mental elements which are unitary ideas that are free to enter into combinations with other elements. The basic mechanism is *chance permutation* of these elements. The use of the term 'permutation' (rather than the more often used term 'combination') draws attention to the order in which elements are combined. The same elements (e.g. musical notes) will have very different effects depending on the order in which they are combined. Once a chance permutation has occurred, some selection must be introduced. Most chance permutations are unstable in that the elements do not cohere; the few that form an inter-related whole are highly stable and Simonton labels these *configurations*. Stable configurations are retained and become new 'chunks' which function as a single element and can thus enter into further permutations.

A new configuration which seems useful has to be further developed into a *communication configuration* before the creative process is complete. The initial chance configuration then is a starting point, e.g. a sketch, an outline, a germinal idea, which must be the basis for a publicly available product, e.g. a painting, a symphony, a scientific paper, and so on. Finally, the product must be perceived as meeting a need by an audience. Particular support for the chance-configuration theory can be drawn from data on the distribution of creative productivity over contributors to particular fields, the relationship between age and creativity and the quantity–quality relationship.

In many fields, the distribution of outputs is such that a few contributors account for a majority of products. Dennis[65] found that the top 10 per cent produced around 50 per cent of contributions, while the bottom 50 per cent produced about 15 per cent of the contributions over many disciplines. Thus, the distribution of number of products per contributor is highly skewed. Simonton[6,28] argues that even if the number of mental elements (n) available for chance permutation is normally distributed, as seems plausible, the number of possible chance permutations (e to the power n) is a highly skewed distribution. Thus, those contributors with more elements will produce disproportionately more configurations and so the observed productivity distributions are consistent with the chance-configuration theory.

The relationships between age and output reported by Lehman[26] have been supported by more recent research.[28,66] The main patterns are that productivity in all fields tends to increase initially with age, reach a peak and then decline more slowly than the initial rise; the onset, peak and rate of decline vary from field to field; and, finally, exceptional output is associated with precocity, longevity and high productivity rates. Simonton[6,28] argues that the typical age–productivity curve reflects the operation of two processes, i.e. production of chance configurations (ideation) and elaboration of chance configurations into creative communications (communication configurations). Ideation is held to occur at a rate proportional to the size of the set of free mental elements which have not yet been combined; while elaboration rate depends in a similar way on the quantity of ideations awaiting conversion into communicable form. Simonton shows that by varying these two rates, the typical age–productivity curves can be produced. In relatively formal disciplines (e.g. mathematics), the rates of ideation and elaboration are high, leading to early peaks; but, in less formalized domains (e.g. history), the rates of ideation and elaboration are low, leading to late peaks and slow declines. Total productivity should be governed by the total number of possible chance configurations of the mental elements which a person brings to the domain. On Simonton's model it can be shown that the greater the number of such combinations that are theoretically possible, the earlier the person will begin to contribute (precocity) and the higher the rate of production will be. The longer the lifespan (longevity) the greater the total contribution (assuming reasonable health).

There appears to be a fairly consistent link between quantity and quality in that the longer the list of products a person has contributed, generally the longer will be that person's list of high quality products. Over a creator's working life, the quality ratio of major to minor works tends to be constant.[67] The 'constant-probability-of-success' rule follows from Campbell's blind-variation model and from Simonton's chance-configuration theory. The stability of creative reputations may partly depend on the existence of multiple high quality products which can support the reputation even when individual products' perceived worth may fluctuate with time. Equally, it is notable that high creatives often have a 'tail' of work which is less highly regarded than the best work of their generally lower ranked contemporaries. As W. H. Auden said, '… the major poet will write more bad poems than the minor', but only because the major poet will tend to write much more than the minor poet.[68]

Overall, Simonton's theory is consistent with a broad range of historical data on productivity and is applicable very broadly over a range of artistic and scientific areas. However, as with Darwin's original theory of evolution, further specification of the means of variation and retention are needed to complete the chance-configuration theory.

The Geneplore model

Finke and colleagues[69–71] have (creatively) invented a new term 'Geneplore' to label their cognitive model of creativity. 'Geneplore' is a selective combination of the words 'generate' and 'explore' and indicates that these processes are central to their theory. They postulate two distinct phases in creative activity: (1) a generative phase in which mental representations called pre-inventive structures are constructed and (2) an exploratory phase in which the pre-inventive structures are interpreted for possible meanings and uses. The process typically involves a number of cycles where either new pre-inventive structures are formed or initial pre-inventive structures are elaborated toward useful solutions. Goal or product constraints may apply to either or both main phases and bias generation or exploration and interpretation.

Support for this model has been drawn from experiments on creative invention[69] which utilize laboratory analogues of invention. In such experiments, subjects are first shown a set of 15 basic object parts, e.g. sphere, half-sphere, tube, bracket, hook and cross. Three different parts were presented by name on each trial and subjects were to imagine combining the parts to make a practical object or device. All three parts had to be used but subjects could vary the size, position or orientation of any part. Objects had to belong to one of eight general categories, such as furniture, transportation, tools and utensils, etc. Three main experimental conditions were explored: (1) subjects were given a category at random but could choose the three parts, (2) the parts were assigned at random but the subjects could choose the category and (3) both the parts and the category were assigned at random. Examples of objects produced are: a shoestring unlacer, a hip-exerciser and a novel hamburger patty maker. The highest rate of products judged creative (i.e. practical and original) was found with randomly assigned categories and parts, sug-gesting that subjects' habitual tendencies and sets may have reduced creativity when free choices of objects or categories were allowed. Retrospective reports indicated that subjects tended to use an exploratory strategy in which they began by constructing interesting (pre-inventive) forms and then tried to interpret these forms rather than starting with the function or category and trying to generate objects to fit. In a further study, subjects were asked simply to combine three randomly chosen shapes into interesting forms without any intended object category being given in advance. After a shape had been generated, subjects were asked to interpret the form as a practical object or device within a randomly chosen category. In other conditions, subjects chose the category in advance or were given a random category in advance of generation. The rate of creative production was highest in the case where no category was specified in advance but was given at random after generation.

The results can be interpreted in terms of the Geneplore model as reflecting the separation of generation and exploration and the benefits of not invoking product or goal constraints too early. The separation of generation and exploration is reminiscent of the separation of idea-generation and evaluation in brainstorming, and the condition in which no goal is given represents an extreme form of such a separation. Notions similar to that of pre-inventive form have also been invoked by Simonton[6,28] in his idea of initial chance-configurations which require elaboration, and Gruber and Davis[72] in their idea of the 'initial sketch' that guides creative work. From the practical point of view, the finding that pre-inventive forms can be useful when produced with no specific goal in mind suggests that inventors could benefit from a playful initial approach in which elements are combined without strong goal constraint. Given a form, often it can be re-interpreted in many ways (as furniture, as tool, as toy, and so on); or as Finke[73] puts it 'Function follows form' rather than the more frequently cited 'Form follows function' in creative invention.

Boden's computational approach: improbabilist and impossibilist creativity

Boden[1,2,74] has argued that there are two broad types of creativity which she labels 'improbabilist' and 'impossibilist'. These in turn can both be divided into psychological/personal and historical creativity. Improbabilist creativity involves generating new and valued products while working within an established rule system which defines a conceptual space of possibilities; impossibilist creativity involves the transformation of conceptual spaces so that new ideas arise which were impossible within pre-transformation spaces. Psychological/personal creativity involves production of ideas new to the individual (though they may have been produced by many others), while historical creativity involves producing ideas which have never been produced by anyone before. Boden points out that historical creativity is a subset of psychological/personal creativity and she focuses on impossibilist psychological/personal creativity. To transform a conceptual space, Boden argues that one must be able to map and explore the space. She points to developmental evidence that children become ever more flexible by using 'representational redescriptions' of lower evel skills.[75] Initially, children develop basic schemas for drawing a man. These schemas are quite rigid and 4-year-olds cannot spontaneously draw a one-legged man because that is outside the schema (or conceptual space). They also have difficulty copying out-of-schema figures. By 10 years of age most children can distort, repeat and omit parts and have greatly transformed their earlier schemas. These transformations develop in a fixed order. Generally, children can change size or shape of an arm before they can insert an extra arm and well before they can draw a man with wings instead of arms.

Larger scale examples may be found in the history of music and mathematics. Post-Renaissance music in the West involved explorations of tonal harmony. Atonal music (Schoenberg) represents a marked transformation of the original tonal space into the atonal space. The transformation fundamentally consisted of dropping the requirement that a piece of music must have a 'home key' from which it starts and must return. Schoenberg dropped this constraint and added new ones (e.g. using every note in the chromatic scale.) A similar case of dropping constraints to develop a new space is found in the move from Euclidean to non-Euclidean geometry which arose from dropping Euclid's fifth axiom.

What type of cognitive architecture might support impossibilist creativity? Boden suggests a hybrid serial/parallel architecture. On this view, long-term knowledge is stored in a connectionist network which can throw up unusual associations, combinations and analogies, while the serial part steadily searches through problem spaces. The network may suggest new problem space through associations and analogies retrieved in response to the task. There are echoes here of the traditional view that the unconscious (the network) is the source of inspiration, and the conscious (the serial system) carries out the more routine work of preparation and verification.[37]

Concluding comment

Overall, the results and theories outlined here indicate that, contrary to the myth of mystery, creative thinking can be empirically investigated and would appear to be explicable in terms of normal cognitive processes suitably marshalled, often in real life cases, over long periods.

References and notes

1. **Boden MA.** *The creative mind.* Weidenfeld and Nicolson, London. 1990.
2. **Boden MA.** *The creative mind,* 2nd revised edn. London: Routledge. 2004.
3. **Albert RS.** Toward a behavioural definition of genius. *American Psychologist,* 1965; 30:140–151.
4. **Stein M.** *Stimulating creativity,* Vol. 1. Academic Press, New York. 1974.
5. **Stein M.** *Stimulating creativity,* Vol. 2. Academic Press, New York. 1975.
6. **Simonton DK.** Creativity, leadership and chance. In RJ Sternberg, ed. *The nature of creativity.* Cambridge University Press, Cambridge. 1988.
7. **Gardner H.** *Creating minds.* Basic Books, New York. 1994.
8. **Roe A.** A psychologist examines sixty-four eminent scientists. *Scientific American,* 1952; 187:21–25.
9. **MacKinnon DW.** The personality correlates of creativity: a study of American architects. In *Proceedings of the 14th Congress of Applied Psychology.* Munksgaard, 1962:11–39.
10. **Barron F.** The disposition toward originality. *Journal of Abnormal and Social Psychology,* 1955; 51:478–485.
11. **Cattell RN.** The personality and motivation of the researcher from measurements of contemporaries and from biography. In CW Taylor, ed. *The 1959 University of Utah Research Conference on the Identification of Creative Scientific Talent.* University of Utah Press. 1959.

12. **Cattell RB, Drevdahl JE.** A comparison of the personality profile (16PF) of eminent researchers with that of eminent teachers and administrators, and of the general population. *British Journal of Psychology*, 1955; **46**:248–261.

13. **Mitroff II.** *The subjective side of science.* Elsevier, Amsterdam. 1974.

14. **Hudson L.** *Contrary imaginations.* Methuen, London. 1966.

15. **Jones E.** *The life and work of Sigmund Freud.* L Trilling L, S Marcus, ed. Hogarth, London. 1961.

16. **Drevdahl JE, Cattell RN.** Personality and creativity in artists and writers. *Journal of Clinical Psychology*, 1958; **14**:107–111.

17. **Jamison KR.** Manic-depressive illness and creativity. *Scientific American*, 1995; **272**:46–51.

18. **Andreasen NC.** Creativity and mental illness: prevalence rates in writers and their first degree relatives. *American Journal of Psychiatry*, 1987; **144**:1288–1292.

19. **Ludwig AM.** Creative achievement and psychopathology: comparison among professions. *Journal of Psychotherapy*, 1992; **46**:330–356.

20. **Ludwig AM.** *The price of greatness: resolving the creativity and madness controversy.* Guilford Press, New York. 1995.

21. **Nettle D.** *Strong imagination: madness, creativity and human nature.* Oxford University Press, Oxford. 2001.

22. **Shapiro PJ, Weisberg RW.** Positive affect and creativity: smptom of psychopathology or component of creative process? *Bulletin of Psychology and the Arts* (APA: Division 10), 2000; 1:58–61. Invited paper for special issue: Creativity and Psychopathology.

23. **Weisberg RW.** Genius and madness? A quasi-experimental test of the hypothesis that manic-depression increases creativity. *Psychological Science*, 1994; 5:361–367.

24. **McDermott JF.** Emily Dickinson revisited: a study of periodicity in her work. *American Journal of Psychiatry*, 2001; **158**:686–690.

25. **Kalian M, Merner V, Witzum E.** Creativity and affective Illness. *American Journal of Psychiatry*, 2002; **159**:675–676.

26. **Lehman HC.** *Age and achievement.* Princeton University Press, Princeton, NJ. 1953.

27. **Lehman HC.** The most creative years of engineers and other technologists. *Journal of Genetic Psychology*, 1966; **108**:263–77.

28. **Simonton DK.** Creative productivity: a predictive and exploratory model of career trajectories and landmarks. *Psychological Review*, 1997; **104**:66–89.

29. **McCann SJH.** The precocity–longevity hypothesis: earlier peaks in career achievement predict shorter lives. *Personality and Social Psychology Bulletin*, 2001; **27**:1429–1439.

30. **McCann SJH.** Younger achievement age predicts shorter life for governors: testing the precocity–longevity hypothesis. *Personality and Social Psychology Bulletin*, 2003; **29**:164–169.

31. **Galenson DW, Weinberg BA.** Age and quality of work: the case of modern American painters. *Journal of Political Economy*, 2000; **108**:761–777.

32. **Ghiselin B.** *The creative process.* University of California Press. 1952.

33. **Koestler A.** *The act of creation.* Hutchinson, London. 1964.

34. **Vernon PE.** *Creativity.* Penguin Books, Harmondsworth, UK. 1970.

35. **Poincaré H.** *Science et methode.* Flammarion, Paris. 1908.

36. **Woodworth RS, Schlosberg H.** *Experimental psychology*, 3rd edn. Methuen, London. 1954.

37. **Wallas G.** *The art of thought.* Jonathan Cape, London. 1926.

38. **Ohlsson S.** Information processing explanations of insight and related phenomena. In MT Keane, KJ Gilhooly, ed. *Advances in the psychology of thinking.* Harvester Wheatsheaf, London. 1992.

39. **Dodds RA, Ward TB, Smith SM.** A review of experimental research on incubation in problem solving and creativity. In MA Runco, ed. *Creativity research handbook*, Vol. 3, Hampton Press, Cresshill, NJ. 2004.

40. **Murray HG, Denny JP.** Interaction of ability level and interpolated activity in human problem solving. *Psychological Reports*, 1969; **24**:271–276.

41. Smith S, Blankenship S. Incubation and the persistence of fixation in problem solving. *American Journal of Psychology*, 1991; **104**:61–87.

42. Yaniv I, Meyer DE. Activation and metacognition of inaccessible stored information: potential bases for incubation effects in problem solving. *Journal of Experimental Psychology: Learning, Motivation and Cognition*, 1987; **13**:187–205.

43. Dorfman J, Shames VA, Kihlstrom JF. Intuition, incubation and insight: implicit cognition in problem solving. In G Underwood, ed. *Implicit cognition.* Oxford University Press, Oxford. 1996.

44. Seifert CM, Meyer DM, Davidson N, Patalano AL, Yaniv I. Demystification of cognitive insight: opportunistic assimilation and the prepared-mind perspective. In RJ Sternberg, JE Davidson, ed. *The nature of insight.* Boston, MA: Bradford Books. 1995.

45. Seabrook R, Dienes Z. Incubation in problem solving as a context effect. *Proceedings of 25th Annual Conference of the Cognitive Science Society*, Chicago, July 31–August 2, 2003.

46. Howe C, McWilliam D, Cross G. Chance favours only the prepared mind: Incubation and the delayed effects of peer collaboration. *British Journal of Psychology*, 2005; **26**:1–28.

47. Osborn AF. *Applied imagination.* Scribners, New York. 1953.

48. Meadow A, Parnes SJ, Reese H. Influence of brainstorming instruction and problem sequence on a creative problem solving test. *Journal of Applied Psychology*, 1959; **43**:413–416.

49. Parnes SJ, Meadow A. Development of individual creative talent. In CW Taylor, F Barron, ed. *Scientific creativity: its recognition and development.* John Wiley, New York. 1963.

50. Taylor DW, Berry PC, Block CH. Does group participating when using brainstorming facilitate or inhibit creative thinking? *Administrative Science Quarterly*, 1958; **3**:23–47.

51. Dunnette MD, Campbell J, Jaastad K. The effects of group participation on brainstorming effectiveness for two industrial samples. *Journal of Applied Psychology*, 1963; **47**:10–37.

52. Bouchard TJ, Jr. Hare M. Size, performance, and potential in brainstorming groups. *Journal of Applied Psychology*, 1970; **54**:51–55.

53. Dillon PC, Graham WK, Aidells AL. Brainstorming on a 'hot' problem: effects of training and practice on individual and group performance. *Journal of Applied Psychology*, 1972; **56**:487–490.

54. Nijstad BA, Stroebe W, Lodewijkx HFN. Production blocking and idea generation: Does blocking interfere with cognitive processes? *Journal of Experimental Social Psychology*, 2003; **39**:531–548.

55. Vallacich JS, Dennis AR, Connolly T. Idea generation in computer-based groups: a new ending to an old story. *Organizational Behaviour and Human Decision Processes*, 1994; **7**:448–467.

56. Kerr DS, Murthy US. Divergent and convergent idea generation in teams: a comparison of computer-mediated and face-to-face communication. *Group Decision and Negotiation*, 2004; **13**:381–399.

57. De Bono E. The Cognitive Research Trust (CoRT) thinking program. In W Maxwell, ed. *Thinking: the expanding frontier.* The Franklin Institute Press, Philadelphia, PA. 1983.

58. De Bono E. *Teaching thinking.* Temple Smith, London. 1976.

59. Edwards J, Baldauf RB. Teaching thinking in secondary science. In W Maxwell, ed. *Thinking: the expanding frontier.* The Franklin Institute Press, Philadelphia, PA. 1983.

60. De Sanchez MA, Astorga, M. *Projecto aprendar a pensor.* Ministerio de Educacion, Caracas. 1983,

61. Kenny LJ. Using Edward de Bono's six hats game to aid critical thinking and reflection in palliative care. *International Journal of Palliative Nursing*, 2003; **9**:105–112.

62. Waks S. Lateral thinking and technical education. *Journal of Science, Education and Technology*, 1997; **6**:245–255.

63. Waks S, Merdler M. Creative thinking of practical engineering students during a design project. *Research in Science and Technological Education*, 2003; **21**:101–121.

64. Campbell D. Blind variation and selective retention in creative thought as in other knowledge processes. *Psychological Review*, 1960; **67**:380–400.

65. Dennis W. Variations in productivity among creative workers. *Scientific Monthly*, 1955; **80**:277–278.

66. Simonton DK. Creative productivity and age: a mathematical model based on a 2-step cognitive process. *Developmental Review*, 1984; **4**:77–111.

67. **Simonton DK.** Creative productivity, age and stress: a biographical time-series analysis of 10 classical composers. *Journal of Personality and Social Psychology*, 1977; **35**:791–804.
68. **Bennet W.** Providing for posterity. *Harvard Magazine*, 1980; **82**:13–16.
69. **Finke RA.** *Creative imagery: discoveries and inventions in visualization.* Lawrence Erlbaum Associates, Hillsdale, NJ. 1990.
70. **Finke RA, Ward TB, Smith SM.** *Creative cognition: theory, research, applications.* MIT Press, Cambridge, MA. 1992.
71. **Ward TB, Smith SM, Finke RA.** Creative cognition. In RJ Sternberg, ed. *Handbook of creativity.* Cambridge University Press, Cambridge. 1999.
72. **Gruber HE, Davis S.** Inching our way up Mount Olympus: the evolving systems approach to creative thinking. In RJ Sternberg, ed. *The nature of creativity: contemporary psychological perspectives.* Cambridge University Press, Cambridge. 1988.
73. **Finke RA.** Mental imagery and creative discovery. In B Roskos-Ewoldson, MJ Injons-Peterson, RE Anderson, ed. *Imagery, creativity and discovery.* Elsevier, Amsterdam. 1993.
74. **Boden MA.** Précis of '*The creative mind*': myths and mechanisms. *Behavioural and Brain Sciences*, 1994; **17**:519–570.
75. **Karmiloff-Smith, A.** Is creativity domain-specific or domain-general? Clues from normal and abnormal development. *Artificial Intelligence and Simulation of Behaviour Quarterly*, August. 1993.

Tall tales on language
and communication

Chapter 13

The more, the merrier: facts and beliefs about the bilingual mind

Antonella Sorace

Introduction

Anyone who has seen a small child switching from one language to another is likely to be amazed—and perhaps envious—at how effortlessly they are able to do this. Stories of immigrant children interpreting for their parents are commonplace, and in some parts of the world it is quite normal for children to be exposed to two or even more languages right from birth. Yet in modern industrial societies, growing up with more than one language is often regarded as 'special'. Bilingualism is still surrounded by false beliefs and misunderstandings, even among the otherwise educated and scientifically minded. Many people are ready to believe that handling two languages at the same time is too much of a burden for the infant's brain, or that the languages compete for resources in the brain at the expense of general cognitive development. The contrast between and these false beliefs and the amazement often expressed by people at how easily children pick up two or more languages has been termed the 'bilingual paradox'.[1]

Why are these beliefs so resilient? Their enduring popularity might have to do, at least in part, with the fact that many people find it difficult to think scientifically about language, and therefore everyone feels entitled to have strong opinions about it: the world is full of linguistics experts. With regard to bilingualism, opinions are unfortunately not restricted to the domain of academic discussion, but often inform decisions—by parents, professional educators, policy makers—that end up affecting children's lives. Many new parents who want their children to speak two languages for family reasons are likely to have heard somewhere that exposure to two languages can cause problems, so they may abandon bilingualism before they even give it a try, or may plan to introduce one of the languages only after the other is 'well established' and then find to their regret that the second language never has a chance. If they successfully establish bilingualism in their pre-school children, they may well be made to feel that they have created a problem by well-meaning primary school teachers, who are often ready to blame bilingualism for any performance problems. In this situation, the parents may abandon successful bilingualism and even make active efforts to re-establish monolingualism to 'cure' the problem. Given the sociological repercussions of these folk linguistic beliefs, it seems valuable to bridge the gap between the scientific approach to the study of bilingual cognition and what many people believe about life with two languages. In this chapter, we try to dissect some particularly strong misconceptions that are still alive and well and affecting the daily lives of bilinguals.

Myth 1: Bilingual children are less intelligent than monolinguals (or, alternatively, bilingual children are more intelligent than monolinguals)

Does knowledge of more than one language make you smarter? Or is it rather a cognitive handicap, at least in the early childhood years? The answer is, quite simply, neither. There is no link between bilingualism and general 'intelligence'. Early research in the 1960s suggested that bilinguals have a cognitive handicap, while subsequent studies in the 1970s seemed to find that bilinguals are more intelligent than monolinguals. More recently, however, both conclusions have been found to be marred by failing to take important sociological and cultural effects into account.[2] The fact appears to be that bilingual children are neither more nor less intelligent than their monolingual peers.

Nevertheless, the experience of dealing with two languages does seem to give bilingual children some cognitive advantages in several domains. Such advantages are particularly evident in tasks that involve cognitive flexibility and the control of attention;[3,4] bilinguals seem to be better at selectively paying attention, at inhibiting irrelevant information and at switching between alternative solution to a problem. In contrast, bilinguals do not seem to have an advantage over monolinguals with respect to functions that depend on the way knowledge is represented. For example, they do not seem to be any better and encoding problems, at accessing relevant knowledge or at drawing logical inferences.

What is the link between enhanced cognitive control and bilingualism? Bilingual speakers must develop a powerful mechanism for keeping the two languages separate, so that fluency in one language can be achieved without intrusions from the unwanted language. Therefore, the bilingual child's constant experience of having two languages available and inhibiting one when the other is activated[5,6] enhances their ability to multitask in other domains. There is also more good news for bilinguals: it has been suggested that some of these cognitive advantages are maintained in old age.[7] If these results are confirmed by future research, it will be possible to conclude that bilingualism provides a defence against the decline of general processing functions that is a feature of normal cognitive ageing.

A further spin-off of bilingualism is higher awareness of language and greater ability to think about it and talk about it. Bilingual children have a greater ability to focus on the *form* of language, abstracting away from meaning. Parents of bilingual children often report that their children engage in 'language play' that may take the form of 'funny accents' or impossible literal translations between one language and another. Many parents also report that bilingual children have more precocious reading skills, and this has recently been confirmed experimentally.[8] Bilingual children recognize symbolic letter–sound correspondences earlier than monolinguals, although this does not appear to be related to greater awareness of the sounds themselves, and it is also a function of the specific languages acquired as well as of the level of proficiency attained.[9]

Because of their experience of selecting languages according to the perceived linguistic competence of the person they are addressing, bilingual children have also been said to have an enhanced 'awareness of the other'. This often goes under the heading of 'Theory of Mind', which is a term used to describe the ability to understand other people's mental states, and more specifically that other people may have beliefs, desires and intentions different from one's own. In the classic 'Sally–Anne' Theory of Mind test,[10] the researcher uses two dolls, 'Sally' and 'Anne'. Each of them has her own basket. Children watch Sally put a marble in her basket and then leave the scene. While Sally is away, Anne moves the marble from Sally's basket into her own. Sally then comes back and the children are asked where they think she will look for her marble. Children pass the test if they say that Sally will first look inside her basket before realizing that her marble is not there; they fail if they say that Sally looks into Anne's basket. The cognitive abilities involved in Theory of Mind normally emerge around the age of 4 in monolingual children; they are permanently impaired in autistic children. Bilingual children develop Theory of Mind, on average, a year earlier than monolinguals, so they succeed in classic false belief tasks at age 3.[11,12] Theory of Mind has also been found to correlate with central executive functions (planning, problem solving, inhibition of habitual responses), so bilinguals' superior performance may be due to their greater ability to suspend their own irrelevant beliefs, rather than to an understanding of other people's mental state. Still, it is remarkable that the experience of dealing with two languages may have such extensive repercussions in so many apparently unrelated domains of cognitive development.

Myth 2: Bilingual children are slowed down in their general cognitive development by the burden of handling two languages

The idea that learning two languages from birth represents a burden is based on the assumption that the brain is naturally predisposed to deal only with one language. However, research in psychology and neuroscience research indicates that there are no foundations to the belief that monolingualism is somehow the biological norm. While it is true that the onset of speech in bilinguals may be slightly later than average, both monolingual and bilingual children go through the same major milestones in language development at approximately the same time. Commonly recognized stages are: babbling (playing with sounds apparently without intending to convey meaning) during the period of roughly 6–12 months; the emergence of single words about the end of the first year; the '50-word stage' at 14–18 months, after which there is a sudden explosion in vocabulary size; the two-word utterance stage at 18–24 months; and the emergence of multiword utterances sometime around the end of the second year. If the brain were set up to acquire only one language, bilinguals would be at a disadvantage: they might be expected to reach the milestones later, or at different times in their two languages. The fact that they follow the same developmental timetable as monolinguals points to the brain's capacity to deal with multiple types of language input.

Very persuasive evidence that the brain can easily accommodate more than one language comes from studies by Petitto and her team.[13] Petitto compared the more common case of bilingual children acquiring two spoken languages with that of hearing children of deaf parents, who were acquiring both a spoken language and a signed language. Her reasoning was that, if exposure to two languages causes delays and confusion, these should be particularly apparent in the sign–spoken bilingual group. What she found was that, as in the case of two spoken languages acquired simultaneously, the signed language and the spoken language follow similar developmental timetables: such babies go through developmental milestones (including a phase of 'babbling with the hands') at about the same time. This shows that babies are not sensitive to speech or sound *per se*, but rather to the abstract patterns and regularities that are encoded by any language in either modality. Petitto's proposal is that children are sensitive to distributional, rhythmical and temporal patterns that uniquely characterize the structure of human language. These patterns are found in any language, whether spoken or signed: so sign–spoken bilingual children are not hampered by exposure to different modalities, and achieve distinct representations in both languages just like bilingual children acquiring two spoken languages.

Myth 3: Bilingual children speak a 'mixed' language in their first years and end up not speaking either language properly

A hopelessly mixed language is the thing that many parents in bilingual families typically fear. Early research on bilingual children actually seemed to show that children are unable to distinguish between the two languages to which they are exposed. The result—it was claimed—is a single unitary system in which both the vocabularies and the grammars of the two languages are fused. Language mixing—it was believed—was a telling sign of this lack of differentiation. Another sign was the fact that in some bilingual children the early words often involve a mix of words taken from both languages, with many referents named by only one word. So, for example, a German–Italian bilingual child might have either *Apfel* or *mela* for 'apple', but not both. This led to the hypothesis that there was a unitary lexicon, which could not contain two words, one from language A and one from language B, for the same referent.

More recent research has completely discredited the idea of the unitary system. First, there are new techniques for studying whether babies can tell the difference between one outside stimulus and another. If you show a child a picture of a ball it will eventually get bored and look away, but if you then show it a picture of a car it will look again. There are now experimental techniques that let us present pictures or sounds to a child until it gets bored, then present it with something subtly different and see if the child notices the difference.[14] Using techniques like these, we have learned that monolingual babies' perceptual abilities are remarkably fine-tuned very early on: they know a lot about what their language sounds like long before they start producing their first words, and even at the age of a few months will notice when someone who was speaking English switches to speaking, say, Japanese. This makes it very implausible that bilingual children do not realize that they are hearing two languages. Indeed, they seem to be even *more* sensitive than monolinguals to a wider range of phonetic contrasts, and they may retain this ability for a longer time than monolinguals, for whom the 'window' of highest perceptual sensitivity to contrasts that are not present in their own language closes around 14 months.

Secondly, research on 'code-switching'—swapping back and forth between languages—shows that bilingual children, like bilingual adults, often switch from one language to another in order to achieve particular communicative effects. For example, even if they are talking in language A, they may switch to language B to report something that somebody said, if the speech they are reporting was originally in language B. Or they may switch because of the topic they are talking about, or simply to play games with their languages. Naturally, this kind of code switching takes place most often when bilinguals are talking to other bilinguals—when they are in what Grosjean[15] has called 'bilingual mode'—not when they are talking to monolinguals. Moreover, code switching is not random but generally obeys a remarkably strict grammar. For example, a Spanish–English bilingual child is much more likely to say 'La house' than 'The casa' (Spanish article + English noun, rather than 'English article + Spanish noun), apparently favouring the combination that is more informative in terms of grammatical features such as gender and number. Far from producing random mixings due to confusion, in other words, bilingual children know when and how it is appropriate to mix their languages.

What about the grammars of the two languages? Do bilingual children import the structures of one language into the other? Sometimes they do (though it is difficult to know whether they are doing so deliberately or not), but most of the time they keep their languages separate. The most interesting counterevidence to the confusion hypothesis comes from research that compares the order of acquisition of grammatical structures in monolingual and bilingual children. There is little evidence that the bilinguals' languages affect each other—they neither speed up nor delay normal acquisition processes. For example, children acquiring a language with complex morphology (grammatical endings, etc.) such as Italian normally start using verb inflections earlier than children acquiring a language with relatively simple morphology such as English. At an age when the English child still says 'Daddy eat cookie' and 'me eat cookie', the Italian child says 'Papà mangia il biscotto', 'Io mangio il biscotto', with the appropriate verb endings. If the two languages affected each other in development, one might expect an English–Italian bilingual child to do one of two things: either to acquire morphology in English earlier than monolinguals (as an effect of Italian) or to acquire morphology in Italian later than monolinguals (as an effect of English). In fact, Italian–English bilingual children do neither: the acquisition of verb morphology happens first in Italian and then in English, following exactly the same schedule as in monolingual children.

Of course this does not mean that the features of one language never show up in the other. One current hypothesis is that 'leakages' between languages occur with constructions where the speaker must both know the grammar and understand the contexts in which a given grammatical choice is appropriate.[16] An example is the possibility of 'dropping' subject pronouns in Italian. In Italian, as in other languages that allow sentences without a subject, subjects can be dropped when it is clear in context who the referent is. So if I say Maria *non c'e', e' andata a casa* (lit. 'Maria's not here, went home') I can omit the pronoun in the second clause because it is clear that I am referring to Maria, who has been mentioned in the previous clause. In other cases, the omission of subject pronouns is blocked for contextual reasons. So if I say '*Maria e Yuri non si capiscono:* **lei** *parla l'italiano, lui no*' ('Maria and Yuri cannot understand each other; she speaks Italian, he does not'), I have to use an explicit pronoun because I am contrasting two different people. English is much simpler in a sense, because it always has a subject, regardless of whether the sentence is referring to an easily accessible referent or not.

Now, bilingual children who acquire Italian and English often use too many explicit pronouns where it would be contextually appropriate to drop them.[17] Why do they do this? If you are a child acquiring Italian, you need to acquire two kinds of knowledge: first, you have to learn that it is grammatical to omit subject pronouns, and secondly, you have to know about the contextual conditions that favour dropping or not dropping subject pronouns. These conditions are sometimes called '*interface conditions*', because they sit at the boundary between the grammar itself and the wider discourse context in which language is used, as represented in Fig. 13.1.

One possibility is that bilingual children have a problem operating with these interface conditions in 'real-time' communication, so they extend the less complicated English system to Italian. The other possibility is that they are more aware of potential

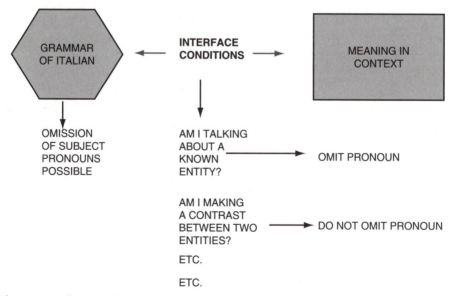

Fig. 13.1 Interface conditions for pronoun selection in Italian.

miscommunication and want to make the sentence as explicit as possible. Bilinguals experience potential miscommunication more often than monolinguals because they learn to adapt their language choice to the person they are addressing. So this 'redundant' feature of bilingual speech may betray a greater sensitivity to potential ambiguity. It is interesting to notice that these interface 'crossovers' from one language to the other are not always from the 'dominant' language to the 'non-dominant language (i.e from the language the child hears or uses more to the one it hears or uses less), but rather from the 'simpler' language to the 'more complex' language. In other words, if one of the two languages offers a simpler way of expressing the same meaning, bilingual children will sometimes import that into the other language.

All in all, then, it appears that children are well aware of the difference between their two languages from very early on, and that each language develops in more or less the normal way, independently of the other. Curiously, however, what is known about bilingualism and the brain looks at first sight inconsistent with this idea. The latest generation of neuroscience studies has taken a serious interest in bilinguals, and particularly in the way the representation of the two languages in the brain is affected by the age at which they are acquired. Several modern neuroimaging studies [such as functional magnetic resonance imaging (fMRI) and positron emission tomography (PET)] indicate that early or simultaneous exposure to two languages from birth results in both languages being represented in the same areas within the left hemisphere, which are normally associated with the native language of monolingual speakers.[18,19] In comparison, exposure to one language and then subsequent exposure to a second results in more bilateral representation, and in the involvement of more distributed frontal lobe areas typically recruited in working memory and inhibitory tasks. According to some models,[20] early bilingualism is neurally distinguished from late bilingualism by its reliance on procedural memory mechanisms, which are implicated in long-established skills, or habits and are not accessible to consciousness; late(r) bilingualism, on the other hand, would mainly be served by declarative memory mechanisms, which are typically used in learning facts and events, and may be explicitly recalled. The brain signatures of these different neural mechanisms are visible in the greater involvement of left frontal ganglia brain areas in early bilinguals, as opposed to the recruitment of temporal lobe areas in later bilinguals.

However, these signatures are not permanently fixed: proficiency in a second language can involve brain reorganization.[21] The flexibility of the brain has also emerged from a study by Mechelli,[22] who analysed structural differences between the brains of bilinguals and monolinguals. The participants in his study had started learning English at various ages and had reached varying levels of proficiency. What he found was that bilinguals have more grey matter than monolinguals—in other words, that they develop a bigger brain in response to exposure to two languages—and that the growth involves a portion of the cortex (the left inferior parietal cortex) that is involved in some verbal fluency tasks and in verbal short-term memory. This happens not only to people who are bilingual from birth, but also to a lesser extent to late bilinguals. So, while it may not be justified to say that bilinguals are more intelligent, it does seem that they may literally have bigger brains.

Myth 4: People cannot learn languages properly after the 'critical period' for language acquisition

Unlike the first three myths, this belief has some basis in fact, but it is still worth taking a closer look. We have seen that simultaneous early exposure to more than one language seems to provide an effortlessly natural path to becoming bilingual. What about older learners? Can they aspire to become fully bilinguals? Also, if they achieve fluency in a second language (as many people do in our increasingly multicultural societies), are they really different from monolinguals? Are there aspects of language that simply cannot be acquired after a certain age?

A theory that has been around for some time[23] maintains that there is a special period for the acquisition of language—a so-called 'critical period'—such that humans are maximally predisposed to acquire language early in life, and complete success at acquiring language can be guaranteed only by exposure during this early period. This seems true enough for the acquisition of a *first* language: if children are not exposed to any linguistic input during the first few years of their life, their language abilities, and especially their grammatical abilities, are irrevocably compromised. We know this from the few 'natural experiments' involving so-called feral children who grew up in conditions of extreme isolation and deprivation; we also know this from recent studies on deaf children of hearing parents, who are often not diagnosed as deaf until 2 or 3 years of age and who therefore are unknowingly deprived of language input up to that point. So why is there a critical period? We still do not have a precise answer to this question, although we have a few good hypotheses. The critical period may be related to the existence of a biological mechanism that is innately geared to the acquisition of language in our species. There may be evolutionary reasons why this mechanism is available in early childhood, when the ability to communicate confers particular advantages in terms of success at survival. In contrast, the advantages of learning languages later in life are not so conspicuous for our species, although they certainly are for us as individuals.

Yet the detailed reasons why the outcome of second language acquisition in adults is different from first language acquisition in children (and from *second* language acquisition in children, for that matter) are far from clear. Are these differences due only to a decline in specific linguistic abilities, or do they result from age-related changes in more general skills, such as memory, for example? After all, second language speakers have been through the process of acquiring language once: why couldn't second language acquisition be helped by 'transferable skills' that are already in place? Moreover, we should not just assume that adults can never attain the levels in a second language that they effortlessly achieved in their first: we do not know exactly how good an adult can become at a second language, or, to put it differently, we do not know what the actual limits of adult second language acquisition are.

One way of addressing this question is to study so called 'near-native' speakers, i.e. people who have achieved the highest level of competence in a second language. These speakers often pass for native speakers, unlike the vast majority of second language speakers who remain recognizably foreign, and in this sense they may be regarded as exceptional. However, exceptions have to be explained: near-native speakers provide us with evidence of what *can* be attained and what cannot, because their learning capacities have been pushed to their limit. So if we compare a speaker who is bilingual from birth with one who has become a near-native speaker of a second language, what do we find? The most obvious difference is that near-native speakers typically differ from early bilinguals because they retain a foreign accent. As we have seen, early exposure to a language seems to play some role in attuning first language acquirers to the phonetic details of their native language. As for grammatical abilities, studies of near-natives consistently point to native-like *knowledge* of syntax and morphology, but that this knowledge can temporarily fail in real-time communication. Near-natives have slower reaction times than native speakers in psycholinguistic experiments, and their comprehension abilities are less tolerant of noisy surroundings. Interestingly, too, problems have been observed in the way near-natives produce and understand sentences that require an interface between grammatical and contextual knowledge.[24] These are the same areas that, as we have seen, are prone to 'leakages' in bilingual children. The difference is that in bilingual children these problems are developmental, and disappear with more exposure; they tend to be permanent in near-natives. If there is a remaining deficit in second language learners who have reached a near-native level, it seems to be the level of the processing abilities required to link different sources of information in fluent use of the second language.[25]

In any case, the comparison between people who are bilingual from birth and even near-native speakers of a second language shows the fallacy of one approach that parents sometimes take to establishing bilingualism—introducing one language first, and waiting until it is established before exposing the child to the other. In all kinds of ways this appears to be the worst mistake one could make. There is no reason to think that children cannot handle acquiring two languages simultaneously, and some reason to think that early bilingualism confers various cognitive advantages. If one of the family languages is introduced after the first one is established, some aspects of it may not be acquired in a native-like way. This is particularly true of the phonetic and articulatory aspect of a 'native accent', which seem to be best acquired within a narrower window of opportunity; but also of some grammatical features for which children are maximally sensitive in the earliest period of their childhood. While children can and often do acquire second languages in later childhood, and often reach native-like mastery in these, the best outcomes are guaranteed by simultaneous exposure. If this is possible, why not go for it? Perhaps equally important, depriving children of exposure to one of the family languages may have other, more sociological, consequences. Children in this situation may feel that the second language is 'less important' than the first, and not really worth speaking.

Children do not know about the cognitive benefits of bilingualism, but they are exquisitely sensitive to the status and prestige of each language within the family and in the outside world. Even if the cognitive windows are still open, closed attitudes may put bilingualism out of reach.

References and notes

1. Petitto LA, Kovelman I. The bilingual paradox: how signing–speaking bilingual children help us to resolve it and teach us about the brain's mechanisms underlying all language acquisition. *Learning Languages*, 2003; 8:5–18.
2. Grosjean F. *Life with two languages*. Harvard University Press, Cambridge, MA. 1982.
3. Bialystok E. *Language processing in bilingual children*. Cambridge University Press, Cambridge. 1991.
4. Bialystok E. *Bilingualism in development: language, literacy, and cognition*. Cambridge University Press, New York. 2001.
5. Green DW. Control, activation and resource. *Brain and Language*, 1986; 27:210–223.
6. Green DW. Mental control of the bilingual lexico-semantic system. *Bilingualism: Language and Cognition*, 1998; 1:67–81.
7. Bialystok E, Craik FIM, Klein R, Viswanathan M. Bilingualism, aging, and cognitive control: evidence from the Simon task. *Psychology and Aging*, 2004; 19:290–303.
8. Petitto LA, Dunbar K. New findings from educational neuroscience on bilingual brains, scientific brains, and the educated mind. Paper presented at the Conference on Building Usable Knowledge in Mind, Brain & Education, Harvard University, October 2004.
9. Bialystok E, Majumder S, Martin M. Developing phonological awareness: is there a bilingual advantage? *Applied Psycholinguistics*, 2003; 24:27–44.
10. Perner J, Lang B. Development of theory of mind, and executive control. *Trends in Cognitive Sciences*, 1999; 3:337–344.
11. Goetz P. The effects of bilingualism on theory of mind development. *Bilingualism: Language and Cognition*, 2003; 6:1–15.
12. Kovácz AM. Bilinguals' advantage in understanding other minds. MSc Thesis. International School of Advanced Studies (SISSA), Trieste. 2005.
13. Petitto LA, Katerelos M, Levy BG, Gauna K, Tetreault K, Ferraro V. Bilingual signed and spoken language acquisition from birth: implications for the mechanism underlying early bilingual language acquisition. *Journal of Child Language*, 2001; 28:453–496.
14. Jusczyk P. *The discovery of spoken language*. MIT Press, Cambridge, MA. 1997.
15. Grosjean F. Studying bilinguals: methodological and conceptual issues. *Bilingualism: Language and Cognition*, 1998; 1:131–149.
16. Müller N, Hulk A. Crosslinguistic influence in bilingual language acquisition: Italian and French as recipient languages. *Bilingualism: Language and Cognition*, 2001; 4:1–22.
17. Serratrice L, Sorace A, Paoli S. Transfer at the syntax–pragmatics interface: subjects and objects in Italian–English bilingual and monolingual acquisition. *Bilingualism: Language and Cognition*, 2004; 7.
18. Wartenburger I, Heekeren HR, Abutalebi J, Cappa S, Villringen A, Perani D. Early setting of grammatical processing in the bilingual brain. *Neuron*, 2003; 37:159–170.
19. Abutalebi J, Cappa S, Perani D. The bilingual brain as revealed by functional neuroimaging. *Bilingualism: Language and Cognition*, 2001; 4:179–190.
20. Ullman M. The neural bases of lexicon and grammar in first and second language: the declarative/procedural model. *Bilingualism: Language and Cognition*, 2001; 4:105–122.

21. **Perani D, Paulesu E, Sebastian-Galles N, Dupoux E, Dehaene S, Bettinardi V, Cappa S, Fazio F, Mehler J.** The bilingual brain: proficiency and age of acquisition of the second language. *Brain*, 1998; 121:1841–1852.
22. **Mechelli A.** Structural plasticity in the bilingual brain: proficiency in a second language and age of acquisition affect grey-matter density. *Nature*, 2004; **431**:757.
23. **Lenneberg EH.** *Biological foundations of language.* Riley, New York, 1967.
24. **Sorace A.** Near-nativeness. In C Doughty, M Long, ed. *Handbook of second language acquisition.* Blackwell, Oxford. 2003:130–151.
25. **Clahsen H, Felser C.** Grammatical processing in first and second language learners. *Applied Psycholinguistics*, 2006; 27.

Chapter 14

The merry vibes of Wintzer: the tale of foreign accent syndrome

Nick Miller

'This baffling disorder'

'Among the strange ailments and disabilities waiting out there to ambush us... is... foreign accent syndrome' forewarned Alexander Chancellor in *The Guardian* newspaper (October 18, 1997). This 'real Twilight Zone stuff' (Barry Didcock, *Scotsman* newspaper March 28, 1997) that robs you of your own accent and causes you to be suddenly changed into a foreigner in your own country (Chancellor again) is described invariably as having affected only a few people worldwide since the early 1900s. This 'mysterious acquisition of a (foreign) accent' (Press release University of Central Florida, November 19, 2003) is hailed as 'not fully understood by neuropsychologists' (BBC news December 20, 1999). Even Linguist List electronic discussion group contributors in 1997 could not shake off the possibility that media reports might be a hoax. Others offer psychiatric reasons as their sole explanation.

These quotes offer a flavour of some of the popular (mis)conceptions about foreign accent syndrome (FAS), which, even allowing for some journalistic licence in oversensationalization to entice the reader, can often steer a path wide of the true mark. As will be argued below, FAS is not so rare as news editors would have us believe, has not affected 'but a handful of people worldwide'; those who study it do have a fair understanding of how it comes about, and that understanding goes rather farther than BBC (December 20, 1999) and ABC (January 3, 2004) news departments' insights that it is 'thought to be linked to the way in which the brain tissue is damaged after a stroke' and it is because victims 'suffered tiny areas of damage in various parts of the brain'. As Didcock, again in the *Scotsman* (March 28, 1997), remarked 'to imply... that Annie B. went to bed sounding like the Queen and woke up talking like Rab C Nesbitt[1] is a gross oversimplification'.

This chapter aims to illuminate what lies behind the FAS label, speculate as to why it should arouse such interest and at the same time engender such confusion.

FAS the basic facts

FAS is the label given to the phenomenon whereby after a neurological incident (stroke; head injury; progressive neurological illness) it sounds as if a person has begun to speak with a foreign accent, or accent of another region of their country. Moen,[2] Miller and colleagues[3] offer recent overviews. The renowned French neurologist Pierre Marie in 1907 gave perhaps the earliest published account when he described a Parisian who now sounded like an Alsatian (person from Alsace!). Arnold Pick (of Pick's disease fame) in 1919 gives us what is probably the second published case, of a Czech whom people now took to be a Pole. Other reports detail Londoners who 'became' Scottish, a Texan mistaken for a New Englander, a Norwegian for a German, Argentinians as Slavs, a Colombian who sounded English and Australians speaking like Japanese.

This is all despite the fact that speakers previously never had a foreign accent, may even have no knowledge of the language their accent is meant to derive from, have never visited nor associated with people from that country or region, and have no other discernible reason why they might all of a sudden speak in such a manner.

Contrary to media claims that FAS is a rare disorder, not a handful but in excess of 50 have been described in the specialist literature. Even this though merely reflects publication bias, and the mounting numbers reported over recent years testify to developments in the linguistics and neuropsychology industry, more latterly the imaging industry too. What is not recorded is the anecdotally reported clinical incidence. Most people who work in neurological clinics will have encountered someone with FAS at some stage. Many cases show only a transient FAS, during the course of recovery or decline of their neurological condition. Those who experience a lasting perceived foreign accent generally do not suffer from impaired intelligibility, so seldom present at clinic (because of their speech) and in consequence remain unrecorded. Absence of intelligibility problems does not of course mean that FAS does not affect the speaker—as will be clear from cases cited below.

FAS the misunderstandings

Why should others, though, be so ready to brand people with FAS as feigners, malingerers, psychiatric cases? When one considers the typical presentation, one maybe should not be so harshly disposed towards those quick to mislabel people with FAS in this way. It can seem baffling, and apart from the apparently bizarre fact that someone out of the blue begins speaking with a foreign accent, other characteristics of FAS do have a tantalizingly mysterious aura and temptingly psychiatric flavour—prime ingredients for media attention and links into the collective psyche regarding suspicions of foreigners, outsiders, people who go native, change allegiance, turn their back on their roots. Why though should FAS attract such scepticism while seemingly equally bizarre sequels of neurological damage such as anarchic hand syndrome, blindsight, jargon aphasia, reduplicative paramnesia, to name but a few, are readily accepted as legitimate behaviours of neurological and not psychiatric origin?

Listeners may sense the accent is not fixed. It alters on a daily basis. Now it sounds more French, now more German. One listener or the speaker themselves may characterize the accent as Polish or Italian, others hear it as Spanish, Irish. More tellingly, an observation we return to later, listeners may label the accent with a general descriptor—Nordic,

British, Slavic, Asian. They do not hear a definite country or dialect. People from the country or region with which the accent is meant to be associated do not perceive it as sounding like their accent.

A further feature bolstering the feeling of relatives, social circle and unquestioning clinicians that a person is presenting with a psychiatric disorder concerns the unmodifyability of the accent. Speakers insist they are unable to modify their accent, despite an ardent desire to do so. Requested to put on a different accent during clinical assessment they struggle in vain. Nevertheless, from one minute or day to the next, it sounds as if speakers are sometimes speaking with their 'foreign' accent, other times have regained their 'normal' accent, only to revert to sounding foreign, but this time Chinese instead of Indian, Welsh not French. Moreover, Added suspicion of a behavioural disturbance may be engendered from superficial observations that this variability is linked to time, place, person or conversational topic changes, not to physiological, or illness-specific patterns of variation. All these traits are straightforwardly interpretable within well-known pictures of neurological disturbances to speech production.

Frequently FAS is the only overt sequel of underlying neurological changes. Speakers' imploring that it is a problem from their stroke are taken with large pinches of salt in the absence of any other sign of illness, or the FAS is deemed an over-reaction to a mild stroke or head injury. FAS seldom affects a speaker's ability to make themselves understood. On this basis, it might not be thought to deliver so serious a fate as befalls many others with communication difficulties in neurological illness. Nevertheless, reported and personal cases are replete with references to the way in which FAS has negatively impacted their life.

Monrad Krohn's wartime Norwegian case made public in 1947 records the community ire suffered by Astrid L after her head injury, as her altered accent aroused suspicions of collaboration with occupying forces. Judi Roberts (ABC News) changed her name to save her family the embarrassment of being associated with what people took to be a psychiatric condition. She became a recluse and agoraphobic from worry of the taunts and questions that greeted her because of her British accent. She even contemplated emigration to Britain—though ironically British speakers listening to her still heard an American. Speakers feel that with the loss of their own accent, a part of them has been robbed, part of their character, of what makes them who they are, has disappeared. The new accent is not them. They speak of the frustration at vainly attempting to modify their speech back to its former patterns. More disturbing for many are the all too ready direct and indirect inferences from friends, family and ill informed clinicians that it is all in the mind, they are putting it on, they have a psychiatric disturbance.

For a few, positive outcomes ensue. A personal case enjoyed the envy of her friends for her 'sexy French' accent. Another woman felt just lucky—considering how her stroke could have left her, having to live with her French accent was a small price to pay. Once more, though, disclosures by speakers concerning effects on their personality are easily misinterpreted as behavioural or personality disturbance. Those cavalierly dismissing their problem as giving them a sexy voice or whatever are readily spoken of as seeking secondary attention or displaying *la belle indifference*, easy hooks for psychiatric misdiagnosis.

Regardless of acknowledgement that FAS generally arises from a genuine organic aetiology, this has not stemmed overheated speculation in sections of the media and some clinical circles about what precisely the organic factor is that leads to FAS. The presenter at BBC Bristol (1998) wondered what (defective) gene might cause FAS, as if one has a gene for each accent one might ever speak. Others have speculated about the site of control of foreign accents in the brain— FAS 'may be indicating that in the human mind there is a separate, independent module for accents' the BBC News on December 20, 1999 fancifully opined.

The search has been on for the key site of the lesion that brings about FAS. The quest for a culprit single lesion site, gene or psycholinguistic process that solves the FAS mystery is a forlorn search since it ignores two obvious facts about speech production. First, speech as a form of motor behaviour is controlled by a widely distributed system of concatenated and interacting neural circuits, systems rendered even more complex through the link of speech (the medium to convey a message) to language (the content of the message), with language itself dependent on another distributed network of interconnections. Little wonder then that FAS cases have been reported with lesions in left frontal, parietal and temporal lobes, right frontal sites, subcortical lesions of the basal ganglia and elsewhere.

The hunt for the key lesion in FAS is equatable to what Michel Paradis[4] labelled the Loch Ness monster approach to second language localization at a time when many naively sought a unique site in the brain where a bilingual speaker's second language was localized. Many claimed to have located the site but, like the sightings of the Loch Ness monster, all these proved to be illusory, failing to stand up to closer scrutiny or attempts by others to find it in the same place. The search was elusive because notions as large and complex as language are not reducible to or analysable as one-dimensional entities.

Linguists have forwarded supposed explanations in terms of altered vowel space, i.e. differences in aspects of the acoustic signal for vowels produced by FAS speakers compared with non-FAS speakers. This though is but a description, not an explanation. It merely means the range of tongue movement and placement have altered, and with it the sounds produced—as happens in several neurological conditions not typically associated with FAS. It leaves unanswered why these changes developed and why one speaker with altered vowel space is perceived as speech disordered, the next as having FAS.

The second factor which precludes the likelihood of pinning down a single factor underlying accent changes in FAS relates to the self same argument in the nature of speech production as the 'localization' of other languages in polyglot speakers. Speech is not a unitary phenomenon. Even from a narrow viewpoint focusing solely on speech output, it emerges from the confluence of many contributory factors. To start to answer what does lie behind FAS, we need to step back and consider some aspects of how speech is produced by the brain and perceived by the listener.

Producing speech

Figure 14.1 lays out some key elements in producing an utterance, emphasizing the diversity of processes involved in producing speech. Note the constantly interactive nature of operations, both within the speaker, and, central to an understanding of FAS, between the sounds the speaker utters and the way in which the listener perceives these. Note too, that because operations are grouped together here in one ellipsis does not indicate that they themselves are unitary processes or are 'localized' in a specific site in the brain. No claim is made here about the exact make up of any of the components illustrated, nor the precise order, interaction of and flow of information through the system. The diagram is purely to portray the multidimensional complexity of speaking.

To convey a message formulated within the meaning and grammar components of language, the speaker needs to identify the sounds that will be required to produce the necessary words. However, sound plans without movement remain silent. Alongside sound specification therefore must come movement specification. Movements need to be executed in such a way as to transmit clearly not just the words intended for the message, but also with the appropriate rate of speech, intonation and tone to transmit the broader meaning of the utterance (informal, formal; quick, slow; angry, patient; doubting...).

Speech is probably the most complex motor act that humans, or any animals, perform—more complex than driving a car, writing, landing upside down on the ceiling. Speech involves coordination across scores of muscles to generate what are perceived as around 14 different sounds per second. It entails at least four major subsystems—respiration, the larynx for phonation, the raising and lowering of the soft palate (or velum) for controlling oral versus nasal resonance, and the oral articulators—lips, tongue and mandible. Figure 14.2 outlines some of the key active and passive articulators engaged in modifying the outgoing air stream from the lungs to produce speech.

Crucially, respiration, phonation and movements of the soft palate, tongue, lips and jaw do not occur in isolation from each other. They are tightly balanced in terms of relative forces, coupled in millimetre-exact spatial configurations and demand millisecond coordination of the on- and offset of their movements in relation to each other.

For instance, in speech production, one of the key differences between what one hears as 'pat' versus 'bat' centres essentially on less than a 100 ms difference in timing between release of the puff of air required to utter a 'b' or 'p' sound and the onset of vibration of the vocal cords (differences in voice onset time in the trade jargon). Likewise, millisecond alterations in the length of the vowel 'a' will determine whether the listener hears 'pat' or 'pad'. The degree of tongue tip closure behind the top front teeth and pattern of release of that closure is central to whether listeners hears 'hit' versus 'hits' versus 'hiss'. Minor deviations in the spatial configuration of the tongue contact and release might cause the listener to perceive not 'hit' but 'hitch' or 'hith', or 'heat' or 'het'. Mistiming of the raising or lowering of the velum, soft palate, would result in such mishearings as thinking that 'manager' was spoken as 'mandager', 'madager' or 'bandager'. Deformation in the spatio-temporal closing configuration of the lips could lead to hearing what

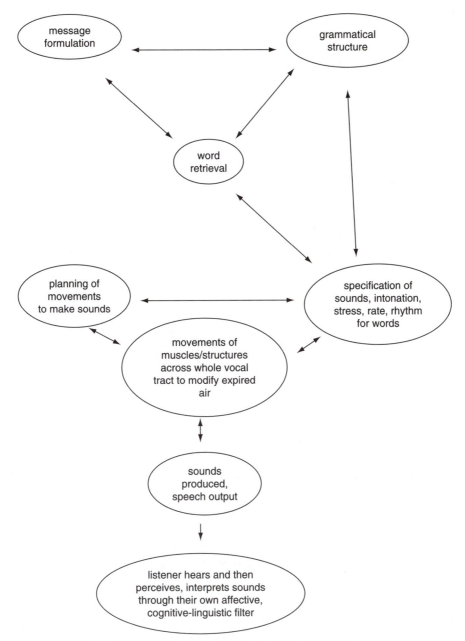

Fig. 14.1 Some chief components and their interaction in producing speech.

sounds like 'Wayne' instead of 'vain' (or vice versa), 'feet' or 'pfeet' instead of target word 'Pete'.

In speech production, it is tempting to think of control in terms of realizing the positioning of the articulators required to produce one sound, followed by the positioning

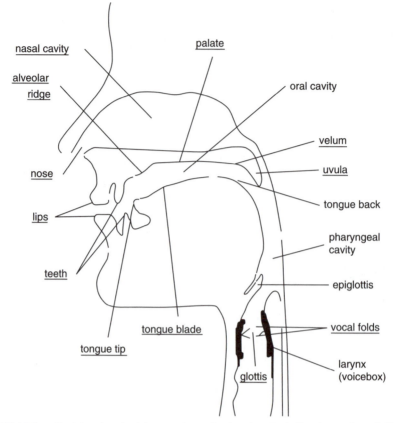

Fig. 14.2 Main articulators involved in speech production (not including lungs/thorax) (from SIL Mexico).

required for the following sound, and so forth. In actual fact, production of strings of sounds consists of complex overlapping on- and offsets of movements of the different articulators. Furthermore, pronunciation of a given sound is not necessarily equal across contexts. Consider how the movements for and sound of 'p' differ in the following words when spoken out loud—pen, happen, ripped, aptly, hipflask, lamp. Attempts to say 'ripped' or 'aptly' with the 'p' pronounced the same as in 'pen' signal something odd about a person's speech, at least in standard British English. Another example: native English speakers produce the 'st' and 'mp' in 'stamp' as an uninterrupted string. If someone utters them as 'sutamup' or astampa', breaking up the close succession of the 'st' and 'mp' and disturbing the architecture of the syllable, their accent is immediately heard as non-normal.

The overlapping of movements and corresponding blending of sounds is manifest in speech in another way, in what is termed sound assimilation. Unless we are imitating Edith Evans acting Lady Bracknell in Wilde's *Importance of Being Ernest* we do not speak of a 'h-a-n-d-b-a-g'. We say 'hambag'. Except in the most deliberate speech no one utters 'th-a-tch-ed-c-o-tt-age' as anything but 'thashcottage'.

Two points are pertinent to FAS here. First, these patterns of assimilation are largely language specific—German speakers, for instance, do not pronounce 'Handball' as 'hamball'. Secondly, when someone does alter expected assimilatory processes it sends powerful messages to a listener—that they are laying unusual emphasis on a sound, word or phrase (the handabag!), or that this is a non-native speaker of the accent or language.

This thumbnail sketch of speech production requires another dimension. Speech production goes beyond concatenations of overlapping movements and sounds. Elements such as pitch, intonation and stress patterns in words and phrases (termed prosody) stretch over whole utterances. Production of these aspects of speech entails a tight balance between control of subglottal air pressure (the force of air being driven out of the lungs) and glottal resistance (the tightness of the vocal cords). Changes in this relationship result in what we hear as differences in stress patterns or intonational rises and falls—the difference between 'that's my coat' versus 'that's my coat'; content versus content; 'yes' or 'you're coming tomorrow' spoken with a questioning intonation versus a statement or imperative intonation. Again, disturbance of the fine balances between sub- and supra-glottal forces and timing leads to distortion in sound production—heard this time as distortions of stress, rhythm and intonation. The speaker might produce what the listener hears as canoe instead of expected canoe, that's my coat? instead of intended that's my coat!, 'what are you doing? spoken with rising intonation on each word separately instead of gradually across the whole phrase.

Perception of rhythm by the listener is a potent factor in recognition of accents. Indeed, studies that manipulate the speech signal, so that listeners hear only the rhythm, and no individual sounds or words, demonstrate that one is able to detect the language being spoken purely on the basis of rhythm. Disruptions to the rhythm from alterations to stress patterns, or from changes to syllable structure (the 'sutampa' example above), and non-familiar intonation patterns are immediately apparent to the listener as something out of the ordinary.

All these distortions, in voice onset time, nasality, length of sounds, changes to coarticulation, stress and intonation arise in neurogenic speech disorders.

Two broad underlying disorders have been linked to cases of FAS—dysarthria and apraxia of speech (see, for example, the volume edited by McNeil: *Clinical management of sensorimotor speech disorders*[5]). Dysarthria labels the speech disorder arising from disruption to speech movements because of neuromuscular changes—abnormally increased or decreased tone in the muscles, rigidity, weakness, fatigueability and discoordination. These changes lead in turn to reduced or erratic rate of movements, under- and over-shooting of movements and discoordination between movements. For their part, these changes result in what listeners hear as distortions and omissions of sounds, altered rhythm patterns to speech and its intonation.

Apraxia of speech is taken to be a disturbance of the programming of speech sounds and movements. There is no alteration to muscle power, tone and coordination. The breakdown is at the stage of specifying, preparing and controlling the movements required to produce a particular string of sounds. In the most severe cases, apraxia of speech renders speakers mute. In mild cases, the listener perceives what are heard as subtle changes to stress patterns, dissolution of expected assimilation processes (the person *does* say hand…bag or handabag, astamup or astampa) and merging of the usually separate distribution of voice onset times across pairs of sounds such as b–p, d–t, g–k, leading to uncertainty over whether someone is saying *pea* or *bee*, *day* or *Tay*, *girl* or *curl*. Distortions of lip closure patterns lead to mishearings such as *vase* for *bars* or vice versa.

Both dysarthria and apraxia of speech may result in dysprosody, i.e. alterations to the stress, rhythm and intonation dimensions of speech. Sentences sound monotone or monoloud; atypical rises and falls of intonation are heard; syllables are missed out of words lending an unexpected rhythm to speech; and stress is placed wrongly. Non-normal pauses between or even within words give a hesitant and dysfluent ring to speech. Certainly these changes feature in dysarthric and apraxic speech. Some argue for a tripartite division, with dysprosody as a third kind of motor speech breakdown. This is not the forum to argue pros and cons. Suffice it to say that neurological changes lead to perceived changes in stress, intonation and rhythm, as well as in individual sounds.

FAS as a neurogenic speech disorder

So, what has all of this to do with FAS? The contention here is that FAS does not arise as a variety of speech motor control breakdown separate from dysarthria, apraxia of speech or dysprosody. The deformation of speech sounds and prosodic production found in FAS are no different from the derailments found in these other speech disorders. There are claims in the earlier literature of cases of FAS without apraxia, dysarthria or dysprosody. These disorders have not always been assessed for and often one has to doubt the validity and reliability of the assessment procedures used.

The distortion of sounds heard in FAS, the altered fluency, the unexpected intonation and stress patterns, the dissolution of normal assimilatory processes (the hambag), the hesitations and self-corrections are all perfectly well understood features of dysarthria, apraxia of speech and problems with prosody. It is therefore quite feasible to interpret FAS speech as a particular manifestation of one of these broad divisions of speech disorder linked to neurological illness.

Further characteristics of apraxia of speech are doubtless what lie behind several of the mistakenly psychiatric flavoured features of FAS. Absence of changes to tone, power, sustainability and range of movement appear to point away from organic origins. A prime finding in apraxia of speech concerns variability of success. Because the problem lies with planning and control and not (as in dysarthria) that muscle weakness or stiffness does not permit realization of the necessary movements for a sound or word, then typically an apraxic speaker will be able to produce a sound flawlessly on one occasion, but not another. One moment they produce a flawless rendition of 'that's my coat', yet in the following utterance seem to say 'datch my goat' or 'cutch me court' for the same target phrase.

Speakers with apraxia of speech are also susceptible to a propositionality effect and closely allied to this what has been variously termed the automatic–volitional, implicit–explicit divide. Asked to count to 5 or recite the days of the week or a well-rehearsed poem or prayer, they succeed. When they are not required to concentrate particularly on what they say, e.g. in an aside, the 'ums' and 'ers' and social formulas of conversation—'morning; lovely day'—pronunciation may be faultless. The same words spoken in a phrase where the speaker has to consider what they wish to say more consciously entails struggle and increased likelihood of mispronunciations—counting up to 5 is accomplished with normal or near normal accent, counting down from 5 elicits a struggling, dysfluent performance with distorted words and sounds. As Isaacs[6] teasingly phrased it 'apraxia is when you can't do what you can do when you try but you can do what you can't do when you don't try'.

Merry vibes of Windsor

There is one snag in arguing that FAS is simply a manifestation of dysarthria or apraxia of speech. If that be so, how come every person with these disorders does not sound foreign? A brief excursion into a key element in evaluation of speech disturbances is in order here—listener perception. It is axiomatic in the field of motor speech disorders that, like beauty and the eye of the beholder, the evaluation of (type, severity, reaction to . . .) a speech disorder is as much in the ear of the listener as it is in the mouth of the speaker.

Two observations are pertinent here. First, while talk above has been of millisecond or millimetre deformations in speech production leading to the perception of altered sounds or intonation and stress patterns, in actual fact listeners' perception of speech is relatively robust to distortions. We still manage to follow when someone speaks quickly or in a very informal manner without so precise articulator contacts; still understand someone over a bad phone line, when they are speaking with a cigarette, hot potato or thumb in their mouth. Such noise in the system usually passes unnoticed. One of the reasons is that as listeners we have certain expectations about what sound must have been intended (we would not normally spend time wondering what 'pfeet' are or who this 'Pete' is when we hear someone say 'he must stand on his own two pfeet/Pete').

However, there are bounds to the distortion that can be tolerated before intelligibility suffers or the speech of an individual is perceived as in some way different. The nature of the transgressions in individual sound realizations, the way someone says a 'w', 'r' or 's' sound for instance, or the way their intonation rises or falls across a phrase, leads us to certain conclusions about them.

We have in our phonological minds a knowledge of the range of normal variation for the sounds, and stress and intonation patterns of our language that count as normal variation, whether the variation is to be ignored as random noise, or whether it will signal something more about the speaker. Part of this knowledge enables us to deduce a range of things about the speaker—they are angry, depressed, in a hurry, old, excited or uninterested. When variability falls outside expected normal bounds, we are further able to build a hypothesis about why—the person has a head cold, laryngitis or lose dentures, they come from another part of the country, they have an idiosyncratic way of pronouncing a particular sound or word, they are not native speakers of the language or they must have a speech impediment.

What though are the crucial factors that say one person's crossing of the normal variation line denotes stranger, while another falls into the realm of disordered speech? The answer lies again with expectations. We harbour notions about which sounds are features of natural languages and which not. We have an impression about which kinds of sound changes are associated with speakers of particular other languages when they speak our own language—either from our own experience of hearing such speech or from popular stage notions about what changes one makes to signify it is a Scottish person talking, a Russian or a Chinese. If someone's speech contains instances that fall in these set categories, then we label them as such—Irish, Japanese, whatever. Distortions that do not match listeners' notions of natural languages are liable to lead them to label the person as having a speech disorder or other explanation (new dentures, frozen face from the dentist's ...). Again, what constitutes a token of disordered speech is likely to be shaped by a listener's personal experience of the types of distortions that divulge a speech impediment and their own threshold of tolerance for the degree of signal deformation before something untoward is perceived.

In act 1 scene 4 of Shakespeare's *Merry Wives of Windsor* Doctor Caius enters proclaiming 'Vat is you sing? I do not like des toys. Pray you go and vetch me in my closet ... a greena box ...'. In J. K. Rowling's *Harry Potter and the Philosopher's Stone* Professor Quirrel greets Potter in chapter 5 with 'P-P-Potter ...... 'c-can't t-tell you how p-pleased I am to meet you,' telling him he teaches 'D-defence against the D-D-Dark arts ...'. We are immediately aware that Shakespeare is intending to convey that Caius is a foreigner and Rowling that Quirrel has a speech impediment. What causes us to accept that *pfeet* is part of normal variation (or even pass over it unaware); 'vat', 'greena box' and 'des' signal a foreign speaker; while 'c-can't t-tell you' denotes a disorder?

In the Shakespeare example, several key features of our perception of foreign accents apply. The sound changes Caius makes fit our preconception in terms of classes of distortion that lead us to hear a Frenchman (but see below). Further, we are tuned to hear a foreigner not from the mispronunciation of every sound in every word. Two or three key distortions are sufficient to prime us. In fact, research shows that people are able to spot foreign accents from millisecond splices of a person's speech. What is more, distortions do not need to occur every time a target sound appears. Later in the same act Caius pronounces 'th', 'wh/w', 'f', 'th' correctly, even whole turns without wavering—not because Shakespeare is being inconsistent, but simply because once we have been primed to perceive someone as a foreign speaker we only have to sense a particular deviation intermittently to uphold our supposition or continue the illusion the writer/speaker intends to plant. Shakespeare intends Caius to be French. However, from the snippets above, many may hear a German or Italian accent, or appreciate that this is a foreign speaker of English, but remain unclear where they might be from.

Again, the parallel is drawn with claims regarding FAS. Not all listeners agree on the precise provenance of the accent, nor the markedness of the accent. Amongst the foreign-accented speech there is also apparently non-foreign accent to be heard. This echoes another observation in reports of people with FAS. In the literature, we read of Parisians who developed an Alsatian accent, Norwegians a German accent, English a Scottish, Americans a British one. Why though are there no reports of British speakers changing to a Lugandan accent, Fijians adopting Finnish speech, Germans sounding to their compatriots like Irish, Italians like Basques?

The interpretation here is that British speakers have no experience and therefore no notion of what a Lugandan speaker of English would sound like, and likewise Italians of Basques or Fijians of Finns. Thus if someone's speech contained elements of these languages that differ from the native speaker's pronunciation, they would more probably be perceived as disordered as opposed to foreign; or, they would be labelled as 'African sounding' or a general area label rather than a specific language origin. In like vein, Germans may have an idea of what German spoken with an Anglo-Saxon accent sounds like, but little finer differentiation according to different underlying varieties of English.

On this basis, one might make some predictions. A person who because of their dysarthria or apraxia of speech produces, say, click sounds, implosives, uvular consonants or nasal vowels, will be perceived as disordered by people who have no experience of languages that utilize these features, but as sounding like a foreigner from such parts by those who do. In as far as different speakers will have varying proportions of natural language, but 'foreign' for any given language, distortions in their speech, then listeners rating speech for gradation of foreignness should produce a continuum from definitely foreign to definitely disordered.

There is one more aspect to Caius's first lines. 'Vat is you sing' contains a grammatical deviation—he does not ask 'what *are* you sing*ing*'. A hitherto neglected factor in the perception of FAS concerns the presence alongside speech distortions of grammatical transgressions. Many speakers with FAS have accompanying mild aphasic problems which can lead to what is heard as foreigner talk. The point further emphasizes that someone's judgement on foreignness may not centre on one individual perceived feature, but stem from the constellation of, for them, tell-tale markers of non-native speech.

Is FAS all?

Not all cases of a foreign accent appearing out of the blue are FAS. Two other origins which feature in differential diagnosis are what has been termed re-emergence of a previous genuine foreign accent, and psychogenic aetiology. There are speakers who previously spoke with a foreign or other regional accent, but who mastered the accent of the new country or region sufficiently to be taken as a local. After stroke or head injury, this previous accent re-emerges. The person now speaks with a foreign/non-local accent as they did previously. The interpretation usually given in these instances is that mastery of a new accent after puberty costs the brain in terms of processing capacity and attention.

When this is impaired in neurological illness, the consequence is that the new accent costs too much, cannot be upheld and lapses to the previous one.

FAS has often been mislabelled as a manifestation of psychiatric disorder. Nevertheless, cases of psychogenic foreign accent do arise. This is not the place to detail all the differential diagnostic steps to tease out neurological from psychological causes. An important point to mention here, though, is that the nature and patterns of changes to speech found in apraxia of speech and the different dysarthrias are well documented, differ in important ways from changes speakers make when attempting to imitate foreign accents and do not lend themselves to feigning. In this way, detailed speech assessment should be able to play a leading role in separating neurological from psychological origins of novel foreign accent.

Typically the onset of FAS speech changes can be linked to a recognizable neurological event or appear alongside other markers or heralds of progressive neurological illness.

Conclusions

The explanation of FAS favoured here has been that it is a manifestation of more common or garden dysarthria, apraxia of speech or dysprosody. Brain damage can alter the fine balance of time and space control in speech production. This leads to distortions of individual sounds and changes to stress and intonation patterns. What sets people with FAS aside from the more typical picture heard in dysarthria and apraxia is that the constellation of distortions arouses echoes in the listener not of disordered speech but of the distortions of their language associated with extant natural languages. In this way, FAS is the disorder par excellence in the ear of the listener and not the mouth of the speaker.

Maybe it should not come as such a surprise that people are quick to label the change as psychiatric in origin, that the accent and the individuals who evidence the change should be found so intriguing and eyed (eared?) with such suspicion. Anarchic hands, phantom limbs, auditory agnosia, mistaking one's wife for a hat are in the mind of the general public perceived as such impossible behaviours that they could only have arisen from brain damage. But why should brain damage change just someone's accent; why should a loyal English person, a patriot American, a staunch Berliner suddenly wish to switch to an Italian, Scandinavian or Bavarian? While someone can learn to conceal their paraesthesiae, reduplicative paramnesia, an altered accent leaps out in every encounter.

For the majority, who understand better what happens under the bonnet of their car or in the back of their television than the operations of the brain, 'Because I had a stroke' for why they sound foreign is met with disbelief. There has to be some other explanation. Accents signal foreigner, stranger, other identities, issues of origin, belongingness, no longer wanting to belong or no longer being the person they were. The wary wives of Windsor, the merry vibes of Wintzer should not be so suspicious of the speaker, though. Distortions of speech may be in the mouth of the speaker, but perception of accents is in the ear of the beholder.

References and notes

1. **Rab C Nesbitt** is a TV character who speaks with, for non-Glaswegians, a barely penetrable Glaswegian accent. As regards varieties of English in the British Isles, it is about as far as one can get from so-called Queen's English.
2. **Moen I.** Foreign accent syndrome: a review of contemporary explanations. *Aphasiology*, 2000; **14**:5–15
3. **Miller N, Lowit A, O'Sullivan H.** What makes foreign accent syndrome foreign? *Journal of Neurolinguistics* (in press).
4. **Paradis M.** The bilingual Loch Ness Monster raises its non-asymmetric head again—or, why bother with such cumbersome notions as validity and reliability? Comments on Evans *et al. Brain and Language*, 2002; **87**:441–448
5. **McNeil M** (ed.) Clinical management of sensorimotor speech disorders. Thieme, NY. 1997.
6. **Isaacs B.** Review of dyspraxia and its management. *Age and Ageing*, 1987; **16**:61.

Chapter 15

Talking with the dead, communicating with the future and other myths created by cold reading

Ray Hyman

Introduction

Christian Dion

Christian Dion is a well-known British psychic. His clients include celebrities both in England and in the USA. He frequently gives readings to callers during radio appearances. Here is a sample of one of his readings that he gave on London Broadcasting on October 27, 1987:

Karen: Hello Christian.

Dion: Hello Karen. How are you?

Karen: Fine thank you. How are you?

Dion: Very good. West Hampstead. Oh, well, very trendy. As usual, we pick out the ten cards[1], plonk you in the middle, and see what we can come up with. A couple of things actually sort of turned up very fast. One is sort of hovering around property concerns and sort of ideas or opportunities to make changes and I'll come back to that.

Karen: Right.

Dion: But is it particularly that within sort of career-stroke-business that you have been contemplating making the bigger changes, so to speak?

Karen: That's right. Yes.

Dion: Yes, because it's like 'shall I, can I'. Now I feel that this has been, if we look back with you over the last two to three months particularly—that's the kind of sort of length of time that it's been sort of revolving around you. And as you go forward from now to sort of the January time, (Karen 'Yes') everything sort of falls into place. (K 'Yes'). But I just want to ask you, apart from yourself dithering, who has actually been trying to sort of dissuade you from either making these changes or putting these changes into effect?

Karen: You mean career prospects?

Dion: Yes.

Karen: Um, somebody in the family.

Dion: Somebody in the family.

Karen: Hmmm.

Dion: Um. Without being rude to them, you're not taking too much notice of them, are you?

Karen: No.

Dion: Good, that's fair enough. Because I don't think... you see I think they're looking at it in a situation that where you are it's like say in a proper job, if you follow me. It's like you know that old expression, 'Oh, you've got a proper job and you're secure and all that kind of thing' (K 'right'). Now I'm not saying that it isn't, but I feel that the opportunities that are lying in front of you, and this is why I think you've been inspired to sort of shift and make changes, are more important in the long term (K 'yes'). Now I do feel that will bring along with it the opportunity or the necessity for you to make a change of your personal home (K 'yes'). Now the only thing I can't say whether this is like selling and then buying one or just moving, because it's only brought a move with it, so I just have to as it comes tell you (K 'Okay'). But I do feel that it will, um, as you go through that period and then pass the January when it's all settled in, it'll enable you to travel more because I just, I just can't pin you down in any way once I get past January. (K 'yes'). It's almost as though you're not here (K 'Right'). I mean I hope to God you are like, but I mean it's like (K laughs) but it's like, it's as though you could be going from here to there, to there, cos it's travel (K 'right') and travelling (K 'yes'). Now that means travel is in the country and travelling is outside–it's just my way of deciphering it (K 'right'). But the only thing you just need to watch a little bit through this month and next month, so we're talking November and December, are sort of nerve conditions, because you've been very sort of electric since about the spring (K 'absolutely'). And I do feel that this has been slightly interconnected with romantic conditions (K 'Absolutely') and it's got (Christian here makes some strange noises with his lips) and you've, you've, you've... I don't know what you've done. I think you just must have blocked it out to be honest (K 'yes') but don't worry about that, because I think if you just follow your good feeling, do the career, the work change, let the move sift into place, and then you'll find that romantic things sort of follow along as you progress through 1988. But it is really a good idea. Has it already been discussed verbally or mentally to go abroad?

Karen: Oh, well I'm actually planning to go away quite soon.

Dion: Abroad?

Karen: Yes.

Dion: Oh, that's alright. And this is to like follow career opportunities?

Karen: Yes, both. Yes.

Dion: Yes, I mean you can go to sort of, bum around for a while, but I just feel as though it's, at the end of it there's some career thing, and I think if you didn't go..let's put it this way, I think if you didn't go I think you'd kick yourself when you were sixty.

Karen: Yes.

Dion: Okay?

Karen: Yes.

Dion: My pleasure.

Karen: Oh, Christian, one last thing. Can I just ask you more about the relationship?

Dion: Hmmm.

Karen: Um ... I'm just not sure what to do about it right now.

Dion: Ah, well. That's why I answered it in the wrapped up way (K 'yes'). Take the career, go for the move, and it will fall itself into place.

Karen: Right, Okay.

Dion: In a nutshell (Here Christian makes a rasping sound).

John Edward

John Edward has become the best known medium on the American landscape. His television show, 'Crossing Over', aired for several years. Edward also has made several guest appearances on the *Larry King Live* show, plus many other popular television venues. He claims to communicate with the dead relatives of his clients and callers. Here is a sample of two readings that he gave to callers on the *Larry King Live* show on October 2, 2003:

Caller: I'm Brenda and ...

Edward: Hey, Brenda, don't—wait. Don't say anything. Brenda, let me just (UNINTELLIGIBLE) I heard your voice and I want to just jump in, if I can. I don't know if your mom has passed, as well. Is there an older female for you has passed?

Caller: Yes.

Edward: OK. And she's got a younger male that she wants me to bring through with her. So I don't know if you have the son figure who's passed or if it's her son-in-law, whoever this is. But the older—the old woman, who I refer to as a female figure above you, has a younger male who is with her. Do you understand this?

Caller: Uh-huh.

Edward: Now, would that be, like, her son, her son-in-law? Who was this guy?

Caller: Probably her son, my father.

Edward: OK. I want you to know that they're coming through together, but I have to let you know that somebody had either their voice box removed or somebody had something with their throat where there's surgery going on here. What is that?

Caller: Yes. That's my grandmother.

Edward: OK. I want you to know also that—you know, this is going to sound kind of general, so all the skeptics, save your letters. I got to say this. There's some type of knitting needles or crochet needles or a metal instruments that would be creatively used. I don't know if those are yours, if those are hers and they're passed down, but there's a joke about them being used for something else. I don't know if somebody was cooking with them or if they made something and they put a knitting needle in something. I have no clue what this is. But it's a joke or it's a tease that comes with this.

And I also want to let you know that besides your dad being there, they're telling me to talk about the person who is now, right now, dealing with something health care-wise. I don't know if they were diagnosed with cancer or if there was an issue that they had a malignancy that they were concerned about. Do you know what he's talking about?

Caller: I can't think of it right now.

Edward: OK. I just want you to know that. Where's Carol?

Caller: Carol?

Edward: With a—.

Caller: I have an Aunt Carolyn.

Edward: OK. Is she still here?

Caller: Uh-huh.

Edward: OK. It might be on that side of the family that somebody just had a scare or there's something going on there. I don't know. All righty? Thank you so much.

King: Thank you. Malibu, California. Hello.

Caller: Hello?

King: Hi.

Caller: Hi. My name is Pamela.

Edward: Hi, Pamela. How are you?

Edward: But I want to stress for you, more than anything...

Caller: Yes?

Edward: ... is that somebody that you're connected to had to put their dog down.

Caller: OK.

Edward: And it's the description that I gave you, and it's going to help them greatly when you share this. Or maybe they're watching this right. They're going to call you when we hang up and go, That's my dog. But it's connected through you.

Caller: OK.

Edward: And I feel like it was—you know, it's the baby of the family. They had no choice. They had to put the dog down. They need to know that the dog was ready to go. It was ill, OK?

Caller: OK.

Edward: So it's very, very important. And also, one last thing. They're telling me to talk about Ellen or Helen. Who is that?

Caller: Ellen or Helen?

Edward: That kind of—yes.

Caller: God, I don't know either of those, either!

Edward: OK. Do me a favor. Remember the names. It's usually their way of pointing me to where we're supposed to go. Thank you.

What is going on?

Christian makes many statements about the caller's situation. He typically describes the caller's status during the recent past, at the time of the reading, and in the future. He might comment on property matters, travel possibilities, career changes, relationships, health and other issues. The caller agrees, disagrees or makes non-commital remarks.

In the late 1980s, the magician David Berglas offered Christian Dion a monetary reward if he could prove that his readings were valid. The late Dr Robert Morris, who occupied the Arthur Koestler chair of parapsychology at the University of Edinburgh, was asked to devise a suitable test of Christian's powers. Morris appeared on an LBC broadcast to discuss his findings. Morris concluded that he could not decide whether Dion's readings were truly valid or not. The problem was that Dion would submit only to tests of the sort that could not be evaluated by scientific procedures. During the same programme, many callers defended Dion. They testified to how Dion's readings—both private and public— had given them information that he could not have gotten through normal means. They also claimed that his predictions had come true.

The same difficulty occurs when we try to assess the validity of John Edward's claims or those of any other alleged psychic. Although the caller or sitter usually wants to hear from a specific relative, Edward frequently conveys messages from a departed person other than the desired one. Edward attempts to provide information that 'validates' that the entity talking through him is someone who was related to the sitter when he or she was alive. Often he throws out names—usually a range of possible names or simply a first letter of a name. Always the names are first names. For some reason, last names never come through.

Dr Gary Schwartz has tested John Edward and other mediums, at the University of Arizona. Schwartz believes that his tests show that Edward and the other mediums were conveying information from the dead relatives that they could not have obtained by normal means. He argues that the evidence supports the hypothesis that John Edward and the other mediums are truly communicating with departed souls. Unfortunately, Schwartz's experiments lack adequate scientific controls such as double-blinding. The data from his experiments pose the same problem of evaluation as do the data from the regular readings by Dion, Edward and other psychics.

The evidence for the validity of psychic readings relies completely on personal valida-tion. The client, caller or sitter decides if the reading is successful. People might conclude that this is as it should be. Who is better than the person getting the reading to decide if it fits? As it turns out, the client's judgement about the accuracy of the reading is unreliable. Psychological research shows that personal validation is useless. To see why, we will begin with an experiment published more than 60 years ago.

The fallacy of personal validation
Crider's test of Margarita

In 1944, the psychologist, Blake Crider, published the outcome of his study of Margarita, 'a professional character analyst'. At the time of the study, Margarita was 30 years old and had been a professional character analyst for 15 years. Crider wrote that Margarita 'has developed a large following of satisfied clients who not only consult her often about their own personality problems but also send their friends for similar analyses and counsel'.

Fig. 15.1 Gypsy Card Reader.

Margarita readily agreed to participate in the study. Margarita saw 16 college students, one at a time, in Crider's office. Margarita looked at the student and wrote down her impression. She wrote down each impression as a series of numbered statements. The number of statements per student ranged from 19 to 25 with an average of 22. While Margarita was obtaining her impressions, Crider had instructed each student to show no reaction. After the analyst finished writing down the statements, she handed the student the set of statements. The student then checked each statement that she or he agreed with.

Crider reports that, 'In seven of the analyses there was no disagreement whatever. Three disagreements occurred in only one analysis. For the 16 analyses there were a total of 364 statements, 22 of which were disagreed with by the students or 96 per cent accuracy'. Crider provides two sample analyses. I list the statements in one sample below:

1. Does not like to take chances.

2. Very-very sensitive.

3. Very self-conscious.

4. Gets along well with the boys.

5. Above-average student.

6. Worries about her studies.

7. Introvert.

8. Overemotional—tries to conceal it.

9. General health good.

10. Love life not in settled stage.

11. Has had broken love affair.

12. Should not be in business world.

13. Appreciates good music.

14. Must always have feeling of security or else is uneasy.

15. Is of generous and cooperative nature.

16. Digestive organs normal.

17. Heart normal.

18. Kidneys normal.

19. Finds it hard to ask favors.

20. Should not be given technical work.

21. Does not like routine either.

22. Very stubborn.

23. Bad temper when aroused, yet does not display it often.

24. This girl would be happiest when being supported.

25. Has many big dreams.

Crider observed, 'Psychologists may say that the statements are mostly complimentary, that they are too general, that they will apply to anyone. However, from what I knew of the students, I was in substantial agreement with the analyses as presented. More interesting is the fact the students were satisfied, and in their discussion with each other following the analyses they were of the opinion that the analyses were surprisingly accurate.'

Margarita obviously impressed Crider. He concluded that her readings provided accurate information about her clients. For this purpose, he relied upon his own acquaintance with each student and the fact that the students were satisfied with their readings. You might find it useful to imagine you were participating in Crider's study. Try hard to set aside what you already know, and treat the reading as if Margarita had written down these 25 statements especially for you. How many of these would you accept as being true of yourself?

Forer's classroom demonstration of gullibility

In 1949, the psychologist, Bertram Forer, published 'The fallacy of personal validation: a classroom demonstration of gullibility'. Forer had read Crider's study and noted that Crider's conclusions relied on accepting his own and the students' subjective impressions of the readings. Forer writes, 'Testing the correctness of inferences about a client by requesting his evaluation of them may be called "personal validation". When the inferences are universally valid, as they often are, the confirmation is useless.'

To test his suspicions about Crider's study, Forer did an experiment with his introductory psychology class. The purpose was 'to demonstrate the ease with which clients may be misled by a general personality description into unwarranted approval of a diagnostic tool'. Forer had previously told his students about his own personality test which he called the Diagnostic Interest Blank (DIB). The students had asked to take the test. Forer obliged.

Forer administered the DIB to the 39 students in his class. He told them he would give each a personality evaluation when he could evaluate the results. The next week, Forer gave each student a typed personality sketch with his or her name written on it. Forer did not tell them that he had handed each of them the identical sketch. He instructed them to read their sketches and then make the following ratings: (1) 'Rate on a scale of zero (poor) to five (perfect) how effective the DIB is in revealing personality'. (2) 'Rate on a scale of zero to five the degree to which the personality description reveals basic characteristics of your personality'. (3) '... check each statement as true or false about yourself or use a question mark if you cannot tell'.

Forer's sketch consisted of 13 statements he had obtained mainly from a news-stand astrology book. Many researchers have used this sketch since Forer's demonstration 55 years ago. It is still used today. Consequently, you should find it interesting to study the 13 statements and decide how well they apply to you. The sketch follows:

1. You have a great need for other people to like and admire you.
2. You have a tendency to be critical of yourself.
3. You have a great deal of unused capacity which you have not turned to your advantage.
4. While you have some personality weaknesses, you are generally able to compensate for them.
5. Your sexual adjustment has presented problems for you.
6. Disciplined and self-controlled outside, you tend to be worrisome and insecure inside.
7. At times you have serious doubts as to whether you have made the right decision or done the right thing.
8. You prefer a certain amount of change and variety and become dissatisfied when hemmed in by restrictions and limitations.

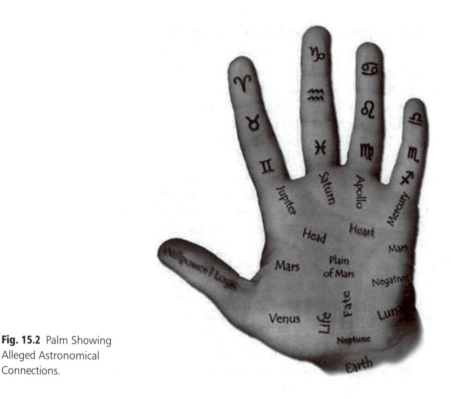

Fig. 15.2 Palm Showing Alleged Astronomical Connections.

9. You pride yourself as an independent thinker and do not accept others' statements without satisfactory proof.

10. You have found it unwise to be too frank in revealing yourself to others.

11. At times you are extroverted, affable, sociable, while at other times you are introverted, wary, reserved.

12. Some of your aspirations tend to be pretty unrealistic.

13. Security is one of your major goals in life.

The students gave the DIB an average rating of 4.31 (remember 5 is perfect). One student gave it a rating of 3 while the remainder rated it either 4 or 5. The students gave the personality sketch an average rating of 4.26. As many as 16 (41 per cent) of the students gave the sketch a rating of 5.

Subsequent research on the Forer effect has not only replicated these findings but also added additional information. An interesting finding is the 'illusion of uniqueness'. I asked you to read the sample analysis from Crider and Forer's sketch. How well did these statements describe you? I think I know. Most of you would probably rate the sketch as descriptive of yourself, but you would not be impressed. This is because you recognize that the statements could apply to everyone. They have universal validity.

The 'illusion of uniqueness' emerged from experiments where people were given the personality sketch under two different conditions. In one condition, the researchers handed the sketch to the subjects and simply told them that the statements are 'generally true of people.' Under these conditions, the individuals rate the sketch, on average, on the 5-point scale as around 3.24. In other words, they accept the sketch as descriptive of themselves but also recognize that the same statements apply to others.

In a second condition, the researchers gave the subjects the same personality sketch. They told them they wrote it specifically for them based on information from a test or other source. Under these conditions, the individuals gave a much higher rating to the sketch. They also claimed that sketch uniquely described themselves as distinct from others. In one experiment, for example, the experimenters told the subjects the goal was to judge the accuracy of astrological horoscopes. The experiment had three conditions. In a control condition, the experimenters gave each subject a horoscope and told them that it was one that was generally true of people. These students rated the horoscope 3.24 on the 5-point scale. A second group gave the astrologer the year and month of their birth. They were then given a horoscope (remember in these experiments, everyone gets the same personality sketch) and told that it was based on the information they had supplied to the astrologer. These students gave the sketch an average rating of 3.76. The third group was treated the same as the second one with the exception that they were also asked to supply the day in addition to the year and month of birth. These individuals gave the horoscope a rating of 4.38.

Two important points emerge from these experiments. One is that people rate a sketch as a more accurate description of themselves, the more they believe that the description was based on information they provided. The second point is that people can read the same sketch in two ways. One is that they can judge it as applying to themselves, but only because the statements apply to everyone. The second is that they can see the sketch as uniquely descriptive of themselves as distinct from others. The difference is not in the personality sketches but in the context in which it is delivered. This is a simple point. However, it has enormous consequences.

Why does it work?

In one sense, the readings given by Dion, Edward and other alleged psychics 'work'. The persons getting the reading, plus observers, agree that it accurately describes their circumstances. Many wealthy and famous individuals are clients. The alleged psychics appear on *Larry King Live* and other television and radio shows. They receive invaluable publicity.

Scientists, psychologists and sceptics, however, focus on another definition of 'work'. They ask for evidence that the 'psychics' are truly producing information from occult and other worldly sources. The first meaning of 'work' relies on personal validation. As Forer and others showed, personal validation is useless as scientific evidence. The second meaning of 'work' requires careful, double-blind studies to rule out non-paranormal reasons for the apparent success of the readings.

Such scientific evidence of validity in the personality area is very difficult to get. Gary Schwartz, for example, has claimed that he has obtained just such evidence to support the claims of Edward and other mediums. In his laboratory, Edward and other mediums gave readings to a sitter (a person who is trying to contact one or more relatives who have passed over.). The sitter then rates the separate statements in the reading as accurate or not. In one experiment, Schwartz reported accuracies of 73–90 per cent. The problem is that these accuracy ratings are meaningless because they were not done double-blind nor were they contrasted with ratings by the same sitters of readings that were not meant for them. Recall the 96 per cent accuracy that Crider attributes to Margarita.

Assessing the scientific validity of character readings is very difficult. This makes life much easier for the alleged psychics. Almost everyone who gets a reading has no access to scientific evidence of its validity. Consequently, they have to rely on personal validation. Personal validation, although scientifically useless, can be quite compelling.

Inherent ambiguity of language

Study the sample readings from Dion and Edward. Do the same with the samples from Margarita and the statements in Forer's sketch. Consider this extract from the beginning of Dion's reading of Karen:

> Dion: A couple of things actually sort of turned up very fast. One is sort of hovering around property concerns and sort of ideas or opportunities to make changes and I'll come back to that.

Dion says that two things come up. 'One is sort of hovering around property concerns.'

'Property' is quite abstract. Just about anything that a person owns can be property such as a house, its contents, and the like. Books, inventions, songs and other creations can be properties. 'Property concerns' is even more vague. Such vagueness and abstractness force the caller to find a concrete fit. Perhaps her boyfriend is in a legal dispute with his siblings over his share of the family estate. Or, maybe, she is trying to find a publisher for a cookbook she has written.

Instead of alluding to 'property concerns', Dion might have said, 'I see that you are trying to find a publisher for the cookbook you have written'. If this were true, it would be impressive. On the other hand, such specific statements increase greatly the possibility of being wrong. If Dion, Edward and other psychics used concrete and precise statements, the client would find it easier to decide if their readings make sense. However, if the psychics did use concrete language, probably none of them would be in business.

Language is inherently ambiguous. Even if Dion and Edward attempted to use more precise and concrete terms in their readings, the sitters would still have room to fit the statements to their unique circumstances. We are victims of the illusion of meaning. The illusion is that the meaning of a statement is entirely contained in the statement. Scholars debate endlessly about the correct interpretation of Hamlet's soliloquy. This illusion is so ingrained in us that we fail to understand that utterances and sentences never completely determine the underlying meaning. At best, the utterances and sentences constrain the possible meanings. The specific meaning conveyed in any situation depends upon context, shared knowledge and understanding between the communicator and listener, and the beliefs and expectations of the listener.

In any communication, then, the listener contributes as much to the meaning of the utterance as does the speaker. In the psychic reading, the meaning comes almost completely from the client or sitter. An example can illustrate this. In 1936, the psychologist Irving Lorge published an experiment on 'prestige suggestion'. Prestige suggestion refers to what happens when experimenters attribute a product or utterance to a famous artist or poet. The subjects rate the same product more favourably if they believe that the creator was important or prestigious. Lorge asked his subjects to rate their approval of quotations by famous individuals. One example was the quotation:

> I hold that a little rebellion, now and then, is a good thing, and as necessary in the political world as storms are in the physical.

Those subjects who were told that the author was Thomas Jefferson approved of the statement and rated it highly. Those who were told that the author was Lenin, disagreed with it and rated it unfavourably. [The true author is Thomas Jefferson.] Lorge concluded that his subjects were acting irrationally. He asked why should the agreement with the identical statement vary depending upon who said it? After all, the content and the meaning of the statement were the same in both cases.

In 1948, the psychologist Solomon Asch published a lengthy critique of Lorge's conclusions. Using a clever research design, Asch showed that Lorge's subjects were reacting to two different meanings. Those who believed that Lenin was the author and believed that Lenin was a ruthless tyrant interpreted the statement as advocating bloody conflicts. According to Asch, this was a rational interpretation given their beliefs about Lenin. Those who were told Jefferson was the author and believed that Jefferson was a democrat and a peace-loving statesman interpreted the statement as advocating political debate and peaceful changes of government. Thus, the identical set of words, according to Asch, had at least two entirely different meanings depending upon the context in which they occurred.

The client, not the 'psychic', creates the meaning

So far we have learned that 'psychic' readings 'work'. What scientific evidence exists does not support the claims for Dion, Edward and other psychic readers. Scientific evidence, however, is irrelevant for the success of mediums, character readers and other alleged psychics. Powerful forces create the illusion of validity. This illusion is so compelling that even scientists and others who should know better become active supporters of the 'psychics' and mediums.

Forer's demonstration of the fallacy of personal validation offers some clues about why 'psychic' readings 'work'. From studies on the Forer effect we know that combining universally valid statements with the appropriate context can create the illusion of uniqueness. Statements that in one context will be recognized as universally valid will be

Fig. 15.3 Palm Reader In Action.

accepted as uniquely self-descriptive in another context. Asch's experiment shows that a change in context can provide a completely different meaning for a given statement.

We have also discussed how language is inherently ambiguous. The illusion of meaning tricks us into believing that the meaning in what Dion or Edward is telling us comes from occult sources or our departed relatives. In ordinary communication, we fail to realize that we contribute much of the meaning. When we are impressed with 'psychic readings', we are unaware that we have contributed all the meaning that we derive from the message.

ELIZA

To understand why the reading works, it does not help to call the clients gullible. I would argue that the client must possess a certain level of intelligence plus creativity for the reading to work. A successful reader gains the active cooperation of the client. The reader can do this in a variety of ways—some subtle and some not so subtle. Before the reading, the 'psychic' implies that reading is a cooperative venture. The 'psychic' will pick up vibes and signs. Sometimes these will have no meaning for the reader, but they often will for the client. The idea is to get the client actively to make sense of what the reader is saying. This active looking for meaning in the reading is similar to what people do in trying to make sense of a work of art, a poem or a novel.

In the 1970s, Joseph Weizenbaum of the Massachusetts Institute of Technology devised his computer program ELIZA. The program apparently enabled a person to converse with a computer. The computer played the role of a Rogerian psychotherapist. The Rogerian technique involves feeding back to the client what he or she has just said in a paraphrased form. In those days people interacted with computers through a Teletype. With ELIZA, the human, playing the role of a patient, typed in comments or questions. ELIZA responded with printed reactions. A typical exchange is as follows:

Patient: Men are all alike.
ELIZA: In what way?
Patient: They're always bugging us about something or other.
ELIZA: Can you think of a specific example?
Patient: Well, my boyfriend made me come here.
ELIZA: Your boyfriend made you come here?
Patient: He says I'm depressed much of the time.
ELIZA: I am sorry to hear you are depressed.
Patient: It's true. I am unhappy.
ELIZA: Do you think coming here will help you not to be unhappy?
Patient: I need some help, that much seems certain.
ELIZA: What would it mean if you got some help?
Patient: Perhaps I could learn to get along with my mother.

ELIZA was a very primitive program even for the 1970s. It employed many tricks and stock phrases. It had no mechanism for understanding sentences. Instead it looked for key words that the patient typed. For example, if the program saw a sentence of the form 'Do you X?' it automatically printed out the response 'What makes you think I X?' When ELIZA could not match the syntax of a given sentence, it could say something non-commital such as, 'Please go on', or 'What does that suggest to you?' Or it could recall an earlier match and refer to it. An example would be. 'How does this relate to your depression?'

Although ELIZA was quite simple, it functioned as an excellent 'psychic' reader. It used stock phrases to cover up when it could not deal with a given question or input. It used the patient's own input to feed back information and created the illusion that it understood, and even sympathized, with the patient. Weizenbaum was startled that the people that tried his program became highly emotionally involved and believed that a sensitive, competent psychotherapist was at the other end of the Teletype. In one case, the lady trying out ELIZA became so involved that she insisted that Weizenbaum leave the room so she could continue with this highly intimate interaction.

Garfinkel

In 1967 the sociologist Harold Garfinkel published a study he had conducted. He told the subjects that the Department of Psychiatry (at Arizona State University) was exploring alternative ways to perform psychotherapy 'as a way of giving persons advice about their personal problems'. Garfinkel's subjects were actual patients who had come to the psychiatric clinic for help with their problems.[2] Each subject was asked to discuss the background of some serious problem on which he or she would like advice. After the subject described the problem, he or she was instructed to ask the 'counsellor' (actually an experimenter) questions that could be answered either 'yes' or 'no'. The experimenter–counsellor was in an adjacent room and remained out of the patient's sight. After each question, and after a suitable pause, the experimenter answered either 'yes' or 'no'. Unknown to the patients, the experimenter's answers had been predetermined by a table of random numbers. The answers did not relate to the questions. Yet, each patient was sure the counsellor fully understood the problem and was providing sound and helpful advice. Indeed, many patients felt this system worked better than the conventional psychotherapy.

Conclusions

'Psychics' who give readings or provide messages from the dead come in two flavours. 'Shut-eyes' are those who believe in what they are doing. They are as much victims of the illusion of validity as are their clients. Shut-eyes make up the vast majority of readers. 'Cold readers' do not necessarily believe in the validity of readings. They deliberately exploit their clients and use a variety of ways secretly to gain information and to convince their clients. I have not emphasized this distinction in this chapter because the readings 'work' equally well for both shut-eyes and cold readers. Cold readers might have a slight edge because they use various ploys to gain facts about their clients.

The readings 'work' because the client is an active participant in the exchange. It is the client who supplies the meaning. The reader gets the credit.

References and notes

1. Christian Dion uses Tarot cards for his readings. Just before he reads a client on the air, he quickly deals out a spread of 10 cards. He uses the classic Celtic Cross.
2. Ethical considerations would prevent such a study from being conducted today.

Chapter 16

Graphology—a total write-off

Barry L. Beyerstein

I wish to propose for the reader's favourable consideration a doctrine which may, I fear, appear wildly paradoxical and subversive. The doctrine in question is this: that it is undesirable to believe a proposition when there is no ground whatever for supposing it true.

Bertrand Russell

It is hard for a scientifically literate person today to imagine how positions of the stars or the creases on one's palms could have any bearing on one's personality, inclinations or abilities. However, oddly enough, many who would sneer at astrology or palm reading still assume that, inasmuch as writing is a form of expressive behaviour, our style of penmanship might reveal something about our psychological make-up. After all, our mannerisms and choice of clothing, jewellery and hair styles seem—at least to some degree—to broadcast something about who we are. Moreover, because writing, aptitudes and personality are all controlled by the brain, the suggestion that they could somehow be related does not seem inherently absurd. Also, since our personalities are obviously unique and handwriting is sufficiently idiosyncratic to allow personal identification (despite the standardized instruction we all receive), many find it at least conceivable that one might reflect the other. Despite their surface plausibility, however, each of these arguments is deeply flawed, as the remainder of this chapter will show.

Graphologists, as handwriting analysts prefer to call themselves, have been quite successful in convincing an uninformed public that their craft is a scientifically respectable technique for assessing someone's personality, abilities and predilections. This misapprehension is reinforced by the unfortunate fact that some large corporations do, as practitioners claim, consult graphologists in personnel matters. Similarly, many people assume that graphology must be legitimate because a few misguided judges have permitted graphologists to give expert testimony in court (here the error lies in the failure of these jurists to make the important distinction, discussed below, between the pseudoscience of graphology and the legitimate forensic field of 'questioned document examination'). Similarities between the two occupations are minimal, but they are often confused by those who fail to do their homework.

Probably the greatest source of unearned credibility for graphology comes from those who came to scoff but remained to pray. Many hard-nosed people have accepted free offers to have their handwriting analysed and found, to their surprise, that the resulting character sketch seemed remarkably accurate. Obviously, any scientific dismissal of graphology will need to explain why there are so many satisfied customers if handwriting analysis is essentially on a par with your next fortune cookie.

This chapter will deal with each of the foregoing issues in due course. Following some definitions and historical background, it will present the logical and scientific objections to graphology. It will then discuss the psychological research on the 'subjective validation effect' which explains why a practice that consistently fails well-controlled empirical tests can still seem utterly convincing to intelligent, educated people who run across it in everyday settings.

What is graphology?

Graphology, or handwriting analysis, is the allegedly scientific practice of determining people's psychological, social, occupational and medical attributes, as well their moral stature, from the configuration of their letters, lines and paragraphs on a page. Graphologists strenuously deny (though there is much evidence to the contrary) that they pay any attention to the contents of the scripts they analyse. They claim to reveal character strengths and flaws, aptitudes and one's state of physical and psychological health, solely from the size, slants, slopes, spacing and other embellishments of the writing itself.

Though today's practitioners are loathe to admit it, graphology has always been a branch of the diverse group of occult practices known as 'character reading'.[1] Since ancient times, people have been fascinated by human diversity and the uniqueness of the individual. As this is the basis on which we apportion life's richest prizes and harshest punishments, those whose fate hangs in the balance have always had an incentive to present an overly favourable face to the world. Consequently, hucksters offering magical formulae for cutting through what these days is euphemistically called 'impression management' have always attracted an eager clientele. Think of the advantages if potential employers, landlords, lenders, spouses, business associates, antiterrorism squads or courts of law could quickly and reliably reveal what someone is *really* like—and all the more so if the object of the probing does not even have to know that anyone is peeking.

At various times, it has been assumed that such a window on anyone's inner make-up could be gained by interpreting the positions of the stars (astrology), the features of the face (physiognomy), the lines on the hand (palmistry), the shape of birthmarks (witches' trials), bumps on the head (phrenology) and, yes...the shape and distribution of one's writing (graphology). Although its modern devotees have done their best to disguise all connections to its occult forebears, handwriting analysis retains, in its origins, underlying rationale, methods and its New Age affiliations, unmistakable ties to all of these magical character reading techniques.[2] Although modern graphologists take offence at being compared with tea leaf readers and psychics, this chapter will show that handwriting analysis has not abandoned its occult beginnings when itinerant conjurers wandered the countryside practising the art. Present-day graphologists claim scientific status but, as we shall see, perusal of their latest texts reveals the same threadbare mix of magical thinking and pseudoscience with which the practice began.

A pseudoscience is a field that seeks the prestige, believability and earning power of the legitimate sciences but lacks their rigour and proven data. Pseudoscientists copy the outward trappings, language and behaviours of genuine scientists, but closer examination reveals them as mere poseurs. What they sell to a largely scientifically illiterate public is occult nonsense repackaged to sound like scientific knowledge. The philosopher and physicist, Mario Bunge[3] has created a useful checklist for identifying pseudosciences. As the remainder of this chapter will show, graphology qualifies on each of Bunge's criteria.

Before supporting this indictment with hard data, let me say that, although I have met some outright frauds and con artists in the nearly 15 years I have been debating graphologists, I freely admit that most practitioners of this faux science genuinely believe what they are doing is valid. The vast majority are what I call 'the sincere but self-deluded'. They have conned themselves as much as anyone else—it may be a sham, but it's not usually a scam. Elsewhere, I have discussed the interesting psychological processes that can make both the sellers and buyers of bogus practices utterly convinced that worthless techniques actually work.[4–6] Although those critiques were primarily aimed at medical and psychological quackery, graphology's followers exhibit the very same errors of reasoning. It should also be noted, as the examples in those earlier papers showed, that sincerity and benign intent in no way prevents one from causing significant harm.

Graphology: a branch of psychology?

Although no reputable textbook in psychological testing or personnel selection treats graphology with anything but disdain, graphologists still claim to be an unfairly maligned branch of psychology. My extensive interactions with graphologists over the years have revealed very few who have even a rudimentary understanding of how a legitimate psychological test should be designed and validated (references listed at the end of this chapter describe how scientifically valid tests are constructed[2,7,8]). A few pro-graphology articles have made it into respectable peer-reviewed journals (for summaries of these papers and the defences put forth by graphologists, see the following references[9,10]) but, on balance, they fall far short of establishing the case, theoretically[11] or empirically.[12] Although graphologists claim persecution from a hostile 'Establishment' bent on preserving its turf, they seem oblivious to the fact that if their techniques really worked, the licensed professionals would long ago have stolen these powerful tools and muscled out the self-credentialed amateurs. Sensitive to their resemblance to fortune tellers, graphologists claim they do not foretell the future. However, what conceivable value could there be in reading the character of a stranger if it were not assumed that the inferred traits would reliably predict how he or she might behave in the future? That is what valid tests are supposed to do.

The terms 'graphology' and 'handwriting analysis' are used interchangeably, but 'Graphoanalysis' refers specifically to followers of the International Graphoanalysis Society (IGAS), late of Chicago, Illinois. The capitalized terms 'Graphoanalysis' and 'Graphoanalyst' denote a particular approach to handwriting analysis, taught by M. N. Bunker, who founded the IGAS in 1929.[13] It became the best established of the graphology training organizations, a status it retained until its bankruptcy in 2003. The society's trade-mark name and its lesson materials were purchased from the bankruptcy receivers by a group of ardent supporters who are attempting to restore the school's faded glories. Although the society never enjoyed the imprimatur of any legitimate academic body, in its heyday, it offered mail-order courses in graphology, held seminars, published its own journal and conferred official-sounding certification on its graduates.

The IGAS was also the most vocal of the competing graphology schools in asserting its scientific status while denigrating similar claims from its rivals. Despite its scientific pretensions, however, the IGAS was too timid to send a representative to debate critics at a 1988 conference sponsored by the Committee for the Scientific Investigation of Claims of the Paranormal—even though the meeting was being held in Chicago, the home town of the IGAS. Another US organization offering certification to paying members is the American Handwriting Analysis Foundation of San Jose, California. The academic merit of the courses offered by stand-alone organizations such as these is apparent from the fact that they are not accepted for transfer credit at accredited institutions of higher learning.

In the UK, similar unaccredited certification is offered by the British Institute of Graphologists (BIG) of Chipping Campden, Glostershire. The BIG grants a diploma to anyone who passes an examination based on courses taught by its 'List of Qualified Members Offering Teaching Services.' The institute's website (http://www.britishgraphology.org/index4.htm) includes 25 acceptable teachers on its roster. Their biographies, also on the website, indicate that none of these teachers (nor the late founder of the BIG, Francis Hilliger) has a position with an accredited university or college. However, one of the approved tutors, according to the biography on the website, 'has taught at Millfield College and Ealing College'. No specifics were given.

I did not try to verify this particular claim, but whenever I have looked into similar claims in the past, the 'teaching' has invariably been of the non-credit, night-school variety, in the colleges' extension programmes, where course offerings are profit driven and their content is not vetted by the faculty in the accredited degree programmes. In the extremely few instances I have found where regular faculty members have accepted the tenets of graphology, they were hired on the basis of their legitimate qualifications to teach other subjects and only after gaining the protection of tenure did they stray into advocacy of the pseudoscience of graphology. Tellingly, these rare instances are almost never in psychology departments, where anyone with the requisite knowledge to secure an appointment in the first place would be likely to know how weak the case for graphology really is.

This kind of isolation from the relevant bodies of research and higher education is one of Bunge's[3] first signs of a pseudoscience. Another is a lack of relevant university degrees among the founders and major proponents of the field. Of the 25 graphology teachers recommended by the BIG on its website, only one lists any degrees at all, an 'honours [i.e. bachelor's level] degree in psychology' (institution unspecified). We can be relatively sure that the rest have not even this minimal background because fringe organizations, desperate for respect, typically highlight any academic qualifications they have because such achievements are so thin on the ground.

To satisfy myself that these deficiencies in relevant areas of higher education are typical of the field as a whole, I generated a random sample of 20 graphology websites that contained biographies of the principals offering services (many of whom were offering to train students in graphology, as well as to advise corporations, the police, government agencies, etc.). Only one of the biographies contained on those websites mentioned holding any accredited university or college degrees. One practitioner listed himself as a graduate of Pepperdine University, a respected institution in southern California, but he neglected to say what field his degree was in—if it had been relevant to his current activities, we can safely assume it would have been underlined, as he did for a spate of other courses on pseudoscientific topics he took from non-accredited institutions. The only other graphologist in my sample who mentioned any post-secondary training at all (except from diploma mills in graphology and other pseudosciences, of course) said she had graduated from a certificate course of study in operating room technology. The school was not specified, and though it was probably a respectable junior college programme for medical assistants, such training would not qualify her to make psychological assessments and provide vocational or psychological advice, which is what she was offering in her website. This widespread lack of academic qualifications in the field is consistent with a revealing answer in the 'Frequently Asked Questions' section of the BIG website:

> Question: Can anyone learn graphology? Do you need any previous qualifications?
>
> Answer: Yes, anyone can learn, providing they are prepared to dedicate themselves and set aside a few hours each week for their studies. But, no, you do not need any prior qualifications, although an ability to discipline yourself is beneficial.

That the BIG's recommended teachers probably got into the field with equally little academic preparation themselves is apparent in the section of the their website detailing the areas of psychology on which applicants for the 'MBIG' diploma will be tested. No pre-requisite courses from accredited institutions were recommended and the only psychological theorists students were advised to be conversant with for the test were Freud, Jung, Adler, Fromm and Maslow. The first four were founders of the psychoanalytic school of personality theory, the least scientific area of psychology. Several critics have even held up psychoanalysis as a classic example of a pseudoscience.[14] As for Abraham Maslow, critics of the humanistic school he helped create find it equally lacking in credibility. Beyond being merely unscientific, critics such as Martin Seligman have accused Maslow and his followers of being hostile toward empirical science.[15]

The BIG website contains no recommended readings such as standard textbooks, even in introductory psychology, let alone any titles in psychological measurement, scientific personality research, organizational psychology, forensic psychology or the many other areas someone offering to advise the trusting public should be conversant with. Not surprisingly, this website, like all the others I have perused, also provides no scientifically credible evidence that graphology works, nor does it cite, let alone rebut, any of the many works mentioned in the present chapter that chronicle graphology's numerous failures and shortcomings. All these sites offer the potential customer in support of their craft are testimonials from satisfied customers.

Ignorance of relevant areas of science, failure to answer serious criticisms and undue reliance on testimonials also rank high on Bunge's[3] criteria for a pseudoscience. Elsewhere, I have discussed at length the reasons why testimonials count for very little as support for any dubious kind of diagnosis or treatment.[4–6]

Backbiting among the various graphological factions is common because there is no independent scientific corpus any one side can appeal to in asserting superiority over the competition. As we shall see, graphologists' attributions have always been nothing more than metaphorical extrapolations to the writer of whatever his or her writing features reminded that particular school's founder of (the basis of all magical divining or augury techniques, as discussed below). Given such unrestricted latitude, the founders of different schools were free to disagree about which signs are tokens of which traits. There are more than 30 graphological societies in the USA alone, many 'using methods which are not easily combined with other systems' (graphologist M. Gullan-Whur, quoted in Nickell[1], p. 28). This lack of standardization is compounded by the fact that many local practitioners simply make up their own intuitive schemes. While there are some concepts common to most systems of handwriting analysis, there are equally notable disputes as to what the various 'signs' in writing actually mean. Take, for instance, two books by internationally known graphologists that I reviewed.[2] One considers a certain way of crossing one's *t*s as indicative of a vicious, sadistic temperament, the other says it is merely a sign of a practical joker. Whose follower do you hope is the one secretly advising your boss?

The origins of graphology

Readers seeking a more detailed history of handwriting analysis should consult the chapter by Nickell[1] on which the following brief summary is based. There are ancient Chinese, Greek and Roman, as well as early Jewish and Christian ancestors of graphology, but its modern incarnation can be traced to the speculations of the seventeenth century Italian physician, Camillo Baldi. The most recognizable forebears of current enthusiasts, however, are to be found among an influential group of Catholic clergy in nineteenth century France. A disciple of that circle, Abbé Jean-Hippolyte Michon, coined the term 'graphology'. Michon founded The Society of Graphology in Paris in 1871 and his several books remain influential in graphological circles today. This is another of Bunge's characteristics of a pseudoscience: undue reliance on a charismatic founder's original texts, coupled with a lack of intellectual ferment in the field and a paucity of theoretical or practical progress. This inevitably leads to an absence of new research breakthroughs. Once again, Bunge's depiction fits graphology, so to speak, 'to a *T*'.

Michon was the founder of the so-called 'analytic' approach (also known as the 'stroke/trait' method) which ascribes specific traits to persons based on isolated 'signs' in their writing, such as where they place their dots on *i*s and crossbars on *t*s, for instance. Michon's student, Crepieux-Jamin broke with his master to become the founder of what is known today as the 'holistic' or 'gestalt' approach. Rather than attending to individual elements of letters, lines, etc., Crepieux-Jamin advocated a more intuitive, impressionistic perusal whereby the analyst absorbs an overall 'feel' for the writer by a vague sort of 'resonance' with the script as a whole. Partisans of the analytic and the holistic approaches to handwriting analysis have perpetuated this schism to the present day.

French graphologists continued to dominate the field until the early twentieth century when they started to be eclipsed by German-speaking authors. At that time, figures such as Preyer, Meyer, Klages and Pulver began to suggest that writing was a subspecies of expressive movement and that mental processes and emotionality could be revealed by analysing this kind of psychomotor behaviour. Realizing that the brain is responsible for both psychological traits and the control of writing, they attempted to justify reading character from writing with the assertion that 'handwriting is brain writing'. This still remains graphology's most prevalent defensive cliché. My detailed critique of this non-sequitur is summarized in a later section of the present chapter.[16]

In the 1930s, the Czech–English graphologist Saudek attempted to introduce more rigorous and mechanized ways of measuring writing movements. Increasing the precision of measures that are of doubtful value in the first place must rank as a dubious contribution, however. In the early 1900s, graphological speculation began to emerge in North America. Following Downey in 1919 and the arrival of the European émigré Klara Roman, Americans such as M. N. Bunker[13] gradually came to the fore. By the 1960s, the then stagnating fortunes of graphology received a boost when it, like astrology and other forms of augury, was embraced by the blossoming New Age movement. The 'New Age' is a marketing umbrella for all things magical and pseudoscientific that grew out of the mystical longings of the so-called 'counterculture' of the 1960s.[17] The vast majority of handwriting analysts continue to be self-taught from popular books or trained by self-accredited correspondence schools or non-credit night-school classes.

Reliable usage figures for graphology are hard to find because many clients fear the ridicule or reproach they could attract if it became known they were basing decisions that materially affect others' lives on methods the scientific community equates with tea leaf reading. Nonetheless, several estimates, including those of the journalist Abby Ellin, writing in the July 18, 2004 edition of the *New York Times*, suggest that it is continuing to grow in popularity throughout North America and Europe. Mainly for historical reasons, graphology seems to enjoy the greatest popular appeal today in France and Israel.

What do graphologists claim to achieve?

If graphologists claimed nothing more than that stingy people might leave narrow margins to save stationery (or that artistic people might write with a more creative flair than the rest of us, or that the correspondence of fastidious people might be a bit tidier than that of their more slovenly peers), I would hardly have wasted my time criticizing them. These are a few places where one's general disposition toward life could conceivably spill over into one's writing, in the same way that such leanings might affect how one tends the lawn or washes up after dinner. In other words, our writing could be just another of the many bits of behaviour that might reflect, in a very general way, how we would go about doing other, *similar* tasks. However, who would be foolish enough to pay a graphologist to interpret such barefaced clues? Besides, such correlations, if any, are much too low to be of any predictive value—presumably the reason for prying into someone's script in the first place. That is to say, while there may be a weak correlation, when computed over a large group of people, between neatness of their writing and their overall level of tidiness, for instance, there are far too many neat-writing slobs and meticulous fashion plates with atrocious penmanship for such a weak correlation to have any predictive value when it comes to making a guess about the future conduct of any *individual*. At any rate, if one wished to prognosticate on the sorts of things that could possibly correlate with handwriting, such as those in the foregoing examples, wouldn't it be more efficient just to observe the writer for a few minutes or perhaps ask his or her room mate for a quick appraisal?

Graphology would hardly have survived as long as it has if all it could offer were the sorts of insights that any bright school kid could produce in a flash, e.g. 'neatness here suggests (perhaps) neatness over there too'. When a test merely measures a sample of the kind of behaviour about which the test giver intends to generalize to slightly broader, but similar, spheres of activity, or asks a straightforward question and simply takes the answer at face value, psychologists say the test has 'face validity'. For example, a test of mental arithmetic will probably have both face and predictive validity if one is about to hire a cashier. Likewise, a glance at someone's writing might be advisable if your organization is seeking a calligrapher. If that is all that graphologists aspired to, I would have been happy to ignore them (though I would still have to warn the public that research shows that untrained people are just as good as trained graphologists at extracting those few things with face validity contained in writing samples).[18] However, graphologists know they will not get rich offering such thin gruel to an anxious public, and indeed they promise more, *much* more.

The question, then, for anyone not wishing to flush good money down the drain is: are there any features of handwriting, discernible only by trained practitioners, that could take us beyond the kind of do-it-yourself face validity ascriptions just discussed? That is, are there signs in writing that could expose a well-hidden disposition to default on loans, spread gossip, cheat on a partner or indulge in pederasty—or that could reveal a guilty conscience or the ability to sell life insurance? Graphologists would have you believe so.

There are few areas of human nature or mental and physical health that graphologists do not feel competent to assess. That a single technique could apply to so many different areas of life flies in the face of virtually everything psychologists have learned about measuring individual differences.[7,8] Following Bunge's criteria,[3] this unfamiliarity with relevant scientific research is, by itself, almost grounds for dismissing graphology out of hand. Nonetheless, graphologists claim to discern temperament (e.g. irritability, sensitiveness, affability, timidity or an explosive temper). They also say they can gauge one's general disposition or way of approaching situations (e.g. self-confidence, egotism, optimism, profligacy, complacency). Moreover, they believe that writing (*per se*, not its content) reveals mental qualities such as intelligence, reasoning ability and intuitiveness, as well as social traits such as introversion, friendliness and dominance. Many special abilities are apparently fair game too, such as musicality. In the workplace, graphologists claim to rate leadership, reliability, diligence, attention to detail, sales ability and propensity to be a team-player (remember that personnel consulting is a major part of most graphologists' business). On the moral and ethical side, graphologists pass judgement on people's honesty, trustworthiness, generosity, piety, cruelty, jealousy, criminal tendencies, sexual deviancy and more.

(Read Box 16.1) Quite a lot for only US$79.95, but there is more to be had. How to judge marital suitability from handwriting occupies a large portion of almost every graphology text or website. Sexuality is also supposed to have a multitude of written signs, as blushingly discussed below. Although graphologists typically demand to know the sex of the writer in advance, they are happy to pronounce on his or her closet sexual orientation and/or deviance, as well as promiscuousness and capacity for intimacy. Could it be that they want to know gender in advance because it is too simple to check the accuracy of such a guess?

Box 16.1 What do graphologists claim they can do?

The following material, on a typical graphology website, shows what well-known graphologists are willing to promise people who sign up for their training courses. Lest you think I cherry-picked a particularly outlandish site, mounted by some obscure outlier in the profession with which to tar other, respectable workers in the field, I draw your attention to the fact that this came from the website of Bart Baggett, one of the two graphologists the FBI turned to for analyses of the handwritten material that accompanied the anthrax spores mailed to US members of Congress in the aftermath of the September 11, 2001 terrorist attacks. As for insights they received, the FBI could have done just as well by asking the person next door to guess what someone deranged enough to mail a deadly pathogen to a politician might be like. The first I heard of this gaff by the FBI was when an amazed reporter for the *New York Times* called me for a comment when the story first broke. Needless to say, I said I was appalled that the FBI did not know that graphology is pure pseudoscience.

Be that as it may, here is a sample of what the graphologist the FBI turned to—Bart Baggett, founder of Handwriting University International and self-professed devotee of another scientifically questionable technique, Neurolinguistic Programming[6,19] (see Chapter 1)—has on offer at his website: http://www.myhandwriting.com/learn/.

Box 16.1 *(continued)*

Urging you to purchase his book and audiotape set, 'How you can analyze handwriting in 10 minutes or less', for the discounted price of only $79.95, Mr Baggett says, and I quote verbatim (ellipses in the original):

   No matter which you choose, you will soon begin to master one of the most accurate and insightful personality methods ever created...and it will change your life like it has changed mine. You will never look at people the same way again. You will experience that...

You have the ability to size up people instantly.

Your own goals, self-esteem, and confidence will grow.

Your romantic relationships will blossom.

Your children's behavior and grades will improve.

You will gain 'instant rapport' with just about everyone.

People will confide in you as never before.

You will earn $100 [per hour] or more in your spare time.

The well-known American graphologist Sheila Lowe (http://www.writinganalysis.com/answers.html#Howdoes) agrees with nearly all other graphologists that they cannot determine the sex of a writer, but, ironically, untrained novices can guess the sex of writers in an anonymous sample with approximately 70 per cent accuracy—something I have confirmed numerous times with my students in classroom projects. Elsewhere, I have suggested possible explanations for these gender/writing correlations.[16] I hasten to add, however, that this offers no support for the other claims of graphology, and anyway, graphologists claim to ignore these signs in writing that are among the very few that actually do correlate with any other aspect of the writer.

   Probably for similar reasons, handwriting analysts will not guess the writer's age, but they are happy to rate slippery attributes such as 'maturity' that offer far more wiggle room if challenged. As the old saying goes, 'you're only young once, but you can be immature forever.'

   The more cynical among us also assume graphologists are trying to tread lightly in the foregoing areas in order not to run afoul of statutes that protect job applicants from discrimination on the grounds of gender, age, ethnicity, etc. If it came to be widely believed that this kind of information could, even potentially, be surreptitiously fed to would-be employers (who, by law, could not use it as an overt hiring criterion), there could be legal repercussions. Though, sad to say, the courts have apparently not objected to use of a personnel selection tool that has no scientific credibility, they have, so several graphologists' websites tell us, found that graphology is non-discriminatory in those areas that the courts do care about. In the USA, graphology is considered a non-discriminatory hiring tool by the Equal Opportunity Employment Commission. For once, I agree. Graphology is non-discriminatory in this regard—it works equally badly for everybody.

Medical diagnosis with graphology

Graphologists' claims to derive medical diagnoses from writing have been alluded to already. My extensive literature search via the US National Library of Medicine has failed to support such claims. A 45-year-old study of handwriting and cancer diagnosis co-authored by the graphologist Alfred Kanfer is the only peer-reviewed paper that proponents of medical graphology have been able to point me to in this area and its relevance to their claims is marginal at best. Although Kanfer and Casten[20] reported a high success rate in using writing to discern those patients with tumours from those in a comparison group, the study offers no real support for the kind of detailed medical diagnoses graphologists claim they can make.

Before we could accept graphologists' claims of this sort, they would have to assure us of the adequacy of their experimental controls. For instance, were the raters adequately blinded; was the comparison group equally sick at the time (from a different disease); and were the groups of comparable age (because cancer rates are higher in older populations—whose writing also tends to deteriorate, even in the healthy); were both taking comparable doses of medications that have motor-impairing side effects, and so on? The lack of subsequent replications and refinements (of Kanfer's or any other medical graphology finding) in the scientific literature is cause for grave doubts.

Certain medical problems can affect writing, but not in the ways that would provide specific diagnoses, as graphologists claim. As a boy, I recall reading a magazine article that showed a series of memoranda written by Franklin D. Roosevelt during the final years of his life. Not surprisingly, the progressive deterioration of his writing was apparent as his health declined. However, this correlation could not say anything useful about the specific nature of Roosevelt's ailments (nor was anything of the sort implied in the article). Also, apropos of the present discussion, Roosevelt's deteriorating handwriting revealed nothing a casual observer of the many photos and newsreels of the president during this time could not have surmised equally well from noting his sunken features, weight loss, stooped shoulders, wan expression, reduced spontaneity, slow movements, etc.

For graphology to have any clinical utility, practitioners would need to show they can produce specific diagnoses that discriminate among the myriad medical conditions that can cause joint stiffness, pained movements, tremors, poor eye–hand coordination, etc., all of which could cause one's handwriting to degenerate. If all graphologists can tell is that the writer might be sick, it would be much cheaper and faster simply to ask the patient how he or she is feeling.

The fact that graphologists, in my experience, do not seem to understand the need to control for the many possible artefacts when trying to establish a claim such as these, ones that could easily produce spurious support for their methods, further underscores the low level of scientific literacy in the field.

Psychiatric and forensic claims of graphology

In the psychiatric sphere, everything from neuroticism and general emotional stability to psychoses, phobias, depression, psychopathy and a host of other clinical symptoms are supposedly all displayed in one's writing. Once again, as with medical claims for graphology, there is no track record of replicated positive findings in the peer-reviewed literature to support practitioners' assertions.

Many of the aforementioned graphological techniques are combined when handwriting analysts go knocking on the doors of the criminal justice system. They claim to expose actual or potential criminal behaviour as well as deceitfulness, lack of self-control, propensity to lie, violence prone-ness and sociopathic tendencies. Graphologists assert that they can help the police apprehend suspects and aid the courts in determining both guilt and appropriate punishment. They also say they can determine a felon's likelihood of recidivism and suitability for parole.

It is bad enough that one might lose a coveted position on the basis of a pseudoscientific character reading, but to have one's standing in the community, and possibly even freedom, jeopardized in this way is frightening indeed. How would you feel being branded a thief because you have 'desire-for-possession hooks' on your *S*s? Bunker, the founder of Graphoanalysis, the self-proclaimed most scientific school of graphology, seriously contends that these 'acquisitive hooks' reveal a disposition to snag others' belongings.[13] McNichol's highly touted graphology text[21] also provides exercises one can do at home to learn how to spot a murderer, a babysitter who might use drugs, and a shop owner inclined to cheat customers. Likewise, Marne's *Sex and crime in handwriting* presents graphological signs for exposing different kinds of criminals.[22] Unfortunately, in the demonstrations in both Marne's and McNichol's books, the supposedly diagnostic signs were all recognized, after-the-fact, in the writing of people the analysts already knew had been convicted of the offences in question. As usual, they offer no evidence that they could reliably identify the guilty parties if given an anonymous pile containing scripts of convicts and upright citizens (and, of course, under conditions that assured the contents of the scripts contained no useful clues, which they typically do—see the 'rich text' problem, below). For example, people in jail typically have less than average levels of education, so spelling, stylistic, grammatical or other content clues in the written material would have to be carefully screened to avoid giving non-graphological cues that could improve the hit rate. Similarly, studies have shown a high incidence of head injuries and neurological problems in incarcerated populations. We know that this could cause various motor problems that could help a graphologist guess at a better than chance rate whether a writing sample came from the prisoners or the comparison group.

Failure to respond to criticism

Since our detailed critique of graphology[23] has been out for more than a decade, I expected that graphologists would at least have begun to rein in some of the more outrageous claims they make in public, even if they have not changed how they operate in private, but I was wrong. I thought they might have ceased by now trying to justify their craft by engaging in the kind of after-the-fact post-diction described in the preceding paragraph, something that makes them look so amateurish in the eyes of scientific critics. However, my recent survey of graphologists' websites indicates they have learned nothing from the critics. For example, they persist in what psychologists call 'confirmation bias'— trying to justify their beliefs by paying attention only to things that support their prior convictions and ignoring or explaining away disconfirming data.[24] Graphologists still try to convince potential customers that what they do is valid by grabbing any attribute of the life of a well-known person that happens to coincide with a graphological sign and say, 'See how accurate graphology is?' They also persist, in these useless exercises, in ignoring the alleged stroke/trait correlations that do not match the famous individual's script.

It was depressingly familiar to go to Anna Koren's website (http://annakoren.com/index.html) and find her still doing the same old things critics long ago warned them about (failure to reassess principles in light of new knowledge is another of Bunge's signs of a pseudoscience[3]). If you visit Koren's website, you will see, for instance, how she picks those attributes of former president Bill Clinton that virtually everybody would already know and then presents them as graphological revelations consistent with his writing style. We call this sort of behaviour 'retrofitting'—it is like shooting an arrow and then drawing the bull's eye around the tip after it has landed. The proper way to proceed would have been for the graphologist to analyse a dozen or more anonymous scripts (stripped of any non-graphological cues, as described above) and then be asked to say which one was Clinton's handwriting.

Ignoring or explaining away failures is another strong sign of a pseudoscience.[3] When one of the most widely agreed upon sign/trait relationships in all of graphology was blatantly contradicted in Bill Clinton's script, Koren failed to draw the unsuspecting viewer's attention to this evidence against her position. She does not tell us that a pronounced backhand slope like Clinton's is claimed by virtually every prominent graphologist to denote an introverted wallflower who shuns social contact (see Fig. 16.1). Despite Clinton's being demonstrably the opposite of what graphology says this feature of his writing indicates, Koren tells us, that Clinton has a strong 'need to belong': 'It is important to him to touch and to be in contact all the time'. Similar obliviousness to disconfirmation is apparent when, having emphasized elsewhere on the website that large letters in one's signature denote power and egotism, Koren has to go through painful gyrations to explain why this extremely charismatic 'people person' who rose to the stature of leader of the most powerful nation on earth not only writes with a backhand slope but seems to have a signature more appropriate to a corner grocer. One wonders what she would have said about the script (minus the 'rich text' items such as the signature and references to the White House in the text, of course) if she had been given it to analyse under blinded conditions, like any competent test of graphology would have required.

When the strokes and the traits they supposedly denote fail to coincide, graphologists typically fall back on the excuse (as Koren does in Bill Clinton's case) that the person's outward appearance belies the true nature within, revealed by infallible graphology, of

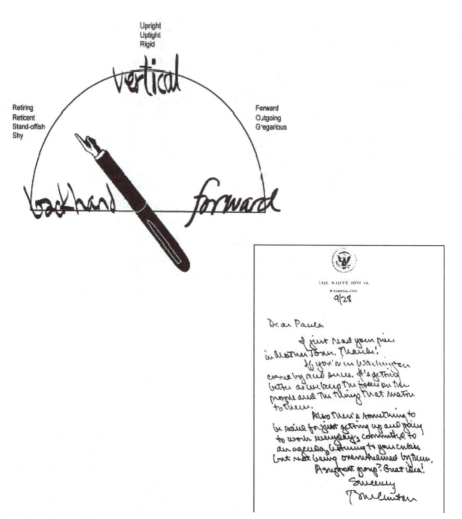

Fig. 16.1 Graphology's engagement gauge: Graphologists claim that one's level of sociability is revealed by the forward, backhand or vertical slant of one's letters. Note that the bashful wallflower Bill Clinton writes with a pronounced backhand slant. (Graphic by Susan Lebo.)

course. A similar lack of falsifiability is what we have come to expect when astrologers and psychics mess up as well. This *post hoc* dodging around failures is another hallmark of pseudosciences.[3] To wiggle out of an apparent disconfirmation in a demonstration that supposedly supports her methods, Koren asks us to believe that Bill Clinton, who is known for his exceptional personal warmth and bonhomie, is merely covering up what he is really like inside, i.e. his writing reveals his *real* but disguised character. According to Koren's psychobabble explanation, Clinton is still the shy little boy from humble Arkansas beginnings, outwardly overcompensating at every turn. I guess the selection committees at Yale University and the Rhodes Scholarship foundation somehow missed that.

Overall, though, Koren displays a fairly positive attitude toward Clinton, and supports it with airtight graphological evidence (derived after she knew whose writing it was, however). The fact that equally prominent graphologists come to opposing views of Clinton's character highlights the subjectivity of graphological judgements. Another famous graphologist who barely even tries to hide his venomous opinion of Clinton finds equally strong evidence in the former president's writing for a depiction that would warm the heart of the most malicious Clinton-hater. Greg Baggett, on his website (http://myhandwriting.com/celebs/clinton.html), paints a typical detractor's view of the ex-president and says he made these attributions all by himself, based on graphology, long before Clinton's impeachment-related problems came to light. According to Baggett, analysis of Clinton's writing reveals 'insatiable sex drives, persistence, ambition, caution, anger at women, and even the tendency to lie and have poor ethics'. Notably, Baggett does not say he discerned all this from the writing before he knew it was Clinton's, or learned what the 'Zippergate' hearings had to say.

Fix your writing, fix your self

The most transparently absurd claim in all of graphology, one so bizarre that not even all graphologists endorse it, is that of 'graphotherapeutics'. According to believers, not only does handwriting unerringly reveal personal attributes but, if you should dislike any of the traits it discloses, you can eradicate them by removing their diagnostic signs from your script.[25] The oh-so-scientific Bunker, founder of the IGAS, devotes a whole chapter to showing how 'changing handwriting will change personality'.[13]

This merely underscores the contention, discussed shortly, that sympathetic magic is the real underpinning of graphology, for the essence of magical thinking is that causes should resemble their effects. For the occultist, cause and effect are thus interchangeable. Case in point: graphotherapists are insisting that personality causes writing causes personality. What better evidence of this could we seek than Bunker's assertion: 'He [Bunker's client] had made a few changes in his writing—not major changes, and he had achieved results'.[13] In this case, the writer with minor retrenchments in his penmanship was miraculously redeemed from his previous persona, that of a suicidal spendthrift. Here we see another common attribute of a pseudoscience, namely that effects are posited which are dramatically disproportionate to the magnitude of their alleged causes. If it sounds too good to be true, it probably is.

In case the reader is inclined to think that such absurdities are mere anachronisms, weeded out by more discerning followers in more recent times, as I write, the British Institute of Graphologists' website, referred to above, still contained the following answer to one of the visitors' frequently asked questions:

Question: What can Graphology be used for?

Answer: As well as the 'traditional' areas of personality assessment for commerce and industry, handwriting analysis may also be used in any area of human activity, or where people interact.

A few examples:

- vocational guidance for those seeking suitable employment or perhaps a job change;
- compatibility in both personal areas of life and business;
- child and family guidance;
- graphotherapy or, therapy through handwriting

Likewise, Greg Baggett, founder of 'Handwriting University International', (http://www.myhandwriting.com/) says he can teach us to 'even use 'grapho-therapy' with your family through our home study courses or live seminars'. This from the graphology school that claims to have 'the best teachers in the world.'

Internal contradictions in graphology

One way philosophers proceed when attempting to refute a doctrine is to show that it contains internal inconsistencies—if its fundamental premises are mutually contradictory, the argument can be dismissed summarily. The underlying doctrines of graphology contain many internal contradictions. This would be fatal for any logical thinker, but apparently not for graphologists. It does have the benefit, however, of allowing them to play both sides of the street. For instance, on the one hand (no pun intended), they say writing is such a sensitive psychological barometer that it varies, moment-to-moment, in relation to subtle mood changes. However, in the next breath, they will tell you writing is so impervious to change that you cannot disguise your true nature by falsifying your script—the real you will still shine through to the handwriting analyst. This is their standard reply to people who rightfully state that features of their writing supposedly crucial to graphologists' diagnostic processes change perceptibly from one writing situation to the next. Graphologists contend that, though the writing looks different to amateurs, it still reveals the same thing to them. A moment later, they say if the writer changes his or her script, the personality will start to match the writing.

Despite such elasticity, graphologists I have tested were willing to draw conclusions from a single, small sample of writing, without any proof that it is the writer's usual hand. They were willing to make quite specific attributions based on subtle nuances of that particular sample, with no attempt to determine that the particular specimen did not differ from the norm. Many offered to make sweeping judgements based on a single signature. Even if the sample had been bigger, we all know that our writing can vary considerably, due to temporary haste, sloppiness, writing posture, desire to make an impression, hand injury, unfamiliar writing instrument, etc. Which specimen denotes the *real* you? Graphologists I have debated claimed that they can tell when they have to compensate for this lack of typicality by attributing something different to the writer from what the signs on the page would normally have implied. They say that because your personality remains the same, the graphologist can still detect the real character traits, but I have never seen in any of their textbooks how this is supposed to be accomplished. Oddly enough, however, if you change your writing at the behest of a graphotherapist, your personality will supposedly change to reflect the new, improved script. This kind of vagueness offers wonderful opportunities to squirm out of wrong attributions, making the system essentially unfalsifiable. On that ground alone, graphology can be excluded from the house of science.[3]

The real rationale underlying the practice of graphology

Present-day handwriting analysts maintain that modern exponents have taken graphology well beyond its occult beginnings when itinerant palm readers and astrologers practised it as a sideline. Unfortunately for their fond hopes, perusal of the latest graphology texts and websites reveals that the seminal concepts in the field remain precisely what they were when the field was born. Claims of scientific improvements notwithstanding, my review of dozens of books touted by well-known graphologists shows that, like all other systems of augury or divination, the underpinnings of graphology remain, as they have always been, the ancient principles of sympathetic magic.[2]

The essence of all magical thinking is sympathetic correspondence or, as it is often stated, 'like begets like'.[26] This is also known in mystical lore as 'The Law of Similarity'. If two things are perceptually similar, magical thinkers assume that this mental resemblance produces some kind of ill-defined 'sympathy' or 'resonance' between the objects themselves. This supposedly links these articles in various ways in the real world, outside the theatre of their own minds. Thus, either member of the pair can then be used to reveal or influence the other via this magical interconnectedness. Sympathy can allegedly be established by physical proximity (so-called 'contact magic'), such as when a psychic attempts to describe the owner of an object by holding the article and absorbing the 'vibrations' its owner somehow imparted to it. Sympathy can also be conceptual or symbolic, such as when tribes hoping to ensure a successful hunt commence by ritualistically 'slaying' carved models of their intended prey. Perhaps the best known believers in sympathetic magic are followers of the Voudon religion (voodoo) who think they can injure adversaries by mutilating their effigies. Needless to say, modern science has found no support for these putative avenues of influence, which must come as a great relief for the many football coaches and political leaders whose likenesses have been subjected to shocking indignities by angry mobs.

Can you picture that?

Where do magical thinkers assume the 'similarity' that breeds 'sympathy' comes from? In the best 'mind-over-matter' tradition, it starts with a process psychologists call 'pareidolia', the ingrained tendency of our sensory systems to impose meaning on random stimuli.[26] Figures 16.2–16.5 present some examples of pareidolia. If you doubt that magical thinking based on pareidolia is still alive and well in the twenty-first century, note the following news report. A ten-year-old, half-eaten grilled cheese sandwich with scorch burns that convinced its owner that the Virgin Mary had miraculously imprinted her face on his lunch, recently sold at auction for US$28 000.[27]

Evolution shaped our perceptual systems for the very important task of detecting patterns, something they must frequently accomplish in our messy world by enhancing weak signals to pull them out of a sea of background noise. A by-product of this very useful ability is that our senses have become so good at extracting patterns that, while they get it right most of the time, they often make sense out of nonsense when they encounter random input. When we look at clouds, smoke, oil slicks, etc., it is almost impossible *not* to 'see' objects in the capricious contours (see Figs 16.2–16.5). Magical thinkers are prone to assume that some occult force put those images, which are entirely in the eye of the beholder, there for the viewer's personal edification. Such was the case in responses to a famous news photo of the smoke billowing from the stricken towers of the World Trade Center on September 11, 2001. Many subscribers were sure they saw the face of the devil or Osama bin Laden clearly revealed in the smoke. Fans of extraterrestrial visitors were guilty of similar exuberance when they claimed to see human-like faces in pictures of the surface of Mars sent back by NASA's Viking orbiter.[28] They were, of course merely shadows, as shots taken later, from a different angle of approach, readily showed.

In the 1950s an entire release of a newly designed Canadian dollar bill had to be recalled because the engraved swirls in Queen Elizabeth's hair reminded a few panicked citizens of the face of the devil (Fig. 16.2). Strong government assurances that Satanists had not infiltrated the Royal Canadian Mint were insufficient to calm those who believed they could be hexed (by contact magic) if they touched these diabolical bills. The government eventually bowed to superstition and had the portrait re-engraved at great cost to the taxpayers.

Astrology provides a classic example of how pareidolia and sympathetic magic are used to assign attributes to strangers.[29] As we shall see, the parallels with graphology are striking. Astrology arose in the dim past when observers of the night sky were reminded of crabs, bulls, twins, and the like, by various clusters of stars. There was nothing inevitable about those particular associations, and different cultures mentally superimposed differ-ent objects on the same constellations, much as different test-takers today see a variety of things in the same Rorschach inkblot. (Ironically, graphologists occasionally try to bolster their credibility by comparing their craft with the Rorschach test, apparently unaware that scientifically minded psychologists consider the Rorschach to have little more validity than graphology or astrology.[30])

For historical reasons, the currently accepted constellation names (which originated in Mesopotamia about 5000 years ago) have been passed down to us—much to the chagrin of astrologers of Chinese and other descents whose ancestors' pareidolia connected the dots somewhat differently. In essence, astrology boils down to the following: (1) the stellar configuration reminded someone of a bull (i.e. 'Taurus'); (2) bulls are plodding, stubborn and obdurate; (3) therefore, those born with this constellation in the appropriate part of the sky are condemned, by sympathetic infusion of these bull-like qualities, to grow up to be dull, loutish drudges as well. On the basis of such reasoning, Ronald Reagan planned important affairs of state!

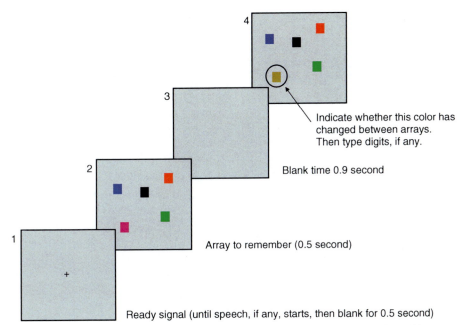

4

Indicate whether this color has
changed between arrays.
Then type digits, if any.

3

Blank time 0.9 second

2

Array to remember (0.5 second)

1

Ready signal (until speech, if any, starts, then blank for 0.5 second)

Plate 1 Illustration of the array comparison procedure of Luck and Voge1 as adapted by Morey and Cowan.

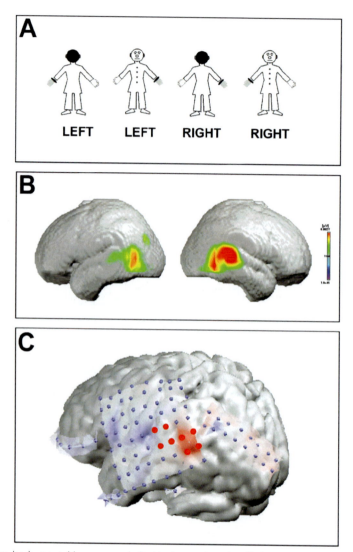

Plate 2 Own-body mental imagery and electrical neuroimaging findings. (A) Four different stimuli as used in the own-body transformation task. Correct responses in the OBT task are indicated below each figure. Front-facing figures simulate the position and visuospatial perspective during spontaneous OBEs and led to longer reaction times in nornmal subjects (see Blanke et al.[46]). (B) A stable map topography was found from >330–400 ms and only in the own-body transformation task (results not shown). This map's duration paralleled the behavioural reaction time differences in the experimental conditions in the own-body transformation task and led to an activation (as estimated by a linear inverse solution) of both temporo-parietal junctions with a right predominance (see Blanke et al.[46]). (C) MRI with the implanted electrodes overlying the lateral convexity of the left hemisphere. The epileptic focus, whose discharge induced an OBE, is indicated by eight red electrodes at the temporo-parietal junction. The figure also depicts the amplitude (in μV) for all implanted electrodes during the own-body transformation task at ~333 ms (blue depicts positive values and red negative values). The most prominent EPs at this latency were recorded over the temporo-parietal junction and partly overlapping with the epileptic focus.

Fig. 16.2 The devil, you say? Pareidolia sinks the Canadian dollar. In the new portrait of the recently crowned Queen Elizabeth II on this 1954 issue of the Canadian dollar bill, some people imagined they saw the face of the devil in the hair waves on the lower right. Superstitious outcries led to the bill being withdrawn and the portrait re-engraved.

The real roots of graphology

Today's graphological notables still rely on the same principles of pareidolia and sympathetic magic to derive a writer's supposed attributes from his or her script.[2] Graphologists have done their best to obscure this fact by embedding their speculations in modern-sounding psychobabble and neurobabble, but one need only compare their 'signs' with the traits they supposedly denote, in the following examples, to see that the basis of their ascriptions is entirely allegorical.[2] Underscoring this pareidolia connection, researchers have discovered a natural tendency for people who know nothing about graphology to make the same kind of spontaneous associations that graphologists do between certain handwriting features and certain personality traits. Novices in one such study came up with similar free associations to elements of letters, etc., that graphology dogma has settled into over the ages. King and Koehler[32] showed non-graphologists scripts and vignettes describing the people who supposedly wrote each specimen. The kind of spontaneous semantic associations to the script features these amateurs came up with were capable of making them think that they saw related features in the characteristics of the people depicted in the character sketches of the alleged writers. However, careful examination of the contents showed that the inferred correlations were illusory. The authors concluded that the 'results [of their study] may partially account for continued use of graphology despite overwhelming evidence against its predictive validity'. Space permits me to present only a limited number of examples of graphological augury (for complete citations and verbatim excerpts, see reference [2]). The examples presented here are paraphrased from texts highly recommended by practicing graphologists.

The founders of every school of graphology I was able to find began with the implicit assumption that whatever metaphors the features of an individual's script bring to mind are necessarily descriptive of the writer as well. This kind of free association, symbolic interpretation and magical extrapolation underlies all divination practices.[31] It remains as central to graphology today as it was when ancient oracles foretold the fates of kings by assuming that their mental associations to the shapes of animal entrails would be re-enacted in the affairs of the realm. For augury, also known as 'skrying' or 'divining', any ambiguous stimulus will do as a starting point—for instance, in another archaic auguring practice, molybdomancy, the oracle would drop molten lead on a flat surface and interpret the shape it assumed as it solidified—the blob, it seems, magically adopts the shape of things to come (see Fig. 16.3). The mystical belief underlying all divination practices is that some 'hidden hand' or occult force will make what would otherwise be just a random outline (smoke, entrails, thrown sticks, etc.) arrange itself in a meaningful design the adept can interpret to reveal hidden knowledge. Graphologist Bart Baggett shows that he believes this when he quotes with approval the popular mystical tome, *The celestine prophecy*, to back up his assertion that 'there are no random events', and hence, 'signs' in handwriting *must* encode personality.

After perusing the following attributions from a variety of prominent graphologists, you can decide for yourself whether handwriting analysis has really abandoned its beginnings in augury and divination. Here is a sample of pareidolia, coupled with allegorical thinking, culled from dozens of graphology textbooks, articles and websites. For details of which prominent graphologist made which of these assertions, see my earlier chapter on the magical origins of graphology.[2]

- ◆ Wide spacing between words supposedly denotes someone who does not mix easily and is therefore prone to be isolated and lonely.
- ◆ Conversely, writers who crowd their words together are so desperate for constant companionship that they are indiscriminate in choosing their friends.
- ◆ Writers whose lines drift upward are 'uplifting' optimists while those whose lines sag downward are pessimists who constantly feel they are being dragged down by the vicissitudes of life.
- ◆ Forward slanting letters denote an outgoing personality, a 'forward' person who is inclined to interact with others. Backhand writing, in contrast, supposedly reveals a reticent, stand-offish individual who prefers to hold back or shy away from social contact (see the Bill Clinton example, in Fig. 16.1). Upright writers are uptight and rigid.

Fig. 16.3 Pareidolia in a solder blob. Molybdomancy is the ancient art of augury where soothsayers interpret the shapes of molten lead as it solidifies after being dropped into a vat of cold water. This is an un-retouched photo of a dropped solder blob retrieved by the author as he was trying to repair his stereo system. He just knew he was about to have a good day when this blob hit his workshop benchtop—until, he burned his finger picking it up, that is. (Photo by Loren Beyerstein.)

- Those with variable letter slants are unpredictable, or, as one of my sources put it, they are people with 'changing inclinations'.
- Writers of unusually large capital *I*'s have large egos and those who write big, 'think big.'
- A past president of a major US graphological association asserts that if a married woman pens her signature with a larger capital on her given name than on her husband's surname, she betrays an unhappy marriage.
- An illegible signature 'reveals a desire to be seen but not known, [to keep] things private'.
- Big letters in a signature denote egotism as a desire for power.
- One of Canada's most prominent handwriting nabobs described in one of her books a writer with crosses on his *t*s that reminded her of little whips, thus revealing his sadistic nature.

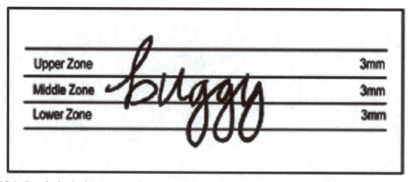

Fig. 16.4 Graphological 'zones'. What writing supposedly reveals to graphologists about the writer is, in part, encoded by how the writer's letters distribute themselves in the three 'zones' shown in this figure. The attribution of characteristics to the writer is made according to metaphorical free associations to terms such as 'high', 'low' and 'middle'. The 'high-minded' 'high-brows' and 'low-down and dirty' low-life supposedly reveal their true natures by unconsciously enlarging parts of their letters that inhabit the upper and lower zones, respectively. After all, heaven is 'up there' and hell is you know where. People whose letters have no prominent features in either the upper or the lower zones are supposed to be practical, 'down-to-earth' types, according to graphological augury. One's sexual prowess is allegedly revealed by how big and bulbous the loops are that dangle below the line. (Graphic by Susan Lebo.)

The so-called 'zones,' shown in Fig. 16.4, refer to 'upper', 'middle' and 'lower' parts of letters. Extra tall upper zones of *t*s, *l*s, *b*s, etc., mean the writer is preoccupied by lofty ideals, the world of ideas, and spiritual pursuits—the head, where thoughts occur, as well as heaven, are 'up' things in the metaphorical world inhabited by graphologists. Exaggerated middle zones denote somebody who's 'down to earth,' preoccupied by practical, worldly concerns. The size of one's lower zone reveals one's obsession with baser stuff, including impolite things that go on 'down there', such as elimination and procreation—see the X-rated section devoted to this, dare I say?, 'below.'

- People who draw the upper, middle and lower sections of their letters equally large have 'a good sense of proportion', says a well-known graphologist.
- Tenacity is shown by ending hooks on the right side of letters, such as the end of the *t*-cross. A person with hooks like this tends to hold on to what is hers. If the hook is in the upper zone, she will cling to her ideas and beliefs. If in the middle zone, she will be tenacious about material items. Don't even ask what a hook in the lower zone means.
- A habitual liar is indicated by loops within loops, inside letters.
- A spendthrift is betrayed by *o*s that, like gaping purses, do not close at the top.
- On the health front, my prominent graphological informants claimed that low writing pressure signals low blood pressure and ragged upper loops are diagnostic of heart disease. Also, a break between upper and lower zones of letters is a sure sign of back problems.

Finally, as I tried to warn you, my all-time favourite ascription is the widely held belief in the graphological community that large, bulbous loops on *g*s, *y*s, etc., i.e. ones that dangle lasciviously below the lines, reveal a strong sex drive. 'If you see a lower loop in the *g* and *y* that is incomplete, know that the sex life is also incomplete', says celebrity graphologist Greg Baggett. I apologize to my readers for the unfortunate sexism here, but I hasten add that I did not invent this phallocentric yardstick, famous and still-revered graphologists did. If you think I jest, check a few graphologists' websites, such as: http://www.handwriting.net/, the website of American Graphological Centers.

All is not lost, graphologically speaking, for the 'other' sex, however. The website of Anna Koren, who advertises herself as, 'a foremost world expert in graphology'—she was the other graphologist consulted by the FBI in our earlier example—proudly displays (with overdrawn anatomical features, for the benefit of those lacking in imagination) her interpretation of the signature of the buxom movie star Jayne Mansfield. Out of purely scientific interest, and assuming you are of legal age, you can look for yourself at: http://annakoren.com/signature1.html. Koren asserts that similar revelations can be gleaned from the signature of Mae West, which she also reproduces, but without the overdrawn anatomical bits so thoughtfully provided in Ms Mansfield's case. In Fig. 16.5, no pun intended—my wife Susan has drawn for your edification her depiction of Koren's analysis of Mae West's signature. We were forced to do this because Koren failed to provide the same titillating details on her website that she did for Ms Mansfield's signature. The monikers of both these famously well-endowed movie stars contain enormous sworls (two of them, no less, for Ms West!) that could only signify you-know-what, according to Ms Koren. Augury by sympathetic magic, or what? At least one can barbecue the ox after examining its entrails. With graphology, all one is left with is what the bull deposited on the trail.

Critiques of the 'official' rationales for graphology

Before presenting graphology's dismal record in empirical tests, let me first dispose of several oft-heard rationalizations from graphologists for why handwriting analysis ought to work.

Handwriting is brainwriting

Yes it is, but walking is also controlled by the brain, so should we henceforth refer to it as 'brainstepping' as Karnes and Leonard[33] wryly suggest? Why would we think that just because something is controlled by the brain, it is necessarily correlated with personality, aptitudes or propensities? That is a hypothesis to be supported with evidence, not glibly assumed at the outset. Vomiting has an associated centre in the brain too. Does that justify using individual regurgitation styles to reveal someone's psychological make-up?

In an earlier chapter,[16] I turned to my background as a biological psychologist to show why research into the neural substrates of writing and personality actually supplies some of the best arguments *against* the validity of graphology. There is simply no evidence,

Fig. 16.5 A prominent graphologist's interpretation of the signature of the movie star, Mae West. This figure was drawn for us according to the interpretation of graphologist Anna Koren, supplied on her website (http://annakoren.com/signature1.html). On this website, there appears a less demure drawing of the signature and most prominent physical attributes of another well-endowed movie star, Jayne Mansfield. (This depiction courtesy of Susan Lebo.)

or even reason to suspect, that the brain mechanisms responsible for writing and those that control temperament and aptitudes could be linked in the lockstep fashion required for graphology to be valid. Research on the physiological bases of personality shows that individual traits are not localized in circumscribed brain areas that could conceivably be attached, one-to-one, to the minute muscle programmes responsible for individual writing features. As I have argued,[16] the graphologists' naïve notions of how the brain controls personality (not to mention their outmoded conceptions of personality itself) are virtually identical to those of the discredited field of phrenology (the pseudoscience that diagnoses traits according to bumps on the head, which are supposedly caused by excess growth of the underlying part of the brain that allegedly controls the trait in question). Graphology would require a brain organization akin to that posited by the phrenologists to make it even remotely plausible. If the brain were organized like that, brain injuries that alter personality should impose predictable and automatic changes in writing features too. Likewise, a brain injury that alters one's handwriting should also warp the patient's personality in its wake. There is not a shred of evidence to support this.

For such a necessary but unlikely brain organization to exist, it would need either to have evolved (and thus be inherited), or to be acquired early in life. Either way, the implications for graphology are daunting. If natural selection shaped brain mechanisms that could cement every character trait to a unique writing movement, graphologists should be able to suggest what possible survival advantages this profligate use of biological resources might have conferred. So far, no graphologist I am aware of has even realized that this is a serious impediment to scientific acceptance of graphology. Moreover, since the ability to write is, at most, 6000 years old and the human brain evolved essentially to its modern form more than a hundred thousand years ago, the putative circuits that would eventually link personality to writing must have evolved for some other purpose. What were these neural pathways selected for initially, and what were the selective pressures pushing the brain in that direction so long before humans got around to inventing writing?

If, instead, one views expression of personality in writing as an acquired skill, the difficulties for graphology are equally sticky. Since writing is unquestionably a learned behaviour, how does the brain unerringly modify every learned writing movement to make it congruent with each of the numerous personality traits a child will grow up to express? What kind of mechanism could conceivably ensure that *everyone* who is destined to be habitually devious will acquire the same neural programme to, say, make *l*-loops in the same way? Do parents ever say, 'Susie, you are obviously gifted with leadership talents; be sure to form your capitals in this way, rather than the way your teacher showed you'?

You have probably noticed that writing varies dramatically across linguistic groups. What differences in genetics or early experience in the various linguistic communities ensure that the infant's brain will develop into the appropriate variant so that it will attach emerging personality traits to quite different movements if the child, by accident of birthplace, should learn to write the Chinese as opposed to the Arabic, Cyrillic, Hebrew or Roman alphabets? Also, what could change in the brain in order to re-connect all those personality traits with brand new writing features if someone who learns one of these scripts as a child then suddenly moves and adopts the one used in a new locale? Writing in all of these different scripts does indeed become personalized, but that individuality arises from biomechanical factors quite different from, and far more interesting than, the graphologists' parochial suppositions.[16] If someone learns to write in a new alphabet, and the graphological signs in the old one and the new one do not jibe, does the person become a multiple personality?

In sum, the graphologists' 'brainwriting' argument is true, but irrelevant to their claims. This rationale would only be necessary if there were a need to explain a proven relationship between writing and other personal attributes. Unfortunately for graphology, much empirical research, reviewed below, says such correlations are illusory in the first place.

Writing is individualized and personality is unique, so each must reflect the other

Aside from the obvious logical flaw in this argument, why should we accept, without good evidence, that any two, admittedly idiosyncratic aspects of a person will necessarily bear any particular relationship to one another? True, forgeries have been exposed and writers of extortion notes convicted on the basis of distinctive penmanship, but does that imply that each of these idiosyncratic writing features is reliably tied to a unique personality attribute of the author (in that person alone, let alone every other writer who uses the same alphabet)? Faces are sufficiently different to serve as personal identification on a driver's licence but the authorities still require that you take a road test before certifying your driving proficiency. At one time, though, it was believed that facial features could reveal other personal attributes. The pseudoscience of physiognomy held that there were uniquely honest faces and criminal faces, generous faces and miserly faces. None but the wooliest New Ager could swallow this today.

To show that not all unique attributes are emblematic of anything in particular, a colleague relates the following story.[33] When he was a graduate student, Ed Karnes trained himself, as a quirky hobby, to identify individuals from the distinctive sound of their footsteps in the long hallway leading to his office. Many a visitor was un-nerved by being welcomed by name, long before he or she came into view. Ed had happened to notice a very subtle, but reliably detectable, personal characteristic. It may be useful for winning bets and amazing one's friends, but would any reasonable person seriously think that, just because it is a unique personal attribute, one's toe-tapping shuffle would be a solid basis for hiring an employee, rejecting a mate or accusing someone of pilfering from the stockroom?

Writing is a form of expressive movement, so it should reflect our personalities

Reviewers of the literature on expressive movements and facial expressions have shown why attempts to shore up graphology by appealing to these data fall short of the mark.[2,16] While it is true that there is legitimate research linking a few global aspects of temperament to certain broad gestural styles, these data offer no comfort to the graphologists who attempt to ride on their coat-tails. Graphologists proudly note that they are mentioned in Allport and Vernon's 1933 classic, *Studies in expressive movement*.[34] They are less likely to tell us that, in the estimate of these respected psychologists, '...the [graphological] terms employed often seem to obscure rather than reveal the personality'.

In fact, the kinds of personal styles found to be loosely related to expressive body movements are much more general than the narrow traits the graphologists claim to infer from writing. A broad tendency to be forceful, irascible or domineering might be readable from certain aspects of body language but, even there, the correlations are too weak to be useful in making the kind of detailed ascriptions in unrelated areas that graphologists attempt. No respectable scientist has ever suggested that something as abstruse as piety, idealism or good business sense was encoded in gestural movements.

Likewise, facial expressions may sometimes betray a lie as it is being uttered (and even that, rather imperfectly as countless successful con-artists will attest), but no competent researcher has suggested that people with a sweeping tendency to be duplicitous have a single gestural manifestation of this or any other long-term inclination of the sort graphologists claim to detect. Moreover, the body and facial movements studied by reputable scientists are unlearned, biologically based social signals, common to all members of our species. Writing, in contrast, is a learned skill that is personally and culturally variable; no one acquires it without instruction. Perhaps most damaging of all to the graphologists' attempts to justify themselves by trying to link themselves to the body language literature is the evidence that such information as can be gleaned from unconscious movements and facial expressions is readable by anyone without formal training—it would be dangerous to enter any bar in town if this were not so. There is no need to pay anyone a fee to interpret what the signals mean.

The police and courts use graphology, so it must be valid

I am tempted to say, 'Ronald Reagan used astrology, so it must be valid', and leave it at that, but there are a few additional lessons to be derived in refuting this old canard. Yes, unfortunately, some misguided officials have employed handwriting analysts in forensic settings, but the practice is not as widespread as graphologists claim. As a group, police officers, lawyers and judges are no more or less prone to erroneous beliefs than anyone else. Faced with difficult decisions where no other method offers certainty (an ideal breeding ground for superstitions), those in the criminal justice system do occasionally get swept up in hopeful nonsense, just like the rest of us (see, for example, Nickell,[35] or the website http://www.csicop.org/specialarticles/police-psychics.html, for a discussion of the disappointing record of police involvement with psychics). The vast majority of police officers and judges do not endorse graphology or psychics, however. Graphologists occasionally offer their services to the police and get a polite hearing, as any citizen is entitled to. For reasons related to the *subjective evaluation effect*, discussed below, some recipients of graphologists' help may well have been more impressed than the performance warranted. Of course, like psychics who claim to solve crimes, a few chance hits by a graphologist, boosted by a bit of charm, embellishment and unabashed self-promotion, can establish a high, but unearned, reputation.

The artificially inflated reputation handwriting analysts enjoy among the general public is largely due to the widespread tendency to confuse the occupation of graphologist with that of a questioned document examiner (QDE). As Dale Beyerstein[11] has observed, nonsense often rides piggy-back on sensible knowledge, and graphology, though it bears only superficial resemblance to scientific document examination, misappropriates the latter's well-deserved prestige.[1,36] Both fields analyse handwriting, but that is where the similarity ends.

A QDE is a scientifically trained forensic investigator who also has considerable knowledge of the history of papers, inks, writing implements, systems of penmanship and styles of expression.[36] QDEs are respected experts who are frequently consulted by the police and the courts. Their *modus operandi* is quite different from that of a graphologist, however. The job of a QDE is to establish the provenance and authenticity of documents, some of which are handwritten. Unlike a graphologist, a legitimate QDE would never attempt to divine the personality of the writer from the script he or she examines. Where appropriate, the QDE will compare the writing in disputed documents with known samples from the hand of the putative author. A typical question for a QDE might be, 'Is this an authentic letter from Mozart to his patron or a clever forgery?' Or, 'Is it likely that the defendant in the dock is the one who wrote this extortion letter?' Questions put to graphologists, on the other hand, are typically of the sort, 'Does this writer harbour a secret resentment of authority?', or 'Does he have larceny in his heart?' You might as well ask, 'Is this writer a vegetarian?'

A QDE will, if need be, carry out chemical assays of the ink, examine the fibres and watermarks of the paper under a microscope, and look for distinctive marks left by different kinds of writing instruments. In addition, a QDE might compare grammar, style and punctuation with social or historical norms, all for the purpose of establishing when, where and by whom a given document was written. The exposure of the infamous 'Hitler Diaries' as forgeries showed QDEs operating at their best.[37] As consultants in litigation or historical disputes, they are asked only to rate the probability that a given person wrote the document in question, not to pass on the guilt, innocence or any other psychological trait of the alleged author. That some QDEs also practise graphology on the side also fuels the confusion in the public mind. Most QDEs, however (including many who have written, thanking me for trying to put the record straight), are just as unhappy at being confused with a graphologist as an astronomer would be if mistaken for an astrologer.

Hard-nosed personnel managers swear by graphologists' usefulness in selecting employees

Some do, but most do not. Regardless, there are many reasons, other than the validity of graphology, that could account for this kind of relatively rare endorsement.[33,38] First, there is ample reason to believe that, even if they are not aware of it, graphologists use other non-graphological clues that could point to the best candidate. For instance, the contents of handwritten application letters are rich in useful biographical information (the 'rich text' problem, referred to earlier). Although graphologists claim to ignore these leads, one well-known study found that students who knew nothing about graphology and were given typed transcripts of the applications rated by graphologists performed just as well as the graphologists who claimed they only looked at the lettering.[18]

I was afforded the opportunity to put this to a direct test, in full public view, when, in 1997, I was invited to do a segment on graphology for Alan Alda's science programme, *Scientific American Frontiers*. By laying a subtle trap for the graphologists the programme hired, we showed quite conclusively that they were drawing inferences from our written answers to questions they posed to us as a means of getting the writing specimens they then proceeded to analyse. This simple demonstration clearly shows, as Jansen[18] found back in 1973, that graphologists do try to pad their hit rates by mining personally revealing contents in the 'rich texts' they analyse. What we did should in no way have impeded their accuracy (which was very poor) if they had been ignoring the 'rich texts', as they claim.

Another unmerited source of satisfaction with graphology stems from the fact that employers rarely give the scripts of all applicants to a graphologist—that would be too time-consuming and expensive. The graphologist usually sees only the scripts of short-listed applicants, those already selected on the basis of superior education, work experience, supervisors' recommendations, etc. Thus it is likely that everyone in this much-reduced pool would be at least adequate for the job. Because the rejects are not given a chance to show what they could do if hired, we have no way of knowing whether they would have performed as well or better than the applicant recommended by the graphologist. Also, of course, the mere fact that a graphologist has anointed the successful candidate may affect later appraisal of performance on the job. Much research on so-called 'halo effects' shows that a recommendation from a trusted source can make average performance seem better than it is and could also make supervisors more apt to excuse shoddy performance as a temporary aberration. The vast literature on 'cognitive dissonance' shows that people who have staked their reputations or significant amounts of money on a course of action, especially if others have questioned its advisability, have strong psychological motives to interpret the outcome as favourable, even in the face of contrary evidence.

Also, in my experience, graphologists often chat up the managers who consult them to see which candidates the employers are already leaning toward. Thus the graphological consultant is often privy to other, conventional information about the applicants and, in many cases, merely reinforces the managers' intuitions.

In scientific tests of the ability of graphologists to recognize job-relevant traits, it is possible to control for the spurious sources of consumer satisfaction discussed above. Klimoski[38] contrasts the methods of scientifically based personnel selection with those of graphologists, reviewing many well-done studies, designed and carried out with the collaboration of well-known graphologists who approved the procedures in advance. In reviewing such tests in the published literature, Klimoski showed that in objective tests, handwriting analysis has fared very poorly in the workplace.

Graphologists must have noticed over the centuries that certain kinds of people write in certain ways

They might have, but they didn't. Systematically tabulating any relationships between personality and features of handwriting is the way a scientific investigator would have gone about it but, as shown above, there is overwhelming evidence that graphology has always followed the rules of augury and divination rather than those of modern personality research. In fact, as Dean et al.[39] document, the founders of graphology couldn't possibly have kept track of the huge number of independently varying combinations of writing and personality variables necessary to be able to extract any such relationships, had they existed in the first place.

Psychologists have shown that, without sophisticated research aids, human cognitive abilities are not capable of tracking the inter-relationships of that many variables simultaneously.[39,40] As it turns out, modern mathematical techniques that would reveal such relationships find none; but even if they had been there, graphologists did not really go about looking for them systematically and the intuitive style they did adopt would have been incapable of extracting any possible signals from the noise. When competent, impartial outsiders tally up both the hits and the misses under controlled conditions, the seemingly impressive track record of graphology evaporates. Let us now turn to that evidence.

The empirical evidence for and against graphology

The foregoing *a priori* reasons for doubt would amount to nothing if graphologists could live up to their claims when tested under adequately controlled conditions. The field's occult beginnings would be irrelevant if it had, in fact, transcended them. The fact that hypnosis has an equally checkered past (and even a few charlatans still in the ranks of its present-day practitioners) bothers no one because its serious supporters rolled up their sleeves and did the painstaking work to determine which claims for hypnosis are sustainable and which are not. Because *some* (but not other) alleged effects of hypnosis have received adequate empirical support, ethical therapists are justified in using it in those restricted realms where it has been shown to work. This example belies the frequent claim that science only rejects graphology and its ilk because of their occult past. In science it is results, not pedigree, that counts. As the great novelist and chemist Primo Levi so nicely put it, 'Science respects what is'. Unfortunately, no such endorsement from working scientists has been forthcoming for graphology.

My task in summarizing the extensive scientific research on graphology has been made quite easy by the superb efforts of Geoffrey Dean[41] who has done an exhaustive review of the literature. In any area of scientific controversy, a single study practically never decides the issue. It is only through the patient accumulation of many experiments, replicated by different investigators with converging methodologies, that a consistent, believable pattern will emerge. As the physicist Victor Stenger said, 'In science, nothing is accepted as true until its appearance becomes commonplace'. Until recently, the most common way of trying to settle disputes in contentious areas was essentially to take a 'box score', i.e. so many studies for conclusion X and so many against, with the preponderance carrying the day. Not all empirical findings should count equally in such a tally, however. Those studies with larger sample sizes, better experimental controls and less noisy data ought to carry greater weight in the grand reckoning. Fortunately, there has emerged a way of factoring such considerations into the overall assessment, and thereby drawing more trustworthy conclusions from multiple studies on a given topic. It is called 'meta-analysis'.[41]

In his review of the empirical research on graphology, Dean applied this mathematical technique for assessing the cumulative effect of over 200 published studies from numerous countries and in several languages. At the end of the day, the 'effect size' (the way a meta-analysis expresses the impact of the experimental variable in question) for graphology amounted to zero.[41]

In his extensive search for empirical evaluations of graphology, Dean[41] unearthed more than 200 studies that had an unambiguous criterion and acceptable methodological rigour. In order to answer questions about the validity of a measure such as graphology, one must have a *criterion* for the trait that is allegedly assessed by the measure in question. If we are evaluating a test that claims to predict superior salesmanship, for instance, the criterion might be the agent's total annual sales or the number of deals closed per number of client contacts. An acceptable test would have to show that those who score highly on the test also tend to score highly on these criterion measures and, of course, that those who do poorly are also at the bottom of the sales charts.

After subjecting the studies that met conventional methodological standards to a meta-analysis, Dean showed an unequivocal failure on the part of graphologists to demonstrate the validity of graphology as a predictor of work performance or personality. Graphology thus fails according to the minimum standards a genuine psychological test must exceed before it can ethically be released for use on a trusting and unsuspecting public. Dean found that no particular school of graphology fared better than any other, belying the smug claims of Graphoanalysis to be scientifically superior to its rivals. In fact, no graphologist of any stripe was able to show reliably better performance than untrained amateurs when guessing about the same traits. In the vast majority of cases, neither group exceeded chance expectancy.

Perusing Dean's accumulated corpus of research, an interesting relationship emerges.[41] The better a given study is with respect to experimental methodology, and the more stringent the peer review process of the journal in which it is published, the more likely it is that the results will be unfavourable to graphology. For this reason, it is not surprising that the majority of studies that find any merit whatever in graphology are published by graphologists themselves, in pamphlets or proprietary journals, or appear in journals that have very high acceptance rates and which charge the authors to publish there.

Of course, graphologists hotly contest these conclusions, claiming that the tests that have belittled their abilities were unfair and irrelevant. The fact remains, however, that, in many of the best studies, graphologists approved in advance the tasks they were tested on and the assessment criteria for success, i.e. they were willing participants until after their poor showing became known. In other tests, the scripts were submitted by researchers who claimed to be ordinary customers seeking help and the graphologists accepted their usual fees—they must have thought they were giving good value for the money or they would not have accepted the business. If not, they would have been intentionally cheating the public. In one of the most rigorous series of studies, by Klimoski and his colleagues[38], the graphologists were so confident they would shine that they even funded the research project themselves. They agreed in advance that what they were being asked to do in the tests was fair and representative of what they do in their everyday practices. Only when the results turned out negatively did the graphologists begin to quibble about the fairness of the tests. They even went so far as to threaten legal action to prevent publication of the embarrassing results.

Summarizing the results of his own research and that of others who have put graphology to the test, Klimoski[38] concludes:

> ...a manager receiving solicitations for graphological services or seeking assistance in personnel decision making would be wise to heed the American credo 'Caveat Emptor'—let the buyer beware.

Why does graphology seem to work?

Faced with the consistently poor showing of handwriting analysis in scientific tests, the typical response from graphologists is, 'I don't need to prove anything to you. I know it works and I have hundreds of satisfied customers to prove it'. Of course, this is the same rejoinder I have received from every medium and Tarot card reader I have debated as well. People pay good money and come back for more—they must be receiving good value, mustn't they? Not necessarily.

If graphology's track record in carefully controlled tests is as poor as critics have demonstrated, how could so many intelligent, well-educated people still believe it has merit? It is now time for complete self-disclosure. I was once a graphologist. When I was 11 years old, I saw a book on handwriting analysis in our local bookshop and, after reading the claims on the dust jacket, I knew immediately that I just had to have it. It required saving up several weeks' allowance, but eventually I could afford it. I quickly set about analysing the writing of my friends, family and neighbours. They were duly impressed, as was I, with the seeming accuracy of my analyses.

Unfortunately, I did not have, at the time, a wise old mentor like the one my friend, Professor Ray Hyman was lucky enough to have when, at an only slightly less tender age, he became enamoured of palm reading. Ray was so impressed that he decided to go professional and began to do palm readings after school at a local arcade. His clientele rewarded him generously for his insight and perspicacity. With such affirmation, it is not surprising that he, like me, came to believe even more firmly in what he was doing. This continued until the aforementioned mentor proposed a simple test. He said, in effect, 'Ray, this week, why don't you try formulating in your head what the palmistry texts say you ought to read from each palm, then tell the clients exactly the opposite of what the textbooks say they should be told? At the end of the week, we'll see, from your earnings and feedback, if your sitters are any less happy with your insights than they have been up 'til now'. Of course, Ray's clientele continued to be just as happy with the accuracy of his insights as the ones from previous weeks. Thus, the seeds of one of academia's most distinguished sceptical careers were planted. Lacking the benefit of such a jaded and worldly advisor, it took me quite a bit longer to see where graphology's apparent accuracy was coming from.

In everyday settings, the pronouncements of graphologists, astrologers, palm readers and psychics can seem remarkably specific and revealing, even though they are not. The spurious sense that something deeply informative has been revealed in a horoscope or in a handwriting, tea leaf or palm reading stems from a form of cognitive slippage known as 'The Barnum Effect'.[42] It is also known as 'The Subjective Validation Effect' or the 'Personal Validation Effect'. Its more colourful name stems from the exploits of the famous American showman, P. T. Barnum, who is reputed to have said not only, 'There's a sucker born every minute'. but also, 'I have a little something for everyone'.

As Furnham[43] demonstrates, people invariably interpret vague, generalizations that are true, in some form, of nearly everyone as if they applied to the particulars of their own lives. Later, they are prone to remember their own embellished version as if it had been literally what was said in the reading or horoscope. The fascinating thing is that we accomplish this 'filling in' with practically no awareness that the apparent specificity comes from our own cognitive interpretation. This is not mere gullibility. It stems, instead, from the overapplication of one of our most useful cognitive abilities—the knack of making sense out of the barrage of poorly connected information we face every day. In fact, we become so good at filling in the gaps to make sensible scenarios from disjointed input that, as we saw earlier in the examples of pareidolia, we sometimes make sense of nonsense.

Simply to decide what many perfectly grammatical sentences actually mean, we often have to draw on our background knowledge to infer what the people who uttered them intended to convey. We do this automatically, without thinking about it. For instance, what do the following sentences mean?

'Visiting relatives can be a drag'.

'Prostitutes are appealing to the minister'.

Obviously, you need to fill in many background details that are not in the sentences themselves in order to arrive at what you think was intended by the speaker. We get so used to making specifics out of generalities in everyday parlance that we do it without realizing it when seers and soothsayers come knocking. Is it any wonder that every generation discovers anew that Nostradamus' flowery language unerringly describes the events of their own era? It is the Barnum Effect, boys and girls. Psychologists have learned a great deal about the social and cognitive factors that make Barnum-type generalities seem so personally relevant and penetrating.[42,43] Have you ever been served a fortune cookie that did not apply to yourself?

The power of the Barnum Effect is so great that an informal demonstration of any personality test, orthodox or not, cannot be taken at face value. Our inquisitive minds will always find a way to make the portrayal seem applicable to ourselves. This is not a result of feeblemindedness; in fact, more intelligent people have an easier time of 'filling in the blanks' convincingly. Therefore, a proper test of any character reader will need to control for the spurious sense of accuracy imparted by the Barnum Effect. So, instead of asking the recipient if the palm reader or astrologer has accurately depicted him or her, a proper test would take many readings done for a large number of clients and remove the names (coding them so they can later be re-attached to the person for whom they were done). After each person had read all the personality sketches, he or she would then be asked to identify his or her own. If the character reader has actually included enough uniquely relevant material in the personality sketch, the group as a whole should be able to do better than chance in choosing their own reading out of the pile. None of the occult or pseudoscientific character reading methods referred to in this chapter has successfully passed such a test.

Another way of showing that the apparent accuracy of unscientific character readings is, like beauty, in the eyes of the beholder can be shown by many studies that have led participants to think they have received a reading done specifically for them. In my own classes, I have demonstrated the Barnum Effect numerous times to my students, both with horoscopes and with graphological analyses. In the case of graphology, I ask each student for a sample of his or her handwriting. I tell them I will be back the following week with a character analysis that I will ask them to evaluate for specificity and accuracy. Although this has always produced very high average ratings (typically over 4 on a 5-point scale) for how well the graphologist had depicted them, the class was unaware (until I told them after they made their ratings) that I only paid to have one sample analysed and they all received the same graphologist's report.

The Barnum Effect can even take in supposedly hard-nosed journalists. In 2005, several media outlets in the UK paid some of Britain's best known graphologists to look at the contents of a scratch pad retrieved from the conference table after Prime Minister Tony Blair attended the recent World Economic Summit. Knowing in advance it was the work of this beleaguered politician whose fortunes were sagging at that moment, the graphologists confidently declared it the output of a reckless, vacillating, incompetent. Blair's open circles revealed an inability to complete tasks, they said—some even detected a hint of suicide prone-ness (both politically and personally). The cream of British graphologists proceeded to expose Blair as someone struggling to concentrate, not a natural leader, unable to keep control of a confusing world, and an unstable man staggering under enormous pressure. No sooner had this been published, but No. 10 Downing Street punctured the balloon by revealing that the handiwork that had been analysed had, in fact, been that of the person sitting next to Blair at the conference table, Microsoft founder Bill Gates, arguably the world's most successful self-made businessman.

The consequences

All of the foregoing would be touchingly naïve, even comical, were it not for the fact that these self-styled experts offer advice in areas that can besmirch people's reputations and have potentially serious effects on their well-being and economic prospects. For instance, in Vancouver, British Columbia, where I live, a prominent graphologist offered to identify, secretly, for pre-emptive action by the school board, the actual *and potential* sexual molesters in the local teaching ranks.[44] Members of the school board's personnel department had actually engaged the graphologist on a pilot project before the elected members of the board found out (thanks to a diligent newspaper reporter) and sent him packing. In doing research for our book, my brother Dale and I found financial institutions who admitted consulting graphologists to determine who were or were not credit-worthy borrowers. We also encountered a number of civic governments and large corporations who defended their employment of handwriting analysts for pre-employment screening of job applicants. Graphologists also say they are competent to help select marriage partners, and there have been press reports that a former member of Canada's National Parole Board had privately consulted her graphologist sister to help select those prisoners who would be safe to release.[2] Similarly, a judge in Denver, Colorado was reported to have used graphology in determining appropriate sentences for convicted felons.[33]

Many graphologists with whom I have dealt have had no compunctions about making potentially devastating predictions as to which employees would steal from the corporation, betray proprietary secrets or become closet alcoholics, drug abusers or security risks. I was told by one graphologist, over the very fine lunch he bought me, that he has a '100% foolproof way' of determining who will become violent on the job. Some handwriting analysts offer to tell clients who secretly submit their spouse's writing if their partners are philandering and, in locales where the police will take them seriously, they are eager to finger supposed criminals. On an internationally aired TV programme, a graphologist once said that my own writing suggested that I had a secret drug problem and that I had probably been sexually molested by my parents.

If this were not bad enough, many graphologists advertise, as a unique benefit of their services, that inquisitive third parties can submit a sample of writing for analysis and act upon the results, without the writer ever knowing the evaluation took place. Wise moves by various governments to restrict polygraph examinations of current and potential employees have been a boon to graphologists who offer prying employers an even more dubious method with which to circumvent this restriction. I even have in my files advertisements for graphology courses that some ignorant officials of state professional psychological associations have approved for continuing education credit for licensed psychologists!

Leaving aside for the moment the question of whether any written signs are ever reliably correlated with other personal attributes, a constant problem I encountered in my extensive review of graphology texts was that, because the attributions are based on symbolism and free association, different schools disagree about which signs are tokens of which traits. Thus, you as a prospective employee or borrower could have your reputation blackened or be denied other significant opportunities if you were unfortunate enough to be secretly assessed by a graphologist of one persuasion but if, by the luck of the draw, your 'true nature' was divined by a disciple of another school, you might have sailed through with ease. Obviously, when the life prospects of unsuspecting people hang in the balance, the use of what would otherwise be a harmless party amusement ceases to be a laughing matter.

In my public lectures on magical character reading, I often encounter someone in the audience who just does not get it. The questioner usually says something like, 'Why don't you lighten up? Graphology may be dumb, but why are you getting so incensed about it? What's the harm?' I sometimes answer such queries by patiently reiterating the unfair consequences discussed above. Other times, I opt for a bit of shock therapy instead. I simply ask the questioner to tell me what the difference is between racism and sexism on the one hand and making attributions based on graphology or astrology on the other. Typically, the audience is stunned that I would make such an outrageous comparison, but then I remind them that what we mean by prejudice is ascribing characteristics to someone we do not know, based on a false means of determining those attributes, and then treating the person differently as a result. Most of us realize by now that skin colour, ethnicity and gender are not valid indicators of honesty, diligence or talent, so we rightly condemn those who use them as criteria for hiring, loaning, renting, dating, befriending or any other form of discrimination. To do so would be objectionable because it is unfair to use scientifically unsupportable criteria to cast aspersions and deny possibly worthy individuals access to things to which they may be entitled (or to give someone else unearned preference on the same disproven grounds). I always emphasize to the questioner that I am definitely not saying that all graphologists or astrologers are bigots, just that what they do is analogous to bigotry because they recommend differential treatment of people based on bogus criteria. Since there is no credible evidence that one's horoscope or, as shown above, a graphologists' personality sketch, is a valid way of knowing what someone is really like, it would be akin to making a racist or sexist slur to treat somebody one way or another based on such flimsy suppositions.

References and notes

1. Nickell, J. A brief history of graphology. In BL Beyerstein, DF Beyerstein, ed. *The write stuff: evaluations of graphology—the study of handwriting analysis*. Prometheus Books, Amherst, NY. 1992:23–28.
2. Beyerstein BL. The origins of graphology in sympathetic magic. In BL Beyerstein, DF Beyerstein, ed. *The write stuff: evaluations of graphology—the study of handwriting analysis*. Prometheus Books, Amherst, NY. 1992:163–200.
3. Bunge M. What is pseudoscience? *The Skeptical Inquirer*, 1984; 9:36–46.
4. Beyerstein BL. Why bogus therapies seem to work. *The Skeptical Inquirer*, September/October, 1997; 29–34.
5. Beyerstein BL. Pseudoscience and the brain: tuners and tonics for aspiring superhumans. In, S Della Sala, ed. *Mind myths: exploring everyday mysteries of the mind and brain*. John Wiley and Sons, Chichester, UK. 1999:59–82.
6. Beyerstein BL. Fringe psychotherapies: the public at risk. *The Scientific Review of Alternative Medicine*, 2001; 5:5–13.
7. Bowman M. Difficulties in assessing personality and predicting behaviour. In BL Beyerstein, DF Beyerstein, ed. *The write stuff: evaluations of graphology—the study of handwriting analysis*. Prometheus Books, Amherst, NY, 1992:203–231.
8. Aiken LR. *Psychological testing and assessment*, 10th edn. Allyn & Bacon, Boston. 2000.
9. Crumbaugh J. Graphoanalytic cues. In BL Beyerstein, DF Beyerstein, ed. *The write stuff: evaluations of graphology—the study of handwriting analysis*. Prometheus Books, Amherst, NY, 1992:105–118.
10. Lockowandt O. The present status of the research on handwriting psychology as a diagnostic method. In BL Beyerstein, DF Beyerstein, ed. *The write stuff: evaluations of graphology—the study of handwriting analysis*. Prometheus Books, Amherst, NY. 1992:55–58.

11. **Beyerstein DF.** Graphology and the philosophy of science. In BL Beyerstein, DF Beyerstein, ed. *The write stuff: evaluations of graphology—the study of handwriting analysis.* Prometheus Books, Amherst, NY. 1992:121–162.

12. **Dean G.** The bottom line: effect size. In BL Beyerstein, DF Beyerstein, ed. *The write stuff: evaluations of graphology—the study of handwriting analysis.* Prometheus Books, Amherst, NY. 1992:269–341.

13. **Bunker M.** *Handwriting analysis: the science of determining personality by graphoanalysis.* Nelson-Hall, Chicago: 1971.

14. **Crews F.** The verdict on Freud. *Psychological Science,* 1996; 7: 63–67.

15. **Seligman M.** Speech delivered at the Lincoln Summit; September, 1999. Available on-line: http://www.psych.upenn.edu/seligman/lincspeech.htm

16. **Beyerstein BL.** Handwriting is brainwriting. So what? In BL Beyerstein, DF Beyerstein, ed. *The write stuff: evaluations of graphology—the study of handwriting analysis.* Prometheus Books, Amherst, NY. 1992:397–418.

17. **Basil R.** *Not necessarily the New Age—critical essays.* Prometheus Books, Amherst, NY. 1988.

18. **Jansen A.** *Validation of graphological judgements: an experimental study.* Mouton, Paris. 1973.

19. **Druckman D, Swets J** (ed.) *Enhancing human performance: issues, theories, and techniques.* National Academy Press, Washington, DC. 1988.

20. **Kanfer A, Casten, D.** Observations on disturbances in neuromuscular coordination in patients with malignant disease. *Bulletin Hospital for Joint Diseases,* 1958; **19**:1–19.

21. **McNichol A.** *Handwriting analysis: putting it to work for you.* Contemporary Books, Chicago, IL. 1991.

22. **Marne P.** *Crime and sex in handwriting.* Constable, London. 1981.

23. **Beyerstein BL, Beyerstein DF** (ed.) *The write stuff: evaluations of graphology—the study of handwriting analysis.* Prometheus Books, Amherst, NY. 1992.

24. **Gilovich T.** *How we know what isn't so: the fallibility of human reasoning in everyday life.* Free Press/Macmillan, NY. 1991.

25. **De Sainte Colombe P.** *Graphotherapeutics: the pen and pencil therapy.* Popular Library, New York. 1972.

26. **Zusne L, Jones W.** *Anomalistic psychology: a study in magical thinking,* 2nd edn. Lawrence Erlbaum Associates, Hillsdale, NJ. 1989.

27. **McMartin P.** Painter finds Jesus on garage door.*The Vancouver Sun.* January 8, 2005; B1, 7.

28. **Carroll, R.** (n.d.) The face on Mars. The Skeptic's Dictionary. Online: www.skepdic.com (accessed December 31, 2004).

29. **Kelly I.** The scientific case against astrology. *Mercury,* Nov.–Dec. 1980:135–142.

30. **Wood JM, Nezworski HN, Lilienfeld SN, Garb HN.** *What's wrong with the Rorschach: science confronts the controversial inkblot test.* Jossey-Bass, New York. 2003.

31. **Loewe M, Blacker C** (ed.)*Oracles and divination.* Shambhala, Boulder, CO. 1981.

32. **King RN, Koehler DJ.** Illusory correlations in graphological inference. *Journal of Experimental Psychology: Applied.* 2000; **6**:336–348.

33. **Karnes E, Leonard SD.** Graphoanalytic and psychometric personality profiles: validity and Barnum effects. In BL Beyerstein, DF Beyerstein, ed. *The write stuff: evaluations of graphology—the study of handwriting analysis.* Prometheus Books, Amherst, NY. 1992:269–341.

34. **Allport GW, Vernon PE.** *Studies in expressive movement.* Macmillan, New York. 1933.

35. **Nickell J** (ed.) *Psychic sleuths: ESP and sensational cases:* Prometheus Books, Buffalo, NY. 1994.

36. **Nickell J.** *Pen, ink, and evidence.* Universities Press of Kentucky, Lexington, KY. 1990.

37. **Harris, R.** *Selling Hitler.* Pantheon Books, New York. 1986.

38. **Klimoski R.** graphology and personnel selection. In BL Beyerstein, DF Beyerstein, ed. *The write stuff: evaluations of graphology—the study of handwriting analysis.* Prometheus Books, Amherst, NY. 1992:232–268.

39. **Dean G, Kelly I, D. Saklofske D, A. Furnham A.** Graphology and human judgement. In BL Beyerstein, DF Beyerstein, ed. *The write stuff: evaluations of graphology—the study of handwriting analysis.* Prometheus Books, Amherst, NY, 1992:342–396.

40. **Dawes RM.** *House of cards: psychology and psychotherapy built on myth.* New York: Free Press, 1994.

41. **Dean G.** The bottom line: effect size. In BL Beyerstein, DF Beyerstein, ed. *The write stuff: evaluations of graphology—the study of handwriting analysis.* Prometheus Books, Amherst, NY. 1992:269–341.

42. **Hyman R.** Cold reading: how to convince strangers you know all about them. *The Zetetic* (now *The Skeptical Inquirer*), 1977; **1**:18–37.

43. **Furnham A.** Hooked on horoscopes. *The New Scientist*, January 26, 1991:33–36.

44. **Beyerstein DF, Beyerstein BL.** General Introduction. In BL Beyerstein, DF Beyerstein, ed. *The write stuff: evaluations of graphology—the study of handwriting analysis.* Prometheus Books, Amherst, NY. 1992:9–18.

Chapter 17

The truth about deception

Aldert Vrij and Samantha Mann

Everybody knows what it is to lie, including young children. This familiarity with lying surely makes us knowledgeable about deception (we will use the terms deception and lying interchangeably). We all know that lying is undesirable. Therefore, of course we do not lie very often ourselves since 'decent people' do not make a habit of lying. We prefer not to be involved with liars. Fortunately, most people do not make good liars. They reveal their deceit by behaving nervously and avoiding eye contact. Hence, just by observing someone's behaviour we can easily spot a liar. We are rather good lie detectors, especially when it comes to our own children, partners and close friends. Correct? Actually no! Every statement mentioned here is a myth rather than a fact, and we will unravel those myths in this chapter. We will start by defining a lie.

What is a lie?

Deception can be defined in many ways. Mitchell's[1] definition is probably one of the most remarkable. He defines deception as 'a false communication that tends to benefit the communicator'. This is a very broad definition and classifies many acts as deceit. For example, from this perspective, several plants, such as the orchid *Ophrys speculum* which dupes male wasps with the illusion of sexual contact, are liars. Mitchell's definition is controversial too. Suppose a boy told his mother that he gave her all the change from the shopping but, unknown to him, a 50p piece was left behind in his pocket. The boy is lying according to Mitchell's definition. However, many people will disagree with this definition. Peterson[2] examined whether people tend to classify 'mistakes' as lies. Participants (both 5-year-olds and adults) were given the following story. A boy witnessed an event involving a green car and is then later asked by his father whether he still remembers the colour of the car. The boy, who thought he remembered but really had forgotten the colour of the car, replies: 'Yes Daddy, I remember. The car was yellow'. Participants were asked whether they thought the boy in the story was lying. The vast majority, 88 per cent of 5-year-olds and 95 per cent of adults, thought the boy was not lying (the remaining 12 per cent of the 5-year-olds and 5 per cent of adults thought the boy was lying). Also, Mitchell's definition only covers *self-oriented lies*, or lies that are told for our own benefit. It would not cover instances that most people would consider a lie, but which are not told to benefit the communicator, or, *other-oriented* lies. For example, when a friend gives us a present that we do not really like, we may lie and pretend that we are really pleased with the gift so as not to offend or upset the present-giver. Mitchell's definition also would not cover instances where we might lie to save a friend from getting into trouble, perhaps providing them with a false alibi. Again, in such instances, the lie would be intended to benefit someone other than the communicator. For many people a core issue of deception is that it is an *intentional* act, or, as DePaulo and her colleagues[3] defined deception: a *deliberate* attempt to mislead others. A boy who misremembers the colour of a car and therefore mentions the wrong colour is not lying, whereas a boy who actually remembers the colour of the car but deliberately reports the wrong colour, is.

Another aspect of deception (apart from being an intentional act) is that it is defined solely from the perspective of the deceiver and not from the factuality of the statement. Thus, a statement is a lie if the deceiver believes what s/he says is untrue, regardless of whether the statement is true or false. We already saw in the example of the boy mistakenly reporting the wrong colour of the car that an untruthful statement is not necessarily a lie. Also, an actual truth could be a lie. Suppose that, unknown to his mother, a child has eaten all the sweets. When he asks for more, his mother, in an effort to pacify him whilst preventing him from eating too much, tells him that he cannot have any more because there are no sweets left. This truthful statement is a lie as long as the mother believes that there are still sweets left.

Reasons why people lie

People lie for different reasons. First, to gain advantage. For example, how many people when selling their car will point out to a potential buyer that the car does not start on cold mornings, and shakes when travelling over 70 miles an hour? Probably not many, as this will lead, at best, to a less attractive offer for their car.

Secondly, we lie to make a positive impression on others or to protect ourselves from embarrassment. For example, some people may deliberately underestimate to their doctor how many units of alcohol and cigarettes they consume, whilst others lie about their real calorie intake when attending Weight Watchers. Many people may lie to present themselves more favourably about issues ranging from their appearance (such as whether their hair colour is natural, or their true weight or age) to giving the impression that they earn more than they do, are more successful than they are or have more friends than they do. Furthermore, people often lie to avoid shame or embarrassment. This can range from an innocent denial to hide spoilt pride, to sex offenders who typically minimize the nature and extent of their sexual offending, because they know how they are perceived by others and so feel ashamed about their activities.[4] Our own research into the secrets kept by undergraduate students revealed that these also often relate to sex. Students reported that issues they prefer to keep secret include still being a virgin, having undergone an abortion or being homosexual. Several also reported having denied fancying a person they, in fact, do fancy.[5] Most typically this would be to avoid feelings of rejection and perhaps humiliation in front of peers, should the object of our affections not reciprocate

Fig. 17.1 Parents may inadvertently encourage their children to lie in order to avoid punishment.

such desires. We also try to hide things that happen to us that we find embarrassing or make us feel that for some reason we are being singled out as 'different'. For example, many children are reluctant to admit that they are bullied at school.

Thirdly, we lie to avoid punishment. Guilty suspects deny their involvement in a crime in their police interviews, teenagers avoid admitting to their parents that they smoke and young children do not mention that they have secretly taken a biscuit. Most of us discover the ability to lie as a means to avoid punishment when we are young children. Lies to obtain rewards probably appear later, followed by lies to protect one's self-esteem. Lewis[6] believes that parents inadvertently encourage children to lie in order to avoid punishment. For example, a 2-year-old girl is told to eat no more biscuits. Later, when her mother asks the girl if she has eaten any more biscuits, she admits that she did have one. Her mother then punishes her. After only a few interactions like this, the child learns that if she admits wrongdoing, she will be punished. Therefore, she starts to lie to avoid punishment. When caught, her mother will tell her that it is bad to lie and that she will be punished if she tells a lie. Now the child faces a dilemma. If she tells the truth about her misconduct she will be punished, but also if she gets caught in her lie she will be punished. She will also soon discover that whilst admitting the truth will guarantee punishment, her parents do not detect all her wrongdoings. Hence, the most viable option for the child is to conceal any misbehaviour, and to only admit to it when it is detected. As soon as children consider the listener's mental state (as they will do by the age of 4), they will become better liars.[7] From that stage, they will realize that in order to lie successfully they must convince another of the veracity of a false statement. In Peskin's study[8], 3- to 5-year-olds were confronted with a competitor who always chose the object for which the children themselves had previously stated a preference. The children were asked to 'think of what to do or to say so that the competitor won't get what you want.' More 5-year-olds (87 per cent) than

3-year-olds (29 per cent) tried to influence the competitor's mental state by pointing to an object they did not like or by concealing information.

As mentioned above, in addition to self-oriented lies told for our own benefit, we also tell lies that are other-oriented for other people's benefit. For example, a pupil tells a teacher that her friend is ill, although she knows that in truth her friend is skiving. Also we might offer a friend a compliment in order to boost their self-confidence.

Finally, people tell lies for the sake of social relationships. These are so-called 'social lies'.[9] If people told each other the truth all the time then conversations could become awkward and unnecessarily rude, and social interactions, including friendships and romantic relationships, could easily be disrupted. In order to maintain a good relationship with colleagues then it is better to say that you would love to but are too busy when they invite you to lunch, than to say that you find them boring and would therefore rather avoid extra time in their company. Similarly, most husbands know better than to criticize their wife's dress explicitly, when aware that she bought it in a sale and cannot return it to the store; and most people would eat a dish that they do not like, with enthusiasm, knowing that a friend has gone to great trouble to cook it for them. Social lies simultaneously serve both self-interest and the interest of others. They serve the interest of others because most people do not like criticism, but do like receiving compliments. They serve self-interest because liars may feel satisfaction when they notice how their lies please other people, or because by telling such lies they can avoid an awkward situation or discussion. Another reason why telling other-oriented lies may not totally be an exercise in altruism is because telling such white lies increases our popularity. People like being with people who make them feel good and, as long as our flattery is not translucent, then it will often make people feel good.

DePaulo[10] published a study where people were asked to keep a diary during a period of 1 week, in which they recorded all of their social interactions and all of the lies they told during those interactions. A social interaction was defined as an exchange with another person that lasted for 10 min or longer. Brief encounters such as greetings in the morning were thus ignored. They found that approximately half of the lies people told were self-oriented, and that about 25 per cent were other-oriented. The remaining 25 per cent served both self-interest and the interest of others. The study also revealed gender differences in the type of lies told (but not in the frequency of lying). Men told more self-oriented lies, whereas women told more other-oriented lies, particularly to other women. In conversations between two women, nearly half of the lies were other-oriented.

How bad is lying?

So, is lying a bad thing? How do you feel yourself about lying? You might feel negatively about lying, but if you give the issue a second thought, you might feel differently. This was the conclusion reached by people participating in the study of Backbier et al.[11] The researchers held group interviews to gain insight into how people view lying in everyday life. Initially, the participants opined negatively about lying, but later they could report many instances in which they had lied themselves, and showed reasoning and understanding of their own lies.

How we feel about deception probably depends on the type of lie told. We may feel bad about telling lies to gain advantage or to avoid punishment. Such lies may well be seen as selfish, disruptive of social life and hurtful to the targets of the lies. This is the stereotypical view of lying; but what about the other lies? How would you feel if you had to be totally truthful all the time and therefore had to expose all of your own embarrassing details, misdemeanours and secrets to others? Or if had to tell your child that you do not like his painting? Or you had to tell your friend that you do not like her haircut? You would probably rather lie in most of these instances, and probably so would most of those to whom you had expressed your true opinions. We typically do not feel guilty at all about telling other-oriented lies or social lies. How would you feel if others were always perfectly honest with you? Of course we probably all like to think that our friends do not lie to us, and that all compliments given to us are in fact a true reflection of what people think of us. However, have you ever considered that if you frequently give empty compliments to others which are readily believed, surely others are doing the same to you? When your friend tells you that she is so envious of your figure, or a neighbour admires how you have redecorated your house, then these may not actually be genuine compliments. Social lies and other-oriented lies are often told to avoid tension and conflict in social interactions and to minimize hurt feelings and ill-will.[10] Social lies and other-oriented lies probably lubricate and improve social relationships. Studies have revealed that both men and women prefer conversations with women more than conversations with men, and the finding that women tell more other-oriented lies than men do probably contributes to this.

How often do we lie?

DePaulo's diary study further revealed that lying is an everyday life event. In their study, 77 psychology students (who are the typical participants in psychology research) and 70 community members participated. Community members lied on average once a day and students just over 1.5 times a day. Only one student and six community members reported having not lied at all during that week. In other words, the vast majority of participants admitted to lying. They also said that their lies were generally not serious, and that they put little effort into planning them. Neither did they worry much about the possibility of being caught. They also experienced little regret about their lies, and the majority indicated that they would tell the lie again if the same situation reoccurred.

Frequency of lying depends on numerous factors, including the personality of the liar, the person to whom the lie is told and the situation in which the interaction takes place.

Personality

One might expect people who try to mould others to suit their own agendas to be frequent liars. Indeed, those manipulative people do tell more lies, especially self-serving lies.

Fig. 17.2 People who are highly motivated to make a good impression on others may lie in order to do so.

However, this does not make them unpopular. In conversations, they tend to dominate but also seem relaxed and confident. They are usually liked more than people low in manipulative skills and are preferred as partners. Manipulators are not the only people to lie frequently. Some people are very much concerned with self-presentation. They pay a lot of attention to how they are perceived by others, and are highly motivated to make a good impression on these others. DePaulo's diary study revealed that one way of making a good impression is to lie. A third group of people found to be frequent liars are sociable people, such as extroverts. The fact that extroverts lie more often than introverts is not just because they tend to socialize more. They tell more lies than introverts in each social interaction they have. Apparently, telling small lies to make oneself look better and make other people feel better appeals more to extroverts than to introverts. The latter might be the reason why sociable people are generally popular and viewed as socially skilled. Rather than calling introverts 'honest', which would be an appropriate label, we call them 'socially somewhat awkward' perhaps because of their tendency to be truthful!

To whom the lie is told

DePaulo's diary study revealed a correlation between telling lies and the emotional closeness of the relationship. In same-sex conversations, people told more other-oriented lies to those they felt intimate with, and more self-serving lies to those they did not feel so close to. Further analyses of DePaulo's diary study,[12] comparing the lies told by community members to spouses, best friends, friends, acquaintances and strangers, showed that the lowest rate of lying occurred in conversations with spouses, while the highest rate occurred in conversations with strangers. However, the results clearly demonstrated that deception occurs in all types of close personal relationships. Although participants said they were predominantly honest in social interactions with their spouses, lies still occurred in nearly one of every 10 social interactions they had with them. Many of those lies were minor. Perhaps a limited amount of trivial lying serves important privacy needs for individuals in such close relationships. Interactions between husband and wife are also often the domain of serious lies. When people were asked to describe the most serious lies they had ever told to someone else, they overwhelmingly reported that the target of these lies were close relationship partners.[13] These lies were often told to cover serious issues, such as infidelities, and were told in order to save the relationship. For a variety or reasons, spouses may believe that the truth cannot be told without threatening the relationship, and so may decide that telling a lie is preferable. They perhaps do so reluctantly. They often feel uncomfortable while lying to their partner, but it is in their view the best option they have, given the circumstances.

People may lie less to their romantic partners (and also to friends) than to strangers due to a desire to be honest to people they feel close to, but there are also other reasons. The fact that friends and partners know more about us limits the topics that are suitable or 'safe' to lie about. For example, we can try to impress strangers at a cocktail party by exaggerating our culinary skills but this is pointless with friends who have experienced our cooking. So, we might lie less because we can see that we will not get away with it.

Although people tend to lie less to those they feel close to, there are exceptions. For example, a consistent finding is that college students lie in up to half of the conversations they have with their mothers on average. Perhaps they are still dependent on their mothers (for example, financially) and sometimes have to lie to secure monetary support. Another explanation is that they still care about what their mothers think of them. They therefore tell their mothers that they do not drink much beer, that they attend all lectures, that they study hard and that they regularly clean their room, in order to avoid upsetting them.

The situation

Robinson and colleagues[14] interviewed undergraduate students of whom 83 per cent said that they would lie in a job interview. Although they believed it was wrong to lie to best friends, they saw nothing wrong in lying if it secured a job. They also thought that to exaggerate skills and abilities in application procedures was expected by potential employers. People not only lie to secure a job, they also lie to find themselves a partner. One study revealed that 90 per cent of participants admitted to being willing to lie to a prospective date, and another study revealed that 40 per cent had told a lie to initiate a date. Also, differences emerge in the types of lie told by men and women during a date. Women more frequently engage in deceptive acts to improve their physical appearance (e.g. 'sucking in' their stomach when around members of the other sex), whereas men tend to feign their earning potential (e.g. misleading members of the opposite sex about their career expectations). These deceptive acts reflect how males and females typically have different preferences in the characteristics they desire in a potential partner. When 50 male and 50 female participants were asked what they look for in a potential partner, men were more likely than women to emphasize the importance of their partner's physical appearance, whereas women were more likely than men to emphasize the importance of their partner's earning capacity.

One possible explanation why frequent lying occurs during dates is that people worry that their 'true self' is not lovable enough to attract a potential partner. They therefore present themselves as they wish they were, or as they believe their potential partner wishes them to be, instead of how they actually are. This might also explain why DePaulo's diary study revealed that people lied relatively often to their romantic partners in the early stages of their relationship. Perhaps they wondered whether their 'true self' was good enough to keep their new partners' attention.

How do we think liars respond?

A considerable amount of research has been conducted into how people believe liars behave. In such studies people are sometimes asked to answer the open-ended question 'How do you think liars respond?' In other studies participants are given a list of possible cues (gaze aversion, fidgeting, smiling, eye blinking, and so on) and asked to indicate for each cue whether, and if so, how, they are related to deception. Those studies have been conducted in numerous Western countries including the USA, Canada, the UK, Sweden, Spain, the Netherlands, Germany and Australia. Both laypersons and 'professional lie catchers' such as police officers have participated in such studies. Despite the variety in research methods, research locations and participants, the findings are highly similar. It thus appears that there are unanimous beliefs among people about how liars respond. By far the most popular cue selected by participants is 'gaze aversion'. The majority of people believe that liars look away. However, there is no evidence for this claim. Research examining how liars actually behave has shown no clear relationship between eye movements and deception.[3] In other words, truth tellers are as likely to break eye contact during conversations as liars. Gaze plays an important role in human interactions. For example, when we attempt to convince others, we tend to look the other in the eye. Gaze is also a sign of dominance. Higher status speakers tend to look more into the eyes of their listeners than do lower status speakers. When listening, the pattern is reversed: lower status listeners look more into the eyes of a speaker than higher status listeners. Gaze is also related to intimacy. When strangers are getting too close to us physically (e.g. in a crowded elevator), we often react by avoiding eye contact. A similar reaction occurs if people ask us questions which we consider to be intimate. Gaze is further related to mental complexity. When we are involved in mentally taxing tasks, such as thinking of an answer to a question, remembering information, planning a reply, etc., it is likely that we avert eye gaze. Gaze aversion also facilitates speech. When speakers are encouraged to continue looking their conversation partners into the eyes, their speech becomes less fluent.

If gaze is not a reliable indicator of deception for adults, it may be an indicator of deceit in our children. Research into how children respond when they lie is rare, primarily for

Fig. 17.3 The notion that gaze aversion and other nervous behaviours are related to deception is commonly expressed in the popular press and even in police manuals.

ethical reasons. In order to examine people's reactions when they lie in scientific studies, it is often necessary to instruct them to lie, which is considered unethical in children. However, the few deception studies which have been conducted with children[15] do not support the claim that children look away when they lie.

There are several factors that contribute to the false belief that gaze is related to deception. First, we mistakenly think that we avert gaze ourselves when we lie. In a study, participants were asked to tell the truth in one interview and to lie in another. These interviews were videotaped. Participants were then asked after the second interview to indicate in a questionnaire how they thought they had behaved in both interviews. These answers were compared with their actual behaviour shown on the videotape, which had been coded and analysed. Results revealed that participants showed the same level of gaze aversion while telling the truth and while lying, although they thought that they had shown more gaze aversion when lying. Secondly, the idea that gaze aversion is related to deception is commonly expressed in the popular press and even in police manuals. Many of us could therefore rightly claim to have read somewhere that liars look away. Unfortunately, such articles are never supported by scientific evidence. Some people say that they believe that specific eye movements, rather than gaze aversion *per se*, are associated with deception. They often refer to 'neurolinguistic programming' (NLP), which is a technique meant to facilitate communication between two people. NLP practitioners pay attention to eye movements as, in their view, it reveals how people are thinking. However, so far there is no scientific evidence to support the idea that deception is related to specific eye movements. Neither have, to our knowledge, the designers of the NLP technique[16] explicitly stated in their writings that observing eye movements could be used as a tool to detect deceit.

More misconceptions about deceptive responses exist. For example, people often believe that liars fidget, i.e. scratch their heads, their wrists or other parts of their body. However, there is no evidence that liars make such movements either.

How do liars respond?

So, how do liars respond then? Research into deception has convincingly demonstrated that there is not a single response uniquely related to deception. That is, there is no particular behaviour which, when displayed, tells us that somebody is lying. Neither is there any particular aspect of liars' speech that conclusively demonstrates that they lie, or any internal bodily (physiological) reaction that we can truly rely upon. In other words, the equivalent of Pinocchio's growing nose does not exist. This does not mean that lies can never be detected. Some responses are more likely to occur during deception than others, although such responses do not occur because someone is lying. They occur because liars experience at least one of three processes: they may feel nervous; they may have to think hard while lying; or they may start to control their behaviour in order to appear honest. Each of these three processes may result in cues which can be noticed by an observer.

Emotions

Two emotions often associated with deception are guilt and fear.[17] People might feel guilty about the fact that they are lying or might be afraid of getting caught in their lie. The idea that liars are nervous and will show cues of nervousness is the most popular view amongst both laypersons and professional lie catchers such as police officers and polygraph examiners. Yet it is a difficult cue to rely upon. First, liars are not always nervous. DePaulo's diary study revealed that people do not feel nervous at all during most of the lies they tell. This is because in most of these lies the stakes (negative consequences of getting caught and positive consequences of getting away with the lie) are low. Therefore, no great harm is done if the lie is detected. The situation might be different when more serious lies are told and when the stakes are high. In high-stake situations, it is really important to the liar that he or she appears convincing and so being in such a situation may well increase nervousness. However, the problem is that truth tellers might also be nervous in such situations, as they too are keen to be believed, particularly if the evidence stacked against them looks ambiguous. A good example of a high-stake situation where a truth teller became very aroused, even more so than a liar, is the biblical story of King Solomon, where two women each claimed a baby as her own. They both appeared before King Solomon, who suggested cutting the infant in half and dividing it between them by way of solution. One mother agreed with this solution whereas the other was distraught. Noticing this arousal in the latter woman, King Solomon realized that she was the real mother and awarded her the child.[18] The fact that truth tellers might be nervous in high-stake situations is a problem polygraph examiners face. Polygraph tests are sometimes conducted in criminal investigations in order to examine whether a suspect is guilty. The polygraph is used in numerous countries all over the world, but less commonly in Western European countries. The polygraph (a composition of the two Greek words 'poly' = many, and 'grapho' = to write) is a measurement device which can display, via ink writing pens onto charts or via a computer's visual display unit, various sorts of bodily activity. The most commonly measured activities are palmar sweating, blood pressure and respiration, and the polygraph is capable of distinguishing even the tiniest fluctuations in these indices. It does this by amplifying signals picked up from sensors that are attached to different parts of the body of the examinee. In the typical use of the polygraph, four sensors are attached to the examinee. Pneumatic tubes are stretched around the person's chest and stomach in order to measure changes in the depth and rate of breathing. A blood pressure cuff placed around the bicep measures changes in blood pressure, and metal electrodes attached to the fingers measure palmar sweating. When a person is aroused, bodily activities increase. Although the polygraph is sometimes called a lie detector, this term is misleading. A polygraph does not detect lies, but arousal which may be the result of telling a lie. Polygraph examiners assume that there is a relationship between arousal and lying. They believe that guilty suspects in particular will be more aroused while answering crucial questions during a polygraph test (i.e. 'Did you shoot Mary James on March 3rd?' compared with control questions (i.e. 'Have you ever tried to hurt someone to get revenge?'), as they may be afraid that the test will reveal their lies. This premise is somewhat naive as truth tellers may also be more aroused when answering the relevant questions, particularly (1) when these relevant questions are emotion-evoking questions (e.g. when the innocent man, Henry James, suspected of murdering his beloved wife Mary James, is asked the above question about his wife in a polygraph test, the memory of his late wife might reawaken his strong feelings about her); and (2) when the innocent examinee experiences fear, which may occur, for example, when the person is afraid that his or her honest answers will not be believed by the polygraph examiner. The latter might have happened in the case of Roger Keith Coleman who was convicted of the rape and brutal murder of his sister-in-law.[18] Coleman insisted that he was innocent, and there were some weaknesses in the case against him. For example, after his conviction, four people came forward to testify that they had heard someone else confess to the crime. In a final attempt to prove his innocence, Coleman asked for a polygraph examination. The polygraph test was administered 12 h before the scheduled execution. It was announced that Coleman failed the test and was put to death later that night. It is perhaps not surprising that Coleman failed the polygraph test. It is difficult to believe that Coleman would have been anything other than extremely aroused when answering the crucial questions during this polygraph test, regardless of whether he was guilty or innocent.

Cognitive load

A second reason why liars may respond differently from truth tellers is when they experience 'cognitive load'. Sometimes it is mentally demanding to lie. Liars have to come up with a story that sounds plausible and convince listeners that they are telling the truth. They have to be sure that they do not contradict facts known to the listeners, and should make sure that they do not contradict themselves when they are asked to elaborate on their stories or repeat what they have said previously. This might make lying more difficult than truth telling, especially when the liar has not prepared a fabricated story in advance. We know from DePaulo's diary study that we often put little preparation into our lies; and even when we do prepare, we might be taken by surprise as it is difficult to foresee every possible scenario. For example, an adulterous partner might be disturbed by his wife whilst talking on the telephone with his mistress, or a malingering employee may have to explain to a colleague what he is doing sunning himself on the beach. Crafty questions might put the prepared liar into a difficult position as well if he has not considered every question that could be asked. Research has revealed that liars display more cues associated with content complexity than truth tellers.[3] For example, liars typically include fewer details in their stories, and make fewer illustrators (illustrators are 'gestures', the movements we make with our arms and hands when we speak) and hand and finger movements than truth tellers. Hand and finger movements are movements we make with our hands and fingers without moving the arms. The reason why such movements decrease while we think hard is that we put all our energy into thinking about what we are saying and thereby neglect body language. Ask somebody what s/he ate 3 days ago, and the chances are high that s/he will decrease in movement while thinking about the answer. Mann and her colleagues[19] examined the behaviour of suspects while they lied and told the truth during their police interviews. They found that suspects showed signs of deceit which could be interpreted as signs of cognitive load. For example, the suspects included more pauses in their speech and blinked less when they were lying compared with when they were telling the truth. Male suspects also moved their hands and arms less while lying. All these cues are indicators of cognitive load. These were high-stakes interviews, as the suspects were suspected of serious crimes such as rape, arson and murder. Hence, getting caught in their lies had serious consequences for these suspects. Nevertheless, they did not show clear signs of nervousness, such as gaze aversion, fidgeting, and so on. The fact that these suspects did not show cues of nervousness does not imply that such cues are never likely to occur in high-stakes situations. Criminals are not average people. Perhaps they experience less fear or guilt while lying, or they might have more experience in lying in high-stake situations than non-criminals. Unfortunately, research into how people respond when they tell high-stake lies is extremely rare. We know that Saddam Hussein did not show nervous responses, such as gaze aversion and fidgeting movements, when he lied in a CNN television interview during the first Gulf War, neither did Bill Clinton display such behaviours while answering crucial questions about his relationship with Monica Lewinsky in his grand jury testimony.[9] However, these are two former Heads of State, and no ordinary people either. There is no research available regarding how ordinary people respond in high-stake situations.

Impression management

Liars may deliberately try to appear honest in an attempt to avoid getting caught. Deliberately attempting to make a positive impression on others is called *impression management*. Effective impression management during deception is not easy. Liars typically have to conceal how they are really feeling or thinking, and therefore they need to act to convey a false impression. It may well be the case that, when attempting to control their behaviour, liars may exhibit 'overcontrol', i.e. displaying a pattern of behaviour that will appear planned, rehearsed and lacking in spontaneity, rather like what happens when some people have their photograph taken. An example of a failed attempt at impression management is Charles Ingram, who was found guilty in the UK of cheating his way to the top prize in the popular TV quiz *'Who wants to be a Millionaire'*. Staff working for the TV programme became suspicious when Ingram and his wife 'had not appeared as jubilant as the newly rich might' after winning the top prize of £1 000 000 (*The Independent*, April 8, 2003, p. 9).

The human lie detector

Sometimes it is easy to detect a lie, e.g. when the liar contradicts facts known to the lie detector. In one real life case (*The Independent*, July 20, 2001, p. 3) Jeffrey Archer, a former British politician later convicted for perjury, asked three journalists to leave his hotel room during a political party conference while he took a call from the Prime Minister. Another politician, who saw the three journalists pacing up and down the corridor, asked them what they were doing. He immediately realized that Archer had lied to the journalists and could not be speaking to the Prime Minister on the phone, because he knew that the Prime Minister was sitting on the conference platform at that very moment. However, in many situations the facts are not known to lie detectors. In these circumstances, different methods of lie detection are required. In principle, there are then three ways to catch a liar. First, by observing their behaviour (gaze, facial expressions, movements, speech rate, and so on); secondly, by listening to their speech (amount of details mentioned, quality of the details mentioned, and so on); and finally, by measuring their physiological responses (heart rate, blood pressure, etc.). Specific equipment (a polygraph) is required for the latter method, making it inappropriate for most daily life situations. We will concentrate on detecting lies via analysing behaviour and speech. People's ability to detect lies has been examined to date in many lie detection experiments. In those experiments, observers are shown a series of videotaped statements made by numerous people about a variety of topics, such as a film they have seen, a person they like or dislike, their attitudes about controversial topics such as abortion or the death penalty, or about an object that they possibly have in their possession. Some statements are truthful and others are deceptive. In the latter cases, for example, the deceptive conditions would involve pretending to have seen a film they have in fact never seen, to like a person they actually dislike, to be in favour of the death penalty when they are actually against it, and deny possessing an object that they know they are holding in one of their pockets. After watching each statement, observers are asked to indicate whether it was truthful or not. In such a scenario, someone has a 50 per cent chance of giving the correct answer by simply guessing. In most studies, people who are not especially trained in lie detection (laypersons) are used as lie detectors, and they are asked to detect truths and lies told by people they do not know and have never seen in their life before. There is no opportunity for the lie detectors to check the veracity of the statement via physical evidence, third parties, etc., so the only sources of information they can use are the non-verbal and verbal behaviour of the target people. The average percentage of correct responses in such studies is 57 per cent, which is only just above the level of chance.[9] In other studies, professional lie catchers, such as police officers, have been used as observers. Again, they were asked to detect lies in people they had never seen before, and had no physical evidence or third party to rely upon. Their average percentage of correct answers was similar to that of laypersons: 55 per cent,[20] suggesting that professionals are not good lie catchers either. In other studies, observers are shown videotaped statements of their friends or partners who lie or tell the truth, but results do not indicate that this task is any easier than detecting lies in strangers.[13] Finally, observers are sometimes asked to make veracity judgements after being shown statements made by children. Even then, people perform at the level of chance.[15] In other words, when we try to detect lies in strangers, friends or children, we do not seem to be any good at it. These findings fit well into the findings of DePaulo's diary study. In her study, liars reported that the vast majority of their lies remained undetected. Not only laypersons, but also professionals face severe difficulties in lie detection. Why is this? Why are we so poor at detecting lies? There are numerous reasons.[9,21] The vast majority of lies are low-stake lies, and so may be more difficult to detect than high-stake lies. There is evidence to support this claim. In their lie detection study, Mann and her colleagues[22] showed police officers videotapes consisting of truths and lies told by suspects in their police interviews. This study is unique as this is the only study where professionals were exposed to high-stake truths and lies. The average percentage of correct answers was 65 per cent, which is higher than the 55 per cent average typically found. However, 65 per cent means that even in those high-stake situations liars often get away with their lies. Another reason why, at least laypersons, in daily life situations, often do not detect lies is that they do not attempt to detect them, if it is not in their interest to do so. We like to be liked and like to receive compliments, so why would we bother to find out whether these compliments are true or false?

Yet another reason why we often fail to catch liars is that we look at the wrong cues. People often rely on gaze aversion to determine whether someone is lying, yet gaze aversion is not a reliable indicator of deception. Our strong reliance upon this unreliable cue explains why research has demonstrated that we are better lie detectors when we can only hear a person, or can only read what that person has said, or are just able to observe that person's body movements without being able to see their face. The moment we cannot see someone's face, we cannot rely on gaze aversion to detect deception, and our performance improves. Related to this is the finding that people become better lie detectors if they do not consciously try to detect deceit! In one study,[23] observers were asked to indicate whether or not each of a number of people had to think hard. These observers were not aware that some of these persons were lying and some of them were telling the truth. Another group of observers were shown the same video clips but instead were told that some of them were lying and were asked to indicate which of them were lying. The findings revealed that the latter group could not distinguish between liars and truth tellers above the level of chance, but the first group, who instead were asked to look for signs of cognitive load, could. Those they indicated as having to think hard were most likely to be liars, and the others were most likely to be truth tellers, hence they could distinguish between liars and truth tellers by looking for cognitive load. An explanation is that the instruction to detect lies resulted in the observers paying attention to unreliable cues to deceit, such as gaze aversion and an increase in movements, whereas the instruction to detect cognitive load resulted in paying attention to more reliable cues such as a decrease in movements.

It could be suggested that people, at least in experimental studies, are poor at detecting lies because they are restricted to passively observing videotapes of the people they are asked to judge. Perhaps actively interviewing those people would make lie detection easier. However, research has demonstrated that actively interviewing does not increase people's ability to detect deceit. In fact, it seems to make matters worse. One reason for this is that active interviewing makes people appear more credulous and this credulity hampers lie detection.

The finding that we do not even seem to be able to detect lies in our partners might sound surprising and perhaps deserves some further explanation. Several reasons contribute to this effect. As relationships become more intimate, partners develop a strong tendency to judge the other as truthful, the so-called *relational truth-bias heuristic*.[24] McCornack and Parks have developed and tested a model to explain this.[25] As soon as the relationship between two people intensifies, they become more confident that they can detect each other's lies ('I know my partner very well, I am able to tell whenever he or she lies'). High levels of confidence will then result in the belief that the other person would probably not dare to lie ('My partner had better watch out, I can detect every lie he or she tells me'). This will result in putting less and less effort into trying to discover whether that person is lying ('I don't really have to worry, my partner does not lie to me anyway'). Obviously, the less effort someone puts into trying to detect deceit, the easier it will be to dupe that person. Anderson[13] provided additional reasons why no link between relationship closeness and accuracy at detecting deception seems to exist. They suggested that when close relationship partners attempt to detect deceit in each other, they bring to mind a great deal of information about each other. This information could well be overwhelming and the lie detector might deal with this by processing the information heuristically (i.e. using general rules of thumb, such as 'He is

Fig. 17.4 The vast majority of lies are low-stakes 'white' lies; we like to receive compliments, so why bother to find out whether these compliments are genuine?

an honest person' or 'He puts a lot of effort into this story, so it probably is true', 'He has no reason to lie about this', and so on) instead of carefully searching for genuine cues to deceit. Another explanation is that in close relationship interactions, the lie detector must simultaneously engage in social behaviour (e.g. the need to appear supportive in those interactions) and social cognition (e.g. decoding possible cues to deception). This might be too much for the lie detector and, as a result, valuable cues may remain unnoticed. A further explanation is that as relationships develop, the partners become more skilled at crafting communications uniquely designed to fool each other. That is, throughout their interactions with their partner, the liar has learned how to tell a lie in such a way that it is difficult for the partner to detect.

Conclusion

We think that your views about deception might well have changed after reading this chapter. Perhaps you think less negatively about the act of deception, and perhaps you agree that lying has more benefits to everyday social life than you initially thought. You may also have changed your mind about how frequently you lie to others and how frequently others might lie to you. Perhaps you were surprised to see how good people are at lying and how difficult it is to spot a liar. We hope that the fact that people often lie (often perhaps to you), and that it is difficult to detect these lies, will not make you feel uncomfortable. In fact, there is no reason to. Many lies told in everyday life are not serious and are meant to smooth social interactions, to protect us from psychological harm, and to make us feel better. In other words, often deception can be viewed as a 'social lubricant', without which our social exchanges would rapidly seize up and rust.

References and notes

1. **Mitchell RW.** A framework for discussing deception. In RW Mitchell, NS Mogdil, ed. *Deception: perspectives on human and nonhuman deceit.* State University of New York Press, Albany. 1986:3–40.

2. **Peterson CC.** The role of perceived intention to deceive in children's and adults' concepts of lying. *British Journal of Developmental Psychology,* 1995; 13:237–260.

3. **DePaulo BM, Lindsay JL, Malone BE, Muhlenbruck L, Charlton K, Cooper H.** Cues to deception. *Psychological Bulletin,* 2003; 129:74–118.

4. **Ahlmeyer S, Heil P, McKee B, English K.** The impact of pornography on admissions of victims and offences in adult sexual offenders. *Sexual Abuse: A Journal of Research and Treatment,* 2000; 12:123–139.

5. **Vrij A, Nunkoosing K, Paterson B, Oosterwegel A, Soukara S.** Characteristics of secrets and the frequency, reasons and effects of secrets keeping and disclosure. *Journal of Community and Applied Social Psychology,* 2002; 12:56–70.

6. **Lewis M.** The development of deception. In M Lewis, C Saarni, ed. *Lying and deception in everyday life.* The Guilford Press, New York, NY. 1993:90–105.

7. **Leekam SR.** Believing and deceiving: steps to becoming a good liar. In SJ Ceci, M DeSimone Leichtman, M Putnick, ed. *Cognitive and social factors in early deception.* Erlbaum, Hillsdale, NJ. 1992:47–62.

8. **Peskin J.** Ruse and representations: on children's ability to conceal information. *Developmental Psychology,* 1992; 28:84–89.

9. **Vrij A.** *Detecting lies and deceit: the psychology of lying and its implications for professional practice.* John Wiley and Sons, Chichester, UK. 2000.

10. **DePaulo BM, Kashy DA, Kirkendol SE, Wyer MM, Epstein JA.** Lying in everyday life. *Journal of Personality and Social Psychology,* 1996; 70:979–995.

11. **Backbier E, Hoogstraten J, Meerum Terwogt-Kouwenhoven K.** Situational determinants of the acceptability of telling lies. *Journal of Applied Social Psychology,* 1997; 27:1048–1062.

12. **DePaulo BM, Kashy DA.** Everyday lies in close and casual relationships. *Journal of Personality and Social Psychology,* 1998; 74:63–79.

13. **Anderson DE, Ansfield ME, DePaulo BM.** Love's best habit: Deception in the context of relationships. In P Philippot, RS Feldman, EJ Coats, ed. *The social context of nonverbal behavior.* Cambridge University Press, Cambridge. 1999:372–409.

14. **Robinson WP, Shepherd A, Heywood J.** Truth, equivocation/concealment, and lies in job applications and doctor–patient communication. *Journal of Language and Social Psychology,* 1998; 17:149–164.

15. **Vrij A.** Deception in children: a literature review and implications for children's testimony. In HL Westcott, GM Davies, RHC Bull, ed. *Children's testimony.* Wiley, Chichester, UK. 2002:175–194.

16. **Bandler R, Grinder J.** *Frogs into princesses.* Real People Press, Moab, UT. 1979.

17. **Ekman P.** *Telling lies: clues to deceit in the marketplace, politics and marriage.* W. W. Norton, New York, NY. 1985.

18. **Ford Ch V.** *Lies! Lies!! Lies!!! The psychology of deceit.* American Psychiatric Press, Washington, DC. 1995.

19. **Mann S, Vrij A, Bull R.** Suspects, lies and videotape: an analysis of authentic high-stakes liars. *Law and Human Behaviour,* 2002; 26:365–376.

20. **Vrij A, Mann S.** Police use of nonverbal behavior as indicators of deception. In RE Riggio, RS Feldman, ed. *Applications of nonverbal communication.* Lawrence Erlbaum Associates, Mahwah, NJ 2005.

21. **Vrij A.** Invited article: Why professionals fail to catch liars and how they can improve. *Legal and Criminological Psychology,* 9:159–181.

22. **Mann S, Vrij A, Bull R.** Detecting true lies: police officers' ability to detect deceit. *Journal of Applied Psychology,* 2004; 89:137–149.

23. **Vrij A, Edward K, Bull R.** Police officers' ability to detect deceit: the benefit of indirect deception detection measures. *Legal and Criminological Psychology*, 2001; **6**:185–197.
24. **Stiff JB, Kim HJ, Ramesh CN.** Truth biases and aroused suspicion in relational deception. *Communication Research*, 1992; **19**:326–345.
25. **Levine TR, McCornack SA.** Linking love and lies: a formal test of the McCornack and Parks model of deception detection. *Journal of Social and Personal Relationships*, 1992; **9**:143–154.

Tall tales on the brain

Chapter 18

The dual-brain myth

Michael C. Corballis

Right-brained adj: 1. Having the right brain dominant. 2. Of or relating to the thought processes involved in creativity and imagination, generally associated with the right brain. 3. Of or relating to a person whose behavior is dominated by emotion, creativity, intuition, nonverbal communication, and global reasoning rather than logic and analysis.

The American Heritage Dictionary of the English Language, 4th edn (2000)

Introduction

Everybody knows about the left brain and the right brain. The left brain is verbal, rational, linear, computational, scientific. The right brain is spatial, intuitive, emotional, creative, artistic. The left brain epitomizes the military–industrial establishment of the West, while the right brain has the glamour and mystery of the East. The left brain is boring, while the right brain is fun.

These notions came to light in the 1960s, largely as a result of research on people who had undergone the so-called 'split-brain' operation for the relief of intractable epilepsy. The basic idea behind the operation was that an epileptic disturbance originating in one side of the brain would be prevented from spreading to the other side, and so causing a major seizure, if the connections between the two sides of the brain were cut. This rather drastic operation was largely successful in at least reducing the frequency and severity of seizures. What was really interesting about these patients, though, was that the two sides of the brain were effectively separated from one another, at least with respect to higher mental functions, so it became possible to assess the capacities of each side without interference from the other.

The leader of this research was Roger W. Sperry, who received the Nobel Prize for his work in 1981. He and his colleagues were able to show that only the left side of the brain could actually name objects or words presented to it, while the right remained speechless.[1,2] The right brain of at least some patients could *understand* language, though, and could direct the left hand (which it controls) to point to the written names of objects it had seen, or point to objects whose names it had seen. The right brain's ability to comprehend language was clearly below that of the left, but this still came as something of a surprise, since a century of research on the effects of damage to the left side of the brain had suggested that the intact right brain had little ability either to understand or to produce language.[2] It is still a matter of controversy as to whether studies of the split brain have painted an accurate picture of right-brain verbal capacities in normal people.

However, what was more interesting was the idea that the right brain might have special abilities of its own, abilities not shared by the left. Until the 1960s, the right brain (or right *hemisphere*) had generally been considered subordinate to the left, and was generally known as the 'minor' or 'non-dominant' hemisphere—a view that was further encouraged by the fact that the left brain controls the right hand, which in most of us is the dominant hand. The split-brain experiments, though, began to reveal a few activities in which the right brain outperformed the left. These were largely spatial, as in matching parts of shapes to wholes, or in imagining shapes in different orientations, or detecting emotion in faces or in speech. The right brain also seemed to be better at identifying melodies, although the left seems to be the more specialized for rhythm, and there is some evidence that professional musicians are more generally left-brain dominant for music. Although the compendium of suggested right-brain functions is quite broad, the advantages are usually slight, and the functions themselves are simple perceptual ones.[3] The most obvious and extreme dominance of the right brain has to do with the control of spatial attention. People with right brain damage often show a striking neglect of the left side of space, in extreme cases failing to dress the left side of the body, or eating from only the right side of the plate, or leaving the left flank ridiculously exposed when playing chess. People with left brain damage seldom show a complementary neglect of the right side of space, and if they do it is usually transitory. These phenomena are usually taken to mean that the left brain can direct attention only to the right side of space, while the right brain can attend to both sides. Although this difference is fairly striking, it scarcely represents a profoundly different style of thought.

These right-brain advantages may have come about simply because of the left-brain's specialization for language, and for related skills such as mathematics. Language occupies a lot of brain space, so the left brain may have forfeited some of its capacity for more elementary functions. True language is almost certainly uniquely human, so the right brain may simply represent the cerebral capacities of both sides of the brain before language came along to destroy the symmetry. This is perhaps a slight oversimplification, since there is evidence for a right-brain advantage for spatial and emotional processing in some non-human species, but even these might be secondary to communicatory functions lodged largely in the left. In any event, Michael Gazzaniga, one of Sperry's original collaborators and a long-time researcher on the split brain, was once moved to remark that 'it could well be argued that the cognitive skills of a normal disconnected right hemisphere without language are vastly inferior to the cognitive skills of a chimpanzee'.[4]

To be fair, it should be said that it is not easy to test the right hemisphere because of its limited verbal comprehension. It may well possess abilities untapped by researchers. Moreover, Gazzaniga's extreme view provoked strong rebuttals from other split-brain researchers, such as Zaidel[5], and Bogen,[6,7] who was one of the surgeons who carried out the split-brain operations in the 1960s. Nevertheless Gazzaniga was not repentant, and

4 years later still insisted 'the vast majority of the cases from all [split-brain] surgical cases reveal little cognitive capacity in their right hemispheres'.[8] In a still more recent survey of the now extensive literature on the split brain, he writes:

> While the right hemisphere remains superior to the isolated left hemisphere for some perceptual and attentional skills, and perhaps also for emotions, it is poor at problem solving and many other mental activities. A brain system (the right hemisphere) with roughly the same number of neurons as one that easily cogitates (the left hemisphere) *is incapable of higher-order cognition*[9] (italics added).

He goes on to argue that the left brain is the seat of what he calls the 'interpreter', which may be likened to the chief executive officer of the mind. The right brain is essentially relegated to routine jobs.

The myth makers

The paucity of evidence did not stop the myth makers, who greeted the right brain as though it were some long-lost but exotic uncle. First off the mark was the surgeon, Joseph Bogen. In a discursive but scholarly review, he suggested that the right brain might be considered to harbour an 'appositional mind', complementary to the 'propositional mind' seated in the left brain.[10] Besides drawing on the neurological evidence, Bogen referred to long-standing notions about the dual nature of the mind, such as the Chinese concepts of *yang* and *yin*, the Hindu distinction between intellect (*buddhi*) and mind (*manas*), Hobbes' notions of directed versus unordered thinking, and the everyday distinction between reason and intuition. Bogen and his colleagues undertook a study comparing different ethnic and racial groups on a battery purported to be sensitive to the different specialized capacities of the two sides of the brain. Among the groups they tested, Hopi Indians were the most 'right-brained', followed by urban Afro-American women, urban Afro-American men, rural whites and urban whites.[11] The idea that primitive peoples might be more right-brained than those from industrialized cultures is a common one, smacking somewhat of eighteenth century Romanticism and the concept of the Noble Savage, and is probably not without a touch of condescension. The 'pernicious myth of the right-brained Indian' is neatly dismantled by a couple of Canadians.[12]

The dual brain was enthusiastically pursued by Robert E. Ornstein in his 1972 best seller *The psychology of consciousness*.[13] Part of Ornstein's message was that society in general, and educationalists in particular, had placed too much emphasis on left-brain thinking, and that there was a need to liberate the creative powers of the right brain. So quickly did this idea grow that in 1977 the editor of *Psychology Today* called it 'the fad of the year', and went on to say that it would soon peter out.[14] A decade later, Lauren J. Harris[15] noted that it was still going strong, and it shows no signs of abating even now. The authors of *Superlearning 2000*, published in 1994, had the audacity to write as follows:

> Yes, it's the left brain/right brain, and you've heard it before. *Superlearning* helped popularize the idea in the early 1980s.[16]

Fig. 18.1 Drawing on the right side of the brain.

In the early 1980s, it had been swilling around in the popular press at least since the publication of Ornstein's book in 1972.

Betty Edward's 1979 book *Drawing on the right side of the brain*, purporting to teach people how to draw by exploiting the spatial and creative powers of the right brain, has been even more successful than Ornstein's book. It has sold over 2.5 million copies, and a second revision, *The new drawing on the right side of the brain* (see Fig. 18.1), was published in 1999. Picking up on Bogen's theme, some anthropologists have argued that differences between the two sides of the brain might explain cultural differences.[17] Even science itself was not immune. In his 1977 book *The dragons of Eden*, the noted cosmologist and popularizer of science, Carl Sagan, portrays the right hemisphere as the creative but paranoid instigator of scientific ideas, often seeing patterns and conspiracies where they do not exist.[18] The role of the rational left hemisphere is to submit these ideas to critical scrutiny.

The duality of the brain was enthusiastically received in educational circles. In 1977, an art teacher, anticipating Betty Edwards, was quoted in the *Los Angeles Times* as saying that the essence of her method was to teach people 'to gain access to the right hemisphere and be able to put it to use for education in general'. Another author chimed in by deploring the emphasis on left-hemispheric values in US schools, and 'the tragic lack of effort to develop our children's right-brain strengths. That potential—a source of equally essential creative, artistic, and intellectual capacity—is at present largely unawakened in our schools'.[19] Suggested ways to enhance right-brain participation in the classroom included being more tolerant of children's wrong answers and of their excursions into dreams and fantasy,[20] and greater use of such meditation devices as transcendental meditation, yoga, Sufi, biofeedback, biorhythms and hypnosis.[21] Zdenek[22] interviewed a number of creative artists and writers, and informed a rather bemused Charles Schulz, the cartoonist, of the ways in which he has been putting his right brain to work; but at least she managed to cheer him up. 'Well, I'm glad you came all the way up here', he said at the end of the interview, 'You helped the sadness go away'.[22]

Perhaps the real reason why these ideas about the two sides of the brain have persisted is that they are good for business. In 1976, a professor in the Faculty of Management at McGill University was moved to write in the Harvard Business Review as follows:

> The important policy processes of managing an organization rely to a considerable extent on the faculties identified with the brain's right hemisphere. Effective managers seem to revel in ambiguity; in complex, mysterious systems with no order.[23]

This kind of thinking has persisted, although whether as a genuine belief or as a plot to sabotage competing business is not clear. It is manifest in such books as Harry Alder's *Right brain manager: how to harness the powers of your mind to achieve personal and business success.*[24] As of 1986, a scheme known as 'whole brain learning' was available on tape for US$195, and provided 'mind–brain expression' through subliminal messages', three hearable by the left brain and four by the right brain. Those interested in the scheme were invited to pay US$1400 to attend seminars so that they might become 'certified in accelerated teaching and learning'.[15] Nowadays, such programs are beamed at us through the Internet—a Google search in late 2004 unearths 3 350 000 references to 'whole-brain learning'. You might also try a website called gocreate.com, which offers the help of right-brain people to get your business going. *The Memphis Business Journal* of October 21, 2002 describes the success of a market research group that dubs itself *The Right Brain People*, who can persuade people to buy things by appealing to the right brain. Programs such as *Superlearning* and *Neuro-Linguistic Programming*,[25,26] which pay extensive homage to the two sides of the brain, continue to attract fee-paying converts and are big business worldwide.

The right brain also managed to infiltrate English literature, a remarkable achievement when it is considered that it has little, if any, language capacity. In 1983, a professor of English published a book entitled *Writing the natural way: using right-brain techniques to release your expressive powers.*[27] Perhaps that was just the beginning; a Google search for 'right brain and literature' in late 2004 turns up 2 930 000 hits. In New Zealand, the syllabus for the teaching of English in schools divides languages into three categories: written language, spoken language and something called *visual* language. This last category seems to include film, television and theatre, as well as posters, computer-generated text and fax machines. It is no doubt in part a concession to political correctness, as well as to the right hemisphere, so that children with little ability in spoken or written language might nevertheless hope to find expression for other talents. They might be better off sticking to rugby. Karl Stead, a distinguished New Zealand novelist, poet and critic, has been watching these developments and foresees dire consequences for the literacy of New Zealand children.[28]

For the ultimate in dual-brain rhetoric applied to literature, though, we can perhaps do no better than turn to the late Poet Laureate, Ted Hughes:

> An explanation for some aspects of the poetic effects of Shakespeare's device is suggested by what is now known of the cooperative inter-activity of the left and right hemispheres of the brain. We are told that, in general, the left side processes verbal language, abstract concepts, linear argument, while the right side is virtually wordless, and processes sensuous imagery, intuitive ideas, spacial [sic] patterns of wholeness and simultaneity ... By nature the two sides presumably live in a kind of happy marriage. A noisily chattering society is supercharged with right-hemisphere right-side participation: music, song, dance, colour, imagery—and a vernacular tending naturally to imagery and musicality ... But, as history demonstrates, the onset of rationality institutes proceedings for a kind of divorce.[29]

Hughes goes on to convince us that Shakespeare had two sides to his brain. There might be something to the idea, since over a century ago Rudyard Kipling wrote the following poem, which appeared in 1901 in *Kim*:[30]

> Something I owe to the soil that grew—
> More to the life that fed—
> But most to Allah who gave me two
> Separate sides to my head.
>
> I would go without shirt or shoes
> Friends, tobacco or bread
> Sooner than for an instant lose
> Either side of my head.

History repeats itself

If that seemed to be remarkable prescience on Kipling's part, I should explain that there was an obsession with the left and right sides of the brain in the latter part of the nineteenth century that eerily foreshadowed that which occurred a century later. In the 1860s, the French physician Paul Broca reported observations from brain-injured patients indicating that the loss of speech (which he called *aphemia*) was associated with damage exclusively to part of the left side of the brain.[31] Shortly afterwards, the German neurologist Karl Wernicke[32] associated the loss of language comprehension with another part of the left brain. These two regions of the left brain, Broca's area in the frontal lobe and Wernicke's area around the junction of the temporal, occipital and parietal areas, are regarded as the two major language areas in the brain.

Even though the left brain was thereafter widely considered the 'major' or 'dominant' hemisphere, there were some who found odd jobs for the right brain to do. The British neurologist Hughlings Jackson[33] speculated that if 'expression' resided in the left brain, then maybe 'perception' occupied the right, an idea that was echoed independently by the French neurologist De Fleury[34] and the Austrian physiologist Exner.[35] Speculation began to mount, however, when the French neuroanatomist Luys[36] noted differences in personality between those with left- and right-brain damage, and suggested that the 'emotion' centre was in the right brain and the 'intellectual' centres were in the left. It had also been observed that hysterical disorders tended to show predominantly left-sided symptoms, implicating the right brain. Although this was first observed by Briquet,[37] even before Broca's observations were made known, it was attributed to Jean-Martin Charcot, well known for his work on hypnosis and hysteria, and was even dubbed 'Charcot's rule'.

By then the game was on. Brown-Sequard[38] argued that the left brain represented 'the life of relations' and the right brain 'the organic life', and pronounced that right-brain damage was likely to lead to 'troubles of nutrition', such as bedsores, oedema, pulmonary congestion and involuntary evacuation of faeces and urine. He went so far as to believe that each side of the brain was a complete brain, each with bilateral control over the whole body, and continued to expand on this theme until well into his old age.[39] Luys[40] maintained that the left brain was the repository of civilization, with the right brain representing the primitive, pre-human side of our nature. Madness was the result of an imbalance, with the right brain assuming dominance. Another influential theorist, Delaunay, associated the left and right sides of the brain with male and female characteristics, respectively, and in 1898 another French physician declared: 'The terms 'male hemisphere' and 'female hemisphere' should render rather well the differences in nature of the two brains, of which one, more intellectual, is more stable, and of which the other, more excitable, is also more rapidly exhausted'.[41]

The dual brain was also used to account for cases of dual personality, with the left brain representing the educated, civilized Dr Jekyll and the right brain the crude, passionate Mr Hyde. One extraordinary case, known as Louis V, apparently suffered paralyses that could be transferred from one side of the body to the other. This transfer was accompanied by changes in personality: 'Louis V, directed by the right hemisphere is a different individual than the Louis V directed by the left hemisphere. The right-sided paralysis [implying right-brain control] only allows the violent and brutal aspects of his character to appear; the left-sided paralysis transforms him into a peaceful boy'.[42]

These claims soon led to therapies directed to one or other side of the brain. A technique known as 'metallotherapy' involved the application of metal discs, and later magnets, to one or other side of the body in order to transfer symptoms from one side to the other, and it was soon claimed that these transfers produced changes in personality and intellect. This was known as 'psychic transfer'.[43] Hypnotic techniques were also developed, especially in France, to hypnotize each side of the brain separately. In one case, the hypnotized person was said simultaneously to express horror on one side of the face and calm contentment on the other through having one side of the brain induced to hallucinate an attack by dogs and the other a pleasant country fete.[44] There were visions of a brave new world in which magnets and hemihypnotic techniques might produce a doubling of mental faculties. John Jackson, one of the founders of the British Ambidextral

Culture Society in 1903, wrote of a new age in which 'each shall be absolutely independent of the other in the production of ANY KIND OF WORK whatever; … if required, one hand shall be writing an original letter, and the other shall be playing the piano, with no diminution of concentration whatever'.[45]

Needless to say, there were spoilsports. From about 1885, Bernheim[46] began a campaign to discredit metallotherapy, claiming that the effects were due entirely to 'suggestion'. Hemihypnosis soon lost credibility because its proponents had naively assumed that one could gain access to a single half of the brain by having the patient cover one eye and directing their attention to the other. In the 1880s there was some confusion as to how information from the eye reached the brain, but it was widely thought that each eye projected wholly to the opposite side of the brain. It was later established that there was partial decussation of the optic tract, so that each eye actually projects to both sides of the brain. By the time this was made clear, the whole fanciful façade of hemihypnosis, metal-lotherapy and assorted dual-brain techniques had collapsed. The historian Harrington[47] states that she could find almost nothing written on the dual brain from 1920 to 1960, when the cycle was destined to repeat itself.

It is entirely to Harrington's credit that this earlier episode is recalled at all. The great majority of researchers on laterality from the 1960s on were oblivious to the fact that they were repeating history, until Harrington revealed all;[39,47] and if history is truly to repeat itself, the present-day phase is likely soon to burn itself out, notwithstanding its resilience over the past 35 years. It is to be hoped that when the next round begins in the 2060s, there is another astute historian who can remind our great-grandchildren of the excesses of the previous two centuries.

What can we learn from history? We have seen that the laterality myths of the late nineteenth century were very similar to those of the late twentieth century, but there was at least one important difference. In the earlier version, the right brain was clearly inferior to the left, and stood for the primitive, uncivilized and dare I say feminine side of our nature. In these respects, of course, it echoed the prejudices of a dominant, 'civilized', male-oriented Europe—'dead white males', to borrow a feminist expression. Small wonder, then, that the right brain, despite the array of functions attributed to it, was referred to as the minor or non-dominant hemisphere—non-dominant, that is, unless some disease caused it to assume dominance and induce madness in the hapless victim. Notwithstanding[8] non-flattering depiction of the right brain as a retarded chimpanzee, modern myth makers are much more respectful of the right brain, even elevating it to a creative genius struggling for release (see Fig. 18.2). This again owes more to the prejudices of the time than to the neurological facts. The 1960s and 1970s were a time of protest, against the Vietnam War, against the military–industrial establishment and against sexism. The right brain became the symbol for the creative, peaceful, exploited people of the East against the brutal Western juggernaut. In the protest slogan 'Make love, not war', the right brain was love, the left brain war.

In homage to the feminist movement, too, the creative, intuitive, feminine side of human nature is associated with the right brain, to be released from the slavery imposed

Fig. 18.2 Releasing the right hemisphere.

by the bullying, masculine left brain. In neuropsychological terms, though, the evidence on sex differences is muddled, to say the least. Women are widely regarded as more intuitive and better able to express emotion than men are, suggesting greater right-brain involvement. However, women are also regarded as more verbal than men, and men more spatially adept then women, yet verbal ability is associated with the left brain and spatial ability with the right. Indeed, in the 1980s, the neurologist Norman Geschwind saw fit to reverse the polarity by arguing that the left brain in males, far from being dominant, was likely to be deficient. He suggested that the male sex hormone testosterone inhibits the early development of the left brain, which might explain why men are more likely than women to be left-handed and to suffer from language disorders such as reading disability and stuttering. The influence of testosterone was also said to increase the likelihood of autoimmune disorders in hapless males and in left-handers.[48,49] In a way, though, Geschwind's theory couples the nineteenth century idea of the brutish, primitive right brain with the more contemporary feminist depiction of men as violent—according to a feminist slogan of the 1980s, 'All men are rapists'. Again we see that the popularity of a theory may owe more to the culture of the age than to neurological evidence. Geschwind's theory has not held up well in the face of research,[50,51] and is already confined to the dustbin of history.

History shows us, then, that the two sides of the brain serve, at least in part, as pegs upon which to hang some of our cultural preconceptions and perhaps explain our inconsistencies (see Fig. 18.3). However, this is a trend that goes much further back than the nineteenth century, except that in the beginning it was not the sides of the brain, it was the hands.

"Good morning, this is William. No, you have his left brain. Just a moment and I'll transfer you."

"Hey dude, this is Bill's right brain. Cool, man. Wicked. Like wow. Party, man, party … Rhubarb, man … rhubarb … rhubarb … spam … spam …"

Fig. 18.3 Making the right contact.

Reading the hands

Throughout history, people of diverse cultures have associated different values with the two hands, or more generally with the two sides of the body. In general, these values are the reverse of those associated with the two sides of the brain, presumably because each side of the body is mapped to the opposite side of the brain. Positive attributes tend to be associated with the right hand and negative attributes with the left, although in some cases the attributes are complementary without being obviously value-laden.

In the Pythagorean table of opposites, recorded by Aristotle, the right was associated with the limited, the one, the odd numbers, the light, the straight, the good and the male, while the left was associated with the unlimited, the many, the even numbers, the dark, the curved, the evil and the female. Many similar examples can be drawn up from quite unrelated cultures.[52] For example, to the New Zealand Maori, the right is the sacred side, the side of the gods, the side of strength and life, while the left is the side of profanity, demons, weakness and death.[53] Also, we should not overlook the Bible:

> And He will set the sheep upon His right hand and the goats upon His left. Then shall the King say to those upon His right, 'Come, ye blessed of my father, and inherit the Kingdom prepared for you from the beginning of the world.' ... Then shall He also say to those on the left, 'Depart from me, ye accursed, into everlasting fire prepared for the Devil and his Angels'. Matthew 25: 33–34; 41.

According to Barsley,[54] there are over 100 favourable references to the right hand in the Bible, and about 25 unfavourable references to the left hand.

The universality of left–right symbolism, with the right nearly always associated with positive attributes and the left with negative ones, no doubt reflects the fact that the majority of people in all human societies are right-handed. It has sometimes been argued that some nation or race of people was predominantly left-handed. In a popular article written in 1956, Trevor Holloway asserted that 'The Antanalas of Madagascar are unique among the races of the world for almost every member of this tribe of 100,000 is left-handed'.[55] I have been able to find no basis for this extraordinary claim. It has also been suggested that the ancient Hebrews must have been left-handed because Hebrew is written from right to left,[56] but up until about 1500 AD there were about as many right-to-left scripts as left-to-right ones, and the gradual predominance of left-to-right writing is almost certainly due to historical events unrelated to handedness.[57] It was also thought for a time that the ancient Hebrews were mostly left-handed because they usually depicted humans and animals in right profile, whereas it is more natural for right-handers to draw left profiles. However, this was probably simply a reflection of the widespread cultural belief that the right side is sacred and the left side profane, and that the left side should be hidden from view. Dennis[58] pointed out that if one considers how the use of the hands themselves is depicted, the evidence for right-handedness in ancient Egypt is comparable with that in modern societies. As long ago as the 1860s, Andrew Buchanan wrote boldly as follows:

The use of the right hand in preference to the left must be regarded as a general characteristic of the family of man. There is no nation, race, or tribe of men on earth at the present day, among whom the preference does not obtain; while in former times, it is shown to have existed, both by historical documents and by the still more authentic testimony of certain words, phrases, and modes of speaking, which are, I believe, to be found in every spoken language.[59,60]

We might qualify this in the light of recent evidence that the great apes may show a population-level preference for the right hand,[61] but this bias is not nearly so extreme as that in the human population, where it seems to be universal across cultures.

A near-universal aspect of left–right symbolism is the association of the right with male and the left with female. To the Maori, *tama tane* refers to the right side, but literally means 'male side', while *tama wahine*, literally 'female side', refers to the left.[53] Hertz also quotes a Maori proverb: 'All evils, misery, and death come from the female element'.[62] Empedocles, the Sicilian argued in the fifth century BC that males were hotter than females and the right hotter than the left, so that sex was determined by relative placement in the womb. Perhaps he was right: Mittwoch[63] reported that in hermaphrodites testes are more likely to be found on the right and ovaries on the left, and she went on to suggest that the same opposing tendencies are present in normal males and females but are overridden by the influence of the sex chromosomes. The association of the female with the left has not always implied disrespect or inferiority, though. In the matriarchal Isis cult of ancient Egypt, honor was accorded to Isis over Osiris, to mother over son, and to night over day, and the Isis procession was led by a priest carrying an image of the left hand.

The symbolic potency of left and right

We may now ask what it is about left and right that inspires such symbolic potency. Perhaps it is in part the sense of paradox that the two hands seem to present: 'What resemblance more perfect than that between the hands', exclaimed Hertz,[62] 'and yet what a striking difference there is!' (p. 89). Part of the paradox is that the two hands are mirror images, and the mirror-image relationship has the paradoxical property that every point on one surface can be mapped uniquely onto a point on the surface of its mirror image, yet the two cannot occupy exactly the same space as previously occupied by the other—except in the trivial case of shapes that are themselves symmetrical. Lewis Carroll, who was obsessed by mirrors, makes the point in *The White Knight's Song*:

And now, if e'er by chance I put
My fingers into glue,
Or madly squeeze a right-hand foot
Into a left-hand shoe ...

The left-hand foot, to use Carroll's quaint terminology, easily slips into the left shoe, but the seemingly identical right-hand foot does not.

However, what Hertz probably had in mind was not the mirror-image relation *per se*, but rather the fact that the difference in the functional capacities of the hands seems to belie their identical structure. You cannot easily tell a person's handedness by inspecting the structure of their two hands, but their handedness is at once apparent if you ask them to write or throw with each hand in turn. Parity, as physicists are wont to say, is not conserved.

I have suggested that this apparent mismatch between function and structure may have encouraged a sort of Cartesian wish-fulfilment.[64] Descartes[65] argued that humans were distinguished from other animals by virtue of a non-material influence that could stimulate the material brain through the pineal gland. The superiority of the right hand over its seemingly identical twin might therefore be taken as a manifestation of this non-material power that sets us apart, and endows us with consciousness and free will.

Something of the sort seems implicit in Gazzaniga's[9] notion of the left hemisphere—driver of the right hand—as the *interpreter*, and source of executive consciousness. This again seems to imply a mismatch between structure and function. One can also detect a whiff of Cartesian wish-fulfilment in the views of Sir John Eccles, who argued that only the left hemisphere of humans is capable of consciousness,[66] and in particular self-consciousness,[67] while the right hemisphere is a mere 'computer' comparable with the brains of other animals. Zangwill[68] dismissed these ideas as 'little more than a rearguard action to save the existence and indivisibility of the soul' (p. 304). Eccles[69] later conceded 'limited self-consciousness to the minor [*sic*] hemisphere' (p. 105).

Of course, one function that we can attribute to the left hemisphere is language itself, but even this is not untainted by Cartesian wish-fulfillment. Descartes considered language to be one of the objective signs of the non-material influence that uniquely endows humans with freedom from mechanical control. This idea was picked up by Noam Chomsky, a neo-Cartesian and the foremost linguist of the late twentieth century:

> ... a chimpanzee is very smart and has all kinds of sensorimotor constructions (causality, representational functions, and so forth), but one thing is missing: that little part of the left hemisphere that is responsible for the very specific functions of human language.[70]

There is nevertheless increasing evidence for systematic asymmetries in the brains of other animals, including left-hemispheric control of vocalization in the lowly frog![71] Recent reviews suggest, in fact, that cerebral asymmetries in other vertebrates closely parallel those in humans,[72,73] and the lateralization for language is uniquely human only because true language is unique, not because lateralization is unique. There are some hardy souls who even challenge the view that language is uniquely human,[74] although the consensus probably remains as articulated by Pinker[75]—namely, that language is an instinct, but a uniquely human one. That said, the point is that Cartesian wish-fulfillment may lead to exaggerated claims, especially of human uniqueness.

The discrepancy between functional asymmetry and structural asymmetry is in any event not an absolute one, since the two sides of the brain are not in fact perfect anatomical mirror images. There are some fairly systematic asymmetries that are at least weakly correlated with left-cerebral dominance for language. For example, Geschwind and Levitsky[76] reported that an area of the brain called the temporal planum, which is involved in language comprehension, is larger on the left than on the right in the majority of people, and this asymmetry is even evident in newborns.[77] These and other anatomical asymmetries of the brain[78] are present in only about two-thirds of human brains, whereas the proportion of people with left-hemispheric dominance for language is probably over 90 per cent.[3] Ironically, it has been reported that the leftward bias in the temporal planum was present in 17 out of 18 chimpanzees, which is a proportion significantly greater than that observed in humans.[79]

On symmetry

In the frenzied attempt to discover asymmetries of the brain, now extended to non-human animals, we are apt to forget that there is a very striking characteristic that we share with most other species—bilateral symmetry. We belong, in fact, to an ancient phylum known as the Bilateria, which established bilateral symmetry as the default condition.[80] This is itself an evolutionary adaptation to a world that is essentially indifferent with respect to left and right. Limbs are symmetrically placed so that movement, whether we walk, run, fly or swim, can proceed in a straight line. Our eyes, ears and skin receptors are symmetrically placed because the events that matter to us are as likely to occur on one side as on the other. Predators or prey may lurk on either side, and an animal with sense organs on one side would be easy meat for an attacker on the other side. Since the brain is largely concerned with inputs and outputs, the symmetry of the limbs and sense organs dictated a symmetrical plan for much of the brain. The psychological consequences of bilateral symmetry are discussed at length elsewhere.[81]

Even in the face of the evidence for the asymmetrical representation of language in the brain, the French physician Pierre Marie was so impressed with the brain's symmetry that he thought that each hemisphere must have at least the potential for language.[82] There is in fact good evidence that if the left brain is incapacitated or removed early in life, the right brain can take over language, with little or no loss of efficiency.[83] At one time it was claimed that people who had undergone total removal of the left hemisphere in early childhood later showed deficits in syntax, supposedly the essence of language and the exclusive preserve of the left hemisphere,[84,85] but this has been disputed on methodological grounds.[86] There is clear evidence that syntax is preserved in at least some cases of people whose right brains have taken over language following incapacitation of the left brain in early childhood.[87,88]

These facts do not suggest that nature has endowed us with a left brain uniquely equipped to perform the special functions of language, and a right brain wired for quite different—some have suggested, *complementary*—functions. Cerebral asymmetry is altogether more fluid than this static picture allows. It seems much more likely that we are endowed with two hemispheres that are ready for almost anything, and that some switch operates early in development to tip the balance toward the left-brained representation of language. That switch may well depend on genetically controlled growth gradients.[89] There is evidence that, between the ages of 2 and 4, the left brain undergoes a growth spurt that may be instrumental in ensuring the syntax is firmly lodged in that side of the brain.[90]

However, if something goes wrong with the switching mechanism, or if the left brain is incapacitated, the faithful right hemisphere is following along behind, ready to oblige.

Another point to note is that, when the right brain does take over language, it does so at the expense of the spatial functions usually associated with that side.[88,91] What this seems to suggest is not that the right brain is intrinsically specialized for spatial function, or for intuition or creativity or any of the other transcendent properties attributed to it, but rather that whichever side of the brain gets burdened with language loses some of its capacity for everything else.[9,89,92,93]

The vexed problem of left-handers

This brings us to that much-maligned minority, the left-handed. Through most of history and in most cultures, the negative associations with the left have meant that left-handedness has been generally discouraged, and there is still many a leftie who was forced to switch to the right hand for writing and/or eating. The American psychiatrist Blau[56] dismissed left-handedness as 'infantile negativism'. Even the sexual identity of left-handers was called into question by Wilhelm Fliess, a colleague[94] and close friend of Freud:

> Where left-handedness is present, the character pertaining to the opposite sex seems more pronounced. This sentence is not only invariably correct, but its converse is also true; where a woman resembles a man, or a man resembles a woman, we find the emphasis is on the left side of the body. Once we know this, we have the diviner's rod for the discovery of left-handedness. This diagnosis is always correct.[95]

Sir Cyril Burt, the British educational psychologist, anticipated Blau in describing left-handers as willful or 'just cussed', and echoed Fliess by noting that 'Even left-handed girls ... often possess a strong, self-willed and almost masculine disposition'. He went on to complete the demolition of left-handers as follows:

> They squint, they stammer, they shuffle and shamble, they flounder about like seals out of water. Awkward in the house, and clumsy in their games, they are fumblers and bunglers at whatever they do.[96]

Among the fumblers and bunglers are Alexander the great, George Bush (41st US President), Julius Caesar, Charlie Chaplin, Charlemagne, Winston Churchill, Cicero, Bill Clinton, Gerald Ford, Benjamin Franklin, Rock Hudson, Goran Ivanisevich, Paul Klee, Rod Laver, Harpo Marx, Michelangelo, Leonardo da Vinci, Paul McCartney, John McEnroe, Martina Navratilova, Ronald Reagan, Peter-Paul Rubens, Babe Ruth, Monica Seles, Ringo Starr, Emperor Tiberius and Harry Truman.

Much of the prejudice against left-handers has dissipated, especially in Western countries. However, left-handers are a little awkward in the house of dual-brain theory. Following his discovery of left-brain dominance for speech, Broca[31] conjectured that in left-handers this would be reversed, and the right brain would be dominant for speech. This became known as Broca's rule. One might then have simply supposed that the left brain

Fig. 18.4 'Sorry mate I'm left-handed'.

would contain the functions attributed to the right brain in right-handers. However, Broca's rule turned out to be wrong, and studies have shown that the majority of left-handers, perhaps as many as 70 per cent of them, are *left*-dominant for speech. To be sure, a higher proportion of left- than right-handers are right-brain dominant for speech, but there is a substantial majority who have speech represented bilaterally.[97] The best explanation for these finding is that most left-handers belong to a minority who do not exhibit the strong lateralizing influence that controls handedness and cerebral asymmetry in most right-handers. In this minority, which includes some right-handers as well, handedness and cerebral asymmetries are determined at random. It has been suggested, but remains unproven, that whether or not this lateralizing influence is expressed depends on a single genetic locus.[98,99]

This poses a problem already for dual-brain theory, since it implies that left-handers do not have brains in which different functions are neatly divided between the two sides of the brain. A glance at the list of left-handers suggests that they are not deficient in creativity or artistic ability. Indeed there are some reasons to believe that left-handers may be slightly superior to right-handers in mathematical and artistic skills, and perhaps slightly inferior in musical and verbal talents (see Fig. 18.4).[100] There is a long but contentious history of claims that left-handers may be slightly more at risk for reading disability and stuttering,[3] while a more bilaterally symmetrical brain may provide a slight advantage in spatial skills[98].

Any advantage of possessing an asymmetrical brain probably has to do with the programming of complex motor skills, such as speech, rather than with the division of mental capacities into packages of opposites. If something as complex as speech involved neural circuits in both sides of the brain, it might be prone to interhemispheric delays and interferences that could potentially create dysfluencies,[92,101] However, there is also evidence that the dominance of one or other side of the brain is achieved by the pruning of the non-dominant side. Annett[98,102] has proposed that this is under genetic control. The hypothesized gene has two alleles (alternative forms), one that prunes and one that does not. In homozygotes with a double dose of the pruning allele, the right brain may be so diminished as to create spatial difficulties to offset any verbal advantage. Conversely, those who lack the pruning allele may have full right-brain spatial function, and are equally likely to be left- as right-handed, but may run the risk of language disorders. The ideal, if you can arrange it, is to be heterozygotic, with one copy of each allele, which minimizes the chances of either spatial or verbal disorder. It may be this so-called heterozygotic advantage that has maintained both alleles in the population, and held the proportion of left-handers roughly constant for at least the last 5000 years.[103]

Another perspective is provided by suggestions that lack of consistent handedness, perhaps due to lack of the pruning allele, is associated with more general deficits in academic ability,[104] and also with a tendency to magical ideation.[105] There is also evidence that schizophrenia is associated with the lack of consistent handedness.[106] Horrobin[107] has argued that in earlier times individuals with schizophrenia were regarded as exceptionally creative and charismatic, but the condition became less adaptive with the rise of animal husbandry and a switch from a fish diet to a diet of red meat. Therefore, the two alleles may express not only the tension between lateralization and symmetry, but the age-old conflict between reason and religion, with its roots in spirituality. According to the dual-brain theory, of course, this is essentially the polarity associated with the left and right brains, respectively, and the suggestion here is that it might be more appropriate to remap the polarity onto lateralized and unlateralized brains, respectively. However, to go too far down this path might be to encourage a new mythology, and I would not wish to do that (unless there were money to be made from it).

Conclusions

We do have asymmetrical brains, and this is a fact of considerable interest and importance. However, our brains are also highly symmetrical, the result of hundreds of millions of years of evolution in a world where the difference between left and right is of virtually no consequence. It is perhaps in the world constructed by humans that the left–right polarity matters most, as in reading and writing, shaking hands in greeting, driving, and so forth, but this is in turn a consequence of our own asymmetry. The most likely explanation for our asymmetrical brains is that certain complex computations are inefficient if constrained by symmetrical circuits, and are better accomplished within a hemisphere than by circuits straddling the hemispheres. The advantages of asymmetrical representation would apply particularly to computations that are not constrained by the forces that led to bilateral symmetry in the first place—namely, linear movement and the ability to detect and react to spatial events in the environment. Spoken language fits this criterion, since it is internally generated and manifest in time, not space.

Even so, the representation of language in the brain is established against a background of structural symmetry, and we have seen that each hemisphere has at least the potential to accommodate it. The asymmetrical representation of language does confer some disadvantages, such as a slight bias toward processing words in the right ear or on the right side of space, and a corresponding bias of spatial attention and spatial processing toward the left side of space. The fact that these biases are slight suggests that bilateral symmetry is still of over-riding adaptive significance. If the left brain were to be totally occupied with language, then we might be easy prey to monsters lurking on the right (politically as well as spatially, perhaps). Shortly after the developments of the 1960s that led to the modern left brain–right brain cult, Brenda Milner, one of the pioneers of modern neuropsychology and a careful researcher of cerebral asymmetry, warned against overemphasizing the asymmetries of the brain at the expense of the considerable overlap in function between the two sides,[108] but her warning has been little heeded.

Given the nature of evolution, it is likely that cerebral asymmetry has been achieved by tinkering with what was already there, rather than by a rewiring of cerebral circuits. The kick needed to give the left brain first option for language may have been as simple as a growth spurt favouring that hemisphere at a critical period in the development of syntax, or it may have been a pruning mechanism that slightly retarded growth in the right hemisphere—or both. It is extremely unlikely that the incremental processes of natural selection somehow managed a rewiring of the cerebral hemispheres so that one became specialized for the complex temporal sequence required for language, while the other was adapted to complementary spatial, intuitive and emotional functions. This is not to say that there are no asymmetries in the way these different functions are represented in the brain; the problem lies in the simplistic notion that the two hemispheres somehow embody opposite ways of thinking, and that the right hemisphere's talents have been subjugated. To understand how the mind works, we need to consider how the brain works as a whole, and it will not do simply to throw our different mental capacities into those convenient bins, the left and right brains.

Does the dual-brain myth do any harm? It is perfectly acceptable to contrast intuition with reason, or holistic thinking with analytic thinking, or emotion with logic, and it might be argued that there is no harm in linking these polarities with the left and right brains. The main difficulty is that reference to the brain can be seen as a legitimizing force to give scientific credence to dubious practices. The idea that there may be hidden talents lying dormant in a subjugated right hemisphere is a powerful and reassuring one—almost as reassuring, perhaps, as the idea of life after death, and ripe for exploitation in much the same way. Unscrupulous therapists, healers and self-proclaimed educators, as well as some who are simply naïve, offer ways to release that hidden potential, and so discover the 'stranger within',[109] whether through music or meditation or electrodes—or breathing through the left nostril for a while.[110] There is always a market for those who would exploit our fears and disappointments.

My *Chambers concise dictionary* (1989 paperback edition) defines a myth as 'an ancient traditional story of gods or heroes, esp. one offering an explanation of some fact or phenomenon'. Except for the word 'ancient', this is not a bad definition of science, where our modern gods are genes and muons and black holes. We do, of course, go beyond the evidence in constructing theories, and the view of cerebral asymmetry I have presented in this chapter no doubt contains its share of myth. The problems arise when we allow the myth to escape from scientific scrutiny and become dogma, and when that dogma creates financial opportunities from charlatans and false prophets. That is what I think has happened to the left and right brains.

References and notes

1. **Gazzaniga MS, Bogen JE, Sperry RW.** Dyspraxia following division of the cerebral commissures. *Archives of Neurology*, 1967; **16**:606–612.
2. **Sperry RW.** Some effects of disconnecting the cerebral hemispheres. *Science*, 1982;**217**:1223–1226.
3. **Corballis MC.** *Human laterality*. Academic Press, New York. 1983.
4. **Gazzaniga MS.** Right hemisphere language following brain bisection: a 20-year perspective. *American Journal of Psychology*, 1983; **38**:525–537.
5. **Zaidel E.** A response to Gazzaniga: language in the right hemisphere, convergent perspectives. *American Psychologist*, 1983; **38**:542–546.
6. **Bogen JE.** The callosal syndromes. In KM Heilman, E Valenstein, ed. *Clinical neuropsychology*, 3rd edn, Oxford University Press, New York. 1993:337–407.
7. **Bogen JE.** Does cognition in the disconnected right hemisphere require right hemispheric possession of language? *Brain and Cognition*, 1997; **57**:12–21.
8. **Gazzaniga MS.** Perceptual and attentional processes following callosal section in humans. *Neuropsychologia*, 1987; **25**:119–133.
9. **Gazzaniga MS.** Cerebral specialization and interhemispheric communication: Does the corpus callosum enable the human condition? *Brain*, 2000; **123**:1293–1326.
10. **Bogen JE.** The other side of the brain. II: An appositional mind. *Bulletin of the Los Angeles Neurological Society*, 1969; **34**:135–162.
11. **Bogen JE, DeZare R, TenHouten WD, Marsh JF.** The other side of the brain: IV. The A/P ratio. *Bulletin of the Los Angeles Neurological Society*, 1972; **37**:49–61.
12. **Chrisjohn RD, Peters M.** The pernicious myth of the right-brained Indian. *Canadian Journal of Indian Education*, 1986; **13**:62–71.
13. **Ornstein RE.** *The psychology of consciousness*. Freeman, San Francisco. 1972.
14. **Goleman D.** Split-brain psychology: fad of the year. *Psychology Today*, 1977; **11**:88–90, 149–150.
15. **Harris LJ.** Right-brain training: some reflections on the applications of research on cerebral hemispheric specialization to education. In DL Molfese, SJ Segalowitz, ed. *Brain lateralization in children*. Guilford Press, New York. 1988:207–235
16. **Ostrander S.** *Superlearning 2000*. Delacorte Press, New York. 1994.
17. **Paredes JA, Hepburn MJ.** The split brain and the culture-and-cognition paradox. *Current Anthropology*, 1976; **17**:121–127.
18. **Sagan C.** *The dragons of Eden*. Random House, New York. 1977.
19. **Garrett SV.** Putting our whole brain to use: a fresh look at the creative process. *Journal of Creative Behavior*, 1976;**10**:239–249.
20. **Brandwein P.** The duality of the brain: a symposium in print with Paul Brandwein and Robert Ornstein. *Instructor*, 1977; **58**:56–58.

21. **Grady MP, Luecke EA.** *Education and the brain (Fastback 108).* Phi Delta Kappa Education Foundation, Bloomington, IN. 1978.

22. **Zdenek M.** *The right brain experience: an intimate programme to free the powers of your imagination.* Corgi, London. 1985.

23. **Mintzberg H.** Planning on the left side and managing on the right. *Harvard Business Review,* 1976; **54:**49–58.

24. **Alder H.** *Right brain manager: how to harness the power of your mind to achieve personal and business success.* Piatkus, London. 1993.

25. This is a thoroughly fake title, designed to give the impression of scientific respectability. Neuro-linguistic programming (or NLP) has little to do with neurology, linguistics, or even a respectable subdiscipline called neurolinguistics.

26. **Bandler R, Grinder J.** *Frogs into princes: neuro-linguistic programming.* Real People Press, Moab, UT. 1979.

27. **Rico GL.** Writing the natural way: using right-brain techniques to release your expressive power. J. P. Tarcher, Los Angeles. 1983.

28. **Stead CK.** The English patient. *Metro,* 1997; **120:**84–90.

29. **Hughes T.** Shakespeare and the goddess of complete being. Faber & Faber, London. 1992.

30. **Kipling R.** *Kim.* Macmillan, London. 1901.

31. **Broca P.** Sur la siège de la faculté du langage articulé. *Bulletins de la Société d'Anthropologie de Paris,* 1865; **6:**377–393.

32. **Wernicke C.** *Der Aphasische Symptomenkomplen.* Cohn & Weigart, Brelau. 1874.

33. **Jackson JH.** Clinical remarks on cases of defects of expression (by words, writing, signs, etc) in diseases of the nervous system. *Lancet,* 1864; **2:**604.

34. **De Fleury A.** Du dynamisme comparé des hémisphères cérébraux dans l'homme. *Association Française pour l'Avancement des Sciences,* 1872;1:834–845.

35. **Exner S.** *Untersuchungen uber die localisation der Functionen in der Grosshirnrinde des Menschen.* Wilhelme Braumuller, Vienna. 1881.

36. **Luys JB.** Recherches nouvelles sur les hémiplégies émotives. *Encéphale,* 1881;1:644–646.

37. **Briquet P.** *Traité clinique et thérapeutique de l'hystérie.* Cited by Harrington 1987[47].

38. **Brown-Sequard Ch.-E.** Dual character of the brain (Toner lecture). *Smithsonian Miscellaneous Collections (Washington, D.C.),* 1877; **15:**1–21.

39. **Harrington A.** Nineteenth-century ideas on hemispheric differences and 'duality of mind'. *Behavioral and Brain Sciences,* 1985; **8:**617–660.

40. **Luys JB.** Etudes sur le dédoublement des operations cérébrales et sur le rôle isolé de chaque hémisphère dans les phénomènes de la pathologie mentale. *Bulletins de l'Académie de Médecine, 2ème série,* 1879;8:516–534, 547–565.

41. **Klippel M.** La non-equivalence des deux hémisphères cérébraux. *Revue de la Psychiatrie,* 1898; 52–57.

42. **Bourru H, Burot F.** *Variations de la personnalité.* J. B. Baillière, Paris. 1888.

43. **Binet A, Feret C.** L'hypnotisme chez les hystériques: 1. Le transfert psychique. *Revue Philosophique de la France et de l'Etranger,* 1885; **19:**1–25.

44. **Dumontpallier A, Magnan V.** Des hallucinations bilaterales à caractère différent suivant le côté effecté, dans le délire chronique; léçon clinique de M. Magnan, et demonstration expérimentale du siège hémilateral ou bilateral cérébral des hallucinations. *Union Médicale, 3ème série,* 1883;35:845–848, 869–875.

45. **Jackson J.** *Ambidexterity or two-handedness and two-brainedness.* Kegan Paul, Trench & Trubner, London. 1905.

46. **Bernheim H.** Notes et discussions. L'hypnotisme chez les hystériques. *Revue Philosophique,* 1885; **19:**311–316.

47. **Harrington A.** *Medicine, mind, and the double brain.* Princeton University Press, Princeton, NJ. 1987.

48. **Geschwind N, Behan P.** Left-handedness: association with immune disease, migraine, and developmental learning disorder. *Proceedings of the National Academy of Sciences, USA*, 1982; **79**:5097–5100.

49. **Geschwind N, Galaburda AM.** *Cerebral lateralization: biological mechanisms, associations, and pathology.* Bradford Books/MIT Press, Cambridge, MA. 1987.

50. **Bishop DVM.** Is there a link between handedness and hypersensitivity? *Cortex*, 1987; **22**:289–296.

51. **Bryden MP, McManus IC, Bulman-Fleming MB.** Evaluating the empirical support for the Geschwind–Behan–Galaburda model of cerebral lateralization. *Brain and Cognition*, 1994; **26**:103–167.

52. **Needham R.** *Right and left: essays on dual symbolic classification.* University of Chicago Press, Chicago. 1973.

53. **Hertz R.** La prééminence de la main droite: etude sur la polarité religieuse. *Revue Philosophique*, 1909; **68**:553–580 (translated in Hertz, 1960).

54. **Barsley M.** *Left-handed man in a right-handed world.* Pitman, London. 1970.

55. **Holloway T.** Left-handedness is no handicap. *Psychology*, 1957; **20**:27.

56. **Blau A.** *The master hand.* American Orthopsychiatric Association, New York. 1946.

57. **Hewes G.** Lateral dominance, culture, and writing systems. *Human Biology*, 1949; **21**:233–245.

58. **Dennis W.** Early graphic evidence of dextrality in man. *Perceptual and Motor Skills*, 1958; **8**:147–149.

59. **Buchanan A.** Mechanical theory of the preponderance of the right hand over the left; or, more generally, of the limbs of the right side over the left side of the body. *Proceedings of the Philosophical Society of Glasgow*, 1862;**5**:142–167.

60. **Wilson D.** Right handedness. *The Canadian Journal*, 1872;**75**:193–203.

61. **Hopkins WD.** Chimpanzee handedness revisited: 55 years since Finch (1941). *Psychonomic Bulletin and Review*, 1996;**3**:449–457.

62. **Hertz R.** *Death and the right hand.* Cohen & West, Aberdeen. 1960.

63. **Mittwoch U.** To be right is to be born male. *New Scientist*, 1977;**73**:74–76.

64. **Corballis MC.** Laterality and myth. *American Psychologist*, 1980; **35**: 284–295.

65. **Descartes R.** *The philosophical writings of Descartes.* J Cottingham, R Stoothoff, D Murdock, ed. and trans. Cambridge University Press, Cambridge. 1985. (Original work published in 1647.)

66. **Eccles JC.** *The brain and the unity of conscious experience.* Cambridge University Press, Cambridge. 1965.

67. **Popper K, Eccles JC.** *The self and its brain.* Springer-Verlag, Berlin. 1977.

68. **Zangwill OL.** Thought and the brain. *British Journal of Psychology*, 1976; **67**:301–314.

69. **Eccles JC.** Mental dualism and commissurotomy. *Behavioral and Brain Sciences*, 1981;**4**:105.

70. **Piattelli-Palmarini M.** *Language and learning: the debate between Jean Piaget and Noam Chomsky.* Harvard University Press, Cambridge, MA. 1980.

71. **Bauer RH.** Lateralization of neural control for vocalization by the frog (*Rana pipiens*). *Psychobiology*, 1993; **21**:243–248.

72. **Bradshaw JL, Rogers LJ.** *The evolution of lateral asymmetries, language, tool use, and intellect.* Academic Press, Sydney. 1993.

73. **Rogers LJ, Andrews RJ** (ed.) *Comparative vertebrate lateralization.* Cambridge University Press, New York. 2002.

74. **Savage-Rumbaugh S, Lewin R.** *Kanzi: the ape at the brink of the human mind.* McGraw-Hill, New York. 1994.

75. **Pinker S.** *The language instinct.* Morrow, New York. 1994.

76. **Geschwind N, Levitsky W.** Human brain: right–left asymmetries in temporal speech region. *Science*, 1968; **161**:186–187.

77. **Witelson SF, Pallie W.** Left-hemisphere specialization for language in the newborn: neuroanatomical evidence of asymmetry. *Brain*, 1973;**96**:641–646.

78. **LeMay M.** Morphological cerebral asymmetries of modern man, fossil man, and nonhuman primates. *Annals of the New York Academy of Sciences*, 1976; **280**:349–366.
79. **Gannon PJ, Holloway RL, Broadfield DC, Braun AR.** Asymmetry of chimpanzee planum temporale: human-like brain pattern of Wernicke's area homolog. *Science*, 1998; **279**:220–221.
80. **Palmer AR.** Symmetry breaking and the evolution of development. *Science*, 2004 **306**:828–833.
81. **Corballis MC, Beale IL.** *The psychology of left and right.* Erlbaum, Hillsdale, NJ. 1976.
82. **Marie P.** Existe-t-il dans le cerveau humain des centres innés ou préformés de language? *La Press Médicale*, 1922; **17**:117–181.
83. **Basser LS.** Hemiplegia of early onset and the faculty of speech with special reference to the effect of hemispherectomy. *Brain*, 1962; **85**:427–460.
84. **Dennis M, Kohn B.** Comprehension of syntax in infantile hemiplegics after cerebral hemidecortication. *Brain and Language*, 1975; **2**:472–482.
85. **Dennis M, Whitaker HA.** Language acquisition following hemidecortication: linguistic superiority of the left over the right hemisphere. *Brain and Language*, 1976; **3**:404–433.
86. **Bishop DVM.** Can the right hemisphere mediate language as well as the left? A critical review of recent research. *Cognitive Neuropsychology*, 1988; **5**:353–367.
87. **Ogden JA.** Language and memory functions after long recovery periods in left-hemispherectomized subjects. *Neuropsychologia*, 1988; **26**:645–659.
88. **Vargha-Khadem F, Carr LJ, Isaacs E, Adams C, Mishkin M.** Onset of speech after left hemispherectomy in a nine-year-old boy. *Brain*, 1997; **119**:159–182.
89. **Corballis MC, Morgan MJ.** On the biological basis of laterality: I. Evidence for a maturational left–right gradient. *Behavioral and Brain Sciences*, 1978; **1**:261–269.
90. **Thatcher RW, Walker RA, Guidice S.** Human cerebral hemispheres develop at different rates and ages. *Science*, 1987; **236**:1110–1113.
91. **Ogden JA.** Visuospatial and other 'right-hemispheric' functions after long recovery periods in left-hemispherectomized subjects. *Neuropsychologia*, 1989; **27**:765–776.
92. **Corballis MC.** *The lopsided ape.* Oxford University Press, New York. 1991.
93. **Le Doux JE, Wilson DJ, Gazzaniga MS.** Manipulo-spatial aspects of cerebral lateralization: clues to the origin of lateralization.*Neuropsychologia*, 1977; **15**:743–750.
94. **Fliess W.** *Der Ablauf der Lebens.* Deuticke, Vienna. 1923.
95. **Fritsch V.** *Left and right in science and life.* Barrie & Rockliff, London. 1968.
96. **Burt CL.** *The backward child.* University of London Press, London. 1937.
97. **Milner B.** Psychological aspects of focal epilepsy and its neurosurgical management. In DP Purpura, JK Penry, RD Walters, ed. *Advances in neurology.* Raven, New York. 1977;**8**:299–321.
98. **Annett M.** *Left, right, hand and brain: the right shift theory.* Erlbaum, London. 1985.
99. **McManus IC.** Handedness, language dominance and aphasia: a genetic model. *Psychological Medicine*, 1985; **8**:1–40.
100. **Smith BD, Meyers MB, Kline R.** For better or for worse: left-handedness, pathology, and talent. *Journal of Clinical and Experimental Neuropsychology*, 1987;**11**:944–958.
101. **Passingham, RE.** *The human primate.* Freeman, San Francisco. 1982.
102. **Annett M.** The right shift theory of a genetic balanced polymorphism for cerebral dominance and cognitive processing. *Current Psychology of Cognition*, 1995; **14**:427–480.
103. **Coren S, Porac C.** Fifty centuries of right-handedness. *Science*, 1977; **198**:631–632.
104. **Crow TJ, Crow LR, Done DJ, Leask S.** Relative hand skill predictsacademic ability: global deficits at the point of hemispheric indecision. *Neuropsychologia*, 1988; **36**:1275–1282.
105. **Barnett KJ, Corballis MC.** Ambidexterity and magical ideation. *Laterality*, 2002; **7**:75–84.
106. **Sommer IEC, Ramsey NF, Kahn RS.** Language lateralization in schizophrenia: An fMRI study. *Schizophrenia Research*, 2001; **52**:57–67.
107. **Horrobin D.** *The madness of Adam and Eve: how schizophrenia shaped humanity.* Bantam Press, London. 2001.

108. **Milner B.** Interhemispheric differences in the localization of psychological processes in man. *Neurology*, 1971;**8**:299–321.
109. **Joseph R.** The right brain and the unconscious: discovering the stranger within. Plenum, New York. 1992.
110. Another secret I can reveal is that lying on the left side enhances right-brain function, and vice versa. Lying through the teeth is best left to the therapist. These revelations are from Ostrander S. *Superlearning 2000*. Delacorte Press, New York. 1994.

Chapter 19

The neurology of the weird: brain states and anomalous experience

Barry L. Beyerstein

> Religious wars and witch crazes throughout history would have been far fewer in number had hallucinations been known as natural phenomena and had men 'possessed by the devil' been considered ill.
>
> Robert L.Thorndike (1934)

> Traces of hallucinations are written on every page of history.
> A. Brierre de Boismont (1859)

Chances are, you believe in the 'doctrine of concordance'. Until Endel Tulving began to chip away at it, so did most of his fellow psychologists. The 'doctrine' is not an edict of the medieval church but, rather, Tulving's term for the assumption that we are almost always aware of what is directing our thoughts, feelings and behaviour at any given moment. Intuitively, it seems that there ought to be close agreement amongst our knowledge and intentions, our conscious deliberations and the decisions we make. Based on introspection, most of us assume that we are automatically aware of all the information we receive and store, the impact it has upon us and its subsequent role in guiding our behaviour. Thus it seems self-evident that, if asked, we could easily point to what motivated a given decision or triggered an emotion or mental image we had just experienced. It certainly feels as though we perform the lion's share of what we do after consciously weighing a list of perfectly transparent options. There is, however, a growing body of research that draws this common sense assumption into question, at least for a large portion of our mental lives. The aim of this chapter is to show that, within the cracks in the doctrine of concordance, there can be found plausible naturalistic explanations for a variety of unusual mental phenomena. Among them are many that believers in the occult have long assumed to be proof of disembodied minds and supernatural powers. Psychologists and neuroscientists today are satisfied that the dramatic subjective experiences dear to mystics and occultists are nothing more than tremendously interesting by-products of the ways our brains produce conscious awareness and control our behaviours in the more ordinary scheme of things.

To agree that the doctrine of concordance does, often enough, accurately describe how we voluntarily extract images from memory, infer the causes of our emotional states and plan and execute our actions does not mean that things always work in such a straightforward way. In drawing attention to the fact that much of what we think and do has non-conscious causes, Freud was undoubtedly right. Where he went off the rails was in his idiosyncratic and scientifically unsupported notions of how these non-conscious mechanisms operate. To his credit, Freud saw these wellsprings of our emotions and motivations as wholly materialistic mechanisms in the brain. Where he erred was his assumption that the forces driving these primitive unconscious structures deep in the brain were primarily sexual and that they operated according to disguised symbolic linkages that could only be deciphered by those steeped in the arcane lore of psychoanalysis. For modern cognitive psychologists, who overwhelmingly reject Freud's conjectures about the exact nature of unconscious processes, there is still ample evidence to suggest that much of our mental processing goes on outside of our immediate awareness and even beyond our introspective ability to reveal it should we wish to do so.[1,2] In fact, it has required a raft of subtle experiments in order for psychologists to infer how these non-conscious influences on cognition, motivation and emotion actually work.[3]

Researchers today see the brain as an evolved collection of semi-autonomous processing units whose specialized functions are assembled into temporary working networks to accomplish particular tasks, much as a conductor calls together different sections of an orchestra depending on which passage they are about to play.[4-6] The self-aware module in the brain, often referred to as 'executive consciousness', is one of the few of these working units to which we have introspective access, i.e. where the doctrine of concordance holds sway. The executive module is responsible for our current state of awareness and for setting the overall behavioural agenda. In service of these conscious plans, it sets in motion non-conscious processes that assemble a temporary bundle of specialized neural units appropriate to the task at hand. Neural processing then proceeds, without further interference from consciousness, to complete the task, at which point this temporary network of modules dissolves and is replaced by another assemblage for the next chore in line.

The executive module is responsible, among other things, for our sense of self and the feeling that this self is 'in control', i.e. that what we do is intentionally governed by our conscious deliberations.[7] Often enough, of course, that is exactly what is happening— we can set plans, weigh options and choose with full awareness to do or not to do something when we focus those attentional mechanisms, which frame the contents of executive consciousness, on satisfying specific demands that we face. On the other hand, research has shown that much more than we typically realize is handled outside of focal awareness and only fed up to this conscious system as a 'done deal', one to which the executive module attaches a feeling, after the fact, of having deliberately chosen to act in this manner. Central to the basic thrust of this chapter is the fact that, occasionally, inputs from various unconscious modules can bypass certain executive functions of the self-awareness system, making the thoughts, emotions or behaviours they initiate seem unwilled, and perhaps even caused by unseen forces external to the individual. When this happens, it may well feel as though some all-powerful but invisible puppeteer is 'pulling the strings' to make us think and behave in mysterious ways.

Along the same lines, very real-seeming images can sometimes be generated, wholly from within the brain, and fed into consciousness. They can have all the vividness and tangibility of percepts generated by any real event that actually transpired in our presence. The emotional significance of such events can seem profound. When oddities like this occur, they often feel quite 'spooky', but psychologists now realize that these episodes are only unusual manifestations of they ways in which our perceptual, memory, emotional and cognitive systems work in more ordinary situations. Before seeing how some of these eerie phenomena could come about, we need to make a brief foray into how our brains direct the affairs of mind under more usual circumstances.

Many odd subjective experiences that some people misconstrue as supernatural events stem from the fact that one of the jobs of executive consciousness is to make as much of our behaviour as possible unconscious, i.e. to practise new skills while we must still pay careful attention to them, in an attempt to make as many behaviours as we can automatic. In this way, the scarce processing capacity of focal awareness can be freed up for attending to those things that do require our moment-to-moment monitoring and deliberation. Driving a car provides one such example: when you were first acquiring this complex and potentially dangerous skill, every aspect undoubtedly demanded, and received, your undivided attention. With practice, however, you automated most of those behavioural routines to such an extent that at some point in your driving career you were probably astounded to realize that you had just driven from point A to point B while listening to the radio, talking to your passenger, reading billboards, planning your itinerary, thinking about your love life, contemplating the meaning of the universe, and whatever else struck your fancy—and all this while operating a potentially lethal vehicle, negotiating your route, obeying the rules of the road, avoiding hazards, and so on, without having been conscious of tending to these various and complicated demands. This is a common every-day example of what psychologists call 'dissociation', the ability of these specialized and well-practised modules of the brain to work independently, carrying out complex assign-ments, initiating behaviours, colouring emotional states, and the like, outside of focal awareness.[8] In mundane examples such as the foregoing, people rarely assume anything uncanny or supernatural has occurred. In other situations, however, the same ability of parts of the brain whose activities we are not monitoring to initiate behaviours that do not feel as though we have willed them, to trigger feelings whose sources we cannot identify or to serve up images or information we cannot recall having experienced before can seem decidedly unnatural. As we shall see, many paranormal beliefs probably have their origins in this ordinary, though perhaps counterintuitive, way in which our brains work.

Understanding that certain attentional and behavioural manipulations (to be discussed below) can cause lapses in communication between the brain systems to which we have introspective access and others that can trigger images, thoughts, feelings and behaviours outside of awareness is a first step in the search for scientific explanations for a number of otherwise puzzling phenomena, ones that are widely attributed to supernatural causes.[9,10] Included in this category are a variety of so-called 'transcendent' states of consciousness, such as religious reveries, mystical 'revelations' and spiritual possession states, as well as the 'born again' experience to which evangelicals aspire.[11-14] Less dramatic examples would include the vague hunches some take to be premonitions, where information we have encountered in the past but lack conscious awareness of can still evoke feelings of unease or unexplainable attractions or repulsions.

Also amenable to this kind of explanation are the phenomena associated with trance mediumship and its modern cousin, 'channelling'. Believers in spiritualism assume that the mental and behavioural manifestations experienced by mediums or channellers in their trances are due to the temporary capture of their bodies and minds by powerful, unseen spirits. Because mediums have no feeling of having willed or directed the images or movements they experience, they are apt to attribute these seemingly spontaneous eruptions to external spiritual control. Psychologists and neuroscientists, however, are satisfied that they are merely further examples of dissociative phenomena that occur when certain manipulations of attention make it possible for unconscious content from one part of the brain to leak into the systems responsible for controlling movements and subjective conscious experience.[8] Thus, notwithstanding the long history of egregious fraud and deception among spiritualists and channellers, there is still reason to believe that at least some of them are sincerely reporting what their 'trances' feel like at the time, even if we reject their belief that the experience was divinely inspired or arose from anywhere but the memory banks of their own brains. One of the mechanisms involved, called 'ideomotor activity', is also responsible for the fact that dowsers and Ouija board afficionados are unaware that they are responding unconsciously to subtle cues and are themselves responsible for making the dowsing rod, planchette or pendulum move in seemingly mysterious ways.[15] (See Hyman, Chapter 15, of this volume for a detailed discussion of these phenomena.)

The doctrine of concordance is so ingrained in folk psychology that apparent violations, such as those discussed above, are apt to evoke the feeling that something supernatural has happened, i.e. that some external force or entity must have usurped control of the 'possessed' person's thoughts, feelings and actions. We can accept that people who have had experiences of this sort are accurately describing what it felt like to them, but we need not necessarily agree that their introspective reports reveal the actual causes. As we have seen, the experience of being controlled or enlightened by occult forces could simply be how it feels when a part of one's own brain that is working outside of conscious awareness initiates mental activities or behaviours without participation of the executive, self-aware level of consciousness.

Anomalistic psychology

In recent decades, there has emerged a field known as 'anomalistic psychology' that is devoted to studying anomalous subjective phenomena that are experienced by ostensibly normal individuals.[8–18] The field is concerned with states of consciousness, of the sort described above, that have traditionally been considered supernatural or paranormal. Since it was founded in 1976, The Committee for the Scientific Investigation of Claims of the Paranormal (www.csicop.org) and its journal *The Skeptical Inquirer* have served as an international clearinghouse for research in this area. Workers in anomalistic psychology are aware that, although a number of aberrant brain states associated with various psychopathologies can produce these kinds of conscious anomalies, similar but temporary warpages of reality can also be produced from time to time by essentially normal brains. Surveys show that spontaneous 'mystical experiences' of this sort occur more frequently in the normal, healthy population than was once thought.[9,10,19] Inasmuch as the basic architecture of the brain, and the conditions that can occasionally cause it to produce awesome subjective experiences, have not changed greatly in the last hundred thousand years, it is likely that dramatic anomalies of consciousness of this sort helped to suggest to our primordial ancestors the existence such magico-religious concepts as powerful spiritual entities, a soul that survives death and the like.[20–22] The fact that these 'transcendent' experiences still effect life-changing conversions today continues to reinforce longstanding beliefs found in nearly all cultures that there are mystical planes of consciousness unfettered by the constraints of the material realm acknowledged by physicists. A recent case of this sort, involving a prominent Canadian politician, shows how powerful such experiences can be. An avowed secularist at the time, Pam Barrett had a transcendent experience during an adverse response to a dental anaesthetic. Taking it to be a divine revelation, she abruptly changed her entire metaphysical stance and the focus of her life.[23] The episode was so overwhelming that she promptly resigned her seat in the legislature, and the leadership of her party, in order to pursue a new career as a full-time promoter of New Age spirituality. If the conditions are right, even giants of rationality such as the late philosopher A. J. Ayer are not immune. Ayer, an eloquent life-long exponent of atheism, had an experience similar to Barrett's during a serious illness. While it was insufficient to shake his doubts about the existence of God, Ayer at least temporarily reconsidered his long-held denial of the existence of an after-life. In the end, he accepted scientific assurances that experiences such as these are quite compatible with the materialist view of mind[9] that explains these dramatic episodes as products of temporarily disrupted brain function (see the discussion of out-of-body experiences and near-death experiences, below).

As might be expected, religionists and scientific materialists have quite a different take on demonstrations that stunning transcendent experiences such as these can be triggered by completely natural manipulations of the brain. Humanists and atheists are apt to say, 'This shows that religious beliefs are just illusions and delusions created by people's misinterpretations of naturalistic, non-spiritual things that go on in our brains'. Theists, on the other hand, respond, 'Isn't it marvelous that God created these mechanisms in our brains for communicating deep truths to us mortals?' Researchers in anomalistic psychology concede that demonstrations that manipulations of the brain can produce all the subjective phenomena traditionally attributed to mystical states does not logically exclude the possibility that there is 'something else', i.e. some purely spiritual aspect of these reveries that is beyond the reach of materialistic science. Most neuroscientists, however, are satisfied that if it looks like a duck, walks like a duck and sounds like a duck, it probably is a duck.[9,10] So far, advocates of mind–brain identity have found no need to posit the existence of a separate non-material mind to account for the mental phenomena put forth by paranormalists in support of their belief in mind–body duality.

The modus operandi of anomalistic psychology

Researchers in the field of anomalistic psychology approach each investigation with the presumption that, unless there are clear indications of pathology or intent to deceive, informants' descriptions of their experiences are probably fairly accurate accounts of what these episodes felt like at the time. Nonetheless, while accepting the subjective believability of such experiences, these researchers start with the working assumption that they are not of paranormal origin. Rather, they are taken, until proved otherwise, to be manifestations of unusual, though not necessarily pathological, states of the brain. These states can be triggered by a variety of causes and, in many instances, investigations reveal that current knowledge in psychology and the neurosciences can provide naturalistic explanations for these arresting subjective interludes. As a bonus, it is hoped that studying these experiences within a naturalistic framework will also expand our knowledge of how the brain ordinarily creates the rich mental model of the external world that we call reality.

When one stops to consider that normal people typically spend about one-twelfth of their lives vividly hallucinating (that is to say, dreaming), it seems less outrageous to suggest that there could occasionally be some leakage of dream-like activity into normal waking consciousness. Neuroscientists have suggested that there are mechanisms that ordinarily suppress full-blown dreams (as opposed to the less vivid and less seemingly real imagery of daydreams) during wakefulness.[24] They have described how the brain's arousal and attentional systems could allow visual images from memory to dominate awareness during dreams but normally not during waking. Interestingly, the neurochemistry of this gating mechanism is affected by a variety of hallucinogenic drugs, which permit waking consciousness to be swamped by highly emotional and very believable dream-like imagery. As we shall see below, a similar opening of the floodgates of sensory memory could occasionally occur during non-drugged wakefulness as a result of a variety of spontaneous or behaviourally induced changes in brain electrophysiology or biochemistry.[25]

Researchers have shown that most people experience bouts of vivid imagery several times during the day.[26] Ordinarily, these daydreams are easily distinguished from perceptions of real events, but, for some people, this kind of imagery can be so compelling that it temporarily supplants the sensory-driven model of reality.[27] Understanding how such illusory but highly believable experiences contribute to belief in paranormal phenomena is a prime concern of those who work in the area of anomalistic psychology.

What are hallucinations?

Hallucinations are sensory experiences that lack external stimulation of the relevant sense organs but seem objectively real. They can be full or partial. Full-blown hallucinations integrate imagery from all sense modalities, feel unwilled by the percipient, and have the detail, vividness and emotional impact that make them utterly convincing.[28,29]

In magico-religious lore, the term 'vision' encompasses essentially what is meant by 'hallucination' but has the further connotation of mystical significance. 'Visions' (or 'voices') supposedly emanate from enlightened beings and are directed specifically to the recipient for his or her edification, i.e. 'a revelation'. History records that many revered figures such as Joan of Arc, Martin Luther, Saint Paul, Jesus Christ, Mohammed and Mozart felt they had been guided in this way, but it also warns us that Adolph Hitler, Attila the Hun, Idi Amin and Charles Manson felt similarly chosen for their special missions. That all *experienced* their voices and visions as 'coming from powers beyond' is uncontestable. It is not equally apparent, however, that these events occurred outside the theatre of their own minds.

Since ancient times, 'visions' of ghosts, demons, angels and deities have fuelled super-natural beliefs and spawned new religions. A close relative is the so-called 'hallucination of presence' where one only senses the nearness of invisible entities.[12] Likewise, as we have seen, so-called 'transcendent', 'near-death' and 'out-of-body' experiences have been taken as evidence for an after-life, higher planes of existence, cosmic consciousness and other mystical states, though they too can have prosaic explanations.[9,10,29–31] Occa-sionally, perception-like insertions can blend with otherwise accurate impressions of the environment, begetting 'sightings' of fairies and assorted monsters of land, sea and air. The space age version of these experiences substitutes sightings of alien spacecraft piloted, according to some, by rapacious crews for the incubi and succubi and the 'old hag' illusions of yesteryear.[12,14] Neuroscientists have begun to look at how aberrations of sensory processes, and the brain's sleep and dreaming mechanisms, in particular, might bring such things about.

Mechanisms of hallucinations

When did you last say to someone, 'I saw it with my own eyes'? In so doing, you were inviting the inference that *it* existed 'out there'—somewhere 'in the real world'. If, instead, you had said, 'I saw it with my own brain', your statement, although closer to the truth, would have lost much of its intended force. That is because it would no longer demand the concession that you had perceived a tangible object 'out there'. Given this opening, the listener might even have the temerity to suggest, 'Couldn't it have been a figment of your imagination?'

Although the statement 'I saw it with my own brain' may have an odd ring, it serves to remind us that the cerebral mechanisms of perception—where sensory events are *really* experienced—are at some remove from the scene of the action. Perceptions are transformations of environmental stimuli encoded in networks of active brain cells.

Quite early in the process, inputs from the brain's memory, emotional and cognitive systems are inserted into the purely sensory stream. As a result, the exact placement of the boundary between raw sensation and the perceptual/cognitive processes responsible for constructing our global awareness of the world is somewhat arbitrary. Perception has sometimes been referred to as 'sensory reasoning' as a way of acknowledging the fact that the final product, our mental model of reality, owes more to cognitive interpretation and embellishment than most people think. As soon as we abandon the notion that our ordinary experience of reality is merely a passive, one-to-one rendition of stimulus characteristics in a camera-like sensory register and realize that the brain's reality model is an active cognitive construction, it becomes easier to see how non-psychotic, non-intoxicated, essentially normal individuals could still, from time to time, be subject to compelling, yet illusory, subjective experiences.

The nineteenth century psychologist Sir Francis Galton emphasized the continuity of all forms of visualization, whether stimulus-driven or memory-driven. Neurologically speaking, sensations, mental imagery, dreams, daydreams and hallucinations are cut from the same cloth. Perceptions are cognitive constructions assembled from raw sense data, seamlessly combined with the images from memory that 'flesh out' all conscious awareness. The relative preponderance of external (sensory) versus internal (memory) inputs to the cerebral mechanisms that assemble our conscious model of reality is constantly shifting. Siegel[29] has emphasized that there is competition between external and internal inputs for access to this central awareness system and that hampering any of the contenders leaves the stage open for domination by its rivals. Marks[26] and Loverock and Modigliani[32] have reviewed studies supporting the conclusion that the same cerebral mechanisms serve perception and imagery. Schatzman[33] reinforced this conclusion by pointing to electroencephalographic (EEG) data from people who can produce extremely vivid hallucinations at will. That visual and auditory hallucinations are correlated with spontaneous activity in the brain areas that mediate perceptions of real sights and sounds has also been confirmed from studies of the effects of localized brain damage and with EEG recordings and with positron emission tomography (PET) and functional magnetic resonance imaging (fMRI) scans.[34]

Because functionally equivalent states of the central awareness system can arise from either memory or sensory sources, it is sometimes possible for dreams, perceptual memories, fantasies and hallucinations to become indistinguishable from real events. Hallucinations result whenever internal events trigger a pattern of brain activity equivalent to that normally generated when sense organs respond to a publicly observable event. Thus, if the brain's awareness mechanisms were to be flooded by neural discharges from memory banks, the experience could feel just as real as if it had been engendered by actual events 'out there'.

How we ordinarily distinguish reality from vivid mental imagery or daydreams and why this ability should occasionally break down are central to an understanding of hallucinations and a variety of ostensibly paranormal experiences.[28,29] The ability of the brain to create illusory experiences so complete as to pass for reality can be seen as a cost we incur in return for the ability to think and remember in the form of complex images, i.e. to conjure up believable tableaux 'in our mind's eye'. In order for imagery to be useful in solving problems and testing out prospective behavioural scenarios in a mental 'dry run', we require neural systems capable of creating a model of the world inside our heads that enjoys considerable veracity. That a representational system of this sophistication should occasionally fool us ought to surprise no one—it is a price we pay for being able to let our ideas die in our stead.

Predisposing conditions

The probability of hallucinating rises with any of several possible functional shifts within the brain's awareness system.[35] One predisposing factor is anything that prompts a move from lexical (i.e. word-based) thinking to imagistic or pictorial thinking. Another is anything that biases the brain's representational system toward its internal sources (memory images) at the expense of sensory information. This could arise because there is a paucity of external stimulation or because the salience of internal activity is amplified by strong motivation or a temporary weakening of the mechanisms that suppress vivid imagery during waking (except, of course, when we engage in visual thinking exercises or daydreaming).

Stress-induced arousal from sources, such as life-threatening accidents or natural disasters, sustained military operations, terrorist attacks or recent bereavement, has also been reported to trigger hallucinations and dissociative states.[8] Likewise, the roles of suggestion and classical (i.e. 'Pavlovian') conditioning have been investigated.[28] In the latter case, conditioned stimuli have been found to evoke hallucinatory images as conditioned responses.

While fears and psychological conflicts often slip into consciousness via the imagistic mode, hallucinations are also sought by some as a source of inspiration, a rite of passage or a way of solemnifying their special status. Prolonged meditation, self-hypnosis, psychoactive drugs, sensory bombardment to the point of physical and emotional exhaustion, various kinds of self-denial and even self-mutilation are all routes that seekers have adopted in this pursuit.[10,17,36] Revival meetings aimed at producing conversions by means of generating what these days is referred to as the 'born again' experience existed long before neuroscientists began to understand what was happening in the brains of people swept up by these rituals.[10,36] Suggestion and strong desire, as in those who fervently seek reassurance that deceased loved ones survive in another realm, are also common instigators of comforting hallucinatory events.

Just as psychedelic drugs and the behavioural manipulations discussed above can trigger hallucinations, so can spontaneous eruptions in the brain. The auras that precede epileptic attacks, particularly of the type known as complex partial seizures or temporal lobe epilepsy, can produce prolonged dreamy states with extremely life-like hallucinations. They are suffused with intense meaningfulness and often with feelings of losing one's autonomy to unseen entities.[10] In the latter cases, complex patterns of behaviour can be initiated that look like they are consciously willed and voluntarily directed, but are in fact robot-like automatisms that lack conscious oversight.[8] Additionally, because various self-protective mechanisms organized in temporal lobe limbic structures can be spontaneously activated by this frequent seizure activity, a very small proportion of these patients become prone to explosive, unprovoked aggressive outbursts. Also, on occasion, it can sometimes lead to development of a form of hyper-religious temperament, to which we will return later in this chapter.

Similarly, the lead up to certain kinds of migraine attacks can produce vivid perceptual, emotional and automatistic effects that could easily be interpreted as not of this world.[9,10,37] These can be accompanied by intense feelings of anxiety, foreboding or joy and absolute certitude. Although migraine-induced trance-like phenomena undoubtedly contributed their fair share to the development of paranormal beliefs in the past (take the Biblical accounts of the prophet Ezekiel's visions, or the ecstatic revelations depicted in the beautiful illuminated manuscripts of the twelfth century mystic nun, Hildegard von Bingen, for example), it is safe to say that most people today would recognize migraine's sometimes bizarre effects on consciousness and behaviour as naturalistic events. There remains, however, a related phenomenon that probably still fuels the supernatural worldviews of many today who may not recognize its intense feelings as a brain-based neurological condition. The condition is known as the 'migraine equivalent', wherein the sufferer experiences all the sensory, visceral and emotional effects of the prodrome and aura that typically precede the horrendous headache, but is spared the headache itself. It is less likely that people today who repeatedly experience these bizarre trance-like states that seem to come out of nowhere, would link them to something naturalistic, such as a variant of the dreaded migraine syndrome. Given the great sense of portent and foreboding that can accompany these dramatic episodes, it seems probable that more than a few sufferers may have developed strong beliefs in occult forces or religious guidance as a result.

Along the same lines, if brain systems other than purely sensory or motor ones were to be spontaneously activated by the sorts of precipitants mentioned above, the subjective effects would be similarly indistinguishable from what one normally experiences when the system in question is triggered by its more usual inputs. Thus, for instance, the feeling of déjà vu that occultists often take to be recollections from a previous incarnation may be nothing more than an occasional false activation of the system in the brain that compares current sensory input with stored memories and initiates a sense of familiarity whenever the two streams overlap to a sufficient extent. Just as we are rarely surprised when this recognition system sometimes fails to be activated by genuinely familiar input, we should not jump to supernatural conclusions when it is occasionally triggered falsely, thereby imbuing novel situations with a spurious sense of familiarity.

Other conditions known to have triggered hallucinatory activity are astonishingly diverse.[13,28,29,33–35] They include sensory deprivation or sensory overload (especially with intense, rhythmic stimuli), extended fasting, dehydration, social isolation or prolonged sexual abstinence. To various toxicities and diseases of the brain can be added oxygen deprivation, hyperventilation, hypoglycaemia and overdoses of common nonprescription drugs, as well as high fever, delirium and extreme pain. Aberrations of the brain's arousal system are also common precipitants, e.g. extended sleep loss, fatigue, hypnagogic and hypnopompic states (hallucinatory reveries occurring at the boundaries between sleep and waking), and narcolepsy and other diseases of the sleep-waking system. Some of the foregoing factors were present during the long solo flight of Charles Lindbergh, the solitary circumnavigations of Joshua Slocum and Francis Chichester, and the polar expeditions of Admiral Richard Byrd—all of whom reported vivid hallucinations during their epic journeys.

Overwhelming the reality-checking processes

Full-blown hallucinations are facilitated by the presence of fatigue and monotony on the one hand, or strong emotions, needs and arousal, on the other. All can hinder the cognitive strategies we normally rely upon to check the veracity of our perceptions.[35] These checks include comparison between sense modalities: 'I see it, but can I also reach out and grasp it?' Likewise, we can check against memory: 'Does this seem familiar?' Or with cognitive appraisal: 'Does this make sense?' As a last ditch, we can enlist the aid of others: 'Did you see *that*?'

Just as some people experience more intense imagery to begin with, others seem to be poorer at judging the differences between real and imagined events. Hence they would be more prone to hallucinate. Situational variables can make the task of reality testing more difficult for everyone under certain conditions. Bentall[28], Reed[12] and Zusne and Jones[14] provide good reviews of research on these cognitive misattributions by which hallucinators mistake their own private mental processes for publicly observable events.

Fantasy-prone personalities

For as many as 4 percent of the healthy population, vivid hallucinations are an everyday occurrence.[38] In an attempt to characterize the 'best-of-the-best' of the hypnotizable population, Wilson and Barber[27] serendipitously uncovered a group of individuals who fantasize with intense realism during a large part of their waking lives. Their hallucinations are sufficiently controllable that they tend not to interfere with their safety, jobs or family lives. Wilson and Barber dubbed these individuals 'Fantasy-Prone Personalities' (FPPs). While fantasizing, they exhibit a reduced awareness of time, place and personal identity, much as if deeply hypnotized, but without any formal induction. They 'see', 'hear', 'smell' and 'touch' (for all intents and purposes, they *live in)* the worlds they fantasize. Their experiences seem so real that FPPs can reach orgasm without physical stimulation, just by imagining a sexual encounter. Most learn early on to conceal their heavy involvement in their fantasy lives for fear of being thought weird or escapist. Because they frequently confuse fantasy and reality, FPPs are apt to hold various paranormal beliefs. Not surprisingly, they are well represented among the mystics, sensitives, mediums and channellers who claim access to higher realities. Spanos and colleagues[39] compared a group of FPPs who were convinced that they had been abducted by aliens with a group who had similar beliefs but did not meet Wilson and Barber's criteria. Interestingly, the researchers found that, at least in this self-selected sample, satisfying the criteria for fantasy prone-ness, by itself, was unlikely to propel someone into the ranks of the self-professed abductees. It required, in addition, a pre-existing and strongly held esoteric worldview infused with beliefs about extraterrestrial creatures and their designs, coupled with the raw material of an experience such as those produced by a bout of sleep paralysis that could be folded into the interpretive scheme and resulting belief structure. Other investigators have also found evidence of fantasy prone-ness among those who believe that they have been abducted by aliens.[40]

Cognitive embellishment and suggestion

We have already seen that our perception of reality is an actively constructed model in our brains. When trauma, drugs, meditative exercises, etc., disrupt the prevailing reality model and release a flood of internal imagery from memory, the same processes of executive consciousness that construct our ordinary sense of reality immediately begin to marshal these chaotic elements into a more coherent (and, hopefully, more predictive and useful) scenario, filling in meanings for the situation as they go. They begin to name, classify and integrate these images, much as happens when we see recognizable objects in smoke, tea leaves, or clouds (see the discussion of pareidolea in Chapter 16). In more ordinary situations, when the stimulus array is sparse and observing conditions are suboptimal, the same cognitive drive to 'make sense' out of whatever we encounter can make honest, intelligent observers impose on a few flashes of light in the night sky visions of space vehicles, complete with portholes and pilots, or turn a wind-rustled curtain into a menacing ghost. In other contexts, it has been pointed out how people with strong imagistic abilities and pressing psychological needs could be influenced by overly suggestive investigators and therapists to create false, but detailed and believable, perceptual 'memories' of ritual satanic abuse, childhood incest as well as alien abductions.[41–43] These people tend to be quite convincing to others because their pseudomemories have all the subjective attributes of true recollections of actual events. Once again, false but fervently believed memories of various sorts become much less puzzling once we realize that memory is much more reconstructive than the doctrine of concordance would have it. Far from storing a perfectly detailed rendition of every experience and replaying it verbatim, the brain stores only skeletons of events which are recreated, with considerable help from inference, when we attempt to recall them. As such, these reconstructions owe more to various psychological traits and needs than we often assume.

As products of active minds, memories, as well as transcendent reveries and hallucinations, reflect the individual's needs, problems and preoccupations. The novelist Ambrose Bierce recognized this when he defined a ghost as 'the outward and visible sign of an inward fear'. By the same token, the resurgence of angel sightings in recent years might be termed an outward manifestation of an inward *hope*. It is for reasons such as these that researchers in anomalistic psychology are less impressed than believers often think they ought to be with eyewitness accounts of aliens, ghosts, lake monsters and the like. Honest, sober, competent people often make sincere but gross errors of perception. The author was once asked by BBC Television to help with staging an intentionally amateurish hoax on the shores of Loch Ness. As tour buses pulled up, a rough log was briefly allowed to float to the surface before being quickly and permanently yanked beneath the water. Earnest young interviewers were on hand to record the eyewitness accounts. Needless to say, what the expectant tourists reported seeing had much more to do with their hopes and expectations than what they actually saw. In a similar vein, researchers have staged a number of intentional UFO hoaxes and found that believers presented with ambiguous, easily debunked stimuli are usually more inclined to support their biases than engage their critical thinking faculties to rule out prosaic explanations before jumping to their preferred conclusions.[29,44]

A century of psychological research has demonstrated that factors as diverse as attention, arousal, belief, desire, context, suggestion, expectancy, fatigue, boredom, stress and even personality influence what we perceive and remember. In light of this and the many payoffs for engaging in 'wishful thinking', it should seem less controversial to assert that 'Believing is seeing' is, in many instances, just as true as the old adage 'Seeing is believing'.

Reality: made to order

Surprisingly, if the cues that help distinguish internally generated images from veridical percepts should become blurred, leading someone to believe she has seen or heard something others dismiss as hallucinatory, this is frequently rejected with the counterclaim that the experience seemed to be of *greater* than ordinary 'realness', i.e. it could not have been illusory because it actually felt 'more real than real'. This hyper-real quality of many hallucinations demands an explanation. It prompted Blackmore[45] to step back and ask the more fundamental question of why anything ever feels real.

Blackmore, in agreement with Siegel,[29] notes that the mental model dubbed 'reality' is that which is most stable, complex and predictive. The candidate with greatest clarity and coherence is ordinarily the model richest in sense data. Under severe psychological stress, physiological trauma or attentional manipulations such as meditation, sensory deprivation or hypnosis, the brain's representational apparatus may lose access to the sense data that are ordinarily its most predictive and useful inputs. So deprived, it begins to search for the next best alternative, usually information stored in memory banks from which it can create seemingly real images. Thus a model from memory becomes 'real' for the time being. If, as during nightly dreams, the brain's reality-testing processes are also disengaged, peculiarities of the temporary model (i.e. hallucination) are less likely to cause its immediate rejection.

To summarize, then, the 'job' of executive consciousness is to construct a mental model of reality from the various inputs at its disposal. In this process, the brain assembles an internal representation of the environment. It takes fragmentary information from the senses and 'fills in' the gaps to produce our global experience of existing in the world around us. As part of the exercise, it also constructs a mental model of one's own body and the self that seems to inhabit it.

If the brain mechanisms that assemble those models should be disrupted, this carefully crafted sense of a self dwelling within a physical body, distinct from the rest of the universe, dissolves. While this could be highly disturbing if it happened spontaneously (which it sometimes does), this feeling of 'one-ness with the universe' is the ultimate goal for mystics. Without understanding why their rituals work, many esoteric movements have independently gravitated to a similar set of physical and psychological manipulations that affect the brain to bring about such experiences.[13,36] Known to acolytes as 'transcendence', 'cosmic consciousness' or 'nirvana', psychologists and psychiatrists call them 'depersonalization' and 'de-realization'. The psychiatrist William Sargant[36] noted that political as well as religious proselytizers throughout history have stumbled (apparently independently) upon a remarkably similar set of rituals for use in their mass rallies to effect conversions, or 'great awakenings', as they have sometimes been called. In the hands of skilled orators and demagogues, these means of producing cathartic, hyperemotional altered states of consciousness leave experiencers utterly convinced that supernatural sanction has been given to whatever religious or political message has been conveyed. Through the ages, these means of altering consciousness by psychosocial mechanisms, coupled with rhythmic movements, sensory bombardment, physical and emotional exhaustion, etc., have proved highly effective in producing converts to whatever dogmas the charismatic holder of the political rally or revival meeting was extolling. We now know something about the effects all these manipulations have in common on mechanisms in the brain.[10,25]

Why do we sometimes confuse fantasy with reality?

Research suggests that the brain can work on several models simultaneously and, in deciding what is 'out there' it confers the accolade of 'reality' on that mental representation which is currently the most stable, complex and coherent. When attention is outwardly directed, that will usually be the model that is most richly supplied with external sense data. Selection among models is necessary because the brain's representational systems not only guide overt behaviours, but also provide the wherewithal for our flights of fancy. In daydreams we can call up images of objects, activities and places that are not present, and in fact may be wholly imaginary. We can place ourselves in the scene, in bird's-eye view, and watch events unfold. If need be, we can even conjure up images of things such as unicorns and trolls that never could have been 'out there'. Given the ease with which we construct detailed mental tableaux that never happened, it should hardly seem mysterious that the brain could occasionally mistake one of them for reality. After all, our nightly dreams often seem terrifyingly real.

Brain mechanisms and esoteric experiences

The neural systems involved in anomalous experiences include various parts of the cerebral cortex and the more primitive 'limbic system'.[46] As I have discussed elsewhere,[9,10] subcortical limbic structures are involved in memory, imagery, motivation, emotion and the spatio-temporal mapping of self and environment. They are responsible for the sense of familiarity and personal meaningfulness that makes some mental representations feel more real than others. If those mechanisms, which both help assemble the reality model and weigh its significance, were to erupt spontaneously, they could concoct a convincing mental panorama and infuse it with a feeling of special realness and importance.

As long ago as the 1930s, the neurosurgeon Wilder Penfield and his colleagues demonstrated that a variety of experiences (some ordinary, but others of the sort that many people accept as supernatural) can be triggered by weak electrical pulses applied directly to the brains of neurosurgical patients.[47] With suitable anaesthesia of the scalp, skull, and the dura mater that covers the brain, the stimulating electrodes can be placed on the exposed surface of the cortex with patients remaining fully awake. In this way, their conscious reports about the effects of stimulation at different points on the cortex can be used to identify the functions of those regions to aid the surgeons' decisions. In some areas of the brain, this stimulation produces extremely vivid memories that feel so real that patients describe them as like re-living the event. Cortical stimulation and, more recently, transcranial magnetic stimulation in normal, non-surgical volunteers,[48] can also elicit otherworldly visions suffused with profound meaningfulness and cosmic importance.[49] It can precipitate feelings of déjà vu, ecstasy or foreboding, as well as estrangement from the body where patients feel as if their spiritual essence is looking down at their bodies from above.

Recently, a neurosurgical team at Geneva University Hospital unexpectedly triggered dramatic hallucinatory experiences of the latter sort while using Penfield's technique to stimulate electrically the parietal lobe of a woman who was undergoing surgery for the diagnosis and treatment of severe epileptic seizures.[49] When the surgeons stimulated a particular site, the angular gyrus in her right hemisphere, she suddenly reported that she was floating above her own body and watching herself while the surgery was proceeding below. The strange experience would recur each time the angular gyrus was stimulated and it stopped each time the current was turned off. Because neither the patient nor the operating staff had discussed this possibility, or expected it to happen, we can assume that the experience was due to disrupting the normal activity of a brain region having to do with creating one's sensed body image, rather than merely the result of suggestion, expectation or vivid imagination. Blanke, the neurosurgeon, and his colleagues also found that electrical stimulation of adjacent parts of the parietal cortex produced other aberrations of sensed body position and size. It seems from demonstrations like these that so-called 'out-of-body experiences' (OBEs) reflect a temporary failure of the responsible part of the brain to integrate spatial information from its various positional sources. Normally, sensors in the muscles, tendons and joints feed positional information into this neural system, along with gravitational and movement information from the vestibular or balance organs in the inner ear, and the all-important spatial data coded by the visual and auditory systems. Thus, an OBE is most probably the outcome of a temporary breakdown in parietal lobe systems that build our experiential model of a self existing in a three-dimensional spatial world. When this happens, due to any of a number of possible causes, as discussed above, the self feels disembodied.[30,31,45]

OBEs often accompany 'transcendent' or mystical experiences induced by a variety of esoteric practices commonly found in the religious tradition.[10] OBEs are frequently the first phase of the 'near-death experiences' (NDEs), reported by as many as a quarter of those who suffer temporary heart stoppage and cessation of breathing following a heart attack.[29-31] The brain has limited supplies of oxygen and nutrients that allow it to continue to function at a somewhat degraded level while the lucky ones undergo cardiopulmonary resuscitation and are revived to tell of the experience. While many people take experiences such as these to be proof of an immaterial mind or soul that can leave the physical body, and as evidence for the existence of an after-life,[50] modern neuroscience views them as complex hallucinations triggered by temporary abnormalities in the brain.[51] It should be noted in passing that the fact that visual memories and dreams often occur in this bird's-eye perspective is an additional reason for concluding that OBEs and NDEs are really vivid, memory-driven hallucinations. Claims that the soul must have really left the body during the OBE, because the person returned with information that could only have been obtained if disembodied consciousness had seen it, remembered it and brought it back, are open to a number of more prosaic explanations.[30]

Interestingly, the limbic system is one of the most electrically volatile parts of the brain, increasing the likelihood that it might spontaneously erupt occasionally, even in normal people. After Persinger[52] developed a way of delivering weak magnetic pulses, through the skull, to the temporal lobes of normal human volunteers, the British psychologist, Susan Blackmore[53] ventured across the Atlantic to try his magnetic brain stimulation technique. She described the experience as follows:

> For the first ten minutes or so nothing seemed to happen .To tell the truth I felt rather daft. Instructed to describe aloud anything that happened I did not know what to say and felt under pressure to say something—anything. Then suddenly all my doubts were gone. 'I'm swaying. It's like being on a hammock'. Then it felt for all the world as though two hands had grabbed my shoulders and were bodily yanking me upright. I knew I was still lying in the reclining chair, but someone, or something, was pulling me up.

> Something seemed to get hold of my leg and pull it, distort it, and drag it up the wall. I felt as though I had been stretched half way up to the ceiling.

> Then came the emotions. Totally out of the blue, but intensely and vividly, I felt suddenly angry— not just mildly cross but that sort of determinedly clear minded anger out of which you act—only there was nothing and no one to act on. After perhaps ten seconds it was gone but later was replaced by an equally sudden fit of fear. I was just suddenly terrified—of nothing in particular. Never in my life have I had such powerful sensations coupled with the total lack of anything to blame them on. I was almost looking around the little room to find who was doing it.

> Of course, I knew that it was all caused by the magnetic field changes but what, I wondered, would I feel if such things happened spontaneously. What if I woke in the middle of the night with all those feelings? I knew I would want, above all, to find an explanation, to find out who had been doing it to me. To have such powerful feelings and no reason for them is horrible. You feel as if you are going mad. If someone told me an alien was responsible and invited me to join an abductees' support group, I might well prefer to believe the idea; rather than accept I was going mad.

The temporal lobe syndrome

Given the profundity of the experiences described above, it is not surprising that some (but definitely not all) patients who suffer temporal lobe injuries develop epileptic activity in this area that can produce major and lasting personality and emotional changes over time. One variant of this syndrome includes a morose personality type preoccupied with religious and moralistic obsessions about the wickedness of the world and an excessive need to lecture others on these shortcomings.[10,54–58] While these patients tend to lose interest in participating in sex themselves, they become obsessed with the perceived sexual dalliances of others. Because the systems in their brains responsible for adding feelings of significance to events they experience has been bumped by the seizure activity into continuous overdrive, everything seems of the gravest consequence. As a result, these patients tend totally to lack a sense of humour, and the gravity of it all frequently compels them to take copious notes at every opportunity (which they intend to condense into great metaphysical tomes).

Comparing temporal lobe symptomology with various historical accounts, it seems likely that at least some of the great religious prophets of old suffered from the kinds of temporal lobe anomalies which can make experiencers feel chosen for a special mission in life.[10,55,58] In more recent times, it has been pointed out that Ellen White, the founder of the Seventh Day Adventist Church—who suffered a serious head injury as a child—displayed many of the characteristics of the temporal lobe syndrome.[59,60] Interestingly, these speculations arose not from secular debunkers but from professionally qualified individuals, such as the paediatric neurologist Delbert Hodder, who are practising members of the church that was spawned by White's supposedly divine 'visions'.

Similar hints that the aftermath of certain brain lesions could produce states of consciousness conducive to the belief that one possesses paranormal powers have surfaced from the research of professionals such as Peter Fenwick, a respected neurologist who is nonetheless sympathetic to various paranormal claims. Fenwick's group conducted a survey and clinical examinations of a sample of London's more prominent psychic mediums.[61] The results showed that, compared with matched controls, the self-described 'sensitives' had an elevated incidence of childhood head injuries and evidence of mild right temporal lobe dysfunction. The authors of the study concluded that these current neurological signs could be related to frequent 'psychic' experiences the sensitives reported, which they believed were supernatural gifts bestowed upon them by higher powers. The suggested involvement of right hemisphere abnormalities in anomalous subjective experiences that may contribute to the formation and maintenance of paranormal beliefs has been studied extensively by a Swiss group headed by the neurologist Peter Brugger.[62] Their studies are part of a growing body of literature which shows that even relatively mild head injuries can result in persistent conscious effects that may be significant contributors to paranormal beliefs.[63] While the relationships are complex and the data somewhat mixed, there is also an emerging a body of research suggesting that there is a genetic contribution to the likelihood that people will interpret anomalous conscious events such as these, or even the milder ones we all experience from time to time, in ways that enhance their religiosity or spiritual leanings.[64]

Possibly resulting from brain differences related to the one described above, psychologists have shown that people who subscribe to strong paranormal beliefs tend to misjudge probabilities to a greater extent than control subjects and are more apt to fall prey to illusory feelings that they had controlled what were in fact chance events.[65]

Faced with a probable instance of hallucination, the prudent investigator should, of course, try to eliminate the various organic and psychopathological causes for such experiences. If none should emerge, however, diagnosticians ought to remember that there are more reasons than is often believed as to why normal people might experience awesome, even life-changing, altered states of consciousness.

Conclusion

In this chapter I have argued that a variety of mental states that occultists consider proof of alternate planes of reality and awesome psychic powers are better explained as unusual but not necessarily pathological states of the brain. These states are experienced as unusually vivid images that are often accompanied by strong emotional content and the feeling that they are caused and directed by powerful external forces. Such experiences are likely whenever induced or spontaneous changes in the brain occur at times when situational variables impair the ability of executive conscious to maintain a coherent sensory-based model of reality. This is exacerbated when, in addition, emotional or cognitive turmoil hampers the normal reality-checking mechanisms of executive consciousness in doing their job.

Since photography and video recorders have become commonplace, people have begun to assume that our senses record everything we experience in the same passive, one-to-one fashion. In fact, research has shown that our subjective awareness, and our memories, are much more constructive and reconstructive than this. The job of executive consciousness is not only to record but also to infer, predict and make sense of the world. As I have tried to show, even at the best of times, much of what goes into this internal model of reality is determined by brain processes working outside of conscious awareness. In so doing, this system, which works tolerably well most of the time, can occasionally manufacture and make sense of things that are not really there. Anything that temporarily impedes the representational system's ability to model the world based on external sense data will send it scurrying about for an acceptable replacement, most often perceptual memories. This can seem real for the time being but, when external sensory data reassert their primacy, this too will pass.

The sheer weight of support for mind–brain identity[9] convinces those of us who work in the area of anomalistic psychology that mind is indeed part of the natural, rather than the supernatural order. This, we are satisfied, applies to its extraordinary as well as its more mundane aspects. Of course, there are many who fervently want mind forever to remain something spiritual and beyond the constraints physics places on mere matter. The anomalous states of consciousness discussed in this chapter will probably remain the occultists' best hope for sustaining their belief in supernatural realms beyond the reach of science. For those constantly on the lookout for something with which to enchant themselves, to suggest naturalistic explanations for various awesome subjective events is to rob them of their specialness, their ability to imply that we humans are above, rather than part of, the natural universe. To those of us of a more materialist bent, the idea that the human brain could have come this far in understanding itself, in both its everyday and its more unusual manifestations, is a source of fascination equal to that of any of the more 'spooky' explanations preferred by believers in the paranormal. What could possibly create more awe and wonderment than the realization that somehow, ordinary chemicals in leaky bags called neurons could create something as marvellous as a thought—or the realization that our brains probably created God, rather than the other way around? The enormity of what is left to discover about both normal and abnormal brain and consciousness is humbling, yet enthralling. A major contributor to the field of anomalistic psychology, Professor Christopher French,[16] nicely summarized why we, its devotees, find it fun to come to work every morning:

> As with most other researchers, my main motivation for working in my chosen field is simply that I find it fascinating. I can think of no other area of study within psychology that covers such a broad range of inherently interesting (and controversial) topics. At one extreme the issues raised in anomalistic psychology are the most profound known to humanity. Are there really paranormal forces at work in the universe? Does consciousness survive the death of the physical body? At the other extreme are more trivial, but highly entertaining, topics such as the methods used by con artists to fool people that they have genuine psychic powers.

What could be more intriguing than that? The author Ann Druyan, widow of the late Carl Sagan, in her usual eloquent manner, encapsulated the feelings of the contributors to the present volume in an answer to those of a persuasion that finds something essentially lacking in the materialist approach to these 'big ticket' questions of existence. In her response to a question during a recent interview (available at www.humanistsnps.com) Druyan said:

> There's a yearning for a spiritual vision of the universe that is not supernatural but which acknowledges that while we may be tiny and not central to the universe, we are part of a great story—much greater than our religious heritage ever conceived. ... To me, there was no greater spiritual awakening than the Enlightenment itself. And I'm convinced that our failure to accept it as a primarily spiritual awakening is a major source of our dysfunction.

References and notes

1. **Bowers KS.** Revisioning the unconscious. *Canadian Psychology*, 1987; 28:93–104.
2. **Kihlstrom JF.** The cognitive unconscious. *Science*, 1987;237:1445–1452.
3. **Farthing GW.** *The psychology of consciousness.* Prentice-Hall, Englewood Cliff, NJ. 1992.
4. **Gazzaniga MS.** Organization of the human brain.*Science*, 1989; 245:947–952.

5. **Oakley D, Eames L.** The plurality of consciousness. In D Oakley, ed. *Brain and mind*. Methuen, London. 1985:217–251.
6. **Ramachandran VS, Blakeslee S.** *Phantoms in the brain: human nature and the architecture of the mind*. Fourth Estate, New York, 1998.
7. **Baars BJ.** The evidence is overwhelming for an observing self in the brain. *Science and Consciousness Review*, 2004;2:1–3.
8. **Lynn SJ, Rhue JW** (ed.)*Dissociation: clinical and theoretical perspectives*. Guilford Press, New York. 1994.
9. **Beyerstein BL.** The brain and consciousness: implications for Psi phenomena. *The Skeptical Inquirer*, 1987; **12**:163–173.
10. **Beyerstein BL.** Neuropathology and the legacy of spiritual possession. *The Skeptical Inquirer*, 1988; **13**:248–262.
11. **Hilgard ER.** *Divided consciousness: multiple controls in human thought and action*. Wiley, New York. 1977.
12. **Reed G.** *The psychology of anomalous experience*, revised edn. Prometheus Books, Amherst, NY. 1988.
13. **Neher A.** *The psychology of transcendence*. Prentice-Hall, Englewood Cliffs, NJ. 1980.
14. **Zusne L, Jones W.** *Anomalistic psychology: a study of magical thinking*, 2nd edn. Lawrence Erlbaum, Hillsdale, NJ. 1989.
15. **Hyman R.** The mischief-making of ideomotor action. *The scientific review of alternative medicine*, Fall/Winter 1999;3.
16. **French C.** Why I study anomalistic psychology. *The Psychologist*, 2001; **14**:356–357.
17. **Cardeña E, Lynn S, Krippner S** (ed.) *Varieties of anomalous experience: examining the scientific evidence*. American Psychological Association, Washington, DC. 2000.
18. **Della Sala S** (ed.) *Mind myths: exploring popular assumptions about the mind and brain*. Wiley, Chichester, UK. 1999.
19. **Greeley A.** *The sociology of the paranormal*. Sage, Beverly Hills, CA. 1975.
20. **Newberg A, d'Aquili E.** *Why God won't go away: brain science and the biology of belief*. Ballantine Books, New York. 2001.
21. **Alper M.** *The 'God' part of the brain*. Rogue Press, New York. 2001.
22. **Stenger VJ.** *Has science found God? The latest results in the search for purpose in the universe*. Prometheus Books, Amherst, New York. 2003.
23. **Goyette L.** *Pam Barrett's afterlife*. Elm Street, Toronto. May, 2000.
24. **Jacobs B.** Serotonin: the crucial substance that turns dreams on and off. *Psychology Today*, 1976; March:70–71.
25. **Mandell A.** Toward a psychobiology of transcendence: God in the brain. In JM Davidson, RJ Davidson, ed. *Psychobiology of consciousness*. Plenum, New York. 1980:379–463.
26. **Marks D.** Mental imagery and consciousness: a theoretical review. In A Sheikh, ed. *Imagery: current theory, research, and application*. Wiley, New York. 1983:96–130.
27. **Wilson S, Barber TX.** The fantasy-prone personality: implications for understanding imagery, hypnosis, and parapsychological phenomena. In A Sheikh, ed. *Imagery: current theory, research, and application*. Wiley, New York. 1983:340–387.
28. **Bentall RP.** The illusion of reality: a review and integration of psychological research on hallucinations. *Psychological Bulletin*, 1990;**107**:82–95.
29. **Siegel R.** *Fire in the brain: clinical tales of hallucination*. Plume/Penguin, New York. 1992.
30. **Ebbern H, Mulligan S, Beyerstein B.** Maria's near-death experience: waiting for the other shoe to drop. *The Skeptical Inquirer*, 1996;**20**:27–33.
31. **Woerlee G.** Darkness, tunnels, and light. *Skeptical Inquirer*, May, 2004;**28**:28–32.
32. **Loverock DS, Modigliani V.** Visual imagery and the brain: a review. *Journal of Mental Imagery*, 1995;**19**:91–132.

33. **Schatzman M.** Evocations of unreality. *New Scientist* 1980; 25 September:935–937.
34. **Manford M, Andermann F.** Complex visual hallucinations: clinical and neurobiological insights. *Brain*, 1998; **121**:1819–1840.
35. **Horowitz M.** Hallucinations: an information-processing approach. In RK Siegel, LJ West, ed. *Hallucinations: behavior, experience, and theory*. Wiley, New York. 1975:163–193.
36. **Sargant W.** *The mind possessed: a physiology of possession, mysticism and faith healing.* Pan Books, London. 1976.
37. **Ardila A, Sancehz E.** Neuropsychologic symptoms in the migraine syndrome. *Cephalgia*, 1988; **8**:67–70.
38. **Lynn SJ, Rhue JW.** 'Fantasy proneness'. *American Psychologist*, 1988;**43**:35–44.
39. **Spanos N, Cross PA, Dickson K, DuBreuil S.** Close encounters: an examination of UFO experiences. *Journal of Abnormal Psychology*, 1993;**102**:624–632.
40. **Nickell J.** A study of fantasy proneness in the thirteen cases of alleged encounters in John Mack's 'Abduction'. *Skeptical Inquirer*, 1996;**20**:18–20, 54.
41. **Loftus E, Ketcham K.** *The myth of repressed memory.* St. Martin's Press, New York. 1994.
42. **Spanos NP.** Multiple identities and false memories: a sociocognitive perspective. APA Books, Washington, DC. 2001.
43. **Baker R** (ed.) *Hidden memories: voices and visions from within.* Prometheus Books, Amherst, NY. 1992.
44. **Simpson D.** A controlled UFO hoax: some lessons. *Skeptical Inquirer*, 1980; **4**:32–39.
45. **Blackmore S.** *Dying to live: near-death experiences.* Prometheus Books, Amherst, NY. 1993.
46. **Joseph R.** The limbic system: emotion, laterality, and unconscious mind. In *Neuropsychology, neuropsychiatry, and behavioral neurology*. Plenum Press, New York. 1990.
47. **Penfield W, Boldrey E.** Somatic motor and sensory representation in the cerebral cortex of man as studied by electrical stimulation. *Brain*, 1937; **60**:389–43.
48. **Johnson CPL, Persinger, M.** The sensed presence may be facilitated by interhemispheric intercalation. *Perceptual and Motor Skills*, 1994; **79**:351–354.
49. **Blanke O, Ortigue S, Landis T, Seeck M.** Stimulating illusory own-body perceptions. *Nature*, 2002; **419**:269–270.
50. **Moody R.** *Life after life: the investigation of a phenomenon—survival of bodily death.* Bantam Books, New York. 1976.
51. **Persinger MA.** Near-death experiences and ecstasy: a product of the organization of the human brain. In Della Sala S, ed. *Mind myths: exploring popular assumptions about the mind and brain.* Wiley, Chicester, UK. 1999.
52. **Cook C, Persinger M.** Experimental induction of the 'sensed presence' in normal subjects and an exceptional subject. *Perceptual and Motor Skills*, 1997;**85**:683–693.
53. **Blackmore S.** Alien abduction. *New Scientist*, 1994; **19**:29–31.
54. **Waxman SG, Geschwind N.** The interictal behavior syndrome of temporal lobe epilepsy. *Archives of General Psychiatry*, 1975;**32**:1580–1586.
55. **Pickover C.** The vision of the chariot: transcendent experience and temporal lobe epilepsy. *Science and Spirit*. September/October, 1999.
56. **Persinger MA.** 'I would kill in God's name:' role of sex, weekly church attendance, report of a religious experience, and limbic lability.*Perceptual and Motor Skills*, 1997; **85**:128–30.
57. **Persinger MA.** Religious and mystical experiences as artifacts of temporal lobe function: a general hypothesis. *Perceptual and Motor Skills*, 1983; **57**:1255–1262.
58. **LaPlante E.** *Seized.* Harper Collins, New York. 1993.
59. **Clapp R.** Was Ellen White merely an epileptic? *Christianity Today*, 1982; **26**:56.
60. **Couperus M.** The significance of EllenWhite's head injury. Adventist Currents. June, 1985. Available on-line at: http://www.sda_egw.com/egw's_head_injury.htm (accessed 19 May, 2005).

61. Fenwick P. Psychic sensitivity, mystical experience, head injury, and brain pathology. *British Journal of Medical Psychology*, 1985;**58**:35–44.
62. Pizzagalli D, Lehman D, Gianotti L, Koenig T, Tanaka H, Wackermann J, Brugger P. Brain electric correlates of strong belief in paranormal phenomena: intracerebral source and regional Omega complexity analyses. *Psychiatry Research: Neuroimaging Section*, 2000; **100**:139–154.
63. Cantagallo A, Grassi L, Della Sala S. Dissociative disorder after traumatic brain injury. *Brain Injury*, 1999; **13**:219–28.
64. Koenig LB, McGue M, Krueger RF, Bouchard TJ. *Journal of Personality*, 2005; **73**:472–488.
65. Blackmore S, Troscianko T. Belief in the paranormal: probability judgements, illusory control, and the 'chance baseline shift'. *British Journal of Psychology*, 1985; **76**:459–468.

Chapter 20

The myth of the clonable human brain

Giovanni Berlucchi

Cloning and the brave new world

The long history of the use of animal embryos in biomedical research has recently been revolutionized by the so-called cloning or nuclear transfer technique. In contrast to the traditional *in vitro* fertilization, obtained with the union of an ovum and a sperm, animal embryos are produced by inserting the engineered nucleus of a somatic cell, for example a mammary gland cell, into an enucleated ovum. When implanted into an appropriately treated uterus, cloned embryos can develop into viable animals having the genetic characteristics of the donor of the nucleus, as in the famous case of Dolly the sheep and a few specimens of other mammalian species.[1] The potential application of the cloning technology to human beings has raised enormous ethical concerns. A cogent case can be made for the employment of the cloning technique for the production of human cells and tissues to be used in the treatment of severe illnesses, but there is a generally justified moral opposition to reproductive cloning, i.e. is to the begetting of children through the implantation of cloned human embryos into a woman's uterus.[2] Among the several reasons why the cloning of a human being appears repugnant to most people, pre-eminent is the conviction that this kind of genetic manipulation may interfere with biological and psychological diversity, and therefore with the distinctiveness and autonomy of the individual. Biological and psychological individuality is part and parcel of human nature, and most human values are corollaries of the concept that each person is unique and identical to him/herself through space and time. Men, women and children are all marked and set apart not only by the characteristics of their bodily structures, but also by the idiosyncrasies of their minds as determined by the unique organization of their brains. If the identity or near-identity of the genes of the developed clone and the somatic cell nucleus' donor means that the two individuals will also share the same personal identity, full human cloning may have the potential for annihilating a person's uniqueness.

Annihilation of personal uniqueness was exactly the purpose of the scientific dictator-ship running Aldous Huxley's *Brave new world*,[3] a fictional society in which the bewilder-ing diversity of men's nature was reduced to some kind of manageable uniformity by a foolproof system of genetic control specifically designed to standardize the human product. By coupling this control with appropriate conditioning paradigms, social stability was achieved by granting members of a largely homogenized mankind a state of physical well-being without conscious experience of suffering and deprivation, but also without freedom, beauty and creativity, and ultimately without the feeling of a unique personal existence.

The natural clones and developmental noise

Are we entitled to believe that human reproductive cloning can eventually implement Huxley's shocking scenario? The answer to this question is that human reproductive cloning could only undermine our genetic uniqueness, not our sense of self or identity, for nothing of what we know about the genetically identical products of nature challenges the facts of individual diversity and uniqueness.[4] From times immemorial nature has being producing genetically identical humans, i.e. monozygotic twins who are born nearly simultaneously with the same genetic endowment, and yet are undoubtedly distinct individuals. A person's identity, individuality or self is the result of that person's genome as much as of his or her unique and unrepeatable life history, including prenatal development in the intrauterine environment. Further, in addition to genetic and environmental influences, there is an independent third source of phenotypic variation which has a major role in ensuring the uniqueness of each individual organism and particularly of each individual brain. Independent of their genetic make-up, persons have different minds arguably because they have different nervous systems, and they have different nervous systems because each nervous system is the unique, irreproducible result of three factors: the genes, the environment and developmental noise.

The term developmental noise denotes the intrinsic variability and randomness of the construction process of the organism. For example, developmental noise is responsible for fluctuating asymmetries, the small and random side differences which occur in symmetrical structures of an organism.[5,6] It is also held responsible for the complex heritability of proneness to major pathologies such as cancer[7] and schizophrenia.[8,9] In brief, all manifest differences between genetically identical organisms that are raised in the very same environmental conditions are thought to result from developmental noise. The most convincing proof of the existence of development noise is provided by unique somatic traits which allow absolute personal identification. Fingerprints are made up by the multiple papillary ridges that cross the epidermis of the palmar surface of the hand and the sole of the foot, and are at their finest on the fingertips. Their function is to increase the gripping ability of hands and feet, preventing slipping, and to sustain tactile discrimination and manipulation with the great density of tactile endings beneath them. The arrangement of the ridge pattern constituting the fingerprints is by itself immutable throughout life and unique to the individual, such that no two fingerprints are exactly alike even in monozygotic twins or in different digits of the same person. Therefore, fingerprints are a more reliable means of personal identification than the so-called DNA fingerprinting, which cannot differentiate monozygotic twins. This does not mean that the fingerprint pattern is not influenced by the genome, since it can be affected by abnormalities of early development, including genetic disorders such as the Down, Turner and Klinefelter syndromes, and possibly schizophrenia as well. However its uniqueness and singularity attest to the action of developmental noise.[10]

Another somatic trait that lends itself reliably to personal identification is the visible pattern of arching ligaments, crypts and ridges of the human iris. Contrary to the odd iridologists' belief that the iris can reveal the state of health of various organs, the textural pattern of each iris remains constant after early childhood.[11] Daugman and Downing[12] used mathematical image analysis to assess the randomness and singularity of the iris patterns on 2.3 million different pairs of eye images. The chance probability of encountering two different irides agreeing on 70 per cent of their features was calculated to be one in 7 billion. What is more important is that isogenic irides, coming from monozygotic twins or even from the right and left eyes of the same individual, were no more similar than those of unrelated persons. Apart from overall form and colour, which are genetically determined, the textural pattern of each iris thus appears to depend on random developmental events that result in a unique structure.[12] It is hard, if not impossible, to conceive a way in which the environment could contribute to such morphological uniqueness.

Individual diversity: between genes and environment

If random developmental events can lead to unique patterns of simple morphological features such as fingerprints and iris texture, it stands to reason that developmental noise can perhaps exert an even deeper influence on the structure of the brain, macroscopic as well as microscopic. Studies on monozygotic twins provide enough information for debunking the myth that identical genes can make identical brains and, by implication, identical minds. It is true of course that monozygotic twins not only look alike, but also seem to think and feel alike. Even when raised in different families, they are undoubtedly quite similar in many psychological traits, to the point of choosing the same occupation, showing preferences for the same brands of hair tonics, toothpaste or cigarettes, and performing the same peculiar antics[13] (Fig. 20.1).

A favourite anecdote which finds its way into most books on evolutionary psychology is that of the female monozygotic twins raised apart who used to enter the ocean backward and just up to their knees.[14] However, the psychological differences between monozygotic twins, whether raised together or apart, are at least as important as the identities. Gould[15] and Lewontin,[16] among others, have eloquently argued against a crude genetic determinism of the mind by referring to evidence of striking mental differences between monozygotic twins. More quantitative and less anecdotal evidence indicates that the concordance on various personality traits is about 50 per cent between genetically identical monozygotic twins, as opposed to 25 per cent between dizygotic twins (who have shared the maternal uterus but have only half of their genes in common), 11 per cent between siblings, who also share half of their genes, and virtually 0 per cent between randomly chosen unrelated individuals. The concordance between monozygotic twins on intelligence tests is even higher, reaching 70 per cent as opposed to 40 per cent or less in dizygotic twins.[13,17] There is thus little doubt that genetics has a strong influence

Fig. 20.1 A humorous representation of the fanciful belief that the mental processes of identical twins raised apart are bound to follow identical courses (cartoon by Charles Addams, from The New Yorker Cartoon Collection, 75th Anniversary, edited by Bob Mankoff, Pocket Books, New York, 1999) © Tee and Charles Addams Foundation.

on the mind, but an even more interesting point is that the 30–50 per cent non-genetic psychological variation between monozygotic twins can hardly be regarded as a *bona fide* effect of the environment. Indeed, the concordance on cognitive and personality measures found between monozygotic twins reared apart is only minimally smaller than that found in monozygotic twins living together.[13]

What then are the causes of psychological variation between monozygotic twins that cannot be accounted for by the overall influence of their family environment, and what are the neural underpinnings of the similarities and differences between their mental processes? One interpretation ascribes non-genetic psychological differences between monozygotic twins to unique non-shared personal experiences that are bound to occur even under strict cohabitation conditions, such as being chased by a dog or receiving an occasional individual reward or punishment from a teacher or parent.[14,18] There seems to be no way to gather direct objective evidence to support this interpretation. Another, alternative view can be traced back to the original suggestion of Hebb[19] that growth of the embryonic and fetal brain and behavioural development alike are bound to be significantly affected by the varying physiological conditions existing in the prenatal uterine environment. With twins, factors such as variations in the position of the fetuses in the womb, in the exchanges between maternal blood and fetal blood, and in the amount of head trauma associated with parturition may all account for mental and cerebral differences which occur in spite of identical genomes. However, there is now ample evidence that the cerebral and mental uniqueness of each monozygotic twin owes more to quite subtle but powerful prenatal vagaries of developmental noise than to the above gross intrauterine influences.

Several years ago, Changeux[20] argued that the complexity of the nervous system is such that already at birth it is virtually impossible for genetically identical twins to possess exactly the same cerebral organization down to the level of the trillions of single synapses that occur in the human brain. He called attention to the experiments on the crustacean *Daphnia magnia*[21] and on the fish *Poecilia formosa*,[22] showing that in the relatively simple nervous systems of these species, animals born by parthenogenesis, thus endowed with the same genes, were distinguishable on the basis of the fine details of the branching of nerve terminals in corresponding sites, though not in terms of number of neurons and major selective interneuronal connections. In considering the development of the nervous system, one has to keep in mind that in addition to cellular differentiation, migration and aggregation processes that apply to the rest of the body, the orderly growth of neuronal axons and dendrites and the formation of highly organized and selective systems of synaptic connections are enormously more complex than the events involved in the genesis of all non-nervous organs. Such complexity greatly expands the fringe of nervous system traits that are not subject to a strict genetic determinism and are therefore open to a more or less pronounced phenotypic variability. Molecules of various types (growth factors, hormones, neurotransmitters, netrins, semaphorins, adhesion molecules, etc.), whether residing in the extracellular matrix or anchored to cell membranes, are essential for directing growing axons and dendrites along appropriate paths to the appropriate targets with which they are to form functioning synaptic relations.[23]

The combinatorial explosion in the number of synaptic connections between several billions of neurons in the large human brain makes it likely that the fringe of non-genetic variability in neural development attains an unsurpassed extent. More specifically, the brains of human neonates are bound to differ with respect to a number of discrete, functionally important features of the pattern of synaptic connections within a shared, species-specific general plan of brain organization which has remained unchanged since the appearance of *Homo sapiens* at least one hundred thousand years ago. This is true not only of genetically different individuals, where brain differences are at least partly determined by different genes, but also of genetically identical twins, where genes alone cannot specify the innumerable intimate details of the overall individual pattern of neuronal interconnections. Given their high inherent variability, the multifarious molecular and cellular aspects of the prenatal development of the nervous system imply that even before being exposed to external environmental influences, each human brain must contain a number of unique and unrepeatable combinations of neuronal interconnections. That major changes in this organization can and do occur after birth as a result of experience and general environmental influences is of course another story. The message here is that if it were possible to bring a newborn baby back to the condition of a fertilized egg in the maternal womb, at least some details of its development, particularly of its brain, would be sufficiently altered to give rise to a perhaps slightly but no doubt significantly different individual with his/her own unique neural machinery for mental activity and behavioural control.

Macroscopic differences between the brains of monozygotic twins

The non-invasive magnetic resonance imaging technique has made it possible to examine and compare the brains of monozygotic twins *in vivo*. Oppenheim *et al.*[24] reported a much greater similarity in the appearance of the corpus callosum between the members of each of five pairs of monozygotic twins than between unrelated individuals, yet subtle intrapair differences in callosal morphology could also be detected. In the members of nine pairs of right-handed monozygotic twins, Steinmetz *et al.*[25] found the typically human side asymmetry whereby the left *planum temporale* is larger than the right, but only in four pairs was the magnitude of this difference consistent between twins. In an additional exceptional pair, one twin showed an inverse difference in favour of the right side. In another sample of 10 pairs of monozygotic twins who were discordant for manual dominance, the intrapair variability in the *planum temporale* asymmetry was even more remarkable, since most of the left-handed individuals showed an inverse or no asymmetry.[25] Another imaging study[26] analysed various aspects of brain morphology in 10 pairs of monozygotic twins and nine pairs of sex-matched dizygotic twins. There was a highly significant 94 per cent intrapair concordance in brain volume in the monozygotic sample, compared with an insignificant 34 per cent intrapair concordance in the dizygotic sample, suggesting that like body size, brain size is under a strict genetic control. In contrast, statistical evidence for heritability of the overall external configuration of the cerebral cortex was low and ill defined, given the far-from-precise concordance in the pattern of cortical sulci and gyri between monozygotic twins, in spite of a greater apparent similarity than in dizygotic twins.

Many more studies aimed at assessing similarities and differences between the brains of monozygotic and dizygotic twins or matched controls have been carried out in recent years. Previous findings of a strict genetic control on the size of the whole brain[26,27] have been confirmed, and the evidence has been extended to select cortical or subcortical regions.[28–31] On the other hand, the existence of considerable differences between monozygotic twins in the surface morphology and therefore in the overall appearance of the brain has also been established beyond doubt. For example, White *et al.*[29] used automated and manual methods to evaluate total brain volume, grey matter, white matter, ventricles, the frontal, temporal, parietal and occipital lobes, cerebellum, thalamus, caudate and putamen in monozygotic twins compared with a matched control sample. They also used measures of surface morphology to evaluate gyral and sulcal curvature, surface area and cortical depth. The cerebral volume regions, including the grey matter, white matter and lobar volumes, as well as the cerebellum were highly correlated ($r > 0.90$) within monozygotic twin pairs. Significant but lower correlations were also found for the cortical depth ($r = 0.84$), caudate ($r = 0.84$), thalamus ($r = 0.75$) and putamen ($r = 0.75$). The lowest correlations within twin pairs were found with regard to surface measures, such as the gyral ($r = 0.63$) and sulcal ($r = 0.58$) curvature indices, the surface complexity index ($r = 0.49$) and the measure of surface area ($r = 0.69$), pointing to a lesser dependence of this aspect of brain morphology on heredity.

Quite recently Mohr et al.[31] obtained three different high resolution magnetic resonance images of the brains of 26 monozygotic twins: whole-brain views, silhouettes and a bird's-eye view of a segment showing the central region. The results led to the conclusion of a considerable intertwin similarity in overall brain shape, supporting the influence of genetic control. On the other hand, the far from negligible differences in sulcal and gyral patterns could only be accounted for by a considerable degree of non-genetic influences. An earlier study[28] had reported that the between-twin differences in surface cortical morphology depend mostly on the superficial or tertiary sulci which develop later than the deeper sulci. The pattern of the latter sulci is relatively stable even across non-related individuals and probably reflects a species-specific plan of cortical folding.

The notion that surface cortical morphology is by no means identical in monozygotic twins receives indirect support from the evidence that it seems easier to distinguish identical twins by looking at their brains than by looking at their faces. Picking out the faces of two monozygotic twins from an array of different faces is a ridiculously easy task, but the performance on a similar task with brain images rather than faces proved considerably more difficult in three studies. While human raters in the study of Bartley et al.[26] were only 50 per cent correct in matching monozygotic twins based on brain morphology, performance was higher in the study of Biondi et al.,[27] reaching a 90 per cent success rate possibly thanks to a larger number of brain surface views. In another study,[31] the success rate in identifying the related twin pair out of a set of five brains was significantly above chance but far from perfect, reaching 75 per cent for whole-brain views and silhouettes and 48 per cent for the view of the central region segment. A computer-based analysis identified brains of twins significantly often as well, but twin matching was again far from perfect, and again better with whole-brain views and silhouettes than with views limited to the central region (Fig. 20.2).

One can argue that the pattern of sulci and scissures of the brain cortex has no functional meaning, and therefore that individual differences in this pattern have no functional meaning as well. There are morphological, physiological and even psychological counterobjections to this argument. Markowitsch and Tulving[32] have called attention to the finding that in neuroimaging studies, peaks of changes in neuronal activity are often observed in or near sulcal fundi, particularly when complex cognitive activities are tested. They have therefore suggested that sulcal and fundal regions of the cortex play a special role in higher cognitive processing. According to Van Essen,[33] the characteristic folding of the cerebral cortex can be explained by the non-random action of tension along axons in the white matter, hence by implication it reflects the connectivity and topology of the underlying neural circuitry. Régis et al.[34] maintain that the variability of the superficial

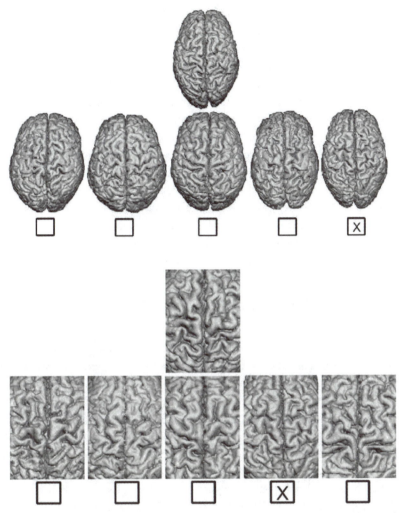

Fig. 20.2 Brains of identical twins do not look identical. In the Mohr et al.'s study 31, observers had to match the image of a single twin's brain at the top with the image of the brain of the other identical twin randomly placed among four different brains below (the cross indicates the correct choice). Performance was far from perfect, especially when only the central region of the brains was used for the test (bottom half of the figure).

appearance of the cortex results from the chaotic behaviour of the folding process, but that this process reflects the differential expression of the surface of cortical areas (i.e. functional areas) from one individual to another. Macroscopic brain features such as the right–left asymmetry of the *planum temporale*[35] and the overall pattern of cortical folding[36] are determined before birth, and therefore cannot be attributed to the action of postnatal environment. Between birth and adulthood, the degree of cortical folding remains virtually constant in spite of a 3-fold increase in brain size.[36] To the extent that individual mental and behavioural characteristics depend on unique specific properties of brain organization, the observed differences in cortical configuration between the brains of monozygotic twins can reasonably be assumed to be major factors of the demonstrable differences in their psychological make-up.[23]

This likely, but still unproven assumption is reinforced by evidence of significant correlations between brain traits and mental traits. In a study by Thompson *et al.*,[37] genetic factors appeared to have a significant, though incomplete influence on cortical structure in Broca's and Wernicke's language areas, as well as in frontal brain regions. There was an association between individual differences in grey matter volume in the frontal cortex and the controversial Spearman's *g* factor, which measures the combined ability to perform tests in different cognitive domains and is regarded by most as an index of general intelligence. It is still a long way from these findings to the assessment of the neural bases, either heritable or non-heritable, of cognition and behavioural control, but the assumption that definite links exist between brain structure and function on one hand, and the mind on the other, is clearly becoming open to scientific investigation. If brain traits correlate with mind traits, and no brain is identical to another brain, no mind can be identical to another mind.

The brain as a social construct

There are two senses in which the brain can be regarded as a social construct.[38] One is that the individual's social environment moulds the anatomic–functional organization of the individual's brain. The other is that in any given historical period, ideas and beliefs about the brain reflect the culture of that period. The current prevailing view of the brain is that the genes predispose a structure of the nervous system which throughout the entire individual's life is partly maintained and partly modified and adjusted by personal experiences and interactions with the environment. A straightforward argument is that since personal identity is psychological identity, and psychological identity is brain identity, it follows that personal identity is brain identity. The implicit equation of a person with his or her brain is made explicit by the laws of several civilized countries which allow organ explantation following brain death. However, some qualifications are needed here, for it may be wrong, even on a strictly biological view, to believe that the mind and the self 'go with' the brain. The brain is interconnected with all the organs of the body not only through the peripheral nervous system, but also by means of chemical messages conveyed to the brain by hormones and other humoral agents. In its turn, the brain sends chemical messages to most body organs through the blood vessels. From a philosophical standpoint, Steinhart[39] has convincingly advocated a biologically realistic theory of personhood based on the brain–body composite and its history rather than on the sole brain. Even in the dreadful locked-in syndrome, where a conscious person cannot emit overt behaviour, the brain continues to receive and process chemical signals from the body in spite of the interruption of most afferent and efferent neural channels.[40] The role of these signals in the maintenance of consciousness is probably far from minor, and the idea that a person may be preserved by transplanting his or her brain in another body is another myth to be dispelled.

The evidence reviewed here suggests that chance events occurring during ontogenesis contribute to the production of unique body/brain composites, each of which will interact with the environment in its own idiosyncratic manner. The idea that genetic manipulation may allow a brain and the mind associated with it to be replicated is preposterous not only because of the sheer impossibility of recreating the detailed vicissitudes of an individual existence, but also because of the uncontrollable nature of the chance events in overall brain development and organization. If nuclear genetic material were available to make a clone of Leonardo da Vinci, and if it were possible to reproduce the conditions in which he grew up and lived, it would be unduly optimistic to foresee that the clone would unfold into a polymath and an artistic genius, and absurd to expect him to paint Mona Lisa and The Last Supper. For all we know, he may not even turn out to be left-handed, as Leonardo instead was, because left-handedness appears to be a chance phenotypic expression in the absence of a gene that biases the direction of handedness toward the right.[41] Individuals lacking the gene and, as a result, the right bias, may develop as either right- or left-handers, which may explain why monozygotic twins can be discordant for

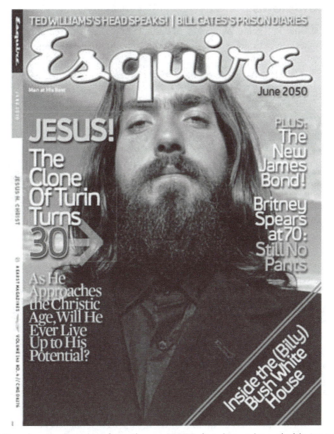

Fig. 20.3 A fictional magazine cover from the year 2050 showing an improbable Jesus Christ cloned by means of DNA sticking to the Turin Shroud.

handedness.[25] The absurdity of the idea that cloning may allow the rebirth of exceptional individuals has been carried to an extreme by religious groups and fictional novels that prospect the 'Second Coming of the Saviour' through the cloning of Jesus Christ. The job would entail the use of cellular remains sticking to the Turin Shroud or from other relics such as blood traces on rusty nails purported to come from the Holy Cross. This grotesque fantasy has lent itself to blasphemous puns and jokes of dubious taste, such as 'from Dolly the sheep to the Shepherd', 'at last we will know God's DNA', 'Jesus' clone will have to develop in a virgin's uterus', and so on (Fig. 20.3).

In conclusion, it has long been recognized that biological evolution by natural selection is predicated on the uniqueness of the biological make-up of the individual and the resulting variability among individuals in sexually reproducing populations. I suggest it is time to acknowledge that a non-genetic inborn variability between the brains of different individuals may in turn help the cultural evolution of the species by the chance production of the cerebral primordia of exceptionally gifted minds, to be nurtured and developed in appropriate environments.

References and notes

1. Paterson L, DeSousa P, Ritchie W, King T, Wilmut I. Application of reproductive biotechnology in animals: implications and potentials. Applications of reproductive cloning. *Animal Reproduction Science*, 2003; 79:137–43.
2. Rhind SM, Taylor JE, De Sousa PA, King TJ, McGarry M, Wilmut I. Human cloning: can it be made safe? *Nature Review Genetics*, 2003; 4:855–864.
3. Huxley A. *Brave new world*. Penguin Books Ltd, Harmondsworth, UK. 1972. (Originally published by Chatto & Windus, 1932.)
4. Brock DW. Human cloning and our sense of self. *Science*, 2002; 296:314–316.
5. Molenaar PC, Boomsma DI, Dolan CV. A third source of developmental differences. *Behavior Genetics*, 1993; 23:519–524.
6. Machin GA. Some causes of genotypic and phenotypic discordance in monozygotic twin pairs. *American Journal of Medical Genetics*, 1996; 61:216–228.
7. Aranda-Anzaldo A, Dent MA. Developmental noise, ageing and cancer. *Mechanisms of Ageing and Development*, 2003; 124:711–720.
8. Petronis A. The origin of schizophrenia: genetic thesis, epigenetic antithesis, and resolving synthesis. *Biological Psychiatry*, 2004; 55:965–970.
9. Singh SM, McDonald P, Murphy B, O'Reilly R. Incidental neurodevelopmental episodes in the etiology of schizophrenia: an expanded model involving epigenetics and development. *Clinical Genetics*, 2004; 65:435–440.
10. Napier J. *Hands* (revised by RH Tuttle). Princeton University Press, Princeton, NJ. 1993.
11. Bito LZ, Matheny A, Cruickshanks KJ, Nondahl DM, Carino OB. Eye color changes past early childhood. The Louisville Twin Study. *Archives of Ophthalmology*, 1997; 115:659–663.
12. Daugman J, Downing C. Epigenetic randomness, complexity and singularity of human iris patterns. *Proceedings of the Royal Society B: Biological Sciences*, 2001; 268:1737–1740.
13. Bouchard TJ Jr. Whenever the twain shall meet. *The Sciences*, 1997; 37:52–57.
14. Pinker S. *How the mind works*. W.W.Norton & Co., New York. 1997.
15. Gould SJ. Individuality. *The Sciences*, 1997; 37:14–16.
16. Lewontin RC. The confusion over cloning. *The New York Review of Books*, XLIV 1997; 16:18–23.
17. McClearn GE, Johansson B, Berg S, Pedersen NL, Ahern F, Petrill SA, Plomin R. Substantial genetic influence on cognitive abilities in twins 80 or more years old. *Science*, 1997; 276:1560–1563.

18. **Gazzaniga MS.** *Nature's mind.* Basic Books, New York. 1992.
19. **Hebb DO.** *A textbook of psychology.* Saunders, Philadelphia. 1966.
20. **Changeux J-P.** *L'Homme heuronal.* Fayard, Paris. 1983.
21. **Macagno ER, Lopresti V, Levinthal C.** Structure and development of neuronal connections in isogenic organisms: variations and similarities in the optic system of *Daphnia magna. Proceedings of the National Academy of Sciences, USA,* 1973; **70**:57–61.
22. **Levinthal F, Macagno E, Levinthal C.** Anatomy and development of identified cells in isogenic organisms. *Cold Spring Harbor Symposia of Quantitative Biology,* 1976; **40**:321–331.
23. **Marcus G.** *The birth of the mind.* Basic Books, New York. 2004.
24. **Oppenheim JS, Skerry JE, Tramo MJ, Gazzaniga MS.** Magnetic resonance imaging of the corpus callosum in monozygotic twins. *Annals of Neurology,* 1989; **26**:100–104.
25. **Steinmetz H, Herzog A, Schlaug G, Huang Y, Jänke L.** Brain (a)symmetry in monozygotic twins. *Cerebral Cortex,* 1995; **5**:296–300.
26. **Bartley AJ, Jones DW, Weinberger DR.** Genetic variability of human brain size and cortical gyral pattens. *Brain,* 1997; **120**:257–269.
27. **Biondi A, Nogueira H, Dormont D, Duyme M, Hasboun D, Zouaoui A, Chantome M, Marsault, C.** Are the brains of monozygotic twins similar? A three-dimensional MR study. *AJNR American Journal of Neuroradiology,* 1998; **19**:1361–1367.
28. **Lohmann G, von Cramon DY, Steinmetz H.** Sulcal variability of twins. *Cerebral Cortex,* 1999; **9**:754–763.
29. **White T, Andreasen NC, Nopoulos P.** Brain volumes and surface morphology in monozygotic twins. *Cerebral Cortex,* 2002; **12**:486–493.
30. **Wright IC, Sham P, Murray RM, Weinberger DR, Bullmore ET.** Genetic contributions to regional variability in human brain structure: methods and preliminary results. *Neuroimage,* 2002; **17**:256–271.
31. **Mohr A, Weisbrod M, Schellinger P, Knauth M.** The similarity of brain morphology in healthy monozygotic twins. *Brain Research Cognitive Brain Research,* 2004; **20**:106–110.
32. **Markowitsch HJ, Tulving E.** Cognitive processes and cerebral cortical fundi. *Neuroreport,* 1995; **6**:413–418.
33. **Van Essen DC.** A tension-based theory of morphogenesis and compact wiring in the central nervous system. *Nature,* 1997; **385**:313–318.
34. **Régis J, Mangin J-F, Ochiai T, Frouin V, Riviere D, Cachia A, Tamura M, Samson Y.** 'Sulcal root' generic model: a hypothesis to overcome the variability of the human cortex folding patterns. *Neurologia Medico-Chirurgica (Tokyo),* 2005; **45**:1–17.
35. **Chi JG, Dooling EC, Gilles FH.** Left–right asymmetries of the temporal speech areas of the human fetus. *Archives of Neurology,* 1977; **34**:346–348.
36. **Armstrong E, Schleicher A, Omran H, Curtis M, Zilles K.** The ontogeny of human gyrification. *Cerebral Cortex,* 1995; **5**:56–63.
37. **Thompson PM, Cannon TD, Narr KL, van Erp T, Poutanen VP, Huttunen M, Lonnqvist J, Standertskjold-Nordenstam CG, Kaprio J, Khaledy M, Dail R, Zoumalan CI, Toga AW.** Genetic influences on brain structure. *Nature Neuroscience,* 2001; **4**:1253–1258.
38. **Eisenberg L.** The social construction of the human brain. *American Journal of Psychiatry,* 1995; **152**:1563–1575.
39. **Steinhart E.** Persons versus brains: biological intelligence in human organism. *Biology and Philosophy,* 2001; **16**:3–27.
40. **Laureys S, Owen AM, Schiff ND.** Brain function in coma, vegetative state, and related disorders. *The Lancet Neurology,* 2004; **3**:537–546.
41. **Corballis MC.** The genetics and evolution of handedness. *Psychological Review,* 1997; **104**:714–727.

Chapter 21

Out on a limb: neglect and confabulation in the study of aplasic phantoms

Peter Brugger and Marion Funk

In this chapter we discuss a phenomenon whose very existence is a matter of debate among today's neuroscientists. Phantom sensations of a limb that was never physically developed are taken as unequivocal evidence, by some researchers, for the innateness of bodily representations, while others consider such sensations the mere product of suggestible minds. We will review the history of ideas concerning 'aplasic phantoms'[1] and attempt to show that, after a long period of neglect of the phenomenon, twenty-first century neuroscience is inclined to consider seriously the reports of some people born without an extremity. Thus, we are in the midst of a particularly exciting transition from one 'scientific fact' (that the body schema is entirely acquired after birth) to another (that at least some components of body schema may be innate or acquired during fetal life). This historical review also reveals how scientists' belief systems concerning phantoms of limbs missing since birth have evolved. Such systems are characterized by a high degree of 'inertia', i.e. they are largely resistant to contradictory evidence. Neglect of such evidence is only one of the dangers to scientific progress. Another, more serious danger is the confabulatory distortion of observations to make them compatible with a currently held belief. Both dangers are still lurking in modern thoughts on aplasic phantoms. We will argue that they can be mitigated by focusing on hypothesis-driven research.

Before addressing the specific issue of aplasic phantoms, we provide a brief introduction to the nature of 'scientific facts' and the gradual integration of new observations into existing theoretical frameworks.

The genesis and development of a 'scientific fact' (Ludwik Fleck)

Ludwik Fleck (1896–1961) worked as a medical doctor in the fields of bacteriology and serology. He is remembered, however, for his sociologically oriented contributions to the philosophy of science, in particular for his studies on the evolution of medical knowledge (for an overview, see Cohen and Schnelle[2]). In 1935, Fleck's treatise *Genesis and development of a scientific fact* was published.[3] Although this book markedly influenced Thomas Kuhn's classic *The structure of scientific revolutions* which appeared just 1 year after Fleck's death,[4] it was not pre-destined to share a similar fame. One reason for the relative neglect of Fleck's work may be that he did not emphasize the revolutionary aspects of science (the sudden shifts in paradigms) as Kuhn did, but rather the slow and gradual transition from one 'scientific fact' to the next. Fleck identified a marked inertia or tenacity of scientists' belief systems ('*Beharrungstendenz der Meinungssysteme*') as responsible for the sluggishness of this transition. What is considered a fact by the scientific community would be protected against disconfirming evidence by various mechanisms, including passive neglect at early stages and later with active distortions. Specifically, Fleck identified three stages in scientists' protection of a certain belief: (1) any contradiction of an existing view seems unthinkable, and incompatibilities remain unnoticed; (2) reports with incompatible observations are suppressed or marginalized; and (3) a contradictory observation is interpreted, with great effort, as supporting the traditional view.[5] This latter stage was identified by Fleck as 'the liveliest stage of tenacity in systems of opinion' (p. 32) and explicitly equated with creative fiction, i.e. the construction of tall tales. The strong longing for a 'harmony of illusions' was made responsible for this cognitive inertia. Although Fleck's terminology may appear flowery from today's perspective, the examples he provided from actual medical research to illustrate each of the above stages are highly convincing. We here attempt to provide further examples of Fleck's scheme of the transition of an observation into a scientific fact, all taken from the history of research on aplasic phantoms.

The existence of aplasic phantoms: a nineteenth century observation

In 1836, physiologist Gabriel Gustav Valentin (1810–1883) published his observations on the 'Subjective sensations of persons born with incomplete extremities'.[6] He labelled 'sensations of integration' what we today call 'phantom sensations'. Such sensations have always fascinated both the popular and scientific mind (for a historical overview, see Finger and Hustwit[7]), but both during Valentin's and more modern times the investigative focus was almost exclusively on phantom limbs after amputation. To our knowledge, Valentin was the first to question persons with congenital limb deficiencies systematically about phantoms of their missing limbs. He was explicit about his reason for doing so: it was an attempt 'to definitely falsify the view that the integration would rely on certain memories of sensation' (p. 330). Apparently, the modern notion that phantom limbs could reflect sensorimotor 'memories' collected during the previous use of the respective limb was already popular in the early nineteenth century. In an examination of four persons born with one incomplete upper limb, he found that all reported phantom sensations which were qualitatively comparable with those described by amputees. For instance, one 19-year-old girl born without a left hand (shortened metacarpal bones, but no phalanges) noted the phantom presence of a regular palm including all five fingers. Valentin was not satisfied by this purely subjective report. He tried to 'objectify' it by administering several behavioural tasks. Thus, he provoked paraesthesias in some of the phantom fingers by prolonged pressure on certain nerves in the stump. As the pattern of innervation in the fingers could not be known by his subjects, the fact that tingling sensations were elicited in the 'correct' phantom fingers was taken as evidence for the genuineness of the reported phantoms. Valentin also designed a length estimation task, later reinvented for the same purpose by other authors.[8] Using the normally developed limb as a reference, subjects were required to indicate the length of the phantoms of their missing limbs. Repeated measurements allowed a systematic determination of the sizes and shapes of reported phantoms.

On the basis of these observations, Valentin concluded that '[the integration of sensation] by persons born with limb dysplasias teaches us that it is out of the question that they could be accounted for by memory or recollective imagery'[9] (p. 334). He speculated about the potential mechanisms of phantom sensations in his patients and proposed that peripheral and central nervous system factors were probably involved.[10] However, he was quick to caution scientists not to accept these speculations as 'an axiom, i.e. the beginning of our ignorance or the borderlines of our knowledge'[11] (p. 334).

Valentin's concern that his findings would be too readily received by the medical community turned out to be unjustified. For more than 100 years, his observations remained entirely neglected, and what was destined to live on instead was the pre-existing axiom that phantom sensations were perceptual–motor memories of limbs once owned. Interestingly, as outlined in the next section, one single sentence in an early twentieth century publication even helped to foster and widely spread the tacit assumption that aplasic phantoms do not exist.[12]

The non-existence of aplasic phantoms: a twentieth century theoretical paper

The First World War sadly provided the observations that allowed Czech neurologist Arnold Pick (1851–1924) to present an overview on pathologies of corporeal awareness.[13] The large number of soldiers injured during the first year of this war offered a 'mass opportunity' (p. 258) to describe various syndromes of distorted bodily perception. Some of these were brought about by brain damage, but Pick's main focus was the phenomenon of phantom limbs following the loss of an extremity. He argued that limbs, like other body parts, would be represented in the brain not only in primary sensory and motor areas, but also at higher associative levels and in a more abstract form. He cited evidence that this central representation of the body, the 'body schema', is continually restructured during a child's development. Acquired information about a limb (postural, tactile, kinaesthetic and visual) would be responsible for the emergence of phantom limbs after amputation—the physical part could be lost, but its representation would persist. To support his argument for the ontogenetic shaping of the body schema, but otherwise entirely parenthetically, Pick mentioned the following fact (the word he used!):

the absence of the phantoms discussed here in cases of congenital [aplasia] or after amputation experienced during early childhood. The amputated part has simply never been represented in the body schema of these particular persons (p. 260).

Nowhere in his text did he state that he had ever examined people with congenital limb deficiencies nor did he cite any empirical data that would have supported his claim. It was a casual note, but for some reason, Pick's 1915 publication was quickly adopted as the key reference to document the non-existence of phantoms in individuals with congenitally absent limbs.[14,15] American psychologist Marianne Simmel (born 1923) helped to spread Pick's reference across language borders.[16–18] She was the first to undertake large systematic case studies on persons with congenitally absent limbs, whose outcome did not convince her of the genuineness of aplasic phantoms (see later). She also complained that the scientific community had failed to notice that Pick's statement was not based on observation.[19] Her complaints may have provoked a sarcastic comment from Vetter and Weinstein:[20] they included Pick's 1915 paper in their tabulation of 19 studies containing data on the incidence of the phenomenon. Demonstratively, the table entry in the column 'total number of cases seen' was, beneath the reference to Pick, the number zero. However, many authors reiterating the claim of the non-existence of aplasic phantoms do not even appear to have read Pick's original report; at least implicitly they introduced it as an empirical study.

Clearly, Ludwik Fleck's description of the first stage in scientists' dealing with a theoretical anomaly is neatly illustrated: any contradiction to the existing view of phantoms as the perceptual correlate of the brain's remembering years of actual limb use seemed unthinkable, and the obvious incompatibilities communicated by Valentin remained unnoticed.[21]

Mild neglect: marginalization of the aplasic phantom

To our knowledge, the first case report on aplasic phantoms to follow those of Valentin was communicated more than three-quarters of a century later by Sohn.[22] His patient was a young woman born without a left forearm and hand (but finger rudiments attached to the stump; Fig. 21.1) who complained of pain in her missing hand.

Sohn, a neurologist by training, provided the following description of his patient's phantom sensations:

The patient, Miss S., a comely girl, aged nineteen years, came to us to be relieved from pain in the stump of her left forearm that had been amputated possibly in utero, a little below the elbow joint. She was free from pain until five years ago, when she began to complain of sticking pains in the stump. At first, the pain was slight, and came at long intervals. Then it began to increase in intensity and frequency, until she was troubled daily with these sharp pains that began in the stump and radiated downward to the fingers of the hand that she never had. She said: 'If the end of the stump was opened a hand would grow out of it, for I am sure there is something inside which wants to come out. It feels as though a lump inside is struggling to get out, and then there is this sticking pain which I feel all the way down to my *fingers*' (p. 960; italics in the original).

Fig. 21.1 Sohn's (1914) patient's forearm stump had at least four rudimental fingers attached to its tip. While the author dismissed her report of phantom fingers as wishful thinking, later studies with similar patients attributed such rudiments a potentially important role in the genesis of aplasic phantoms (see text).

Sohn, apparently unaware of Valentin's 1836 contribution, recognized the significance of his observation when he noted that all traditional theories on phantom sensations inevitably failed to account for the phantom sensations reported by his patient. However, his own attempts to explain the genesis of the girl's aplasic phantom remained unconvincing, at least from a neurological perspective. After having pointed out that the 'only mildly erotic' girl, whose 'libido is neither deep nor lasting' (p. 960) was obsessed with the idea that her deformity would act as a barrier to marriage, he concluded: 'Therefore I do not hesitate to assume that the subjective sensation of pain in the fingers and the consciousness of a hand are equivalent to a wish fulfilment' (p. 961).

With this 'explanation' of aplasic phantoms, i.e. wish fulfilment, stage 2 according to Fleck's scheme of the development of scientific facts was realized: an observation is no longer entirely suppressed, but its potential impact is only partially recognized and its significance thus downplayed. Specifically, recasting subjects' reports of concrete sensations into mere fantasies marginalized the phenomenon under investigation and thus removed any need to adjust the theory with which it seemed to conflict. We deal here with the issue of wishful thinking and suggestibility at some length, because these interpretations have often been forwarded in the literature on aplasic phantoms and are not entirely unfounded. We hope to show, however, that some characteristics of aplasic phantoms are hardly of a self-serving nature, and that simple methods exist to circumvent gross suggestibility effects in the investigation of phantom sensations.

As far as Sohn's comely girl is concerned, one is indeed tempted to wonder whether a *painful* phantom could ever be the result of wishful thinking. Similar concerns about the validity of the wish-fulfilment argument have been mentioned in the literature. Thus, Weinstein and Sersen noted that the relative over-representation of certain phantom parts over others (e.g. the hallux over the calf) could hardly be explained by differential psychological needs for different body parts.[8] They also stated that the report of one of their patient's of a vivid awareness of a phantom calf with two toes separated from one another by a gap could 'scarcely be considered a fantasy worth its salt' (p. 909). Likewise, Ramachandran introduced the case of a 20-year-old woman with both arms missing since birth.[23] He noted that the unnatural shortness of this woman's arm phantoms and the fact that they felt rigid rather than freely moveable argue against wish fulfilment as a phantom-generating factor. We entirely agree with these authors. As Skoyles correctly pointed out, however, the observation of a deformed or dysfunctional aplasic phantom does not only invalidate the argument of psychological needs, but clearly it is also not readily compatible with a genetic basis of body schema—'innate' limb representations would supposedly result in normal rather than distorted phantom limbs.[24]

One further observation seems at variance with the view of aplasic phantoms as mere wish-fulfilling fantasies. It is the triggering, in dysmelic persons, of the phantom percept by superficial injury to the stump. In three out of the four cases communicated by Saadah and Melzack, the very first occurrence of a phantom was induced by such peripheral stimulation.[25] One person, born without a left forearm and hand, had a horse riding accident at age 16. She lost her prosthesis and fell on the tip of her stump, which developed a small haematoma requiring minor surgery. Shortly afterwards, she became aware of a phantom forearm with a complete hand, including fingers—for the first time in her life. Although by no means common, the appearance of aplasic phantoms following stump injury suggests that previously dormant and competing representations may be released by 'overriding' the acquired representation of a limb which had been established and continuously reinforced by tactile and visual impressions'.[26] Such an interpretation was also provided for the first-time experience of aplasic phantom sensations after stump manipulations in a more controlled environment. Xue treated two persons with congenital limb dysplasia with acupuncture (for reasons unrelated to this condition).[27] On being needled in the left stump region, a 24-year-old woman with shortened forearms and deformed hands (wrists and thumbs missing) felt a sudden prolongation of her arm that took on the shape of a regular upper limb with a hand and five fingers (Fig. 21.2A). The other patient, also a 24-year-old woman, had been born with a left forearm measuring only 10 cm and ending in a cone-like stump with five tiny papillary prominences. Acupuncture produced a similar sensation of stump prolongation. However, when the phantom had reached an estimated length of 3 cm, the patient became so frightened that she refused to continue the stimulation procedure (Fig. 21.2B).

The view that aplasic phantoms are the product of an examiner's suggestive inquiry is somewhat related to the interpretation of aplasic phantoms as wishful thinking on the part of the patient. The power of suggestion is in fact known from accounts on phantom

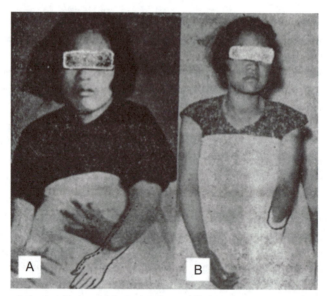

Fig. 21.2 In people born with incomplete or deformed limbs, phantom sensations are sometimes elicited after minor injuries to the stump. The two women shown here experienced phantom limbs, for the first time in their lives, during irritation of the arm stumps during acupuncture. (Reproduced, with permission, from Xue[27].)

limbs in adult amputees,[28] and the concerns raised by Skoyles appear especially warranted as they addressed early observations in *children* with congenital limb deficiencies.[8,24,28–31] Skoyles emphasized the high vulnerability of child testimony to leading questions and situational demands, including the 'length estimation game' to obtain measurements of the size of a phantom (see above). In 1990, Scatena approached the argument of suggestibility from a completely different angle.[32] He summarized previously published evidence that some parents were '*more* than unaware' (p. 1228) of their (aplasic or amputated) child's phantom sensations and would strongly discourage any report of such fantasies.[33]

Although the mere subjective report of aplasic phantoms does not establish them as a scientific fact, many behavioural investigations have ruled out suggestion as a major force in their genesis. Thus, we admire Valentin's selective provocation of paraesthesias in some, but not other, phantom fingers (see above). The elegance of this procedure is only matched by its simplicity. Alternative methods to demonstrate the reality of a subjective sensation while minimizing the potentially confounding effects of a subject's suggestibility will be discussed later.

From neglect to confabulation: theoretical accounts of the aplasic phantom

During the second half of the twentieth century, more case studies of aplasic phantoms surfaced in the literature. Some were single case studies, for instance Poeck's often cited report of an 11-year-old girl born without both forearms and hands who experienced

Table 21.1 Comprehensive list of published reports on aplasic phantoms; not included are cases of persons with limb aplasia who experienced phantom sensations only after major stump surgery

Studies	No. of phantoms/no. of aplasic persons examined	Cumulative no. of cases with aplasic phantoms
Sohn, 1914;[22] Mikorey, 1952;[36] Poeck, 1964[29]; Ramachandran, 1993;[23] Grouios, 1996;[37] Brugger et al., 2000[38]	1/1 each	6
Burchard, 1965[34]	1/17	7
Kooijman et al., 2000[39]	1/27	8
Simmel, 1961[17]	2/27	10
Xue, 1986[27]	2/2	12
Wilkins et al., 1998[40]	2/17	14
Valentin, 1836[6]	4/4	18
Saadah and Melzack, 1994[25]	7/75*	25
Weinstein and Sersen, 1961[8]	5/30	30
Weinstein et al., 1964[31]	13/71	43
Melzack et al., 1997[35]	15/76	58

*Only four of the seven cases reporting phantoms were described.

vivid phantom hands with a complete set of fingers that helped her to solve simple arithmetic problems at school.[29] However, beginning with Simmel ($n = 27$) and Weinstein and Sersen ($n = 30$), group studies were also published, which allowed the first rough estimation of the incidence of phantoms among persons with limb aplasia.[8,17] Different authors' estimates depended on the exact definition of what constituted a 'phantom' and varied between around 6 per cent (one out of Burchard's 17 subjects[34]) to 18 per cent (13 out of 71 subjects of Weinstein et al.[31]). This latter figure comes close to the 20 per cent incidence reported in the largest group study ever published (76 people born with absent or malformed limbs; 15 with phantoms).[35] Table 21.1 lists these and additional contributions and shows that, to date, between 50 and 60 cases of aplasic phantoms have been described.

One might think that these numerous observations which contradict the predominating theoretical notion of phantoms as perceptuomotor 'memories' would have prompted a revision of the theory to accommodate the observed facts. Instead, great efforts were undertaken to fit the observations to the traditional theory—Fleck's stage 3 of the transition of an observation to a scientific fact is realized.

Briefly, we provide three examples of attempts to explain aplasic phantoms within the framework of the traditional theory despite having opposing evidence available at the time. All three attempts did not incorporate the innate representation of body schema as a postural–kinaesthetic model of body shape and limb movement dynamics. It is not our intention to ridicule these attempts; we only wish to point out their common flaw, namely that the hypothesized mechanism could have been falsified by observations already available at the time of their formulation. This is what we mean by 'confabulation' in the present context: once neglect of contradictory data is surmounted, there is often a tendency hastily to create new 'theories' which do not readily promote global insights. In the context of the present volume, if a very big tall tale has been around for a long time, the creation of small tall tales often accompanies its demise.

Example one: the aplasic phantom as a product of stump characteristics

In 1961, Simmel interviewed 27 people with aplasia or dysplasia of the upper limbs about phantom sensations.[17] Two persons reported such sensations, both were 10-year-old girls. While the first girl was born with a completely absent forearm below the elbow (no finger rudiments attached to the stump), the second was born with an incomplete hand. Specifically, while a 'rudimentary thumb [was] present with some voluntary motion' (p. 469), the fingers were absent. Simmel dismissed the first girl's report about phantom finger sensations as due to the suggestive nature of the interview. She interpreted the second girl's report about finger phantoms (mainly the little finger) as an illusory extrapolation of enhanced thumb motility into extracorporeal space: 'The kinesthetic stimulation resulting from such abnormally great excursion may possibly provide a sufficient condition [...] which, under the special circumstances here, culminates in the experience of a "phantom finger"' (p. 470). Simmel was probably correct in pointing out that cases of completely absent limbs must be investigated separately from cases with rudimentary preservation of distal body parts attached to the stump ('intercalary aplasia'[41]). However, she failed to notice that her proposal was at variance with Valentin, who had explicitly stated 'I have to note here that the feelings of integration are more vivid in individuals who lack all peripheral parts, e.g. all fingers, than in those that are more completely organized in this regard, i.e. who still have a thumb or thumb plus first digit' (p. 331).[6] Thus, Simmel's proposal may at least have some theoretical validity with respect to the case published 1914 by Sohn (see Fig. 21.1).[22] It must inevitably fail, however, to account for the aplasic phantoms reported by people with complete aplasia of an entire limb.

Example two: the aplasic phantom as a representation of the contralateral limb

Burchard found indications for aplasic phantoms in only one out of the 17 cases examined[34] (two more persons reported having felt the congenitally absent hand during their dreams[42]). This individual was a 36-year-old woman born with a forearm only 9 cm long and with no hand. She occasionally felt a prolongation of the stump, so vivid that she would touch its physical tip to ascertain that the felt forearm was only a creation of her mind (note the similarity of this 'growing-out-of-the-stump phantom' with the cases of Sohn[22] and Xue,[27] described above). Fifteen of Burchard's patients had strictly unilateral limb defects (including the woman with the fleeting phantom percept), and the author speculated (p. 370) that aplasic phantoms would be mediated by information about the existing limb that reached the deafferented cortex from homotopic areas of the contralateral hemisphere. This idea was later elaborated on by Grouios, who introduced the case of a 12-year-old boy born without a right elbow and forearm and reporting phantom sensations of the missing hand and fingers.[37]

> It seems that the upper and lower limbs in people with congenital limb deficiency are linked in the brain as a result of frequent co-activation. Hence, sensory input of the left upper limb, for example, projects not only to the somatosensory cortex of the right cerebral hemisphere but—by identified or unidentified commissural pathways—to mirror-symmetrical points in the left cerebral hemisphere. It thus contributes to a weak formation of the cortical representation of the right upper limb' (pp. 503–504).

The conceptualization of an aplasic phantom as the phenomenal awareness of the mirror limb is not without experimental support from the literature on amputation phantoms,[43] from reports on referred sensations from a normal to an anesthetic hand[44] and from work on the cross-modal integration of somaesthetic and visual information in limb observation tasks.[45] However, the generalizability of this theory is limited; clearly, it cannot account for reports of aplasic phantoms in people with *bilateral* absence of upper and/or lower limbs.[8,25,29] We emphasize that the theoretical importance of cases of bilateral limb aplasia was already noted in this specific context by Valentin in the year of 1836.[6]

Example three: the aplasic phantom generated from a schema for hand-mouth coordination

A novel theoretical contribution to the issue of aplasic phantoms was provided 1998 by Gallagher *et al.*[46] These authors suggested a very specific mechanism for the formation of phantom percepts in individuals with limb aplasias, i.e. the activation of an innate schema for hand–mouth coordination. The empirical data on which Gallagher *et al.*'s proposal rests comes from investigations of human fetal behaviour. Not only are right upper limb preferences already determined at around 10 weeks of gestation,[47,48] but the precision of hand-to-mouth movements for thumb sucking, from their very first occurrence around week 12,[49] suggests an innate schema representing these movements. Gallagher *et al.* proposed that evocation of this schema coordinating the hand and mouth could give rise to sensations of a hand even in the absence of a hand; specifically, they suggested that activation of the mouth part of the schema would always be accompanied by activation of the hand part of the schema. 'Activation of the expanded face-representing neural map may also reactivate the indigenous limb-representing neurons and thus cause the phantom experience' (p. 59). We note that Gallagher *et al.* were the first to ground a hypothesis that an innate component of body schema is responsible for aplasic phantoms on empirical findings. However, these authors did not address cases of phantoms in persons with congenitally absent *lower* limbs. In fact, their tabular overview of published reports on aplasic phantoms meticulously and comprehensively lists cases of upper limb phantoms (explained by their theory) but omits cases of aplasic phantom legs and feet, even if these had been described by the same original authors.[31] Again, this theory may have its merits, but it clearly cannot account for all observational data from the clinical literature on aplasic phantoms.

An experimental approach to aplasic phantoms: the case of AZ

When I (PB) met AZ for the first time, I did not know what to think about the nature of the detailed and vivid phantom sensations she reported. The then 44-year-old university-educated woman had been born without forearms and legs (Fig. 21.3). Her upper arms are conically shaped and about 25 cm long. Importantly, they lack any appendages representing rudiments of more distal parts of an upper limb. X-rays confirmed the complete absence of both elbow joints. AZ skillfully uses her upper arms to steer her electric wheelchair, grasp objects, typewrite and eat (with the aid of a fork or spoon attached to a ring placed on her right upper stump). AZ's thighs measure about 10 cm long, are

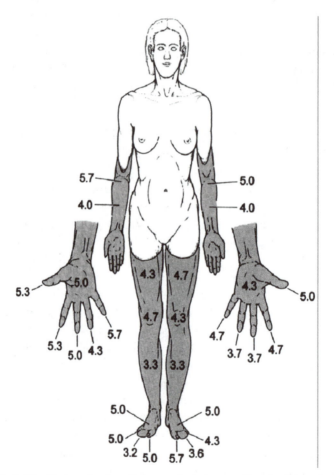

Fig. 21.3 Subject AZ with her phantom limbs as shaded areas. The numbers refer to vividness ratings for different parts of the phantom (from zero = no awareness to 6 = most vivid awareness). Note the more pronounced vividness for the right compared with the left hand and the lack of differentiation between the three middle toes that appeared 'lumped together' according to her report. (Reproduced from Brugger et al.[38])

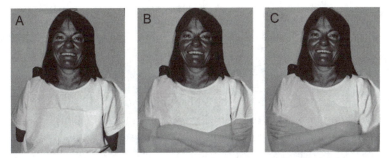

Fig. 21.4 Subject AZ (A) reported that she occasionally folded her phantom arms 'as normal people do'. Having folded them on command, she indicated that the left was on top of the right (B). On being asked to fold her phantom arms 'the other way round' (i.e. to put the right on top of the left; C) she immediately showed an expression of discomfort and commented that this posture 'feels extremely awkward'.

free from any rudimental appendages, and X-rays showed dysplasic hip articulations and very short proximal femurs.

AZ reports that she has been aware of a complete body for as long as she can remember. Specifically, she provided vividness ratings of different body parts that indicated greater awareness for hands and feet compared with lower arms and lower legs, and also seemed to reflect 'right-handedness'[50] (Fig. 21.3).

What convinced me that AZ's phantom sensations are more than a mere reflection of some unspecific, general body knowledge was the manner in which she folded her phantom arms. AZ indicated that she would spontaneously adopt a particular posture, although infrequently, during daily life.[51] When I requested that she deliberately fold her arms, she adopted the posture within seconds and answered my question as to which phantom arm was on top of the other without hesitation: the left rested on the right (Fig. 21.4B). I then asked her to fold the arms 'the other way around' such that the right arm would rest on the left. She did so, again within a few seconds, and spontaneously exclaimed: 'My gosh, I would never do it this way—this feels extremely awkward!' Nearly all individuals have a clear preference for arm folding, one option dominating the other almost 100 per cent of the time. It appears that AZ has a comparably strong preference, despite the physical impossibility, but consistent with evidence for a genetic basis of an individual's preferred pattern of arm folding.[52]

Apart from this anecdotal observation, a large number of more 'objective' data testify to the reality of AZ's aplasic phantoms. We briefly mention data pertaining to the functional neuroanatomy of AZ's phantoms. First, indications for a cortical representation of her hands and feet were obtained by functional magnetic resonance imaging (fMRI). Specifically, AZ's premotor and parietal cortices were activated bilaterally when she repeatedly moved her phantom hand while laying in the MRI scanner.[38] In contrast to observations in amputees,[53] the primary sensorimotor cortex remained silent during these phantom movements (but were activated by movements of the stumps). Secondly, we used transcranial magnetic stimulation (TMS), a procedure that allows the transient enhancement (or impairment, depending on the frequency of stimulation bursts) of functions of a circumscribed cortical area. We applied TMS over AZ's hand area of the sensorimotor cortex.[54] After each train of stimulation, we asked AZ to report any sensation she might feel in any part of her body, including her phantom body parts. TMS consistently elicited sensations in the contralateral phantom fingers and hand. The relationship between the stimulated scalp regions and the triggered phantom sensations did not disclose a well-organized somatotopic organization with distinct regions for fingers, hands and forearms as is the case in normal individuals, but instead a representation of phantom body parts dispersed over large parts of the cortex.[38]

We consider the findings from simple behavioural tasks to be more impressive evidence for the genuineness of AZ's aplasic phantoms than the results of these neuroimaging and neurophysiological investigations. For instance, we presented AZ with line drawings of hands and feet, with fingers and toes pointing either up or down.[38] The drawings were presented tachistoscopically on a computer screen, and AZ was required to press a left-sided response key with her left upper stump for pictures of left body parts and a right-sided key for right body parts. She solved this task as accurately as control persons and, importantly, her reaction times were much faster for hands and feet whose fingers and toes, respectively, pointed up than for those presented 'upside-down'. This differential reaction time effect was also observed in the control persons and has been documented in a large literature on laterality decisions to visually presented body parts.[55] It is interpreted as reflecting an implicit 'reaching' movement of the observer, i.e. the matching between the visually presented hand and a representation of one's own hand. This process is fast as long as the fingers are pointing upwards and one's own hand can easily match the pictured hand, as if slipping into a glove. However, an imagery rotation of one's hand is required when the drawing is rotated 180°, a time-consuming mental manipulation associated with longer decision times. The fact that AZ showed this rotation effect speaks for an intact representation of hands and feet in her parietal cortex, reportedly activated during similar hand laterality decision tasks in subjects born with intact bodies.[56] In 2001, these findings were replicated and significantly extended by Funk, who showed that AZ's hand laterality decisions were constrained by the biomechanical limitations of wrist joints, as is the case for individuals with a lifelong experience with physical wrist movements.[57] The performance of a person who was born without arms, but had never experienced any phantom sensations (CL), was not constrained by biomechanical limitations.[57]

The comparison of CL's (a 43-year-old journalist) with AZ's performance in a paradigm known as 'apparent motion of body parts'[58] also revealed intriguing findings. In this paradigm, subjects observe pairs of photographs depicting a human model. The two pictures of a pair differ from one another only in the posture of a single limb, for instance a hand in the sample stimulus in Fig. 21.5. If the two pictures are repeatedly flashed on the screen in rapid succession (with an interstimulus interval of less than half a second), observers will invariably perceive the limb move along the shortest trajectory of apparent motion, a trajectory which, however, is impossible to execute due to anatomical limitations. With longer interstimulus intervals, observers begin to perceive the trajectories that

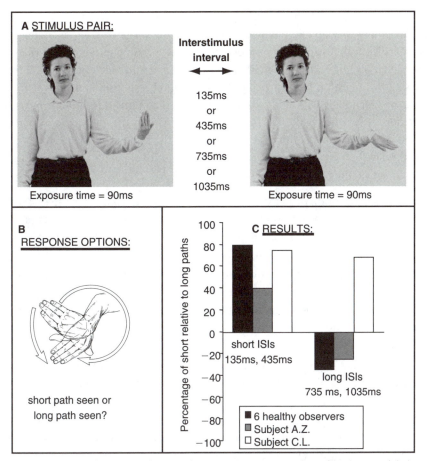

Fig. 21.5 Sample stimulus pair in the experiment on apparent motion of body parts (A), here of a hand around the wrist, with the response options (B). The performances of subjects born with intact bodies, as well as for AZ and CL (a man born with a body similar to AZ but without a history of phantom sensations) are shown (C; data from Funk et al.[60]). See text for explanation.

are biologically possible for a given limb. In other words, what is seen during high flash rates is entirely determined by the visual system; there is no dialogue with those regions of the brain that 'know' about the specific laws that constrain human limb movements. These laws determine one's apparent motion percept only when the brain is given enough time to integrate the purely visual with body schema information. In line with this interpretation, neuroimaging data have revealed motor and parietal cortex involvement at slow flash rates, but only visual cortex activation at brief interstimulus intervals.[59]

As shown in Fig. 21.5, AZ showed the same flash rate-dependent perception of short versus long apparent motion trajectories as individuals with limbs, while CL, who had never experienced phantom sensations of his congenitally absent arms or hands, perceived the short, anatomically impossible trajectories at all interstimulus intervals.[60] It thus appears that the subjective feeling of having arms and hands is more decisive for the behaviour in this task than is the physical development of these body parts. While these data show that aplasic phantom sensations can constrain the visual analysis of limb movements, they cannot address one of the most pressing questions, i.e. why some people with limb aplasia develop phantom sensations and others do not. We are currently addressing this question by comparing the behavioural responses and brain activation patterns of individuals with and without phantom sensations during limb movement observation. It is conceivable that individual differences in the automatic matching of observed movements to the imagined execution of the same movements[61] may play a role in the development of aplasic phantoms in a minority of people with limb aplasia.

Taken together, the results of our experiments with AZ ...

- ... allow a falsification of all three theoretical proposals to account for aplasic phantoms (see above), at least in their most general form: AZ has neither upper nor lower limbs, nor does she have any rudiments of distal body parts attached to her stumps, yet experiences phantoms of all missing body parts.

- ... rule out that her phantoms are the product of wishful thinking or 'pure' imagination; mere fantasies cannot account for preferred postural patterns of arm folding (Fig. 21.4) or the distinctive pattern in motor reaction times to picture body parts that reflect time-consuming, biomechanically constrained motor imagery processes.

- ... suggest that AZ's brain stores sensorimotor representations of hands and feet that are automatically activated during motor imagery conditions (fMRI experiments) and on visual observation of other people moving their limbs (experiment on apparent motion of body parts).

- ... do *not* solve the puzzle about the genesis of aplasic phantoms. They can only help to shape future empirical research.

Out on a limb: the balance between neglect of and confabulations about an observation

In this chapter, we attempted to illustrate Ludwik Fleck's scheme of the genesis of a 'scientific fact'[3] with examples from the literature on phantom sensations in people with congenitally missing limbs. This subject matter is a burning issue within the philosophy of science because currently held opinions on this topic still vastly diverge. Some scientists do not have any tale to tell about aplasic phantoms, while others report rather tall tales. The group one belongs to in this debate depends on one's inclination to attend to an observation that contradicts established knowledge. On the level of sensory detection, similar individual differences exist in observing an event pop out against a uniform background. Signal detection theory describes an observer's reaction towards a faint sensory signal as a function of his criterion to consider the signal as distinct from the sensory noise in which it is embedded.[62] In the context of scientific discovery, the 'signal' is an anomaly within an orderly theoretical framework. A conservative response criterion will hinder its detection—Fleck's 'tenacity of systems of opinion' comes into play (Fig. 21.6,

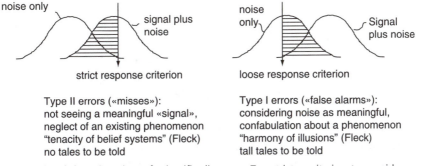

Fig. 21.6 A signal-detection view of scientific discovery. Too strict a criterion to consider a new observation as meaningful prevents scientists from making new discoveries (left-hand side). On the other hand, too loose a criterion leads to the hasty acceptance of an observation as a scientific fact and to the confabulatory overinterpretation of the existing evidence (right-hand side). Adopted from Brugger and Taylor.[63]

left panel). In contrast, a less conservative response criterion will prevent a scientist from missing an important anomaly, but this heightened awareness comes at a price, i.e. an enhanced susceptibility to assume the presence of an anomaly where in fact there is none, or to exaggerate the anomalous character of an observation (Fig. 21.6, right panel).

In the context of aplasic phantoms, Abramson and Feibel noted that some persons born without a limb may not report phantom sensations since they were not asked about their presence. 'That it [the phenomenon of aplasic phantoms] had not been more frequently observed would be puzzling were it not that physicians are least prone to ask about something that they cannot see, feel, hear, or smell' (p. 100).[64] We agree that the failure to ask questions most probably diminishes the frequency of positive responses. As surprising as it may seem, even twenty-first century authors do not necessarily consider it worthwhile to ask their subjects with limb amelia whether they had ever experienced phantom sensations.[65] Other authors did ask the question, and were quick to generalize from five participants' negative responses that phantom sensations are 'quite possibly nonexistent in congenital amputees' (p. 210).[26,66]

On the more confabulatory side of the tale about aplasic phantoms are overinterpretations of clinical and research findings. We again cite from Abramson and Feibel, who contended that '...a structural basis for the phantom experience is encoded in the DNA. We are born with a full-blown potential for imaging body parts' (p. 99).[64] Although a genetic component of body schema was proposed (see especially Melzack[67]), we have to be aware that agreement about the genuineness of aplasic phantoms does not automatically imply agreement about a genetic basis of corporeal awareness. Even if an infant's aplasic phantoms could ever be 'objectified' a few moments after birth, this should not necessarily be taken as evidence for a genetic hard-wiring of a four-limbed body; 'innate' must not be equated with 'genetically determined'. As alluded to earlier, there is an extensive limb use during fetal life, and the possibility that a representation of a physically absent limb may be formed *in utero* by use of the contralateral limb cannot be dismissed.

As persons with aplasic phantoms most frequently indicate that they had been aware of phantom sensations for as long as they can remember, the first few years of life may be decisive, even in cases of bilateral aplasia. Concretely, early experience with functional prosthetic devices must be considered as an important factor for the formation of an awareness of limbs.[31,68] We have also mentioned potential contributions of a neuronal system matching action observation and action execution. There is in fact anecdotal clinical evidence for phantom limb sensations being triggered by the observation of other people moving their limbs (amputation phantoms, Henderson and Smith;[69] aplasic phantoms, Melzack et al.[35]). However, the crossmodal visual–somaesthetic genesis of phantom limbs by long-term limb observation cannot dictate the presence or absence of phantom sensations. After all, not all sighted persons with limb aplasia report aplasic phantoms.[70]

These issues illustrate that research on the nature of aplasic phantoms would greatly benefit from a close collaboration between scientists from different disciplines such as embryology, developmental psychology and cognitive neuroscience. There *is* a tale to be told here, but it should be told in the tradition of Valentin, who in all modesty stated that his own contribution was to introduce 'the facts that mattered to physiology and psychology equally importantly (p. 329)' and without confabulatory explanations.[6,71]

Acknowledgements

This chapter celebrates the foundation of the Ludwik Fleck Zentrum at the Collegium Helveticum in Zürich, July 7, 2005. Part of the work described here was funded by the Swiss National Science Foundation (grant no. 3100-67168.01 to PB). We thank Kristen I. Taylor (Basel) and Marianne Regard (Zürich) for helpful comments.

References and notes

1. Although somewhat imprecise, we will use this term instead of the more accurate, but rather lengthy expression 'phantoms of people with limb aplasia'. 'Aplasia' indicates that an organ or tissue did not develop. Related terms are amelia/dysmelia, which refer to the complete/partial absence of skeletal parts of a limb, and phocomelia, indicating the attachment of a hand/foot directly to the trunk or to the upper arm/leg. For an overview on the classification and incidence of various congenital limb deficiencies, see Froster-Iskenius UG, Baird PA. Amelia: incidence and associated defects in a large population. *Teratology*, 1990; 41:23–31.
2. **Cohen RS, Schnelle T.** (ed.) *Cognition and fact. Materials on Ludwik Fleck.* Reidel, Dordrecht, The Netherlands, 1986.
3. **Fleck L.** *Genesis and development of a scientific fact.* University of Chicago Press, Chicago/London. 1979 (original: *Entstehung und Entwicklung einer wissenschaftlichen Tatsache. Einführung in die Lehre vom Denkstil und Denkkollektiv.* Schwabe, Basel, Switzerland. 1935).
4. **Kuhn T.** *The structure of scientific revolutions.* University of Chicago Press, Chicago. 1962.
5. 'wird mittels grosser Kraftanstrengung dem Systeme nicht widersprechend erklärt'
6. **Valentin G.** Über die subjectiven Gefühle von Personen, welche mit mangelhaften Extremitäten geboren sind. *Repertorium für Anatomie und Physiologie*, 1836; 1:328–337.
7. **Finger S, Hustwit MP.** Five early accounts of phantom limb in context: Paré, Descartes, Lemos, Bell, and Mitchell. *Neurosurgery*, 2003; 52:675–686.

8. **Weinstein S, Sersen EA.** Phantoms in cases of congenital absence of limbs. *Neurology*, 1961; **11**:905–911.

9. „... so lehren die an den mit verstümmelten Extremitäten Geborenen evident, dass von Gedächtnis- oder Erinnerungsvorstellungen bei eben dieser Erscheinung gar nicht die Rede sein kann.'

10. We had hoped to be able to summarize Valentin's theoretical thoughts in more detail. We must admit, however, that the neurophysiological terminology used during the first half of the nineteenth century was not entirely penetrable to us.

11. Literally, the full passage reads: 'Das Letztere ist zu merkwürdig, als dass man sich damit begnügen sollte, den so paradoxen aber durch die mannigfachsten Erfahrungen so fest begründeten Satz als Axiom, d.h. den Anfang unserer Unwissenheit oder die Grenze unseres Wissens aufzustellen'. Note Valentin's colourful definition of the term 'axiom', which already acknowledges the relativity of a 'scientific fact'!

12. It is rarely possible to track down the origin of a 'tall tale' with a precision comparable with the one of the myth that aplasic phantoms do not exist (see, however,[18]). We know of only one instance, the 'Popeye spinach myth', whose unique source is even less ambiguous (Skrabanek P, McCormick J. *Follies and fallacies in medicine.* Tarragon Press, Glasgow. 1989).

13. **Pick A.** Zur Pathologie des Bewusstseins vom eigenen Körper. Ein Beitrag aus der Kriegsmedizin. *Neurologisches Centralblatt*, 1915; **34**:257–265.

14. **Cronholm B.** Phantom limbs in amputees. *Acta Psychiatrica et Neurologica Scandinavica*, 1951; **72**:1–310.

15. **Weiss AA.** The phantom limb. *Annals of Internal Medicine*, 1956; **44**:668–677.

16. **Simmel M.** On phantom limbs. *Archives of Neurology and Psychiatry*, 1956; **75**:637–647.

17. **Simmel ML.** The absence of phantoms for congenitally missing limbs. *American Journal of Psychology*, 1961; **74**:467–470.

18. In fact, Simmel's 1961 article 'The absence of phantoms for congenitally missing limbs' (*American Journal of Psychology*, **74**:467–470) was later erroneously cited by Ramachandran and Hirstein as the historical origin of the myth regarding the absence of aplasic phantoms (Ramachandran VS, Hirstein W. The perception of phantom limbs: the D.O. Hebb Lecture. *Brain*, 1998; **121**:1603–1630).

19. **Simmel ML.** Developmental aspects of the body scheme. *Child Development*, 1966; **37**:83–95.

20. **Vetter RJ, Weinstein S.** The history of the phantom in congenitally absent limbs. *Neuropsychologia*, 1967; **5**:335–338.

21. Interestingly, Valentin's (1836[6]) thoughts were received outside of the mainstream scientific literature. The German philosopher Carl du Prel (1839–1899) discussed them at length in his half-visionary, half-occult monography on the nature of the human soul (Du Prel C. *Die monistische Seelenlehre. Ein Beitrag zur Lösung des Menschenrätsels.* Ernst Günthers Verlag, Leipzig. 1888).

22. **Sohn DL.** The psychic complex in congenital deformity. *New York Medical Journal*, 1914; **100**:959–961.

23. **Ramachandran VS.** Behavioral and magnetoencephalographic correlates of plasticity in the adult human brain. *Proceedings of the National Academy of Sciences, USA*, 1993; **90**:10413–10420.

24. **Skoyles JR.** Is there a genetic component to body schema? *Trends in Neuroscience*, 1990; **13**:409.

25. **Saadah ES, Melzack R.** Phantom limb experiences in congenital limb-deficient adults. *Cortex*, 1994; **30**:479–485.

26. **Flor H, Elbert T, Mühlnickel W, Pantev C, Wienbruch C, Taub E.** Cortical reorganization and phantom phenomena in congenital and traumatic upper-extremity amputees. *Experimental Brain Research*, 1998; **119**:205–212.

27. **Xue C-C.** Acupuncture induced phantom limb and meridian phenomenon on acquired and congenital amputees. *Chinese Medical Journal*, 1986; **99**:247–252.

28. According to an anecdotal report (Hebb DO. The American Revolution. *American Psychologist*, 1960;**15**:735–745), a surgeon, upset by 'unrealistic complaints' about phantom sensations, used to prepare his patients for an amputation with the following words: 'Tomorrow morning I am going

to cut your leg off, and it's going to be *off*, understand? And no damned nonsense about it' (p. 741). He received significantly (1 per cent significance level) fewer reports of postoperative phantoms compared with without these instructions. We dare to suggest that in this context the number of *reports about* a phenomenon is a weak indicator of the *actual prevalence* of the phenomenon.

29. **Poeck K.** Phantoms following amputation in early childhood and in congenital absence of limbs. *Cortex*, 1964; 1:269–275.

30. **Poeck K.** Phantome nach Amputation und bei angeborenem Gliedmassenmangel. *Deutsche Medizinische Wochenschrift*, 1969; **94**:2367–2374.

31. **Weinstein S, Sersen EA, Vetter RJ.** Phantoms and somatic sensation in cases of congenital aplasia. *Cortex*, 1964; 1:276–290.

32. **Scatena P.** Phantom representations of congenitally absent limbs. *Perceptual and Motor Skills*, 1990; 70:1227–1232.

33. Such parental discouragement also inhibited AZ, the aplasic person we ourselves have been working with (see later), from talking about her phantoms during childhood.

34. **Burchard JM.** Zur Frage nach der Natur von Phantomerlebnissen bei angeborener Gliedmassenverstümmelung. *Archiv für Psychiatrie und Nervenkrankheiten*, 1965; **207**:360–377.

35. **Melzack R, Israel R, Lacroix R, Schultz G.** Phantom limbs in people with congenital limb deficiency or amputation in early childhood. *Brain*, 1997; **120**:1603–1620.

36. **Mikorey M.** *Phantome und Doppelgänger*. JF Lehmanns, Munich. 1952.

37. **Grouios G.** Phantom limb perceptuomotor 'memories' in a congenital limb child. *Medical Science Research*, 1996; 24:503–504.

38. **Brugger P., Kollias SS, Müri RM, Crelier G, Hepp-Reymond M-C, Regard M.** Beyond re-membering: phantom sensations of congenitally absent limbs. *Proceedings of the National Academy of Sciences, USA*, 2000; **97**:6167–6172.

39. **Kooijman CM, Dijkstra PU, Geertzen JHB, Elzinga A, van der Schans CP.** Phantom pain and phantom sensations in upper limb amputees: an epidemiological study. *Pain*, 2000; **87**:33–41.

40. **Wilkins KL, McGrath PJ, Finley GA, Katz J.** Phantom limb sensations and phantom limb pain in child and adolescent amputees. *Pain*, 1998; **78**:7–12.

41. **O'Rahilly R.** Morphological patterns in limb deficiencies and duplications. *American Journal of Anatomy*, 1951; **89**:135–193.

42. The issue of phantom sensations during dreams has been addressed by many authors writing about aplasic phantoms, beginning with Valentin (1836). A detailed study of the phenomenon in amputees is found in Frank B, Lorenzoni E. Experiences of phantom limb sensations in dreams. *Psychopathology*, 1989; 22:182–187.

43. **Jacobson E.** Electrical measurements of neuromuscular states during mental activities. VI: A note on mental activities concerning an amputated limb. *American Journal of Physiology*, 1931; **96**:122–125.

44. **Sathian K.** Intermanual referral of sensation to anesthetic hands. *Neurology*, 2000; **54**:1866–1868.

45. **Funk M, Brugger P.** Visual recognition of hands by persons born with only one hand. *Cortex*, 2002; **38**:860–863.

46. **Gallagher S, Butterworth G, Lew A, Cole J.** Hand–mouth coordination, congenital absence of limb, and evidence for innate body schemas. *Brain and Cognition*, 1998; **38**:53–65.

47. **Hepper PG, McCartney GR, Shannon EA.** Lateralized behaviour in first trimester human foetuses. *Neuropsychologia*, 1998; **36**:531–534.

48. **Hepper PG, Wells DL, Lynch C.** Prenatal thumb sucking is related to postnatal handedness. *Neuropsychologia*, 2005; **43**:313–315.

49. **DeVries JIP, Visser GHA, Prechtl HFR.** Fetal motility in the first half of pregnancy. In Prechtl HFR, ed. *Continuity of neural functions from prenatal to postnatal life*. Spastics International Medical Publications. 1984:46–64.

50. Various action imagery tasks confirmed a better representation of right- compared with left hand use (see Poeck K. Zur Psychophysiologie der Phantomerlebnisse. *Nervenarzt*, 1963; **34**:241–256, for

opposite findings in a case of aplasic phantoms of both upper limbs). Moreover, AZ consistently holds a pen with the right side of her mouth while writing. Tachistoscopic testing indicated a left hemisphere dominance for language. In this context, we would like to comment on the potential importance of hemispheric dominance for language in people born with only one hand: preliminary data suggest a regular left hemispheric superiority in those born without a left limb, but an absence thereof in people born without a right upper limb (Brugger and Funk, in preparation). These data may help to answer fundamental questions about the ontogenesis and possible co-evolution of right-handedness and language lateralization (Corballis MC. From hand to mouth: gesture, speech, and the evolution of right-handedness. *Behavioral and Brain Sciences*, 2003; **26**:199–260).

51. Similar observations exist of leg amputees' habit to cross their legs (e.g. Riddoch G. Phantom limbs and body shape. *Brain*, 1941; **64**:197–222).

52. **McManus IC, Mascie-Taylor CGN.** Hand clasping and arm-folding: a review and a genetic model. *Annals of Human Biology*, 1979; **6**:527–558.

53. **Ersland LG, Rosén G, Lundervold A, Smievoll AI, Tillung T, Sundberg H, Hugdahl K.** Phantom limb imaginary fingertapping causes primary motor cortex activation: an fMRI study. *NeuroReport*, 1996; **8**:207–210.

54. The existence of anatomically preserved hand knobs in AZ's primary sensorimotor cortex is by no means self-evident. Early neuroanatomical studies indicated sensorimotor cortex atrophy in the hemisphere contralateral to a congenitally missing hand (Gowers WR. The brain in congenital absence of one hand. *Brain*, 1879; **1**:386–390) or at the level of the spinal cord in a case of congenital absence of all four limbs (Nordmann M, Lindemann K. Tetraperomelie und Zentralnervensystem. *Virchows Archiv für Pathologische Anatomie und Physiologie und für klinische Medizin*, 1940; **306**:175–182). While these early reports are compatible with more recent observations (e.g. Stoeckel MC, Jörgens S, Witte OW, Seitz RJ. Reduced somatosensory hand representation in thalodomide-induced dysmelia as revealed by fMRI. *European Journal of Neuroscience*, 2005; **21**:556–562), other authors did not find any structural abnormalities in the brains of people with congenitally absent limbs (e.g. Hamzei F, Liepert J, Dettmers C, Adler T, Kiebel S, Rijntjes M, Weiller C. Structural and functional abnormalities after upper limb amputation during childhood. *NeuroReport*, 2001; **12**:957–962). To our knowledge, more fine-grained, morphometric analyses of cortical hand areas in people born without hands and, importantly, *as a function of presence/absence of aplasic phantoms*, have not yet been performed.

55. **Sekiyama K.** Kinesthetic aspects of mental representations in the identification of left and right hands. *Perception and Psychophysics*, 1982; **32**:89–95.

56. **Bonda E, Petrides M, Frey S, Evans A.** Neural correlates of mental transformations of the body-in-space. *Proceedings of the National Academy of Sciences, USA*, 1995; **92**:11180–11184.

57. **Funk M.** Mentale Rotation von Händen und körperfremden Objekten: Untersuchungen mit Kindern und Erwachsenen mit und ohne kongenitalem Handmangel. Unpublished diploma thesis. Department of Experimental and Developmental Psychology, University of Zürich. 2001.

58. **Shiffrar M, Freyd JJ.** Apparent motion of the human body. *Psychological Science*, 1990; **1**:257–264.

59. **Stevens JA, Fonlupt P, Shiffrar M, Decety J.** New aspects of motion perception: selective neural encoding of apparent human movements. *NeuroReport*, 2000; **11**:109–115.

60. **Funk M, Shiffrar M, Brugger P.** Hand movement observation by individuals born without hands: phantom limb experience constrains visual limb perception. *Experimental Brain Research*, 2005; **164**:341–346.

61. **Rizzolatti G, Fogassi L, Gallese V.** Neurophysiological mechanisms underlying the understanding and imitation of action. *Nature Reviews Neuroscience*, 2001; **2**:661–670.

62. **Tanner WP, Swets JA.** A decision making theory of visual detection. *Psychological Review*, 1954; **61**:401–409.

63. **Brugger P, Taylor KI.** ESP: Extrasensory perception or effect of subjective probability? *Journal of Consciousness Studies*, 2003; **10**:221–246.
64. **Abramson AS, Feibel A.** The phantom phenomenon: its use and disuse. *Bulletin of the New York Academy of Medicine*, 1981; **57**:99–112.
65. For recent under-documentation see Nico D, Daprati E, Rigal F, Parsons L, Sirigu A. Left and right hand recognition in upper limb amputees. *Brain*, 2004; **127**:120–132.
66. The other extreme is exemplified in statements such as 'the majority of congenitally missing limb patients report phantom sensations' (Kamping S, Lütkenhöner B, Knecht S. Shifting of cortical somatosensory areas in a man with amelia. *NeuroReport*, 2004; **15**:2365–2368, p. 2365), without providing a single reference to any study that would support this claim (but, instead, to half a dozen studies denying the existence of aplasic phantoms).
67. **Melzack R.** Phantom limbs and the concept of a neuromatrix. *Trends in Neurosciences*, 1990; **13**:88–92.
68. **Price EH.** A critical review of congenital phantom limb cases and a developmental theory for the basis of body image. *Consciousness and Cognition*, 2006; **15**:310–322.
69. **Henderson WF, Smyth GE.** Phantom limbs. *Journal of Neurology, Neurosurgery, and Psychiatry*, 1948; **11**:88–112.
70. **Abramson and Feibel** (1981, p.101; [64]) pointed out that only an aplasic person with phantoms who was born blind could invalidate the view that visual signals would be decisive in shaping the aplasic phantom experience.
71. 'Ich begnügte mich, die für Physiologie und Psychologie gleich wichtigen Facta nackt hinzustellen, ohne mich auf kritische Beleuchtung oder Erfindung von Erklärungsversuchen einzulassen'.

Chapter 22

Imagery and blindness

Cesare Cornoldi and Rossana DeBeni

When we speak of mental images we refer to representations of objects in our mind and typically to representations experienced in a visuospatial form. Think of your last holiday or a beautiful scenario, for example a sunset on the beach, with white sand and green palm trees bending towards the water: is the image vividly present in your mind? Can you see the palms, the sea, the sun? Even if your image can include the memory of other sensory experiences, the sound of the waves, the salty smell of the sea and the feel of the fresh air on your skin, the most salient aspects of your image are surely associated with what you saw. By definition, this central portion of the image is visual and seems to be based on the visual experience, which is not, however, available to the totally congenitally blind. Thus an apparently logical consequence would be that *blind people cannot have mental images*. However, this is in fact a myth since a modern concept of mental imagery is less strict in placing the visual experience as the necessary condition for the ability to generate mental images. This latter idea is also based on the observation that blind people themselves report having mental images and on the widely spread assumption that humans tend to compensate for their deficits. The latter assumption has generated an opposite paradoxical myth whereby *blind people may have mental images as clear as, as efficient as or even better than sighted people*.

The mental image concept

Mainly based on sensory experiences, we may represent (imagine) objects and contexts in the visuospatial component of our working memory system in a format which shares many features with perceptions. In many circumstances of our life, the retrieval and generation of mental images from memory represents a useful tool, such as, for example, when we orient ourselves in a familiar environment using a visuospatial mental map, or when—before leaving for a holiday—we imagine the optimal luggage arrangement in the boot of the car.

Mental images have been considered very similar to percepts in our mind. A debate is still running on the hypothesis that imagery and perception share not only functional properties but also common mechanisms. This hypothesis has guided the revival of studies on mental imagery in the second part of the twentieth century. The analogical view of perception and imagery was supported by results deriving from the execution of certain mental operations using imaginal and perceptual representations. The mental rotation of visuospatial configurations[1] or tasks requiring the mental scanning of imagined stimuli showed that visual mental images are subject to the constraints of the physical world. However, according to a constructive view of mental imagery,[2] a mental image is less modality specific than the corresponding perception. Furthermore, the content of the evoked mental images may consist of more layers than the corresponding sensory perception. Thus we could imagine a dear friend or the long hours before obtaining a result of an exam with deep emotional involvement, and hence produce a specific emotional mental image, but also reconstruct it as a mental image involving many modalities simultaneously. The constructivist view of mental imagery is not particularly popular either in common sense or scientific psychology: based on a strong analogical view, people tend to think that individuals who have never had a visual experience cannot generate a type of image sharing the same properties with the mental images sighted people experience as visuospatial images (we will refer to them in this chapter with the simple expression of 'mental images').

The case of totally congenitally blind individuals

The issue of mental imagery and blindness is particularly critical in the case of individuals both congenitally and totally blind. In this case, no visual trace based on visual experience is stored in the person's memory. If mental imagery is based on the mechanisms and on the contents of visual sensory experiences, blind people should not be able to generate mental images.

This, however, contrasts with congenitally blind people often reporting imagery rich in visual elements. There have also been reports showing that blind people tend to use linguistic expressions referring to a visual experience (e.g. 'I lost sight of you' or 'See you tomorrow') more often than sighted people do, including expressions which directly refer to a visual act (e.g. 'Let's go and watch TV'). Blind people's dreams also often include visual elements.[3] One blind person, for example, told us of their anxiety after a dream in which they clearly saw a disturbing puddle of blood on a concrete floor. Is it possible for someone who has never seen with their physical eyes, nonetheless to be able to see with their mind's eye?

Mental imagery is a subjective experience defined by specific phenomenological properties. However, the impression of having a mental image is not proof that a specific representation with imaginal properties has in fact been generated. It has been suggested that mental images are penetrable, i.e. affected by the ideas people have of their representations.[4,5] Fastame *et al.*[6] stressed that, in order to demonstrate that blind people process and use mental images, it is not sufficient to believe in their assertions, even if these are detailed descriptions of what they can mentally represent. Hence, in order to argue that congenital blindness does not prevent the use of mental imagery, convergent evidence is needed. First, it is necessary to show that mental representations generated in the absence of a visual experience share the same properties with mental images created by sighted individuals. Secondly, it is necessary that the absence of vision produces specific predictions concerning peculiar features and limitations which can be found in the blind but not in the sighted people's mental images.

In conclusion, the interest in studying mental imagery in totally congenitally blind individuals offers the possibility not only of knowing the mental world of the blind, but also to understand whether it is really possible for people without a visual experience to generate mental images and, if so, which are the specific features of those images.

Experimental studies of mental imagery in the blind

To develop experimental studies of mental imagery in the blind, one of the first objectives that cognitive psychologists had to achieve was to design tasks requiring mental imagery strategies in which congenitally blind people could be compared with sighted individuals. This issue was tackled by several researchers, by adapting cognitive experimental paradigms for use with blind people.

The development of new specific experimental tasks largely contributed to the investigation of mental imagery in congenital blindness. For instance, a meaningful contribution came from a methodology that requires firstly a tactile exploration of the stimuli and then the creation of a mental representation that is stored in visuospatial working memory. By using this experimental procedure, many authors have showed that the tactile exploration of a pattern of stimuli is sufficient to generate mental images in congenitally blind people.[7,8]

Other researchers investigated the qualitative aspects characterizing mental images processed by blind and sighted people.[3,9,10] For instance, it was found that in carrying out mental rotation tasks, the performance of blind people is subject to the same characteristics as that of the sighted, i.e. the time taken in order to judge the identity of two spatial configurations differently oriented in the third dimension depends on the size of the angle required for rotating the figure in order to make them overlap.[11] Furthermore, it was found that memory organization of items based on perceptual features, mental scanning and colour representations produced similar patterns of performance both in the blind and in the sighted.[10]

The use of mental imagery in word recall

Do the blind have mental images? If so, are those images identical to the images generated by the sighted and do they give the same type of memory advantage?

In the study of imagery and blindness, one of the main areas studied by experimental psychologists and by ourselves concern memory.[12] This particular area of research was the focus of a long research project we started about 30 years ago. Our first goal was to see if the use of mental imagery would facilitate memory in blind people to the same degree as in sighted people. To achieve this aim, we used a number of different experimental approaches. One of these consisted of asking blind and sighted people to imagine a number of objects placed in a series of locations. For example, participants were asked to imagine a newspaper in a post office, a shirt in a church and a mug at a crossroads. We would then mention the location and ask participants to remember the corresponding object. We thus found that the use of mental imagery facilitated memory to the same extent both in the blind and in the sighted participants.

Another experimental scenario required participants to form bizarre images which would establish a relationship between two objects. In another still, we suggested the use of a 'chain mnemonic technique' in which a series of words presented are remembered by forming an image relating two words/elements at a time. So, for example, given the series of words 'table, train, cat, flower, stone etc.', participants are invited to imagine a train placed on a table, a train running over a cat, a cat smelling a flower, and so forth.

All these mnemonic procedures were used equally successfully by blind and sighted individuals, the former amply reporting the use of mental imagery throughout.

When we asked participants how it was possible for them to have such precise mental images given they were unable to see, the standard response was: 'Well doctor, *you* can have a somewhat imprecise picture of the train station, because once you are there, looking at it, you can check it and resolve the inconsistencies. But we have to have an extremely clear image of it, or else we get lost'.

However, due to the type of experience blind people can have, some stimuli, i.e. concrete words evoking a mental image of an object actually experienced by the blind person (i.e. with HI, high imagery value) produce a better performance than stimuli that can evoke a mental image but that cannot be associated with a direct personal experience, for example the item 'tower' (HINE, high imagery not experienced).[13]

The pattern of results found in the HINE condition was further investigated by De Beni and Cornoldi[14] and Tinti et al.[15] These researchers replicated the early findings confirming that blind people have difficulty in recalling HINE words, but, if we take into account their limited knowledge of the world, their performance was less impaired than expected.

In another series of studies, differences between sighted and blind participants in the use of mental imagery was investigated by comparing their performance in recalling sequences of verbal information. It is well known that the loci mnemonics—which consists of imagining locating a series of stimuli along a well known path—improves memory performance and offers the possibility of preserving information as regards the material's order of presentation. Do blind people have the same type of advantage? Are they able to imagine pathways and associate locations with to-be-memorized items? Is this advantage also present if a location must be imagined interacting with more than one item? In a series of studies,[14,16] we asked sighted and blind participants to use loci mnemonics in order to retrieve a list of 20 single, pair or triplets of words. Each single, pair or triplet had to be imagined interacting with a different location along a mental pathway. We found that non-sighted people took advantage of the loci mnemonic technique to the same extent as the sighted participants, both showing an advantage when using this technique as compared with a word rehearsal strategy. Moreover, although the congenitally blind participants could generate complex interactive mental images, they had difficulty in creating a single mental representation containing different stimuli. The difficulty met by the blind in memorizing triplets was not due to a generic increase in the memory request. In fact, according to Tinti and colleagues,[15] when complex mental images are processed and used in an auditory format, non-sighted people are not impaired.

Mental imagery and spatial configuration recall

Another area of study with the congenitally blind concerns their use of mental images in the recall of spatial arrays, for example processing of mental pathways and memory for locations in matrices (e.g. 4 × 4, 5 × 5 matrices, etc.). It has been shown with sighted participants[17] that in this type of task visualization produces a better performance than language. For example, it is easier to memorize a location in a 5 × 5 matrix rather than memorizing its verbal description (the second cell in the third row...). It has been shown that blind people can be as good as the sighted in this type of task.[17,18] These results help to reject the hypothesis that the blind individual's memory performance is improved by the use of mental images because the depth of processing is increased rather than by the fact that they use specific representations.

More recently,[19] we have even been able to show a superiority of the blind over the sighted in the memorization of an actual pathway explored with the aid of a stick (sighted participants were blindfolded). The pathway consisted of a 15 m trail composed of six segments of different lengths, forming a total of five 90° angles. Having reached the end of the trail, participants had to return directly to their supposed starting point and then point to various locations specifying the distance from their own. Participants were also asked to draw the path. In all these aspects, the congenitally and totally blind individuals performed significantly better than the sighted.

It could be argued that the blind are more familiar with exploring their surroundings using this method, thus placing the sighted individuals at a disadvantage. If no specific advantage pertaining to blindness existed, but there was simply an advantage in the exploratory process in the dark, the non-congenitally but totally blind individuals should show the best performance on this task, since they would benefit both from having had the experience of vision, thus helping in the formation of adequate spatial representations, and from the experience of exploratory behaviour in darkness. Having checked this aspect, the authors found there was no difference between the congenitally and non-congenitally totally blind individuals, but both were superior in this task to the sighted individuals.

These results relate back to a traditional concept frequently associated with a common-sensical view, which maintains the existence of compensatory mechanisms for specific handicaps. According to this framework, persons with a specific cognitive handicap may be able to develop certain competencies in other substitute areas, to compensate for their deficiencies. In the past decades, the 'compensatory' concept sparked a number of criticisms. For example, it was objected that to insist on the idea of compensation was neither kind nor appropriate because it emphasized the idea of a deficit needing compensation. Furthermore, given that certain capabilities form the basic characteristics of individuals, it was considered rather naive that it would be possible to alter them in any significant way. These objections have been gradually overcome especially by a more pragmatic and realistic view which conceives of an individual's capabilities as the result of the interaction between basic characteristics and the environment. Furthermore, reporting on the compensatory mechanism is now limited to specific cases. In accordance with results reported with blind people, Ronberg showed the extraordinary competencies developed by (certain, but not all) deaf people in the comprehension of non-verbal communication and lip-reading.[20]

The constructivist theory of generated images

How can we best explain the apparently paradoxical results regarding the image pro-duction of blind people? A first, impulsive, reaction may be to return to a propositional theory whereby blind people are as capable as the sighted in producing mental images because, in fact, mental images do not exist. In other words, images exist only as subjective experiences (given that no one can question that man does in fact have the experience of a mental image), but does not exist as a mental function. This position would not, however, be justified given the many results both qualitative and quantitative showing that when we imagine we are actually doing something different from when we are simply thinking without imagining.

The alternative is a corrected version of the analogical theory where the view that a mental image is identical to either the one perceived or that left immediately after observation, is abandoned. In other words, the perception of the table we may have at present and the image we may have of it from the immediately preceding perception are different from the image we may generate, using the elements from memory. In the latter case, the imagination uses elements derived from previous experiences in a constructive manner.

Using the example of the table, try to imagine not having seen it for a while and that you must build its image in mind. Are you sure the image will correspond to the perceived object? Surely it will be imprecise, perhaps poorer in perceptual detail but richer in associations. Are you sure you will use only visual elements? Probably without realizing you will also take into consideration motor experiences such as your movement around the table, or perhaps you will consider auditory experiences connected with moving it or else the perception of its weight. It is not unlikely that within your image there will also be elements of evaluation (e.g. it may be considered a precious object, because it is an antique and you have paid a lot for it) or emotions (the table being associated with sweet memories). All these elements are quite typical associations because they concern the common experiences connected with that table. It thus logically follows that when the memory of the table is activated, the other associated memories are also brought up.

The mental image generated from long-term memory is of the reconstructive type, both incomplete and rich in elements emerging from different sources.

Obviously with sighted people, the main source of the experience is usually, but by no means exclusively, visual. With blind people, the mixture of elements used would be different from those for sighted individuals, yet, in fact, it is not so dissimilar as to produce a functionally and experientially different result.

The possibility of 'seeing' an object with our mind's eye seems to require that we have first experienced it in the perceptual world. This may be considered true if we refer to memory images, but we could also create original and total new representations in our mind, not based on real perceptual representations. This assumption, also held by Hobbes, maintains that the generation of images is due to a combination, often new and original, of percepts stored in memory. The memory images can be generated on the basis of information retrieved from long-term memory. Cornoldi *et al.*[2] called this type of mental image 'a generated image', and distinguished it from a representation directly derived from a recent experience or from a well-learned sensory pattern, called 'a visual trace'. According to their constructivist view, generated images are the result of the combined synthesis of long-term memory information coming from different sources which may be penetrated by beliefs, emotions and conceptual knowledge.

The constructivist view of mental imagery assumes that images generated from information in long-term memory must be distinguished from perceptions and visual traces resulting from a very recent visual experience (see Table 22.1). Visual traces and generated images are different in terms of access, source of information, degree of required

Table 22.1 Differences between a visual trace and a generated image

	Visual trace	Generated image
Access	Direct	Generated
Sources	Visual perception only	Different modalities
Access for blind people	Impossible	Possible
Attention	Very low (pre-attentive)	Usually high
Represented object	Phenomenic object	Generated object
Perception analogy	Almost complete	Partial
Main characteristics	Sensorial/phenomenic	Perceptual/semantic
Role of LTM	Marginal	Substantial
Process penetrability	Almost none	Substantial
Modality of loss	Similar to sensorial processes	Similar to memory processes
Interference	Visual similarity	Similar processes, attentional requests
Capacity limitations	Storage	Storage and processing
Age-related modifications	Minimal	Substantial

attention, type of representation, degree of analogy to perception, main characteristics, role of the LTM (long-term memory), process penetrability, modality of loss, interference, capacity limitations, age-related modifications and access for blind people.[2] In particular, blind people may generate images (although with specific features and limitations), whereas they cannot have visual traces.

The limitations of imagination without perception

We have thus noted that mental images are not equivalent to pure perception and that the absence of perception does not inhibit the generation of mental images. It follows that even blind people can evocate mental images since we have maintained that the visual experience is but one ingredient of an image.

Is it therefore possible that the image of a blind person shares the same characteristics of the sighted person's image? No, it is not.

Studies on blind people's mental images have concentrated on exploring their peculiarities. For example, it has been shown that blind people perform better with images pertaining to an auditory experience than with images of objects depending more heavily on the visual component. Further limitations regard a fundamental principle of visual perception which allows a simultaneous vision of multiple elements.

This 'multiple, parallel elaboration' is partially possible also in other sensory modalities (for example one can simultaneous place his/her two hands on two objects thus permitting a multiple and parallel tactile exploration), but this is undoubtedly more difficult. It follows that blind people's multiple images, which cannot rely on prior experiences, are impaired.

The hypothesis of a difficulty in processing multiple simultaneous representations in blind people was tested by comparing their performance in the memorization of one or more items associated with each location with that of sighted people.[14,21] Thus participants were invited to memorize either a single object (e.g. a television) or three objects (e.g. a television, a dog and a book) in association with a location (e.g. a square).

What would you do if you had to imagine a TV, a book and a dog, in a square? A possible solution would be, for example, to imagine a familiar square, with a TV placed on the edge of its fountain and the screen showing a dog holding a book in its mouth.

Obviously people are free to choose the image that best suites them, but the important feature is the creation of an image which simultaneously presents all the required elements, so that when asked 'What was in the square?' the entire image will be immediately present, facilitating the recall of all three associated elements.

Sighted people are very good at this task. When asked to remember objects associated with a location with the aid of this method, people would on average recall 15 out of a total of 20 single words presented in association with a location, and an average of 40 of the 60 presented words in the case of the triplets. This was not the case, however, for blind people. With the single words blind people performed on a par with sighted participants, remembering on average 15 objects. However their performance did not improve when the simultaneous image of three objects was required: on average, they remembered only 15–20 of the 60 objects presented.[14,21]

The hypothesis of a specific difficulty in multiple and parallel elaboration of images in blind people could also explain their difficulty in processing three-dimensional spatial representations. In a series of studies requiring totally congenitally blind and sighted participants to imagine movements, the performance of the two groups was often comparable when using 2D matrices but differences, favouring sighted individuals, emerged in 3D tasks[17,22,23] Moreover, it was found that blind people were more impaired in the faster conditions. Concerning speed, Juurmaa and Lehtinen-Railo[24] and Rieser, Guth and Hill[25] suggest that blind people are slower in those tasks requiring a modification of their spatial mental representations and also when a judgement on orientation and distance is required. The blind individuals' slowness could be due to the lack of suitable exploration strategies useful in carrying out the different tasks.[26] Conversely, other researchers[27] hypothesized a different cerebral organization that regulates the generation and the use of mental images in the blind.

The lower speed and the particular difficulty blind people showed in processing the third dimension could be explained in different ways, for example with reference to a specific difficulty with the vertical dimension, a more limited capacity—compared with the sighted—to rely on the pattern's border or a greater involvement of active visuospatial working memory components[28,29] According to other results, an important difference between blind and sighted people is that the former seem to ignore the rules of perspective,[30,31] although other studies found that drawings carried out by blind people unexpectedly contained notions of spatial perspective.[32,33]

However, the hypothesis of a difficulty in multiple simultaneous processing in blind people also seems able to explain the third dimension problem, since people may be helped in the processing of 3D patterns by the simultaneous representation of the horizontal and the vertical solution of the pattern. Further evidence concerning this hypothesis comes from the observation that blind people show particular difficulties compared with sighted controls when they have to remember two separate matrices, whereas this is no longer the case when the information is collected in a single matrix.[18]

Conclusions

In conclusion, the notion that blind people cannot have mental images is a myth. In our view, mental images can be generated from different sources of information which do not necessarily have to include the results of actual visual experiences. These mental images are representations with specific features and cognitive effects which differentiate them from other non-imaginal representations. Congenitally blind people generate mental images which show the same cognitive effects as those created by sighted people.

However, the opposite notion that blind people compensate for their sensory deficits by generating images superior to those of sighted people is also a myth. In general, blind people's mental images present a series of limitations related to those cases where a prior visual experience could be useful in their production. This does not exclude that, in particular cases, blind people may have visuo spatial images superior to those of sighted people.

References and notes

1. Shepard RN, Metzler J. Mental rotation of three dimensional objects. *Science*, 1971; **171**:701–703.
2. Cornoldi C, De Beni R, Giusberti F, Massironi M. Memory and imagery: a visual trace is not a mental image. In M Conway, S Gathercole, C Cornoldi, ed. *Theories of memory*. Psychology Press, Hove, UK. 1998:87–110.
3. Kerr NH. The role of vision in 'visual imagery' experiments: evidence from congenitally blind. *Journal of Experimental Psychology: General*, 1983; **112**:265–267.
4. Cornoldi C, De Beni R, Giusberti F. Meta-imagery: conceptualization of mental imagery and its relationship with cognitive behavior. *Psychologische Beitrage*, 1997; **38**:484–499.
5. Pylyshyn ZW. What the mind's eye tells the mind's brain: a critique of mental imagery. *Psychological Bulletin*, 1973; **80**:1–24.
6. Cornoldi C, Fastame M, Vecchi T. Congenitally blindness and spatial mental imagery. In Y Hatwell, A Streri, E Gentaz, ed. *Touching for knowing*. Benjamins, Amsterdam, 2003:173–187.
7. Carreiras M, Codina M. Spatial cognition of the blind and the sighted: visual and amodal hypotheses, *Current Psychology on Cognition*, 1992; **12**:51–78.
8. Klatzky RL, Golledge RG, Loomis JM, Cicinelli JG, Pellegrino JW. Performance of blind and sighted persons on spatial tasks. *Journal of Visual Impairment and Blindness*, 1995; **89**:70–82.
9. Marmor GS. Age at onset of blindness and the development of the semantics of colour names. *Journal of Experimental Child Psychology*, 1978; **25**:267–278.
10. Zimler J, Keenan JM. Imagery in the congenitally blind: how visual are visual images? *Journal of Experimental Psychology: Learning, Memory and Cognition*, 1983; **9**:269–282.
11. Marmor GS, Zaback LA. Mental rotation by the blind: does mental rotation depends on visual imagery? *Journal of Experimental Psychology: Human Perception and Performance*, 1976; **2**:515–521.
12. Jonides J, Kahn R, Rozin P. Imagery instructions improve memory in blind subjects. *Bulletin of the Psychonomic Society*, 1975; **5**:424–426.
13. Cornoldi C, Calore D, Pra Baldi A. Imagery ratings and recall in congenitally blind subjects. *Perceptual and Motor Skills*, 1979; **48**:627–629.
14. De Beni R, Cornoldi C. Imagery limitation in totally congenitally blind subjects. *Journal of Experimental Psychology: Learning, Memory and Cognition*, 1988; **14**:650–655.
15. Tinti C, Galati D, Vecchio MG, De Beni R, Cornoldi C. Interactive auditory and visual images in the blind. *Journal of Visual Impairment and Blindness*, 1999; **93**:579–583.
16. Cornoldi C, De Beni R, Roncari S, Romano S. The effects of imagery instructions on totally congenitally blind recall. *European Journal of Cognitive Psychology*, 1989; **1**:321–331.
17. Cornoldi C, Cortesi A, Preti D. Individual differences in the capacity limitations of visuospatial short-term memory: research on sighted and totally congenitally blind people. *Memory and Cognition*, 1991; **19**: 459–468.
18. Vecchi T, Tinti C, Cornoldi C. Spatial memory and integration processes in congenital blindness. *Neuroreport*, 2004; **15**:2787–2790.
19. Tinti C, Adenzato M, Tamietto M, Cornoldi C. Visual experience is not necessary for efficient survey spatial cognition: Evidence from blindness. *The Quarterly Journal of Experimental Psychology.* 2006; **59**:1306–132.

20. De Beni R, Cornoldi C, Anderson M, Magnussen S, Ronberg Y. Memory and expertise. In S Magnussen, T Helstrup, ed. *Everyday memory*. Psychology Press, Hove, UK. (In press).

21. De Beni R, Cornoldi C. The effects of imaginal mnemonics on congenitally totally blind and on normal subjects. In D Marks and D Russel, ed. *Imagery*. Human Performance Associates, Dunedin, New Zealand. 1985:54–59.

22. Cornoldi C, Bertuccelli B, Rocchi P, Sbrana B. Processing capacity limitations in pictorial and spatial representations in the totally congenitally blind. *Cortex*, 1993; 29:675–689.

23. Vecchi T, Monticelli ML, Cornoldi C. Visuo-spatial working memory: structures and variables affecting a capacity measure. *Neuropsychologia*, 1995; 33:1549–1564.

24. Juurmaa J, Lehtinen-Railo S. Visual experience and access to spatial knowledge. *Journal of Visual Impairment and Blindness*, 1994; 88:157–170.

25. Rieser JJ, Guth DA, Hill EW. Sensitivity to perspective structure while walking without vision. *Perception*, 1986; 15:173–188.

26. Thinus-Blanc C, Gaunet F. Representation of space in the blind: vision as a spatial sense? *Psychological Bulletin*, 1997; 121:20–42.

27. Stuart I. Spatial orientation and congenital blindness: a neuropsychological approach. *Journal of Visual Impairment and Blindness*, 1995; 89:129–141.

28. Cornoldi C, Vecchi T. Mental imagery in blind people: the role of passive and active visuo-spatial processes. In M Heller, ed. *Touch, representation, and blindness*. Oxford University Press, New York. 2000:143–181.

29. Cornoldi C, Vecchi T. *Visuo-spatial working memory and individual differences*. Psychology Press, Hove, UK. 2003.

30. Arditi A, Holtzam J, Kosslyn S. Mental imagery and sensory experience in congenital blindness. *Neuropsychologia*, 1988; 26:1–12.

31. Heller MA, Calcaterra JA, Tyler LA, Burson LL. Production and interpretation of perspective drawings by blind and sighted people. *Perception*, 1996; 25:321–334.

32. Kennedy J. Haptic pictures. In W Schiff, E Foulke, ed. *Tactual perception*. Academic Press, New York, 1982:303–333.

33. Kennedy J. *Drawing and the blind: pictures to touch*. Yale University Press, New Haven. 1993.

Chapter 23

Something wicked this way comes: causes and interpretations of sleep paralysis

Christopher C. French and Julia Santomauro

Introduction

Consider the following account from Herman Melville's *Moby-Dick* (as cited in Herman,[1] p. 578). The main protagonist, Ishmael, describes his experience as follows:

> ... and slowly waking from it—half steeped in dreams—I opened my eyes and the before sunlit room was now wrapped in outer darkness. Instantly I felt a shock running through all my frame; nothing was to be seen and nothing was to be heard; but a supernatural hand seemed placed in mine. My arm hung over the counterpane, and the nameless, unimaginable silent form or phantom, to which the hand belonged, seemed closely seated by my bedside. For what seemed ages piled on ages, I lay there, frozen with the most awful fears, not daring to drag away my hand; yet ever thinking that if I could but stir it one single inch, the horrid spell would be broken.

Similar episodes also appear in F. Scott Fitzgerald's *The Beautiful and Damned* published in 1922[2] and in Ernest Hemingway's short story *The Snows of Kilimanjaro*, written in 1938.[3] Are such accounts merely a product of the creative imagination of the novelist or might similar experiences happen to real people in everyday life?

Now take a look at Fig. 23.1. It illustrates a famous painting known as *The Nightmare*, painted by Henry Fuseli in 1781.[4] This rather surreal and disturbing image shows a beautiful woman sleeping on her back. Perched upon her chest is a grotesque demon, his full weight pressing down upon her. In the background, a horse with staring eyes peers at the scene through parted curtains. The whole scene has an unreal and oppressive quality that truly lives up to the picture's title. Again, is this artistic depiction based upon nothing more than Fuseli's vivid imagination?

Compare these artistic accounts with the following account from Katy Haley, a British psychology student who experiences episodes such as the following on a regular basis:

> I am lying on my back in bed with my eyes seemingly open and feeling just as I would if I were awake. I can see that my bedroom door is open and I try to turn my head to focus more clearly but I am unable to move. It is at this point that I begin to sense some sort of presence beyond the bedroom door. I am straining in order to see what is coming, and then she appears. She has wild reddish hair and is short in stature. She seems to glide across the floor dragging her feet as she

THE NIGHTMARE.

Fig. 23.1 *The Nightmare*, 1781, by Henry Fuseli. This painting is one of the first ever artistic representations of sleep paralysis. Note the supine sleeping position, and the grotesque visual hallucinatory creatures, one of whom is sitting on the victim's chest.

moves. I am terrified, I still cannot move and I know that she is going to try to kill me. She reaches the bed and climbs up onto my chest; she puts her hands around my neck and starts to strangle me. At this point there is no doubt in my mind that the situation is real, she is really strangling me and I feel the pressure of her hands around my neck. I cannot move, then all of a sudden I wake up, but it is so difficult to remain awake that I immediately fall asleep again. Then the process is repeated again and again sometimes up to 12 times in one night.

Here is an example that was reported to us by a 35-year-old academic psychologist:

These days it's pretty much always the same. It's when I'm going off to sleep. I never have them in the middle of the night, I never have them waking up, always when I'm going off to sleep. There are some sensations I feel sometimes, almost like a charge in my head, but that happens when I'm falling off too. What happens is my eyes are open and usually I get the sense that something in the room is happening, so it's more like apprehension, it's a sort of belief that something's going to go off. And then a shape gathers, a sort of [. . .] small black cloud gathers and it's the devil. . . a monster. And it comes onto me and I can feel its weight and basically the belief is that it's holding me and that it's going to drag me down into an abyss. I can feel sensations on my body, it's multi-sensory. I can sort of smell it too. I feel sensations in my body, like in a lift, I feel like I'm going down. I can't move, certainly. Well I try but it never works. Usually all I can do is make a kind of hum in my throat and try to make a feedback cycle, make that louder, as it gets louder the more awake I get, the more I can do until I can eventually perhaps shout. And that wakes me up, properly wakes me up.

Clancy[5] presents several cases, including that of Mike, a 44-year-old computer programmer:

> I woke up around 3 a.m. and couldn't move. I managed to open my eyes and there were creatures in the room with me. I saw shadowy figures around the bed. Then I felt this pressure like pain in my genitals. I must have fallen asleep again, because the next thing I remember it was morning. I woke up in a state of shock. (Clancy,[5] p. 34).

Mike, in common with several other cases discussed by Clancy, believed that his experience was best explained in terms of him having been abducted by aliens.

Other cultures have different interpretations for such experiences. Hinton et al.[6] (pp. 54–55) provide the following account from a Cambodian refugee:

> [...] 48-year-old Krauch usually saw a black shape moving towards his body and, once it reached him, it seemed to wrap around him, severely impeding breathing. Krauch believed that the shape was either a demon or a ghost. In the week prior to his most recent clinic visit, Krauch had a new [nocturnal] visitor: a demon with fangs who held a nail-studded club. While Krauch was attempting to fall asleep, this new demon walked up to his side; he tried to move but couldn't. The demon pushed down on Krauch's chest with one hand, making him feel extremely short of breath. The demon then raised the club with the other hand, as if about to swing it down on Krauch's head; with its fangs protruding ominously close, the demon stood like this—one hand pushing down on Krauch's chest, the other holding the club above his head—for about two minutes. Then, just as the creature started to swing the club, Krauch was able to move. He sat up, seized by terror. For five minutes he felt his heart beat frantically, his ears rang, and his vision was blurry. [...] Krauch thought the being wanted to steal his soul by killing him directly or by scaring his soul out of his body.

It appears then that the fictional account with which we introduced this chapter may well be based upon a real-life experience. The real-life accounts are certainly at least as terrifying as the fictional account!

Are the people who report such experiences all suffering from some kind of severe psychopathology? Or, worse still, are they really being visited in the night by ghosts, demons and aliens? The answer is almost certainly 'neither'. They are experiencing a phenomenon known as *sleep paralysis*. Although sleep paralysis is, as we will see, a fairly common experience, it is not widely recognized or understood either by members of the general public or by medical professionals.

The most commonly experienced feature of sleep paralysis is that of being in a state between sleep and wakefulness and realizing that one is unable to move. This state lasts for anything between a few seconds and a few minutes. On its own, it is quite frightening, but it is worse when it is accompanied, as it often is, by any of the other common features of sleep paralysis. These include a sense of presence, a feeling of pressure on the chest, difficulty breathing, and visual and auditory hallucinations. The visual hallucinations include such things as grotesque monsters, demons, animals, or lights moving around the room, even though the sufferer appears to be able also to see their normal surroundings. The auditory hallucinations may include voices, footsteps, heavy objects being dragged, and mechanical sounds such as humming or vibrating. The sufferer may also report unusual bodily sensations such as floating or sinking, and the episode may even develop into an out-of-body experience.

The purpose of this chapter is to present a review of what we currently know about sleep paralysis in terms of its prevalence, how our understanding of the phenomenon has developed historically, probable causes of sleep paralysis and the ways in which the phenomenon has been interpreted cross-culturally. Finally, we suggest some strategies for preventing and coping with sleep paralysis.

Definition and description of sleep paralysis

The international classification of sleep disorders, Revised[7] (p. 166) offers the following definition:

> Sleep paralysis consists of a period of inability to perform voluntary movements at sleep onset (hypnagogic or predormital form) or upon awakening, either during the night or in the morning (hypnopompic or postdormital form).

Sleep paralysis is classified as an REM (rapid eye movement) sleep parasomnia; that is, an undesirable sleep disturbance that occurs during sleep that is characterised by the kind of rapid eye movements (REMs) typically associated with dreaming.[8]

During an episode of sleep paralysis, the individual is fully conscious and aware that it is not possible to move limbs, head and trunk, and there may also be respiratory difficulties.[9] When a person experiences their first episode of sleep paralysis they may think that they are dying.[10] In addition to this, the individual may experience acute anxiety and hypnagogic or hypnopompic hallucinations. Hypnagogic hallucinations are simply hallucinations that are experienced while falling asleep; hallucinations experienced upon waking up are termed hypnopompic hallucinations. These hallucinations can be visual and/or auditory and are often vivid and terrifying.[10]

Sleep paralysis usually occurs when the individual is lying on a bed and is unlikely to occur if the individual is in an uncomfortable sleeping position such as sitting upright.[10] An episode of sleep paralysis can last between a few seconds and a few minutes, and ends suddenly. It can end either spontaneously, because of intense effort to break the paralysis by the person experiencing it, or by the touch or voice of another person.[11] Immediately after an episode of sleep paralysis there may be numbness or tingling in the hands and feet and there is the possibility of relapse if the individual does not get up and move around. The fully conscious state accompanied by paralysis, breathing difficulties and vivid hallucinations constitutes a truly terrifying experience for the sufferer.

It is important to differentiate sleep paralysis from other unpleasant sleep-related phenomena with which it is often confused. The first of these is simply a bad dream, often referred to in modern times as a nightmare. The main difference between a bad dream and sleep paralysis is that during the latter sufferers have the extremely strong impression that they are actually awake and may well be aware of being able to perceive their surroundings accurately, even though such perceptions may also include auditory and visual hallucinations. Also, of course, in dreams one typically feels subjectively that one can move around within the dream, even though in fact the muscles of the body are paralysed during dreams, presumably to prevent one from actually executing the actions of the dream. Although bad dreams of all kinds are typically referred to as *nightmares* nowadays, sleep paralysis corresponds to the classical usage of the term, by which it was meant to denote a nocturnal attack by an evil spirit or demon during which the attacker would attempt to crush the terrified victim.

This is illustrated in the following account from Macnish[12] (cited by Liddon,[13] p. 88):

> Imagination cannot conceive the horrors it [The Nightmare] frequently gives rise to, or language describe them in adequate terms ... Everything horrible, disgusting or terrifying in the physical or moral world is brought before him in fearful array; he is hissed at by serpents, tortured by demons, stunned by the hollow voices and cold touch of apparitions ... At one moment he may have the consciousness of a malignant demon being at his side; then to shun the sight of so appalling an object, he will close his eyes but still the fearful being makes its presence known; for its icy breath is felt diffusing itself over his visage, and he knows that he is face to face with a fiend. Then, if he looks up, he beholds horrid eyes glaring upon him, and an aspect of hell grinning at him with even more hellish malice. Or, he may have the idea of a monstrous hag squatted upon his breast—mute, motionless and malignant.

Jones,[14] in his classic psychoanalytical work *On the nightmare*, emphasizes that the word *nightmare* originally referred to the fiendish nocturnal visitor involved, sometimes also known as a *night-fiend* or *night incubus*. He described the three cardinal features of the nightmare as (1) a sense of agonizing dread; (2) the feeling of pressure on the chest causing difficulty in breathing; and (3) bodily paralysis. It is clear that Jones was attempting to provide a psychoanalytic account of what we now call sleep paralysis in contrast to the modern, less precise, usage of the word *nightmare*. Unfortunately, however, psychoanalytic accounts are impossible to test scientifically and they will not therefore be discussed further in this chapter.

Another phenomenon that is often confused with sleep paralysis is that of the night terror, *Pavor nocturnus*. The latter involves the sleeper apparently awakening in a state of great agitation and terror, often with a loud scream. The sufferer typically makes strenuous efforts to escape from the source of this terror. The main differences between sleep paralysis and night terrors are that the latter does not involve any paralysis and the sufferer typically has no recollection whatsoever of the episode upon awakening properly. Also, night terrors occur most commonly during childhood whereas sleep paralysis is more common in adulthood. Finally, night terrors occur during the first third of the night with spontaneous awakenings from stage 3 or 4 sleep (see below), whereas the psychophysiological pattern of activity associated with sleep paralysis is quite different as we will see.

Prevalence of sleep paralysis

Sleep paralysis is a common symptom of narcolepsy which is a sleep disorder affecting approximately 0.02–0.05 per cent of the population.[8] Narcolepsy consists of a tetrad of four major symptoms:

Table 23.1 Examples of reported incidence rates of isolated sleep paralysis illustrating the wide range of estimates obtained

Study	Sample	Incidence
Goode[11]	359 American adults (231 medical students, 53 nursing students, 75 inpatients)	5%
Ness[16]	69 adults, Newfoundland	62%
Fukuda et al.[17]	635 college students, Japan	40%
Wing et al.[18]	603 undergraduates, Hong Kong	37%
Spanos et al.[19]	1798 Canadian students	21%
Cheyne et al.[20]	870 university students, Canada	29%
Kotorii et al. [21]	8162 Japanese citizens	40%

1. Sleep attacks—overwhelming episodes of drowsiness or sleep.
2. Cataplexy—sudden loss of muscle tone usually triggered by a strong emotion.
3. Sleep paralysis—consciously experienced paralysis whilst falling asleep or waking up.
4. Vivid hypnagogic hallucinations—vivid hallucinations at sleep onset.

People who experience narcolepsy do not necessarily experience the symptom of sleep paralysis but approximately 17–40 per cent do,[7] and 20–40 per cent experience vivid hypnagogic hallucinations.[15] Many narcoleptics who experience sleep paralysis will do so several times per month and some of them will experience it every time they fall asleep.

However, it is important to emphasize that sleep paralysis is also experienced by people who do not have narcolepsy. This is termed isolated sleep paralysis (ISP) to indicate that the person is not experiencing it as a symptom of narcolepsy. Reported prevalence rates based upon interview or, more commonly, questionnaires vary greatly (see Table 23.1). According to *The international classification of sleep disorders*, Revised,[7] 40 per cent of people will experience ISP at least once in their lifetime. Furthermore, between 3 and 6 per cent of the population will experience ISP more often, and some will experience it severely (episodes occurring at least once per week) and chronically (for 6 months or longer).[7]

It is unclear whether the wide range of prevalence rates reported across different ethnic groups reflects genuine underlying genetic differences in susceptibility to ISP across these groups or is better explained in terms of other factors, such as the description of the phenomenon supplied to respondents or the actual wording of the questions used in the surveys to assess prevalence. For example, it appears to be the case that higher incidence rates are reported from cultures in which ISP is already widely recognized as a non-disease, such as Japan and Newfoundland.[22] Fukuda[23] highlighted the importance of the actual wording used in a study in which different samples of Japanese respondents were given questionnaires that differed by only a single word or phrase, i.e. the word or phrase used to refer to sleep paralysis. When the phenomenon was referred to as *kanashibari*, the traditional folklore term used in Japan, 39.3 per cent reported having experienced it. When it was referred to as *transient paralysis*, only 26.4 per cent gave positive answers. These biases were especially strong amongst female respondents. About 30 per cent gave positive responses when the neutral term *condition* was used.

It is also unclear whether or not there are differences between the sexes in terms of susceptibility to sleep paralysis. Some studies have reported higher incidence in males,[11,16] some in females,[17,21] and others find no differences between the sexes.[24] There is general agreement, however, regarding the typical age of onset. Attacks usually begin in adolescence or young adulthood, although earlier and later onset has been reported.[17,18]

There is evidence to suggest that people suffering from panic disorder are more prone to attacks of sleep paralysis than non-sufferers.[25–27] Once again, however, the reasons for this association are unclear. On the one hand, it may be that both sleep paralysis and panic disorder share the same underlying biological basis. On the other hand, it may that those suffering from anxiety disorders have more disrupted sleep patterns as a consequence of their anxiety and that it is the sleep disruption, not the anxiety disorder *per se*, that directly causes the higher incidence of sleep paralysis. Such an explanation may also account for some of the differences found between ethnic groups. As Paradis and Friedman[27] point out, higher rates of sleep paralysis were found amongst African-American participants than among whites, especially if they also suffered from panic disorder. The African-Americans also reported higher levels of stress, resulting from such factors as poverty, racism and acculturation, that may have disrupted sleep patterns.

Medical and scientific understanding of sleep paralysis

Sleep paralysis was first described in the medical literature in 1876 by Weir Mitchell,[28] an American neurologist: 'The subject awakes to consciousness of his environment but is incapable of moving a muscle; lying to all appearance still asleep. He is really engaged in a struggle for movement fraught with acute mental distress; could he but manage to stir, the spell would vanish instantly'.

Sleep paralysis was first reported to be associated with narcolepsy and cataplexy in the 1920s.[29] The term sleep paralysis was coined by Wilson around 1925, but before and since sleep paralysis has had various different terms used to refer to it including 'nocturnal hemiplegia', 'nocturnal paralysis', 'sleep numbness', 'delayed psychomotor awakening', 'cataplexy of awakening' and 'postdormital chalastic fits'.[11]

In the mid 1900s, several researchers suggested that sleep paralysis was a form of epilepsy because of certain features it shared with some types of epileptic seizure.[30,31] However, subsequent investigations using electroencephalographic (EEG) recordings have shown conclusively that no epileptic discharges occur during episodes of sleep paralysis.[10] Polysomnograph (PSG) recordings (i.e. EEG, eye movement and other types of psychophysiological activity recorded during sleep) show patterns of activity during sleep paralysis that are generally similar to those found during normal REM sleep.

The neurophysiology of sleep and sleep paralysis

PSG recordings have provided researchers with an objective way of measuring brain activity during sleep and have enabled the identification of different stages of sleep, the first four of which are not associated with REMs and are thus collectively referred to as NREM (non-rapid eye movement) sleep. As we go through stages 1–4 of sleep, heart rate, breathing rate and brain activity progressively slow down. The progression through these stages takes approximately 60–90 min and then the cycle reverses and continues via stage 3 and stage 2 sleep and then enters REM sleep that lasts for 10–15 min. REM sleep appears to be associated with dreaming. Following REM sleep the person would typically re-enter stage 2 sleep and then cycle through the other sleep stages again. Each complete cycle takes approximately 90–100 min. Early on, sleep is dominated by stage 3 and stage 4 sleep, but towards the end of sleep stage 4 sleep shortens and REM sleep extends.[32]

Sleep paralysis can be considered to be an intrusion of REM sleep characteristics into wakefulness, i.e. the muscles of the body are deeply relaxed (they cannot be moved) and the dream-like element of any associated hallucinations may result from the brain activity typical of this sleep period. Wakefulness has occurred but the body and part of the brain are still in REM sleep. It is therefore understandable that sleep paralysis can be experienced upon waking up from REM sleep. However, if a person normally enters stage 1 sleep upon sleep onset and if sleep paralysis is associated with REM sleep, then why do people often experience sleep paralysis when falling asleep? Interestingly, it has been found that narcoleptics who experience the symptoms of sleep paralysis, cataplexy and/or hypnagogic hallucinations often enter REM sleep directly after they have fallen asleep.[33] This is termed a sleep-onset REM period (SOREMP). Furthermore, when researchers woke up narcoleptics with the symptoms of sleep paralysis, cataplexy and/or hypnagogic hallucination during various stages of sleep, they discovered that sleep paralysis was regularly reported when the person was woken up from a SOREMP. However, sleep paralysis was not reported if the person was woken up from NREM sleep or if they were woken up from REM sleep that occurred after a period of NREM sleep.[34]

SOREMPs are also found in people without narcolepsy. They usually occur after disruption of the sleep–wake cycle (such as irregular sleep habits, jetlag, shiftwork or sleep deprivation) or after interruption of the NREM–REM sleep cycle.[35] It is possible to induce a SOREMP by waking the person up at a particular point in the sleep cycle.[36] Researchers in Japan elicited SOREMPs in participants using this sleep interruption method, and 9.4 per cent of induced SOREMPs elicited an episode of ISP.[35] This research suggests that sleep paralysis is related to REM sleep and in particular REM sleep that occurs at sleep onset.

Situational factors that may be related to the occurrence of ISP include the position in which the person sleeps. In a large-scale survey, Cheyne[37] found that although only 13–19 per cent of people reported normally falling asleep in the supine position (lying face-up on their back), it was by far the most common position to be in during ISP. People who experienced ISP in the middle or towards the end of the night were more likely to experience it in a supine position than those who experience it at the beginning of the night. It is possible that episodes of ISP that occur later in the night are due to brief micro-arousals during REM sleep as a consequence of obstructive sleep apnoea caused by adopting the supine position. This argument is supported by the fact that Ohayon et al.[38] had previously reported an association between the occurrence of sleep paralysis and obstructive sleep apnoea.

One of the most detailed neuropsychological models of sleep paralysis is that proposed by Cheyne et al.[39] On the basis of factor analyses of data from questionnaires on the phenomenology of sleep paralysis, Cheyne et al. identified three factors that grouped together commonly reported symptoms of such episodes. They also speculated upon the likely neurophysiological substrate associated with each of the three factors, basing their arguments largely upon the activation synthesis theory of dreaming.[40,41] According to the activation synthesis theory, inhibitory activation of REM-off cells in reciprocal interaction with REM-on cells initiates REM sleep. Motor output is inhibited by these brainstem mechanisms and sensory input is blocked. Internally generated quasi-random activity is synthesized by the forebrain cortical centres into meaningful patterns.

The first factor in the model of Cheyne et al.[39] is labelled Intruder, and consists of the sensed presence, extreme fear, and visual and auditory hallucinations. They argue that the experience of the Intruder begins with the sense of presence and extreme fear caused by brainstem-induced activation of the amygdala. Neuroimaging studies[42,43] have indicated significant activation in the amygdala during REM dreams. Under normal circumstances, the amygdala is involved in emergency reactions, causing a heightened state of vigilance and a lowering of detection thresholds for threat cues in the environment.[44] In evolutionary terms, this clearly aids survival. The subcortical thalamoamygdala pathway quickly provides a coarse-grained analysis of potential threats that is sufficient to cause attention to be switched from ongoing activities to scanning the environment. Reciprocal projections from the amygdala to the association cortex enhance more detailed analysis of the potential danger, allowing assessment of the true level of danger and the initiation of fight or flight if appropriate. Normally, this entire sequence, from alerting response to confirmation or disconfirmation of threat, takes only a fraction of a second, but the state of alert apprehension at the onset of sleep paralysis is likely to last much longer, from a few seconds to even minutes, because there is no external source to allow resolution of the perceived threat. According to Cheyne et al., this state of heightened fear and alertness may well be perceived as a sense of presence. As time goes on, efforts to disambiguate the perceived threat, mainly based upon the reciprocal interaction between thalamocortical and amygdalocortical pathways, will produce increasingly elaborate interpretations based upon exogenous input (e.g. ambient sounds, shadows, etc.) and endogenous dream-like imagery. The end result will be vivid auditory and visual hallucinations of a terrifying nature.

The second factor identified by Cheyne et al.[39] was labelled Incubus and comprised feelings of pressure on the chest, difficulty breathing and pain. This factor was substantially correlated with Intruder. It is argued that this cluster of experiences reflects the fact that sufferers may try to control their breathing (e.g. to take a deep breath) during sleep paralysis and thus become aware that voluntary control of breathing is no longer possible. Even though there is no real danger of suffocation because involuntary breathing will continue normally, it is understandable that the sufferer may interpret this inability to take voluntary control as an indication of pressure on the chest and may well feel that they are choking. As already stated, apnoea associated with the adoption of a supine sleeping position may also be a factor. Painful spasms might occur as a consequence of strenuous efforts to breathe. Both *Intruder-* and *Incubus*-type experiences imply an 'other' who is present and threatening, with the qualities of a monitoring, stalking predator.[45] Given the symptoms described, it is not surprising that a significant minority of sufferers, especially women, spontaneously describe their experience as feeling very much like being raped or sexually assaulted.

The third factor identified was labelled as *Unusual Bodily Experiences*, and consisted of flying/floating sensations, out-of-body experiences and feelings of bliss. The experiences associated with bodily orientation and movement in space often involve the perception of strong inertial forces acting upon the sufferer, described variously as 'rising, lifting, falling, flying, spinning, and swirling sensations or similar to going up or down in an elevator or an escalator, being hurled through a tunnel, or simply accelerating or decelerating rapidly' (Cheyne *et al.*[39], p. 331). Some respondents report feeling that they were forcibly pulled or sucked out of their bodies prior to full-blown out-of-body experiences. During normal consciousness, superior and medial vestibular nuclei play a role in coordinating eye and head movements, in association with cerebellar, cortical and thalamic centres. It is known that pontine centres controlling the sleep–wake cycle are closely associated with such vestibular nuclei in the brainstem.[46] Cheyne *et al.* propose that activation of the vestibular nuclei, in the absence of correlated head movements and retinal images, is interpreted as floating or flying. The conflicting interpretations of simultaneously floating or flying above one's bed while at the same time lying upon it is sometimes resolved by a splitting of the phenomenal self and the physical body, i.e. an out-of-body experience. Although sleep paralysis is typically associated with intense fear, feelings of bliss are sometimes reported by those whose experience involves this aspect. Some people also report seeing their own physical body from above (referred to as *autoscopy*).

Cross-cultural interpretations of sleep paralysis

Although there is still much to learn about sleep paralysis from a medical and scientific perspective, in recent years real progress has been made. It should come as no surprise, however, to realize that this vivid and terrifying experience has more often been interpreted in spiritual than scientific terms.[47,48] Consideration of the various ways in which sleep paralysis has been interpreted in previous eras and in other contemporary cultures provides a fascinating insight into the way in which the same core experience can be interpreted within the context of a variety of different belief systems and can also be shaped to some extent by such belief systems. A recent special issue of the journal

Fig. 23.2 Nocturnal visitation by an incubus, in the form of a bird.

Transcultural Psychiatry was devoted entirely to this topic in recognition of the special opportunity it offers to study the interaction of culture and physiology.[49]

From a historical perspective, Davies[50] presents a convincing case that many accusations of witchcraft probably had their roots in episodes of sleep paralysis. It also seems likely that sleep paralysis episodes were at the core of the belief in the Middle Ages that demons would sometimes enter a victim's bedroom and have sex with the sleeper against his or her will. The female version of this demon was known as a *succubus* whereas the male version was known as an *incubus* (see Fig. 23.2). The Latin word 'incubus' literally means 'one who presses or crushes'.

Even in contemporary cultures, however, such spiritual interpretations of sleep paralysis are still prevalent. In Newfoundland, for example, the experience is commonly referred to as an attack by the 'Old Hag' who comes and sits on the sleeper's chest.[16,47] The Japanese refer to the same core experience as *kanashibari*[17] and again interpret the experience as a spiritual attack. The following quotation from Dressler (cited by Ness,[16] pp. 34–35) illustrates the interpretation adopted by people living near St Lucia in the West Indies:

> The attack comes at the time that an individual is just falling asleep or just waking up, and the individual's sensations include a pressure on the chest, inability to move, and anxiety ... (the experience) is referred to as *kokma*. A *kokma* is a spirit of a dead baby that haunts an area, and will attack people in bed. They jump on your chest and clutch at your throat. To get rid of them the attacked person struggles to cry out, or in some way gets another person's attention, who will scare off the *kokma* ... The informants who have given me a description of *kokma* have always talked

about the babies actually clutching at their throats ... the attacks are always by dead, unbaptized babies. The *kokma* cannot be controlled, they 'grab' people just for the hell of it.

Culture-specific interpretations of sleep paralysis are also to be found amongst the Chinese, who refer to it as 'ghost oppression',[18,51] and amongst the Inuit of Canada, who believe that sleep paralysis can result from attack either by shamans or by malevolent spirits.[52,53] De Jong[54] describes how different culturally determined interpretations of sleep paralysis affect the ways that psychiatric patients from Guinea Bissau, the Netherlands, Morocco and Surinam react to such episodes.

Hinton *et al.*[6] present a fascinating but disturbing analysis of the complex ways in which sleep paralysis is experienced and interpreted by Cambodian refugees. Many of the refugees (42 per cent) were suffering from current sleep paralysis (i.e. at least one attack per year) and all of those suffering from sleep paralysis also suffered from panic attacks. Almost half (45 per cent) of the refugees suffered from post-traumatic stress disorder (PTSD) and two-thirds of the PTSD sufferers also suffered from sleep paralysis compared with only 22.4 per cent in the non-PTSD group. Sleep paralysis is associated with elaborate belief systems amongst the Khmer refugee population. For example, it is believed that one's soul may be dislodged from one's body when one is frightened and that fear can directly cause illness, insanity and even death. It is easy to see how a vicious circle is then set in place. The sufferers believe that the fact that they have had an episode of sleep paralysis indicates that they must be in a weakened state and thus prone to such attacks. This frightens them further, leading to disrupted sleep patterns that are likely actually to produce the very attacks that are feared so much.

In Cambodian, sleep paralysis is referred to as *khmaoch sângkât* (literally, 'the ghost pushes you down'). Most of the episodes experienced by the refugees involve visual hallucinations of a threatening figure approaching, and the actual content of this hallucination is often influenced by the nature of previous traumas experienced during the Pol Pot occupation. The type of supernatural attacker that is hallucinated is also influenced by the elaborate culture-specific beliefs of the refugees. Some of the attackers are believed to be (and perceived as) supernatural beings that were never human (house spirits, demons or the god of death). Sometimes the attackers are believed to be the spirits of deceased humans, such as those who died a 'bad death', those who are still too emotionally attached to the living and are thus reluctant to be reborn, and those who committed evil acts during their lives. Dying a 'bad death' would include such examples as being murdered, hanging oneself, not receiving a Buddhist death ritual or a fetus dying in the womb. The hallucinated figures often appear to be either the victims or perpetrators of wartime atrocities. One particularly gruesome supernatural being that appears in some episodes is known as an *ap*. As Hinton *et al.*[6] (p. 61) describe it, 'An *ap* appears to be a normal human during the day. However, at night, when the person lies down, the head floats forth from the body with the intestines and liver dangling down—the head separates from the body in order to scout for blood to feed on, such as the blood of a placenta. On occasion, the *ap* may attack a person, making that individual very ill'.

The level of distress likely to be caused by episodes of sleep paralysis can thus be seen to be related to the interpretation given to the episodes. That interpretation will depend upon both the belief system of the sufferer and the actual content of any hallucinations that accompany the episode. As a consequence of top-down processing, however, the belief system of the sufferer is likely to have a direct influence upon determining that very content.

Perhaps the most alarming potential consequence of sleep paralysis is the idea put forward by Adler[55,56] that, among Hmong refugees in the USA, episodes of sleep paralysis may have been the cause of sudden unexpected nocturnal death syndrome (SUNDS). From the late 1970s until the early 1990s, over 100 Southeast Asians died mysteriously in their sleep, with a particularly high incidence amongst male Hmong refugees. The cause of death baffled medical experts, despite having investigated a range of possible causative factors including heart disease, toxicology, nutrition, metabolism and genetics. Evidence suggested that the victims did have some abnormalities of the cardiac conduction system but this still did not account for the fact that deaths from SUNDS were only thought to have occurred amongst the refugees once they had reached the USA (typically within the first 2 years of arrival) and the victims were almost always male.

Adler[55,56] argues convincingly that the direct cause may well have been episodes of sleep paralysis, interpreted by the Hmong as potentially lethal nocturnal spiritual attacks. Back in their countries of origin, the Hmong would typically respond to any such attacks by engaging in rituals to ward off the attacking spirits, but such rituals were not feasible in their new country. The predominance of male victims is explained by two main factors. First, the Hmong belief system explicitly holds that the male head of the household, who is also the spiritual leader of the family, would be the prime target for any attacking spirit. Secondly, although all Hmong refugees suffered greatly from the stresses of being displaced to an alien culture, this was felt particularly strongly by the males who were no longer able to function effectively in their traditional patriarchal roles of head of the family and spiritual guide and protector. Evidence showed that many of the victims of SUNDS had suffered in the past from sleep paralysis. The belief among the Hmong was that one might be able to ward off one or two such attacks but that in the absence of remedial action such as appropriate rituals and sacrifices, the spirit would return, causing increasing terror until ultimately death would result. It cannot be emphasized too strongly that episodes of sleep paralysis are, in themselves, terrifying but essentially harmless. However, it does appear that under the particular and tragic circumstances of the Hmong refugees over this period, such episodes may have resulted in death, due to the interaction of a particular belief system and certain minor cardiac abnormalities.

The latest cultural interpretation of sleep paralysis is one that has particularly taken hold in modern Western societies. Many people in such societies take seriously the notion that if you have experienced the symptoms of sleep paralysis, you may well have been abducted by aliens and they have simply wiped your memory for the rest of the episode. For some sufferers, particularly those who were worrying that the episode might be an indication that they were losing their sanity, such an explanation may be quite appealing.

They may then decide to undergo hypnotic regression in the mistaken belief that this is a reliable technique to unlock hidden or repressed memories. As a result, they may well end up with a vivid and detailed story of being the victim of a full-blown alien abduction that they now believe to be an accurate account of events that really did take place. In fact, it seems much more likely that the narrative is based upon false memories.[57–59] The mistaken idea that the symptoms of sleep paralysis may actually be indicators of alien abduction is widespread within the UFO literature and has been popularized in books, magazines, TV programmes and films. One of the most notorious examples of the promotion of this idea is the widely publicized claim by Hopkins et al.[60] that some 3.7 million Americans have probably been abducted by aliens. This claim was based upon the totally unjustifiable assumption that if respondents to a questionnaire on unusual personal experiences endorsed at least four of five items relating to common symptoms of sleep paralysis, this in itself was an indication of probable alien abduction. Although other factors are also involved in explaining the alien abduction experience, sleep paralysis seems to be central to many such claims.[61–63]

Strategies for preventing and coping with sleep paralysis

Although the causes and interpretations of sleep paralysis make it a fascinating topic from an academic point of view, this is of little comfort to anyone who actually suffers from repeated attacks. Unfortunately, there is a dearth of studies directed at evaluating the most effective strategies for preventing or, at the very least, coping with sleep paralysis. What follows are a few practical suggestions that readers might like to try if they are themselves suffering from repeated ISP attacks. It has often been noted that simply learning that there is a recognized phenomenon known as sleep paralysis often brings a great deal of comfort to sufferers. It is not at all uncommon for individuals to suffer in silence with this condition, afraid to tell family and friends of the terrors that visit them in the night for fear of ridicule. They may even fear that they are suffering from some kind of serious mental illness. To learn that sleep paralysis, although terrifying, is typically quite harmless and that they are not alone in having such experiences is often a great comfort in itself. It is not uncommon for the frequency of the attacks to diminish as a direct result of learning more about the condition, presumably because the sufferer no longer feels so anxious about going to sleep and thus their sleep patterns are less disturbed. There is a great need to educate the public and, even more so, healthcare professionals about the nature of sleep paralysis. Sometimes serious misdiagnoses can take place as a result of ignorance.

From what we already know about the factors that predispose sufferers to have sleep paralysis attacks, some of the practical advice that can be offered is fairly obvious. We know that sleeping in a supine position makes attacks more likely,[37] so this should be avoided wherever possible. Sufferers should avoid going to sleep in this position and should turn over onto their sides if they awake during the night and find themselves on their backs. In extreme cases, sufferers might even consider trying to sleep sitting up.

Another possibility would be to adapt a technique that is sometimes effective in avoiding the supine sleep position in people suffering from obstructive sleep apnoea. A tennis ball or two is sown into a pocket on the back of the sufferer's nightwear, making the supine position too uncomfortable to adopt.

It is also clear that anything that disrupts the sleep cycle (e.g. jetlag, shiftwork, stress) may also increase the frequency of attacks. Obviously, it may not be possible to eliminate such factors altogether, but they should be minimized if at all possible. Individuals suffering from affective disorders that may disrupt their sleeping patterns have been reported to show a reduced incidence of sleep paralysis attacks if their affective disorder is effectively treated. For example, Paradis et al.[64] reported that of 11 patients suffering from both panic disorder and recurrent ISP, five reported improvements with respect to the latter following cognitive–behavioural treatment directed only at the former. They speculate that 'a decrease in panic symptoms leads to an improvement in quality of sleep, which in turn, may lead to a reduction in ISP episodes' (p. 74).

Clearly, anything else that is likely to disrupt the sleep cycle, such as excessive intake of caffeine, alcohol or cigarettes, should also be avoided, and a healthy diet should be adopted, along with plenty of exercise. Regular hours of going to bed and getting up should be maintained. Ironically, it has been reported that Hmong men often tried to prevent attacks by setting their alarm clocks so as to sleep in a series of short intervals in an attempt to avoid going into a deep sleep, during which they believed they were at heightened vulnerability. In fact, this practice is likely to lead to SOREMPs and actually makes an attack more likely.

A number of medical treatments have been employed in order to try to reduce the frequency of ISP attacks.[65] These include the prescription of tricyclic antidepressants such as imipramine and clomipramine, serotoninergic agents such as L-tryptophan (with or without amitriptyline), and more exotic forms of treatment, such as the application of weak time-varying electromagnetic fields.[66] Terrillon and Marques-Bonham[65] suggest that taking melatonin may also reduce the frequency of ISP by better controlling circadian rhythms. However, they acknowledge that there is at present no proven medical treatment for reducing the frequency of ISP attacks.

If the sufferer is unable to prevent the attacks, what advice can be offered with respect to helping to cope with them when they do occur? People often develop their own strategies for trying to bring the episodes to an end. Often this involves trying to move the extremities, such as fingers or toes, or even one's tongue. During REM, the smaller muscles are not as completely paralysed as the major muscles and even the slightest movement is often enough to break the spell, even though it takes a huge effort of will. Some people recommend moving the eyes rapidly from side to side. It is also a good idea to try to get up and move around after an episode as this reduces the chances that one will experience another episode immediately upon going back to sleep.

Some people have found that they are able to adopt the opposite strategy. Rather than fighting against the experience, they simply give in to it, let it happen and try to learn to enjoy it. Terrillon and Marques-Bonham[65] (p. 117) quote with approval the following account from an electronic mailing list devoted to 'Awareness during Sleep Paralysis' (ASP):

> I just wanted to let you all know about my first ever pleasant ASP! It happened on Saturday night, and I felt all the usual sensations (buzzing, being pushed down/dragged) but wasn't scared and just let it happen. After a while I felt like I was being lifted from the bed, and next thing I knew I was 'floating' near the top of my wardrobe. I looked down at my bed and could see that it was unmade, but there was no one in it. I also remember being very excited, and pleased that this was such a non-threatening experience!

Not all sufferers are able to overcome the intense fear that is a typical component of ISP and to just 'relax and enjoy it', but those that are can actually get to a point where they look forward to and value their sleep paralysis episodes. We do know of at least one case where one unintended consequence of the decision to try to learn to relax during the next sleep paralysis episode and to enjoy the out-of-body experience was that the sufferer never had another episode again—presumably because she had stopped worrying about them!

As we have already described, sufferers for whom the experiences are interpreted in terms of some kind of spiritual attack are likely to benefit from whatever traditional practices are said to prevent further attacks. This is, of course, not to endorse such interpretations, but if such practices relieve stress for the sufferer they are likely to be effective by allowing for better quality sleep.

Conclusions

Although the nature of sleep paralysis is becoming clearer, there is still a lot to learn about this puzzling phenomenon. We already understand enough, thanks to PSG studies, to know that sleep paralysis represents a unique altered state of consciousness. Consideration of the different interpretations of the same core phenomenon cross-culturally provides a unique opportunity to assess the interaction between biology and culture, and the myriad ways in which this can be reflected in folklore and religious beliefs. The belief system of the sufferer provides a context for interpretation of the experience and also influences the content of the experience directly in the many societies that have a culture-specific interpretation of sleep paralysis.

The very fact that this surprisingly common experience is hardly recognized either by the public or by health professionals within modern Western societies is worthy of comment. It seems likely that this situation reflects the fact that the experience itself seems so alien to our modern, largely secular, view of the world that individuals are reluctant to talk about their own experiences of sleep paralysis. Consequently, health professionals are only rarely exposed to patients for whom repeated attacks of sleep paralysis are causing real anxiety and distress. Unfortunately, when this situation does arise, they are often unable to advise such patients because they themselves are ignorant of the nature of sleep paralysis. There is clearly a need for wider education on this topic among such professionals. There is also an urgent need for more systematic research into the most effective ways of preventing and coping with sleep paralysis.

References and notes

1. Herman J. An instance of sleep paralysis in *Moby Dick*. *Sleep*, 1997; **20**:577–579.
2. Schneck JM. Sleep paralysis in F. Scott Fitzgerald's *The Beautiful and Damned*. *New York State Journal of Medicine*, 1971; **71**:378–379.
3. Schneck JM. Disguised representation of sleep paralysis in Ernest Hemingway's 'The Snows of Kilimanjaro'. *Journal of the American Medical Association*, 1962; **182**:318–320.
4. Schneck JM. Henry Fuseli, nightmare, and sleep paralysis. *Journal of the American Medical Association*, 1969; **207**:725–726.
5. Clancy SA. *Abducted: how people come to believe they were kidnapped by aliens.* Harvard University Press, Cambridge, MA. 2005.
6. Hinton DE, Pich V, Chhean D, Pollack MH. 'The ghost pushes you down': sleep paralysis-type panic attacks in a Khmer refugee population. *Transcultural Psychiatry*, 2005; **42**:46–77.
7. American Sleep Disorders Association. *The international classification of sleep disorders, revised: diagnostic and coding manual.* American Sleep Disorders Association, Rochester, MN. 1997.
8. Lavie P, Pillar G, Malhotra A. *Sleep disorders: diagnosis, management and treatment.* Dunitz, London. 2002.
9. Dahlitz M, Parkes JD. Sleep paralysis. *Lancet*, 1993; **341**:406–407.
10. Hishikawa Y. Sleep paralysis. In C Guilleminault, WC Dement, P Passouant, ed. *Advances in sleep research*, Vol, 3. Spectrum, New York. 1976:97–124.
11. Goode GB. Sleep paralysis. *Archives of Neurology*, 1962; **6**:228–234.
12. Macnish R. *The philosophy of sleep.* Appleton and Co., New York. 1834.
13. Liddon SC. Sleep paralysis and hypnagogic hallucinations. *Archives of General Psychiatry*, 1967; **17**:88–96.
14. Jones EM. *On the nightmare.* Hogarth Press, London, 1931.
15. Broughton RJ. Narcolepsy. In MJ Thorpy, ed. *Handbook of sleep disorders.* Marcel Dekker, Inc., New York and Basel. 1930:197–216.
16. Ness RC. The Old Hag phenomenon as sleep paralysis: a biocultural interpretation. *Culture, Medicine and Psychiatry*, 1978; **2**:15–39.
17. Fukuda K, Miyasita A, Inugami M, Ishihara K. High prevalence of isolated sleep paralysis: kanashibari phenomenon in Japan. *Sleep*, 1987; **10**:279–286.
18. Wing YK, Lee ST, Chen CN. Sleep paralysis in Chinese: ghost oppression phenomenon in Hong Kong. *Sleep*, 1994; **17**:609–613.
19. Spanos NP, McNulty SA, DuBreuil SC, Pires M, Burgess MF. The frequency and correlates of sleep paralysis in a university sample. *Journal of Research in Personality*, 1995; **29**:285–305.
20. Cheyne JA, Newby-Clark IR, Rueffer SD. Relations among hypnagogic and hypnopompic experiences associated with sleep paralysis. *Journal of Sleep Research*, 1999; **8**:313–317.
21. Kotorii T, Kotorii T, Uchimura N, Hashizume Y, Shirakawa S, Satomura T, Tanaki J, Nakazawa Y, Meada H. Questionnaire relating to sleep paralysis. *Psychiatry and Clinical Neurosciences*, 2001; **55**:265–266.
22. Fukuda K. Sleep paralysis and sleep-onset REM period in normal individuals. In RD Ogilvie, JR Harsh, ed. *Sleep onset: normal and abnormal processes.* American Psychological Association, Washington, DC, 1994:161–181.
23. Fukuda K. One explanatory basis for the discrepancy of the reported prevalences of sleep paralysis among healthy respondents. *Perceptual and Motor Skills*, 1993; **77**:803–807.
24. Wing YK, Chiu H, Leung T, Ng J. Sleep paralysis in the elderly. *Journal of Sleep Research*, 1999; **8**:151–155.

25. **Allen D, Nutt D.** Co-existence of panic disorder and sleep paralysis. *Journal of Psychopharmacology*, 1993; 7:293–294.
26. **Bell CC, Hildreth CJ, Jenkins EJ, Carter C.** The relationship of isolated sleep paralysis and panic disorder to hypertension. *Journal of the National Medical Association*, 1988; 80:289–294.
27. **Paradis CM, Friedman S.** Sleep paralysis in African Americans with panic disorder. *Transcultural Psychiatry*, 2005; 42:123–134.
28. **Mitchell S.** On some of the disorders of sleep. *Virginia Medical Monthly*, 1876; 2:769–781.
29. **Wilson SAK.** The narcolepsies. *Brain*, 1928; 51:63–109.
30. **Ethelberg S.** Symptomatic cataplexy or chalastic fits in cortical lesions of the frontal lobe. *Brain*, 1950; 73:499–512.
31. **Aird RB, Gordon NS, Gregg HC.** Use of phenacemide (phenurone) in the treatment of narcolepsy and cataplexy. *Archives of Neurolology and Psychiatry*, 1953; 70:510–515.
32. **Kalat JW.** *Biological psychology*, 5th edn. Brooks Cole, Pacific Grove. 1995.
33. **Hishikawa Y, Kaneko Z.** Electroencephalographic study on narcolepsy. *Electroencephalography and Clinical Neurophysiology*, 1965; 18:249–259.
34. **Hishikawa Y, Tabushi K, Ueyama M, Hariguchi S, Fujiki A, Kaneko Z.** Electroencephalographic study in narcolepsy: especially concerning the symptoms of cataplexy, sleep paralysis and hypnagogic hallucinations. *Proceedings of the Japanese EEG Society*, 1963; 52–55.
35. **Takeuchi T, Miyasita A, Sasaki Y, Inugami M, Fukuda K.** Isolated sleep paralysis elicited by sleep interruption. *Sleep*, 1992; 15:217–225.
36. **Miyasita A, Fukuda K, Inugami M.** Effects of sleep interruption on REM–NREM cycle in nocturnal human sleep. *Electroencephalography and Clinical Neurophysiology*, 1989; 73:107–116.
37. **Cheyne JA.** Situational factors affecting sleep paralysis and associated hallucinations: Position and timing effects. *Journal of Sleep Research*, 2002; 11:169–177.
38. **Ohayon MM, Priest RG, Caulet M, Guilleminault C.** Hypnagogic and hypnopompic hallucinations: pathological phenomena? *British Journal of Psychiatry*, 1996; 169:459–467.
39. **Cheyne JA, Rueffer SD, Newby-Clark IR.** Hypnagogic and hypnopompic hallucinations during sleep paralysis: neurological and cultural construction of the night-mare. *Consciousness and Cognition*, 1999; 8:319–337.
40. **Hobson JA, McCarley RW.** The brain as a dream state generator: an activation synthesis hypothesis of dream process. *American Journal of Psychiatry*, 1977; 134:1335–1348.
41. **McCarley RW, Hobson JA.** The form of dreams and the biology of sleep. In BB Wolman, ed. *Handbook of dreams: research, theories and applications*. Van Nostrand-Reinhold, New York. 1979:76–130.
42. **Maquette P, Péters J-M, Aerts J, Delfiore G, Degueldre C, Luxen A, Franck G.** Functional neuroanatomy of human rapid-eye-movement sleep and dreaming. *Nature*, 1996; 383:163–166.
43. **Hobson JA, Stickgold R, Pace-Schott EF.** The neurophysiology of REM sleep dreaming. *NeuroReport*, 1998; 9:R1–R14.
44. **LeDoux J.** *The emotional brain*. Simon & Schuster, New York. 1998.
45. **Cheyne JA.** The ominous numinous: sensed presence and 'other' hallucinations. *Journal of Consciousness Studies*, 2001; 8:133–150.
46. **Hobson JA, Stickgold R, Pace-Schott EF, Leslie KR.** Sleep and vestibular adaptation: implications for function in microgravity. *Journal of Vestibular Research*, 1998; 8:81–94.
47. **Hufford DJ.** *The terror that comes in the night: an experience-centered study of supernatural assault traditions*. University of Pennsylvania Press, Philadelphia. 1982.
48. **Hufford DJ.** Sleep paralysis as spiritual experience. *Transcultural Psychiatry*, 2005; 42:11–45.
49. **Hinton DE, Hufford DJ, Kirmayer LJ.** Culture and sleep paralysis. *Transcultural Psychiatry*, 2005; 42:5–10.
50. **Davies O.** The nightmare experience, sleep paralysis, and witchcraft accusations. *Folklore*, 2003; 114:181–203.

51. **Yeung A, Xu Y, Chang DF.** Prevalence and illness beliefs of sleep paralysis among Chinese psychiatric patients in China and the United States. *Transcultural Psychiatry*, 2005; **42**:135–145.
52. **Law S, Kirmayer LJ.** Inuit interpretations of sleep paralysis. *Transcultural Psychiatry*, 2005; **42**:93–112.
53. **Bloom JD, Gelardin RD.** Eskimo sleep paralysis. *Arctic*, 1976; **29**:20–26.
54. **De Jong JTVM.** Cultural variation in the clinical presentation of sleep paralysis. *Transcultural Psychiatry*, 2005; **42**:78–92.
55. **Adler SR.** Sudden unexpected nocturnal death syndrome among Hmong immigrants: examining the role of the 'nightmare'. *Journal of American Folklore*, 1991; **104**:54–71.
56. **Adler SR.** Ethnomedical pathogenesis and Hmong immigrants' sudden nocturnal deaths. *Culture, Medicine and Psychiatry*, 1994; **18**:23–59.
57. **French CC.** Alien abductions. In R Roberts, D Groome, ed. *Parapsychology: the science of unusual experience.* Arnold, London. 2001:102–116.
58. **French CC.** Fantastic memories: the relevance of research into eyewitness testimony and false memories for reports of anomalous experiences. *Journal of Consciousness Studies*, 2003; **10**:153–174.
59. **Holden KJ, French CC.** Alien abduction experiences: clues from neuropsychology and neuropsychiatry. *Cognitive Neuropsychiatry*, 2002; **7**:163–178.
60. **Hopkins B, Jacobs DM, Westrum R.** *Unusual personal experiences: an analysis of the data from three national surveys conducted by the Roper Organisation.* Bigelow Holding Corporation, Las Vegas, NV. 1992.
61. **Appelle S, Lynn SJ, Newman L.** Alien abduction experiences. In E Cardeña, SJ Lynn, S Krippner, ed. *Varieties of anomalous experience: examining the scientific evidence.* American Psychological Association, Washington, DC. 2000:253–282.
62. **McNally RJ, Clancy SA.** Sleep paralysis, sexual abuse, and space alien abduction. *Transcultural Psychiatry*, 2005; **42**:113–122.
63. **Spanos NP.** *Multiple identities and false memories: a sociocognitive perspective.* American Psychological Association, Washington, DC. 1996.
64. **Paradis CM, Friedman S, Hatch M.** Isolated sleep paralysis in African Americans with panic disorder. *Cultural Diversity and Mental Health*, 1997; **3**:69–76.
65. **Terrillon J-C, Marques-Bonham S.** Does recurrent isolated sleep paralysis involve more than cognitive neurosciences? *Journal of Scientific Exploration*, 2001; **15**:97–123.
66. **Sandyk R.** Resolution of sleep paralysis by weak electromagnetic fields in a patient with multiple sclerosis. *International Journal of Neuroscience*, 1997; **83**:153–163.

Tall tales on the mind

Chapter 24

The power of the full moon. Running on empty?

Eric H. Chudler

It is the very error of the moon;
She comes more near the earth than she was wont,
And makes men mad.

William Shakespeare, *Othello*, act 5, sc. 2, l

Look! Up in the sky! It's a bird. It's a plane. No. It's just the moon. However, not just any moon. It is a full moon (Fig. 24.1), capable of causing accidents, psychosis, suicide and animal rage. At least that is what the media would have us believe—that the full moon can somehow influence our behaviour; but what does the research show? Is there an association between the full moon and abnormal behaviour? If such an association exists, then should we alter our behaviour according to the lunar cycle to minimize risks to our physical and mental health? If there is no such association, then why is the belief that the full moon can control behaviour so prevalent in many areas of the world?

History

The moon has played a role in literature, superstition and medicine for centuries. Ancient Roman and Greek scholars, including Plutarch, Pliny the Elder and Hippocrates, all linked the moon to mental illness.[1] Indeed, mental illness has been referred to as 'lunacy', a word derived from the Latin 'luna' meaning moon. English authors, such as Charles Dickens, John Milton, Lord Byron, Percy Bysshe Shelley and William Shakespeare, have all written about the disturbing effects of the moon on behaviour.[1] The moon has even influenced English law.[2] For example, Sir William Hale, who went on to become chief justice of England in the 1600s, believed that the moon had the ability to influence brain disorders, especially dementia. In the mid 1700s, Sir William Blackstone in *Commentaries on the laws of England*, mentioned the influence of the moon on mental state when he wrote:

> A LUNATIC, or *non compos mentis*, is one who has had understanding, but by disease, grief, or other accident has lost the use of his reason. A lunatic is indeed properly one that has lucid intervals; sometimes enjoying his senses, and sometimes not, and that frequently depending upon the change of the moon.

Fig. 24.1 Full moon.

England's Lunacy Act of 1842 also distinguished between behaviour that was normal 2 weeks before the full moon, but abnormal 2 weeks after the full moon.

More violence, more suicides, more accidents, more aggression: does the full moon really bring out the worst in people? The belief that the moon influences behaviour has led people to label the phenomenon as 'The Lunar Effect'. These beliefs, that were so widespread throughout Europe hundreds of years ago, are still prevalent today, even within the medical and mental health professions.

The published data

Although anecdotal reports of abnormal behaviour during the full moon may make good newspaper copy, they do not carry much scientific support. Moreover, widespread acceptance of a belief does not make the belief true. Published research studies have investigated the relationship between the phase of the moon and abnormal behaviour by focusing on several general themes including (1) crime, aggression and violence; (2) mental illness, for example, anxiety, depression, psychosis and suicide; (3) emergency room (A&E) and hospital admissions; (4) drug overdoses; and (5) motor vehicle and other accidents. These retrospective studies have used quantitative methods to search for correlations between the phase of the moon and the frequency or severity of specific behaviours.

Aggression/criminal behaviour

The influence of the moon on aggressive and criminal behaviour has received a great deal of media attention. The frequencies of homicides in Dade County, Florida, have been reported to increase significantly around the full and new moons.[3] Further investigations by the same researchers, however, were unable to find a significant relationship between homicide rate and lunar phase in Cyahoga County, Ohio. Similarly, no significant relationships were found for homicide rates and lunar phase in Texas.[4,5] Differences in these results have been attributed to using the time of death rather than the time of injury to define when a homicide took place.[6] Although a few studies have found clustering of the number of assaults and other crimes around the time of the full moon,[7–9] these results have been difficult to replicate.[10] Police records indicate that there is no correlation between the number of arrests for violent crimes and the lunar cycle.[11] Furthermore, the frequency of violent behaviour in a captive prison population does not vary with moon phase.[12]

Although it is commonly assumed that emergency telephone operators are busier during the full moon, data do not support this belief.[13] For example, no association between the phase of the moon and 361 580 calls for police assistance has been found.[14] Victims of violence are also not admitted to the hospital more frequently during the full moon.[15] Nevertheless, police officers continue to believe more strongly in the power of the full moon and hold stronger opinions about the lunar effect than pedestrians and psychiatric workers.[16]

Investigations about a lunar influence on aggressive non-human animal behaviour have also failed to produce convincing results. In one study, for example, the frequency of animal bites peaked during the full moon.[17] However, this study examined only 10 lunar cycles and did not control for weekends or holidays. When adjustments for weekends were made, research has failed to find a relationship between the frequency of dog bites and the cycles of the moon.[18,19] It is important to note the day of the full moon because people do appear to be at a higher risk for being bitten by a dog on weekends and during non-winter months.[19]

Mental illness

Mental health professionals commonly believe that the moon can alter human behaviour. For example, 81 per cent (21 of 26 respondents) of the mental health professionals surveyed agreed with the statement 'I think the moon makes some people act weird or crazy'.[20] Crisis centre workers also believe more strongly in the lunar effect than non-crisis centre workers.[21] Anecdotal stories and news accounts of increased antisocial psychiatric patient behaviour, suicide attempts, telephone calls to mental health crisis centres and admissions to psychiatric hospitals during the full moon help to reinforce these beliefs in the general public. However, most studies do not provide evidence of increased psychiatric disturbances during the full moon. For example, telephone calls to crisis intervention centres[21–24] and college counselling centres[25] do not increase in frequency during the full moon. The number of psychiatric hospital admissions,[26,27] frequency of medical consultations for anxiety and depression[28] and the use of psychiatric services[29] are also not correlated with lunar phase. Although one study reported more frequent misbehaviour by developmentally delayed, institutionalized women on the day of the full moon,[30,31] violence and aggression by hospitalized psychiatric patients[32] and agitated behaviour by nursing home residents[33] are not observed more often during the full moon.

Suicidal behaviour also does not occur more frequently during the full moon. In fact, a significant increase in recorded suicides around the new moon, but not around the full moon, has been reported.[34] A significant relationship between any phase of the moon and successful suicides or suicide attempts has not been found in several studies.[35–40]

Data about the relationship between self-poisoning and moon phase are conflicting. Intentional consumption of poison has been found to increase during the new moon and decrease during the full moon,[41] increase on days of the full moon[42] or show no relationship with the lunar cycle.[43] The cultural significance of the full moon (see below) may contribute to the positive association between self-injurious behaviour and lunar phase.

Accidents

Emergency room nurses and physicians also hold strong beliefs about the lunar effect. Of 25 emergency department nurses surveyed, 20 (80 per cent) responded that they believed that the moon affected their patients and their mental health; 16 of 25 (64 per cent) of the emergency department physicians surveyed held similar beliefs.[44] These nurses also believed that lunar influences created a more stressful work environment and, therefore, that they should be compensated with higher wages during these periods.[44] Such workers, therefore, could be motivated by possible financial gain by believing in a lunar effect or by reporting such beliefs in the lunar effect when completing a survey. Hospitals, however, are not plagued by excessive accidents or errors during the full moon. Analyses of hospital records have failed to find a correlation between medication errors, treatment errors, falls and other 'untoward events' and lunar phase.[45] There is also no association between surgical complications (e.g. pain, mental health, patient complaints) and lunar phase.[46]

Despite the beliefs of medical personnel, data show that emergency departments are not unusually burdened with cases and there are no increases in emergency department admissions during the full moon. Examination of emergency department and hospital records of trauma, cardiac, respiratory and neurological cases has failed to find an increase in the number of cases during the full moon phase.[47–55] The number of patients who arrive to the hospital by ambulance also does not vary with the phase of the moon.[53] On the other hand, emergency departments do appear to be busier on Mondays than on other days of the week.[47]

Research that claimed an increase in vehicular accidents[56] during the new and full moon phases has been critiqued because of a variety of errors made by the investigators.[57] Moreover, when these data were reanalysed and controls for day of the week and holidays were included, the lunar effect disappeared.[14] Other data show no association between the number and severity of vehicular accidents with moon phase.[58] Still other studies have reported that traffic accidents occur least often on the day of the full moon,[59] and that traffic accidents involving property damage and personal injury show no relationship with the phase of the moon.[60]

Drug abuse

Just as emergency departments are not unusually busy with trauma and other cases, they are also not troubled by an abnormal number of drug abuse cases during the full moon.[61,62] This is also reflected in the absence of a relationship between the number of toxicology requests processed by hospital laboratories and lunar phase.[62]

Box 24.1 Moon facts

- The distance from the moon to the Earth varies from 356,410 km (221,438 miles) to 406,697 km (252,681 miles). The average distance between the Earth and moon is 384,400 km (238,855 miles).
- The equatorial radius of the moon is 1737 km (1080 miles).
- The circumference of the moon is 10,916 km (6783 miles)
- The surface area of the moon is 37.9 million km^2.
- The mass of the moon is 7.35×10^{22}.
- The first lunar landing occurred on July 20, 1969, at 4.18 p.m. (EDT) when the Apollo 11 Lunar Module touched down on the moon at Tranquility Base. At 10.56 p.m., astronaut Neil Armstrong touched one foot to the moon's surface.

Citation: National Aeronautics and Space Administration (Accessed July 14, 2006), http://solarsystem.jpl.nasa.gov/planets/

Possible mechanisms

It is readily apparent from the published data that studies indicating a positive relationship between abnormal behaviour and lunar phase are difficult to replicate. Although a few studies show increases in the frequency of unusual behaviour during the full moon, most studies show no relationship or a decrease in the frequency of abnormal behaviour at the time of the full moon. The inability to replicate these experimental data is a major problem faced by those who study the relationships between lunar phase and behaviour. A significant relationship should be replicable by different investigators using similar methodologies.

Rotton and Kelly[10] and Campbell[63] discuss the methodological problems inherent in many lunar effect studies and the methodological differences that make comparisons of the results from different data samples difficult. Some failures to replicate findings may be related to differences in experimental design. For example, some studies consider a few days before and after the full moon as a full moon period, while other studies restrict their investigations to only those behaviours on the day of the full moon. The number of moon cycles used to analyse lunar effects has also differed greatly among studies. Some investigators have collated data from moon phases extending 10 or more years, while others used data from only a few cycles of the moon. Limiting the observation period to only a few moon cycles may result in specific moon phases falling frequently on holidays or weekends, thus influencing the results. Nevertheless, a meta-analysis of 37 lunar effect studies has revealed that only 1 per cent or less of the variance in abnormal behaviour could be attributed to the phase of the moon.[10]

Several excellent discussions and critiques of the mechanisms by which proponents of the lunar effect have suggested that the moon could alter behaviour have been published.[10,63,64] Such mechanisms include (1) a gravitational effect; (2) increased moonlight; (3) weather effects; (4) ozone effects; and (4) imperceptible stimuli such as geomagnetic forces, extremely low frequency electromagnetic waves and air ions. To date, none of these mechanisms have sufficient experimental data to account for a lunar effect. For example, the gravitational effect theory proposes that water in the human body, like water in the ocean, is influenced by the gravitational pull of the full moon. The problem with this hypothesis is that the moon has negligible effects on the human body, certainly much less than other earthly bound objects.[63,65] Moonlight provides a weak source of illumination and is nothing more than reflected sunlight.[64] Therefore, behaviours affected by moonlight should also be affected by other light sources, including that of the sun.

Although the majority of studies have failed to find evidence to support the belief that the full moon affects behaviour, the large body of negative data does not prove the absence of an effect. As the expression goes, *the absence of evidence is not the same as evidence of absence.* However, the burden of proof for the existence of a lunar effect lies with experimental evidence. Experiments must be designed to test the hypothesis that the full moon can influence behaviour. Perhaps the most common error made by lunar effect proponents is that of assigning cause to correlative data. In other words, even if the correlation between moon phase and the frequency of a behaviour is statistically significant, this does not mean that a particular moon phase *caused* the change in behaviour. As students of elementary statistics learn: *correlation does not mean causation.* Correlational studies are not sufficient to demonstrate causation. Experiments to test hypotheses regarding the mechanisms by which the lunar effect may work have not been conducted and may be difficult. As suggested by Rotton and Kelly,[10] 'Without observing individuals on a planet without a moon (say, Venus), there is no way investigators can conclude that phases of the moon affect behavior'. Alternatively, studies could be designed to investigate possible lunar effect mechanisms, for example by comparing how behaviour changes on full moon days when the moon can be seen (clear nights) with that when the moon cannot be seen (cloudy nights). Similarly, the influences of ozone, extremely low frequency electromagnetic waves and charged ions, on behaviour could be tested in humans and other animals.

Why the myth persists

Despite the absence of evidence for the lunar effect, many people continue to believe that the full moon can affect behaviour. With few exceptions, data that negate the lunar effect rarely pique the interest of the media. Therefore, the public is denied access to an abundant body of literature that has failed to support the lunar effect. This lack of information may help propagate the belief in a relationship between the full moon and behaviour such that the belief becomes a self-fulfilling prophecy. In other words, if people believe that the moon affects behaviour, they may interact with others in ways to produce a relationship that then reinforces their belief. For example, if police officers believe that the full moon causes violent behaviour, they may stop more drivers for aggressive driving or make more arrests on days of the full moon. Nurses and physicians who believe in the lunar effect may treat patients differently on the day of the full moon.

Some people may go out of their way to mark the day of a full moon. They may highlight the day of the full moon on a calendar or alert co-workers to the next occurrence of a full moon. This heightened awareness of the full moon may also serve to direct attention toward events that occur during the full moon and may even motivate some people to act irresponsibly on days of the full moon. Heightened awareness of the full moon may also contribute to selective memory of strange events that occur. Although an accident or an unusual event may occur during a full moon, similar unusual events are likely to happen at other times during the lunar cycle. However, only those strange events that occur during the full moon will be remembered because of the significance that people have placed on this period of the lunar cycle.

Raison et al.[66] have advanced a novel hypothesis suggesting that moonlight may have affected sleep–wake patterns before the widespread use of artificial light. They point out that moonlight was important to many human social activities prior to the 19th century and suggest that people slept less on full moon days than on other days. Such an alteration in sleep patterns may have resulted in sleep deprivation that then led to cognitive and emotional changes including mania. Relationships between the full moon's light and these abnormal behaviours may have been recognized by people before the invention of gas and electrical lighting. Therefore, although moonlight has little value to most contemporary human activities, stories about the full moon and abnormal behaviour may have been carried over into modern times.

Cultural influences may also contribute to the persistence in the belief of the lunar effect. For example, the wonder and mystery of the full moon is instilled in children as they learn to read. Popular children's books such as *Goodnight Moon*,[67] *Where The Wild Things Are*,[68] *Goodnight, Goodnight*[69] and *Moongame*[70] all draw attention to the moon in their storylines. The moon has also been worshiped by cultures throughout the world, with moon goddesses and gods taking a prominent position in many religious beliefs. For example, the full moon holds a special place in the Hindu religion and is celebrated as 'purnima'. It is interesting to note that a significant increase in the incidence of poisoning on the day of the full moon was found in a study conducted in India[42] although the number of poisonings of people of the Hindu religion in this study is unknown. The full moon is linked to the time of festivals and celebrations in other cultures. For example, many Buddhist holidays, such as the Buddhist New Year, Vesak (Buddha Day), Magha Puja Day (Sangha Day) and Asalha Puja Day (Dhamma Day), take place on days of the full moon. In Korea, Taeborum is celebrated on the first full moon of the lunar year and in Thailand, the Loy Krathong festival is celebrated on the day of full moon in the

12th lunar month. The Jewish holiday of Passover also starts on the night of a full moon. Furthermore, calendars based on the lunar cycle are still used around the world. For example, the Hebrew, Islamic and Chinese calendars are all tied to the lunar cycle.

Summary

Newspaper editors who publish stories about the lunar effect, law enforcement officers who insist people act strangely on days of the full moon and healthcare workers who maintain that the moon influences their patients all provide fuel to perpetuate the belief that the phase of the moon affects behaviour. Examination of the many studies that have searched for a relationship between the full moon and abnormal behaviour, however, shows that the engine that drives these beliefs is running on fumes.

References and notes

1. Oliven JF. Moonlight and nervous disorders. *American Journal of Psychiatry*, 1943; **99**:579–584.
2. Guiley RE. Moonscapes. *A celebration of lunar astronomy, magic, legend and lore*. Prentice Hall Press, New York. 1991.
3. Lieber AL, Sherin CR. Homicides and the lunar cycle: toward a theory of lunar influence on human emotional disturbance. *American Journal of Psychiatry*, 1972; **129**:69–74.
4. Pokorny AD. Moon phases, suicide, and homicide. *American Journal of Psychiatry*, 1964; **121**:66–67.
5. Pokorny AD, Jachimczyk J. The questionable relationship between homicides and the lunar cycle. *American Journal of Psychiatry*, 1974; **131**:827–829.
6. Garzino SJ. Lunar effects on mental behavior. A defense of the empirical research. *Environmental Behaviour*, 1982; **14**:395–417.
7. Lieber AL. Human aggression and the lunar synodic cycle. *Journal of Clinical Psychiatry*, 1978; **39**:385–387; 390–393.
8. Tasso J, Miller E. The effects of the full moon on human behavior. *Journal of Psychology*, 1976; **93**:81–83.
9. Thakur CP, Sharma D. Full moon and crime. *British Medical Journal*, 1984; **289**:1789–1791.
10. Rotton J, Kelly IW. Much ado about the full moon: a meta-analysis of lunar-lunacy research. *Psychology Bulletin*, 1985; **97**: 286–306.
11. Forbes GB, Lebo GR Jr. Antisocial behavior and lunar activity: a failure to validate the lunacy myth. *Psychological Reports*, 1997; **40**:1309–1310.
12. Simon A. Aggression in a prison setting as a function of lunar phases. *Psychological Reports*, 1998; **82**:747–752.
13. Frey J, Rotton J, Barry T. The effects of the full moon on human behavior: yet another failure to replicate. *Journal of Psychology*, 1979; **103**:159–162.
14. Templer DI, Brooner RK, Corgiat MD. Geophysical variables and behavior: XIV. Lunar phase and crime: fact or artifact. *Perceptual Motor Skills*, 1983; **57**:993–994.
15. Coates W, Jehle D, Cottington E. Trauma and the full moon: a waning theory. *Annals of Emergency Medicine*, 1989; **18**:763–765.
16. Rotton J, Kelly IW, Elortegui, P. Assessing belief in lunar effects: known-groups validation. *Psychological Reports*, 1986; **59**:171–174.
17. Bhattacharjee C, Bradley P, Smith M, Scally AJ, Wilson BJ. Do animals bite more often during a full moon? Retrospective observational analysis. *British Medical Journal*, 2000; **321**:1559–1561.
18. Chapman S, Morrell S. Barking mad? Another lunatic hypothesis bites the dust. *British Medical Journal*, 2000; **321**:1561–1563.
19. Frangakis CE, Petridou E. Modelling risk factors for injuries from dog bites in Greece: a case-only design and analysis. *Accident; Analysis and Prevention*, 2003; **35**:435–438.

20. Vance DE. Belief in lunar effects on human behavior. *Psychological Reports*, 1995; 76:32–34.
21. Wilson II JE, Tobacyk JJ. Lunar phases and crisis center telephone calls. *Journal of Social Psychology*, 1990; 130:47–51.
22. Byrnes G, Kelly IW. Crisis calls and lunar cycles: a twenty-year review. *Psychological Reports*, 1992; 71:779–785.
23. De Voge SD, Mikawa JK. Moon phases and crisis calls: a spurious relationship. *Psychological Reports*, 1977; 40:387–390.
24. Michelson L, Wilson J, Michelson J. Investigation of periodicity in crisis intervention calls over an eight-year span. *Psychological Reports*, 1979; 45:420–422.
25. Weiskott GN. Moon phases and telephone counseling calls. *Psychological Reports*, 1974; 35:752–754.
26. Climent CE, Plutchik R. Lunar madness: an empirical study. *Comprehensive Psychiatry*, 1977; 18:369–374.
27. Gorvin JJ, Roberts MS. Lunar phases and psychiatric hospital admissions. *Psychological Reports*, 1994; 75:1435–1440.
28. Wilkinson G, Piccinelli M, Roberts S, Micciolo R, Fry J. Lunar cycle and consultations for anxiety and depression in general practice. *International Journal of Social Psychiatry*, 1997; 43:29–34.
29. Amaddeo F, Bisoffi G, Micciolo R, Piccinelli M, Tansella M. Frequency of contact with community-based psychiatric services and the lunar cycle: a 10-year case register study. *Social and Psychiatric Epidemiology*, 1997; 32:323–326.
30. Hicks-Caskey WE, Tusell DR. Effect of the full moon on a sample of developmentally delayed, institutionalized women. *Perceptual Motor Skills*, 1991; 72:1375–1380.
31. Hicks-Caskey WE, Potter DR. Weekends and holidays and acting-out behavior of developmentally delayed women: a reply to Dr. Mark Flynn. *Perceptual Motor Skills*, 1992; 74:344–346.
32. Owen C, Tarantello C, Jones M, Tennant C. Lunar cycles and violent behaviour. Australia. New Zealand. *Journal of Psychiatry*, 1998; 32:496–499.
33. Cohen-Mansfield J. Full moon: does it influence agitated nursing-home residents? *Journal of Clinical Psychology*, 1989; 45:611–614.
34. Jones PK, Jones SL. Lunar association with suicide. *Suicide and Life-Threatening Behaviour*, 1977; 7:31–39.
35. Garth JM, Lester D. The moon and suicide. *Psychological Reports*, 1978; 43:678.
36. Gutierrez-Garcia JM, Tusell F. Suicides and the lunar cycle. *Psychological Reports*, 1997; 80:243–250.
37. MacMahon K. Short-term temporal cycles in the frequency of suicide, United States, 1972–1978. *American Journal of Epidemiology*, 1983; 117:744–750.
38. Maldonado G, Krause JF. Variation in suicide occurrence by time of day, day of the week, month, and lunar phase. *Suicide and Life-Threatening Behaviour*, 1991; 21:174–187.
39. Mathew VM, Lindesay J, Shanmuganathan N, Eapen AV. Attempted suicide and the lunar cycle. *Psychological Reports*, 1991; 68:927–930.
40. Rogers TD, Masterton G, McGuire R. Parasuicide and the lunar cycle. *Psychological Medicine*, 1991; 21:393–397.
41. Oderda GM, Klein-Schwarz W. Lunar cycle and poison center calls. *Journal of Toxicology, Clinical Toxicology*, 1983; 20:487–495.
42. Thakur CP, Sharma RN, Akhtar HS. Full moon and poisoning. *British Medical Journal*, 1980; 281:1684.
43. Jacobsen D, Frederichsen PS, Knutsen KM, Sorum Y, Talseth T, Odegaard OR. Self-poisoning and moon phases in Oslo. *Human Toxicology*, 1986; 5:51–52.
44. Danzl DF. Lunacy. *Journal of Emergency Medicine*, 1987; 5:91–95.
45. Bonk JR, Don't pass the buck! The full moon is not responsible for an increase in the occurrence of untoward events in a hospital setting! *Journal of Psychiatric Nursing and Mental Health Services*, 1979; 17:33–36.
46. Holzheimer RG, Nitz C, Gresser U. Lunar phase does not influence surgical quality. *European Journal of Medical Research*, 2003; 8:414–418.

47. **Allen JL.** Emergency admissions and lunar cycles. *Journal of Emergency Nursing,* 1986; **12**:85–88.

48. **Alves DW, Allegra JR, Cochrane DG, Cable G.** Effect of lunar cycle on temporal variation in cardiopulmonary arrest in seven emergency departments during 11 years. *European Journal of Emergency Medicine,* 2003; **10**:225–228.

49. **Benbadis SR, Chang S, Hunter J, Wang W.** The influence of the full moon on seizure frequency: myth or reality? *Epilepsy and Behaviour,* 2004; **5**:596–597.

50. **Butler S, Songra A, Hardee P, Hutchison I.** The moon and its relationship to oral and maxillofacial emergencies. *British Journal of Maxillofactory Surgery,* 2003; **41**:170–172.

51. **Eisenburger P, Schreiber W, Vergeiner G, Sterz F, Holzer M, Herkner H, Havel C, Laggner AN.** Lunar phases are not related to the occurrence of acute myocardial infarction and sudden cardiac death. *Resuscitation,* 2003; **56**:187–189.

52. **Stair T.** Lunar cycles and emergency-room visits. *New England Journal of Medicine,* 1978; **298**:1318–1319.

53. **Thompson DA, Adams SL.** The full moon and ED patient volumes: unearthing a myth. *American Journal of Emergency Medicine,* 1996; **14**:161–164.

54. **Wolbank S, Prause G, Smolle-Juettner F, Smolle J, Heidinger D, Quehanberger F, Spernbauer P.** The influence of lunar phenomena on the incidence of emergency cases. *Resuscitation,* 2003; **58**:97–102.

55. **Zargar M, Khaji A, Kaviani A, Karebakhsh M, Yunesian M, Abdollahi M.** The full moon and admission to emergency rooms. *Indian Journal of Medical Sciences,* 2004; **58**:191–195.

56. **Templer DI, Brooner RK, Corgiat MD.** Geophysical variables and behavior: VI. Lunar phase and accident injuries: a difference between night and day. *Perceptual Motor Skills,* 1982; **55**:280–282.

57. **Kelly IW, Rotton J.** Geophysical variables and behavior: XIII. Comment on 'lunar phase and accident injuries': the dark side of the moon and lunar research. *Perceptual Motor Skills,* 1983; **57**:919–921.

58. **Laverty WH, Kelly IW, Flynn M, Rotton J.** Geophysical variables and behavior: LXVIII. Distal and lunar variables and traffic accidents in Saskatchewan 1984–1989. *Perceptual Motor Skills,* 1992; **74**:483–488.

59. **Alonso Y.** Geophysical variables and behavior: LXXII. Barometric pressure, lunar cycle, and traffic accidents. *Perceptual Motor Skills,* 1993; **77**:371–376.

60. **Laverty WH, Kelly IW.** Cyclical calendar and lunar patterns in automobile property accidents and injury accidents. *Perceptual Motor Skills,* 1998; **86**:299–302.

61. **Halpern SD, Mechem CC.** Declining rate of substance abuse throughout the month. *American Journal of Medicine,* 2001; **110**:347–351.

62. **Sharfman M.** Drug overdose and the full moon. *Perceptual Motor Skills,* 1982; **50**:124–126.

63. **Campbell DE.** Lunar-lunacy research. When enough is enough. *Environmental Behaviour,* 1982; **14**:418–424.

64. **Culver R, Rotton J, Kelly IW.** Geophysical variable and behavior: XLIX. Moon mechanisms and myths: a critical appraisal of explanations of purported lunar effects on human behavior. *Psychological Reports,* 1988; **62**:683–710.

65. **Myers DE.** Gravitational effects of the period of high tides and the new moon on lunacy. *Journal of Emergency Medicine,* 1995; **13**:529–532.

66. **Raison CL, Klein HM, Steckler M.** The moon and madness reconsidered. *Journal of Affective Disorders,* 1999; **53**:99–106.

67. **Brown MW.** *Goodnight Moon.* Harper & Row, New York. 1947.

68. **Sendak M.** *Where The Wild Things Are.* Harper & Row, New York. 1963.

69. **Rice E.** *Goodnight, Goodnight.* Greenwillow Books, New York. 1980.

70. **Asch F.** *Moongame.* Scholastic, New York. 1984.

Chapter 25

Ouija, dowsing and other seductions of ideomotor action

Ray Hyman

Introduction

In 1992, I served as an expert witness for the state of Oregon. The state had accused four chiropractors of using an unproven medical device. This device consisted of a block of wood with an embedded concave plastic surface. The plastic surface served as a 'rubbing plate'. In diagnosing a client, the chiropractor would use his left hand to palpate the patient's spine. Simultaneously, he would move the fingers of his right hand back and forth across the rubbing plate. The chiropractors claimed that whenever their left hand touched a problematic spot on the patient's spine, the friction on the rubbing plate would increase and the fingers would 'stick' on the rubbing plate.

The district attorney asked me to make a videotape to illustrate the psychological principles that made the rubbing plate seem to work. I used two groups of student volunteers. I explained to the first group that an Oregon doctor had created the rubbing plate to amplify the sensitivity of our perceptions. I spread 10 playing cards faces up on a table. Some were red and some were black. I told the students that the red cards reflected light from the long end of the visual spectrum. The black cards reflected very little light, but what they did reflect contained equal amounts from all parts of the spectrum. Normally, I continued, the human senses cannot detect the difference between these two types of emission. However, the rubbing plate can enhance our sensitivity to these differences.

I demonstrated by passing my left hand back and forth, about a foot above the face-up playing cards. Meanwhile, I was rubbing the fingers of my right hand on the rubbing plate. My fingers glided smoothly over the plastic surface whenever my hand passed over a black card. My fingers would 'stick' when my left hand was over a red card.

I asked each student, in turn, to try the experiment. To their surprise, their fingers would also glide smoothly when their left hand was over a black card. The fingers of their right hand would stick when their left hand was over a black card. I then dismissed the first group and brought in the second group. I told them the same story that I told the first group. However, the fingers of my right hand would now stick when my left hand was over a black card. They would slide smoothly when my left hand was over a red card.

In both groups, the students' fingers stuck on the rubbing plate when their left hand was over the colour of the card that had apparently caused my fingers to stick. In the first group it was the red card and in the second group it was the black card. Obviously, they had all been influenced by what they saw me do. If they believed the red card would cause their fingers to stick, it did. If they believed the black card would cause their fingers to stick, it did.

After the experiment, I interviewed each student. Everyone insisted that they had not consciously controlled their fingers. They believed that the sticking of their fingers was controlled from a power outside of themselves. One student, who was from Africa, became terrified when her fingers began to stick. She insisted this was the work of the Devil. I spent considerable time trying to reassure her that the sticking sensation was nothing but a normal, unconscious psychological reaction. Demonic powers were not involved.

The extended family

I made this video to emphasize a simple, but important point. Under a variety of circumstances, our muscles will behave unconsciously according to an implanted expectation. This seems obvious. Yet this simple fact has been the source of much misunderstanding and self-deception. We have very strong illusions that we have conscious control over our actions. So when our bodies do things that we did not consciously initiate, we look for causes outside ourselves. This attribution of our unconscious behaviour to external sources has created much mischief and grief throughout history. In the next section, I will provide some examples of this mischief.

A simple idea; enormous consequences

The magic pendulum

Perhaps you have experimented with the dowsing rod. Or maybe you have consulted the ouija board (Fig. 25.1). Maybe you have sat around a small table with some friends. You may have been amazed when, with all your hands pressing lightly on the table top, the table appeared to take on a life of its own. It began to gyrate and move around the room dragging you and friends along with it. Possibly you may have played with the pendulum or 'sex detector'. If so, you know how compelling the experience can be. The planchette pointed to letters and spelled words that were meaningful. The table's antics were spooky. The pendulum moved in ways that were informative. Yet, you probably were sure that you or your friends were not the source of these antics.

If you have not had such experiences, then you might find it useful to try the following experiment. Take a small weight such as a key or ring and suspend this weight from a string or chain. A length of 1 or 2 feet is just about right. Hold the end of the string between the tips of your right fingers opposite to where you attached the weight. Stand erect and suspend the weight from your outstretched arm. With your free hand, impart a swinging motion to the weight. As the weight is swinging back and forth, forget your

Fig. 25.1 Ouja board.

fingers and your arm. Concentrate upon the swinging weight. Want the weight to begin gyrating in a clockwise circle. Concentrate and imagine that it is doing so. For most of you, the pendulum will begin gyrating in the expected clockwise circle. With a little practice, you can concentrate and get the pendulum to reverse its course and gyrate in a counterclockwise direction. In the same way you can will the ring to move back and forth in a pendulum fashion, etc. If this experiment has worked for you, you have experienced the same phenomenon that for centuries has baffled wise persons and convinced them that supernatural forces were in play.

The Latin historian Ammianus Marcellinus, who died in AD 390, gave the first detailed account of the pendulum. The authorities had captured a band of conspirators who were planning the assassination of the Emperor of the East. In his confession, a conspirator described how his group determined the name of the emperor's successor. A priest held a thread from which was suspended a ring. He held the ring over a disk, around the edge of which were printed the letters of the alphabet. The pendulum, oscillating in the priest's hand, pointed out, successively, the letters T,H,E, and O. This was sufficient to inform the conspirators that the emperor's successor would be Theodorus.

People have continued to use the magic pendulum since the Roman times. Notice that the very first account includes the elements of the ouija board.

Michel Eugene Chevreul

In the late eighteenth and early nineteenth centuries, several scientists began using the magic pendulum as a scientific instrument. They wrote books on its behaviour and its ability to react differently to magnetic poles and chemical substances. In 1808, Professor Gerboin of Strassburg wrote a book on the use of the pendulum for chemical analysis. The French chemist Michel Eugene Chevreul had read Gerboin's book and other writings on the pendulum's ability to analyse the composition of chemical compounds. These writings intrigued, him, but he was sceptical. In 1812 he decided to experiment with the pendulum.

He began by holding the pendulum over a dish of mercury. To his surprise, the pendulum moved according to Gerboin's description. He carried out additional tests. To see if a physical force was responsible for the pendulum's movement, he placed a glass plate between the ring and the mercury. The oscillations diminished and then stopped. He removed the glass plate and the pendulum's movements resumed. Chevreul next decided to see if the pendulum moved because he could not hold his arm steady. When he rested his arm on a support, the movements diminished but did not stop entirely.

Finally, Chevreul did what none of his predecessors had thought of doing. He conducted the equivalent of what today we would call a double-blind trial. He blindfolded himself and got his assistant to interpose or remove the glass plate between the pendulum and the mercury without his knowledge. Under these conditions, nothing happened. Chevreul concluded, 'So long as I believed the movement possible, it took place; but after discovering the cause I could not reproduce it'.

Chevreul's experiments with the pendulum showed how easy it is 'to mistake illusions for realities, whenever we are confronted by phenomena in which human sense organs are involved under conditions imperfectly analyzed'. Chevreul used this principle of expectant attention to account for the phenomena of dowsing, movements of the magic pendulum, and table turning, which was then the fad among spiritualists.

Michael Faraday and table turning

By the 1850s, table turning (also called table tilting or table rapping) had become the rage among spiritualists, both in North America and in Europe. A small group of 'sitters' would sit around a table with their hands resting upon its top. After a period of expectant waiting, they would hear a rap or the table would tilt upon one leg. Sometimes the table would sway and begin moving about the room, dragging the sitters along. Occasionally, sitters would claim that table levitated off the floor. Allegedly, the spirits of the departed relatives caused these movements. In some sessions, the spirits would communicate with the sitters by tapping a number of times. The spirits and the sitters would use a code for this purpose. In one version, for example, the sitters would slowly recite the alphabet. They would then record the letter at which the table rapped. Then they begin reciting the alphabet again and record the second letter at which the table rapped. In this laborious manner, the spirits created messages for the sitters.

In 1853, England's most famous scientist, Michael Faraday, published his study of table turning. Faraday obtained the cooperation of participants who he knew to be 'very honourable' and were also 'successful table-movers'. Faraday quickly discovered that the table would move in the expected direction even if one person were seated at the table. This greatly simplified his investigation. The first task was to see if the table moved because of known forces such as electricity or magnetism. He found that sandpaper, millboard, glue, glass, moist clay, tinfoil, cardboard, vulcanized rubber and wood did not interfere with the table's movements. He concluded that, 'No form of experiment or mode of observation that I could devise gave me the slightest indication of any peculiar force. No attraction, or repulsion...nor anything which could be referred to other than mere mechanical pressure exerted inadvertently by the turner'.

By now Faraday suspected that his sitters were unconsciously pushing the table in the desired direction. The sitters, however, insisted that they were not the source of the table's movements. So Faraday devised an ingenious arrangement to pin down the cause of the movement. He placed four or five pieces of slippery cardboard, one on top of the other, upon the table. The sheets were attached to one another by little pellets of soft cement. The bottom-most sheet was attached to a piece of sandpaper that rested against the table top. The edge of each layer in this cardboard sandwich slightly overlapped the one below. To mark their original positions, Faraday drew a pencil line across the exposed edges of the cardboard sheets on their under surface. The stack of cardboard sheets was secured to the table top by large rubber bands. This insured that when the table moved, the sheets would move with it. However, the bands allowed sufficient play to permit the individual sheets of cardboard to move somewhat independently of one another.

The sitter placed his hand upon the surface of the top cardboard layer and waited for the table to move in the direction previously agreed upon. Faraday reasoned that if the table moved to the left, and the source of the movement was the table and not the sitter, the table would move first and drag the successive layer of cardboard along with it. The bottom layer would move first and the top layer would move last. If this were the case, the displaced pencil marks would reveal a staggered line sloping upwards from left to right.

On the other hand, if the sitter unwittingly moved the table, his hands would push the top cardboard layer to the left and the remaining layers of cardboard would be dragged along successively. This would result in the displacement of the pencil marks from left to right from the top down. As Faraday observed, 'It was easy to see by the displacement of the parts of the line that the hand had moved further from the table, and that the latter had lagged behind—that the hand, in fact, had pushed the upper card to the left and that the under cards and the table had followed and been dragged by it'.

Faraday added another interesting phase to his experiment. He attached a pointer to the cardboard layers so that if the sitter were pushing the table to the left, the pointer would point to the left. On the other hand, if the table were initiating the movement, the pointer would point to the right. When the sitter could not see the pointer, the table still moved and the pointer pointed to the right. This simply reinforced what Faraday had already discovered. The sitter was the source of the movement. However, when he allowed the sitter to see the pointer, the table no longer moved. Faraday concluded:

> But the most valuable effect of this test-apparatus is the corrective power it possesses over the mind of the table-turner. As soon as the index is placed before the most earnest, and they perceive—as in my presence they have always done—that it tells truly whether they are pressing downwards only or obliquely; then all effects of table-turning cease, even though the parties persevere, earnestly desiring motion, till they become weary and worn out. No prompting or checking of the hands is needed—*the power is gone*; and this only because the parties are made conscious of what they are really doing mechanically, and so are unable unwittingly to deceive themselves.

More variations on the same theme
Robert Hare and the spiritscope

Faraday's report convinced most scientists that table turning and related phenomena did not stem from new physical forces or occult powers. Robert Hare, an eminent professor emeritus of chemistry at the University of Pennsylvania, had read Faraday's report with great interest. The *Philadelphia Inquirer* asked Hare for his comments. In his letter to the newspaper on July 27, 1853, Hare firmly rejected the possibility that an exotic force could cause the movement of the tables. He wrote, 'I recommend to your attention, and that of others interested in this hallucination, Faraday's observations and experiments, recently published in some of our respectable newspapers. I entirely concur in the conclusions of that distinguished expounder of Nature's riddles'.

A Mr Amasa Holcombe and a Dr Comstock replied to Hare's letter and invited him to attend a table turning session. Comstock appealed to Hare's sense of fair play by asking him to observe and test the phenomena for himself rather than rely upon Faraday's report. Hare accepted the invitation and attended a 'circle' at a private house. Hare described his experience as follows:

> Seated at a table with half a dozen persons, a hymn was sung with religious zeal and solemnity. Soon afterwards tappings were distinctly heard as if made beneath and against the table, which, from the perfect stillness of every one of the party, could not be attributed to any one among them.

Apparently, the sounds were such as could only be made with some hard instrument, or with ends of fingers aided by nails.

I learned that simple queries were answered by means of these manifestations; one tap being considered as equivalent to a negative; two, to doubtful; and three, to an affirmative. With the greatest apparent sincerity, questions were put and answers taken and recorded, as if all concerned considered them as coming from a rational though invisible agent. Subsequently, two media sat down at a small table (drawer removed) which, upon careful examination, I found present to my inspection nothing but the surface of a bare board, on the under side as well as upon the upper. Yet the taps were heard as before, seemingly against the table. Even assuming the people by whom I was surrounded to be capable of deception, and the feat to be due to jugglery, it was still inexplicable. But manifestly I was in a company of worthy people, who were themselves under a deception if these sounds did not proceed from spiritual agency.

Hare described other phenomena he experienced in subsequent sittings. He insisted that normal agency could not explain the antics of the table. His personal experiences with table turning convinced him that Faraday's findings could not account for what he had witnessed.

To the dismay of his scientific colleagues, Hare began a programme of research into spirit communication. His remarkable book of 1855 has the equally remarkable title: *Experimental investigations of the spirit manifestations, demonstrating the existence of spirits and their communion with mortals, doctrine of the spirit world respecting Heaven, Hell, morality, and God. Also the influence of scripture on the morals of Christians.* Hare stated that before he began investigating spiritualism he was a materialist and atheist. His book describes his investigations that convinced him of the reality of the spirit world. During these experiments he discovered he had mediumistic powers. He could communicate with the spirit world. Hare claimed that he could communicate with his departed relatives. Also, he could communicate with the spirits of George Washington, John Quincy Adams, Henry Clay, Benjamin Franklin, Lord Byron and Isaac Newton.

To simplify communicating with the spirits, Hare invented what he called a spiritscope. This consisted of a pasteboard disc larger than a foot in diameter. Around its circumference he attached the letters of the alphabet in a haphazard order. He attached an arrow to the centre of the disc so that it could move and point to various letters. Hare mounted the disc vertically on a table. For his initial test, a medium sat opposite him at the table. The disc was oriented with its back to the medium such that Hare could see the arrow and the letters while the medium could not. The medium sat with her hands on a surface above the table which, through a system of pulleys, cords and weights, was attached to the arrow. Thus, slight pressures of the medium's hands would cause the arrow to move and point to letters.

Facing the disc and the medium, Hare began by asking if any spirits were present. The arrow pointed to the letter Y (indicating 'yes'). Hare next asked the spirit to provide the initials of his name. The index pointed to R and then to H. Hare then asked, 'My honored father?' The index pointed to Y. Harried did several more experiments with similar results. Because the letters were arranged in a haphazard order around the disc and because the medium could not see the disc, Hare assumed the medium could not be controlling the actions of the arrow. Furthermore, because only Hare, not the medium, knew the answers to the questions Hare was sure that the answers came from a spiritual source.

Apparently Hare never fully grasped the key message of Faraday's experiment: that honest, intelligent people can unconsciously engage in muscular activity that is consistent with their expectations. Although the medium sitting opposite Hare could not see the letters or the arrow, she was looking directly at Hare as he was observing the behaviour of the pointer. The case of Clever Hans, which I discuss next, is just one of many that show that people frequently give clues about what they are thinking or observing without realizing it. These subtle clues can guide the behaviour of other individuals, including animals. Sometimes these individuals consciously detect such clues and use them to deceive the unsuspecting emitter. More often, the person being guided by the clues is just as unconscious of them as is the individual providing them. Thus, people often unwittingly provide clues about their thoughts, and others can unwittingly respond to such clues.

Hare stared at the moving arrow with strong expectations about where it should point. Under these conditions, the probability is high that Hare unwittingly made some bodily sign when the arrow reached the expected letter. This sign could cue the medium about when to stop pressing down on the surface. She could have consciously detected the sign. Yet as we will see when we discuss Clever Hans, it is just as likely that she could have reacted unwittingly to the signs from Hare.

Although, I will not discuss the ouija board, the action of the planchette follows the same principles underlying the other examples we have discussed. Notice that Hare's spiritscope is an early forerunner of the ouija board.

Clever Hans

In 1904 perhaps the biggest celebrity in Berlin was a Russian trotting horse known as Clever Hans (Fig. 25.2). The public sang his praises in songs, articles and books. His picture appeared on postcards and liquor labels. Children's toys were made in his image. A committee investigated Hans. It consisted of a circus manager, several educators, a zoologist, a veterinarian, a physiologist and the famous psychologist Carl Stumpf. The committee reported that it was baffled. It maintained that no trickery or known cues were involved. Educators declared that Hans had achieved the intellectual and educational stage of a 14-year-old child.

The horse's owner and trainer, Herr Von Osten, declined to profit from Hans's fame. He refused several lucrative offers to exploit the talents of his pupil. At regular intervals, Von Osten gave the public free exhibits of Hans's abilities. During these exhibits, Von Osten, approximately 70 years of age and a former arithmetic school teacher, stood proudly at the horse's right. He occasionally rewarded Hans with carrots that he kept in his pockets.

Hans could answer almost any question put to him in German. He could count to 100. He could do basic arithmetical operations including those involving compound fractions

A horse is a horse, of course: Wilhelm von Osten and Clever Hans.

Fig. 25.2 Clever Hans.

and decimals. He could spell words, identify persons and objects by name, designate the pitch of musical notes and even express a like or dislike for certain kinds of music. Hans, of course, could not talk in the vocal sense. He responded to questions by tapping with his hoof, shaking his head or walking over and pointing with his nose to letters on a board or objects on a rack. What convinced even the most sceptical observers, was that Hans could often perform quite successfully without his owner.

The psychologist Oskar Pfungst, a student of Carl Stumpf, got permission to do his own investigation of Hans. Pfungst began by making friends with Hans. Then, in the owner's absence, he put questions to Hans. To Pfungst's amazement, the horse answered each question correctly. He was baffled. He knew he was neither coaching nor signalling the horse. Yet, with no-one else present, Hans went through his paces with precision. At this point, Pfungst could have behaved like the investigators who had preceded him. He could have stopped and admitted that he could provide no normal explanation. Pfungst, however, was both a determined and thorough investigator.

Pfungst conducted a series of further tests. This time he asked questions for which he did not know the answer and ones for which he did know the answer. He discovered that Hans could give correct answers only when the questioner knew the answer. Hans, then, was only as intelligent as his questioner. Obviously Hans was picking up clues from the questioner. What were these clues and how was Hans detecting them? Pfungst eliminated auditory and tactual cues without impairing the horse's accuracy. The horse balked and became unruly when he tried to block Hans's ability to see him. After patient, and sometimes dangerous interaction with the unruly horse, Pfungst showed that Hans depended upon visual cues from the questioner.

So Hans was apparently responding to visual clues. No matter how hard he tried, Pfungst could not detect any clues that he might be providing the horse. He kept himself perfectly still, made sure not to change his expression, and avoided any other possibility for signalling. Yet, Hans answered his questions correctly. Again Pfungst was stumped. He brought in other questioners and watched them closely as they posed problems for Hans. Hans also answered their questions correctly. Yet Pfungst could detect no discernible clues. He persisted and eventually he discovered the clues. Hans was responding to postural cues from the questioner. These clues were so subtle it was almost impossible for a human to detect.

When the questioner asked a question, he or she focused upon Hans's hoof that tapped out the answer. To focus on the hoof, the questioner typically tensed and leaned ever so slightly forward. This turned out to be the clue that Hans used to begin tapping. When Hans had tapped the appropriate number of times, the questioner would slightly relax and almost imperceptibly raise his/her head. This was the clue that Hans used to stop tapping. Later, Pfungst built an apparatus to measure the extent of these involuntary movements. Many were less than 1 mm in extent.

Pfungst carried out additional investigations of Hans. Perhaps the most interesting one was where Pfungst took the role of Clever Hans. He would get a questioner to stand beside him and merely think of a number. Pfungst tapped with his right hand, much like Hans tapped with his hoof. As he did so, he carefully watched the questioner out of the corner of his eye. When he thought he detected a slight relaxation or other indication from the questioner, he would stop tapping. Pfungst tried this experiment with 25 different persons who ranged in age from 5 upwards. None of these individuals was aware of the purpose of the experiment and none discovered what Pfungst was looking for. All insisted they had not consciously given any clues about their number.

The results were striking. All but two of the persons gave the same involuntary head movements when Pfungst's tapping reached the correct number. Until Pfungst explained what was going on, they were amazed that Pfungst could apparently read their minds.

Muscle reading and mind reading

For centuries horses have reacted to the tension and relaxation of their masters. Beginning around 1870, some humans found that they could emulate horses in this respect. They discovered that they could start, stop and turn in response to unspoken commands of another person. Although such an achievement is taken for granted when done by horses, the humans who did this called themselves 'mind readers'. They made their living by giving demonstrations before awed spectators. In a typical performance, the demonstrator would arrange for the audience, in his absence, to hide an object in the lecture hall. Then the demonstrator would return, grasp the hand of an audience member, and pull this person along as he roamed the hall in search of the hidden item. Usually, the demonstrator succeeded. The demonstrators called this 'mind reading'. Sceptics called it muscle reading. They believed that the demonstrator was picking up unconscious clues from the degree of resistance in the volunteer as he was dragged about the lecture hall.

In the 1920s, Eugene de Rubini from Moravia created a sensation in the USA with his telepathic demonstrations. Rubini's feats were much like those of the earlier mind readers. The earlier mind readers, however, held the hand of a 'transmitter' to find a hidden object. Rubini, however, performed similar feats without physical contact. Psychologists at the University of California published their investigation of Rubini in 1921. They found that Rubini could find an object or person mentally chosen by a 'transmitter'. Rubini had no contact with the transmitter. The transmitter always walked behind and somewhat to the side of Rubini. Rubini's ability did not deteriorate when the investigators eliminated possible auditory clues by using ear plugs. Rubini, however, refused to be blindfolded. Finally he agreed to wear blinders. The blinders allowed him to see straight ahead but not out of the side of his eyes. Under these conditions, he could not see the transmitter. Under these conditions, Rubini's performance dropped to chance level.

The California investigators did not carry out further studies on Rubini. Like Hans, Rubini had to see his transmitter to produce the correct response. Like Hans, we can assume that Rubini was picking up unconscious clues from the transmitter. Rubini would get clues from the movements of the transmitter and the distance between the transmitter and Rubini as the latter tried to home in on the target. We can safely make this assumption because such 'mind readers' still perform these feats today and some have written explanations on how they achieve success.

Again, I should emphasize that although the transmitter unconsciously emits signals, the receiver ('mind reader') may pick up those signals either consciously or unconsciously. From what I can tell, Rubini was aware that he needed to see the transmitter. I believe, however, that he was unaware of the specific clues he was using.

Medical consequences

This chapter has covered a wide range of false beliefs created by the simple fact that people can unwittingly behave or unwittingly react to others' behaviour. Yet, this is only a sample. Many other examples exist. The rubbing plate that I described at the beginning of the chapter is just one of many black boxes or quack medical devices that involve this principle. The Abrams' devices, Ruth Drown's instruments, George de la Warr's machine and a host of radionic machines fall into this family. More recent examples depending upon the principles discussed in this chapter are applied kinesiology, facilitated communication and recent revivals of Traditional Chinese Medicine.

Ideomotor action

Although both Chevreul and Faraday recognized the general principle underlying the examples in this chapter, William B. Carpenter was the first to give it a name. In 1852, he called it ideomotor action, which he defined as the 'influence of suggestion in modifying and directing muscular action'. Carpenter wanted to show that a variety of currently popular phenomena had natural rather than supernatural origins. Under the rubric of ideomotor action, Carpenter included dowsing (Fig. 25.3), the magic pendulum, certain

Fig. 25.3 Dowsing.

aspects of mesmerism, table turning and Reichenbach's 'Odylic force'. Carpenter did not question the reality of the phenomena, nor the honesty of the people who were involved. He disputed only the explanation. He argued that, 'All the phenomena of the 'biologized' state, when attentively examined, will be found to consist in the occupation of the mind by the ideas which have been suggested to it, and in the influence which these ideas exert upon the actions of the body'.

William James, the Harvard physician turned psychologist, elaborated upon Carpenter's idea. He asserted that ideomotor activity was the basic process underlying all volitional behaviour. He wrote, 'Wherever a movement unhesitatingly and immediately follows upon the idea of it, we have ideomotor action. We are then aware of nothing between the conception and execution. All sorts of neuromuscular responses come between, of course, but we know nothing of them. We think the act, and it is done; and that is all that introspection tells us of the matter'. James saw ideomotor action as 'simply the normal process stripped of disguise'. He concluded that, 'We may then lay it down for certain that every [mental] representation of a movement awakens in some degree the actual movement which is its object; and awakens it in a maximum degree whenever it is not kept from so doing by antagonistic representation present simultaneously to the mind'.

By making ideomotor action the basic psychological process, James came close to some recent ideas about the role of the unconscious in instigating behaviour. Recent findings suggest that many of our actions are initiated before we are conscious of intending to make them. Yet, we have the illusion that we have consciously decided to make that action. Work on automatic behaviour also suggests that many of our actions are triggered or initiated outside awareness. Conscious control can enter the picture however in consciously suppressing such automatically instigated actions. This is consistent with how James wrote about the role of ideomotor action.

Persuasion versus conviction

The false beliefs generated by ideomotor action can be quite compelling. Even individuals who are familiar with ideomotor action have argued for the validity of the phenomena even if ideomotor action is involved. For example, today many dowsers accept ideomotor action as a partial cause of the rod's movement. Some of these dowsers argue that a true dowser can suppress the ideomotor response and, by that, allow the true dowsing force to control the rod. Others, with more sophistication, accept that ideomotor action is the direct cause of the movement of the dowsing rod, the pendulum, the planchette and in other cases. These latter proponents claim that the unconscious source that triggers the rod's or the pendulum's movement is itself under the control of occult forces.

Such arguments imply that there is an actual correspondence between the movement of the rod and its target. The studies by Faraday, Chevreul, Pfungst and others fail to detect any validity of these actions. Many phenomena that entail ideomotor action have been investigated with controlled scientific procedures. Those that have, however, have consistently failed to show validity. Many scientific studies have tested dowsing, both in the laboratory and in the field. No study that met adequate scientific standards has shown any validity for dowsing. The controlled studies of facilitated communication consistently show it is the facilitator and not the autistic child who is the source of the communication.

Some philosophers used to distinguish between persuasion and conviction. Conviction comes from the kind of evidence—logical and scientific—that should convince us. Persuasion is a compelling belief in the truth of a claim lacking convincing evidence. Ideomotor action is a most persuasive force.

Conclusions and lessons

We have had the evidence to understand the effects of ideomotor action for more than 150 years. Yet, the phenomenon remains surprisingly unknown, even to most scientists. This ignorance contributes to embarrassing examples of otherwise competent scientists supporting invalid and dangerous systems such as applied kinesiology, facilitated communication and therapeutic touch.

To conclude, I will list some features that characterize nearly all the systems involving ideomotor action.

Ideomotor action. All systems using the rubbing plate, the dowsing rod, the magic pendulum, the ouija board and related techniques depend on an almost undetectable motor movement, amplified into a more noticeable event. The impetus arises from one's own subtle and unperceived expectations. Elaborate and grandiose theories are then devised to explained the observed effects.

Projections of the operator's actions to an external force. This is a primary property of ideomotor systems. Although the operator's own actions cause the fingers to stick, the rod to move or the pendulum to rotate in a given direction, the operator attributes the cause to an external force. Subjectively that is what it feels like. Lacking a sense of volition, the operator credits unknown forces, radiations or other ethereal emanations.

The cause of the action is attributed to forces that are new to science and revolutionary.

Delusions of grandeur. The proponents also see themselves as revolutionary saviours of humanity.

Delusions of persecution. Self-styled revolutionaries assert that orthodox scientists dismiss their discoveries merely out of envy, pigheadedness, conformism or unwillingness to credit brave outsiders who are not part of the scientific establishment.

To be forearmed is to be disarmed. Proponents of quack devices and procedures argue that they are aware of ideomotor action and the role of expectancies. This awareness, they assert, immunizes them from its effects. Unfortunately, as has been shown repeatedly, being aware of ideomotor action does not make you immune from its effects. Indeed, the opposite is apt to be the case. The proponent becomes a victim to the 'illusion of invulnerability.'

Self-sealing belief systems. Once the proponent becomes convinced that his favourite system 'works', a variety of psychological forces come into play. These forces or self-serving biases protect the belief system from falsification.

Chapter 26

Inducing out-of-body experiences

Olaf Blanke and Gregor Thut

Introduction

In an out-of-body experience (OBE), people seem to be awake and feel that their 'self', or centre of awareness, is located outside of the physical body. It is from an elevated extracorporal location and perspective that the subjects who undergo an OBE experience seeing their body and the world. The following example from Irwin[1] may illustrate what subjects experience during an OBE:

> I was in bed and about to fall asleep when I had the distinct impression that 'I' was at the ceiling level looking down at my body in the bed. I was very startled and frightened; immediately [afterwards] I felt that, I was consciously back in the bed again.

An OBE is minimally defined by the presence of three phenomenological characteristics: disembodiment (location of the self outside one's bodily borders), the impression of seeing the world from an elevated visuospatial perspective (extracorporal, but egocentric visuospatial perspective) and the impression of seeing one's own body (autoscopy) from this elevated perspective.[2-4] This is shown in Fig. 26.1.

Next to disembodiment, extracorporeal perspective and autoscopy, further characteristics of abnormal self processing during an OBE can be defined. Agency (or the feeling of being the agent of one's actions and thoughts) is localized at the position of the elevated, disembodied self. Moreover, the feeling of ownership (or of inhabiting one's body) is abnormal as the self that hovers over the autoscopic body is only rarely localized within a second own body.[1,3,5] Based on these characteristics, OBEs challenge the experienced spatial unity of self and body or the experience of a 'real me' that resides in one's body and is the subject of experience.[6-9] This has also been suggested by psychologists[1,3,10] and neurologists.[4,11-13] These authors argued that OBEs are culturally invariant neuropsychological phenomena or deviant self models due to abnormal brain activation patterns whose scientific investigation might lead to a better understanding of the processes mediating the self under normal conditions. Understanding how the brain generates the abnormal self during OBEs is particularly interesting since OBEs are not only found in clinical populations,[4,11-13] but also appear in approximately 5 per cent of the healthy population[1,3] and have been described in the majority of the world's

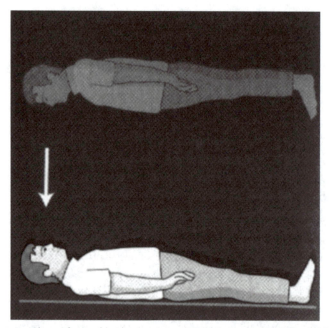

Fig. 26.1 Phenomenology of out-of-body experience (OBE). During an OBE, the subject appears to 'see' himself (bottom figure) and the world from a location above his physical body (extracorporeal location and visuospatial perspective; top figure). The self is localized outside one's physical body (disembodiment). The direction of the subject's visuospatial perspective during an OBE is indicated by an arrow (modified from Blanke 2004[74]).

cultures.[14] Moreover, several behavioural techniques have been described that are supposed to enhance the occurrence of OBEs.[3] Although these techniques are quite diverse, they have some common characteristics and emphasize (1) a state of physical relaxation; (2) sensory deprivation; (3) mental imagery with respect to one's own body (bodyshape, size, weight or position); as well as (4) a state of elevated concentration and absorption as being important for the induction of an OBE.[3] Yet, despite a large number of publications on OBEs, there are to date only few scientific investigations on the cognitive and neural basis of OBEs, probably because they generally occur spontaneously, are of short duration and happen only once or twice in a lifetime.[2,3]

The present review will focus on recent neurological and neuroimaging findings with respect to OBEs as well as on experimental techniques that have been used to induce OBEs artificially. This was done in order to investigate OBEs scientifically and to induce them experimentally in the research laboratory for the understanding of corporeal and self-awareness.

OBEs induced by neurological disease

The description of several neurological patients with OBEs due to brain damage has allowed a description to be made of the aetiology, associated phenomenology and anatomy of OBEs.[4,11,13–16] OBEs have mainly been observed in patients with lesional and non-lesional epilepsy as well as migraine. Neurological authors have observed disturbed own-body processing in patients with OBEs. First the frequent association of vestibular sensations and OBE was reported,[11] whereas others[12] proposed that a paroxysmal vestibular dysfunction might be an important mechanism for the generation of OBEs. More recently, the importance of vestibular mechanisms in OBEs was underlined by their presence in all patients with OBEs[4] and by the fact that vestibular sensations were evoked in one patient at the same site where higher currents induced an OBE[17] (see below). In addition to vestibular disturbances, it has been reported that OBE patients may also experience paroxysmal visual body part illusions such as phantom limbs, supernumerary phantom limbs and illusory limb transformations either during the OBE or during other periods related to epilepsy or migraine.[4,11,17–19] Lesion analysis based on magnetic resonance imaging (MRI) showed involvement of the temporo-parietal junction in three OBE patients[4] (Fig. 26.2; cases 1, 2a and 3). This was also found in another recently reported OBE patient[20] (case 1). Moreover, OBEs can also be induced by electrical stimulation of the temporo-parietal junction, pointing to the importance of this region in the generation of OBEs[17] (see below). A recent review of all previously reported OBE cases of focal neurological origin (also including the earlier cases reported by Daly,[21] Lunn[19] and Devinsky et al.[11]) found that OBEs were related in 75 per cent of cases to right hemispheric brain damage.[16] Lesion overlap analysis of OBE patients with focal brain damage or focal electroencephalogram abnormalities is illustrated in Fig. 26.2.

Based on these neurological findings, a model of OBEs has recently been proposed[4] suggesting that during an OBE the integration of proprioceptive, tactile and visual information of one's body fails due to discrepant central representations by the different sensory systems. This may lead to the experience of seeing one's body (autoscopy) in a position (i.e. on a bed) that does not coincide with the felt position of one's body (i.e. under the ceiling; see the above quoted example). As OBEs are also characterized by disembodiment and elevated visuospatial perspective, these authors speculated[4] that an additional vestibular dysfunction is present in OBEs. They suggested that OBEs are related to an integration failure of proprioceptive, tactile and visual information with respect to one's own body (disintegration in personal space) and to a vestibular dysfunction leading to an additional disintegration between personal (vestibular) space and extrapersonal (visual) space. Both disintegrations were proposed to be necessary for the occurrence of an OBE. The neurological data also suggest that OBEs are due to a paroxysmal cerebral dysfunction of the temporo-parietal junction in a state of partially impaired consciousness or awareness due to epilepsy or migraine.[4]

Importantly, these clinical findings have allowed the complex phenomenon of the OBE to be linked with multisensory disintegration and deficient own-body processing at the temporo-parietal junction. This is not trivial, as these findings may help to demystify OBEs and facilitate the formulation of precise research hypotheses about the sensory, cognitive and neural mechanisms of OBEs. The neuroscientific investigation of OBEs may also turn out to be useful in defining the functions and brain structures mediating aspects

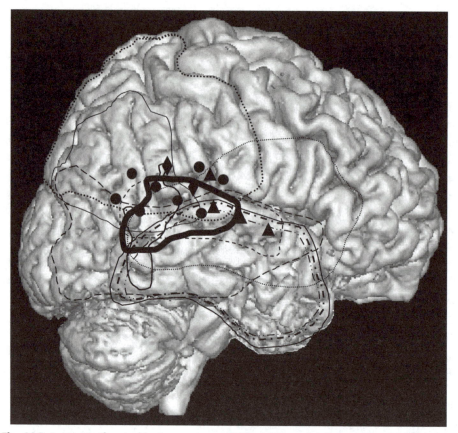

Fig. 26.2 Anatomy of out-of-body experience (OBE). MRI-based lesion overlap analysis of 13 previously reported OBE patients due to focal brain damage including patients from Penfield and Erickson[22] (n = 1), Penfield[23] (n = 1), Daly[21] (n = 1), Lunn[19] (n = 1), Devinsky et al.[11] (n = 5), Blanke et al.[4] (n = 3) and Maillard et al.[20] (n = 1). The data for all patients are drawn on the MRI (right hemisphere) of one of the patients from the study of Blanke et al.[4] (only two OBEs were due to left hemisphere interference). All lesions were estimated based on the anatomical results in the respective study (except the study by Blanke et al. where the lesions were transformed to Talairach space). Thus, when the lesion location (or the epileptic focus) was described as right temporal, we marked the whole temporal lobe for that patient; if the lesion was characterized as left fronto-temporal, parts of the fronto-temporal lobe were marked. The region of maximal overlap is indicated by the red area and was found on the right temporo-parietal junction.

of the normal self such as corporeal awareness, embodiment, egocentric visuospatial perspective and self-consciousness.[9,16]

OBEs induced by electrical brain stimulation

Before reviewing recent neuroimaging data about the temporo-parietal junction's implication in corporeal awareness and self processing, we will first report what is known about the artificial induction of OBEs by focal electrical stimulation of the human brain.

Recently, a patient has been reported[17] in whom OBEs, vestibular sensations and visual body-part illusions were induced by direct electrical cortical stimulation of the right hemisphere. In this patient, who underwent intracranial pre-surgical epilepsy evaluation for intractable seizures, focal electrical stimulation at currents of 3.5 mA for 2 s induced an OBE that lasted for 2 s and was characterized by disembodiment, elevated visuospatial perspective and autoscopy. In this OBE, the patient experienced that her self was localized under the ceiling (almost touching it with 'her' back) and looking down on her body that was lying motionless on the bed. Repeated stimulations induced identical OBEs in the intrigued and surprised patient who had never experienced an OBE previously. Interestingly, smaller currents at this site (2.0–2.5 mA) led to vestibular sensations.[17] The OBEs in this patient were induced whenever she looked straight ahead (without fixation of any specific object). If she fixated her outstretched arms or legs during electrical stimulation there were no OBE's, but she had the impression that the inspected body part was transformed, leading to the illusory, but very realistic, visual perception of limb shortening or illusory limb movement if the limbs were bent at the elbow or knee (currents of 4.0–4.5 mA). Finally, with closed eyes, the patient had neither an OBE nor a visual body-part illusion, but perceived her upper body as moving towards her legs.[17] These data suggest that visual illusions of body parts and visual illusions of the entire body such as autoscopic phenomena might depend on similar functional and anatomical mechanisms, as argued by others.[13,18]

Wilder Penfield has described two further pre-surgical epilepsy patients (cases G.A.[22] and V.F.[23]) who have reported experiences strongly resembling OBEs while undergoing electrical cortical stimulation.[24] Below we discuss phenomenological, methodological, anatomical and epileptogenic differences and similarities between these patients and the above-described patient of Blanke et al.[17] Regarding phenomenology, only little information has been provided by Penfield for patient V.F.,[23] who exclaimed 'Oh God! I am leaving my body'. It is thus not known what exactly this patient experienced or whether he was able to describe his experience more precisely (i.e. with respect to autoscopy, extracorporal visuospatial perspective or associated vestibular sensations). It was also not reported whether it was possible to reproduce the patient's experience. The sensation of 'leaving his body' was induced by electrical stimulation within the sylvian fissure at a depth of 2 cm on the surface of the superior temporal gyrus close to the insula. The region of stimulation was within the patient's epileptic focus where he had been operated on before. The stimulation that evoked the 'OBE' also elicited a concurrent seizure that was characterized initially by an unpleasant taste followed by swallowing movements, mental confusion and slow electroencephalogram waves of 4 Hz. It was during this latter ictal period that the patient exclaimed that he was 'leaving his body'. Interestingly, stimulation at a site 1 cm posteriorly to the 'OBE'-inducing site elicited illusory whole body movements described as if he would be standing up or spinning around (resembling the patient's habitual aura). The descriptions of patient G.A.'s experiences[22] are even less similar to full-blown OBEs and were rather illusory whole-body and contralateral arm movements. Thus, G.A. exclaimed that 'I feel queer' and asked 'Am I here?' and described that she felt as if she was floating away and as if her left arm was moving. These experiences were reproducible, but induced at four different sites including the supramarginal gyrus and the superior temporal gyrus. G.A. suffered from focal epilepsy due to right hemispheric atrophy and local microgyria in the frontal, upper and lower postcentral areas associated with contralesional corporeal atrophy. In conclusion there are not sufficient phenomenological details to classify these patients' experiences unambiguously as OBEs. In addition, both patients of Penfield might have had substantial cortical reorganization at the site whose stimulation resulted in an OBE since the epileptic focus was either very close to or directly at the stimulation site. This was not the case in the patient of Blanke et al.[17] Despite these differences between the two patients of Wilder Penfield and the patient of Blanke et al.,[17] there are a number of striking phenomenological similarities including disembodiment, vestibular sensations and visual body part illusions. Furthermore, both previously reported cases of electrically induced 'OBEs' were observed after stimulation of the right hemisphere at the temporo-parietal junction, matching patient 3 of Blanke et al.[17] Note that although the total number of stimulation-induced 'OBEs' is very low, it might be significant that OBEs have never been reported following electrical stimulation of the left hemisphere. Right hemisphere predominance is also suggested by neurological lesion data[16] (see Fig. 26.2).

Neurocognitive mechanisms of OBEs

Neuroimaging studies support the role of the temporo-parietal junction in many of the functions that are relevant for or dysfunctional in OBEs. These are vestibular processing, multisensory integration as well as the perception of human bodies or body parts. The core region of the human vestibular cortex[25,26] is situated at the temporo-parietal junction including the posterior insula, and brain damage in this area has been associated with vestibular sensations and dysfunctions.[27,28] Several neuropsychological and neuroimaging studies suggest the implication of the temporo-parietal junction and cortical areas along the intraparietal sulcus in combining tactile, proprioceptive and visual information in a coordinated reference frame.[29] Interestingly, the temporo-parietal junction codes multisensory conflict between visual and proprioceptive information about one's arm position as proposed in the above OBE model for the entire body.[30] The temporo-parietal junction and the extrastriate body area are also involved in many different aspects of processing with respect to the human body including the perception of body parts,[31] the entire body[32,33] as well as biological motion.[34,35] Importantly, some of these 'visual body' areas are modulated not only by visually presented human bodies or body parts, but also by limb movements (without visual feedback), suggesting their role in multisensory own-body perception.[33] The temporo-parietal junction has also been involved in cognitive functions that are closely linked to self processing and OBEs such as egocentric visuospatial perspective taking,[36] agency (the feeling of being the agent of one's actions and thoughts)[37–39] and self–other distinction (the capacity by which one distinguishes between oneself and other conspecifics).[38–42] This is of relevance as during OBEs one's visuospatial perspective and one's sense of agency are localized at the position of the disembodied self that is hovering above the physical body. In other words, during an OBE the self is experienced as looking at the (autoscopic) body from a third (or other) person's visuospatial perspective and position. Furthermore, the temporo-parietal junction is the classical lesion site in patients with visuospatial neglect,[43] a clinical condition, which has been shown to disturb the patient's egocentric spatial relationship with extrapersonal space and visuospatial perspective taking.[36] Neuroimaging studies in healthy observers have also revealed activation of the temporo-parietal junction during egocentric visuospatial perspective changes in healthy subjects.[40,44] Moreover, it has been shown that mental activities such as agency and self–other distinction activate the temporo-parietal junction.[45]

The relationship of some of these aspects of the self with the three essential phenomenological characteristics of the OBE (disembodiment, visuospatial perspective and autoscopy) and own-body processing at the temporo-parietal junction has been investigated in a recent study by our team.[46] We used a mental imagery task with respect to one's own body (modified from[47,48]). Schematic human figures in front or back view (see Fig. 26.3A) were presented to healthy subjects and to an epileptic patient with OBEs, who were asked to indicate whether the schematic figure's left or right hand was marked. The subjects were also instructed only to give their response after having imagined themselves in the depicted position and visual perspective of the figure.

In the healthy subjects, we observed a selective activation of the bilateral temporoparietal junction that was stronger and longer when subjects imagined the position and visual perspective that is generally reported by people experiencing spontaneous OBEs (front-facing figures; see Fig. 26.3B). Importantly, in the epileptic patient with OBEs originating from the temporo-parietal junction, the results revealed a functional activation of the seizure focus during mental transformations of her body and visual perspective mimicking her OBE percepts (see Fig. 26.3C) directly linking OBEs, mental own-body imagery and the temporo-parietal junction. Based on these results, we argued that the temporo-parietal junction might be a crucial structure for the conscious experience of the normal self mediating spatial unity of self and body as well as one's egocentric visuospatial perspective, and that impaired processing at the temporo-parietal junction may lead to the experience of abnormal selfs such as OBEs.[46]

In summary, although many other cortical areas such as prefrontal cortex, anterior cingulum, postcentral gyrus, precuneus, occipito-temporal junction, insula and superior parietal lobule[30,34,35,40,45,49] have been shown to play a role in self processing, the reviewed neuroimaging data on body and self processing as well as our data on OBEs suggest that the temporo-parietal junction is a key neural locus for self processing that is involved in multisensory body-related information processing as well as in processing of phenomenological and cognitive aspects of the self. Interestingly, the above-mentioned studies show that techniques that have been used to induce OBEs and the phenomenology of OBE may be combined with classical neuropsychological paradigms of mental imagery and neuroimaging methods to examine the neural correlates of OBEs and the self. Ideally,

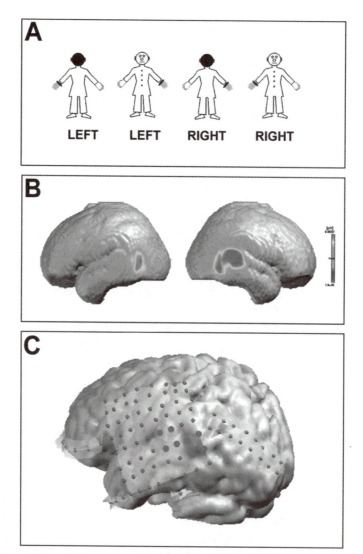

Fig. 26.3 Own-body mental imagery and electrical neuroimaging findings. (A) Four different stimuli as used in the own-body transformation task. Correct responses in the OBT task are indicated below each figure. Front-facing figures simulate the position and visuospatial perspective during spontaneous OBEs and led to longer reaction times in normal subjects (see Blanke *et al*.[46]). (B) A stable map topography was found from >330–400 ms and only in the own-body transformation task (results not shown). This map's duration paralleled the behavioural reaction time differences in the experimental conditions in the own-body transformation task and led to an activation (as estimated by a linear inverse solution) of both temporo-parietal junctions with a right predominance (see Blanke *et al*.[46]). (C) MRI with the implanted electrodes overlying the lateral convexity of the left hemisphere. The epileptic focus, whose discharge induced an OBE, is indicated by eight red electrodes at the temporo-parietal junction. The figure also depicts the amplitude (in μV) for all implanted electrodes during the own-body transformation task at ~333 ms (blue depicts positive values and red negative values). The most prominent evoked potential at this latency were recorded over the temporo-parietal junction and partly overlapping with the epileptic focus. (*See colour plate section*)

these techniques may also be combined to induce OBEs artificially in healthy subjects as has previously been done for the induction of illusory phantom limbs.[50,51] Artificially induced OBEs (or illusory whole-body phantoms)[52] would have the great advantage of allowing the investigation of corporeal awareness and self processing for the entire body. The possibility of scientifically inducing OBEs is discussed below with respect to some behavioural conditions and transcranial magnetic stimulation (TMS).

Combining TMS with cognitive neuroscience to induce OBEs

TMS is a non-invasive technique to excite or inhibit transiently relatively circumscribed areas of the human brain.[53] It is frequently used as a research tool in the study of human brain physiology and function.[54,55] Originally conceived as an alternative method to the non-invasive, but painful technique of transcranial *electrical* stimulation,[56] transcranial *magnetic* stimulation has also proven useful in cognitive neuroscience as an important extension of current neuroimaging procedures such as functional MRI (fMRI) or positron emission tomography (PET).[55,57] During TMS, a strong, relatively focal and rapidly changing magnetic field is applied adjacent to the scalp, in order to stimulate electrically a given cortical area through electromagnetic induction. Because the magnetic field penetrates the cranium unimpededly, the stimulation is almost painless and normally well tolerated by the subjects. The induced current in the neural tissue underlying the magnetic stimulation coil transiently disrupts normal functioning of the stimulated area, which provides an important supplement to functional neuroimaging procedures such as fMRI or PET. Whereas functional neuroimaging reveals the areas that are active during a given task, disruption during TMS shows that a given area is not only active but also necessary for task performance.[58]

Using TMS in this disruptive mode, we have recently extended our finding of selective temporo-parietal junction activation when subjects mentally transform their body position into the position that is frequently reported by subjects with OBEs (front-facing figures; see above). We showed that interference with the temporo-parietal junction by TMS impaired this mental body transformation task in healthy subjects relative to magnetic stimulation of a control site[46] (see Fig. 26.4A).

Furthermore, this functional interference by temporo-parietal junction stimulation was task specific, i.e. was not observed for mental transformations of the own-body position into back-facing figures (not matching the classically experienced 'OBE position', see Fig. 26.4B) and also not observed for a control task that implicated mental spatial transformations of external objects such as letters (adapted from classically used mental rotation paradigms; see Fig. 26.4C, D). Thus, interference by temporo-parietal junction stimulation with own-body transformations did not generalize to other, non-body spatial imagery tasks. It is worth mentioning that while TMS over the temporo-parietal junction selectively interfered with performance in the imagined body transformation task, TMS over the control site (consisting of the intraparietal sulcus region) impaired mental object-based transformations (see Fig. 26.4A versus C). This altogether was interpreted to support the notion that the temporo-parietal junction plays an essential role in the

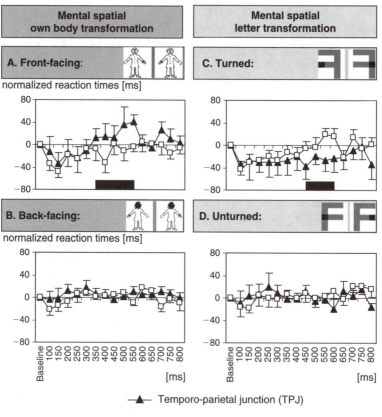

Fig. 26.4 Own-body mental imagery and TMS findings. TMS was used in its disruptive mode to probe the implication of the temporo-parietal junction in mental own-body transformations. A single TMS pulse was applied (1) over the temporo-parietal junction (black triangles) or (2) over a control site (intraparietal sulcus = white squares), while subjects were asked (i) mentally to transform their own body into a visually presented, schematic human figure (left panels) or (ii) to perform a control task consisting of mental spatial transformations of an external object, i.e. the letter 'F' (right panels). For further details, see text (and Blanke et al.[46]). Reaction times were recorded (y-axis, reaction time normalized to baseline) as a function of 15 visual stimulus–TMS pulse onset asynchronies (x-axis, 100–800 ms). (A) When subjects were mentally transforming their own body into front-facing figures, temporo-parietal junction stimulation at 350–550 ms interfered with task execution (prolonged reaction times) relative to TMS over the control site (intraparietal sulcus). (C) When subjects were mentally transforming the letter 'F', an opposite effect was found. Intraparietal sulcus stimulation at 450–600 ms prolonged reaction times relative to TMS over the temporo-parietal junction. This indicates a double dissociation of mental own-body and object-based transformations with respect to the site of TMS interference. (B and D) No effects were observed for mental spatial transformations into back-facing figures or of unturned letters. Data modified from Blanke et al.[46]

generation of OBEs as well as the mental imagery of one's own body position, i.e. in the updating of body position in space, egocentric perspective taking and corporeal awareness.[46]

The converging evidence that a temporo-parietal junction dysfunction might play a role in OBEs of neurological origin raises an interesting question. Is it possible to induce OBEs also in healthy volunteers through non-invasive TMS of the temporo-parietal junction? Of particular interest in this regard are situations in which TMS can be considered to operate in a productive rather than disruptive mode, i.e. when TMS is generating a discernible peripheral response or conscious percept. This is the case for TMS over the motor cortex, which induces a muscle twitch in the contralateral face, arm or foot depending on the site of TMS relative to somatotopic organization.[59] Other productive effects of TMS include transient paraesthesia in the upper or lower extremities in response to stimulation of contralateral sensorimotor cortex,[59–61] as well as stationary or moving phosphenes in the peripheral or bilateral visual fields in response to stimulation of visual areas V1–V5, respectively.[62–65] Finally, and most closely related to the present issue, TMS over motor cortex has also been reported to induce a 'sense of movement' when actual motor responses were ischaemically blocked.[66,67] (Recently, the cortical origin of this kinaesthetic, body-part illusion has been questioned.[68]) To the best of our knowledge, TMS has never evoked productive effects when applied to higher order association cortex, such as the temporo-parietal junction, temporal cortex or the prefrontal cortex. However, given that direct electrical cortical stimulation of this area can elicit OBEs[17] and given that OBEs can occur spontaneously in the healthy population,[1,3] we argue that TMS over the temporo-parietal junction is also likely to evoke OBEs in healthy subjects when TMS is applied in specific experimental settings.

It has been suggested that OBEs result from a disturbance of on-line integration of various body-related sensory inputs (proprioceptive, tactile, visual and vestibular) that normally provide a three-dimensional, dynamic representation of the body in space, combined with a prominent graviceptive vestibular dysfunction.[4] We hypothesize that TMS could eventually interfere with such processes and hence lead to OBEs or related illusory sensations in conditions in which proprioceptive, tactile, visual and graviceptive vestibular inputs are weak or ambiguous. Interestingly, vestibulo-sensory illusions frequently occur during weightlessness on space missions and the low gravity phase of parabolic flights, and include the feeling of falling down, being upside-down, the sensation of self- and surround motion, or the sensation that fixed real visual targets move downwards.[69–71] Also, temporary peripheral nerve block in neurologically healthy subjects can lead to a transiently impaired sense of ownership of the deafferented limb in spite of residual perception of position or posture or residual sensations of this limb.[72] Although weightlessness cannot be simulated in a laboratory, other techniques might be used to modulate vestibular and other sensory input and interfere with the subject's orientation regarding body position in space. For instance, mental relaxation techniques leading to a sense of lightness and floating might be used to modulate vestibular, proprioceptive and tactile processing (relaxation). A supine position on a surface that equally distributes gravity forces over the body might help to achieve this goal. For further disorientation in space, visual and auditory input should be prevented by blindfolding the subjects and using a soundproof room (sensory deprivation). Relaxation and sensory deprivation have previously been reported to facilitate the occurrence of OBEs,[3] as introduced above. Moreover, additional weak vestibular stimulation (either physiological or galvanic) might be considered. Overall, this might facilitate the induction of discrepant central representations of the subject's body by the different sensory systems, suggested to be the neural basis of OBEs. Finally, there might be specific subpopulations of healthy subjects who are particularly prone to OBEs and hence its induction through TMS, given that some personality scores assessed through questionnaires on dissociative experience, hypnotic susceptibility and fantasy proneness have been found to relate to OBEs.[5]

Conclusion

In science, the most challenging phenomena are often the ones we take for granted in our everyday lives. An excellent example is the self and the experienced spatial unity between self and body that is challenged by OBEs.[7,9] The evidence from neurological patients experiencing OBEs and thus the striking dissociation between self and body suggests that OBEs are culturally invariant phenomena, which can be investigated scientifically. The neuroscientific study of the self is in its infancy and there are currently no established models, very few data and often not even the vocabulary to describe neuroscientific notions of the self.[73] The investigation of OBEs and related mechanisms at the temporo-parietal junction might thus allow an improvement in our neuroscientific models of self and body. Although many other cortical areas are involved in self processing, recent neuroimaging studies suggest a key role for the temporo-parietal junction in OBEs and many aspects of body and self processing, such as the integration of multisensory bodily information, the visual perception of human bodies, biological motion perception, self–other distinction, agency and perspective taking.[4,16,45] It is hoped that the experimental induction of OBEs and related experiences in healthy subjects will further our understanding of the central mechanisms of corporal and self-awareness much as previous research was successful with respect to the investigation of ownership of limbs by inducing an embodiment of artificial limbs in healthy subjects.[50,51]

References and notes

1. Irwin HJ. *Flight of mind: a psychological study of the out-of-body experience.* Scarecrow Press, Metuchen, NJ. 1985.
2. Green CE. *Out-of-body experiences.* Hamish Hamilton, London. 1968.
3. Blackmore SJ. *Beyond the body. An investigation of out-of-body experiences.* Heinemann, London. 1982.
4. Blanke O, Landis T, Spinelli L, Seeck M. Out-of-body experience and autoscopy of neurological origin. *Brain,* 2004; 127:243–258.
5. Alvarado CS. Out of body experiences. In E Cardena, SG Lynn, S Krippner, eds. *Varieties of anomalous experiences.* American Psychological Association, Washington, DC. 2000:183–218.
6. Shoemaker S. Self-reference and self-awareness. *Journal of Philosophy,* 1968; 65:555–567.

7. Neisser U. The five kinds of self-knowledge. *Philosophical Psychology*, 1988; **1**:35–59.

8. Gallagher S. Philosophical conceptions of the self: implications for cognitive science. *Trends in Cognitive Sciences*, 2000; **4**:14–21.

9. Metzinger T. *Being no one.* MIT Press, Cambridge, MA. 2003

10. Palmer J. The out-of-body experience: a psychological theory. *Parapsychology Review*, 1978; **9**:19–22.

11. Devinsky O, Feldmann E, Burrowes K, Bromfield E. Autoscopic phenomena with seizures. *Archives of Neurology*, 1989, **46**:1080–1088.

12. Grüsser OJ, Landis T. The splitting of 'I' and 'me': heautoscopy and related phenomena. In Cronly-Dillon Jr, ed. *Visual agnosias and other disturbances of visual perception and cognition.* MacMillan, Amsterdam. 1991:297–303.

13. Brugger P, Regard M, Landis T. Illusory reduplication of one's own body: phenomenology and classification of autoscopic phenomena. *Cognitive Neuropsychiatry*, 1997; **2**:19–38.

14. Sheils D. A cross-cultural study of beliefs in out-of-the-body experiences, waking and sleeping. *Journal of the Society for Psychical Research*, 1978; **49**:697–741.

15. Brugger, P. Reflective mirrors: perspective taking in autoscopic phenomena. *Cognitive Neuropsychiatry*, 2000; **7**:179–194.

16. Blanke O, Arzy S. The out-of body experience, self, and the temporo-parietal junction. *The Neuroscientist*, 2005; **11**:16–24.

17. Blanke O, Ortigue S, Landis T, Seeck M. Stimulating illusory own-body perceptions. *Nature*, 2002; **419**:269–270.

18. Hécaen H, Ajuriaguerra J. L'Héautoscopie. In *Méconnassiances et hallucinations corporelles.* Masson, Paris. 1952:310–343.

19. Lunn V. Autoscopic phenomena. *Acta Psychiatrica Scandinavica*, 1972; **46**:118–125.

20. Maillard L, Vignal JP, Anxionnat R, Taillandier T, Vespignani L. Semiologic value of ictal autoscopy. *Epilepsia*, 2004; **45**:391–394.

21. Daly DD. Ictal affect. *American Journal of Psychiatry*, 1958; **115**:171–81.

22. Penfield W, Erickson TC. *Epilepsy and cerebral localization.* Charles C. Thomas, Springfield, IL. 1941:122–124; 261–265.

23. Penfield W. The twenty-ninth Maudsley lecture: the role of the temporal cortex in certain psychical phenomena. *Journal of Mental Science*, 1955; **101**:451–465, 458–460.

24. Tong F. From Penfield to present. *Trends in Cognitive Sciences*, 2003; **7**:104–106.

25. Lobel E, Kleine J, Leroy-Wilig A. Functional MRI of galvanic vestibular stimulation. *Journal of Neurophysiology*, 1999; **80**:2699–2709.

26. Fasold O, von Bevern M, Kuhberg M, Ploner CJ, Vilringer A, Lempert T, Wenzel R. Human vestibular cortex as identified with caloric vestibular stimulation by functional magnetic resonance imaging. *Neuroimage*, 2002; **17**:1384–1393.

27. Smith BH. Vestibular disturbances in epilepsy. *Neurology*, 1960; **10**:465–9.

28. Brandt T. Central vestibular disorders. In *Vertigo. Its multisensory syndromes.* Springer, London. 2000:146–167.

29. Calvert GA, Campbell R, Brammer MJ. Evidence from functional magnetic resonance imaging of crossmodal binding in the human heteromodal cortex. *Current Biology*, 2000; **10**:649–657.

30. Leube DT, Knoblich G, Erb M, Grodd W, Bartels M, Kircher TT. The neural correlates of perceiving one's own movements. *Neuroimage*, 2003; **20**:2084–2090.

31. Bonda E, Petrides M, Frey S, Evans A. Neural correlates of mental transformations of the body-in-space. *Proceeding of the National Academy of Science, USA*, 1995; **92**:11180–11184.

32. Downing PE, Jiang Y, Shuman M, Kanwisher N. A cortical area selective for visual processing of the human body. *Science*, 2001; **293**:2470–2473.

33. Astafiev SV, Stanley CM, Shulman GL, Corbetta M. Extrastriate body area in human occipital cortex responds to the performance of motor actions. *Nature Neuroscience*, 2004; **7**:542–548.

34. Grossman E, Donnelly M, Price R, Pickens D, Morgan V, Neighbor G, Blake R. Brain areas involved in perception of biological motion. *Journal of Cognitive Neuroscience*, 2000; 12:711–720.

35. Beauchamp MS, Lee KE, Haxby JV, Martin A. Parallel visual motion processing streams for manipulable objects and human movements. *Neuron*, 2002; 34:149–159.

36. Farrell MJ, Robertson IH. The automatic updating of egocentric spatial relationships and its impairment due to right posterior cortical lesions. *Neuropsychologia*, 2000; 38:585–595.

37. Farrer C, Frith CD. Experiencing oneself vs another person as being the cause of an action: the neural correlates of the experience of agency. *Neuroimage*, 2002; 15:596–603.

38. Farrer C, Franck N, Georgieff N, Frith CD, Decety J, Jeannerod M. Modulating the experience of agency: a positron emission tomography study. *Neuroimage*, 2003; 18:324–333.

39. Chaminade T, Decety J. Leader or follower? Involvement of the inferior parietal lobule in agency. *Neuroreport*, 2002; 13:1975–1978.

40. Ruby P, Decety J. Effect of subjective perspective taking during simulation of action: a PET investigation of agency. *Nature Neuroscience*, 2001; 4:546–50

41. Ruby P. Decety J. What you believe versus what you think they believe: a neuroimaging study of conceptual perspective-taking. *European Journal of Neuroscience*, 2003; 17:2475–2480.

42. Ruby P, Decety J. How do you feel versus how do you think she would feel? A neuroimaging study of perspective taking with social emotions. *Journal of Cognitive Neuroscience*, 2004; 16:988–999.

43. Halligan PW, Fink GR, Marshal JC, Vallar G. Spatial cognition: evidence from visual neglect. *Trends in Cognitive Science*, 2003; 7:125–33.

44. Maguire EA, Burgess N, Donnett JG, Frackowiak RS, Frith CD, O'Keefe J. Knowing where and getting there: a human navigation network. *Science*, 1998; 280:921–924.

45. Decety J, Sommerville JA. Shared representations between self and other: a social cognitive neuroscience view. *Trends in Cognitive Science*, 2003; 7:527–533.

46. Blanke O, Mohr C, Michel CM, Pascual-Leone A, Brugger P, Seeck M, Landis T, Thut G. Linking OBEs experience and self processing to mental own body imagery at the temporo-parietal junction. *Journal of Neuroscience*, 2005; 25:550–557.

47. Ratcliff, G. Spatial thought, mental rotation and the right cerebral hemisphere. *Neuropsychologia*, 1979; 17:49–54.

48. Zacks J, Rypma B, Gabrieli JD, Tversky B, Glover GH. Imagined transformations of bodies: an fMRI investigation. *Neuropsychologia*, 1999; 37:1029–1040.

49. Zacks JM, Ollinger JM, Sheridan MA, Tversky B. A parametric study of mental spatial transformations of bodies. *Neuroimage*, 2002; 16:857–872.

50. Botvinick M, Cohen J. Rubber hands 'feel' touch that eyes see. *Nature*, 1998; 391:756.

51. Ehrsson HH, Spence C, Passingham RE. That's my hand! Activity in premotor cortex reflects feeling of ownership of a limb. *Science*, 2004; 305:875–877.

52. Brugger P. From phantom limb to phantom body. In G Knoblich, I Thornton, M Grosjean, M Shiffrar, ed. *Perception of the human body inside out*. Oxford University Press, Oxford. 2006:171–210.

53. Hallett M. Transcranial magnetic stimulation and the human brain. *Nature*, 2000; 406:147–50.

54. Chen R. Studies of human motor physiology with transcranial magnetic stimulation. *Muscle Nerve*, 2000; 9: S26–32.

55. Walsh V, Cowey A. Transcranial magnetic stimulation and cognitive neuroscience. *National Neuroscience Reviews*, 2000; 1:73–79.

56. Barker AT, Jalinous R, Freeston IL. Non-invasive magnetic stimulation of human motor cortex. *Lancet*, 1985; 1:1106–1107.

57. Pascual-Leone A, Walsh V, Rothwell J. Transcranial magnetic stimulation in cognitive neuroscience—virtual lesion, chronometry, and functional connectivity. *Current Opinion in Neurobiology*, 2001; 10:232–237.

58. **Theoret H, Pascual-Leone A.** Transcranial magnetic stimulation and the study of cognition. In K Hugdahl, ed. *Experimental methods in neuropsychology*, Kluwer Academic Publishers, Boston. 2003:173–195.

59. **Amassian VE, Cracco RQ, Maccabee PJ, Cracco JB, Henry K.** Some positive effects of transcranial magnetic stimulation. *Advanced Neurology*, 1995; **67**:79–106.

60. **Amassian VE, Somasundaram M, Rothwell JC, Britton T, Cracco JB, Cracco RQ, Maccabee PJ, Day BL.** Paraesthesias are elicited by single pulse, magnetic coil stimulation of motor cortex in susceptible humans. *Brain*, 1991; **114**: 2505–2520.

61. **Cohen LG, Topka H, Cole RA, Hallett M.** 1991. Leg paresthesias induced by magnetic brain stimulation in patients with thoracic spinal cord injury. *Neurology*, 1991; **41**:1283–1288.

62. **Meyer BU, Diehl R, Steinmetz H, Britton TC, Benecke R.** Magnetic stimuli applied over motor and visual cortex: influence of coil position and field polarity on motor responses, phosphenes, and eye movements. *Electroencephalography and Clinical Neurophysiology*, 1991; **43**:121–134.

63. **Kammer T.** Phosphenes and transient scotomas induced by magnetic stimulation of the occipital lobe: their topographic relationship. *Neuropsychologia*, 1999; **37**:191–198.

64. **Kammer T, Beck S, Thielscher A, Laubis-Herrmann U, Topka H.** Motor thresholds in humans: a transcranial magnetic stimulation study comparing different pulse waveforms, current directions and stimulator types. *Clinical Neurophysiology*, 2001; **112**:250–258.

65. **Cowey A, Walsh V.** Magnetically induced phosphenes in sighted, blind and blindsighted observers. *Neuroreport*, 2001; **11**: 3269–3273.

66. **Amassian VE, Cracco RQ, Maccabee PJ.** A sense of movement elicited in paralyzed distal arm by focal magnetic coil stimulation of human motor cortex. *Brain Research*, 1989; **479**:355–360.

67. **Brasil-Neto JP, Valls-Sole J, Pascual-Leone A, Cammarota A, Amassian VE, Cracco R, Maccabee P, Cracco J, Hallett M, Cohen LG.** Rapid modulation of human cortical motor outputs following ischaemic nerve block. *Brain*, 1993; **116**:511–525.

68. **Ellaway PH, Prochazka A, Chan M, Gauthier MJ.** The sense of movement elicited by transcranial magnetic stimulation in humans is due to sensory feedback. *Journal of Physiology*, 2004; **556**:651–660.

69. **Gurovskiy NN, Bryanov II, Yegorov AD.** Changes in the vestibular function during space flight. *Acta Astronautica*, 1975; **2**:207–216.

70. **Von Baumgarten RJ, Baldrighi G, Shillinger GL, Harth O, Thuemler R.** Vestibular function in the space environment. *Acta Astronautica*, 1975; **2**:49–58.

71. **Kornilova LN.** Orientation illusions in spaceflight. *Journal of Vestibular Research*, 1997; **7**:429–439.

72. **Paqueron X, Leguen M, Rosenthal D, Coriat P, Willer JC, Danziger N.** The phenomenology of body image distortions induced by regional anaesthesia. *Brain*, 2003; **126**:702–712.

73. **Kircher T, David A.** *The self in neuroscience and psychiatry.* Cambridge University Press, Cambridge. 2003.

74. **Blanke O.** Illusions visuelles. In *Neurophtalmologie*. Masson, Paris. 2004:147–150.

Chapter 27

Can mind conquer cancer?

Barry L. Beyerstein, Wallace I. Sampson,
Zarka Stojanovic and James Handel

The human understanding is no dry light, but receives an infusion from the
will and affections; whence proceed sciences which may be called 'sciences
as one would'. For what a man had rather were true he more readily
believes. Therefore he rejects difficult things from impatience of research;
sober things, because they narrow hope; the deeper things of nature, from
superstition; the light of experience, from arrogance and pride, lest his mind
should seem to be occupied with things mean and transitory; things not
commonly believed, out of deference to the opinion of the vulgar.
Numberless in short are the ways, and sometimes imperceptible, in which
the affections colour and infect the understanding

Francis Bacon

Introduction

Critics have argued that there is very little in the so-called 'New Age' that is actually
new.[1] The worldview of its adherents is a collection of ancient, scientifically dubious
ideas repackaged and vigorously marketed in modern-sounding jargon.[2,3] New Age
thinking contains a number of recurrent threads. The first is its promotion of emotive,
as opposed to objective, truth criteria (i.e. how one *feels* about something determines
its veracity). Second, is its epistemological relativism—any sincerely held belief is said
to be unassailable. This is coupled with a sustained attack on the idea that objectivity
is humanly possible and that evidence could ever be more than mere opinion. Thirdly,
New Age proponents wish to re-establish the human-centredness of the physical universe
that was so rudely trounced by Copernicus, Darwin and the giants of the Enlightenment.
Fundamental to this reversion to a spiritual view of the physical realm is the belief that
personally relevant moral laws govern the workings of the natural world, rather than
purely mechanistic ones. Because these spiritual forces supposedly factor one's moral
standing into their operation, New Age adherents generally assume that when bad things
happen, the recipient somehow had it coming—a form of blaming the victim. Conversely,
when fortune smiles, this is taken as comforting proof of the beneficiary's worthiness.

As we shall see, these themes arise frequently in the healthcare arm of the New Age movement, 'complementary and alternative medicine' (CAM). CAM supporters have reverted in various ways to pre-scientific, vitalistic doctrines, such as 'subtle energies', 'life forces' and the belief that sickness and health are tied to one's moral stature—in other words, they are one's just deserts. In challenging the bedrock assumption of scientific medicine that diseases are mechanistic and organ specific, CAM has also championed the notion that mental powers strongly affect disease and recovery. This has led to the rejuvenation, in various guises, of a concept that gained popularity in the nineteenth century in the wake of the influential 'positive thinking' movement. In the medical sphere, this was known as 'the mind cure'—the promise of conquering disease through spirituality and uplifting thoughts.[4] The teachings of Christian Science were an outgrowth of this movement. Today, the most prominent exponents of the mind cure include inspirational writers such as Bernie Siegal[5] and the late Norman Cousins.[6]

Academic interest in the effects of emotional states on health and disease dates back to the early twentieth century, with Charcot's theory of somatization and Freud's theory of conversion hysteria.[7,8] The idea that one's mental state could affect the onset, progression and remission of cancer was an outgrowth of such thinking, e.g., Lawrence Le Shan, quotes Carl Jung's observation: '.... I have in fact seen cases where the carcinoma broke out... when a person comes to a halt at some essential point in his individuation or cannot get over an obstacle... An inner process of growth must begin [or] the outcome can only be fatal'.[9]

Given the extreme subjectivism of the New Age worldview and its strong belief in magical forces, it is not surprising to find that most adherents are great fans of the idea that the powers of mind can over-ride inconvenient laws of physics or physiology ('You create your own reality', they say.). Not wishing to forego the prestige and earning power of science, however, many New Age entrepreneurs copy the trappings, if not the substance, of genuine sciences. CAM, for example, is riddled with pseudo-scientific theories and doubtful methods for which practitioners claim to have empirical support.[10,11]

CAM is a collection of health practices derived from anecdotal or uncontrolled clinical observations and traditional folkways, and heavily influenced by ideological and utopian beliefs. CAM's magico-religious roots are plain to see when major proponents cite scriptures as proof of the reciprocal connection between the body and the mind,[12,13] This is deemed sufficient to prove the proposition that any deterioration of one's spiritual well-being can stimulate disease, while its amelioration may prevent sickness and augment cure. Although some of CAM's interventions undoubtedly enhance patients' subjective quality of life, many invoke physiological mechanisms that are scientifically implausible, if not discredited outright. These treatments remain in the marketplace despite the accumulation of negative evidence because of the ideologically and economically driven advocacy of those who profit from their sale. Both sellers and buyers can maintain belief in the efficacy of these therapies because of the ubiquitous placebo effect, coupled with a variety of face-saving rationalizations and cognitive distortions that help preserve cherished metaphysical and sociopolitical dogmas in the face of contrary evidence.[14]

That said, it is only fair to give credit where a modicum is due. It is true that some good has come from CAM's promotion of the alleged powers of mind in medicine, however overblown it may have been. This orientation has encouraged less extreme researchers with better methodological skills to delve into those areas of healthcare where psychosocial factors can make a difference. While one can point to many logically flawed and poorly executed studies done by advocates of spirituality in medicine (such as those concerned with the alleged medical benefits of intercessory prayer[15,16]) and various critiques and refutations of such findings,[17,18] it is still the case that New Age health advocates have had a hand (though a far from unique one) in encouraging certain lifestyle changes that can enhance one's health. Whether this makes up for the harm they cause by opposing universal vaccination, selling worthless (and sometimes dangerous) nostrums or diverting sick people from therapies that really work is another matter. Be that as it may, their assertion that one should take more responsibility for one's own health is hardly controversial any more. New Age medical proponents have also done some good by popularizing those aspects of what they call 'mind–body medicine' (such as certain relaxation techniques) that can claim some scientific support. The critical issue, usually lost on CAM advocates however, is knowing where to stop.

A common rhetorical ploy of New Age devotees is to arrive at a nonsensical conclusion by riding on the coat-tails of proven knowledge. Starting with uncontested facts, they stretch them by barely perceptible increments until the unwary listener is seduced into accepting total hogwash. For instance, the notion that psychological factors can affect physiological processes, and thereby influence certain aspects of one's health, would surprise few who know anything about modern physiology. The possible routes for interactions between brain mechanisms that produce thoughts and feelings and various processes within the autonomic nervous system, the endocrine system and the immune system are well known. The question is how big are these effects and how far can they be stretched to support CAM's more outlandish claims?

Modern neuroscience is founded on a materialist view of consciousness—the proposition that mind equals brain function. If perceptions, memories and emotions are physical states of the brain, there is nothing mystical about the notion that that these physiological processes could influence equally physical processes in other organs. What is in dispute is not whether these interactions could affect one's health, but rather in what ways and to what degree. As always, however, the burden of proof is on the claimant, and many such claims have far outstripped the evidence.

A review of research in the area of mental effects on health was recently published by the respected psychologist, Oakley Ray.[19] In summarizing known points of interaction among neural, endocrine and immune processes, Ray's review cites a number of areas in which researchers have documented the influence of psychosocial processes on the onset and remission of certain diseases. Except in those cases where direct links can be shown, the researchers cited by Ray should not be lumped together with the fringe elements of CAM, who stretch the results of legitimate investigators to untenable lengths. There is much to recommend in Ray's article, which serves to remind us that the dramatic successes of physiologically based interventions in the last hundred years have tended to overshadow a number of psychological contributions to the onset and alleviation of some diseases. Nonetheless, it is unfortunate that Ray's review continues to cite favourably certain papers claiming to have found strong mental effects on outcomes in patients with cancer, ones that have come under increasingly heavy fire in recent years. It is those widely believed but flawed assertions that we wish to address in this chapter.

The assertions in question are that one's state of mind affects susceptibility to cancer, its rate of progression and how long an afflicted patient will survive. While uncontrolled observations of cancer patients lent some initial plausibility to these claims, most oncology researchers have remained sceptical. In frequently cited anecdotal accounts, cancer remission has been attributed to intercessory prayers, visits to shrines and so-called 'psychic surgeons', conversion to Christian Science and force-feeding.[20] However, since virtually all diseases can go into welcome, though rare, spontaneous remission, the fortuitous coincidence of any holistic ritual with such a remission provides unearned support for the treatment's allegedly curative powers. The far more numerous cases where these interventions produce no benefit receive no such publicity. Also, of course, since feeling better is not the same as getting better, subjective improvement following an inert but uplifting treatment is often mistaken for cure. Inasmuch as the putative mechanisms of remission cited by CAM advocates remain only speculative, it is prudent to demand far better evidence before assuming that these happy events represent anything more than random occurrences.

Mind and disease

Interest in possible effects of consciousness on health over the last 30 years eventually grew to encompass a variety of degenerative conditions. Belief in powerful mental effects on cancer was buoyed by a renewed appreciation in the public at large of the importance of personal, social and humanistic aspects of medicine that had tended to be marginalized by its dramatic technological innovations. Growing acceptance of psychosocial contributors to ill health eventually led to calls for a new conceptual model of disease, popularized by George Engel as the 'bio-psycho-social' model.[21] The idea that this might extend to a mind–cancer link gained legitimacy through a number of influential articles and presentations in the 1970s. For example, the oncologist T. R. Miller offered the following encouragement during his 1977 delivery of the prestigious James Ewing lecture:

> Clinicians have long been aware of the influence of the neuro-endocrine axis and the action of the hypothalamus on the humoral immune response in the origin and course of cancer. Little attention has been paid, however, to the psycho-physiologic aspects of cancer. These psychosocial effects may be related to hypothalamic activity, the autonomic nervous system, and neuro-endocrine activity. More attention should be paid to the manipulation of the psyche in the prevention and management of cancer.[22]

The growth of the field of psycho-neuro-immunology provided proponents of the mind–cancer link with a theoretical basis for their speculations. As its name implies, psycho-neuro-immunology studies the interactions among mental states, the central and autonomic nervous systems, the endocrine system and immune responses.[19]

The hypothalamic–pituitary–adrenal (HPA) axis was suggested to be part of a 'stress circuit,' a feedback-controlled system by which the brain and the endocrine glands respond to stressors.[23] The hypothalamus (part of the brain's limbic system, discussed in Chapter 19, which recognizes and responds to threats) secretes releasing hormones that act on the pituitary gland, situated at the base of the brain. This initiates the release of adrenocorticotrophic hormone (ACTH) into the bloodstream. ACTH is carried around the body, eventually reaching receptors in the adrenal glands. The adrenals then release epinephrine (adrenalin), norepinephrine (noradrenalin) and cortisol. These hormones affect various organs throughout the body and act as feedback signals to the brain's limbic system, which is also involved with the control of motivation and emotion. A number of studies point to the fact that immune responsivity can be impeded by stimulating this stress circuit,[19] but does this really affect cancer rates?

At this point, the argument becomes more speculative. Some advocates of mind–body medicine suggest that lack of psychological well-being furthers the development of cancers because there are tumour-enhancing effects of the endocrine and immune responses initiated by activating the HPA axis.[24] On this basis, it was proposed that teaching patients coping strategies and alleviating depressed moods could foster cancer regression by reversing the same mechanisms.[25–28]

By the late 1970s, the concept that consciousness plays a role in cancer had become firmly embedded in clinical as well as popular thinking. The reasoning typically went as follows: if psychosocial support could improve quality of life by enhancing the patient's outlook, self-esteem and self-control, then this improved emotional state should be reflected in his or her medical status (because disease status is influenced by the strength of the immune response, which can be suppressed by negative emotional states). By extension, proponents argued, patients who are helped to feel better about themselves will have improved immune responses that will fight malignant cells and thereby lengthen patient survival. Few informed people doubt that psychosocial support can improve a sick person's quality of life, but some therapists became convinced that quality of life and patient longevity after cancer diagnosis necessarily go hand in hand. Unfortunately, as we shall see, such a desirable outcome has proved hard to demonstrate.

Despite the surface plausibility of the mind–cancer hypothesis, when researchers performed large-scale surveys matching indices of psychological well-being with cancer incidence, no strong associations emerged. Much research has been devoted to the topic, but it remains difficult to tease apart the direct versus indirect effects of behavioural, let alone mental, effects on immunity, and thereby, allegedly, on cancer onset or progression. In a meta-analysis, combining over 85 investigations, Miller and Cohen found no reliable support for the hypothesis that psychosocial interventions significantly affect the immune parameters that have been suggested to have an impact on cancer.[29]

Support is also lacking for the proposed underlying mechanism by which psychological factors are supposed to foster the growth of malignacies, i.e. that mental suppression of the immune system reduces the surveillance that weeds out incipient tumour cells in the body.[30,31] The cancer expert Saul Green has argued that the past 20 years of research indicates that cancer is the result of cell mutation that is impossible for the immune system to detect. To our immune systems, Green says, a cancer cell is still 'self', (i.e. it still displays normal antigenic surfaces) and therefore thrives in the body despite a normal, healthy immune system.[30] Tests of hypotheses that environmental stressors and one's emotional reactions to them could affect cancer genesis or growth (by means of psycho-neuro-immunological mechanisms) have produced conflicting results, the more recent ones tending to be negative. The overall picture does not favour a causal relationship between clinical depression or psychosocial influences and cancer.

Even if a relationship did exist between psychological factors and cancer rates, it would be difficult to demonstrate because the stress response varies substantially from person to person. Genetic differences in the HPA axis lead some people to under-respond to stress and others to over-respond. Attributing tumour growth to environmental stress levels is further hampered by the fact that the concept of stress itself is so varied that patients who are grouped together in studies of this sort will have been exposed to many different kinds of allegedly detrimental pressures, and researchers have shown that there is great variability in what is perceived to be stressful by different individuals.

Factors such as genetics, age, sex, quality of medical care, socio-economic status, carcinogen type, viruses, bacteria and a range of other variables all correlate in various ways with the onset of cancer. The interplay among these variables is extremely complex, and many suggested cause–effect relationships are still topics of debate. This lack of academic consensus has largely escaped the public, which remains enthusiastic about the protective and curative powers of mind, as do many researchers who continue to search for reliable effects. As shown below, properly controlled studies have provided little support for the proposed relationship between psychological processes and onset or remission of cancer.

Early speculations about psychological effects on the genesis or suppression of cancer received some initial support from work with non-human species.[32,33] Although early animal studies found that some cancers were sensitive to hormones and stressors in the environment, those findings failed to translate into useful therapies in the clinic. Moreover, they failed to lead to advances in understanding of the basic mechanisms of human cancer.[30] Consequently, the focus of research on how psychological interventions might affect the clinical course of cancer shifted from animal studies to controlled human trials. Before turning to those human studies, let us briefly examine the animal literature that is often cited in support of the stress–cancer link.

Experimental stress and animal tumours

A number of studies with non-human animals reported stress to be associated with more rapid tumour growth or increased numbers of 'takes' of transplanted tumours (i.e. viable incorporations of malignant cells into the host).[32,33] Since an exact analogue of psychological stress in humans is not readily achieved with non-human animals, these studies used surrogate methods such as rotation, restraint, crowding, noxious stimuli, etc., the specific stress-like qualities of which were difficult to quantify or standardize. In the final analysis, one could not be certain that the hypothesized kind of stress in these studies was the only irritant being delivered. Not surprisingly, the results varied, with some studies actually showing *reduced* tumor formation in the stressed animals. Some animal studies that looked for augmented cancer growth in stressful environments did show the predicted effect, but some showed the exact opposite, while others found no effect at all. Probably because of this inconsistency in the literature, one major oncology text included no section on stress effects on animal tumours.[35]

Another hindrance to any attempt to generalize animal results to human clinical applications has been that most of these studies were conducted with rodents and employed chemically or radiation-induced tumours, or transplanted tumours, instead of spontaneous neoplasms that would have more closely approximated the human clinical picture.[30,31] As a result, a number of researchers have begun to question the ease with which the results of cancer research in rodents can be generalized to humans.[36] Because the animal findings, though somewhat encouraging, did not translate into effective interventions for humans, the focus of mind–cancer research shifted instead to trials with actual patients.

Human clinical observations

The 'cancer personality'

Over the years, various treatment providers have claimed that cancer patients tend to be more depressed and withdrawn than other sick people, suggesting that certain character types may predispose people to carcinogenesis. Le Shan traced anecdotal observations in favour of such a link as far back as the late 1700s.[9,28] However, because the microscopic criteria for the diagnosis of cancer did not exist before the late 1800s, such attributions would have been subject to considerable error. In more recent times, some clinicians have claimed to see a tendency in cancer patients to respond to adversity by suppressing their emotions and falling prey to hopelessness and resignation.[24,26,27] In general, it was suggested that those who would eventually develop cancer tend to be overly passive and defensive. Vulnerable people were described as unassertive, conflict avoidant, compliant and excessively patient and appeasing. These traits, it was claimed, are likely to foster feelings of helplessness, leading to clinical depression.[37,38] The tendency to suppress emotional expression in the vulnerable groups was thought to make them poorer at dealing with stress. The suggested mechanism with respect to cancer was that people with this kind of psychological make-up are prone to exaggerated stress responses, clinical depression and resulting immune deficiencies that lower their body's natural ability to suppress malignant cells.

Looking at the broad picture, there has been little support for earlier claims that certain clusters of personality variables constitute a cancer-prone profile (the so-called 'Type C' personality). Studies using improved methodology in Australia[39] and the Netherlands[40] found no association between these personality factors and the incidence of breast cancer.

A major prospective study conducted in Sweden also found no support for the hypothesis that certain personality traits are associated with cancer risk.[41] The authors concluded that there is little evidence that psychological coping styles play an important part in survival from or recurrence of cancer. Most recently, Scottish researchers[42] conducted a major review of the literature concerning differences in psychological coping styles and survival and recurrence in patients with cancer. The authors concluded that most of the studies that investigated the alleged benefits of a 'fighting spirit' or the detrimental effects of a helpless/hopeless attitude found no significant associations with survival or recurrence. The evidence that other coping styles play an important part was also weak. Positive findings tended to be confined to small or methodologically flawed studies; lack of controls for potential confounding variables was common.

Depression and cancer

Initial impressions that psychological depression seemed to affect vulnerability to cancer probably reflected the ease with which cause can be confused with effect when observations are made in an uncontrolled manner. If a relationship of this sort exists, critics responded, it is likely to be a moderating one at best. For example, dysphoria and stress might decrease patients' appetite or sleep, which, in turn, could lower immune responses, through malnutrition and fatigue. Without adequate controls for these possible confounds, it is impossible to say whether any immune decline that might be found is the result of any mental state *per se*, or even whether this decline is responsible for (as opposed to merely correlated with) the progression of the cancer.

A frequently cited longitudinal study of the interactions among various physical and psychological risk factors and the development of mammary cancer later in life did find their presence to have some predictive value.[38] However, the effects of both physical and psychological variables were seen to be largely over-ridden by hereditary factors. The data pointed to a relationship between the number of risk factors and the likelihood of developing cancer, but the authors placed the primary importance on the *synergistic* effects of hereditary, psychosocial, economic and personality factors in development of cancer. Among the three groups of cancer patients classified according to risk profiles devised for this study, the mortality of low-risk patients on follow-up was only 0.35 per cent, medium risk-patients had a 2.8 per cent mortality rate and high-risk patient mortality was 8.5 per cent. Thus, despite the statistical significance of the psychological risk factors identified in this study, the actual mortality rates in the different classes of patients were unusually low, even in the highest risk group.

Ironically, Derogatis and colleagues reported, in the 1970s, that cancer patients who survived longer were *more* anxious, symptomatic and dysphoric than those who succumbed earlier (who tended to have more positive outlooks and lower levels of hostility).[43] These observations were widely quoted by supporters who tried to link psychological factors and cancer, although they rarely acknowledged that the direction of the effect was paradoxical. These results are hard to reconcile with the alleged medical (as opposed to psychological) benefits of teaching patients to resolve anxieties, achieve better psychological adjustment and develop a more cooperative outlook by means of psychosocial support.

Retrospective studies of patients who already have a disease are fraught with problems that make it difficult to attribute causes. Thus, Borgelt and colleagues at the Danish Institute of Cancer Epidemiology designed a prospective study that followed 8527 people to see whether depressive feelings were risk factors for cancer.[44] These researchers looked for psychological effects on development of smoking-related, alcohol-related, virus-related, immune-related and hormone-related cancers. Even though people with high depression scores showed higher rates of behaviours that put them at increased risk for cancer (such as tobacco consumption and low physical activity), no association was found between the severity of depressive symptoms and enhanced risk of developing cancer. In fact, the authors found that those at the highest end of their depressive scale had a slightly decreased risk for cancer.

Despite the disappointing trends in research attempting to link psychological factors to the onset of cancer, one thesis seemed to retain some promise, however. Some reports in the 1990s appeared to show an effect of psychosocial support on the progression of cancer, an effect apparently reflected in patient longevity. Some earlier researchers had found a positive correlation between quality of life scores and survival rates, though most did not. For instance, a study conducted by the US National Cancer Institute's Cancer and Leukemia Group B, in 1996, collected demographic and psychosocial measures for 280 female cancer patients. No relationship was found between psychosocial indicators and cancer course or survival.[45] A major study by Cassileth evaluated patients with cancer, looking for effects of personal and external life-event factors. It found no association with the course of cancer, survival or time to disease recurrence.[46]

Against this generally negative backdrop, a few, more positive, results managed to capture the popular imagination and develop a life of their own. Two in particular were widely quoted in the media and quickly incorporated into influential textbooks, despite subsequent difficulties in replicating their results. As discussed below, the initially encouraging findings seem to have been due to a combination of relatively small sample sizes, chance variation and possible artefacts introduced by the experimental design or its implementation. Although a number of studies indicate that psychosocial support can improve adjustment and quality life in cancer patients, evidence that it has a direct effect on tumour growth or patient survival remains slim.

Claims that psychosocial support increases longevity in cancer patients

A 1989 paper from Stanford University, published in the prestigious journal, the *Lancet*, captured headlines around the world because of its unexpected discovery that patients with metastatic breast cancer enrolled in a psychosocial support programme lived twice as long as a group of control patients who had been placed on a waiting list.[47] The mean survival duration of the control group was 16.6 months from discovery of the metastasis, whereas the patients given group psychotherapy lived, on average, a further 36.6 months post diagnosis. The study had originally been designed to see if improved adjustment due to psychological support affected how well patients cope with their symptoms.[48] Longevity had not originally been an outcome measure in the study—the differential survival times emerged from a retrospective analysis of the data in the researchers' 10-year database. This news, however welcome, was at odds with earlier studies in the literature and then-current opinions of most cancer experts. These doubts were temporarily quelled when further analysis by the Stanford researchers revealed no significant differences between the treatment and control groups for a number of prognostic factors that might have explained the different survival rates.[49]

However, other important prognostic indicators were not included in this retrospective analysis, such as patients' performance status (a way of quantifying cancer patients' general well-being). Nonetheless, the report fit the growing mind–body Zeitgeist and thus became a touchstone for those bent on reviving the notion of the 'mind cure'. It took nearly a decade before alternative explanations for the published results started to circulate widely. The alternatives included the possibility that chance occurrences had skewed the results (something that should always be considered when claims are based upon relatively small samples and *post hoc* analyses) and certain methodological anomalies, discussed below. Some of the latter were actually alluded to in the original *Lancet* publication but had escaped the notice of most critics.

Mind–body enthusiasts were also buoyed by another study, conducted at UCLA, that seemed to support the Stanford conclusions.[50] This study, of Stage I melanoma patients, also received wide publicity because of its unanticipated, upbeat findings. Also in a retrospective analysis, 6 years into the study, it too showed a difference in survival between control patients and those who had attended a series of support group meetings. As with the Stanford study, longevity had not been an original interest of the UCLA researchers, and, unfortunately, by the time the study had run its full 10-year course, the apparent survival benefit of the psychological intervention was no longer statistically significant.[51]

The popular persistence of these optimistic reports is remarkable. They continue to be widely cited in spite of later doubts as to their reliability—the reasons for which we will now examine.

Methodological concerns regarding the results

In hindsight, there were clues in the two studies under discussion that should have cast doubt on their conclusions about psychological support and cancer survival. Both the 1989 Stanford study and the 1996 UCLA study contained anomalies that should have immediately suggested alternative interpretations of their results.

With regard to the Stanford study published in the *Lancet*, a number of such concerns were eventually voiced. The study was originally designed to measure the effects of psychotherapy on adjustment and other psychological indicators of patient well-being; the effect on patient survival was unpredicted and discovered only on retrospective examination of the data, 10 years after the study began. In science, it is considered proper to report results such as these, but, because unpredicted *post hoc* observations have a high chance of being due to random fluctuations, it is considered inadvisable to base strong conclusions upon them until they have been independently replicated by researchers who posit the same finding as a *predicted* outcome of a *planned* experimental manipulation.

The authors of the Stanford study reported the mean survival times, rather than the medians, as is customary in this type of research (because a few atypical outliers can skew the means considerably). The median survival durations of the experimental and control groups differed by only 2 months, a difference that would hardly have received the attention the mean difference was accorded.

Although the authors' subsequent comparison of several antecedent predictors of outcome suggested the treatment and control groups had been adequately matched, other symptom clusters that would have bolstered this claim, such as overall functional status of the patients, weight loss, pain reports, etc., were not recorded.

The randomization procedure for assigning patients to the psychotherapy and control groups was not described in the original *Lancet* publication. Random assignment to intervention versus non-intervention status is essential in any clinical study to avoid capitalizing on differences that could affect the outcome if patients with better or worse prognostic indicators were placed disproportionately in one group or the other. Any deviation from a strictly blinded, random assignment procedure opens the door for subtle, unintentional biases that could make the groups appear different upon follow-up, even if the experimental therapy is ineffective. The authors stated in the article that, 'More subjects were randomly assigned to therapy ($n = 50$) than to control ($n = 38$) to ensure enough patients for group work'.[47] This statement raises a number of concerns. First, there was no explanation for how such a distribution was arrived at with a totally random, blinded assignment procedure. The protocol for assigning patients to their respective groups was not published, nor was the procedure by which patients were randomized to achieve the desired ratio. In a personal communication, one author of the *Lancet* paper stated that the intended ratio was 2:1 favouring therapy, and the assignment had been conducted by drawing straws (D. Spiegel, personal communication to W. Sampson, October 1997). The possibility that there may have been anomalies in the patient assignment procedure seems more likely when we consider the slight odds of obtaining a ratio of 50:38 with an assignment regimen geared to produce a two to one split (note that we are not claiming intentional bias here). The binomial probability of that ratio occurring by truly random assignment is 0.06. While that outcome is not in itself extremely unlikely, it reduces the weight that should have been given to the study's conclusions until they were independently replicated.

It took many years for most sceptics to notice the oddity that no patient in the Stanford control group lived beyond 4 years, whereas national and regional survival data on metastatic breast cancer patients at the time of the study showed about 19 per cent alive after 5 years and 7–8 per cent at ten years.[52,53] Thus, we must ask, 'What is the probability that all control patients from an adequately randomized sample of this nature would have died within 4 years?' The binomial probability of all 38 patients dying before 10 years is only 0.018. In concentrating on the divergence of the survival curves between the experimental and control groups, both supporters and critics initially failed to recognize that the allegedly improved survival curve for the psychotherapy group was, in fact, nearly identical to the averages published for all patients with the same diagnosis in huge cancer databases such as the Survival, Epidemiology and End Results (SEER)[52] and National Cancer Institute (NCI) reports[53] for that period (the majority of whom would not have received this kind of group therapy). In other words, an alternative interpretation of the Stanford data would be that the treatment group's longevity was unaffected by the psychological interventions and the control group was somehow atypical vis-a-vis the SEER/NCI patient populations. Overall, one small probability (6 per cent probability that purely random assignment would have produced the stated assignment ratio) was compounded by another (1.8 per cent probability of a control group representative of the 'normal' population of breast cancer patients surviving as long as reported). Hence, a more likely explanation for these findings is that the sample of patients studied was not representative of the general population of such patients, and/or unknown confounding factors affected the assignment of patients. Similar but non-statistical explanations were suggested by Fox in a series of articles and letters.[54,55] Fox suggested that an aberrant control group was probably responsible for the difference in longevity between it and the group that received group psychotherapy. This anomaly was also pointed out by Lawrence A. William within the first week of publication of the *Lancet* article, and subsequently repeated in a 1997 article.[56] Similar doubts were expressed by Sampson in a 1997 critique.[56]

In the other widely heralded project, the 1996 UCLA study referred to earlier[50,51], 68 Stage I melanoma patients were randomly assigned to a 6-week course of psychosocial therapy, or to a no treatment control group, and followed for 6 years. Both cancer recurrence (13/34) and death (10/34) were more common in the controls than in the treatment group (7/34 and 3/34, respectively). Difficulties with the UCLA study were similar to those in the Stanford one, however. The differences in recurrence and survival rates were unpredicted and found retrospectively, the numbers of participants were fairly small and multiple end points were possible (another way of capitalizing on chance variations that can make a therapy seem more effective than it is). Additionally, only 25 per cent of the interventions delivered in the experimental group involved psychosocial support and it was provided for only 6 weeks. This is arguably far too short a time for the reported effects of a psychosocial manipulation to be seen, as it is generally agreed that several sessions are required simply to build rapport between patients and staff and among the group participants themselves.[57]

More importantly, questions were raised once again concerning the adequacy of the control group in the UCLA study. Five-year survival in the treatment group was about 92 per cent, whereas in the control group it was only about 72 per cent. SEER data from the same decade show an overall 92 per cent survival at 5 years for all patients diagnosed with Stage I melanoma.[52] The binomial probability of a representative sample of Stage I melanoma patients from a typical population having a 5-year survival rate of only

72 per cent is about 0.001. The overall survival at 5 years for the entire cohort in the UCLA study was 57 of 68. The binomial probability of a truly representative sample of Stage I melanoma patients having that survival rate is only 0.007. Thus, it seems likely that the entire cohort was unrepresentative of the usual population with this diagnosis, and/or the control group was probably anomalous in some important way.

In summary, both of these widely quoted studies suffered from similar shortcomings. The most plausible conclusion, therefore, is that their reported improvements in survival, attributed to psychosocial support, were due to undetected experimental artefacts, and that biomedical factors are, in fact, the dominant contributors to patient survival.

Failed attempts at replication

One or two studies almost never settle an important scientific controversy; it is the overall track record that counts. As the physicist Victor Stenger nicely put it, 'In science, nothing is accepted until its appearance becomes commonplace'. Several studies have attempted to reproduce the findings reported in the *Lancet* study, but none has been able to do so unequivocally. Both it and the UCLA study discussed above contradicted other reports, published both before and afterwards, that showed no increased survival among cancer patients attributable to participation in psychological support groups. The widely publicized positive articles contradicted earlier studies such as one that found that when late stage cancer patients were provided with counselling, comprised purely of social support, they did not survive significantly longer than the late stage patients who did not receive counselling.[57] This is consistent with three other reports that soon followed the Stanford and UCLA publications, which showed no survival advantage for patients given group or other psychotherapy.[58–60] Another study, by Gellert *et al.*,[61] employing the case–control method, compared the 'exceptional' cancer (ECaP) group therapy patients of Dr Bernie Siegel (a major proponent of the curative effects of psychological interventions) with matched patients who received no group therapy. This 10-year follow-up study of the effects of psychosocial support on breast cancer patients did not show 'significant favorable impact on survival'[61(p.66)]. A Canadian study that attempted carefully to repeat the exact experimental conditions in the original *Lancet* study[60] was unsuccessful, as was another attempt at precise replication.[61]

In contrast, some studies have reported shorter average survival in cancer patients who received group therapy. For instance, a study of cancer patients at the Bristol (UK) Self-help Centre found that participants who attended psychological support groups actually survived for a shorter time than controls.[62] This should not be construed to mean that the intervention was harmful, however, because this project used self-selected volunteers, and assignment to the two groups was not random. Another study reported similar but mixed findings.[63] Although the control and psychological intervention groups were carefully matched, when survival times were compared, the patients without the psychological intervention survived longer. The two subsets of the intervention group, which were supervised and unsupervised by a social worker, had mean survival times of 70.7 and 62.0 months, respectively. However, the control group had a mean survival time of

82.4 months. When the authors separated the breast cancer patients in their sample in order to compare them with the *Lancet* study's patients, all of whom had that diagnosis, they found no difference between those receiving psychosocial support and those that did not.

A few studies seemed to offer partial support for the value of psychological interventions, but odd patterns in the data reduce their ability to counter the generally negative trend. One study from Germany, for example, showed a short-term survival advantage at 2 years in a group of gastroenterological cancer patients receiving group therapy, compared with controls that did not attend such groups.[64] Unexplainably, however, this advantage was present in only one of the four groups defined by the anatomical locus of their cancer. Another study occasionally cited in support of psychological effects on cancer longevity is that of McCorkle *et al.*[65] It compared survival rates between older post-surgical cancer patients who received home care visits by advanced practice nurses (APNs) versus those who received the usual follow-up care. The researchers found no difference in survival among early stage cancer patients, but the 2-year survival for late stage patients in the intervention group was 67 per cent compared with only 40 per cent in the control group. The authors also mention, however, that some patients in the control group died of causes they described as related to, but not directly due to cancer. Because social support (comprised of only three visits and five telephone calls over a 4-week period) represented only 16 per cent of the total services provided by the APNs, the study does not claim, as others have sometimes stated, that social support itself was responsible for the improved longevity figures.

A study conducted at the University of Southern California[66] is often listed as evidence for a positive effect of social support on longevity, but closer scrutiny once again reveals cause for doubt.[67–69] This study employed three types of nursing support, including a single home visit to check on drug therapy compliance. There was no structured or group psychosocial support involved. The study found that survival correlated only with compliance rates of taking prescribed medications, which improved in response to the nurses' visits.

In response to the generally negative attempts at replication, some supporters called for larger scale trials, arguing that real but small effects might have failed to reach statistical significance due to the inadequate sample sizes of the non-supportive studies—a problem known as 'lack of statistical power'. Rather than undertake such an expensive and time-consuming endeavour, researchers at the University of Toronto decided to pool eight previously published randomized trials into a meta-analysis, which can partially compensate for sample size problems in the individual studies that are combined. Their meta-analysis included 1062 cancer patients who received psychosocial support with the aim of prolonging their survival.[72] It failed to find any significant differences between intervention and control groups, neither in patients with metastatic breast cancer nor in those suffering from all other types of cancer.

The aforementioned studies represent substantial evidence against the notion that psychosocial support improves the length of survival in cancer patients. Since the Stanford and UCLA studies appeared, no controlled study to date has shown a direct influence of psychosocial intervention on increased longevity in cancer patients. Several meta-analytical studies have found no evidence to support this claim, and the proposed mechanism underlying the hypothesized relationship between psychosocial support and survival in cancer patients remains only speculative.[70–74] Thus, the overall picture strongly suggests that more than simple social support is necessary for improved survival in cancer patients.

The mounting evidence recently against the claim that psychosocial interventions can intercept or retard tumour growth has caused a shift in emphasis among researchers in the area, back to where it all began, i.e. helping patients cope with their disease. It is now more commonly claimed that psychosocial support can be beneficial in helping patients deal with pain, loneliness and psychological symptoms, and that improved psychological adjustment may increase adherence to treatment.[75,76] However, even these results are inconsistent. Some studies report no improvement in the quality of life or any other significant differences between psychological intervention and control groups. For instance, Edmonds et al. found that a weekly psychological intervention over a period of 8 months resulted in no significant improvement in quality of life for metastatic breast cancer patients.[77] Other studies show mixed results with different intervention techniques within the psychosocial support model, such as cognitive–behavioural therapy, coping skills training or supportive–expressive group work. These techniques have been shown to help improve the functional adjustment and perception of cancer-related symptoms for some patients but not for others. Owen and colleagues[73] have criticized the multi-component interventions that have been used in psychosocial support programmes for patients, calling it the 'kitchen-sink approach', because such confounding of experimental variables makes it difficult to determine which components of these interventions are most effective for specific types of cancer.

Conclusion

Given the weakness of the case for psychological contributions to the onset and alleviation of cancer, we must ask what has kept the notion alive so long. Once again, it appears that the appeal of implausible ideas and unlikely findings is embedded in the social milieu of the times, the so-called 'Zeitgeist'. The popular resurgence of comforting beliefs in the miraculous powers of the mind spilled over from New Age, postmodernist circles to affect thinking in many areas of academia.[2,3] Academic medicine was not immune to these trends and some researchers were swept along by the mentalistic revival. Concerted attempts to re-insert a spiritual dimension into science led some academics to question the purely mechanistic approach that distinguished scientific medicine from its vitalistic forebears. Despite good intentions, some lost sight of the fact that the checks and balances of the scientific method evolved, in large part, to reduce the impact of our human propensity to see what we want to see and believe what we want to believe. In the case of alleged mind–cancer effects, demonstrations of a psychological impact on the progression of some other diseases paved the way for an overly credulous acceptance of a mind–cancer link. While research has demonstrated that psychological factors play a larger role in many diseases than most medical researchers once thought, the extension of these findings to the mechanisms of cancer turns out to have been overly enthusiastic.

The resurgence of the mentalistic Zeitgeist resulted in a new orthodoxy in some quarters that promoted acceptance of weakly supported ideas, and their dogged defence in the face of more believable evidence to the contrary. Investigators' attempts to confirm the new, upbeat orthodoxy were accepted if supportive, while contrary results were either dismissed or rationalized away.[78,79]

Questioning established positions in science can lead to important breakthroughs, as long as the alternatives are backed up with convincing evidence. Such was the case in the recent awarding of the Nobel Prize in medicine to Marshall and Warren for proof that stomach ulcers owe more to a common bacterium than to psychosocial stress, the previously dominant position.[80] The difference between Marshall and Warren's case and many of the forays of 'mind–body medicine' is that, in the former instance, the outsiders eventually persuaded the rightly sceptical scientific community with hard evidence, rather than merely asserting that it must be so because it is consistent with an attractive philosophical outlook.

The Nobel Laureate Rita Levi-Montalcini noted the existence, even in mainstream science, of what she calls 'the law of negative regard of information ... facts that fit into a preconceived hypothesis attract attention, are singled out, and remembered. Facts that are contrary to it are disregarded, treated as an exception, and forgotten'.[81] In more borderline areas of investigation, this effect is even greater, because experimental controls are typically weaker and subjective appraisals hold greater sway. With respect to suggested effects of mental state on cancer, the usual situation found in the scientific community was reversed. In this instance, the postmodernist influence on academic medicine, instead of promoting rejection of information contrary to old, established theory, led to rejection of information contrary to a new and attractive, though unlikely, proposition. Information from flawed studies was accepted, reinforcing the questionable assertion that one's state of mind directly affects the progression of cancer.

Improbable but stimulating ideas often receive more attention than established, though less interesting ones. This is now the case with widely held attitudes toward CAM, a large part of which is devoted to the 'mind cure' of days gone by. Theories and claims long regarded as doubtful now have multiple champions who assert that a new and exciting reversal of mainstream opinion has occurred. As a result, the scientific establishment has had thrust upon it the burden of disproof—the inverse of the conventional scientific practice in which advocates must supply adequate evidence for claims before they are accepted. Establishment of the National Center for Complementary and Alternative Medicine (NCCAM) within the US National Institutes of Health has provided huge sums of money for advocates to promote various scientifically questionable notions, including alleged spiritual effects on disease. Although the founders of the NCCAM promised to apply conventional standards of proof to evaluate the worth of various non-scientific treatments, little in the way of newly validated therapies has been forthcoming.[82] This despite the centre's annual budget of over US$100 000 000. When the director of the NCCAM was challenged at a news conference to point to a single 'alternative' therapy that had been scientifically verified as a result of this huge outlay, he could not think of one. None of this surprises critics, because they have long asserted that CAM is founded on belief rather than evidence and that CAM is, in fact, hostile to empirical evaluation of its claims.

High rates of literacy and mandatory education have done little to reduce the prevalence of supernatural, irrational and occult beliefs in modern societies. Polls consistently report high levels of such beliefs, even among well-educated people. Why should this be? Psychologists assert that it is because our brains did not evolve to be 'truth seeking machines'[83,84] Natural selection, which shaped the brain, and hence the ways we ordinarily think, works on reproductive success, not any automatic respect for the truth. Alcock[83] explains that the human brain evolved to be a belief-generating machine that takes sensory input, filters and organizes it in relation to our existing memories and emotional feelings, and produces beliefs that tend to be consistent with those we already hold. Thus, our innate way of forming judgements is just as capable of producing false but useful (i.e. survival-enhancing) beliefs as objectively true ones. True or false, they tend to be held because they are functional in our lives, not because they are necessarily accurate. Irrational beliefs are created in the same way as any other belief we may hold, most of which are accepted on the basis of the authority we accord to the source.

Critical thinking abilities, on the other hand, are acquired through training and practice; they are not innate. We must *learn* to test our reasoning and to mistrust our gut feelings and intuitions, especially when they reinforce our cherished attitudes and aspirations. At the same time, our society teaches us that certain things are 'off limits' for this kind of scrutiny and should be accepted on intuition and faith. Thus, we are often inconsistent in how we bring our critical skills to bear. If new data are supportive of our core beliefs, we tend to test them less stringently than those that challenge our fundamental worldview. Although we often get it right in spite of these impediments, there are also times when deeply held metaphysical beliefs cause us to impose patterns on input that are not really there. Not surprisingly, those patterns tend to be congruent with our pre-existing beliefs, hopes and expectations. As a result, we sometimes make sense out of nonsense.

As the philosopher Bertrand Russell wisely advised, 'What we need is not the will to believe, but the wish to find out'. Those who followed Russell's dictum have found little to support the notion, however comforting it may be, that the scourge of cancer is greatly affected by our state of mind.

Acknowledgment

We are indebted to Dr Jan Willem Nienhuys of Einthoven University, the Netherlands, for his invaluable help with statistical calculations presented in this chapter.

References and notes

1. Basil R. (ed.) *Not necessarily the New Age*. Prometheus Books, Amherst, NY. 1982.
2. Sokal A, Bricmont J. *Intellectual impostures*. Profile Books, London. 1997.
3. Gross PR, Levitt N. *Higher superstition. The academic left and its quarrels with science*. John Hopkins University Press, Baltimore, MD. 1998.
4. Beyerstein BL. Whence cometh the myth that we only use ten percent of our brains? In S Della Sala, ed. *Mind myths: exploring everyday mysteries of the mind and brain*. John Wiley & Sons, Chichester, UK, 1999:1–24.
5. Siegel B. *Love, medicine & miracles*. Harper-Collins, New York. 1986.
6. Cousins N. *Head first: the biology of hope and the healing power of the human spirit*. Dutton, New York. 1989.
7. Shorter E. *From paralysis to fatigue*. Macmillan, New York. 1994.
8. Showalter E. *Hystories: hysterical epidemics and modern media*. Columbia University Press, New York. 1997.
9. Le Shan LL. Psycholological states as factors in the development of malignant disease: a critical review. *Journal of the National Cancer Institute*, 1959; **22**:1–18.
10. Beyerstein B, Downie S. Naturopathy. *Scientific Review of Alternative Medicine*, 1998; **1**:10–18.
11. Stevens P. Magical thinking in complementary and alternative medicine. *Skeptical Inquirer*, 2001; **25**:32–37.
12. Kaufman Y. *Psychoneuroimmunology: the science connecting body and mind*. Available online: http://chabadstanford.org/pages/wisdom_center/Article/Print/61.html
13. Dossey L. Prayer is good medicine: how to reap the healing benefits of prayer. Harper, San Francisco. 1996.
14. Beyerstein BL. Alternative medicine and common errors of reasoning. *Academic Medicine*, 2001; **76**:10–17.
15. Cha KY, Wirth DP, Lobo R. Does prayer influence the success of *in vitro* fertilization-embryo transfer? Report of a masked, randomized trial. *Journal of Reproductive Medicine*, 2001; **46**:781–787.
16. Byrd RC. Positive therapeutic effects of intercessory prayer in a coronary care unit population. *Southern Medical Journal*, 1988; **81**:826–829.
17. Flamm BL. Faith healing confronts modern medicine. *Scientific Review of Alternative Medicine*, 2004; **8**:9–14.
18. Krucoff MW, Crater SW, Gallup D, Blankenship JC, Cuffe M, Guarneri M, Krieger RA, Kshettry VR, Morris K, Oz M, Pichard A, Sketch MH, Koenig HG, Mark D, Lee KL. Music, imagery, touch, and prayer as adjuncts to interventional cardiac care: the Monitoring and Actualisation of Noetic Trainings (MANTRA) II randomised study. *Lancet*, 2005; **366**:211–217.
19. Ray O. How the mind hurts and heals the body. *American Psychologist*, 2004; **59**:29–40.
20. Achterberg J, Dossey L, Gordon JS, Hegedus C, Herrmann MW, Nelson R. *Mind–body interventions*. Available online: http://www. naturalhealthvillage.com /reports/rpt2oam /mindbody.htm
21. Engel G. The need for a new medical model: a challenge for biomedicine. *Science*, 1977; **196**:4286–4288.
22. Miller TR. Psychophysiologic aspects of cancer: the James Ewing lecture. *Cancer*, 1977; **39**:413–418.
23. Bock R, Weeks M. Stress system malfunction could lead to serious, life threatening disease. National Institutes of Health News Releases, September 2002 Available online: http://www.nichd.nih.gov/new/releases/stress.cfm
24. Solomon GF, Amkraut AA, Kasper P. Immunity, emotions and stress with special reference to the mechanisms of stress effects on the immune system. *Psychotherapy and Psychosomatics*, 1974; **23**:209–217.
25. Riscalla LM. Consciousness: an added dimension in the treatment of cancer. *Journal of the American Society of Psychosomatic Dentistry and Medicine*, 1975; **22**:71–80.
26. Simonton OC, Simonton S, Creighton M. *Getting well again*. JP Tarcher, Los Angeles. 1978.

27. **Sommer SJ.** Mind–body medicine and holistic approaches. *Australian Family Physician,* 1996; 25:1233–1241.

28. **LeShan LL.** *You can fight for your life.* M. Evans & Co., NY. 1997.

29. **Miller GE, Cohen S.** Psychological interventions and the immune system: a meta-analytic review and critique. *Health Psychology,* 2001; **20**:47–63.

30. **Green S.** Can alternative treatments induce immune surveillance over cancer in humans? *Scientific Review of Alternative Medicine,* 2000; 4:6–9.

31. Stress does not uniformly accelerate tumor growth. *Cancer Letters,* 2001; **10**:11–15.

32. **Amkraut A, Solomon GF.** Stress and murine sarcoma virus (Moloney) induced tumors. *Cancer Research,* 1972; 32:1428–1433.

33. **DiBerardino MA, King TJ.** Renal adenocarcinomas promoted by crowded conditions in laboratory frogs. *Cancer Research,* 1965; 25:1910–1912.

34. **Baker DG.** Influence of a chronic environmental stress [cold] on the incidence of methylcholanthrene-induced tumors. *Cancer Research,* 1977; 37:3939–3944.

35. **De Vita V, Hellman S, Rosenberg SA.** *Cancer: principles and practice of oncology.* Lippincott, Philadelphia. 1996.

36. **Corpet DE, Pierre F.** How good are rodent models of carcinogenesis in predicting efficacy in humans? A sytematic review and meta-analysis of colon chemoprevention in rats, mice and men. *European Journal of Cancer,* 2005; 41:1911–1922.

37. **Grossarth-Maticek R, Eysenck HJ.** Personality, stress and disease: description and validation of a new inventory. *Psychological Reports,* 1990; 66:355–373.

38. **Grossarth-Maticek R, Eysenck HJ, Boyle GJ, Hebb J, Costa SD, Diel IJ.** Interaction of psychosocial and physical risk factors in the causation of mammary cancer and its prevention through physiological methods of treatment. *Journal of Clinical Psychology,* 2000; 56:33–50.

39. **Burke MA, Goodkin K.** Stress and the development of breast cancer: a persistent and popular link despite contrary evidence. *Cancer,* 1997; 79:1055–1059.

40. **Bleiker EM, van der Ploeg HM.** Personality factors and breast cancer development: a prospective longitudinal study. *Journal of National Cancer Institute,* 1996; 88:1478–1482.

41. **Hansen PE, Floderus B, Frederiksen K, Johansen C.** Personality traits, health behavior, and risk for cancer: a prospective study of a Swedish twin cohort. *Cancer,* 2005; 103:1082–1091.

42. **Petticrew M, Bell R, Hunter D.** Influence of psychological coping on survival and recurrence in people with cancer: systematic review. *British Medical Journal,* 2005; 325:1066–1076.

43. **Derogatis LR, Abeloff MD, Meliseratos MHS.** Psychological coping mechanisms and survival time in metastatic breast cancer. *Journal of the American Medical Association,* 1979; 242:1504–1508.

44. **Borgelt C, Christensen J, Prescott E, Grønbæk G, Koch ME, Johansen C.** Vital exhaustion and risk for cancer: a prospective cohort study on the association between depressive feelings, fatigue and risk for cancer. *Cancer,* 2005; 104:1288–1295.

45. **Tross S, Herndon J 2nd, Korzun A, Kornblith AB, Cella DF, Holland JF, Raich P, Johnson A, Kiang DT, Perloff M, Norton L, Wood W, Holland JC.** Psychological symptoms and disease-free and overall survival in women with stage II breast cancer. Cancer and Leukemia Group B. *Journal of National Cancer Institute,* 1996; 88:629–631.

46. **Cassileth BR, Lusk EJ, Miller DS, Brown LL, Miller C.** Psychosocial correlates of survival in advanced malignant disease. *New England Journal of Medicine,* 1985; 312:1551–1555.

47. **Spiegel D, Kramer H, Bloom JR, Gottheil E.** Effects of psychosocial treatment on survival of patients with metastatic breast cancer. *Lancet,* 1989; 2:888–891.

48. **Spiegel D, Bloom JR, Yalom I.** Group support for metastatic cancer. A randomized outcome study. *Archives of General Psychiatry,* 1981; 38:527–533.

49. **Kogon MM, Biswas A, Pearl D, Carlson R, Spiegel D.** Effects of medical and psychotherapeutic treatment on the survival of women with metastatic breast cancer. *Cancer,* 1997; 80:225–230.

50. Fawzy FI, Fawzy NW, Hyunh C. Malignant melanoma. Effects of an early structured psychiatric intervention, coping, and affective state on recurrence and survival 6 years later. *Archives of General Psychiatry*, 1993; 50:681–689.

51. Fawzy IF, Canada AL, Fawzy NW. Malignant melanoma: effects of brief, structured psychiatric intervention on survival and recurrence at 10-year follow-up. *Archives of General Psychiatry*, 2003; 60:100–103.

52. Miller BA, Reis LAG, Hankey BF, Kosary CL, Harras A. Devesa SS, Edwards BK. SEER *Cancer statistics review*, 1973–1990. National Cancer Institute. NIH No. 93-2789. 1993.

53. Rosen PP, Groshen S, Saigo PE, Kinne D, Hellman S. Pathological prognostic factors in stage I (T1N0M0 and stage II (T1N1M0) breast carcinoma: a study of 644 patients with median follow-up of 18 years. *Journal of Clinical Oncology*, 1989; 7:1239–1251.

54. Fox BH. Some problems and some solutions in research on psychotherapeutic intervention in cancer. *Supportive Care in Cancer*, 1995; 3:257–263.

55. Fox BH. A hypothesis about Spiegel *et al.*'s 1989 paper on psychosocial intervention and breast cancer survival. *Psycho-oncology*, 1998; 7:361–370.

56. Sampson WI. Inconsistencies and errors in alternative medicine research. *Skeptical Inquirer*, 1997; 21:35.

57. Linn MW, Linn BS, Harris R. Effects of counseling for late stage cancer patients. *Cancer*, 1982; 49:1048–1055.

58. Cunningham AJ, Edmonds CV, Jenkins GP, Pollack H, Lockwood GA, Warr D. A randomized controlled trial of the effects of group psychological therapy on survival in women with metastatic breast cancer. *Psycho-oncology*, 1998; 7:508–517.

59. Goodwin PJ, Leszcz M, Ennis M, Koopmans J, Vincent L, Guther H, Drysdale E, Hundleby M, Chochinov H, Navarro M, Speca M, Hunter J. The effects of group psychosocial support on survival in metastatic breast cancer. *New England Journal of Medicine*, 2001; 345:1719–1726.

60. Edelman S, Lemon J, Bell DR, Kidman AD. Effects of group CBT on survival time of patients with metastatic breast cancer. *Psycho-oncology*, 1999; 8:474–481.

61. Gellert GA, Maxwell RM, Siegel BS. Survival of breast cancer patients receiving adjunctive psychosocial support therapy. *Journal of Clinical Oncology*, 1993; 11:66–69.

62. Bagenal FS, Easton DF, Harris E, Chilvers CED, McElwain TJ. Survival of patients with breast cancer attending Bristol Cancer Health Center. *Lancet*, 1990; 336:606–610.

63. Ilnyckyj A, Farber M, Cheang MC, Weinerman BH. A randomized trial of psychotherapeutic intervention in cancer patients. *Annals RCPSC*, 1994; 27:93–96.

64. Kuchler T, Henne-Bruns D, Rappat S, Graul J, Holst K, Williams JI, Wood-Dauphinee S. Impact of psychotherapeutic support on gastrointestinal cancer patients undergoing surgery: survival results of a trial. *Hepatogastroenterology*, 1999; 46:322–335.

65. McCorkle R, Strumpf NE, Nuamah IF, Adler DC, Cooley ME, Jepson C, Lusk EJ, Torosian M. A specialized home care intervention improves survival among older post-surgical cancer patients. *Journal of the American Geriatric Society*, 2000; 48:1707–1713.

66. Richardson JL, Shelton DR, Kraio M, Levine AM. The effect of compliance with treatment on survival among patients with hematological malignancies. *Journal of Clinical Oncology*, 1990; 8:356–364.

67. Spiegel D. Healing words. *Journal of the American Medical Association*, 1999; 281:328–1329.

68. Spiegel D. Psychological distress and disease course for women with breast cancer. *Journal of the National Cancer Institute*, 1996; 88:629–631.

69. Spiegel D, Kramer H, Bloom J. A tale of two methods: randomization versus matching trials in clinical research. *Psycho-oncology*, 1998; 7:371–375.

70. Chow E, Tsao MN, and Harth T. Does psychosocial intervention improve survival in cancer? A meta-analysis. *Palliative Medicine*, 2004; 18:25–31.

71. **Meyer T, Mark MM.** Effects of psychosocial interventions with adult cancer patients: a meta-analysis of randomized experiments. *Health Psychology*, 1995; **14:**101–108.

72. **Edelman S, Craig A, Kidman AD.** Can psychotherapy increase the survival time of cancer patients? *Journal of Psychosomatic Research*, 2000; **49:**149–156.

73. **Owen JE, Klapow JC, Hicken B, Tucker DC.** Psychosocial interventions for cancer: review and analysis using a three-tiered outcomes model. *Psycho-oncology*, 2001; **10:**218–230.

74. **Ross L, Boesen EH, Dalton SO, Johansen C.** Mind and cancer: does psychosocial intervention improve survival and psychological well-being? *European Journal of Cancer*, 2002; **38:**1447–1457.

75. **Clipp EC, Hollis DR, Cohen HJ.** Considerations of psychosocial illness phase in cancer survival. *Psycho-oncology*, 2001; **10:**166–178.

76. **Fukui S, Koike M, Ooba A, Uchitomi Y.** The effect of a psychosocial group intervention on loneliness and social support for Japanese women with primary breast cancer. *Oncology Nursing Forum*, 2003; 30:823–830.

77. **Edmonds CVI, Lockwood GA, Cunningham AJ.** Psychological response to long term group therapy: a randomized trial with metastatic breast cancer patients. *Psycho-oncology*, 1999; **8:**74–91.

78. **Spiegel D.** Cancer and depression. *British Journal of Psychiatry*, 1996; **30:**109–116.

79. **Spiegel D.** Psychosocial intervention in cancer. *Journal of the National Cancer Institute*, 1993; **85:**1198–1205.

80. **Atwood KC.** Bacteria, ulcers, and ostracism: *H. pylori* and the making of a myth. *Skeptical Inquirer*, November 2004. Available on-line: http://www.csicop.org/si/2004–11/bacteria.html

81. **Levi-Montalcini R.** *In praise of imperfection*. Basic Books, New York, 1988.

82. **Atwood KC.** The Ongoing Problem with the National Center for Complementary and Alternative Medicine. *Skeptical Inquirer*. September 2003. Available on-line: http://www.csicop.org/si/2003–09/alternative-medicine.html

83. **Alcock J.** The belief engine. *Skeptical Inquirer*, 1995; **19:**255–263. Available on-line: http://www.csicop.org/si/9505/belief.html

84. **Sutherland S.** *Irrationality: why we don't think straight*. Rutgers University Press, New Brunswick, NJ. 1992.

Chapter 28

The elusive search for a 'gay gene'

Fernando Saravi

Science can tell us how things are, but not how they ought to be. Nevertheless, scientific research is influenced by politics and by group interests and values, and this is indeed true about research on homosexuality, in particular on its origin (aetiology). The two main views may be called the essentialist (inborn) and the constructionist/developmental.

Essentialist hypotheses about the aetiology of homosexuality—largely addressing male homosexuality—understandably focus on brain development, since sexual orientation is a neuropsychological phenomenon. Additionally, there are no physical characteristics allowing reliable identification of a person's sexual orientation. The main organic developmental hypotheses for which there is some evidence include those focusing on neuroendocrine mechanisms, on fraternal birth order and on genetics.

As a whole, journalistic coverage of research on the aetiology of homosexuality has been plagued by misrepresentation, lack of critical discussion on limitations of reported studies and, last but not least, defective follow-up—a trend to report just 'positive' findings while failing to give proportionate coverage to later studies which refute them.

A gay brain?

A 1991 work by Simon LeVay published in *Science* got exaggerated attention from the popular press and prompted some wild speculations.[1] On August 30, 1991, the *Los Angeles Times* featured the story with the subtitle 'Researcher's findings offer the first evidence of a biological cause for homosexuality'. Actually this was not true, as a Dutch study reporting a neuroanatomical difference between heterosexual and homosexual men had been published in 1990.[2]

Time magazine ran a story which included some critical remarks and took notice of the Dutch 1990 study. Nonetheless, it ended with the following politically loaded remarks:

> Over the years much research on homosexuality has been motivated by a desire to eradicate the behavior rather than understand, let alone celebrate, diversity (…) LeVay and others hope their work will enable humans to view homosexuality the way other species seem to see it: as a normal variation of sexual behavior.[3]

LeVay examined the small interstitial nuclei of the anterior hypothalamus (INAH) in post-mortem brains of 19 homosexual men, 16 supposedly heterosexual men and six putatively heterosexual women. All homosexual men, six 'heterosexual' men and one woman had died of acquired immunodeficiency syndrome (AIDS). One of the nuclei, the INAH3, was found to be larger in heterosexual men than in either homosexual men or the women. Many criticisms were raised against the study. The sample was small; the staining method was unreliable; AIDS might have caused changes in the nuclei; and no check was performed to confirm the sexual orientation of supposedly heterosexual people. Furthermore, taking into account the plasticity of the brain, it is conceivable that sexual behaviour was the cause of the anatomical difference instead of the reverse. Thus, the precise connection between INAH3 and human sexual behaviour remains unknown. In subhuman primates, destruction of an area homologous to human INAH3 did not result in homosexual behaviour[4].

Retrospectively, though, the major problem with LeVay's study is that it has never been independently replicated. Byne et al. confirmed that the INAH3 is indeed larger (and has 60 per cent more neurons) in men than in women. Later they performed a post-mortem study in 34 supposedly heterosexual males [24 positive for human immunodeficiency virus (HIV)], 34 supposedly heterosexual women (nine positive for HIV) and 14 HIV-positive homosexual men. The difference in INAH3 volume between heterosexual and homosexual HIV-positive men did not reach statistical significance. Neuron density (number per mm^3) and total neuronal number were similar in both groups and larger than in women.[5] Unfortunately, lack of confirmation of LeVay's findings went largely unnoticed by the general public.

Look at your fingers!

In 2000, wide press coverage was granted to a brief communication published in *Nature*.[6] Williams et al. measured finger length in men and women, both heterosexual and homosexual. The 2D:4D ratio, i.e. the ratio between the length of the index finger and the ring finger, had been found to be lower in men than in women, and negatively correlated with adult testosterone plasma level.[7] The *Nature* report also found that the 2D:4D ratio was lower ('significantly more masculine') in lesbian women compared with heterosexual women. No such difference according to sexual orientation was found in males. However, regardless of sexual orientation, men with two or more older brothers had as a group a lower 2D:4D ratio than those without older brothers (older sisters did not affect the results). This was related to previous research showing that the probability of male homosexual orientation increases with the number of older brothers, the so-called fraternal birth order effect.[8]

Bad reporting of Williams et al.'s results was inaugurated by *Nature* itself, as follows: 'This ratio, then, is a measure of foetal androgen exposure'. Again, after noting that homosexual women had lower 2D:4D ratios than heterosexual women, it added: 'Oddly, the results for gay men are similar...' This assertion is simply false. Another report stated that the 2D:4D ratio 'is almost certainly a product of androgen levels (...) in the womb',[9] adding that the 'same prenatal influences may affect behavior and sexual identity throughout life'.

Actually, the *Nature* report provided no data on intrauterine androgen exposure. An independent study later measured testosterone (androgen) in the amniotic fluid of 33 pregnant women, and 2D:4D ratios in their children (18 males and 15 females). No significant correlation was found in either gender between testosterone level and 2D:4D ratios.[10]

Other studies have yielded utterly contradictory findings, to the point that a hypothetical journalist wishing to write a story on this issue today would face these bewildering facts: the 2D:4D ratio has been reported variously to be both higher or non-significantly different in homosexual women compared with heterosexual women, higher, lower or non-significantly different in homosexual men compared with heterosexual men, with a larger difference in either the right or the left hand.[11]

It is in the genes, isn't it?

The notion that homosexuality may be inherited has a long history, with highs and lows. It was held by pioneer German sex researchers Richard von Krafft-Ebing and Magnus Hirschfeld. Later zoologist Richard B. Goldschmidt advanced a hypothesis of a genetic 'metamorphosis' in homosexual people, which was developed by others, notably including Theo Lang (1898–1957). Lang suggested that homosexual men were genetically females who, because of a developmental disorder, obtained prenatally the anatomy of males.[12] This hypothesis received a fatal blow when it was found that the Y chromosome determines male sex, and it is present in both heterosexual and homosexual males.

Nevertheless, the general public finds the notion of a genetic cause of homosexuality a tantalizing idea, and a number of studies suggest that both male and female homosexuality runs in families.[13] This does not necessarily mean that it is genetic, or otherwise inherited, since of course families also share common environmental factors. Furthermore, from research in the past decades it currently seems clear that homosexuality is not inherited following a simple, monogenic Mendelian pattern of dominant and recessive genes which explains traits such as eye colour and diseases such as Huntington's chorea. Genetic influences on same-sex attraction must be subtler, and therefore evidence for them has to be sought through more complex approaches, which as a rule depend on a number of assumptions and do not lend themselves to straightforward interpretations.[14]

Identical (monozygotic) twins share the same hereditary genetic endowment. Thus, for any genetically determined trait they have the same phenotype; in other words they are 100 per cent concordant for that trait, with few known exceptions.[15] Dizygotic (non-identical) twins and any other pair of sibs are in average 50 per cent concordant for most traits, including gender. If sexual orientation is determined at least in part by genetic factors, the expected concordance rate (percentage sharing the same trait) is expected to be higher in monozygotic twins than in dizygotic twins or any other pair of sibs. This is actually the case; nevertheless, knowing the sexual orientation of a monozygotic twin does not allow an accurate prediction of the other's sexual orientation. Thus, it is worth noting what the *New York Times* OpEd columnist Nicholas Kristof wrote about twin studies of sexual orientation:

> Still, while the data has [sic] problems, it is piling up (. . .). Earlier this year, the journal Personality and Individual Differences published an exhaustive review of the literature entitled 'Born Gay?' After reviewing the twin studies, it concluded that 50 to 60 percent of sexual orientation might be genetic.[16]

This is simply not true, as we shall see soon. Initial studies on monozygotic twins, now regarded as flawed, reported concordance rates for sexual orientation close to 100 per cent. Later studies have found concordance rates for homosexuality of around 50 per cent for both male and female monozygotic twins.[17]

Even these better designed studies probably overestimated concordance rates, because subjects were recruited through advertisements, in HIV clinics and 'Gay Pride' festivals. The problem here is ascertainment bias: a homosexual twin may be more likely to volunteer for a study if he knows that his twin brother is also homosexual. In some cases, sexual orientation of one twin was only assessed through the other (volunteer) twin report. Additionally, the samples were relatively small.

More reliable estimations of concordance come from studies based on large twin registries. Even here some methodological problems remain. For example, since these studies rely on voluntary participation, it may well be that those who agree to enter the study are in some sense different from those who do not; and then, there is the confounding factor of environmental influences, both shared and not shared by the twin pairs. Anyway, as a rule, registry studies have yielded lower concordance rates (about 20–30 per cent) than those relying on convenience samples.

Actually, what the above-mentioned *New York Times* OpEd presented as the conclusion of reviewers Rahman and Wilson is taken from the middle of the section on Heritability and Genetics after reviewing studies with non-random samples. They immediately added 'However, [these studies] suffer the methodological problem of ascertainment bias', and proceed to discuss more reliable twin studies, which as a whole provide consistently lower estimates. Furthermore, Rahman and Wilson did not state that '50 to 60 percent of sexual orientation might be genetic'. but that 'around 50–60% of the variance in sexual orientation is genetic'.[18]

When it comes to the genetic factors influencing homosexuality, an estimate of heritability is sought for. By definition, heritability (abbreviated h^2 or a^2) is the proportion of the total variance of a given trait (phenotype) which is explained by (additive) genetic effects.[19] The total variance is the sum of heritability plus environmental variance, which in turn may be further divided into shared and non-shared environmental effects. One relevant condition to achieve valid estimates is independence of genetic and environmental factors. If they are not independent, part of the total variance will depend on their interaction.

Even within registry twin studies, estimates of heritability of sexual orientation are widely variable. According to Mustanski *et al.*, the first study of this kind (on male twins only) yielded a heritability of just 14 per cent, while shared and non-shared environmental effects accounted for 38 and 46 per cent of the variance, respectively.[20]

A second twin registry study found that non-shared environment (which includes random measurement error) had the largest single effect both for males and females. The heritability was 48 per cent for women, but zero for men.[21] A third study on American monozygotic twins, dizygotic twins and non-twin sibling pairs yielded sexual orientation heritability estimates ranging from 28 to 65 per cent.[22]

A larger study recruited almost 1900 twin pairs from the Australian National Health and Medical Research Council Twin Register. Monozygotic twin concordance was 20 per cent for men and 24 per cent for women. Evidence was furnished for a genetic influence in two variables (childhood gender non-conformity and continuous gender identity) related to sexual orientation. The authors stated:

> Consistent with several studies of siblings (...), we found that sexual orientation is familial. In contrast with most prior studies of sexual orientation, however, ours did not provide statistically significant support for the importance of genetic factors for that trait. This does not mean that our results support heritability estimates of zero, though our results do not exclude them either.[23]

Finally, in a separate analysis of the same data, taking into account more indicators of sexual orientation and their covariance produced estimates of heritability of 30 per cent in males and 50 to 60 per cent in females.[24]

Thus, registry twin studies yield mean heritability estimates for sexual orientation ranging from zero to 60 per cent, in most cases larger in women than in men. It should be noted that heritabilities for behavioural traits and social attitudes are often around 50 per cent. Some examples are humility, criminality, emotional stability, altruism, alcoholism and substance abuse.[25] Heritability will be high in settings where environmental factors do not account for a large part of variation, while it will be low where environmental factors do have a large effect. At any rate, the important point is that 'heritable' does not mean 'inherited.'

Looking for specific candidate genes

The human genome contains about 25 000 protein-coding genes, but relatively few of them might be expected to influence sexual orientation. The gene coding for the androgen receptor was a likely candidate, for several reasons. First, genetic males with mutations in this gene may develop a complete androgen insensitivity syndrome. These persons are phenotypically female and uniformly display sexual attraction towards men. Secondly, the gene is located in the X sex chromosome, which a male always receives from his mother (the father contributing a Y chromosome), and some evidence suggests maternal influences on male sexual orientation. Thirdly, the gene comes in several versions (alleles), and one or more of them could be related to homosexual orientation. This, however, was not substantiated by research findings. Homosexual brothers have the same probability to have the same or a different allele, and the structure of variable sequences does not differ significantly between homosexual and heterosexual men.[26]

Because, paradoxically, oestradiol is necessary for normal male brain differentiation, another candidate was the gene of the enzyme aromatase (CYP19), which transforms testosterone into oestradiol. Again, the results of a study on whether CYP19 gene variants influence male sexual orientation were negative. The authors concluded that 'naturally occurring variations in the CYP19 gene do not play a major role in individual differences in this trait'.[27]

Since thus far the search for specific candidate genes for sexual orientation has been unsuccessful, it is not surprising that it has not made it to the headlines. This contrasts with the great fanfare granted to a paper which, with a less direct approach, did find something.

The 'gay gene', at last?

To date, the paradigm of exaggerated, unbalanced media reaction to a scientific paper on sexual orientation was that caused in 1993 by a report linking male homosexuality to the X chromosome. The team led by Dean H. Hamer performed pedigree studies in 110 families of homosexual male volunteers and found a high prevalence of homosexuality among males in their maternal line, namely brothers, maternal uncles and sons of maternal aunts. These relatives were homosexual in 13.5, 7.3 and 7 per cent, respectively, which was significantly higher than the 2 per cent estimated for the general population.

One obvious explanation for transmission through the maternal line was that the genes involved were located in the X sex chromosome. Each body cell of the mother has two X chromosomes, but the female gamete (oocyte) carries only one. This single X chromosome is actually a composite of both maternal X chromosomes formed through a process known as recombination. With DNA markers it is possible to determine whether a given section of the son's X chromosome comes from one member of the maternal pair or from the other. In principle, a pair of brothers have a probability of 0.5 (50 per cent) of sharing a given section of their X chromosome.

In a subgroup of the sample of homosexual males (40 families, each with two homosexual brothers) the X chromosome was scanned through identification of a set of 22 markers called microsatellites, which are very short DNA segments highly variable (polymorphic) among different subjects. No locus of the short arm of the X chromosome was shared with higher than chance frequency. However, a set of five loci located in the region Xq28 (band 8 of region 2 of the long arm of chromosome X) was shared by each member of 33 out of 40 pairs. The statistical probability that this coincidence might be due to chance was about 0.1 per cent.[28]

A *Science* press release on the day before the report was published started the popular media craze. A National Public Radio dramatic announcement was framed as a question: 'Is a team of scientists at the National Institutes of Health on the trail of a gene that causes homosexuality?' On the same day (15 July 1993), the National Organization of Gay and Lesbian Scientists and Technical Professionals issued a press release entitled 'Scientific freedom and the ethics of a discovered genetic link to homosexuality'. The statement said:

> Our reaction as gay and lesbian scientists is mixed. On the one hand, we are pleased that there is now scientific support that sexual orientation has an immutable component. On the other hand, this work raises the spectre of the various possibilities of screening for such components.[29]

It should be noted that these mixed feelings have lingered to this day. This explains, at least in part, why some homosexual persons and groups endorse this kind of research while others (e.g. www.queerbychoice.com) bitterly denounce it.[30]

On July 16, 1993, as the report was being published, the *USA Today* article 'Is there a gay gene?' began thus: 'A predisposition to homosexuality appears to be written into the very genes of some men. And they get the key genes from their mothers'. The *Wall Street Journal* was even more misleading: 'Research points toward a gay gene'. Slightly more cautious, the *New York Times* announced 'Report suggests homosexuality is linked to genes'.

The cover of the July 26, 1993 *Newsweek* issue read: 'Born gay? Science finds a genetic link'. The article bore the title 'Does DNA make some men homosexual?' The authors suggested that phrases calling homosexuality 'a lifestyle choice' or a 'sexual preference' may be 'scientifically wrong'. While noting that the research actually 'hasn't found the gene that makes some men gay', and that this could take years, they went on to say: 'But eventually, biologists hope, they will learn how such a gene works, in men as well as in women'. *Time* magazine included the study among the best 1993 science reports. As a whole, the British press was more cautious. Still, the *Daily Telegraph* published an article with the alarming title 'Claim that homosexuality is inherited prompts fears that science could be used to eradicate it'.[31]

Although most news reports included some caveats, they conveyed as a whole the impression that the finding of a specific gene which caused homosexuality was close at hand. The following comments, written by a British scientific editor on the aftermath of this media hype, are still current today:

> The reporting on the 'gay gene' work, though not the original report itself, conveys ... [a] set of misconceptions—those about the genetic determination of complex, human traits. While Hamer *et al.* were careful to stipulate ... [the limitations of the study], most of the press was content to report this as a finding of either 'a gay gene' or 'the gay gene'. General discussions in the television, radio and newspaper reports were conspicuous for their absence of a discussion of the concept of heritability and the fact that all complex traits, both behavioural and physical, necessarily have both genetic and environmental components in their determination.[32]

To get some perspective, some aspects of Hamer team's findings worth mentioning are given below.

1. In the pedigree studies, not a single family showed a pattern consistent with Mendelian inheritance of homosexuality. This argues against a single gene strongly influencing homosexual orientation, even in this restricted sample.
2. The pedigree analysis assumed a rather low (2 per cent) base rate of male homosexuality (that of the population at large). Thus a probability significantly higher than 2 per cent in a given family would suggest an inheritance pattern.

However, if the actual base rate is 4 per cent or higher, then the results of pedigree analysis (and further analyses based on them) are no longer significant.[33]

3. The study identified markers, not genes as such. It just suggested that some genes located in region Xq28 might be somehow related to homosexuality. Additionally, the influence of these genes could be rather direct (e.g. promoting gender non-conformity) or very indirect, e.g. enhancing sensitivity to environmental influences.

4. No single set of markers was common to all 33 pairs of homosexual brothers; rather, each member of these pairs shared the same set of markers in Xq28, which in turn were different from the set of the other pairs.

5. Seven pairs of homosexual brothers did not share the same markers in Xq28.

6. The study had no controls, nor did it address the very important question on whether heterosexual brothers share the markers in Xq28 with their homosexual sibs. Also, since genotyping was not blinded to sib status, researcher bias was possible.

7. Linkage studies are unable to produce an association in the general population. An association is a relationship between a particular allele and a trait or a disease. For example, an allele A is associated with a trait T if present in 20 per cent of the general population but in 70 per cent of persons with trait T. Associations have genetic and non-genetic causes. A linkage is a specific relationship between genetic loci (not phenotypes or alleles) within families. Thus linkage by itself cannot prove an association in the general population.

8. About 60 genes have so far been identified in Xq28, but to date not one of them has been pinpointed as a likely candidate for influencing sexual orientation.

Rise and fall of the 'gay gene'

Despite the above-mentioned facts, the study by Hamer *et al.* made it into the authoritative Online Mendelian Inheritance in Man (OMIM) database on August 30, 1993.[34] Dr Hamer even wrote a book for lay people with the subtitle 'The gay gene and the biology of behaviour'. In contrast to his cautious remarks to the media, in the book he claimed:

> No one had ever been able to *prove* that homosexuality was swayed by genes, however, until our study offered the most convincing evidence to date that sexual orientation was genetically influenced (...) We didn't invent a new idea; we just showed it was true.[35]

Saying that they actually showed that homosexuality is 'swayed by genes' is true is obviously a long jump from the report's careful conclusions. Furthermore, in science it always takes more than a single report definitely to *prove* any claim. This is particularly true in a field so complex as behavioural genetics. As noted in the Research News of the same issue of *Science* where Hamer's paper was published: 'The field of behavioural genetics is littered with apparent discoveries that were later called into question or retracted'.[36]

Later Hamer was charged with 'research improprieties', specifically excluding pairs of brothers whose genotype was against the main reported finding. An investigation by the

Federal Office of Research Integrity was supposed to be going on in 1995, but it produced no public report.[37]

Indirect support for a link to the X chromosome was furnished in 1995 by a study of 133 families of homosexual males and females, which also included data from the literature for another 116 families.[38] Male (but not female) homosexuals had far more maternal aunts than maternal uncles, yielding for the maternal line a total of 310 uncles versus 628 aunts (49 per cent). The author attributed this difference to 'fetal wastage' of the mother's male sibs. He compared the uncle/aunt ratio with those found in the descent of Xq28-linked disorders. Since no such disorders were found in probands, and no genetic analysis was performed, the proposed explanation remains conjectural.

In the same year, Hamer and co-workers published a follow-up study in another series of families with pairs of gay brothers or pairs of lesbian sisters. In this case heterosexual sibs were also studied. The results for linkage between Xq28 markers and sexual orientation in 32 gay brother pairs were still significant but less impressive than in the 1993 study. No linkage was found for 36 pairs of lesbian sisters and 12 heterosexual brothers.[39]

This time the media response was more cautious. National Public Radio announced 'Research suggests genetic link to homosexuality'. One story was entitled 'X chromosome again linked to homosexuality'; and the *U.S. News & World Report* asked once more whether there is a 'gay gene'.

Coming from the same research team, the new study could hardly be regarded as an independent replication. Then, researchers from the Clinical Neurogenetics branch of the National Institutes of Health presented data on 54 male homosexual sibling pairs, but were unable to confirm a link between Xq28 and homosexuality.[40] First author Alan R. Sanders reportedly stated: 'No marker data reached statistically significant criteria'.

In 1999, Canadian researchers led by George Rice published yet another study in *Science*. They studied 52 pairs of homosexual brothers, finding no evidence for linkage to markers in Xq28. Rice and colleagues wrote:

> Because our study was larger than that of Hamer *et al.*, we certainly had adequate power to detect a genetic effect as large as was reported in that study. Nonetheless, our data do not support the presence of a gene of large effect influencing sexual orientation at position Xq28.[41]

In a Technical Comment published by *Science* shortly thereafter, Hamer raised criticisms against the new study, while defending his own.[42] The answer by Rice and colleagues stated that Hamer's group findings could not be replicated even combining the data of Sanders *et al.* with their own. The OMIM database entry on homosexuality updated its information including a reference to the Canadian study, adding: 'These results do not support an X-linked gene underlying male homosexuality'.

Furthermore, two well designed, independent studies found no increased frequency of homosexual maternal uncles or in sons of maternal aunts compared with the respective paternal relatives, arguing against a maternal link.[43]

The 'gay gene': demise or multiplication?

The Xq28 story is not yet over, though. The results of the first genome-wide scan of male homosexuality, by Mustanski *et al.* (including Hamer), were recently published. They scanned 456 members of 146 unrelated families, all of them with two or three homosexual brothers. One-third of the families included heterosexual siblings. Half of the families were those studied in Hamer's 1993 and 1995 papers, while the remainder had not been previously reported. In the latter, evidence of maternal transmission was not required.[44]

In this study, the linkage to Xq28 in the previously reported families was substantially lower than in the original studies, a finding which the authors attribute to lower scan resolution and a lower number of markers located close to the X chromosome tip. On the other hand, the sample as a whole showed no evidence of linkage, raising 'the possibility of etiologic heterogeneity for the proposed Xq28 locus'. In other words, the Xq28 locus might still be linked to homosexual orientation in some men, but not in others (perhaps most).

A press release by the University of Illinois at Chicago stated that Mustanski 'has identified several areas that appear to influence whether a man is heterosexual or gay'. The leading author reportedly asserted: 'There is no one "gay" gene. Sexual orientation is a complex trait, so it's not surprising that we found several DNA regions involved in its expression'. Actually this is an overstatement. The genome-wide scan had low resolution, and did not find any region with a statistically significant linkage using established criteria.[45]

One locus at 7q36 qualified as 'suggestive linkage', while the other most likely candidates at chromosomes 8 and 10 fared even worse. Therefore, contrary to Mustanski's confident statement, no DNA region involved in the expression of sexual orientation has actually been positively pinpointed. At most, the identified regions are candidates for future localized scans with higher resolution, which if positive will be just the beginning.

Embryonic mouse gender identity

Sexual differentiation may start right after conception, even before implantation occurs.[46] Some female (XX) and male (XY) nerve cells may develop differently even before the development of the gonads. Sex chromosome gene expression has been found to differ in normal mice, as well as in genetically engineered mice.[47] Then, a study by Phoebe Dewing *et al.* found that early sexually dimorphic gene expression in the brain is not restricted to the sex chromosomes. In the embryonic mouse brain, they identified 54 genes that have differential expression according to sex, before gonadal differentiation. However, the authors noted: 'The mechanisms by which these genes act on neural development and behaviour, either independently or synergistically with sex hormones, are still to be determined'.[48] This qualification, however, went largely unnoticed by press reports.

The *Los Angeles Times* announced 'Brain study focuses on gender identity', although the story itself got the facts quite right. In contrast, Reuters ran an article with the title 'Sexual identity hard-wired by genetics, study says' which confidently asserted: 'Sexual identity is wired into the genes, which discounts the concept that homosexuality and transgender sexuality are a choice, California researchers reported on Monday'. Co-author Eric Vilain was thus quoted: 'Our findings may explain why we feel male or female, regardless of our actual anatomy. These discoveries lend credence to the idea that being transgender (...) is a state of mind'.[49] Actually the report fell short of finding a cause for transsexualism or homosexuality. Indeed, it is a bit hard to believe that mouse embryos possess such a thing as sexual identity.

A riddle solved?

If homosexuality is largely genetic, its persistence in time is difficult to explain from an evolutionary viewpoint, since survival depends on reproductive success. How, then, does homosexuality remain stable in a given population? Several hypotheses have been advanced, some more convincing that others.[50]

Recently, a paper from researchers of the University of Padua (Padova) attracted a large amount of attention from the press. An article from the Agence France Press stated:

> While acknowledging that the Nature versus Nurture debate about homosexuality will continue to rage, the authors believe they may have resolved one of the enigmas about homosexuality.
>
> This is the so-called Darwinian paradox (...). The answer could lie in Xq28, for the mothers of homosexuals could be exceptionally fertile.[19,51]

The story in the *Daily Telegraph*, 'Gays linked to women's fertility' began stating: 'Homosexuality is a natural side-effect of genetic factors that help women to have more children, a study suggests today'. Headlines in some scientific publications were more disturbing. For example, the *Nature*'s News title read 'Mother's genetics could influence sexual orientation. Genes could increase male homosexuality while boosting female reproduction'. The article stated that the findings 'suggest that the mothers and maternal aunts of [male] homosexuals have a genetic advantage—but one that reduces reproduction when passed to male offspring'. The first author of the study, Andrea Camperio-Ciani, reportedly said: '...we have found that there might be a set of genes that, in males, influences homosexuality but in females increases fecundity (...) whatever the genes are, the X chromosome is almost certainly involved'.[52]

The *New Scientist*'s title bluntly stated 'Survival of genetic homosexual traits explained'. Camperio-Ciani told *New Scientist*: 'We have finally solved this paradox. The same factor that influences sexual orientation in males promotes higher fecundity in females'.[53]

The study did not actually perform a direct assessment of any genetic variable. Ninety eight self-identified homosexual men and 100 self-identified heterosexual men paired by age (about 33 years old) anonymously reported their own sexual orientation and those of their relatives, and demographic data about their families. Homosexual men reported more homosexual subjects in their maternal line than in their paternal line, and a small but statistically significant higher mean fecundity in women of their maternal line. Mothers of homosexual men had a mean fecundity of 2.69 while those of heterosexual men had a mean fecundity of 2.32. The survey also found evidence for a fraternal birth order effect (see above). The number of homosexual relatives in the maternal line accounted for just 14 per cent of the variance in sexual orientation, while the number of older male brothers accounted for an additional 7 per cent.[54]

Several points are worthy of mention. First, although higher female fertility in the families of homosexual men was the major point of the whole study, it seems that the number of sibs did not account for a significant portion of the variance, an intriguing fact to say the least. Secondly, as already noted, other studies have not found an increased incidence of homosexuality in the maternal line of homosexual men. The possibility that homosexual men are better acquainted with relatives from their maternal line was not considered. Thirdly, as the authors noted, almost 80 per cent of the variance in sexual orientation was not accounted for by the factors considered. They wrote: 'Indeed, it is still possible that the higher incidence of homosexuality in the maternal line results from culturally, rather than genetically, inherited traits'. If this is the case, it is hard to see why they failed to gather relevant information, for example, about family dynamics and attitudes toward child bearing and rearing. In the absence of this information, to hail this work as a breakthrough on the genetics of homosexuality is highly misleading.

Beyond DNA: epigenetics of sexual orientation

Epigenetics studies changes in DNA function which do not involve alteration of its sequence of bases (mutations). Although most people think of the DNA molecule as a bare double helix, in cell nuclei DNA is found in chromatin, half of which is made of protein, mostly histones. Epigenetic changes involve reversible methylation of the DNA bases and several chemical changes in the associated histones. Epigenetic traits may be transmitted from parents to their offspring by genomic imprinting. Through this process, only the copy (allele) inherited from the mother, or that inherited from the father, is expressed. Almost 80 imprinted genes have been identified in humans.[55]

Imprinting of male and female germ cells is sexually dimorphic. A well-known epigenetic phenomenon in females is the inactivation, in each cell, of one member of the pair of X chromosomes. Inactivation provides gene dose compensation between females (XX) and males (XY) for X-linked genes, whose overexpression would be catastrophic in the early female embryo. Whether the X chromosome inherited from the father or that inherited from the mother is inactivated seems to be a random process, but in some diseases preferential inactivation of one or the other (skewing) has been found.

An explanation invoking imprinting for male to female transsexualism was advanced by Green and Keverne.[56] A male transsexual is a man whose gender identity is female, despite his genetic and phenotypic sex. In a large series on 417 male to female transsexuals and 96 female to male transsexuals, a disparate maternal aunt/uncle ratio was found in the former but not in the latter. The authors subdivided the male transsexuals into homosexual (attracted to men), heterosexual, bisexual and asexual (not experiencing sexual attraction towards persons of either sex). Although the disparity in male to female transsexuals was not nearly as high as that found by Turner in male homosexuals, still it was statistically significant. No significantly disparate ratio in the paternal line was found for either group of transsexuals. The asexual subgroup had significantly more paternal uncles than aunts, but the authors did not discuss this finding. Furthermore, they predicted that 'homosexuality and transexuality have the same biological pre-disposition, but are expressed differently as a consequence of developmental relationships'. However, neither the homosexual nor the bisexual subgroups showed a significant difference in maternal aunt/uncle ratio; the only transsexual subgroup showing a significantly disparate ratio was curiously the *heterosexual* one. The authors provided no explanation of this fact, which at first sight is at odds with their hypothesis.

Afterwards Bocklandt and Hamer also suggested that male homosexuality could involve maternal 'incorrect imprinting', causing in the male offspring increased expression of feminizing genes, decreased expression of virilizing genes, or both.[57] They provided evidence for this hypothesis at the 2004 Annual Meeting of the American Society of Human Genetics.[58] They assessed X chromosome inactivation in 96 mothers of homosexual men and in 100 women matched by age and ethnicity, and found a significantly different X inactivation skewing. A larger proportion of mothers of homosexual men (14 per cent) than control women (<3 per cent) showed more than 90 per cent inactivation of one X chromosome, or 'extreme skewing'. The distribution of skewing was bimodal in mothers of homosexual men, but normal in control women. Only about 4 per cent of daughters of women with extreme skewing showed skewing themselves. The abstract also mentions a full genome scan on 146 homosexual brother pairs, which found significant linkage to the 10q26 locus only on the maternal allele. Additionally, they studied male-oriented and female-oriented rams to identify, through a cross-species comparison, candidate genes influencing sexual orientation.

Although not yet published in a peer-reviewed journal, this study was quickly reported by *New Scientist* with the titles 'The strange case of the skewed X chromosomes' and 'Mother's genetic skew linked to gay sons'. The account said:

> Bocklandt suspects that whatever is causing the skewed methylation of the X chromosome also affects the methylation of certain genes on the chromosomes the women pass on to their sons. Women might not be resetting their own 'I like males' program, he told a meeting...[59]

While interesting, the findings of Bocklandt *et al.* prompt several observations. First, although the difference in skewing between mothers of homosexual men and control women was significant, still 86 per cent of the former did not show extreme skewing, and the distribution was bimodal. This suggests that if skewing in mothers is related to male homosexuality, this might be restricted to a subgroup of male homosexuals only. Secondly, apparently the mothers with skewed X inactivation and their offspring were healthy. This is remarkable, since skewing has been found in women who are carriers for several X-linked diseases. Also, a skewed inactivation pattern has been reported in women with ovarian cancer, breast cancer and idiopathic recurrent spontaneous abortion. Thirdly, in the recently published genome-wide scan of male sexual orientation, the linkage to the locus on chromosome 10 did not reach significance, and actually it did not even fulfil established criteria for suggestive linkage. Fourthly, in the context of previous research (see above) it would be interesting to know the maternal aunt/uncle ratio in the studied families.

An open epilogue

While there is general agreement that homosexuality, like other complex human traits, is the result of multiple factors, in recent years many studies have assessed different organic developmental hypotheses. While few, if any, of these studies have supplied definitive answers about the origin of male homosexuality, it is possible that interesting new findings may be brought to light in the not-so-distant future.

While the notion of a single 'gay gene' overwhelmingly driving same-sex attraction has been largely forsaken, exploration of more complex models is being actively pursued. Bocklandt *et al.* will perform a genetic study in twins, and a team led by Alan R. Sanders will perform a genome-wide scan in 1000 male homosexual brother pairs with generous sponsorship from the National Institutes of Health.

One problem with current research on the origin of homosexuality is the paucity of well-conducted, powerful studies which simultaneously address organic developmental and socio-cultural factors. Another problem is the deficit on organic developmental factors influencing female homosexuality. The relatively few studies which have been carried out are somewhat disappointing.[60] Since female homosexuality is obviously within the range of human behaviour, there must be a role for genetic factors, even if these factors turn out to be different from putative genetic effects underlying male homosexuality.

As developments in this research subject unfold, I would just beg higher accuracy and balance in their media coverage.

References and notes

1. LeVay S. A difference in hypothalamic structure between heterosexual and homosexual men. *Science*, 1991; 253:1034–1037.
2. Swaab DF, Hofman MA. An enlarged suprachiasmatic nucleus in homosexual men. *Brain Research*, 1990; 537:141–148.
3. Gorman C. Are gay men born that way? *Time*, 9 September 1991.
4. Byne W. The biological evidence challenged. *Scientific American*, 1994:50–55.
5. Byne W, Tobet S, Mattiace LA, Lasco MS, Kenether E, Edgar MA, Morgello S, Buchsbaum MS, Jones LB. The interstitial nuclei of the human anterior hypothalamus: an investigation of variation with sex, sexual orientation, and HIV status. *Hormones and Behavior*, 2001; 40:86–92.
6. Williams TJ, Pepitone ME, Christensen SE, Cooke BM, Huberman AD, Breedlove NJ, Breedlove TJ, Jordan CL, Breedlove SM. Finger-length ratios and sexual orientation. *Nature*, 2000; 404:455–456.
7. Manning JT, Scutt D, Wilson J, Lewis-Jones DI. The ratio of 2nd to 4th digit length: a predictor of sperm numbers and concentrations of testosterone, luteinizing hormone and oestrogen. *Human Reproduction*, 1998; 13:3000–3004.
8. The latest review paper in this topic (a copy of which was kindly sent to me by the author) is Blanchard R. Quantitative and theoretical analyses of the relation between older brothers and homosexuality in men. *Journal of Theoretical Biology*, 2004; 230:173–187.

9. **Hall CT.** Finger length points to sexual orientation; anatomy quirk called possible biological cue. *San Francisco Chronicle.* March 30, 2000.

10. **Lutchmaya S, Baron-Cohen S, Raggatt P, Knickmeyer R, Manning JT.** 2nd to 4th digit ratios, fetal testosterone and estradiol. *Early Human Development*, 2004; 77:23–28.

11. **Robinson SJ, Manning JT.** The ratio of 2nd to 4th digit length and male homosexuality. *Evolution and Human Behavior*, 2000; 21:333–345. McFadden D, Shubel E. Relative lengths of fingers and toes in human males and females. *Hormones and Behavior*, 2002; 42:492–500. Rahman Q, Wilson GD. Sexual orientation and the 2nd to 4th finger length ratio: evidence for organizing effects of sex hormones or developmental instability? *Psychoneuroendocrinology*, 2003; 28:288–303. Putz DA, Caulin SJC, Sporter RJ, McBurney DH. Sex hormones and finger length. What does 2D:4D indicate? *Evolution and Human Behavior*, 2004; 25:182–199. Lippa RA. Are 2D:4D finger-length ratios related to sexual orientation? Yes for men, no for women. *Journal of Personal and Social Psychology*, 2003; 85:179–188.

12. **Dietrich MR.** Of moths and men: Theo Lang and the persistence of Richard Goldschmidt's theory of homosexuality. *History and Philosophy of the Life Sciences*, 2000; 22:219–247.

13. **Mustanski BS, Chivers ML, Bailey JM.** A critical review on recent biological research on human sexual orientation. *Annual Review of Sex Research*, 2002; 13:89–140.

14. **Strachan T, Read AP.** *Human molecular genetics*, 2nd edn. BIOS Scientific Publishers, Oxford. 1999. Chapter 12. Available on line at http://www.ncbi.nlm.gov/books/

15. In fact, monozygotic twins (and any pair of sibs) have genetic differences in their immune system (e.g. repertoire of antibodies), somatic cell mutations, mitochondrial DNA and, if female, in the pattern of X chromosome inactivation.

16. **Nicholas D, Kristof ND.** Gay at birth? (OpEd) *The New York Times.* October 25, 2003.

17. **Bailey JM, Pillard RC.** Genetics of human sexual orientation. *Annual Review of Sex Research*, 1993; 6:126–150.

18. **Rahman Q, Wilson GD.** Born gay? The psychobiology of human sexual orientation (Review). *Personality and Individual Differences*, 2003; 34:1337–1382.

19. **Strachan T, Read AP.** *Human molecular genetics*, 2nd edn. BIOS Scientific Publishers, Oxford. 1999. Chapter 19. http://www.ncbi.nlm.nih.gov/books/bv.fcgi?rid=hmg.chapter.2455

20. **Buhrich N, Bailey JM, Martin NG.** Sexual orientation, sexual identity, and sex-dimorphic behaviors in male twins. *Behavioral Genetics*, 1991; 21:75–96.

21. **Hershberger SL.** A twin registry study of male and female sexual orientation. *Journal of Sex Research*, 1997; 34:212–222.

22. **Kendler KS, Thornton LM, Gilman SE, Kessler RC.** Sexual orientation in a U.S. national sample of twin and non-twin sibling pairs. *American Journal of Psychiatry*, 2000; 157:1843–1846.

23. **Bailey JM, Dunne MP, Martin NG.** Genetic and environmental influences on sexual orientation and its correlates in an Australian twin sample. *Journal of Personal and Social Psychology*, 2000; 78:524–536.

24. **Kirk KM, Bailey JM, Dunne MP, et al.** Measurement models for sexual orientation in a community twin sample. *Behavioral Genetics*, 2000; 30:345–356.

25. See Rushton JP, Fulker DW, Neale MC, Blizard RA, Eysenck HJ. Altruism and genetics. *Acta Genetica Medica et Gemellologica (Roma)*, 1984; 33:265–271; Martin NG, Eaves LJ, Heath AC, Jardine R, Feingold LM, Eysenck HJ. Transmission of social attitudes. *Proceedings of the National Academy of Sciences, USA*, 1986; 83:4364–4368; van den Bree MB, Johnson EO, Neale MC, Pickens RW. Genetic and environmental influences on drug use and abuse/dependence in male and female twins. *Drug and Alcohol Dependence*, 1998; 52:231–241.

26. **Macke JP, Hu N, Hu S, Bailey M, King VL, Brown T, Hamer D, Nathans J.** Sequence variation in the androgen receptor ene is not a common determinant of male sexual orientation. *American Journal of Human Genetics*, 1993; 53:844–852.

27. **DuPree MG, Mustanski BS, Bocklandt S, Nievergelt C, Hamer DC.** A candidate gene study of CYP19 (aromatase) and male sexual orientation. *Behavioral Genetics*, 2004; 34:243–250.

28. **Hamer DH, Hu S, Magnuson VL, Pattatucci AM.** A linkage between DNA markers on the X chromosome and male sexual orientation. *Science*, 1993; **261**:321–327.

29. **Diamond R.** National Organization of Gay and Lesbian Scientists and Technical Professionals Press Release, July 15, 1993. http://www.qrd.org/qrd/origins/1993/nih.genetic.study-NOGLSTP-07.15.93

30. See also Dahl E. Ethical issues in new uses of preimplantation genetic diagnosis. Should parents be allowed to use preimplantation genetic diagnosis to choose the sexual orientation of their children? *Human Reproduction*, 2003; **18**:1368–1369.

31. See Conrad P, Markens S. Constructing the 'gay gene' in the news: optimism and skepticism in the US and British press. *Health*, 2001; **5**:373–400.

32. **Wilkins AS.** Jurassic Park and the 'gay gene': the new genetics seen through the distorting lens of the media. *FASEB Journal*, 1993; **7**:1203–1204.

33. **Schüklenk U, Stein E, Kerin J, Byne W.** The ethics of genetic research on sexual orientation. *Hastings Center Report*, 1997; **27**:6–13.

34. **OMIM** Homosexuality 1, HMS1, # 306995. Created by Victor A. McKusick on August 30, 1993; last update by A. Lopez, May 7, 1999. http://www.ncbi.nlm.nih.gov/entrez/dispomim.cgi?id=306995

35. **Hamer D, Copeland P.** *The science of desire. The gay gene and the biology of behavior.* Simon & Schuster, New York. 1994. The quote is from the Touchstone reissue, 1995: 20; italics are theirs. It appears to me that Dr Hamer has a taste for writing books based on tiny evidence. His latest work is entitled *The God gene: how faith is hardwired into our genes* (Doubleday, New York. 2004). Reviews: Zimmer C. Faith-boosting genes. *Scientific American*, 2004: 110–111. Mohler A. 'The God gene': bad science meets bad theology. http://www.beliefnet.com/story/154/story_15458.html

36. **Pool R.** Evidence for homosexuality gene (Research News). *Science*, 1993; **261**:291–292.

37. **Horgan J.** Gay genes, revisited. *Scientific American*. November 1995:26.

38. **Turner WJ.** Homosexuality, type 1: an Xq28 phenomenon. *Archives of Sex Behavior*, 1995; **24**:109–134.

39. **Hu S, Pattatucci A, Patterson C, Li L, Fulker D, Cherny S, Kruglyak L, Hamer D.** Linkage between sexual orientation and chromosome Xq28 in males but not females. *Nature Genetics*, 1995; **11**:248–256.

40. **Sanders AR, Guroff JJ, Gershon ES, Gejman PV.** Genetic linkage study of male homosexuality. Poster Presentation # 149, Annual Meeting of the American Psychiatric Association, Toronto (Ontario), Canada, 1998. Abstract (not very instructive): http://www.psych.org/edu/other_res/lib_archives/ archives/ meetings/1998_nra.pdf

41. **Rice G, Anderson C, Risch N, Ebers G.** Male homosexuality: absence of linkage to microsatellite markers at Xq28. *Science*, 1999; **284**:665–667.

42. **Hamer DH.** Genetics and male sexual orientation (Technical Comment). *Science*, 1999; **285**:803a; Rice G, Risch N, Ebers G. Reply to Dean H. Hamer. *Science*, 1999; **285**:803a.

43. **Bailey JM, Pillard RC, Dawood K, Miller MB, Farrer LA, Trivedi S, Murphy RL.** A family history study of male sexual orientation using three independent samples. *Behavioral Genetics*, 1999; **29**:79–86; McKnight J, Malcolm J. Is male homosexuality maternally linked? *Psychology Evolution and Gender*, 2000; **2**:229–252.

44. **Mustanski BS, DuPree MG, Nievergelt CM, Bocklandt S, Schork NJ, Hamer DH.** A genomewide scan of male sexual orientation. *Human Genetics*, 2005; **116**:272–278. Published online January 12, 2005. DOI 10.1007/s00439-004-1241-4.

45. **Lander E, Kruglyak L.** Genetic dissection of complex traits: guidelines for interpreting and reporting linkage results. *Nature Genetics*, 1995; **11**:241–247. See also Kruglyak L, Daly MJ. Linkage thresholds for two-stage genome scans. *American Journal of Human Genetics*, 1998; **62**:994–996.

46. For early evidence see Erickson RP. Does sex determination start at conception? *Bioessays*, 1997; **19**:1027–1032.

47. For a recent review see Arnold AP. Sex chromosomes and brain gender. *Nature Review Neuroscience*, 2004; **5**:1–8.

48. **Dewing P, Shi T, Horvath S, Vilain E.** Sexually dimorphic gene expression in mouse brain precedes gonadal differentiation. *Molecular Brain Research*, 2003; **118**:82–90.

49. Sexual identity hard-wired by genetics, study says. *Reuters*, October 20, 2003.

50. See the discussion on pp. 1343–1349 of Rahman and Wilson (2003)[11]. Also Miller EM. Homosexuality, birth order, and evolution: towards an equilibrium reproductive economics of homosexuality. *Archives of Sexual Behavior*, 2000; **29**:1–34; Berman LA. *The puzzle. Exploring the evolutionary puzzle of male homosexuality*. Godot Press, Wilmette, IL. 2003.

51. Agence France Presse English. Maternal genes, family size linked to homosexuality, study says. October 13, 2004.

52. **Hopkin M.** Mother's genetics could influence sexual orientation. *Nature News*, published online October 12, 2004; DOI: 10.1038/news041011-5.

53. **Coghlan A.** Survival of genetic homosexual traits explained. *New Scientist*, 2004; **13** October. http://www.newscientist.com/article.ns?id=dn6579

54. **Camperio-Ciani A, Corna F, Capiluppi C.** Evidence for maternally inherited factors favouring male homosexuality and promoting female fecundity. *Proceedings of the Royal Society B*, 2004; **271**:2217–2221.

55. See Gene Imprint Com, http://www.geneimprint.com/databases/?c=clist

56. **Green R, Keverne EB.** The disparate maternal aunt-uncle ratio in male transsexuals: an explanation invoking genomic imprinting. *Journal of Theoretical Biology*, 2000; **202**:55–63.

57. **Bocklandt S, Hamer DH.** Beyond hormones: a novel hypothesis for the biological basis of male sexual orientation. *Journal of Endocrinology Investigation*, 2003; **26**:8–12.

58. **Bocklandt S, Horvath S, Vilain E, Hamer DH.** Extreme skewing of X chromosome inactivation in mothers of homosexual men. *Human Genetics*, 2006; **118**:691–694.

59. **Motluk A.** The strange case of the skewed X chromosomes (NewScientist.com news service). *New Scientist*, November 6, 2004. http://www.newscientist.com/article .ns;jsessionid=JJNLEIENPCGP?id =mg18424721.600

60. **Veniegas RC, Conley TD.** Biological research on women's sexual orientations: evaluating the scientific evidence. *Journal of Social Issues*, 2000; 56:267–282.

Chapter 29

To sleep, perchance to REM? The rediscovered role of emotion and meaning in dreams

Mark Solms and Oliver Turnbull

Dreams are hallucinations and delusions that we all experience. Indeed, they have long been regarded as a 'normal' form of psychosis, implying that an account of the dream process should lead to better understanding of mental illness.[1] This view is paralleled by a widespread folk-psychological belief that dreams carry some sort of 'meaning', including the tantalizing possibility that they can be interpreted—somehow 'decoded' to understand ourselves better. In the twentieth century, this widespread belief entered the scientific arena—albeit controversially—through the psychological theories of Sigmund Freud.[2] Some aspects of Freud's model are, of course, very well known. However, many aspects are less well understood.

Freudian dream theory, and sleep protection

A central aspect of Freud's theory, and the easiest to test, is the hypothesized link between dreams and emotion. Freud claimed that dreams begin when an idea in the sleeper's mind is linked to a powerful motivational state. This emotionally charged state is, of course, an *activating* force, and hence apt to arouse the sleeper to wakefulness. The dream, Freud argued, is an attempt to 'transform' the emotionally charged mental process into something other than real—purposive—action, and hence to maintain the state of sleep. The dream creates the *illusion* of motivated action. The dream, therefore, plays the role of *guardian*, or protector, of sleep. This set of ideas—about emotional arousal and its disturbing effect on sleep—are a clear and uncomplicated proposal about the causal underpinning of the dream state. They are also so simple that it is always surprising to read, from writers that should know better, that psychoanalytic ideas are 'untestable'.

There is, of course, more to Freud's theory, which relates to the *way* in which the arousing impulse is transformed—an act that he suggested is completed by a 'censor'. The transformation, Freud claimed, typically involves a modification of some aspects of the original impulse. The modified aspect is, however, 'symbolically' linked to the original. For example, thoughts of sexual activity are transformed into imaging of dancing—where the factor of intimate physical activity is retained, but the ideomotor specifics are toned down. Any transformation of this type would, of course, require retrospective reconstruction of the process—reverse-engineering the transformation—to establish the true cause (the latent content) of the experienced dream (the manifest content). Like all reverse-engineering inferences, such reconstructions are difficult to test[3]—but in principle they are no less testable than inferences about the verbal substitutions that cause semantic paraphasias and neologisms.

Neuroscience and Freud's model

How, then, has Freud's dream theory fared in the crucible of neuroscientific research? This chapter outlines the long and curious journey of the neuroscientific evaluation of Freud's dream model. For many years the central claim that dreams are somehow motivated was not readily accessible to investigation by neurobiological methods. However, the middle of the twentieth century saw the discovery of the physical state now known as rapid eye movement (REM) sleep. This state—and its neurobiological basis—appeared to contradict the central tenet of Freud's model: dreams appeared to be caused by automatic brain processes that have nothing to do with emotion and motivation. In the last decade, however, this conclusion has been reversed: recent findings have revealed that dreaming and REM sleep are dissociable states, controlled by distinct (but interactive) brain mechanisms. REM sleep is generated by a 'mindless' brainstem switch, but dreaming is generated by a forebrain *motivational* system.

These newer findings appear to support central claims of Freudian dream theory: so that few neuroscientists today would still assert—as we once did—that dreams are 'motivationally neutral'.[4] Rather, it is now widely accepted that 'dream emotion is a primary shaper of plots'.[5]

To begin our journey, we must first consider some of the practical aspects of dream research. The methodological problems that arise when studying dreams seem to explain a great deal of the ebb and flow of support for Freud's claims about the 'meaning' of dreams.

REM sleep

REM sleep is widely known as 'dreaming sleep'. However, as we shall learn, it is a mistake to equate the two phenomena. The conflation of REM sleep with dreaming is one of the most substantial errors that has arisen from methodological impropriety in this field.

When the REM state was first discovered in the 1950s, the scientists involved[6] immediately suspected that it was the physiological correlate of dreaming. This was because the REM state consists of a period of physiological arousal in the context of otherwise quiescent sleep, just as the dream state involves conscious mental activity in the context of otherwise unconscious sleep. During REM, it is not only the eyes that are active. The electroencephalogram (EEG), which is a measure of electrical activity in the brain, revealed that although you are sleeping, your brain is in a state of heightened activation approaching full wakefulness. There is also arousal of other bodily systems. You begin to breathe rapidly, your heart rate increases and your genitals (in both males and females) become engorged.[7] One is thus highly excited, in several ways, during REM sleep. In contrast, however, skeletal muscle tone *drops* dramatically (with the exception of the musculature controlling eye movements). This effectively paralyses the sleeper. This cycle occurs roughly every 90 min in humans, so that we spend some 25 per cent of our sleeping hours in the REM state.

The easiest and most obvious way to test the hypothesis that the REM state is the physiological equivalent of dreaming is to wake people up during REM and non-REM sleep, and compare the frequency of dream reports found in the different awakenings. The first time this hypothesis was tested, it was immediately obvious that many more dream reports are obtained from REM than non-REM awakenings. Today, half a century after this issue was originally investigated, there remains some controversy about the exact percentages. Is it, as the Shakespeare quotation in the title suggests, only 'perchance' that we dream in sleep—even in REM sleep? The strongest claim is that 90–95 per cent of awakenings from REM sleep produce dream reports, whereas only 5–10 per cent of awakenings from non-REM sleep produce equivalent reports. Most authorities would agree on a conservative 80:20 (REM:non-REM) dream report ratio.

Taking into account the fallibility of human memory in general, let alone memory for *dreams* (which are particularly difficult to recall), it would have been unreasonable for early investigators to expect a 100 per cent dream recall rate from REM sleep awakenings and a 0 per cent rate from non-REM awakenings. Under the circumstances, the (roughly) 80:20 ratio that *was* observed was therefore interpreted as a near-perfect correlation, and the hypothesis was taken as confirmed: REM sleep and dreaming were thereafter considered to be literally the *same thing*, viewed from two different observational perspectives.

This equation provided an apparently valuable scientific foothold—although it later proved to be an unfortunate simplification. By making the assumption that the REM state is synonymous with the dream state, scientists believed they had in their grasp an objective measure of the presence or absence of dreaming. As a consequence, they could carry out objective experiments on perhaps the most subjective of all mental functions—a psychological phenomenon which simply cannot be independently observed by the investigator, and yet provided the theoretical bedrock for the whole discipline of psychoanalysis (which at that time totally dominated American psychiatry). The fact that not only humans but *all mammals* display the REM state made it possible for neuroscientists to go one step further: now they could identify the *brain mechanisms* underlying the REM state (read: dream state) by means of animal experiments which were ethically unacceptable in humans. This is where the slippery slope began, for no matter how close the homologue may be between the REM state in humans and other mammals, we have no way of knowing whether the same applies to their *dreams*. The moment investigators switched from studying human to animal physiology, the concomitant study of dreams (*per se*) was perforce abandoned.

The biological basis of REM sleep

The main thrust of the ensuing investigations took the form of lesion studies. A French neuroscientist called Jouvet carried out the first key experiments by performing a series of ablation studies.[8] Although REM sleep occurs in a wide variety of animals, cats were the main targets of this research—partly because their brain are so similar to ours, but no doubt also because they sleep for so much of the day! Jouvet made a series of slices through the neuraxis of the cat, starting at the highest level of the frontal lobes and moving progressively downwards toward the brainstem. He then systematically investigated the effects on the sleep cycle. He wanted to determine the key lesion site that would obliterate REM sleep. To his surprise, he found that you could effectively detach the entire forebrain from the brainstem, and the REM state would still remain intact, and punctuate non-REM sleep with the same monotonous regularity. The critical incision occurred only in the middle regions of the primitive brainstem, at the level of the pons. Subsequent investigators confirmed that REM sleep can only be obliterated entirely by creating fairly large lesions in the pons ([9], see Fig. 29.1). In short, these studies demonstrated that, whatever REM sleep was, it was causally generated by structures in the pontine brainstem.

The implications of this finding were enormous. Since the forebrain is the seat of all our higher mental functions, the early investigators concluded that REM sleep (read: dreaming) is an entirely 'mindless' activity. This raised serious questions for any psychological theory of the causation of dreams, not least among them being the Freudian theory that dreams are caused by motivated states of mind. Below is a quote from one of the most influential papers in the field:

> If we assume that the physiological substrate of consciousness is the forebrain, these facts completely eliminate any possible contribution of ideas (or their neural substrate) to the primary driving force of the dream process.[4]

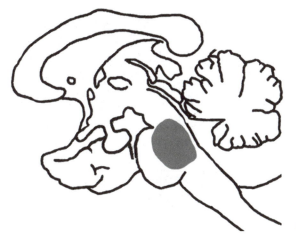

Fig. 29.1 Pontine brainstem.

Links between REM sleep, consciousness and emotion

The role of the pons and other nearby brainstem structures in creating 'core' consciousness[10] is not incompatible with the notion that dreams are 'mindless'. Nobody denies that dreaming is a *state of mind*; that you are *conscious* while you are dreaming. The same applies to the fact that many dreams are strongly *emotional* experiences. Although the role of brainstem structures in generating emotional states was not yet discovered,[11] the role of the reticular formation in generating *consciousness* was known at that time. However, whether these links were understood or not was immaterial; the early investigators did not deny that dreams *took the form* of conscious, emotionally charged experiences; what they asserted was that the mental aspect of dreaming was not *causal* of the dreams. Dreams, they argued, are caused by something happening in the pons, that switches on absolutely *automatically*, every 90 min or so, regardless of your state of mind. Since nearby brainstem structures were also known to regulate eye movements, heart rate and breathing, it seemed perfectly obvious that REM/dreaming was just a basic physiological state. The biological reason for this pontine clockwork was (and remains) unknown, but it was confidently assumed that dreams were merely a secondary by-product (or *epiphenomenon*) of this causal physiological process.

Philosophically minded readers might well have problems with this type of reasoning. You might well ask whether it ever makes sense to claim that a physiological process *causes* a mental event, and vice versa, or whether it makes sense to claim that some neurophysiological events are mindless while others are not. From the standpoint of dual-aspect monism, for example,[12] every neurophysiological event is simultaneously a mental event. However, although the early neuroscientific investigators of REM dreaming did not address such issues in any depth, they were able to claim that since the generation of REM is an automatic, pre-programmed process, its unconscious mental correlate is as 'motivationally neutral'[4] as the brainstem mechanism that generates your heart beat.

The neurochemistry of REM

By the mid-1970s, Hobson and colleagues[13] had narrowed the search for the pontine 'dream-state generator' (as they called it) to a set of precisely defined nuclei within the pons. In that year they published a famous paper in which they argued that the REM state is switched on and off by two groups of reciprocally interacting nuclei, one of which excretes a neurotransmitter which switches it on, and the other two neurotransmitters

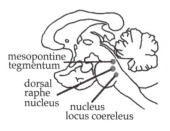

Fig. 29.2 Mesopontine tegmentum.

which switch it off. Although they gradually changed their minds about the specifics of the anatomy, their argument was that the key neurons which switch REM sleep *on* lie in the meso-pontine tegmentum (see Fig. 29.2). Shortly before the onset of REM, these neurons fire rapidly and they stay highly active throughout the REM phase. These neurons excrete the neurotransmitter acetylcholine. They are therefore described as *cholinergic* cells, and the REM state is considered to be a cholinergically driven phenomenon.

At the transition between REM and non-REM sleep, two other sets of neurons, in the dorsal raphe nucleus and the nucleus locus coeruleus, start firing rapidly (Fig. 29.2). The dorsal raphe excretes the neurotransmitter serotonin, and the nucleus locus coeroleus excretes noradrenalin (norepinephrine). When these nuclei become active, the cholinergic system simultaneously (in fact *consequently*, due to reciprocal inhibition) switches off. This switches off the REM state, and the sleeper falls back into non-REM sleep, with a mellowing surplus of serotonin and noradrenalin flowing around the brain. Some 90 min later, these two groups of nuclei reciprocally switch their function again—such that the levels of serotonin and noradrenalin drop, and acetylcholine increases—and the excited REM state re-appears.

So, according to this model, acetylcholine switches the REM state on and switches non-REM sleep off. Serotonin and noradrenalin switch non-REM sleep on and switch the REM state off. For obvious reasons, this model was named *the reciprocal interaction model*. This physiological account of REM sleep is extremely compelling. Some 25 years after it was first proposed, it still completely dominates the field of sleep research. By the 1970s, then, some the great mysteries surrounding sleep and dreaming appeared to be resolved.

Dreams are froth?

Two years after they proposed the reciprocal activation model, Hobson and McCarley[4] published a second paper, which contained a second model—this time not a model of REM sleep but rather one of *dreaming* itself. This seemed to be a legitimate extension of the first model, because REM sleep and dreaming were thought to be essentially the same thing. They called their second model the *activation synthesis model*. The *activation* aspect of the model argues (no surprise here)—that dreaming is activated by cholinergic mechanisms in the pontine brainstem. As we have noted already, this activation—which actually *causes* dreaming—is thought to be 'motivationally neutral'. The *synthesis* aspect of the model argues that the forebrain, thus activated, frantically attempts to piece together (or synthesize) the meaningless conscious representations (memory images, thoughts and feelings) that are randomly stimulated from below. Again, note that the forebrain's contribution to the process is passive, secondary to a brainstem-driven process—hence the notion that the dreams themselves are epiphenomenal to the REM state. From the forebrain's point of view, images are being activated during REM as if it were wide awake and experiencing something. It therefore does the only thing it can do, which is to string the images together into a self-world *episode*. In Hobson and McCarley's memorable phrase, the forebrain makes 'the best of a bad job' by trying to create a sensible experience during REM sleep out of the intrinsically 'inchoate' images thrown up by the brainstem. The essential implication is this: dreams are *inherently* meaningless. Freud had a term for this sort of theory, which actually existed in a speculative form in 1900. The expression was '*Traume sind Schaume*', which literally translates as 'dreams are froth'.[14]

This phrase epitomizes Hobson and McCarley's conception of dreams. Their work posed a clear threat to Freudian psychoanalysis, and Hobson wasted no time in pointing this out at the 1976 meeting of the American Psychiatric Association. After Hobson's presentation, a vote was taken among the membership of the APA as to whether Freud's dream theory was still scientifically tenable, in the light of Hobson's findings. At that time, the APA was still dominated by psychiatrists sympathetic to psychoanalysis. Nevertheless, the vote went overwhelmingly against Freud—suggesting that this was the end of the road, scientifically speaking, for Freud's account of the dreams. Given that Freud saw dreams as the 'royal road' to an understanding of the unconscious mind, this had serious implications for psychoanalysis in general. It is no exaggeration to suggest that the tide turned decisively against psychoanalysis in America at that fateful 1976 meeting.

The dreams of cats

However, as the attentive reader will recall, the activation synthesis theory embodied a critical methodological flaw. Hobson and McCarley's dream theory rested heavily on the *assumption* that dreaming and the REM state are *synonymous*. The finding that the REM state *co-occurs* with dreaming in humans, and the fact that the REM state also occurs in cats (and rats), led to a series of experiments on the brains of these lower mammals which sought to identify the brain mechanisms that generate REM sleep (read: dreaming). Having done so, and having demonstrated conclusively that only large pontine brainstem lesions obliterate REM sleep, the next logical step would be to check whether these lesions also obliterate *dreams*. After all, it was the association of REM sleep with dreaming that made it so interesting in the first place. The problem was, of course, that it is impossible to ask a cat (or a rat) whether it is dreaming or not. Some cat-lovers might believe that they *do* know when their beloved pets are dreaming, but everyone knows that it is dangerous to infer the content of an inner mental state from the form of an external behaviour!

Nevertheless a reliable method for checking the assumption that the REM state and dreaming are synonymous was available all along, by simply investigating the causal link in those who *can* provide a subjective report. However, once the assumption that REM and dreaming were synonymous was formed, it had become such a truism that nobody in neuroscience seemed to even think of checking it, and attention shifted to animal research.

A reliable method for linking a psychological function with a brain structure is the *clinico-anatomical method*, which formed the basic methodological building-block of all human neuropsychology. This well established tool was introduced to neuroscience by Pierre Paul Broca in 1861. The *clinical* side of this method involves making an observation that a mental function is lost following a focal brain lesion. In Broca's famous case, it was language that was lost (in the disorder known as aphasia). The *anatomical* side of the clinico-anatomical method involves ascertaining the precise location and extent of the brain damage that caused the loss of the mental function in question. In Broca's time, investigators had to wait for autopsy information to make this kind of observation. Subsequently this research could be conducted with living human subjects, using brain imaging technology.[15]

The autopsy of Broca's patient, Leborgne, revealed an area of damage on the lower left-hand side of the frontal lobe. Broca concluded that this is the neurological substrate of the ability to speak—because, when it is damaged, language is lost. This turned out to be a slightly oversimplified conclusion. Today we know that other parts of the brain participate in a complex functional system subserving speech and language (see any undergraduate neuropsychology text for more information); but even these other components of the neural substrate for language were identified using the clinico-anatomical method. From 1861 onwards, therefore, the guiding principle in neuropsychology has remained the same: in order to demonstrate that activity in a certain part of the brain is the neural correlate of a specific mental function, it is necessary to link damage to that region to a deficit of that function.[16] Jones[17] demonstrated this necessary correlation (using lesion studies) for REM sleep in rats; and subsequent sleep researchers confirmed that this clinico-anatomical correlation held good for humans as well (in cases with naturally occurring lesions). The link between the pons and *REM sleep* is thus clearly established—in humans and other animals. However, it is only in humans that the link with *dreaming* could be established—or refuted.

REM and dreams are not synonymous

Astonishing as it may seem in retrospect, the equation 'REM sleep = dreaming' was subjected to systematic clinico-anatomical scrutiny only 40 years after the association between REM sleep and dreaming was discovered; and when it was, it was found to be seriously wanting. In a 1997 study, six patients who had sustained damage to the REM-generating regions of the pons were asked whether or not they were still dreaming, and their answer was a clear '*yes*'. More than 40 other patients, in contrast, with damage to two specific parts of the *forebrain*, nowhere near the critical REM-generating structures (see below), *did* experience a cessation of dreaming following brain damage—but in these patients *the REM state was preserved*.[18]

Non-REM dreams

The discovery that pontine brainstem damage does not produce a loss of dreaming in humans led neuroscientific researchers belatedly to take account of previously neglected observations which seemed to point in the same direction (derived from other methods, more suited to human dream research than research on cats and rats). The main victim

of this neglect was the work of David Foulkes (a Chicago psychologist) and his collaborators. Foulkes focused on non-REM dreams which, according to classical teaching,
were supposed to be extremely rare. What he found was that by simply re-phrasing the
question that subjects are asked upon awakening in the sleep laboratory, and saying 'what
was passing through your mind?' rather than 'were you dreaming?', subjects reported that
they were experiencing complex mentation during non-REM sleep on some 50 per cent of
awakenings. However the REM = dream theorists were quick to point out that *dreaming*
is not the same as *thinking*.

Our attention therefore shifts to the 5 or 10 per cent of occasions on which subjects
report fully fledged dreams in non-REM sleep. These dreams are, it turns out, no different
from the dreams of REM sleep. Even Hobson (who has the most to lose from such findings) confirmed that these non-REM dreams are 'indistinguishable by any criterion' from
REM dreams.[19] In fact, some REM = dreaming theorists believed that these *were* actually
REM dreams, which were misattributed to non-REM sleep due to the aforementioned
vagaries of human memory.[20] Foulkes then showed that this assumption was clearly
incorrect.[21] He observed that you are most likely to have dreams in non-REM sleep just
after you have fallen asleep, during what is known as the *sleep-onset* phase of non-REM
sleep (more technically known as descending stages 1 and 2). On awakenings during these
first few minutes after falling asleep, subjects report dreams some 70 per cent of the time.
Most people do not remember these dreams when they wake up in the morning, for
obvious reasons, but we have all had the experience of dozing off briefly and then waking
up (often with a start) from a dream. These dreams occur *before* you have entered your
first REM period (in fact, roughly 90 min before). The 70 per cent of non-REM dream
reports that are obtained from the sleep onset phase therefore cannot be misremembered
REM dreams.

Antrobus and his colleagues made a related observation, at the opposite end of the sleep
cycle.[22] They demonstrated that the closer you get towards awakening in the morning,
i.e. at the end of a night's sleep, after the last REM phase (more technically: in the rising
morning phase of the diurnal rhythm), the more likely you are to obtain a REM-like non-
REM dream report. This is called the 'late morning effect'. The implications of this finding
are similar to those for sleep-onset dreaming: the *further away* from the last REM period
you get, the more likely you are to have a non-REM dream. In the classical 'reciprocal
interaction model', these transitional phases between wakefulness and sleep (sleep onset
and the late morning) were described—physiologically speaking—as *maximally distinct
from the REM state*: they were characterized by very high levels of noradrenalin and
serotonin and very low levels of acetylcholine. Clearly, dreaming is *not* causally dependent
on the unique physiological characteristics of the REM state. However, most non-REM
dreams do share *another* crucial characteristic with the REM state, which probably casts
important light on their true causal physiology. We shall mention this characteristic in a
moment.

Before doing so, it is worth asking in passing why the findings contradicting the REM =
dreaming doctrine were neglected for so long. The answer may have something to do with

the difference between 'brain' observations (concerning the state of a piece of physical tissue), and 'mind' observations (concerning the contents of subjective reports). The reactions of the scientific community to findings in dream research, and perhaps other aspects of neuroscience, have often been distorted by the fact that we are more prepared to accept evidence derived from precisely measurable physiological and anatomical variables than from the complicated sphere of clinical and subjective reports. Understandable as this bias may be, the example of dream research shows that it is essential for modern neuroscientists to take serious account of data derived from *both* observational perspectives in the mind–body equation.

Dreams and arousal

The feature that most non-REM and REM dreams have in common is *arousal*. Shortly after you fall asleep your brain is still relatively aroused, as you begin the gradual decline from full wakefulness into sleep.[23] As mentioned earlier, the REM state is likewise characterized, perhaps above all, by sustained periods of (cholinergic) brain arousal interrupting an otherwise quiescent sleep state.[24] The rising morning phase, too, is characterized (indeed defined) by relative arousal—albeit hormonally rather than cholinergically mediated. The *three* periods of sleep during which you are most likely to experience a dream, therefore, are characterized not by the unique physiology of the REM state (which characterizes only one of the three periods) but by *various* types of arousal. This suggests that a certain *amount* rather than a certain *type* of arousal is a necessary pre-condition for dreaming.

In the activation synthesis theory, the arousal that generates dreams was not only thought always to be of the same type (i.e. *cholinergic* arousal), it was also thought always to arise from the same place (namely, the *pons*). If this were true, it might still be possible to claim that dreams are 'mindless' and 'motivationally neutral'. However, in fact good evidence exists which suggests that dreams can be causally generated by *forebrain* mechanisms.

Dreams and epilepsy

There is a form of epilepsy which involves *partial* seizures that are entirely localized to the limbic regions of the forebrain. Partial seizures occur when the abnormal neuronal activity which causes a seizure does not spread to the rest of the brain (which causes seizures to *generalize*, usually into the familiar form known as 'tonic–clonic convulsion'). Partial seizures reflect their localization: if epileptiform neuronal firing occurs in the visual cortex of the right occipital lobe, the seizure takes the form of flashes of light (or 'phosphenes') in the left visual field; if the abnormal activity is in the left motor cortex, the seizure takes the form of twitches in the right arm or leg. Similarly, when epileptiform brain activity is localized to the *limbic* parts of the forebrain, which subserve emotional and memory functions (e.g. the amygdala and hippocampus), the resultant seizure takes the form of a *complex mental experience* (e.g. reminiscence accompanied by a strong feeling of emotion). This (limbic) form of partial seizure is called *complex*-partial to distinguish it from the elementary sensations and movements that are characteristic of the *simple*-partial seizures described previously.

Seizures occur quite frequently during sleep, and typically during the non-REM phases—which are characterized by rythmical, slow waves of electrical activity of a kind that are apt to trigger seizures in predisposed brains. These assume various forms (depending on the location and extent of the epileptogenic focus) but not infrequently they take the form of complex-partial seizures. This implies (by definition) that the abnormal brain activity causing the seizure is *wholly confined to the limbic regions of the forebrain*. Specifically, the seizure focus does not spread to the core brainstem structures that regulate the sleep cycle (if it did, the resultant seizure would be neither complex nor partial). It is therefore of considerable interest to observe that these non-REM seizures are frequently accompanied by dreams. In fact, they are typically associated with highly distinctive dreams which take the form of recurring nightmares (this reflects the involvement of limbic emotional and memory mechanisms). Given what we know about the underlying physiology of these dreams (which are in fact seizures— unequivocally *caused* by focal activation of specific limbic forebrain structures during non-REM sleep) we may confidently conclude that the arousal mechanism that triggers dreams is not *necessarily* located in the brainstem at all. Dreaming, it seems, can be triggered by arousal of *any type* arising from *any place*—including the emotion- and memory-generating structures of the limbic forebrain. This casts further, serious doubt on the assertions of the old pons–REM dream theorists who claimed that the activation of ideas, memories and emotions cannot be the primary 'driving force' of the dream process.

What is the primary driving force of the dream process?

If it is no longer tenable to assert that the pontine brainstem contains the primary causal generator of dreaming, then what *is* the causal mechanism of dreams? We said earlier that clinico-anatomical studies revealed that lesions of the pons did *not* cause cessation of dreaming (evidence *against* an exclusive causal role for the pons), but we also said that lesions in two forebrain regions *did* have that effect. Perhaps *these* regions contain the long-sought 'dream state generator'.

The first of these regions is the transitional zone between occipital, temporal and parietal cortex, at the back of the forebrain in the functional unit for receiving, analysing and storing information. Lesions in this area (on *either* side of the brain) produce a total cessation of dreaming.[25] The other region with this property is the *white matter* of the *ventromesial* quadrant of the *frontal lobes*. Damage to this area of the brain (on *both* sides simultaneously) also produces a total cessation of dreaming. Damage to other parts of the brain causes other characteristic changes in dreaming (e.g. increased frequency of dreaming, increased nightmares, defective visual dream imagery). This suggests that these regions, too, form part of the complex functional system that generates dreams.

The parts of the brain in question include the entire *limbic system* (including all the limbic components of the frontal and temporal lobes, but excluding their higher cognitive components) as well as most of the *visual system* (excluding the primary visual areas). However, these structures are of secondary interest; it seems more likely that one of the two structures that are *essential* for the generation of dreams (i.e. either the occipito-temporo-parietal junction or limbic frontal white matter) embody the 'primary driving force' behind dreaming.

Functional imaging findings

We said earlier that clinico-anatomical findings nowadays are typically checked against functional imaging findings for accuracy. This is in keeping with the view that scientific conclusions regarding something as complicated and experimentally elusive as human mental life should—wherever possible—be confirmed by multiple, converging methods of investigation before they can be accepted with confidence.

Through functional brain imaging, it is possible to obtain a radiological representation of the brain of a healthy, living subject, and observe where neural activity is greatest during certain mental states. In the last few years this procedure has been applied to sleep and dreaming by a number of pioneering investigators. The definitive study in this regard was published by Alan Braun from the NIH in Washington. Braun and others[26] used positron emission tomography (PET) to investigate what the brain looks like during REM sleep—the time when one is *most likely* to be dreaming.[27]

When investigating the state of the brain during REM sleep, one is probably imaging two different states simultaneously. The first is the REM state and the second is dreaming. There is a (roughly) 80 per cent chance that dreaming will occur during REM, so the average of data spread across several REM phases will almost certainly also capture the dream state.[28] The average picture that emerges is therefore a combination of the dreaming and the REMing brain. Not surprisingly, then, Braun found that the pontine brainstem mechanisms that switch on the REM state were highly active during REM sleep. More interesting is what *else* he found.

The activation synthesis theory would have predicted that the brainstem activation of REM should globally activate the entire forebrain—thereby generating the random sensory, motor, emotional, memory and thought images that comprise the supposed 'froth' of dreams. This is not what Braun found. Instead, he observed that only highly specific parts of the forebrain were activated during REM dreaming, while other parts were completely inactive (see Fig. 29.3). This is evidence of a striking pattern of dissociation between the levels of activation of various parts of the forebrain during sleep, suggesting that dreams are constructed by specific forebrain mechanisms. Moreover, the parts of the forebrain that Braun found were most active during dreaming were precisely the parts that obliterated or otherwise altered dreaming when they were damaged by brain lesions—and vice versa, the least active parts were the parts that had no effect on dreaming when damaged.[29] Braun therefore observed the very same pattern of dissociation that

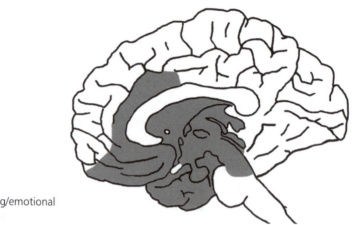

Fig. 29.3 Dreaming/emotional brains.

the lesion studies had found: the parts of the forebrain involved in the construction of dreams are the entire *limbic system* (including all the 'limbic' components of the frontal and temporal lobes, but excluding their 'higher cognitive' components) and most of the *visual system* (excluding primary visual 'projection' cortex). This implies, among other things, that the brain mechanisms underlying dreams share crucial components with the brain mechanisms of emotion.

An aside on emotion

There is now a convincing body of evidence in emotion research that there are a relatively small number (likely to be between four and six) basic emotion systems.[11] One of these is a system, closely associated with pleasurable states, which runs from the transitional area between brainstem and forebrain to the limbic components of the frontal and temporal lobes (closely linked to nearby basal forebrain nuclei—especially the nucleus accumbens). It appears to be a non-specific motivational system, engaged in looking for something to satisfy needs. There are also a range of emotion systems associated with other emotions— primarily the negative ones of sadness, anger and fear (mediated by structures such as the amygdala, hypothalamus and rostral brainstem). All of these emotional systems (together with the hippocampus, which subserves episodic memory, and parts of the visual system) are highly active during REM dreaming; but which of them provides the 'primary driving force' of dreaming?

The primary driving force, revisited

We said earlier that a certain degree of *arousal* was a necessary pre-condition for dream- ing. We also said that two *forebrain* structures are essential for the generation of dreams (i.e. the occipito-temporo-parietal junction and the limbic frontal white matter). One of these two regions, we said, therefore probably reveals the 'primary driving force' behind dreaming.

While arousal is a *necessary* pre-condition for dreaming, it is not a *sufficient* condition to produce dreaming. We know this to be the case from the observation that patients with damage in the occipito-temporo-parietal junction or the limbic frontal white matter cannot dream, no matter how aroused they may become during sleep (even in the REM state). The necessary and sufficient conditions for dreaming are (1) forebrain arousal and (2) integrity of the occipito-temporo-parietal junction and limbic frontal white matter. So, which of the latter two structures delivers the primary driving force? One way of addressing this question is to consider what else these two structures are known to do.

There is abundant evidence to suggest that the occipito-temporo-parietal junction (or the inferior parietal lobule) is heavily implicated in the generation of visuospatial imagery.[30] It is therefore no surprise that it should be implicated in dreaming, which is, after all, a special type of visuospatial imagery. A decade ago, there was little reason to suspect that the limbic frontal white matter had a function obviously implicated in dreaming. However, it is of some interest that an earlier, largely ignored, literature had pointed to a link of exactly this sort.

Frontal lobotomy and dreaming

From the 1940s until the 1960s, the surgical procedure of frontal lobotomy (surgical disconnection of the prefrontal lobes) was performed on thousands of patients for the treatment of serious mental illness, especially schizophrenia. In the early days, this procedure involved a near-total disconnection of the prefrontal lobes from the rest of the brain. This certainly seemed to reduce psychotic symptoms—especially the so-called 'positive' symptoms of schizophrenia, such as delusions and hallucinations—but it also produced a range of debilitating side effects. The most commonly reported adverse effects were inertia and apathy, intellectual decline, personality change and post-operative epilepsy. The patients who underwent these operations lost not only their psychotic symptoms but also a great deal of what it means to be human.

For these reasons, the surgeons involved modified the procedure. They developed a more limited operation that damaged a far smaller region of the brain, with the intention of achieving the same therapeutic benefit without the side effects. Several different approaches involving different parts of the frontal lobe were attempted. They finally settled on the white matter of the ventromesial quadrant of the frontal lobes[1,31] This modified procedure was called *ventromesial leucotomy*, and involved using a custom-designed surgical 'leucotome' to create bilateral lesions beneath the ventromesial surfaces of the frontal lobes (Fig. 29.4).

The area targeted by this modified procedure is exactly the same area that the lesion studies mentioned above discovered was essential for the preservation of dreaming. In fact, we should say *re*-discovered, for incredible as it may seem, the practitioners of frontal leucotomy had already observed in the 1950s that the operation resulted in a cessation of dreaming in the vast majority of patients.[32] Psychiatrists knew this long ago but, after the operation fell out of use, the knowledge was never transferred to the neuroscience

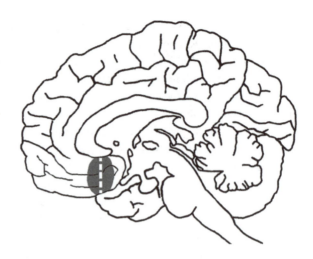

Fig. 29.4 Frontal leucotomy.

literature. One of them even went so far as to observe that preservation of dreaming after the operation was a poor prognostic sign—such that continued dreaming seemed to indicate that the psychosis had not been successfully treated (see Solms[29]). So, we may conclude that whatever it is that generates positive psychotic symptoms might well be the primary 'driving force' behind dreams. As already noted, many psychiatrists have observed that dreams and psychotic illness must somewhere share a common mechanism.

Drugs and dreaming

There are a number of reasons why the psychosurgical treatment of schizophrenia fell out of favour, including ethical considerations. However, it is widely accepted that the most important reason for the shift was the development of *pharmacological agents* which were just as successful at controlling positive psychotic symptoms (if not more so) with fewer side effects. These drugs are the 'major tranquillizers', also referred to as 'neuroleptics' or 'antipsychotics'. Psychiatrists still employ versions of these drugs today for the treatment of schizophrenia. All of these agents have one core feature in common—they block *dopamine* transmission, and mesocortical–mesolimbic dopamine (D2) transmission in particular.[33] These pathways course through exactly the area of white matter that was targeted in ventromesial leucotomy. For this reason, some neurobiologists have irreverently remarked that antipsychotic drugs function as 'chemical leucotomies'.[34]

A little earlier, we pointed out that one of the basic emotion systems is embedded in precisely the same pathways. This is the dopaminergic system associated with wanting and seeking. Antipsychotic medications therefore block activity in this system, just as the old ventromesial leucotomy procedure did.[35] This treats the positive symptoms of schizophrenia because, although this is not well understood why, overactivation of this dopamine system seems to generate hallucinations and delusions. This association is demonstrated, among other things, by the fact that pharmacological *stimulation* of this system can artificially produce psychotic symptoms in psychiatrically normal subjects. *Cocaine* and the *amphetamines* are two other classes of pharmacological agent that act on this dopamine system. Modest doses of both of these drugs produce a great boost of energy, and increased interest in objects in the world. This is consistent with increased activation of the wanting/seeking system.[1,36] With sustained use, in higher doses, a 'stimulant psychosis'[37] is initiated. Long before dosage levels produce psychosis, however, users develop the feeling that some events in the world have a special 'significance' for them, and they exhibit a degree of suspiciousness about the behaviour of others. In more extreme states, patients almost invariably become paranoid, and sometimes suffer auditory hallucinations. Such stimulant psychoses can be rapidly and effectively treated by the administration of the antipsychotic medications usually given to schizophrenics.

The same thing can happen with the administration of dopamine agonists (stimulants) in the treatment of Parkinson's disease. The drug *L-dopa*, for example, is notorious for inducing psychotic symptoms. On this basis, Ernest Hartmann and colleagues[38] conducted a study iatrogenically which might be considered a direct test of the hypothesis that the mesocortical–mesolimbic dopamine (seeking/wanting) system is the 'primary driving force' of dreams. He administered L-dopa and a placebo to neurologically and psychiatrically normal subjects, shortly after the first REM period. The effect was immediate and dramatic. The subjects who received the L-dopa experienced a massive increase in the frequency, vivacity, emotional intensity and bizarreness of dreaming. The frequency, density and length of their REM periods, in contrast, was completely unchanged. This provides further evidence for the dissociation between dreaming and REM sleep discussed above, and suggests that the dopaminergic seeking/wanting system might well be the 'force' we have been looking for.[39]

In summary, when the seeking/wanting system is damaged, patients lose interest in objects in the world, dreaming ceases and positive psychotic symptoms (hallucinations and delusions) decrease. Conversely, when the system is stimulated, energy levels increase, dreaming increases and psychosis may ensue. There are therefore a series of clear links between dreaming, psychosis and the operation of the seeking/wanting system.[40] In Hobson's original argument against the Freudian dream theory he said: 'these facts completely eliminate any possible contribution of ideas (or their neural substrate) to the primary driving force of the dream process' and he argued that the real driving force behind dreams was 'motivationally neutral'. In the light of the present-day neuroscientific evidence, it seems quite inappropriate to claim that dreams are not caused by 'ideas' and that they are instigated by a 'motivationally neutral' process.[4] On the contrary, dreaming and motivated ideas (akin, perhaps, to Freudian 'wishes') appear to be inextricably interlinked.

Visual areas involved in dreaming

We have said that there is a second forebrain area that appears to be critical for dreaming, but it seems less likely that this area is the primary *driving force* behind dreams. The role that the occipito-temporo-parietal junction plays in the dream process is not entirely clear. It may well be that lesions to these sites produce loss of dreaming because of their role in mental imagery. If the patient loses the ability to generate a mental image, then inability to dream seems a logical consequence. If this argument is valid, the effects of this second lesion site are of less theoretical interest than the important role of motivation in dreams.

A more significant finding is the *isolated loss* of visual dream imagery (or *aspects* of visual dream imagery, such as colour or movement) after damage to the brain's higher visual areas. This suggests something about the 'direction of flow' of visual information processing in dreams. The visual regions of the brain can be regarded (as a first-pass simplification) as involving three hierarchically organized zones. First, an area more or less directly connected to the retina, known as primary visual cortex, lies at the back of the occipital lobes. This region is the 'input' end of the system. In front of this zone lies the 'middle' part of the system which is dedicated to a range of specialized visual processing tasks (Fig. 29.5). Colour and motion processing, object recognition, and so on appear to depend on this zone. Finally, the highest level of the visual system runs the most abstract aspects of visual processing, which are also dependent upon several other sensory modalities. This zone is involved in arithmetic, writing, constructional operations and spatial attention. It represents the 'output' end of the normal visual system.

Damage to the lower zone—the primary visual area—causes cortical blindness. Visual consciousness ceases, because the 'input' end of the system is disrupted. Damage to the middle zone causes more complex disorders of visual processing. These patients lose the ability to perceive colour, or movement, for example, or they lose the ability to recognize specific objects, or faces. Damage to the higher zone—the occipito-temporo-parietal junction—does not affect visual perception *per se*, but rather causes more abstract disorders which transcend concrete perception: acalculia (inability to calculate), agraphia

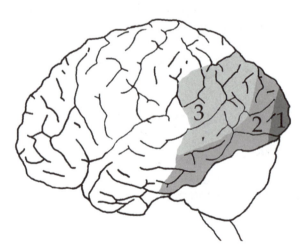

Fig. 29.5 Visual areas.

(inability to write), constructional apraxia (inability to construct) and hemispatial neglect (inability to attend to one side of space).

In *dreaming*, however, this hierarchy seems to be reversed. Damage to the primary visual cortex has (perhaps surprisingly) no effect on dreaming at all. Although these patients cannot see in waking life, they see perfectly well in their dreams. It appears that this aspect of the system is no longer the 'input' end. Damage to the middle zone of the system causes exactly the same deficits in dreams as it does in waking perception: these patients continue to dream in various sense modalities, especially somatosensory and auditory, but their visual dream imagery is deficient in specific respects. For example, they no longer dream in colour, or they dream in static images (loss of visual movement) or they cannot recognize any of the faces in their dreams. Damage to the higher zone in the occipito-temporo-parietal junction, on the other hand, produces complete loss of dreaming. Remember in normal waking life damage here does not affect perception *per se*, only higher visual cognition, i.e. damage to the part of the system that is the 'output' end in normal waking life seems to function as the 'input' end during dreaming.

This inverted relationship has been proposed in the cognitive neuropsychological literature as a suitable model for the organization of the imagery system in waking cognition.[41] It seems to apply equally well in the case of dreaming. Freud called this mode of organization 'regression', and wrote that 'in dreams the fabric of thought is resolved into its raw material'.[42]

A summary of the neurobiology of dreams

The following description of the mechanism of dreaming integrates the evidence reviewed above. Some speculation is required, however, to fill in the gaps, although this will no doubt be less of a problem in the near future, as research in this exciting area is proceeding apace.

First and foremost, dreaming depends upon a critical degree of activation of the basic mechanisms of core consciousness. If this endogenous source of consciousness is not active, you cannot have a dream. It does not appear to matter what the trigger of the activation is. Frequently, it is simply the residue of waking thoughts, as you drift off to sleep. The most reliable trigger is the REM state, which provides a sustained source of activation at regular intervals throughout sleep. As you begin to wake up, hormonal mechanisms gradually activate the forebrain. All these triggers activate (or 'prime') consciousness, which is a necessary pre-condition for dreaming, but is not dreaming itself.

The arousal of the motivationally charged seeking/wanting system, which drives our appetitive interest in the object world, appears to begin the dream process proper. It is probably accurate to say that *an arousal stimulus only triggers dreaming proper if it attracts appetitive interest*. When this happens, the subjective feeling is something along the lines of: 'what could this be? I want to know more about this'.

Activation of the seeking/wanting system during sleep is commonly, but not exclusively, triggered by the REM state. A thought process occurring during any stage of sleep can presumably also activate the seeking/wanting system. This thought process could be linked to an episodic memory from the previous day, or even just a feeling. If the memory or feeling activates the interest of the seeking/wanting system, this would be enough to begin the dream process. This explains the observation that although *most* dreams occur at sleep onset, during REM sleep, or just before waking, it *is possible* to have a dream almost anytime during the night—even during deep (stage 4) sleep. Recall, in this context, that these non-REM dreams are indistinguishable from REM dreams.

When you sleep you cannot go about purposively exploring or seeking what you are interested in. This sort of behaviour is incompatible with sleep, and it is probably for this reason that we dream. It seems a reasonable hypothesis that *the dream occurs instead of a motivated action*, i.e. instead of doing something in the real world, you have a dream. The frontal lobes (the principal 'action' systems of the brain) are normally a central 'scene of action' in waking cognitive activity. However, this system is dormant, i.e. inhibited or underactivated, during dreaming sleep. The 'scene of action' of cognitive activity therefore shifts to the posterior forebrain, with activation of the parietal, temporal and occipital lobes. This is experienced as imaginative perception and cognition—which, however, differs from waking thought in that it is unconstrained by frontal executive control. In the absence of the ability of the prefrontal lobes to programme, regulate and verify our cognition, emotionally and motivationally charged, subjective experience becomes bizarre, delusional and hallucinated.

In our dreams, the focus of motivated cognition is therefore redirected from the goal-directed action systems, and shifts toward the perceptual systems—especially the visuospatial aspects of perception. The functional anatomy of dreaming therefore shares some properties with that of schizophrenic psychosis.[43] One substantial difference is that in schizophrenia it is primarily the *audioverbal* component of the perceptual systems that is activated, rather than the visuospatial. The basis of this difference is unknown.

Dreams as the guardians of sleep

In addition to claiming that dreams were motivated by wishes, Freud famously argued that they 'serve the purpose of prolonging sleep instead of waking up—that dreams are the guardians of sleep, and not its disturbers'.[44] This means that the sleeper is 'protected' from the disturbing influence of motivational urges that arise during sleep. This hypothesis seems reasonable in the light of what we have learned above. However, reasonable hypotheses are frequently proved wrong; so untested hypotheses have limited value in science. One of the criticisms most frequently thrown at psychoanalysis is that its core hypotheses are untestable—but it appears that this aspect of dream psychology is open to direct empirical assessment. Now that we know that certain unfortunate individuals with damage to specific parts of their brains are unable to dream, the sleep protection hypothesis can easily be tested. Non-dreaming neurological patients should experience more disturbed sleep than (say) neurological patients with equivalent degrees of brain damage in whom dreaming persists.

Thus far we have been able to gather some preliminary data on the question, by simply asking patients who do not dream whether the quality of their sleep is better or worse than before their neurological problems began. The data collected so far (on a sample of 361 patients) supports Freud's sleep protection theory at the required levels of statistical significance.[45] However, a sleep laboratory study (instead of a bedside assessment) is required before this issue can be addressed with confidence. Consistent with this claim, a single case recently investigated by Bischof and Basseti[46] diagnosed sleep maintenance insomnia.

Dream censorship

People who misunderstand Freud's theory of dream censorship[47] claim that the theory predicts that the (inhibitory) frontal lobes should be more active during dreams than waking life, rather than less (which is what they are). However, Freud's dream theory states only that the 'censorship' function of the executive ego is *not completely inactive* during sleep, not that it is *more active* during sleep than in waking life. In fact, according to Freud's theory, it is the *weakened* state of the inhibitory systems of the mind that makes our instinctual drives so unruly during sleep, and causes us to think the things we do in our dreams, which would be inconceivable in our waking lives. The theory therefore predicts exactly what functional brain imaging suggests, namely that the inhibitory systems of the brain are *relatively* but not *completely* inactive during dreaming sleep.[48] However, this is far from proving Freud's censorship theory correct.

Freud's theory was designed to explain the differences between two components of the dream process. On the one hand, the manifest (or 'explicit') content of the dream is often illogical and bizarre. On the other hand, the patient's associations with the individual elements of the dream suggest that the underlying, latent (or 'implicit') content of the dream involved a motivational impulse which was not at all illogical or bizarre. In this regard, the neuroscientific evidence is compatible with Freud's model. Freud went on to question why the two levels of dream content differed so dramatically. His answer, of course, was the censorship. Here he may have been wrong. The apparent illogicality and bizarreness of dreams may be due to the inherently 'regressive' nature of the dream process. The mere fact that the system is forced to function in the way that does, where the executive systems of the frontal lobes cannot programme, regulate and verify the output of the posterior forebrain, may well produce the difference between the latent and manifest contents—with no need to introduce the additional function of censorship. The symbolic transformations that Freud drew attention to might, therefore, simply be the product of unconstrained parietal lobe mechanisms operating in reverse, 'resolving the fabric of thought into its raw material', as it were.

However, the unbiased observer would agree that the neuroscientific evidence does not yet have a decisive bearing on this important question. The available evidence cannot tell us whether the distortions that appear to be introduced between latent and manifest dream thoughts are tendentiously motivated or not. For now, we shall have to rely on purely psychological techniques to assess the validity of this aspect of Freud's dream theory. Although multiple, converging lines of evidence are desirable in science, certain types of psychological question cannot be pertinently answered by neuroscientific methods.

In conclusion, modern neuroscience has come to understand a great deal about the biological basis of dreams, particularly the brain regions and attendant psychological processes that appear to be most central to the dreaming state. This knowledge is *broadly consistent* with Freud's psychoanalytic theory of dreams—although these are some aspects of his theory has been not been addressed as directly as we might like. We also know that the neural mechanisms of dreaming appear to overlap, in several important respects, with the neural mechanisms of certain core features of psychosis—especially the positive symptoms such as hallucinations. This confirms a long-standing hunch harboured by Freud (and many others) to the effect that understanding dreams might provide us with a key to understanding mental illness in general. Dreams truly do appear to be 'the insanity of the normal man', and are apparently closely linked to issues of motivation and personal meaning.

References and notes

1. For a survey of prominent scientists who have shared this view, see Gottesman C. Neurophysiological support of consciousness during waking and sleep. *Progress in Neurobiology*, 1999; 59:469–508.
2. Freud S. *The interpretation of dreams*. Standard edition. Vols 4 and 5. London: Karnac Books. 1900.
3. Reverse-engineering arguments are, for example, commonplace in evolutionary biology—as in the problem of why elephants have trunks.
4. Hobson JA, McCarley R. The brain as a dream state generator: an activation-synthesis hypothesis of the dream process. *American Journal of Psychiatry*, 1997; 134:1335–1348.
5. Hobson JA, Pace-Schott EF, Stickgold R. Dreaming and the brain: toward a cognitive neuroscience of conscious states. *Behavioral and Brain Sciences*, 2000; 23:793–842.
6. Aserinsky E, Kleitman N. Regularly occurring periods of eye motility and concomitant phenomena during sleep. *Science*, 1953; 118:273–274. Dement W, Kleitman N. Cyclic variations in EEG during sleep and their relation to eye movements, body motility, and dreaming. *Electroencephalography and Clinical Neurophysiology*, 1957; 9:673–690.
7. In fact, penile erection during REM sleep is so reliable that it provides the basis for one of the most widely used investigations of male impotence.
8. Jouvet M. Neurophysiology of the states of sleep. *Physiological Reviews*, 1967; 47:117–177.
9. Jones B. Elimination of paradoxical sleep by lesions of the pontine gigantocellular tegmental field in the cat. *Neuroscience Letters*, 1979; 13:285–293.
10. See, for example, Damasio A. *Descartes' error*. Grosset/Putnam, New York 1994; Damasio A. *The feeling of what happens*. William Heinemann, London. 1999.
11. See Panksepp J. *Affective neuroscience: the foundations of human and animal emotions*. Oxford University Press, New York. 1998.
12. See Solms M, Turnbull OH. *The brain and the inner world: an introduction to the neuroscience of subjective experience*. Karnac Books, London. 2002.
13. Hobson JA, McCarley R, Wyzinki P. Sleep cycle oscillation: reciprocal discharge by two brainstem neuronal groups. *Science*, 1975; 189:55–58.
14. Freud S. *The interpretation of dreams*. Standard edition. 1900:133 (in the English translation) and p. 138 (in the original German). London: Karnac Books.
15. Computerised axial tomography (CAT or CT) and magnetic resonance imaging (MRI).

16. Today it is possible to go further, and check the clinico-anatomical correlation by ensuring that exercising the function in question is linked with increased metabolic activity in that same region (using PET imaging and fMRI).

17. Jones B. Elimination of paradoxical sleep by lesions of the pontine gigantocellular tegmental field in the cat. *Neuroscience Letters*, 1979; **13**:285–293.

18. Solms M. *The neuropsychology of dreams*. Lawrence Erlbaum Associates, Mahwah, NJ. 1997; Solms, M. Dreaming and REM sleep are controlled by different brain mechanisms. *Behavioral and Brain Sciences*, 2000; **23**:843–850.

19. Hobson JA. *The dreaming brain*. Basic Books, New York. 1998.

20. A similar claim has recently been advanced by Tore Nielsen. A review of mentation in REM and NREM sleep: 'covert' REM sleep as a possible reconciliation of two opposing models. *Behavioral and Brain Sciences*, 2000; **23**:851–866. Nielsen speculates that although these dreams occur during NREM sleep, as defined by the standard physiological criteria endorsed by the field for over 30 years, they are probably generated by intrusions of REM physiology into the non-REM state. According to Nielsen non-REM dreams are therefore actually 'covert' REM dreams. Hobson (2000, p. 952), so enthusiastically grasped Nielsen's lifeline to his theory that he actually went so far as to assert that 'all of sleep is REM sleep, more or less'! Hobson JA. Dreaming and the brain: the ghost of Sigmund Freud haunts Mark Solms's dream theory. *Behavioral and Brain Sciences*, 2000; **23**:951–952.

21. Foulkes D. Dream reports from different stages of sleep. *Journal of Abnormal and Social Psychology*, 1962; **65**:14–25.

22. Kondo T, Antrobus J, Fein G. Later REM activation and sleep mentation. *Sleep Research*, 1989; **18**:147.

23. The contribution that these remnants of wakefulness make to dreaming may be one source of what Freud (1900) called the 'day residues' in dreams.

24. This striking co-existence of heightened brain activation with ongoing sleep led the early investigators of what later came to be known as 'REM sleep' to call it 'paradoxical sleep'.

25. Solms M. *The neuropsychology of dreams*. Lawrence Erlbaum Associates, Mahwah. 1997; Solms M. Dreaming and REM sleep are controlled by different brain mechanisms. *Behavioral and Brain Sciences*, 2000; **23**:843–850.The *precise* location of these lesions in the posterior cortex is still uncertain: see Yu CK. Neuroanatomical correlates of dreaming: the supramarginal gyrus controversy (dream-work). *Neuro-Psychoanalysis*, 2001; **3**:193–202.

26. Braun A, Balkin T, Wesenten N, Carson R. Regional cerebral blood flow throughout the sleep-wake cycle. *Brain*, 1997; **120**:1173–1197; Braun A, Balkin T, Wesenten N, Gwadry F. Dissociated pattern of activity in visual cortices and their projections during human rapid eye movement sleep. *Science*, 1998; **279**:91–95.

27. Other investigators have carried out similar studies, and all have produced findings compatible with Braun and colleagues. There have, as yet, been no functional imaging studies of the brain during sleep onset, or the late morning, when dreaming is *dissociated* from the REM state, due to technological constraints. However, these constraints will soon be removed when fMRI technology is applied to dreaming sleep.

28. With PET imaging (for technical reasons) it is necessary to study the *average* picture.

29. Solms M. *The neuropsychology of dreams*. Lawrence Earlbaum Associates, Mahwah. 1997.

30. Any basic neuropsychology text will provide a good survey, though for a specific review of imagery findings see Kosslyn S. *Image and brain*. MIT Press, Cambridge, MA. 1994.

31. For a review see Walsh KW. *Neuropsychology: a clinical approach*. Churchill-Livingstone, Edinburgh. 1985:158–168.

32. For a review of these findings, see Solms[29] pp. 45–53.

33. For a review see any general psychopharmacology text, for example Lickey ME, Gordon B.. *Medicine and mental illness: the use of drugs in psychiatry*. Freeman & Co., Washington DC. 1997. Snyder SH. *Drugs and the brain*. Scientific American Library, New York. 1999.

34. **Panksepp J. Mood changes. In P Vinken, G Bruyn, H Klawans, ed.** *Handbook of clinical neurology,* Vol. 45. Elsevier, Amsterdam. 1985:271–285.

35. The system is not *typically* described by psychiatrists as a wanting/seeking system—this term is employed only by those working on the neurobiology of emotion. However, both literatures know this set of pathways as the mesocortical–mesolimbic ascending dopamine system. Psychiatrists often describe it as the D2 (or D2-family, or second dopamine) system. Different disciplines have developed separate terminologies to describe the same neuroanatomical and neurochamical systems.

36. **Kapur S.** Psychosis as a state of aberrant salience: a framework linking biology, phenomenology, and pharmacology in schizophrenia. *American Journal of Psychiatry,* 2003; **160**:13–23.

37. For example, see Snyder SH. *Drugs and the brain.* Scientific American Library, New York. 1999:138–140.

38. **Hartmann E, Russ D, Oldfield M, Falke R, Skoff B.** Dream content: effects of L-DOPA. *Sleep Research,* 1980; **9**:153.

39. This conclusion is still hotly contested by Hobson and his school. For an overview of the current arguments for and against, see Harnad S, Pace-Schott E, Blagrove M, Solms M (ed.) *Sleep and dreaming: scientific advances and reconsiderations.* Cambridge University Press, New York. 2002.

40. In this context, it is of some interest that Freud [Freud S. (1924). *Neurosis and psychosis.* Standard edition 19, p. 149; Freud, S. (1940). *An outline of psychoanalysis.* Standard edition 23, p. 141) believed that psychotic states resulted from an overwhelming of the ego by the libidinal (appetitive) drives (i.e. by the system that motivates our interest in objects in the world). Freud's position is therefore quite consistent with the fact that some aspects of psychosis (no less than dreams) appear to flow from an overactivation of the seeking/wanting system. A full discussion of this interesting possibility is beyond the scope of this chapter.

41. It is sometimes referred to as 'backward projection', see Kosslyn S. *Image and brain.* MIT Press, Cambridge, MA. 1994; see also Zeki S. *A vision of the brain.* Blackwell, Oxford. 1993.

42. Freud[2] p. 543.

43. **Silbersweig D.** Mesolimbic activity associated with psychosis in schizophrenia. Symptom-specific PET studies. *Annals of the New York Academy of Sciences,* 1999; **877**:562–574.

44. Freud[2] p. 223.

45. **Solms M.** New findings on the neurological organisation of dreaming: implications for psychoanalysis. *Psychoanalytic Quarterly,* 1995; **64**:43–67.

46. **Bischof M, Bassetti CL.** Total dream loss: a distinct neuropsychological dysfunction after bilateral PCA stroke. *Annals of Neurology,* 2004; **56**:583–586.

47. Solms[29] p. 63.

48. **Hobson JA.** The new neuropsychology of sleep: implications for psychoanalysis. *Neuro-Psychoanalsyis,* 1999; **1**:157–183.

Index